Voices of Torah

A Treasury of Rabbinic Gleanings
on the Weekly Portions, Holidays,
and Special Shabbatot

Voices of Torah

A TREASURY OF
RABBINIC GLEANINGS
ON THE WEEKLY PORTIONS,
HOLIDAYS, AND
SPECIAL SHABBATOT

Edited by
Hara E. Person

Introduction by Kenneth J. Weiss

CENTRAL CONFERENCE OF AMERICAN RABBIS
5771   NEW YORK   2011

Library of Congress Cataloging-in-Publication Data

Voices of Torah : a treasury of rabbinic gleanings on the weekly portions, holidays, and special Shabbatot / edited by Hara E. Person ; introduction by Kenneth J. Weiss.
p. cm
ISBN 978-0-88123-159-5 (pbk. : alk. paper)
1. Bible. O.T. Pentateuch—Commentaries. I. Person, Hara.
BS1225.53.V65 2011
222'.107—dc23
2011019258

Copyright © 2011, Central Conference of American Rabbis
Printed in U.S.A. All rights reserved. No portion of this book may be copied in any form for any purpose without the written permission of the Central Conference of American Rabbis.

15 14 13 12 11   6 5 4 3 2 1

CCAR Press, 355 Lexington Avenue, New York, NY 10017
(212) 972-3636 ccarpress@ccarnet.org
www.ccarpress.org

Contents

Introduction	vi	**EXODUS**	**145**
Acknowledgments	xi	Sh'mot	147
		Va-eira	159
GENESIS	**1**	Bo	171
B'reishit	3	B'shalach	183
Noach	15	Yitro	195
Lech L'cha	27	Mishpatim	207
Vayeira	39	T'rumah	219
Chayei Sarah	53	T'tzaveh	231
Tol'dot	65	Ki Tisa	241
Vayeitzei	77	Vayak'heil/P'kudei	253
Vayishlach	89		
Vayeishev	101	**LEVITICUS**	**267**
Mikeitz	113	Vayikra	269
Vayigash	123	Tzav	279
Va-y'chi	135	Sh'mini	287

Tazria/M'tzora	299	**ADDITIONAL READINGS**	551
Acharei Mot/K'doshim	313	Rosh HaShanah	553
Emor	329	Yom Kippur	557
B'har/B'chukotai	341	Sukkot	563
		Chol HaMo-eid Sukkot	571
NUMBERS	357	Sh'mini Atzeret / Simchat Torah	577
B'midbar	359		
Naso	371	Chanukah	585
B'haalot'cha	383	Tu BiSh'vat	591
Sh'lach L'cha	395	Purim	595
Korach	407	Shabbat HaGadol	599
Chukat/Balak	419	Pesach	601
Pinchas	435	S'firat HaOmer	603
Matot/Mas'ei	445	Chol HaMo-eid Pesach	607
		Seventh Day of Pesach	615
DEUTERONOMY	457	Eighth Day of Pesach	617
D'varim	459	Yom HaShoah	619
Va-et'chanan	469	Yom HaAtzma-ut	621
Eikev	477	Shavuot	623
R'eih	485	Tishah B'Av	631
Shof'tim	491		
Ki Teitzei	501	Glossary	635
Ki Tavo	511	Permissions	647
Nitzavim/Vayeilech	521		
Haazinu	537		
V'zot Hab'rachah	549		

Introduction:
So That Torah Speaks through Us

Is Torah timeless . . . or just old-fashioned and out-of-date? This volume offers an answer to that question. To begin, let's consider a sampling of "truths" embedded in (and gleaned from) our ancient Torah. We learn that

- Fitness is about the *entire* body . . . not least of all the tongue.
- *Chameitz* can be found in our homes . . . and in our very lives.
- Our world comes about by design . . . thus there must be a Designer.
- The sukkah teaches us a profound lesson: your life, too, is frail . . . celebrate now!
- Korach's sons "did not die"; they might well be with us still . . . fomenting discontent.
- "You were strangers in the land of Egypt"; you know the feeling . . . so affirm even the stranger's holiness.

Torah is deeper than deep. It touches each person differently because each of us is created different and unique. It also is true that we tend to reach more deeply into—and appreciate—Torah's innumerable levels of meaning, significance, and relevance differently (and more profoundly?) with the passage of our years. Torah's text does not change, but our openness to it and our ability to draw perspective from it does evolve as we read and reread it, year by year.

In anticipation of each Shabbat, rabbis probe the assigned Torah portion, seeking to find truths that are no less true now than they've ever been, wisdom that speaks to our times, anomalies that are as puzzling now as they were when Torah was first written down, questions still in need of answers. As rabbis, our goal and our passion are to transmit and interpret Torah and its insights, week in and week out, to our twenty-first-century congregants.

Drawing forth wisdom and life lessons from Torah is an ancient Jewish practice, and we Reform Jews have engaged in this pursuit since our Movement's first days. Since 1995, such efforts have been published in the monthly *Newsletter* of the Central Conference of American Rabbis (CCAR). Originally called "Makshim," meaning "difficulties," "toughies," "questions," "problems," or "wrinkles," these commentaries later were known as "Likkutim," meaning "gleanings," a name inspired by the most important collection of Torah teachings from Rabbi Nachman of Bratzlav (1772–1810). Recently, these writings have been renamed "Voices of Torah".

Those who were responsible for this monthly page of Torah explorations as editors/columnists were, in order, Rabbis Lawrence S. Kushner, Stephen E. Cohen, Sheldon J. Marder, Kenneth J. Weiss, Alan S. Cook, and Amy R. Scheinerman. A number of others contributed one or more pieces to this effort.

Torah is a literature, a people's (indeed, a civilization's) history, a philosophy, a guide to wisdom and human experience, a set of rules and mores and values; it is replete with deeds, rituals, and beliefs that Jews from one age to the next at times follow and at other times reject. Read from cover to cover, year in and year out for a lifetime, Torah is the Jew's foundation, basis, and touchstone. Torah contains what we need to build a worthy and purposeful life—all we have to do is to tap into it and apply its richness. Torah is so much more than a book (or even five books!) . . . Torah is where Jews live.

"Gleanings" (using the name most commonly associated with these explorations of Torah) is based on a fundamental Jewish affirmation that Talmudic-era Rabbi Ben Bag Bag put into these words: "Turn it [the Torah] and turn it again, for everything is in it . . . contemplate it . . . grow gray and old with it and don't swerve from it, for you can have no better rule than this" (*Pirkei Avot* 5:26). Torah is like a multifaceted gemstone: as one holds it and turns it this way and that, a new facet, a new perception, a new beauty or color or clarity or depth presents itself—each different, one from the other. Another apt image is a flame of fire: view it from above or below or from different angles, or just watch it as it consumes its fuel, and what you'll see will be variations—endless aspects—innumerable semblances. Torah is just like that, so "turn it and turn it again. . ."

We who were deeply involved in the creation of these writings were also sensitive to the ancient Rabbis who urged Jews to "find a teacher and acquire a friend" (*Pirkei Avot* 1:6) with whom to study. Originally created for today's rabbis who are one another's teachers and companions, the Torah explorations published here now enable us to open up and broaden our circle of students who might, with this volume as a start, one day become Torah teachers. Each reader can "turn it and turn it again," and with each turning gain new perspectives, ask new questions, perhaps find (and transmit) never-before-considered solutions to life's continuous perplexities.

It is a custom to conclude each chapter of *Pirkei Avot* (Sayings of the Ancestors) with a quote from a particular Mishnah (*Makkot* 3:16). Included in this Mishnah are these words: *L'fichach hirbah lahem Torah u'mitzvot*, "Therefore God has given them a copious Torah and many commandments." The Hebrew word *hirbah*—often translated as "copious" or "many"—is, like Torah itself, open to interpretation. *Hirbah* is related to a verb meaning "to increase" or "to multiply" and to a noun meaning "vast" or "numerous". This single word sheds light on why Jews engage in this sort of Torah study: since the beginning of Jewish time, we Jews have uncovered "numerous" (indeed, ever more) ways in which Torah informs the lives of every generation of our people, a "vast" and growing source of understandings that are embedded in Torah's words. We Jews find guidance in Torah as we face life's opportunities and challenges; with each passing year, with each annual Torah cycle read, probed, and contemplated, we garner ever more truths from the vast treasure trove of human (and divine) experiences that are the "stuff" of Torah.

Let's look at one gleaning as an illustration of what this volume will impart to you: God is speaking to Moses at Mount Sinai: "Let them [the Israelite people] make Me a sanctuary that I may dwell among them" (Exodus 25:8). Was God implying here that Mount Sinai was where God lived and that the people should build a sanctuary there? If so, when they left that mountain, would the link with God be broken? No (this gleaning suggests), God's message was: I will be with you **wherever** you find yourselves—whether in the desert sanctuary or (later) on the Temple Mount or (later still) in neighborhood synagogues and in every Jewish home (called *mikdash m'at*, "small sanctuaries"). Torah's lesson, once again, is as new as it is old—God tells the Jewish people: When you leave Mount Sinai, you'll bring Me with you. Even now, in every generation, wherever **you** dwell, **I** will (continue to) dwell among you . . . I'm as accessible and as close to you as the place where you pray and live.

Torah continues to speak **to** us, and it must continue to speak **through** us. May the "voices of Torah" included in this volume touch your hearts, challenge your minds, and motivate you to probe our Torah tradition and reach ever more deeply into it. With this volume and its offerings, may you discover new understandings and identify new gleanings that you can transmit to those you teach and befriend, so that yours will be a new voice for our ageless Torah.

Kenneth J. Weiss

Acknowledgments

The first thank-you goes to all those who carefully tended this project, which took root in the *CCAR Newsletter* over the years. As editors and writers, they shaped these thoughtful commentaries on the *parashiyot* and, in so doing, provided a magnificent resource for all CCAR members. A warm thank-you to Melanie Aron, Jeffrey Ballon *z"l*, Michael Boyden, Henry Bamberger, Herbert Bronstein, Ari Cartun, Paul Citrin, Stephen Cohen, Alan Cook, Yossi Feintuch, Mordecai Finley, Janice Garfunkel, Elaine Glickman, Larry Kushner, Steven Kushner, Richard Levy, Janet Marder, Sheldon Marder, Joshua Minkin, David Novak, Jim Ponet, Louis Rieser, Amy Scheinerman, Kenneth J. Weiss, and Stephen Wylen. The CCAR is deeply appreciative of the contribution they have made and grateful for their permission to reprint the commentaries here.

It seemed like a shame to keep this vast archive of commentary to ourselves, and so we made the decision to combine all the commentary and produce it in a format that we could share with others interested in the study of Torah. We hope this collection sheds new light on old questions and offers challenging new insights.

The support of Rabbis Steven A. Fox, CCAR Chief Executive, Deborah Prinz, and Lennard Thal cannot go unremarked upon, as well as that of CCAR Press Chair Lance Sussman. A special thanks goes to Kenneth (Kenny) Weiss, who was particularly supportive of this project and has been a great cheerleader from the start. Our rabbinic interns Sara Newman and Jillian Cameron both played important roles in preparing this material and helped whip it into shape. Debbie Smilow, as always, worked her magic on an unruly manuscript and helped the project move forward. Thanks also to copy editor Debra Hirsch Corman and proofreader Michael Isralewitz.

Genesis

בראשית *B'reishit*

(Genesis 1:1–6:8)

B'reishit
Lawrence S. Kushner, 1995

Why, if the sun, the moon, and the stars were created on the fourth day of the Creation sequence, did the Creator make light on the first day? How does one do that?

Why, of all animals, was it a snake that got Eve and Adam in trouble? Would the story be as effective if it were, for instance, say, a talking chicken? And why, if Adam blamed Eve, did Eve blame the snake and not Adam?

B'reishit
Lawrence S. Kushner, 1996

In the traditional understanding of Genesis 1 and 2, the two stories are not from different sources but are different ways of telling the same story. Putting the Documentary Hypothesis aside for a moment, what might be learned from placing the creation of humanity last in one account and first in the next, from mentioning the arising of a mist in one story but not in the other, from the creatures of earth and sky preceding Adam's creation in one story and created as a possible *eizer k'negdo* (helpmate) in the second? If God created man and woman simultaneously in God's image, as Genesis 1 suggests, what does it mean that woman was taken from Adam in Genesis 2? If Genesis 1 and 2 are the same story with different emphases or lessons, how might you tell the story a third way to emphasize yet a different lesson?

B'reishit: The Tree of Knowledge of Good and Evil
Stephen E. Cohen, 1997

None of the sages of *B'reishit Rabbah* speak openly of the Tree of the Knowledge of Good and Evil "symbolizing" a general realm of forbidden knowledge; they speculate only about actual species—wheat, grapes, figs.

B'reishit Rabbah **15:8**   Rabbi Yosei said, "They were figs. It is like the story of a prince who slept with one of the concubines. When the king heard of it, he threw the prince out of the palace. The prince went knocking on the doors of each of the concubines, and none would let him in, except the one with whom he had slept. She opened her door and received him. So too, when the first man ate from the tree, the Holy One threw him out of the garden, and he went from one tree to another, but none would receive him, except the fig tree, whose fruit he had eaten. She opened her door and received him, as it says, 'They sewed fig leaves together and made loincloths' (Gen. 3:7)."

Comment   Several of the medieval *m'forshim* (commentators)—and modern commentators as well—believe that the Knowledge of Good and Evil refers to sexual knowledge. Rabbi Yosei may be guiding us, indirectly, toward that idea by using a frankly sexual parable to help identify the mysterious fruit. Do you think so?

B'reishit: Whose Land?
Stephen E. Cohen, 1998

In this midrash, transmitted by Rashi, we may detect a sensitivity on the part of at least certain rabbis to the ancient (and enduring) accusation that in conquering the land of the Canaanites, we were simply stealing their property.

Rashi Rabbi Yitzchak said: God might well have begun the Torah with "This month shall be for you . . ." (Exod. 12:2). For what reason does the Torah open with the story of Creation? Because of the principle expressed in the verse "The strength of His deeds He related to His people, to give them the inheritance of nations" (Ps. 111:6). So that if the nations of the world say to Israel, "You are thieves; you conquered the lands of the seven nations," they will be able to reply, "The entire earth belongs to the Holy One. He created it, and gave it to whomever He saw fit. By His will He gave it to them, and by His will He took it from them and gave it to us."

Comment Does this teaching not lead directly to the conclusion that all territorial conquest is God distributing land according to the divine will? Would Rashi say that there is no such thing as "stealing" on a national level?

B'reishit
Mordecai Finley, 1999

If prophecy is fruit from the Tree of Life, and the fruit is pressed into wine for our personal use through *t'shuvah* (repentance), then what do we make of the fruit of the Tree of the Knowledge of Good and Evil and the exile resulting from that fruit being eaten? According to the *Zohar*, Adam HaRishon, the first person, ate from the Tree of Knowledge of Good and Evil purposefully; he sought not prophecy, but experience, to know vagaries of good and evil, compassion and judgment, right and wrong. He became like "*Elohim*," not like "*Adonai*." Adam HaRishon became like the emanation from *Adonai* called "*Elohim*," the aspect of the Godhead that creates differentiated reality. Adam HaRishon was now like *Elohim* in now being ontologically rooted in the world of differentiation, but without the intrinsic connection to the Godhead—in him, the Tree of the Knowledge of Good and Evil was separated from the Tree of Life. Ingesting the fruit of the Tree of Knowledge of Good and Evil separates Adam HaRishon from the Tree of Life, and places him in the worlds of husks (*k'lipot*)—masks and veils. Some say, and the *Zohar* agrees (1:36b) that the tree was in the form of a fig tree, and in a homeopathic-like urge, he cleaved to the shadow-making power (the leaves) of the very tree that plunged him into the shadows.

B'reishit
Sheldon Marder, 2000

The power of language is at the heart of Adam's naming of the birds and beasts in Gen. 2:19–20, and so it is in a poem that alludes playfully and poignantly to these verses: Louise Gluck's "The Gift" (*Descending Figure*, Ecco Press, 1981). Here the poet (a professor at Williams College, whose poetry has won the Pulitzer Prize and the National Book Award) evokes the excitement of a child's discovery of language—as we, too, experience anew the primal power of language in reading aloud the opening chapters of Genesis.

> Lord, You may not recognize me
> speaking for someone else.
> I have a son. He is
> so little, so ignorant.
> He likes to stand
> at the screen door, calling
> *oggie, oggie*, entering
> language, and sometimes
> a dog will stop and come up
> the walk, perhaps
> accidentally. May he believe
> this is not an accident?
> At the screen
> welcoming each beast
> in love's name, Your emissary.

B'reishit: A Design Requires a Designer!
Kenneth J. Weiss, 2001

"In the beginning of God's creating" (Gen. 1:1—R. E. Friedman).
   "When God began to create" (Gen. 1:1—JPS).

A heretic once came to Rabbi Akiva and asked him, "Who created the world?" "The Holy Blessed One," he replied. "Give me a clear proof," the heretic said. "What are you wearing?" asked Rabbi Akiva. "A garment." "Who made it?" "The weaver." "I do not believe you," said Rabbi Akiva, "give me a clear proof." "In which way can I prove it? Do you not know that the weaver made it?" "And yet you do not know that the Holy One created the world," retorted the rabbi. The heretic departed.

Rabbi Akiva's pupils said to him, "How was your answer clear proof?" He replied, "My disciples, just as a house testifies that there is a builder, and the garment a weaver, and the door a carpenter, so does the world testify that God created it" (*Midrash T'murah*).

The Rambam, in his time, encountered—and dispatched—a heretic who brought a similar challenge.

Extending the logic, the world we know came about either by design or by accident—one of these has to be true! If begun by accident, there are no meaningful conclusions to draw. If, however, the world was created by design, then there had to have been a Designer. If there is an ongoing and unfolding design in the continuing function of the world, then there must be a living, omnipotent Designer. The Rambam story ends as follows: "When examining how perfectly all (the world's) features exist and interact, anyone can tell that it was formed by an All-Knowing Creator"—only a Designer can create a design!

B'reishit
Kenneth J. Weiss, 2002

"I will make an *eizer k'negdo* for him" (Gen. 2:18b).

Eizer k'negdo—JPS translates this as "a fitting helper." Eve (as she is soon thereafter named) is created to "help" Adam, from whose rib or "side" she emerges.

Richard Elliot Friedman, in his *Commentary on the Torah* (HarperOne, 2001) offers—and justifies—a different take on this Hebrew phrase. Friedman teaches that *eizer* can mean "strength" as well as "helper." He references R. D. Freedman, who first suggested that *eizer* is "in parallel with '*oz*,' another word for 'strength,' as in, for example, Psalms 46:2. See also *Azariah* (2 Kings 14:21) and *Uzziah* (2 Chronicles 26:1) as alternative names for the same king." Given all this, Professor Friedman suggests that *eizer k'negdo* "may very well mean 'a corresponding strength.' If so, it is a different picture from what people have thought, and an intriguing one in terms of recently developed sensitivities concerning the sexes and how they are pictured in the Torah. In Genesis 1, man and woman are both created in the image of God; in Genesis 2, they are corresponding strengths." These two accounts emphasize the "essential equality of worth and standing" of the two sexes.

Are *oz* and *eizer* identical, synonymous, or (at least) "in parallel," as Friedman posits? Could be: the *Tanach* texts cited above seem to support that premise. Whimsy may bolster Friedman too: whereas Adam existed from the time he received "the breath of life" (Gen. 2:7), Eve might suggest that he only started to live when she (his *eizer!*— his *oz?*) entered it. Furthermore, the *ezrat nashim* (women's gallery in Orthodox synagogues) might also be referred to as *oz nashim*— the place from which the women lend their strength to communal worship.

"A corresponding strength": people who love can understand and feel it.

B'reishit
Kenneth J. Weiss, 2003

"When God began to create . . . the earth being unformed and void" (Gen. 1:1–2).

Biblical scholars—from classical to modern—seek to justify why Torah begins with the story (stories!) of Creation. Richard Elliot Friedman (*Commentary on Torah*, HarperOne, 2001) paraphrases Rashi's claim that "Torah could have begun with the first commandment to Israel—the commandment to observe Passover . . . rather than with creation." Torah begins with Creation, suggests (Friedman on) Rashi "in order to establish God's ownership of all the world."

Friedman adds his take: Torah doesn't start with a commandment because Torah's purpose—beyond transmitting commandments—is also to tell stories, in this instance, the story of Creation. Furthermore—here in *B'reishit*, we find an accounting of the "relationship between the creator and all the families of the earth ... crucial background to the story of Israel."

I'd like to weigh in: why does Torah begin where it does—with an account of Creation? It does so, I believe, because Torah's writers—inspired, sensitive, insightful—needed to record for themselves and their listeners/readers how everything that was had come to be.

They saw a world: ordered, dependable, beautiful. It was there from the first day their youthful minds could apprehend it. It had been there for their parents. It was right in front of them and all around them when they opened their eyes each morning. In patterned ways, it changed with the flow of seasons and years. By God's grace, it fed and nurtured, clothed and protected them.

Torah's writers sought to account for, to explain, and to preserve how Creation happened. Through their words in *B'reishit*, we sense their praise and gratitude to Creation's Creator.

With what else **could** *Tanach* have started?

B'reishit
Kenneth J. Weiss, 2004

Sidrah B'reishit portrays grandeur itself: beginning and renewal, a celebration of who we are, why God created us.

And yet, imbedded within even this most exalted of human stories are examples of humankind's darker side:

- Having defied God regarding the "fruit of the tree in the middle of the garden" (Gen. 3:3), Adam and Eve first hide, then cast blame away from themselves when God confronts them. Soon thereafter...
- Cain and Abel—the first sons—exemplify (nay, create!) sibling rivalry. In and after Eden, our ancestors reveal predilections that move God to express regret at humanity's creation (Gen. 6:6). Then along comes Noah...

B'reishit
Alan Cook, 2005

"Ten things were created on the eve of the Sabbath in the twilight: the mouth of the earth, the mouth of the well, the mouth of the ass, the rainbow, the manna, the rod, the *shamir,* the writing, the writing tool, and the tablets" (*Pirkei Avot* 5:6).

One could dwell on any one of the items that the Rabbis list in *Pirkei Avot*. But let us consider particularly the first two objects on this list.

The mouth of the earth is understood by commentators to refer to the passage in במדבר (*B'midbar*) when Korach and his fellow rebels descend to Sheol. But there is an earlier incident in which the earth "speaks": following Cain's murder of Abel, God proclaims, "Your brother's blood cries out to Me from the earth!" (Gen. 4:10).

As for the mouth of the well, it is said to have sustained the Israelites during their sojourn in the desert, providing them with a fairly consistent water supply. Tradition connects Miriam to this well.

But what connects Cain and Miriam? Cain famously proclaims, "השומר אחי אנכי?" (*Hashomeir achi anochi?* "Am I my brother's keeper?" [Gen. 4:9]), taking the attitude of "every man for himself." He denies that he has any responsibility toward his own family, let alone to the community at large.

By contrast, Miriam's tacit answer to Cain's question is "yes!" She first appears on the scene in the role of her brother's protector, watching over baby Moses as he is taken from the Nile and adopted by Pharaoh's daughter. Later, she expands this familial responsibility into an acknowledgment of her responsibility to כלל ישראל (*K'lal Yisrael*, "the community of Israel").

May we all strive to be less like Cain and more like Miriam, reaching out to all our brothers and sisters, and acknowledging that we are, indeed, their keepers.

With gratitude to Rabbi Ray Zwerin for inspiring these thoughts.

B'reishit
Alan Cook, 2006

Intelligent design or evolution? What should a good Jew believe in? Does accepting the premise of Creation as described in the Book of Genesis preclude us from giving any credence to Darwinism?

Consider one of the first questions that children often ask as they seek to make sense of the world around them: "Why is the sky blue?"

Eric Cornell, the winner of the 2001 Nobel Prize for Physics, noted that there are at least two possible answers that can be given to that question—answers that help to frame the debate over intelligent design. We may say, "The sky is blue because of the phenomenon known as Rayleigh scattering," or we may say, "The sky is blue because blue is the color that God wants it to be."

The two answers are valid, and they are not necessarily mutually exclusive. A person of faith may choose to believe that Rayleigh scattering is simply the means that God has used to make the sky the color that God desires it to be.

Good science has nothing to say about God. Similarly, the concept of intelligent design adds nothing to the field of science.

Rather than continually attempting to pit science and faith against each other, perhaps we can come to accept that there can be multiple answers to the same question, depending on one's understanding, one's interest, and one's field of discipline.

B'reishit
Amy Scheinerman, 2007

Actress Shelley Winters quipped, "I think onstage nudity is disgusting, shameful, and damaging to all things American. But if I were twenty-two with a great body, it would be artistic, tasteful, patriotic, and a progressive religious experience." Are shame and humility quaint by-products of a bygone era or necessary elements in a moral society?

Upon God's creation of Eve, Torah informs us, "The two of them were naked, the man and his wife, yet they felt no shame" (Gen. 2:25), confirming that the people have not yet eaten from the Tree of

Knowledge of Good and Evil. Adam and Eve are prototypes for the human race; their life stories reflect human development. Here we see them as young, innocent children, unaware of their sexuality, unconcerned with their bodies. They feel neither humility nor shame at being naked because they have no reason to believe it wrong. Shame and humility will emerge when they acquire moral discernment.

Micah taught the importance of walking humbly with God (Micah 6:8), which R. Elazar bar Tzaddok interpreted as discretion in both dress and comportment (Babylonian Talmud, *Sukkah* 49b). Unfortunately, the focus of צניעות (*tz'niyut*, "modesty") became restrictions on women's clothing and public voices. צניעות (*tz'niyut*) is about setting appropriate boundaries: listening to others, not merely promulgating our own opinions; following the lead of others and not always insisting upon being in charge; respecting other people's right to privacy and not insisting upon hearing their secrets as an entitlement of friendship.

B'reishit
Amy Scheinerman, 2008

If *Gan Eden* is a perfect universe, why does Adam have responsibilities for tending and tilling the garden? Why isn't a perfect garden totally self-sustaining? What is this *parashah* teaching us about our relationship to the world?

Gan Eden is the picture of perfection. It contains all that is needed to sustain life: abundant food, verdant beauty, peaceful creatures, a regulated climate. Yet as we quickly learn, the picture of perfection is not the same as genuine perfection. Life in the garden lacks challenge, purpose, and meaning. Eve's courage in trading immortality for moral insight meant that humanity could be born and generations come to be.

The one set of tools Adam took with him from the picture-perfect garden into the world beyond included the rake, hoe, and shovel: the tools with which he tended and tilled the garden in his role as steward. These are the tools that remind him that the role of humans with respect to the earth is as caretakers. Even in a world of abundant resources, our primary role is as stewards.

Our attitude should not be takers but rather givers. Given that the most fundamental human characteristic is selfishness, this is a marvelous and important lesson for our personal, family, communal, and global relationships. For far too long we have seen the world as our garden of delights, here to provide us with sensual satisfactions. We cannot continue in that way: we are the tenders and tillers. "Behold My works! See how beautiful and commendable they are! Take care not to corrupt and destroy My universe, for if you do, there will be no one to repair it after you" (*Kohelet Rabbah* 7).

B'reishit
Amy Scheinerman, 2009

"A river issues from Eden to water the garden, and it then divides and becomes four branches" (Gen. 2:10).

The garden is watered by a river originating in Eden, but outside the garden. This garden does not depend upon rainfall or irrigation, but rather enjoys a constant stream. In turn, the world outside Eden is watered by the branches of the primordial river.

The *Zohar* (181a) comments: "Just as a fountain or a water source fills a mighty stream, and from thence sources of rivers extend and flow on every side, so here: through one fine, subtle channel that is not known, that great river emerges and gushes forth, and from thence sources and streams extend, and they are filled with it. This is [the meaning of] 'Who sends forth springs into the streams' (Ps. 104:10)."

For the *Zohar*, the river issuing from Eden is God, the wellspring of life, effusively flowing, perpetually watering the world, the source of life and consciousness. The branching rivers and channels are the *s'firot*. The garden it waters is human consciousness, where life blossoms and grows, a world of differentiation, where all is interrelated and abides in dynamic existence. Our overwhelming need is balance and equilibrium in all the spheres of our lives.

For the kabbalists, God is constantly flowing into our world, continuously accessible. When we cause disequilibrium—in our lives, in our families and communities, in the environment—everything is affected. When we achieve balance, blessings flow outward to all.

The *Zohar* helps us see the interconnectedness of all.

Can we learn to locate the points and causes of imbalance and correct them?

נח Noach

(Genesis 6:9–11:32)

Noach
Lawrence S. Kushner, 1995

Why, if Noah built the ark himself, does the text specify that God shut him inside it? He couldn't close the door behind himself? The grammar seems more appropriate for a jailer than for a savior.

Noach
Lawrence S. Kushner, 1996

As a rabbinic student, Stephen Arnold gave a sermon suggesting that Gen. 6:14, *aseih l'cha teivat*, should emphasize the *l'cha*: "Make of yourself an ark." How might you tell the rest of the Noah story if you saw it as an allegory of how individuals should care for each other? What is gained, what is lost, by such an interpretation?

Traditional readers of this *parashah* see it as an integrated whole, despite the seeming contradiction between the seven pairs of clean animals and two pairs of unclean in some verses, and two pairs of every animal in others. One interpretation of this seeming discrepancy is that it reminds us that though some animals have preference in terms of eating and sacrifice, all animals are equally precious in God's sight. Does this interpretation have merit? Why should animals have been punished, as humans were, for the earth's violence?

Noach: The Raven
Stephen E. Cohen, 1997

Noah's dove has become a universal symbol of hope and deliverance, but what does the raven represent? Tractate *Sanhedrin* offers this depiction of the first-chosen bird, who refuses to fly far, but never returns to the ark

Babylonian Talmud, *Sanhedrin* 108b   Resh Lakish said: The raven brought an irrefutable charge against Noah. He said, "Your Master hates me and you hate me. Your Master hates me—of the pure species, He commanded you to take seven; of the impure only two. You hate me—you don't touch the species of seven, but send from a species of two. If I am struck by the sun, or by the cold, will the world not be lacking a creature? Or perhaps you have 'need' of my wife?"

Comment   The raven seems to stand for the "difficult" individual—the arguer, the sarcast, the outcast. Why **did** Noah choose the raven first?

Noach: The Flood of the Soul
Stephen E. Cohen, 1998

In this characteristic Chasidic treatment by Elimelech of Lizhansk, the waters of the Flood story are taken as a metaphor for the "ebb and flow" of our spiritual life.

Noam Elimelech   On Gen. 8:5: "The waters were going and diminishing [*haloch v'chasor*] until the tenth month." The waters refer to the Holy Torah, which is called "water," as in "All who are thirsty, go to the water!" (Isa. 55:1). It is the holiness and cleaving/*d'veikut* that are in a person, but that are impossible to experience constantly. At moments, one goes/*holeich* in *d'veikut*, and at others one is diminished/*chasor*. That is, one is cut off from *d'veikut*, as in the phrase, "He wanted to fetch water but could not" (Jerusalem Talmud, *Sanhedrin* 6:23). And the continuation of the verse, "until the tenth month/*chodesh*," means "until the tenth rung is renewed/*nifchadeish* within us." The tenth rung is supernal holiness, as in the verse "The tenth shall be holy" (Lev. 27:32).

Comment   One gets the sense from this particular teaching that the "ebb and flow" of *d'veikut* is independent of any spiritual "work" that we might or might not do. Are we, like Noah, fated to bob up and down on the surface of the flood, watching and waiting for the waters to rise or fall?

Noach
Mordecai Finley, 1999

After the destruction, Noach sought to correct the sin of Adam Ha-Rishon, who ate not the fruit of prophecy, which unites us to God, but the fruit of mere experience, which separates us from God. In the *Noach* narrative, one stream of thought in the *Zohar* now identifies the fruit of the Tree of Knowledge of Good and Evil as grapes from the vine (1:73a–b). The esoteric meaning of the story holds that the vine was exiled from Eden along with Adam. Noach had the vine and replanted it after the Flood. He planted the vine and drank of the wine (of the Tree of Knowledge of Good and Evil). According to the *Zohar*, "When Noach came to examine the sin of Adam HaRishon, he came not to cleave to it, but to understand/know it [*i'minda*] and to fix the world, but could not." And because of this, the *Zohar* continues, *vayishkar vayitgal*, he became intoxicated with these supernal matters and uncovered secrets of the world, creating breaches that had been closed (see the *Y'did Nefesh* commentary to the *Zohar*). This wine, by the way, was the same wine that the sons of Aharon drank in Torah portion *Sh'mini*.

Noach
Sheldon Marder, 2000

"Noah was a righteous man; he was blameless in his age; Noah walked with God" (Gen. 6:9). What does it mean to "walk with God"? What is piety? Our tradition answers in diverse ways.

For instance, "Noah walked with God" is reread by *Targum Onkelos* as "Noah walked in the fear of God" ("בדחלתא דיי הליך נח"),

probably to remove any taint of anthropomorphism from the text. "Fear of God"—one of the hallmarks of the Wisdom tradition—is one of those "old-time religion" phrases that offends, even alienates, many contemporary Jews. Onkelos's rationale, however, would likely win back points.

K'li Yakar sees "Noah walked with God" as Noah's rejection of the spirit of his times. "Noah did not turn to other Gods," says K'li Yakar; thus Noah piously distinguished himself spiritually from his contemporaries. Boldly asserting our Jewish principles is not controversial, in theory, but the assertion of our differences can be a thorny issue in many of our communities.

According to Rashi, "walked **with** God" implies the familiar notion that Noah was weaker than Abraham. Abraham "walked **before**" God, which is to say, he was self-sustaining in his righteousness. Noah, a lesser soul, required God's support in order to be a righteous person. How do Jews today feel about spiritual hierarchies? Tolerance for such thinking is tested even further by Rabbeinu Bachya (as documented by Hillel Zeitlin and cited in *Iturei Torah*), who sees in Gen. 6:9's description of Noah an ascending hierarchy of character and spirituality: (1) איש, *ish*, "man," (2) צדיק, *tzadik*, "righteous," (3) תמים, *tamim*, "pure," (4) את האלהים התהלך נח, *et haElohim hithalech Noach*, "Noach walked with God." This fourth and highest level—"walking with God"—means that Noah possessed an "eternal attachment of the mind to the Creator of all, who gives life, blessing, and happiness."

But Yitav Lev sees "walking with God" very differvently. Noah is portrayed here as an accomplice with *Midat HaDin* (the attribute of strict justice), siding, as it were, with *Midat HaDin*, instead of praying compassionately to annul the decree that would destroy all life. Here we have a Noah who is part of the establishment, when he should have been questioning authority.

Where does all this leave us? Such diversity of interpretation challenges us to think about why some theologies from the past make us squirm, and why others still inspire and sustain us. What does it mean, **in our age**, "to walk with God"? What is the nature of the God-centered enterprise in Reform life today? How do we define piety?

Noach: Primal Needs
Kenneth J. Weiss, 2001

"And God saw the earth, and, here, it was corrupted, because all flesh had corrupted its way on the earth" (Gen. 6:12—R. E. Friedman).

I never knew how important the ocean was to me until I moved away from it twenty-one years ago. Only then (and increasingly over time) did I come to realize that the sea—uniquely—renews me. I began to refer to my visits to the coast as a "primal" necessity. The cycle of the tides, the ceaseless rhythm of the waves, the interplay between the hue of the sky and the color of the water, these move and refresh me.

Why do so many people feel the pull, the lure, the renewing impact of the seas? *Parashat Noach* offers one possible answer.

In the first verses of this *parashah* we read that the *eretz* (Gen. 6:11ff.) was corrupted. Richard Elliott Friedman notes that the word *eretz* can mean "land" or it can mean "earth." In this context, "it refers to all the earth but still applies just to the dry land, and not the sea" (Richard Elliot Friedman, *Commentary on the Torah,* HarperOne, 2001). Thus, "all flesh [that] had corrupted its way on the earth" (Gen. 6:12) refers to life on land, not the living things in the sea.

How do we know this? Perhaps because God sent a flood in response to all the corruption. Had God sought to destroy the sea creatures as well as all life on dry land, it is reasonable to conclude that a different mode of destruction would have been employed.

Since every living thing on dry land (except those aboard the ark) was destroyed in the *mabul* (flood), earth's seas in the days of Noah were one source of renewed life. We, too, turn to the seas when our lives feel threatened, corrupted. Today as in Noah's time, the seas' gift is renewal.

Noach
Kenneth J. Weiss, 2002

"Noah did . . ." (Gen. 6:22; see also 7:5, etc.).

Noah stood out in his generation because he did something! He did his job, built an ark, was active and industrious in a generation characterized by sloth. *That's* why he's characterized as "blameless in his age."

The story of Noah suggests the importance of staying busy, getting involved. At the beginning of the *parashah*, we learn that "the earth became corrupt . . . [and] was filled with lawlessness" (Gen. 6:11). So, God "decided to put an end to all flesh" (Gen. 6:13). Why the corruption and the lawlessness? Rabbi Aryeh Leib Zunz of Plotsk explains: idle hands. "According to the midrash, [Noah's contemporaries] needed to sow their fields only once to obtain crops for the next forty harvests." So, God contrived to make "life on earth difficult so that [each person would] be forced to labor mightily" and continuously just to survive. Folks would have little time (or energy!) left to sin.

It didn't work! Even after the ark, the flood, the rainbow, and the promise, Babel suggests that nothing really changed: the tower offers just another example of idle hands engaging in frivolous projects.

Noah comes out looking pretty good against the backdrop of his contemporaries. Back then, pretty good was good enough: Noah (*NoaCH*) found favor (*CHeiN*) in God's eyes.

Noach
Kenneth J. Weiss, 2003

"Thus *Adonai* scattered" (Gen. 11:8). In *Parashat R'eih*, human free choice is affirmed: "See, I set before you blessing and curse" (Deut. 11:26).

This message resonates when we read the story of Babel. God—thoroughly disgusted with the "Babelites" and their tower—first confounded human speech, then "scattered [the people] over the face of the whole earth" (Gen. 11:8). God's presumed goal: to ensure that folks could never again choose to create anything so ill-advised.

But questions abound:

- Did God act too hastily, too severely?
- After destroying the tower, why couldn't God have concluded with a severe "tongue-lashing" for its builders: next time, I expect you to do better?

- Yom Kippur's primary message is verbalized in the *Ki Vayom Hazeh* prayer ("on this day atonement shall be made for you . . . you shall be cleansed from all your sins before the Lord"). By multiplying languages and scattering the human race, did God thereby make "atonement" and "cleansing" impossible?

The God of *Parashat Noach* was a short-tempered God. In Noah's time, God (אלהים, *Elohim*) "decided to put an end to all flesh" (Gen. 6:13). In punishing the people of Babel, God (יהוי, *Adonai*) made communication and understanding infinitely more difficult . . .
 . . . **we** have yet to recover from Babel's punishment.

Noach
Kenneth J. Weiss, 2004

Depravity is the offspring of corruption, lawlessness, self-aggrandizement. The human inclination to turn away from—or even dismiss—moral law is fertile soil in which all of this takes root, becomes verdant.

Sidrah B'reishit could be subtitled "The Beginning . . . of the End!" God creates the world. From the outset, humankind seems genetically programmed to deflect criticism, deny culpability, and focus on self ("me") rather than on community ("we"). After creating, God rests on the first Shabbat, permitting humankind to evolve (devolve?). Thus, "The Lord [clearly!] saw how great man's wickedness on earth [was], and how every plan devised by his mind was nothing but evil all the time" (Gen. 6:5).

Parashat Noach might be subtitled "The Consequences of Benign Neglect." Left on our own, lacking both divine guidance and human (religious/moral) leadership, humankind's profligacy brings society (as it was then configured) to the brink of extinction: a worldwide flood would "wash away" the ubiquitous stain of moral decay. Given another chance, however, a new—post-deluvian—generation accomplishes nothing more praiseworthy than a vain, misguided tower.

B'reishit tells of creation and splendor compromised by individual acts of moral failure. *Noach* shows how—despite human decadence—God resolved to create a beautiful and moral world.

Then God realizes what's (who's) missing . . .

Noach
Alan Cook, 2005

"Noah was a righteous man; he was blameless in his age; Noah walked with God" (Gen. 6:9).

David Maine's *The Preservationist* (St. Martin's Griffin, 2005) retells the Noah story from the viewpoint of each of the key players. Each has a different perspective on what they are living through and what it means. Noah's daughter-in-law, called Bera, is perhaps the most pensive of the bunch. While Japheth, for instance, seems engrossed in the idea that "we'll have a hell of a story for the grandkids," Bera (Shem's wife) is much more philosophical. "Why me and not them?" she wonders. "Why them, and not me?"

Noah never had such thoughts—at least, not according to the *p'shat* of the text. Rabbi Y'hudah, commenting on the qualifier בדרתיו (*b'dorotav*, "in his age") in Gen. 6:9, states, "In his own generation he was righteous, but had he been in the generation of Moses, . . . he would not have been righteous."

Noah did not consider the needs of others. He did not warn his neighbors or urge them toward תשובה (*t'shuvah*, "repentance"). He never questioned why he had been chosen to be spared, while others would be destroyed.

When tragedy befalls us, we are quick to ask, "Why me?" We should be willing to ask the same question when we find ourselves richly blessed.

May the "unhappy, storm-tossed ones" of the Gulf Coast continue to find healing, comfort, and peace.

Noach
Alan Cook, 2006

"Everyone on earth had the same language and the same words" (Gen. 11:1).

What must existence have been like in the days before Babel? If we are to take literally the idea that everyone had "the same words," this implies that all thought and acted in a uniform manner. Everyone marched in lockstep with one another.

As Vivian Paley writes in her book *White Teacher* (Harvard University Press, 2000), about her experiences with one of the nation's first integrated kindergarten classes, "homogeneity is fine for a bottle of milk, but not for a classroom." We might add, ". . . and not for a society either." We need diversity of viewpoints and of expression in order to have a vibrant and free culture.

Reform Judaism ostensibly embraces such heterogeneity. We try to make our congregations and institutions open and welcoming places, accepting of those from all walks of life. But occasionally we need to take a step back and examine whether we, in fact, are succeeding in such endeavors. For instance, are we empowering our constituents to examine our tradition and make informed choices about how to shape their Jewish lives? Are we conflating liberal Judaism with liberal politics, thereby disenfranchising a significant portion of our people?

To paraphrase Voltaire, we may not always agree with our neighbors, but we must defend their right to hold their beliefs. The story of Babel may not be telling us to lament the loss of unity in the world. Rather, it may be encouraging us to celebrate our diversity.

Noach
Amy Scheinerman, 2007

It's been heading steadily downhill: the exile from גן עדן (*Gan Eden*), the murder of Abel, the tower of Babel. Leo Tolstoy, mystic and novelist, surveying the corruption of human society and the carnage of human history, commented that any intelligent person would conclude that the corruption of the world is so overwhelming that it must surely be obliterated soon. Torah tells us God agrees. Cosmic order does not necessarily result in human social order. Our modern global economy breeds competition, aggression, and concern for the bottom line. "He who dies with the most toys wins."

Enter Stephen Post and Jill Neimark, who, in their new book *Why Good Things Happen to Good People: How to Live a Longer Healthier, Happier Life by the Simple Act of Giving* (Broadway, 2008), provide social research suggesting that in fact goodness—generosity, compassion, forgiveness, love, and nurturance—improve health, increase longevity, and enhance the quality of life. Martin Seligman, in *Learned Optimism: How to Change Your Mind and Your Life* (Vintage, 2006) and *Authentic Happiness: Using the New Positive Psychology to Realize Your Potential for Lasting Fulfillment* (Free Press, 2004), writes that virtue begets "the good life," including improved health and happiness.

The Flood narrative is about starting over, a new beginning for humanity. Post, Neimark, and Seligman offer a roadmap for a new beginning. Fanciful depictions for children of the ark and its cheerful inhabitants happily bobbling along a global sea seem oblivious of the death and devastation the Flood wrought. Can we understand the story as the death of one approach to living life in favor of nurturing a very different approach—the one characterized by the covenant of Abraham that follows the Flood?

Noach
Jeffrey Ballon, 2008

Noah was introduced to me as my bar mitzvah *sidrah* before I could legitimately hold a shot aloft and say *"l'chayim."* Many *Shabbes* minyanim in those days were punctuated with marinated onions, herring, and "Wild Turkey." In such an atmosphere, a *bocher* could learn a *bissel* Torah. But time passed before the study would go beyond the ark. The undertone was hidden from me as much as the real stories of the men who comprised the minyan. The siddur, the camaraderie, and the schnapps covered their pain.

Similarly, Noah the vintner, the drinker, indeed the drunkard, was never discussed. A few drinks might be acceptable to one still begetting at the age of five hundred, but passing out naked in your tent is a bit over the top. This was well beyond social drinking. When Noah's sons found him naked, they put a cloak around their shoulders and backed into the tent to cover their father's nakedness. They turned their back on the problem and tried to cover it up: this is denial.

Parashat Noach gives Torah's first clue about the necessity for Al-Anon, the support group for people who love alcoholics. Some congregations have made their minyan a place of healing for those who struggle with addictions. The Rush Center of the Johnson Institute (*www.rushcenter.org*) educates rabbis and congregations about addiction and recovery. Mindy Agler, the wife of our colleague in Boca Raton, works with the center, and she can be reached at *maglerlmhc@yahoo.com* for further help in relieving the anguish caused by this problem.

Noach
Joshua Minkin, 2009

"Let us make ourselves a name [*shem*], so that we will not be scattered all over the face of the earth" (Gen. 11:4). Creating institutions that bear our name is one way we strive to achieve immortality. Carnegie Hall and Rockefeller Center are both monuments to their wealthy namesakes.

We see this concern already in the Torah with regard to the daughters of Zelophechad, who petition for the right of daughters to inherit, to maintain their family name: "Why should the name of our father be done away from among his family because he has no son?" (Num. 27:4). Fundraisers know that plaques and honorific inscriptions work.

Nachmanides, the thirteenth-century mystical commentator, says that the word *shem* should be understood as referring to God, suggesting that the tower builders were saying: let us show how important we are, how we are able to control the world through our technology, how God-like we are. The results were disastrous.

Their hubris mirrors our own. We pollute the earth with poisons and change the chemistry of the atmosphere and oceans, imagining that our God-like technology will resolve problems caused by our shortsightedness and greed. It is already too late to avoid many of the consequences. The sea level is already rising. Our weather patterns are already changing.

We can be like Noah, listening to God's warnings and building an ark to the next generations, or we can be like *dor hamabul* (the generation of the Flood), ignoring the warnings and failing to plan for the imminent dangers they chose to ignore.

לֶךְ-לְךָ *Lech L'cha*
(Genesis 12:1–17:27)

Lech L'cha
Lawrence S. Kushner, 1995

"Go forth from your land" (Gen. 12:1).

Rashi says it means, "For your own benefit and reward." But if God assured Abraham that this would be for his own benefit and reward (win the lottery), then what kind of a difficult test is it? And why would this be the first of the ten trials by which Abraham was tried?

"And behold, a great, dark horror fell upon him" (Gen. 15:12).

The language, "a great, dark" is redundant; it makes no sense. Can there be a great darkness and a tiny darkness? Isn't all darkness equally dark?

"And you will go to your fathers in peace" (Gen. 15:15).

Rashi says that by saying "to your fathers," it means that Abraham would go to his father, Terah, who was an idolater! This teaches that Terah must therefore have repented of his ways. But isn't it more likely that Terah remained obdurate in his idolatry? But then how could Terah be rewarded with the Garden of Eden together with Abraham, his son?

Lech L'cha
Lawrence S. Kushner, 1996

Debby Friedman's song *L'chi Lach* is popular with us all. Yet this is not the name of this *parashah*. Why not? God does speak to Sarah, albeit seemingly through messengers (though sometimes the messengers are called God) — why did not God call Sarah also to "go forth"?

Abraham tries to pass Sarah off as his sister twice (and Isaac tries it once with Rebekah). Is this a test of Sarah as well as of Abraham — and what, besides chastity, is being proved? To what degree is Sarah responsible for Abram's accumulation of wealth (Gen. 12:16)?

Lech L'cha: Sarai's Plan
Stephen E. Cohen, 1997

Nachmanides emphasizes, quite tenderly, the love and regard that Abram and Sarai had for each other when Sarai brought Hagar to Abram. He is bluntly direct, however, in passing judgment on the first Jewish couple when their plan fell apart.

Ramban "She took" (Gen. 16:3), to inform us that Abram did not hurry to do this thing, but waited for Sarai to bring her to him. And the text says, "Sarai, Abram's wife" (Gen 16:3), to suggest that Sarai did not despair of their marriage, nor did she distance herself from him, for she was still his wife, and he was still "her husband" (Gen. 16:3). But she desired that Hagar also be his wife, and so it says "to be his wife" (Gen. 16:3) — not a concubine, but a true wife. All of this shows the great honor that Sarai paid to her husband. "And Sarai oppressed her, and she fled from before her" (Gen. 16:6). Our mother sinned in oppressing her, and Abram did also in allowing it. And God heard Hagar's affliction and made her son a "wild man," who would afflict the descendants of Abram and Sarai with every manner of affliction.

Comment Does Ramban believe that Sarai's plan was basically sound or fundamentally flawed?

Lech L'cha: Abram's Castle
Stephen E. Cohen, 1998

The original author of this famous midrash probably regarded Abraham as the first to recognize the "illuminated," "activated" quality of the world. The Eitz Yosef supercommentary, without changing a single word of the aggadah, sees Abraham as the first to be perplexed by the suffering and destruction in the world.

B'reishit Rabbah   Rabbi Yitzchak said: A parable of one who traveled from place to place. And he saw a castle *doleket* [translated either "illuminated" or "burning"]. He said, "Can it be that this castle has no owner?" The owner of the castle looked out at him and said, "I am the owner of the castle." Thus, when our father Abraham said, "Can it be that this world has no owner?" it was then that the Holy One looked out at him and said, "I am the owner of the world."

Eitz Yosef   The point of the parable is one who sees a beautiful, well-ordered building perceives and acknowledges that there is a lord and master of the castle and that a wise architect designed it. But when he [the traveler] saw the castle burning, then he thought that the owner had abandoned it, until the owner declared, "I am the lord of the castle, and it is my intention that it burn, as a punishment for the wicked."

Comment   What theological principles emerge from the two different translations of *doleket*? Compare the imagery here to the story of the call to Moses, at the Burning Bush.

Lech L'cha
Mordecai Finley, 1999

Adam HaRishon sundered the lower worlds from the higher in his search for experience, not the holy. Noach breached the worlds even more in his attempt at repair—it seems that any ulterior search for the Holy, even for repair, can disrupt the world of spirit. The only authentic search, it seems, is to know God. In knowing God, we repair the breaches and nourish the upper worlds. In the *Zohar*, the sealing of the covenant with Abraham is the moment of the reversal of the bicosmic entropy. When the world is no longer emptying of meaning because of the breaches, restoration occurs. The *Zohar* in portion *Lech L'cha* says that the world was created through covenant, the covenant of fire; the word *B'reishit* is rearranged to *b'rit eish* (covenant of fire). Adam dismembered that covenant, as Noach violated his. In circumcision, Abraham uncovers himself to God, and God uncovers God's self to Abraham, as we see in the opening words of the next portion, *Vayeira*, words that occur immediately after circumcision. The holy lights that were the garments of Adam and Eve, until they dressed themselves in the shade of the Tree of Vagaries, were now given to Abraham as his garment.

Lech L'cha
Sheldon Marder, 2000

Midrash T'hillim (11:21) observes that Abraham's and Sarah's devotion to Torah was complete: "The two of them observed the Torah from *alef to tav*." Therefore, asserts the midrash, Psalm 112 was composed about Abraham, and Prov. 31:10–31 was composed about Sarah—for these depictions of the righteous man and the righteous woman "go from *alef to tav*"—they are alphabetical acrostics. Might *Lech L'cha*, therefore, be an opportunity to recall in our worship the ancient practice of reading a "haftarah" from the Book of Psalms—in this case, Psalm 112 (and, to expand the custom just a bit, *Eishet Chayil*)—in addition to the Prophets?

The same midrash goes on to teach that Abraham did not observe the Torah out of compulsion, rather, in the words of Ps. 112:1, *b'mitzvotav chafeitz m'od*, "ardently devoted to God's commandments." Abraham discovered the pure delight of doing what God wants. Does the verse speak, in a special way, to the powerful religious experience of the *b'nei mitzvah* who enter the congregation on *Shabbat Lech L'cha*?

Lech L'cha
Kenneth J. Weiss, 2002

"And *YHVH* said to Abram, 'Go'" (Gen. 12:1).
"And God tested Abraham" (Gen. 22:1).

Abraham was tested—many times! Two of Abraham's severest tests—it might be argued—are foundational passages in our two *parashiyot*. In *Lech L'cha*, YHVH is addressing Avram. In *Vayeira*, *Elohim* addresses Avraham. And yet, the two passages—the two tests—are eerily similar in literary syntax / word flow, as a note in R. E. Friedman's *Commentary on the Torah* suggests. Let me illustrate as follows:

> "Go from your land [*mei-artz'cha*] and from your birthplace [*mimolad'tcha*] and from your father's house [*mibeit avicha*] to the land that I'll show you." (Gen. 12:1)

> "Take your son [*et bincha*] your only one [*et y'chid'cha*] whom you love Isaac [*et Yitzchak*] and make him a burnt offering on one of the mountains I'll show you." (Gen. 22:2)

In the passage from chapter 12, the *mi* prefix characterizes the tripartite pattern. In the excerpt from chapter 22, note the word *et* three times. These passages do more than relay information: we learn not only what Abraham is being asked to do, the way in which he is being tested. We learn also of the drama, we feel the angst—the growing angst (Friedman sees in the three-part construction an "ascending order of difficulty") as God slowly pulls back the curtain to let Abraham (and us!) in on the full impact of the tests of faith here presented.

> Now Avram: you'll leave your land, but not only that—you'll leave your birthplace as well, but not only that ... Now Abraham: take your son, but not only that—it's the one you love (best), but not only that ...

The threefold structure of both of these passages is surely worthy of note and consideration. The undefined future venue in both—a place that "I will show you," is also cause for pause. Finally, in both texts, blessing is the reward for successfully passing the tests (see Gen. 12:2 and 22:17).

Is that how God has set up the world? Are we tested and then rewarded with blessing when we pass the test? Are we blessed only if we pass the test?

No, says Jewish tradition and belief. Though blessing comes to the patriarch as he proves and reproves the totality of his faith in

God, a culminating passage—yet another threefold text—affirms the availability, indeed the unconditional constancy, of God's blessing for all of us at any time, in all times. Here (the *Birkat Kohanim* in Numbers 6) God blesses the people *lishmah* (for its own sake). Through Aaron and his sons, God's choicest blessing—in three distinct phrases (no coincidence here, I suggest!)—is extended to one and all: in all circumstances, without precondition. *Y'varech'cha Adonai v'yishm'recha....* "Thus they shall link My name with the people of Israel, and I will bless them" (Num. 6:27).

Lech L'cha
Kenneth J. Weiss, 2003

Vayaavor Avram, "Abram passed through" (Gen. 12:6).

Joe is brand-new to our retirement community—new and lonely. My parents have just moved into a full-care senior residence. Life—even in its latter stages—requires transitioning from one experience/place/situation to a new and (often radically) different one.

Abram experienced this. "Go forth," he is told: separate yourself from all you know; go "to a place that I will show you" (Gen. 12:1). So, at seventy-five, Abram departed the homeland of his youth for "a place he did not know."

Abram grew to know what Joe and my parents Charlotte and George continue to learn: so long as we live, transition is a constant.

One Hebrew root—ע-ב-ר—captures this concept. Since one of Abram's ancestors is Eber (עבר), perhaps successful transition between life's stages was built into Abram's gene code.

Presenting Abram, our paradigm. Know that, for us as for him, life requires episodic, and often difficult, transitions. Abram didn't just move physically: he transitioned from one of his life's stages to the next—and did so with grace and conviction.

Abram's the best. Perhaps that's why he's called אברם העברי (*Avram HaIvri*): Abram the Transitioner (Gen. 14:13).

Lech L'cha
Kenneth J. Weiss, 2004

All those mistakes, Avram—those worlds I created then had to destroy.

Then I fashioned this world . . . perfection, or so it at first seemed. Step by step, stage by stage, I unfolded My creation. Adam and Eve were given everything—an idyllic existence, a place of beauty and plenty: a Sabbath world. In fashioning humanity, I knew—of course—that there were inherent risks. With the gifts of soul and mind came the innate human capacity for making choices. Temptation and misstep followed: a symbolic tree, a conniving serpent.

Yes: they chose—foolishly, recklessly. Eve and Adam chose to defy; Cain chose to kill Abel; a whole generation chose to descend into immorality, profligacy. Sadly, the flood purged (only) the symptoms; it could not touch the disease. That ludicrous tower in Babel was proof that nothing had changed.

So, Avram, make no mistake: I truly need you—a human being—to be My partner. *Lech . . . lech*: "Go, (please) go" to a land that I will show you. Leave your birthplace; come to where you are needed. Together, we will tackle the disorders at the core of the human psyche. I once regretted creating humankind (Gen. 6:6). But together we can transform their inclination toward evil.

Go . . . go now!

Lech L'cha
Alan Cook, 2005

"O Lord God, what can You give me, seeing that I shall die childless" (Gen. 15:2).

After all of the promises that God has made to Abraham, and after all of the faith that Abraham has shown, something still bothers Abraham. What good are all of these promises as he gets up in years? He can't "take it with him," and he has no child to inherit all of the fortune that has been guaranteed to him. Who will carry on his name? What will be his legacy for the future?

Abraham's question is steered as much by emotion as it is by practicality. We all want a way to be remembered. We all want to know that our good name will live on long after we are gone. We want to achieve not only biological continuity, but also psychological survival. We wish to have our personalities live on in our children.

Abraham recognizes that he has been a part of something unique — a new way of looking at the world. His question is not meant to be petulant; it merely asks whether the great experiment of ethical monotheism and the wondrous relationship between God and man will endure beyond his lifetime.

Thankfully, it does endure. Yet it also evolves. Though we worship the same God as Abraham, we bring to our worship our own perceptions, and our own needs.

Lech L'cha
Alan Cook, 2006

There are nine *sidrot* in the Torah that derive their names from imperative verbs. Yet we are taught that these commands are issued not as harsh imprecations, but rather because the individual (or group) being spoken to stands to derive some benefit from acting upon the instruction.

This is particularly true in *Lech L'cha*. Though it is difficult for Abram to leave behind all that he has ever known, it will be beneficial to him as he becomes the progenitor of a great and prosperous nation.

Abram does not know where his journey will lead him; nonetheless, he is courageous enough to take the first steps because he has faith that God will deliver according to the promise that has been made.

We have much to learn from Abram's willingness to take this chance. We, too, are called to go forth, to explore our world and to try to make the most of it. We do not always know what fate has in store for us; we cannot foresee our destiny. But there is one thing of which we can be sure: we will get nowhere if we do not take the first steps.

Let us be willing to heed the call to go out and realize our full potential. Let us take the necessary first steps. After all, it is for our own good.

Lech L'cha
Amy Scheinerman, 2006

The *parashah* opens with Avram's call, initiating the covenant, and closes with his circumcision, fulfillment of the mark of the covenant. Avraham is depicted as a man of infinite trust in God, a model to be revered. What effect does a figure of this stature have on those around him? What constitutes religious greatness: Is it one's spiritual communion with God? one's involvement with family and community? or a balance between the two?

Eve Penner Ilsen explores these questions in "A Tale of Reb Nackhum Chernobler" in *Because God Loves Stories: An Anthology* by Steve Zeitlin (Touchstone, 1977). Reb Nakhum's selfless devotion to God seen through his wife's eyes is selfish dedication to his own piety at the expense of his family's suffering. Reb Nakhum loves God deeply but takes his family for granted. He chooses poverty and privation, and they are forced to live with his choice. We might cheer his moral victory in controlling his temper, until we consider his wife, Sarah. Abraham appears in the same mold, until we consider his Sarah, who endures privation, imprisonment, perhaps even rape, and the terror of losing her only child, all that her husband might fulfill his religious quest.

Ilsen is understandably disturbed by the story of Reb Nakhum, as we might be with the account of the *Akeidah*. She offers us a *tikkun*, an alternative ending in which Sarah teaches Nakhum that piety and God's covenant are far broader in their concerns than the holy man realized. So, too, the Sarah of our *parashah*.

Lech L'cha
Amy Scheinerman, 2007

When God commands Avraham to circumcise himself and all the males in his household as a sign of the covenant, Avraham does not respond verbally.

Midrash, however, tells us that Avraham took a detour on his way to the performance of this mitzvah. *B'reishit Rabbah* 42:8 (also 3) tells us that Avraham went first to seek the advice of three friends, Aner, Eshkol, and Mamre. Aner said, "You are already one hundred years old, yet you would inflict this pain on yourself?" Eshkol said, "Why should you make yourself distinguishable from your enemies?" Only Mamre encouraged Avraham to fulfill God's commandment: "When did God not stand by you—in the fiery furnace, in famine, and with the kings? Will you not obey God in this matter?"

Of late we see an upsurge in Jews opposing circumcision. They often speak as Aner and Eshkol, expressing concerns about pain, "mutilation," and looking different that are easily opposed on intellectual grounds but more difficult to address on the underlying emotional level. (One wonders how they respond to research documenting that circumcision protects against cancer, urinary tract infections, a variety of sexually transmitted diseases, and HIV, not to mention that lidocaine, a topical analgesic, may be used for the procedure.)

For well over three millennia, we have circumcised our sons. It is a mark of distinction and identity, connecting Jewish males to the larger Jewish community, generations past, and God. The response of Mamre still holds sway: as God has maintained us despite trials and tragedies, so should we continue.

Lech L'cha
Michael Boyden, 2008

If *Parashat B'reishit* is the tale of the creation of the world, then *Parashat Lech L'cha* describes the birth of the Jewish people.

What does *Lech l'cha* mean? It is generally translated as "Go forth." So why not just *lech*? Perhaps it means "Go **to yourself**." In that sense, Abraham is called upon by God to discover his true self, just as he will later be addressed with the same words when commanded to take Isaac to Mount Moriah.

In both cases Abraham is required to step out of his normal routine, albeit Rashi explains the call to mean "Go for your well-being and for your good," but it is not always easy to change established patterns and take the risks involved in moving forward, even if it is for our own good.

Perhaps the Torah is emphasizing the difficult choices that have to be made by spelling it out in such detail: "Leave your land, your birthplace, and your father's home."

Note, however, that it is his "father's home" that he is called upon to leave and not his own. "Go to yourself" will require Abraham to find his own identity and discover his true home elsewhere.

But the call to Abraham is also a reminder that to be Jewish is much more than to fulfill our own destiny, or even to be part of a faith community. To be a Jew involves a trifocal identity that includes not only God but also people and Land. And that is why Israel must inevitably play a key role in our lives as Jews and as teachers.

Lech L'cha
Louis Rieser, 2009

Maimonides and the midrash offer contrasting descriptions of the journey facing Abraham.

The *Mishneh Torah*, *Avodah Zarah* 3:1, describes Abraham: "When this giant was weaned, he began to roam around in his mind, while he was still small, and began to think by day and by night. . . . His mind roamed in search of understanding till he achieved the true way and understood out of his own natural intelligence."

This Abraham was a self-taught philosopher who studied the world from his youth and devised his understanding from the strength of his own intelligence. Confident in his truth, Abraham engaged those around him in dialogue until "thousands and myriads gathered round him and became part of his household, and he implanted in their hearts this great principle."

Midrash HaGadol 12:1 opens with the tale of Abraham breaking the idols in his father's shop, then moving progressively from worship of the earth to the sky, from the sun to the moon. Abraham hops from place to place adopting new beliefs only to be disappointed by them. Finally he concludes, "Unless there were someone in charge, this would not happen. It is not right to bow down to these, but to the One in charge." Then God reveals Godself to Abraham. Abraham seeks consistency, but bounces from god to god before finding God.

Two Abrahams: one who methodically and intellectually develops his faith; one who discovers her home only after a (disappointing?) journey of experience. Which are you? Do you recognize these Abrahams in your community?

וירא Vayeira

(Genesis 18:1–22:24)

For additional commentary on *Vayeira*, see "Rosh HaShanah."

Vayeira
Lawrence S. Kushner, 1995

Vayeira alav Adonai, "And there appeared to him, the Lord" (Gen. 18:1).

The Or HaChayim, noting the Hebrew syntax, asks: Why does the Torah put the one who sees before the One who is seen? One would expect the logical sequence to be as the English translation customarily renders it: "And the Lord appeared to him."

"And he said, my lords, if I have found favor in your eyes, please do not travel on past your servant" (Gen. 18:3).

The Babylonian Talmud, *Yoma* 28b, says that "Abraham, our father, kept the whole Torah." But if the Torah had not yet been given, how could he know the commandments?

"And God tested Abraham" (Gen. 22:1).

The merit of Abraham, who bound his son on the altar, was based on an awesome deed. But what did Abraham really do that was so extraordinary? Wouldn't any Jew do the same? After all, if the Holy One of Being, in all God's awesome power, appeared to you, wouldn't you also do whatever God commanded?

Vayeira
Lawrence S. Kushner, 1996

This is a *parashah* about God's appearances, appropriate to its title. What do God's appearances in the announcement and fact of Isaac's birth (chaps. 18, 21), the visitation upon Sodom and Gomorrah (chap. 19), Abraham and Sarah in Abimelech's house (chap. 20), and the *Akeidah* (chap. 22) have in common? How do they differ? Which, if any, are closest to our experiences of God's manifestation?

To what extent is chapter 21 a preparation for chapter 22—Abraham helps Hagar take Ishmael into a confrontation with death in the wilderness, Abraham himself takes Isaac to such a confrontation on Mount Moriah? What does Abraham learn from the Ishmael experience—does he apply it to the *Akeidah*?

Vayeira
Lawrence S. Kushner, 1996

B'reishit Rabbah suggests that Isaac was about thirty-seven years old at the time of the *Akeidah* and thus was a full and willing participant ("And the two of them walked together" [Gen. 22:6]). Do the moral issues change depending on whether he is a little boy or an adult?

If, as the midrash suggests, Abraham knew that God's promise of uncountable progeny through Isaac was immutable, is his willingness to ascend the mountain just playing a game with God, as God did with him at Sodom and Gomorrah (God knew that there would not be ten righteous people in the city)? Or is this the ultimate act of faith—to believe that God would not go back on the covenant and so to risk everything on that faith, trusting that he will find out in the end why God asked him to do it? Is Abraham's faith a model for us?

Vayeira: Isaac's Question
Stephen E. Cohen, 1997

Yalkut Shimoni and Ibn Ezra present opposite views of the father-son bond in the *Akeidah*.

Yalkut Shimoni   Isaac said to his father, "*Abba*, bind my hands and my feet, for the instinct to live is strong. When I see the knife, I may struggle and cause you to injure me, spoiling the sacrifice."

Ibn Ezra   The most reasonable estimate is that Isaac was about thirteen years old. And his father forced him, and bound him against his will, and his father hid the secret from him in saying, "God will see to the lamb for the offering." For if he had said, "You are to be the sacrifice," Isaac might have fled.

Comment   Ibn Ezra's stark reading of the story is at odds with nearly all other traditional commentaries on the *Akeidah*. Would the story still have its place of honor in the tradition if the mainstream had followed his version of the telling?

Vayeira: At the Last Moment
Stephen E. Cohen, 1998

What did Abraham feel in the moment of reprieve, stopped by the angel at the last possible second? Shockingly, Rashi depicts Abraham struggling to carry out his mission to completion.

Rashi   "Do not send forth your hand"—to slaughter. Then Abraham said, "If so, then I have come here for nothing. I will wound him and draw forth from him a measure of blood." The reply: "Do not do anything/*m'uma*." Do not make a blemish/*mum*.

Comment   How can Rashi imagine Abraham resisting the command to stop? Was this also a moment of testing for Abraham?

Vayeira
Mordecai Finley, 1999

Assembled and paraphrased from the *Zohar*, portion *Vayeira*, 97b–98a: What is the meaning of the verse, "The buds appear in the land, the time of pruning/song [*hazamir*] has arrived, the voice of the *tor* [turtledove] is heard in our land" (Song of Songs 2:12)? The world yearns to sing to God—it was created with that latent power. When Adam HaRishon was created with his power of uniting upper and lower worlds, the buds appeared on the earth, and the voice of God could be heard. But when Adam sinned, the earth was cursed—thorns and thistles replaced the buds. Noach was an *ish adamah* (man of the earth), but he, too, violated the hidden realms, and the strength of the earth departed. With Abraham, the "blossoms appear on the earth." The time of pruning—of circumcision—releases the song. The pruning, the cutting away of the branches of *orlah* (forbidden produce, also foreskin), allows the voice that emits from the innermost realms to be heard and is now divided up into *milim* (words) from the power of the covenant of *milah* (circumcision). The *kol* (voice) becomes *dibur* (speech), Torah revelation, with its discreet *milim*/words.

The buds that appear in the land are the fruit that will ripen into the prophecy that Israel will hear at Sinai, but . . . we will not be able to hear them really, until we press them in press of our work, not in the desire for gnostic experience, or even knowing the upper secrets for repair of those worlds.

It is only when the *tor* (תור) that is heard in the land as "guide, mystical knowledge" (from *latur*) becomes *tor-HaShem*, "the guide to/of God," that the prophecy may be drunk. We eat from the Tree of Life, we drink from the desire to fill ourselves with God, not to be masters of upper worlds.

On Simchat Torah, second-day Sh'mini Atzeret, we rejoice in the Tree of Life, we drink the wine of Noach, and because of our attachment to the covenant, we reunite worlds cast asunder.

Vayeira: Standing with God
Elaine Rose Glickman, 1999

In assigning to Abraham his tenth and most difficult trial, God seems to command instant and unquestioning obedience. "Take your only beloved son Isaac, go to Moriah, and offer him there as a burnt-offering" (Gen. 22:2). Yet God does not demand, "*Kach*/Take"; rather,

God asks, *"Kach-na /* Please take." Why would an all-powerful, all-knowing God say "please" to Abraham?

Babylonian Talmud, *Sanhedrin* **89b**   "And God said, 'Take—*na*—your son'" (Gen. 22:2). R. Shimon bar Abba said *na* is used only as the language of petition, or request. This may be compared to a king of flesh and blood who had triumphed in many wars, for he had a great soldier. In later days, he would be confronted with another tremendous battle. He said to his soldier, "I implore you to stand by me in this war—lest someone say there was no meaning in the former battles." So the Holy One, blessed be God, said to Abraham, "I have tried you through several trials, and you have withstood them all. Now stand with Me in this trial, lest it be said that there was no meaning in the former trials."

Comment   God's beseeching attitude suggests that our actions in times of difficulty affect God tremendously. How is our understanding of God's partnership with humanity reflected in R. Shimon bar Abba's teaching? How can we—like Abraham—stand with God?

Vayeira
Sheldon Marder, 2000

Mishnah Taanit notes that one of the insertions in the *Amidah* for a fast day is: "The One who answered Abraham on Mount Moriah will answer you and will hearken to the sound of your crying this day. Blessed are You, *Adonai*, the redeemer of Israel." What is meant here by "answered Abraham"? Does Abraham pray in Genesis 22?

According to one midrash (cited in *Book of Legends/Sefer HaAggadah: Legends from the Talmud and Midrash*, ed. Hayyim Nahman Bialik and Y. H. Rawnitzky, Schocken, 1992, last paragraph on p. 31): When Abraham reached out to pick up the knife, "his mouth fell wide open with weeping as a great cry of anguish erupted from him. Then, his eyes blinking frantically, he looked up to the Presence and pleaded in a rising voice, 'I lift mine eyes to the mountains, whence will my help come?'" (Ps. 121:1).

Why did the Rabbis, who celebrated Abraham as the ultimate symbol of silent submission to God's will, present this other Abraham, a man churning with raw emotion—frenzied and desperate, crying out for God's help?

Vayeira: Hineni V'ni—Hineni Avi!
Kenneth J. Weiss, 2001

"And he said, 'I am here [*hineni*], my son.' ... And the two of them went on together [*yachdav*]" (Gen. 22:7–8).

Abraham and Isaac: it took both of them for there to be a *yachdav* relationship, for *hineni* to have been spoken, heard, and understood. Even in the most difficult of times—at the extremes of human pathos—two people who share such a relationship can find strength and support in the bond that is defined by the word *hineni*.

Kierkegaard suggests that Abraham—by a leap of faith—found a way to overcome his doubts, to know in his deepest place that God would *not* demand Isaac's life. Could not this leap have been born out of their *hineni* bond? Is not a loved and fully trusted partner often central to another's healing, to a reaffirmation of life's purpose and goodness?

Does not Kohelet remind us that "two are better off than one ... for should they fall, one can raise the other" (Eccles. 4:9–10)? Might not Abraham and Isaac *both* have fallen under the weight of their terrible fears and doubts, had they not found in each other a partner to help the other stand and not collapse?

Delva Seavy Rebin writes, "Caring we cannot do just for ourselves, it grows when it's shared with others ... and it can save lives" (*Chicken Soup for the Surviving Soul: 101 Stories of Courage and Inspiration*, Health Communications, 1996, p. 192).

"*Hineni v'ni*"—*hineni avi*: "*vayeilchu sh'neihem yachdav.*"

"Here I am, my son"—Father, I'm here: "and the two of them went on together."

Vayeira
Kenneth J. Weiss, 2003

"The two of them walked on together" (Gen. 22:8).

New teenage drivers in California, at high risk behind the wheel, may not drive unless a parent or other adult (over twenty-five years old) accompanies them. Too few parents enforce this law for their own children.

Abraham and Isaac model a diametrically different behavior. On a day when his son's safety was at risk, Abraham literally refused to leave his side. For days, they rode together. For hours they walked together. Abraham would not let anything separate them: they would stay close, they *would* face the future together. At their time of peril, father and son reaffirmed—reinforced—their filial bond.

The key to the survival of family life and Jewish values is togetherness: parents teaching, parents modeling; children watching and listening—being molded by two loving hearts, four firm hands: parents and children walking life's path together.

Today, too many parents too often walk away from their kids: they give them too much freedom (call it "license"), too much money (call it a "payoff"), too much responsibility (call it "abrogation").

Parents must *want* to walk (and to drive!) with their children. Then children will want the same and the two will traverse life's path together. Be assured of this: the path is well marked. It was blazed by our ancestors who taught us how to be together, to walk together—and even what to say along the way.

Vayeira
Kenneth J. Weiss, 2004

We heard from our parents who heard from their parents—stories about a beautiful, perfect world; a garden not far from our birthplace: an unspoiled paradise. We learned that the first of our species were given everything they could need or want. We asked ourselves how we might have acted differently had we been Eden's first citizens. We affirmed that God would have been happier with our conduct than

God was with theirs. Had we been there, "The Tree" would have remained untouched, the serpent would have gone unheeded. Had we given life to the world's first children, we would have taught them family love, not sibling rivalry. Indeed, Noah might well have inherited a whole different (a wholly better!) world than the one whose destruction he survived.

Over the years, we came to understand many important lessons that prepared Abraham and me to be God's partners. We learned of the mitzvah of hospitality; we learned of evil and punishment through the experience of Sodom and Gomorrah; we learned of family dysfunction by experiencing it ourselves as we wrestled with the place of Ishmael and his mother Hagar.

Ultimately, we learned what pain *really* was: the (threatened) loss of our beloved son Isaac.

Additionally, we sensed what God already knew: that the world depends as much on human intervention as it does on divine direction . . . we knew we would "Go" when we were called.

Despite our humanness, God needed us as partners—to speak God's words, to teach and inculcate God's ways so that humanity could understand and live by them. When God commanded us to help, we could only assent.

Vayeira
Alan Cook, 2005

"Lot's wife looked back, and she thereupon turned into a pillar of salt" (Gen. 19:26).

Why did Lot's wife look back? Sometimes what is behind us seems more comforting than that which lies ahead. Change may appear distasteful; it involves learning new tasks, adjusting to a new way of doing things. The landscape that stretches out before us may appear foreign and frightening, compared to the one that is already familiar.

What would we have done in this situation? Would we have been prepared to forge ahead and look to distant horizons, or would we also have felt a pull from the familiar and turned around to get one final glance?

It is undeniably important to remain conscious of our past. But we must not get mired in it. If we insist on continually looking back, we may become like Lot's wife: a stationary, immobile pillar of salt. If instead, we can bring ourselves to move forward and openly embrace new opportunities, we will be well-equipped to face our future.

This is the difference between Abraham's family and Lot's. Abraham explored new possibilities; Lot stuck to the tried and true. Abraham set out for unchartered territory, "and Lot went with him" (Gen. 12:4). Lot settled in familiar territory, while Abraham "moved his tent" (Gen. 13). And then Lot's wife turned back to look upon the destruction of her home.

When life presents us with such challenges and possibilities, will we be more like Abraham, or more like Lot?

Vayeira
Amy Scheinerman, 2006

Tradition holds that Avraham underwent ten trials. The first and last are recorded in *Vayeira*.

Each is introduced by לך (*l'cha*), "go." However, the first word that comes to mind in reading the *Akeidah* is "fanaticism."

Numerous midrashim imagine Avraham eager to sacrifice Yitzchak on Mount Moriah, the awe-filled locus for the awe-full event. In some, Avraham actually completes the sacrifice despite the *malach*'s attempt to stay his hand. In one Avraham draws a log of blood; in another he completes the sacrifice and Yitzchak spends a year in the yeshivah of Shem and Ever. This midrash might well function to explain how Yitzchak, having experienced *t'chiyat hameitim* (resurrection), could have authored the second *b'rachah* of the *Amidah*, but we cannot help but ask whether Avraham, who challenged God concerning the fate of Sodom and Gomorrah but did not utter a word of protest concerning God's command to sacrifice Yizchak, was a religious fanatic.

Seymour Panitz, in his clever and insightful midrashic novel *Abraham and Sons* (Devora Publishing, 2001), posits that Yitzchak was the religious fanatic in the family, and the *Akeidah* was a complex and clever scheme concocted by Avraham and Ishmael to satisfy Yitzchak's religious fervor without compromising his life.

We see in our world examples of religious fanaticism, bent on death and destruction, failing to recognize the image of God in those who are different from themselves. Torah, midrash, and Panitz's version all confirm the need to diffuse fanaticism.

Vayeira
Amy Scheinerman, 2007

The High Holy Day theme of balancing justice and mercy returns. Concerning God's plan to destroy Sodom and Gomorrah, *B'reishit Rabbah* 39:6 tells us that Avraham reminds God of the divine promise not to bring another catastrophic deluge. What God contemplates is equivalent, Avraham implies. Rabbi Levi expands "Shall not the Judge of all the earth do justice" (Gen. 18:25) to include, "If you want the world to endure, there can be no absolute justice. If you want absolute justice, the world cannot endure. Yet you hold the cord by both ends, desiring both the world and absolute justice. Unless you relent a bit, the world will not endure."

Burton Visotzky, in *The Genesis of Ethics*, tells us that the experience of negotiating on behalf of the righteous in Sodom and Gomorrah taught Avraham the futility of bargaining with God, who holds all the cards. Accordingly, Avraham raises no protest when God commands him to bind his son Yitzchak as an offering.

Yet we revere Avraham for his attempt to negotiate with God. Amidst a lengthy invective concerning idolatry, Torah comments: לא תעשון כן ליהוה אלהיכם (*Lo taasun kein l'Adonai Eloheichem*), "Do not worship *Adonai* your God in like manner" (Deut. 12:4). The פשט (*p'shat*, "simple meaning") is that Israel should not worship God using pillars, idols, sacred posts, or any other manner employed by the Canaanites to worship their deities. The Kotzker Rebbe, Menachem Mendel, interpreted the seemingly superfluous כן (*kein*, "thus" or "yes") to teach us that we should not live our Jewish lives only saying כן to God. Rather, questioning and challenging minds are essential to genuine כונה (*kavanah*, "intentionality"). Our covenant requires no less.

Vayeira
Michael Boyden, 2008

Parashat Vayeira includes the well-known tale of Abraham's plea to God to save the lives of the inhabitants of Sodom and Gomorrah. "Will You sweep away the innocent along with the guilty?" he pleads (Gen. 18:23).

Whereas the *p'shat* has Abraham turning to God and saying, "Shall not the Judge of all the earth deal justly?" (Gen. 18:25), the midrash takes the interrogative *hei* with which the verse begins and turns it into a definite article: "The Judge of all the earth will not exercise justice." As *B'reishit Rabbah* puts it, "If You want a world, there cannot be justice, and if You want justice, then there will be no world."

While the efforts that Abraham is prepared to invest in order to save these two wicked cities may seem admirable, one cannot help but notice the marked contrast between his actions here and the way he behaves later in the same *parashah*.

As *Parashat Vayeira* draws to a close, we read how Hagar and Ishmael are expelled without mercy and how Abraham takes his son Isaac to sacrifice him on Mount Moriah. In both cases, Abraham responds to God's call without protest. Where is the fighter for human rights who earlier exclaimed, "Will You sweep away the innocent along with the guilty?"

Is it that, in the case of Ishmael and Isaac, Abraham is prepared to set aside ethical considerations, seeking to justify his actions by saying that he is just obeying orders? Or is it that he is prepared to go to extreme lengths to save others, while leaving the members of his family alone to fend for themselves?

Vayeira
Amy Scheinerman, 2008

As we read the *Akeidah*, Yitzchak's passivity in the face of his father's passion is painfully clear. Midrash does its best to suggest Yitzchak acts not only in obedience to his father, but according to his own priorities, and therefore possesses the will to resist the *satan*, but Torah's account of Yitzchak's later life undermines this effort.

In *Finding Meaning in the Second Half of Life: How to Finally, Really Grow Up* (Gotham, 2006), Jungian psychoanalyst James Hollis explores the terrain of midlife and provides guidance for navigating the turbulent emotional topography that prevents many of us from realizing our authentic selves, a journey that requires us to separate from the expectations and values of our parents in order to live our true destiny. His book resonates with the *Akeidah*, from the early question, "How is it possible that I can be in my world, and that of my parents at the same time?" to his prescient observation that "serving a past image unconsciously may very well prove to be that oldest of religious heresies—*idolatry*! Idolatry is often a comforting artifact of the ego, but it is an impediment to the renewing agenda of the soul." Hollis's book is a guide for renewal and spiritual rebirth through psychological and spiritual maturation.

Torah suggests that Yitzchak did not find meaning in the second half of life, overcome and overwhelmed as he was by living his father's values and agenda and nearly forfeiting his life to them. Hollis contends that many of the maladies of modern life—depression, addictions, crises of every stripe—bespeak our need to find our own path and destiny. Would that Yitzchak had had this book!

Vayeira
Amy Scheinerman, 2009

Rabbi Mendel of Satanov taught that one of the essential qualities of a *lev tov* (good-hearted person) is the *midah* of *dan k'kaf z'chut* (giving the benefit of the doubt).

In Genesis, chapter 20, Avraham tells Avimelech of Gerar that Sarah is his sister, as he told the pharaoh of Egypt in chapter 12. The pharaoh is afflicted with a plague to warn him that Sarai is a married woman. Avimelech, however, learns of Sarah's status in a dream.

Upon awakening, Avimelech turns directly to God, the source of his dream, asking the eternal theodicy question, "O Lord, will You slay people even though innocent?" (Gen. 20:4). To Avraham, Avimelech says, "When I did this, my heart was blameless and my hands were clean" (Gen. 20:5). God responds that Avimelech's blameless heart is well-known and hence the dream was provided to keep him from doing and experiencing harm. The Torah exonerates Avimelech, but Rashi does not. Drawing on *B'reishit Rabbah* 52:6, Rashi comments on Gen. 20:6: "It is true that from the start you did not intend to sin, but there is no cleanness of hands here. It was not because of you that you did not touch her; rather, I spared you from sin."

It seems that although Avraham assumes the worst (he tells Avimelech in Gen. 20:11, "I thought surely there is no fear of God in this place, and they will kill me because of my wife"), Torah is willing to give Avimelech the benefit of the doubt. Yet later commentators line up behind Avraham. Why is this? Is it human nature to presume the worst about strangers? Is this a presumption concerning people in power? Where are the proper boundaries to the principle of *dan k'kaf z'chut*?

חיי שרה *Chayei Sarah*
(Genesis 23:1–25:18)

Chayei Sarah
Lawrence S. Kushner, 1995

"Hear / understand / listen / hearken to me" (Gen. 23:6, 8, 11, 13, 14).

We are used to reading these verses as a (mere) bargaining ritual in which everyone does his best to avoid suggesting that the land can actually be sold for money. But if this is a mere exercise, why all the repetition of *sh'ma-eini*, and the emphasis on remarks being made "in the ears of the Hittites"? What do Abraham, the Hittites, and Efron want each other to hear? And which (if any) translation of *sh'ma* above seems the appropriate one? [Do we learn anything about **the Sh'ma** from this passage?]

"Afterward Abraham buried Sarah his wife in ['into'? Why *el* and not *b'*?] the cave of the field of Machpelah before . . . Hebron" (Gen. 23:19).

Much is made of the fact that Moses's burial place is unknown. Why is the burial place of the First Family so specifically identified? Look at all the trouble that would have been avoided on the West Bank if the place had not been identified! Did God learn from the "mistake" of Machpelah in Moses's case?

"His servant, the elder of his house" (Gen. 24:2).

Tradition assumes, from Gen. 15:2, that the *eved* (servant) who seeks a wife for Isaac is Eliezer. Why then does the text call him only *ha-eved*? What might be suggested in Gen. 14:12–14 by the *eved*'s deciding on the signs for identifying Isaac's prospective wife, rather than asking God or Abraham? Would you choose a spouse by such signs?

Chayei Sarah
Lawrence S. Kushner, 1996

In Gen. 24:12ff., Abraham's servant conceives a test to identify the woman he should choose for Isaac's wife. Why does Abraham not come up with this idea himself? This mission makes it absolutely clear that Isaac or his line will inherit Abraham's house and not the servant (see Gen. 15:2). What are we to learn from the servant's altruism?

Chayei Sarah: Old Age
Stephen E. Cohen, 1997

K'li Yakar notes that the text comments that Abraham was "old, advanced in years" (Gen. 24:1), but that he had been described the same way thirty-seven years earlier (Gen. 18:11).

K'li Yakar From the birth of Isaac until Sarah's death, it was a "triple-braided cord," for Abraham's life-force was increased both by virtue of his wife and by virtue of his son Isaac. And throughout all those days he stood upright and did not weaken (as is common for the elderly), for those were days of joy and blessing for him. But before Isaac's birth, he had no joy except from his wife, and after Sarah's death, he had no joy except from his son. Therefore these two moments in Abraham's life were equivalent to each other.

Comment Is it healthy or neurotic to regard our own vitality as the "sum" of the lives around us?

Chayei Sarah: Timely Death
Stephen E. Cohen, 1998

The first two metaphors offered in this midrash, by R. Y'hudah and R. Abahu, contrast death from old age, which is both natural and acceptable, with premature death, which is unnatural and wrong. The aggadah that follows, however, suggests that there is a hidden, divine wisdom at work when God "rises early" to take us.

***B'reishit Rabbah* 62:5**   What is the difference between early death and the death of the elderly? R. Y'hudah says: This oil lamp—when it goes out by itself, it is beneficial for both the oil and for the wick. But when it is extinguished beforehand, it is evil for both the oil and the wick. R. Abahu said: This fig when it is picked at the proper time, it is beneficial for both the tree and the fruit. But when it is picked too early, it is harmful for both the tree and the fruit. R. Chiya (others say R. Akiva and others say R. Chalafta) and his students used to rise early and sit and learn under a certain fig tree. They noticed that the owner of the tree would rise early and pick the fruit. They said, "Perhaps he suspects us of stealing his fruit," and they moved to another spot. He came after them and said, "My masters! The mitzvah with which you honored me, of sitting and learning under my fig tree, is lost to me!" They replied, "We thought that you might suspect us." He reassured them and they returned to their place. The next day he rose up early again, but did not pick; the sun blazed and the fruit rotted. They said, "The owner of the fig tree knew the proper time to pick, and the Holy One knows the proper time for the righteous to depart from the world. As it is written, 'My beloved went down to his garden, to the bed of spices' [Song of Songs 6:2]."

Comment   In your experience, have mourners been comforted by the notion that God had "gathered up" their departed loved one?

Chayei Sarah
Morrison Bial, 1999

"The life of Sarah" (Gen. 23:1). Why is the account of the death of Sarah called "the life of Sarah," just as Jacob's death is told in *Va-y'chi*, "and he lived"? Their days on earth were so filled with life that when they died all we could see was the intensity of their lives.

"Was a hundred and seven and twenty years" (Gen. 23:1). R. Akiva told his students that Esther was queen over 127 provinces (Esther

1:1). Akiva said that Sarah was rewarded for her faithfulness by having her distant daughter become a mighty queen and savior of her people. We would say that it was just a coincidence, but Akiva had a reason. His age was that of Roman cruelty. Being a Jew meant persecution. Why continue? So that even if we do not see a reward for our faithfulness, our progeny will.

"To weep for her" (Gen. 23:2). The Sages said that meant to eulogize her. Abraham's eulogy, beginning with "a woman of valor," was so beautiful that his family remembered it and centuries later Solomon included it at the end of Proverbs (Eliyahu Kitov, *Sefer HaParashiyot*, p. 289).

"Cave of Machpelah" (Gen. 23:9). Why was Abraham so intent on that parcel of land? Midrash tells us that he entered the cave while chasing a lamb. He was struck by the marvelous aroma and realized that this was the tomb of Adam and Eve and the proper burial place for himself and his family. This sounds like a story of no worth, but it is significant: If the tomb of Adam and Eve was blessed with such an aroma, it means that they died in God's good odor. Which means no Original Sin. If God could forgive the first errant pair, He could certainly forgive their children.

"Four hundred shekels" (Gen. 23:15). This was an exorbitant sum, and Ephron knew he had Abraham in a vise. He could not refuse any amount after his fervent plea. Abraham bought an otherwise useless cave while Jacob would later pay one-quarter of the sum for land to dwell on (Gen. 33:19).

"Ten camels" (Gen. 24:10). Why ten camels? Each camel was led or ridden by one of Abraham's servants. The men were now Jews and thus they formed a minyan.

Chayei Sarah
Sheldon Marder, 2000

"Abraham gave everything he had to Isaac" (Gen. 25:5). What did Abraham give his son? Said R. Nehemiah: He gave him the blessing as a legacy. For the Holy One had said to Abraham, "'And be a blessing.' The blessings are given into your possession to bless whomever you desire." And Abraham gave them to Isaac (*B'reishit Rabbah*, according to Rashi).

What do we give our children? "In their great love," writes Yehuda Amichai, "my parents saved me from disappointment, / from pain and sorrow. Now I am left with their savings / plus the pain I would like to spare my children.... / My mother was a prophet and didn't know it.... / My father was God and didn't know it..." (*Open Closed Open*, Mariner Books, 2006).

Parents as mythic figures. What do parents know—what *can* they know—about the legacy they leave? Can parents ever grasp what they are and what they will come to represent in the lives of their children?

Davar acher: "And Abraham breathed his last and he was gathered to his kin" (Gen. 25:8). Again, Amichai:

> When a man dies, they say "He was gathered unto his fathers."
> As long as he is alive, his fathers are gathered within him,
> each cell of his body and soul a delegate from one of his
> thousands of fathers since the beginning of time.
> (*Open Closed Open*, Mariner Books, 2006).

Like a well-crafted poem, *Chayei Sarah* begins with the death of one parent and ends with the death of the other. Like a great poem, it leaves us reflecting on what is most precious and, at the same time, incomprehensible.

Chayei Sarah: More Than Yesterday, Less Than Tomorrow
Kenneth J. Weiss, 2001

"Isaac ... raised his eyes.... Rebekah raised her eyes.... Isaac ... took Rebekah ... she became his wife, and he loved her" (Gen. 24:63–64, 24:67).

Isaac and Rebekah were taken with one another. He was vulnerable: mourning for his dead mother, traumatized still in the wake of events known ever after as the *Akeidah*. She was ready: she acceded to Eliezer's request that she accompany him from her birthplace to Canaan to become the wife of his master Abraham's son.

Did they fall in love? No—they did not fall in love: one might fall off a horse or off a cliff. One can fall down. A couple might, as Rabbi Reuven Bulka teaches, fall into infatuation, but they—over time—must rise if they are to reach the level of true love. Perhaps Torah hints at this when it tells us that Isaac and Rebekah both raised their eyes as they approached one another. Bulka would say that infatuation ended before it began. Love is a rising—their eyes hint at that truth.

Love, I teach my couples, is of the mind ever so much more than it is of the heart. Thus, true love is a decision: the decision to commit to another, and to tend to and deepen that commitment forever.

Samson Raphael Hirsch writes that "the wedding is not the summit but only the seed of future love." Love must grow after the marital vows are spoken—and it will grow if the decision to commit to and love the other is reaffirmed and strengthened daily. My wife wears a pendant, its message: "I love you *yoteir me-etmol, pachot mimachar* (more than yesterday, less than tomorrow)"—and that is love.

Chayei Sarah
Kenneth J. Weiss, 2002

"Isaac . . . took Rebekah as his wife" (Gen. 24:67).

We really were meant for each other. Although distant cousins (geographically and by bloodline), the parallels in our lives cannot be written off as coincidences.

Significant males negatively impacted us both: Isaac's *n'shamah* (soul) was damaged at Moriah. His dad's virtual silence as they ascended; the knife poised to slay him; the unbridgeable chasm that opened between son and father in the aftermath—these scarred Isaac forever. My father is best characterized as—reticent. His mother—my grandmother Milcah—was a much more central figure in my family than he ever was. Then there's my brother Laban, whose deceitfulness I witnessed even in Eliezer's presence.

Both of us were shaped by strong and influential mothers. My mother let me determine whether I'd marry Isaac or not. When I resolved to do so, she blessed me as few have ever been blessed (Gen.

24:60). Isaac's mother Sarah was his haven in a world of turmoil. Despite her age, Sarah was his *ima* (mother) in every sense of the word: her very tent symbolized her maternal nurturing. With her death the tent sat empty—until I came along.

Both of us made difficult decisions at crucial, transitional times. At Moriah, Isaac knew where he had to be, knew what he had to do: he chose to face and overcome God's test of faith. I, too, faced a difficult decision. No—not at the well (watering the camels came naturally: my instincts and values impelled me so to act). The difficult decision came later, when I determined to leave my family and home to marry a stranger in a strange land.

We were indeed one another's *bashert*! On "Day One," I knew it; we both did. Marrying, we grew our love and shared our life stories. Thus we learned that God had planned our union all along.

Chayei Sarah
Kenneth J. Weiss, 2003

Last Shabbat, we read that "Abraham and Sarah were old, advanced in years" (Gen. 18:11).

Yet, despite their ages, this couple still had plenty of living to do. Indeed: they had yet to experience the destruction of Sodom and Gomorrah, an encounter with Abimelech the king of Gerar, the birth of Isaac, the expulsion of Hagar and Ishmael, and—ultimately—the *Akeidah*.

Throughout their years together, Sarah and Abraham's strong, nurturing marriage protected them both from the ravages of time.

Then Sarah died. Abraham mourned the loss of his life's partner, bewailed the loss of the mutual love that kept them both youthful.

Kyla Epstein Schneider pictures Abraham weeping as he thinks back over all they shared: "She wandered from land to land with me. She went hungry with me. She spent most of her life childless and struggled with my need for an heir. And in her last days, she had to confront the fact that I would bring her son up to Moriah as a sacrifice to God" (*Living Torah: Selections from Seven Years of Torat Chayim*, ed. Elaine Rose Glickman, URJ Press, 2005).

Having lost Sarah and her restorative presence, Abraham felt the weight of the years, as we read in **our** *parashah* (Gen. 24:1), "Abraham was **now** old."

Chayei Sarah
Kenneth J. Weiss, 2004

"I am a . . ." (Gen. 23:4).

Abraham—whose descendants would one day lay legitimate claim to the Land of Israel—introduces himself to the Hittites of Hebron as גר ותושב (*ger v'toshav*)—in R. E. Friedman's translation "an alien and a visitor."

The word גר (*ger*) is descriptive of more than an individual's socio/legal status. The word's various English nuances depict the complex reality of feeling like—and living as—an alien. The verb from which גר is derived (גור) can be translated as "to dwell." It can also mean "to fear" and "to quarrel." Though Sarah's death precipitated Abraham's meeting with the Hittites, we know little about Abraham's state of mind; surely, he was still mourning his loss. We can imagine some level of trepidation evoked by his audacious bid to purchase a burial place from the Hittites. We can also affirm that there was—if not a quarrel—at least a "respectful disagreement" over whether the land would become his as a gift or through purchase (see Gen. 23:9–15).

Beginning with Abraham, Jews have experienced alienation in many lands, among many peoples, Egypt being the paradigm. Zipporah and Moses named their Egyptian-born son גרשום (Gershom), "an alien in a foreign land" (Exod. 2:22). Later, Moses urged our ancestors never to forget their Egyptian vassalage: Upon entering Canaan, recite, "My father . . . went down to Egypt and was alienated there [ויגר שם, *vayagar sham*]" (Deut. 26:5).

Jews are commanded "to know the soul of [i.e., to identify with] the גר. . . ." Why? Because if we are ever mindful that we "were aliens in the land of Egypt" (Lev. 19:34, etc.), we will actually feel their fear—their insecurity—and thus "feel" our moral obligation to love, welcome, and comfort גרים (*gerim*) in our own midst. An alien is never at home, never free of fear, never far from quarrel (or outright abuse), ever targeted for conversion. In our brilliant "holy tongue," a single verb goes to the heart—and the depth—of how Abraham felt (how anyone feels) being an alien.

Chayei Sarah
Alan Cook, 2005

In a much-acclaimed episode of *The Mary Tyler Moore Show*, Chuckles the Clown, a local children's television host, dies unexpectedly in a freak accident. When Mary and her friends hear the news, they are struck by the silliness of the circumstances surrounding Chuckles' death, and they find themselves coping with the loss of their friend by making jokes about the incident. This continues through the funeral service, until the preacher notices Mary laughing and asks her to share her memories of the laughter that Chuckles brought to all. At that invitation, Mary bursts into tears.

In moments of grief, each individual responds differently. Some are consumed by waves of sadness, others smile as they remember precious times shared with their dear departed. When his beloved wife passes on, Abraham marks the moment by taking time לספד לשרה ולבכתה (*lispod l'Sarah v'livkotah*), "to mourn for Sarah and to bewail her" (Gen. 23:2). He then goes about other important business.

The miniscule כ that appears in the word *v'livkotah* in the Torah scroll is considered by the Baal HaTurim to be an indication that Abraham mourned for just a brief period. It is not that Abraham was unaffected by his loss; he merely recognized that he could not allow his grief to become all-consuming, lest it prevent him from accomplishing significant tasks.

Mourners should be afforded the opportunity to grieve in the manner that they see fit, for as long as they desire. But when they rejoin our communal circle, let us encourage them to recall their loved ones not only with tears, but occasionally with laughter. For while "weeping may tarry with the night, joy cometh in the morning."

Chayei Sarah
Amy Scheinerman, 2006

Oscar Wilde said, "Romance should never begin with sentiment. It should begin with science and end with a settlement."

When Avraham sends Eliezer to Haran to find a wife for Yitzchak, Eliezer pursues his task with scientific determination, designing a strategy to determine the inner character of the women he meets. He cements the deal with an impressive settlement of silver, gold, and garments for Rivkah (perhaps not what Wilde meant by "settlement").

Yet the passage seems purposefully tinged with romance. When Eliezer and Rivkah arrive in *Eretz Yisrael* we read וישא עיניו (*vayisa einav*, "[Yitzchak] raised his eyes" [Gen. 24:63]) and then ותשא רבקה את עיניה (*vatisa Rivkah et eineha*, "Rikvah raised her eyes" [Gen. 24:64]). When the language seems almost comical—ותפל מעל הגמל (*vatipol mei-al hagamal*, "she fell from her camel" [Gen. 24:64])—Rashi draws on *Targum Onkelos* and Ps. 37:34 to disavow us of the *p'shat* in favor of "gracefully alit from her camel."

Moreover, the passage is bracketed by two episodes in the life of Avraham that reinforce a romantic interpretation: Avraham's purchase of *M'arat HaMachpelah* (the Cave of Machpelah) to bury his beloved Sarah, and his marriage to Keturah, which Rashi tells us was actually remarriage to Hagar, called here Keturah (meaning "fragrance" or "incense") because her deeds were as pleasing as incense and because she had remained chaste since the day she separated from Avraham long ago.

We value rationalism, aesthetics, and mysticism. Does a romantic reading of this passage detract from the Torah's theme of divine providence or even levelheaded Jewish thinking? Does it diminish the seriousness of Eliezer's fulfillment of Avraham's directive, and Yitzhak's marriage to Rivkah? Or perhaps, is the message that all our human proclivities can be marshalled in service of God?

Chayei Sarah
Amy Scheinerman, 2007

Nearing the end his life, Avraham entreats his servant Eliezer to find a wife for Isaac: "I will make you swear by the Lord, the God of heaven and the God of the earth, that you will not take a wife for my son from the daughters of the Canaanites among whom I dwell, but will go to the land of my birth and get a wife for my son Isaac" (Gen. 24:3). As Abravanel astutely points out, if Avraham's objection to the Canaanites concerns their idolatrous practices, Nahor and Betuel are no better, and perhaps not preferable to Aner and Eshkol, whom Avraham esteems. *Midrash HaGadol* attempts to answer this question by explaining that Avraham is in the proselytizing business and feels it is important to begin with his own kith and kin, who are more promising proselytes. The midrash has Avraham quote Isaiah, "From your own flesh to not hide yourself" (Isa. 58:7).

The Ran (Rabbi Nissim ben Reuven of Girondi) explains that Avraham's concern is not the beliefs of Aner and Eshkol, as opposed to Nahor and Betuel, but rather the evil deeds of the Canaanites compared with those of Terah's people (see Lev. 18:3). The Ran held that beliefs, however misguided, are not hereditary, but growing up witnessing evil deeds leaves a lasting impression that is transmitted from one generation to the next. Rabbi Samson Raphael Hirsch adds: the influence of the Canaanites will be more potent since Isaac lives among them.

Perhaps this is why Torah notes "the God of heaven and the God of the earth"—the influences of ideas and behavior are both significant to consider in so many arenas today.

Chayei Sarah
Janice Garfunkel, 2009

Have you noticed how matriarchal Genesis is? It is true that the "founders" of Judaism are the three patriarchs—three men—but it was their mothers and not their fathers who determined who carried the mantle.

Abraham had two sons. Did his firstborn, Ishmael, become the standard-bearer of the new faith? No, Sarah's firstborn and only son, Isaac, did (and the Holy One made it clear that being the son of Abraham was not sufficient to secure the tradition; the heir must be the son of Sarah). Isaac had two sons. Did his firstborn and preferred son, Esau, get to inherit the birthright? No, Rebekah's favorite, Jacob, did; Rebekah made sure of that. The mother's plans (and the divine prophecy she received when pregnant) overrode primogeniture. Jacob grew up and had twelve sons of his own with four women. Did Jacob's firstborn, Reuven, become the focus of the last fourteen chapters of Genesis? No, but Rachel's firstborn (not her second), Joseph, did.

Sarah, Rebekah, and Rachel determined the early direction and formation of the Hebrew people; it was the women of Genesis who anointed our patriarchs.

So perhaps our Jewish cultural trait of strong "bossy" (e.g., powerful) women originates as long ago as the first families of the Hebrew people. May we go from strength to strength!

תולדות *Tol'dot*

(Genesis 25:19–28:9)

Tol'dot

Lawrence S. Kushner, 1995

V'rav yaavod tza-ir, "And the older shall serve the younger" (Gen. 25:23).

This is God's answer to Rebekah's question in v. 22, *lamah zeh anochi* ("why do I exist?"), suggesting that Rebekah's purpose is to make sure that her elder son serves the younger. Isn't Rebekah only fulfilling God's charge to her by showing Jacob how to acquire the blessing Isaac wants to give Esau? If so, why do we view Rebekah so negatively? Should Rebekah have interpreted God's answer differently?

"She is my sister" (Gen. 26:7).

Didn't Abraham tell Isaac about his misadventures with this story? Critical theory, of course, holds that the three sister-wife accounts represent a common story in different local versions. More interesting is the traditional view that this incident was enacted three times, by father and son. *Vayeilchu sh'neihem yachdav* ("And the two of them walked on together" [Gen. 22:8]) appears only in the *Akeidah*, but does it apply here as well? Why is this encounter so crucial that Isaac and Rebekah must experience it as well as Abraham and Sarah?

"And Esau hated Jacob" (Gen. 27:41).

The Torah tells us to honor and revere our father and mother and not hate our brother in our heart. Esau clearly obeyed the filial mitzvah (or did he do so only toward his father?) but violated the fraternal one. While the Torah seems neutral, even positive, about Esau, Rabbinic literature is distinctly negative. Does this suggest that the fraternal relationship is more important than the filial one?

Tol'dot
Lawrence S. Kushner, 1996

The Rabbis, determined to see Esau as unworthy of the rights of inheritance, interpret Gen. 35:28 (*tzayid b'fiv*) as "entrapment—i.e., lying—was in his mouth," leading him to say the things that made Isaac love him. Is there any evidence of this in the text? Why do the Rabbis feel Isaac is naive—or over-trusting? Is this a positive or a negative quality?

Isaac *m'tzacheik* with Rebekah (Gen. 26:8). In Gen. 24:64, Rebekah literally falls off her camel upon seeing Isaac. Isaac is the only patriarch described in such a sensual fashion. He also knows how to pray effectively (Gen. 25:21) and work hard (all the well digging). What are we to learn from this variety of character traits?

The midrash argues that because Isaac knowingly gives Jacob his blessing in Gen. 28:3–4, this demonstrates that Isaac really wanted to bless him, canceling out the deception of the previous chapter. Do you agree?

Tol'dot: To Give Blessing
Stephen E. Cohen, 1997

In the text, Isaac's blessing follows upon the physical act of being fed. The following two comentaries reflect further upon the elaborate "dance of blessing" that transpires between father and son, Isaac and Jacob.

Baalei Hatosafot "And he brought wine" (Gen. 27:25). But where did he get the wine? We do not find that his mother gave him wine. The angel Michael brought him wine from the Garden of Eden. This was the wine of Blessing, which we also find with Abraham, when Melchizedek, king of Salem, brought forth wine and bread. And there too, after drinking, he blessed him (Gen. 14:18–19).

Sforno "And he smelled the smell of his clothes" (Gen. 27:27). To expand his soul through the pleasure of smell.

Comment Does the giving of blessings usually require a physical interaction of give and take between the one giving and the one receiving the blessing? Or is this specific to the personalities of Isaac and Jacob?

Tol'dot: The Fragrance of Eden
Stephen E. Cohen, 1998

Although the Rabbis of the midrash inhabited a world distant from the nomadic life of the patriarchs, they were much closer to the sights and smells of the world of the Torah than we are today.

B'reishit Rabbah "And he kissed him and he smelled the smell of his clothes and he blessed him" (Gen. 27:27). R. Yochanan said: There is no smell worse than the smell of washed goatskins, yet the text says, "He smelled the smell of his clothes and he blessed him"? In the moment that our father Jacob went to his father, the fragrance of Eden entered with him.

S'fat Emet Our Sages have commented, "There is no smell worse than that of goatskins. The fragrance of Eden entered with him." But we must ask, "What is the smell of his clothes?" The point is that each person through their actions acquires garments for their soul. By means of righteous actions, we earn garments for our soul in the world-to-come, and in this world we may receive a whiff of that clothing that our soul wears in the Garden of Eden. This is the meaning of "he smelled the smell of his clothes," and of the comment that the fragrance of Eden entered with him. Isaac saw that Jacob was attached to the divine source, and so he blessed him.

Comment Are R. Yochanan and the S'fat Emet each, in their own way, attempting to make sense of the "stink" of Jacob's behavior?

Tol'dot
Morrison Bial, 1999

"For she was barren" (Gen. 25:21). Is there a lesson in the fact that all three patriarchs had wives who were barren? It took a miracle for Sarah to bear a son, and both Rebekah and Rachel had to be prayed for before they could bear. Meanwhile the wives who did bear children readily were disparaged: Hagar and Leah get short shrift.

"And the children struggled together within her" (Gen. 25:22). Rashi speaks of the unborn Esau wanting to attend pagan rites whereas Jacob wanted to attend the yeshivah of Shem and Ever. Rashi forgot that the Talmud says that each fetus is instructed in the Torah by an angel. Just before it is born, the angel slaps it on the upper lip—which forms the indentation there—and all is forgotten. However, this makes later study easier as the paths in the brain are set (Babylonian Talmud, *Nidah* 30b). So the prenatal Jacob did not have to go to the yeshivah; he had his own private angelic tutor.

"Isaac loved Esau" (Gen. 25:28). Torah says the love was born as Esau supplied Isaac with venison. Some rabbis were not satisfied. R. Menachem Mendel of Kotzk maintained that Esau donned tallit and *t'fillin* and wore *payot* and led the daily minyan services to dupe his father. Yet Esau's pride made him hate the truly pious Jacob. The casting of biblical worthies as ultra-pious Chasidim of the eighteenth century results from the rabbis' conviction that this was the only Jewish way.

Tol'dot
Sheldon Marder, 2000

"When Isaac was old" (Gen. 27:1). While marveling at Abraham's and Isaac's similarities (both were blessed, both were called "old," both had a righteous son and a wicked son, and both had wives who were barren), the midrash wonders: Why were the matriarchs, Sarah and Rebekah, barren? Because, according to several sages, God desired their prayer. The Holy One said, "They are rich, they are beautiful—if I give them children, they won't pray [אינן מתפלוֹת]" (*Tanchuma, Tol'dot*, sec. 9).

Is the midrash suggesting that parenthood should not come so easily—not as easily, say, as good looks and good fortune? Might this midrash point to the value of self-judgment and self-examination [S. R. Hirsch's interpretation of להתפלל (prayer)]—entailing a thorough consideration of one's motives and readiness—before becoming a parent? Does the underlying logic of this midrash insist on a relationship with God as a prerequisite to parenthood? How is our spirituality enriched by becoming a parent? And how is our parenting enriched by developing a deeper relationship with God?

Tol'dot: *Lamah Zeh Anochi!* Rebekah's Inner Turmoils
Kenneth J. Weiss, 2001

"If it's like this, why do I exist?" (Gen. 25:22—R. E. Friedman).

In her youth, Rebekah seemed secure, self-assured: at the well with Eliezer, in her father's house as she—without hesitation—declared her willingness to move to Canaan and become Isaac's wife, in Sarah's tent where love began. Then, her troubles started; she knew turmoil in her roles as a woman, wife, mother.

- First, when Rebekah wished to become pregnant, she learned that she was infertile. Only after Isaac prayed to *YHVH* on her behalf could she conceive (Gen. 25:21).
- Second, her pregnancy was not an easy one. A difficult pregnancy caused her to wonder if there was a purpose to this endless inner turmoil. "If it's like this, why do I exist?" *YHVH* responded by telling her, "Two nations are in your womb, and two peoples will be dispersed from your insides" (Gen. 25:23—R. E. Friedman): you'll have twins.
- One interpreter, Simcha Bunim of Przysucha suggests that—before God revealed that she was carrying twins—Rebekah "thought she was bearing only one child, and therefore she assumed that the convulsive movements when she passed by houses of study and heathen temples were indicative of the struggle between the good impulse and the evil impulse in her (unborn) child." Rebekah, in other words, was agitated by the

"inner struggle that she thought was taking place within her (single unborn) child. Good or evil . . .": which impulse would prevail? (*Kol Simchah*).
- Rebekah's turmoil extended for many more years, through her sons' unfolding competition and her involvement in it.

The question *"Lamah zeh anochi?"* might well have been on Rebekah's lips often, as her life seemed to carry her from one struggle to the next. That question—asked still today by people in extremis—challenges the fundamental goodness of life. Ellen Frankel's *The Five Books of Miriam* sums up the attitude of a person beset by turmoil. Rebekah (midrashically) recalls, "Mine was an elemental cry, familiar to all of us: why is this happening to me? After my kindness by the well, did I deserve such a cruel fate . . . ? This was not why I left my homeland and my family" (HarperOne, 1997, p. 41). How often have we heard—or said—the same thing?

Tol'dot
Kenneth J. Weiss, 2002

"A source of bitterness to Isaac and Rebekah" (Gen. 26:35).

Though he was their firstborn son, both his mom and dad knew that Esau could never be given the "innermost blessing" that ought to have been his. He just wasn't suited—by temperament or intellect; he was incapable of upholding the covenant, transmitting the promise.

In fact, Esau disqualified himself! His natural predilections and life-choices undermined his claim: he had base appetites, selling his birthright for a single meal. Later he married two Hittite women. (Because his parents objected to union with Canaanites? If so, Esau here confirms his innate lack of judgment.)

That's why Rebekah and Isaac both acted so as to bypass Esau's hereditary right to the blessing. For her part, Rebekah remembered God's words to her: "The older shall serve the younger" (Gen. 25:23). Conspiring with Jacob years later to "fool" the blind Isaac was merely fulfillment of God's intention that Esau must serve and not lead.

Isaac—for his part—undoubtedly knew that it was Jacob standing before him to be blessed. His own words—taken together—affirm his astuteness and purpose:

"Which of my sons are you?" (Gen. 27:18)
"How did you succeed so quickly [in the meal preparation]?" (27:20)
"Come closer that I may feel you." (27:21)
"The voice is the voice of Jacob, yet the hands are the hands of Esau." (27:22)
"Are you really my son Esau?" (27:24)

Isaac knew! Though his eyes could not see, his vision was uncompromised! And Rebekah, perspicacious as ever, also (always) knew. Individually, they acted. Indeed: that old couple—each other's "missing piece"—were "in cahoots"!

Tol'dot
Kenneth J. Weiss, 2003

Near the end of *Parashat Chayei Sarah* are the words ואלה תולדות ישמעאל (*V'eileh tol'dot Yishmael*, "This is the line of Ishmael"); we read of Ishmael's children (interestingly, there were precisely twelve sons). Despite his forced exile and close encounter with death, Ishmael survived.

Beginning this week's *parashah*, we read, in virtually identical terms, ואלה תולדות יצחק (*V'eileh tol'dot Yitzchak*, "This is the line of Isaac"). Isaac—like his half-brother—also survived.

The Torah's commentators seem to undervalue Isaac in comparison to his father Abraham and son Jacob: he was not a "mover and shaker."

Thus, it's easy to miss a key point: Isaac actually **survived** the trauma of the *Akeidah*; furthermore, he married and became a father. Isaac **persevered** despite the traumas of his youth, which could well have damaged his soul, compromised his mental stability. How strong and resilient the human spirit can be, has ever been.

Do you know why this portion was given the name *Tol'dot* (תולדות)? Precisely to emphasize that the scarred Isaac actually endured and **had** children . . . isn't that comparable to anything accomplished by his father or his son?

Tol'dot
Kenneth J. Weiss, 2004

Expectant parents—modern or ancient—are (usually) thrilled to learn that a child is coming into their lives. Yet, we read nothing of Rebekah and Isaac's excitement or anticipation upon learning she has conceived. All we learn is how arduous her pregnancy is—a foretaste (a cause?) of difficulties yet to unfold.

Torah inventories the striking differences between Esau and Jacob. Far from identical, they are barely "fraternal." When the first was born, "**they** called his name Esau" (Gen. 25:25). When his brother emerged "**he** called his name Jacob" (Gen. 25:26). So, who were "they," and who was "he"? Moshe Chayim of Sadikov—grandson of the Baal Shem Tov—suggests that "deceit [as personified by Esau] attract[ed] many followers," whereas "truth [i.e., Jacob] [had] a much smaller number of adherents." From (just after) birth, the twins' lives irrevocably diverge.

As less-than-thrilled parents, Isaac and Rebekah (models of parental dysfunction) exacerbated their sons' dissimilarity: whereas "Isaac loved [past tense] Esau . . . Rebekah loves [present tense] Jacob" (Gen. 25:28). Isaac's love was contingent on past deeds (what have you done for me lately?). Rebekah's love was not contingent at all: she loves (only?) her youngest son—period.

It's really no wonder that the brothers took opposite directions in life. From Torah's perspective, that development was a forgone conclusion. It didn't start when Jacob deceived Esau into relinquishing his birthright for a bowl of stew. It didn't end with their "reunion" decades later. It hasn't ended yet!

Tol'dot
Alan Cook, 2005

Roosevelt Grier is six foot six. He was a linebacker for the New York Giants and a tackle for the Los Angeles Rams. Working as a bodyguard, he subdued Robert F. Kennedy's assassin. And in 1974, he recorded the song "It's All Right to Cry," for the *Free to Be You and Me* album.

That last item on Grier's resume doesn't exactly fit our stereotypical image of machismo. By the same token, if we were to read the beginning of our *sidrah*, without knowing the outcome of the story, we would expect Esau, the "skillful hunter, a man of the outdoors," to be the victor, rather than Jacob, "a mild man" (Gen. 25:27).

But Jacob was not weak; he simply showed his might in nonconventional ways. *Pirkei Avot* 4:1 teaches, "Who is mighty? One who conquers his inclinations; as it is said: 'One who is slow to anger is better than a strong man, and one who controls his spirit is more honored than a conqueror of a city' [Prov. 16:32]."

Strength is not always measured by physical power. It is also important to be strong in character, to be slow to anger, to share our feelings with others, and to lead a moral life. These are the traits that Malachi had in mind when he proclaimed, "Jacob I have loved, but Esau I have rejected" (Mal. 1:2–3).

The way in which an individual exhibits such qualities is the true measure of a man.

Tol'dot
Amy Scheinerman, 2006

How do we traverse the tension between long-term good and short-term wrong? Midrash ascribes to Rivkah insight during her pregnancy that Yaakov is God's choice to carry the covenant forward. Yet are theft and deception necessary and permitted? Does Yaakov cheat Esav and deceive Yitzchak with ease, or does his conscience trouble him?

Torah rarely provides details about its characters' state of mind or feelings, and we must deduce them from the subtle hints and our own intuition.

B'reishit Rabbah finds a hint of Yaakov's reluctance: "He went and took and brought to his mother—under duress, bent over and weeping." So, too, we know that others disapprove of Yaakov's role in the affair. *Tanchuma* (*Vayeitzei* 1:1) hints at the price Yaakov pays, envisioning him arising the morning after his mistaken marriage to Leah and accusing her, "Daughter of the Deceiver! Why did you deceive me?" Leah responds, "And you—why did you deceive your father?"

Torah seems to suggest that Yaakov atones the night before his reunion with Esav, when he wrestles with the איש (*ish*, "man") and sustains permanent injury. "Offenses committed by a person against another person are not remitted until the one makes restitution to the other and appeases him," Rambam wrote in the *Mishneh Torah, Hilchot T'shuvah* 2:9, and so Torah confirms: "Your name shall no longer be יעקב [Yaakov, 'supplanter'] but ישראל [Yisrael], for you have striven with beings divine and human and have prevailed" (Gen. 32:29). Yaakov's long exile and permanent injury constitute his atonement.

Is it enough to prevail and arrive at the desired goal if we do not act ethically along the way?

Tol'dot
Amy Scheinerman, 2007

In contrast with Avraham, about whose birth, childhood, and even early adulthood Torah is silent, we learn of Yitzchak's impending conception and are present for his *b'rit milah* and weaning. When Yaakov and Esav are born, we have a front-row seat for both their gestation and birth. The contrast between the newborn twins could not be more stark: Esav is hairy all over, already the ruddy-complexioned hunter and outdoorsman. It is as if Esav emerges from the womb fully formed. Yaakov, in contrast, arrives holding his brother's heel, but that is all we know.

Traditional commentaries use this description (Gen. 25:24–26) to contrast Esav's robust physicality and his attendant base and violent proclivities, with Yaakov's spiritual and intellectual attributes, associated with a sensitive, religious soul.

There is another way to view the twins. In Esav we see little or no growth or change. He remains who he is throughout life, a man of the earth. Yaakov, however, undergoes enormous growth and development. As a youth, he is a selfish and spoiled lad, far from admirable. Yet in time Yaakov grows into his potential, a reminder of our ability to realize our potential. Perhaps Yaakov's name connotes not so much his grasping for Esav's heel, as his reaching out for growth in his life. For this reason, Yaakov is worthy of admiration and emulation.

Tol'dot
Janice Garfunkel, 2008

This *parashah* wrestles with the concept of masculinity in a way that still resonates with us today, thousands of years after it was written.

Twins are born. One represents a stereotyped "ideal" of masculinity: ruddy, hairy, an outdoorsman and hunter, a man of appetites—one would imagine Esau as muscular, a "doer" rather than a thinker, a fighter, a jock—basically, a guy with a lot of testosterone. The other twin is literally a mama's boy, the favorite of his mother, a dweller in tents, a maker of stews—we imagine Jacob to be more of an ectomorph, studious and thoughtful. We can easily imagine a pale Jacob wearing a slender black suit and hat, sitting in a poorly lit *shtiebl*, swaying over a text of Talmud, or leaning over a computer terminal, writing his PhD thesis.

What is amazing is that this ancient narrative favors the ectomorph, the one with less testosterone, more like the stereotype of a woman. It favors yin over yang. Calm over impulsive. Deliberate over brawny. Dare we say female over male?

Jewish men can be jocks, soldiers, mechanics. But somehow, incredibly, the imprimatur of the preference of Jacob over Esau has stayed with us from our birth as a people to this day. We still prefer our men to be doctors rather than boxers.

Tol'dot
Amy Scheinerman, 2009

"Give me some of that red stuff to gulp down, for I am famished" (Gen. 25:30).

Esav is *ayeif*. Is he merely physically famished? Or is he also hungering spiritually? If Esav is physically famished, should Yaakov not recognize that *ein kemach, ein Torah*? If Esav is hungering spiritually, is this because he is inherently limited or because no one has helped him develop his spiritual potential? In either case, what can justify Yaakov's treatment of his brother and womb-mate? Yaakov's immediate response, "First sell me your birthright" (Gen. 25:31), and subsequent coercion of Esav to swear an oath relinquishing the birthright, certainly sound like one brother taking unfair advantage of the other. Yet Torah comments that Esav "spurned the birthright" (Gen. 25:34).

Perhaps the answer is in the fullness of Gen. 25:34: "Yaakov then gave Esav bread and lentil stew; he ate and drank, and he rose and went away; thus did Esav spurn the birthright." Esav did not express appreciation to God either before or after eating—a sign that Esav's worldview did not extend beyond his immediate, material existence and needs. As Maurice Samuel wrote in *Certain People of the Book* (URJ Press, 1977), "Esau was a huntsman, nothing but huntsman, delivered up, heart and soul, body and spirit. . . . He despised his birthright as a civilized man, and how much more his birthright as the son of Isaac and the grandson of Abraham!" Surely such a one is incapable of recognizing the bigger picture of God's covenant and carrying it through to future generations.

Yet, should the covenant be entrusted to one who schemes and cheats to achieve his success?

Life delivers up few unblemished, fully qualified, heroic leaders. Rather, life delivers talented and ambitious human beings whose failings are often near the surface. This raises important questions about how we discern and respond to what is good and what is not within ourselves, and how we do the same with the leaders in our communities and institutions.

ויצא Vayeitzei

(Genesis 28:10–32:3)

Vayeitzei
Lawrence S. Kushner, 1995

According to Masoretic tradition (see also *Minchat Shai* and Maimonides' commentary to chapter 8 of *Hilchot Sefer Torah*), in *Parashat Vayeitzei*, unlike in any other *parashah* in the Torah, there are neither *p'tuchot* nor *s'tumot*, spaces. The entire *parashah* is one long paragraph. Why?

Rashi, commenting on Gen. 28:11, "And he came upon a place and spent the night there, for the sun had set," points out that by a word analogy, *vayifga* (came upon) in our verse and *tifga* (plead) in Jer. 7:16, we may conclude that Jacob prayed. According to the Babylonian Talmud, *B'rachot* 26b, Jacob established the evening prayer. Rashi explains that the Torah does not write the customary word for praying, *vayitpaleil*, in order to teach us that the earth shrank before Jacob's steps (cf. Babylonian Talmud, *Chulin* 91b). But what does the earth shrinking have to do with establishing the evening prayer?

Y'hudah Aryeh Lieb of Ger, upon reading, "And Jacob awoke from his sleep. . . . Shaken, he said, 'How awesome is this place! This is none other than the house of God and that is the gateway to heaven'" (Gen. 28:16–17), wonders why Jacob was overcome with awe and reverence. Wouldn't a more reasonable reaction be one of security and self-importance?

Vayeitzei
Lawerence S. Kushner, 1996

Since God intended that Jacob would be preferred over Esau, why does he seem to be so sorely tried in this *parashah*—is it punishment for his tricking Esau? But his mother told him to do it. Should he have disobeyed her? (The fifth commandment does not say, "Obey your father and mother.") And why should Rachel and Leah, innocents both, be punished with such rivalry? Do Jacob and his wives grow from their sorrows?

Vayeitzei: Darkness and Intimacy
Stephen E. Cohen, 1997

In the classic midrash, the stage is set for Jacob's dream/vision of the *sulam* (ladder) by a miraculous early setting of the sun.

B'reishit Rabbah 68:10 "For the sun had set [*ki va hashemesh*]" (Gen. 28:11). Our rabbis punned: Do not read *ki va hashemesh*, rather, read it *kiba hashemesh* [God extinguished the sun]. This teaches that the Blessed Holy One caused the sun to set unusually early, in order to speak with our father Jacob privately. This is like the story of the intimate friend of the king, who occasionally comes to visit him. The king commands, "Extinguish the candles; extinguish the lanterns. For I desire to speak with my friend privately."

Comment How does darkness enhance intimacy—between humans, and between humans and God?

Vayeitzei: The Kiss of Torah
Stephen E. Cohen, 1998

Here is Nachman of Bratzlav at his virtuosic best—spinning a shimmering web of Torah, Talmud, commentary, and his own theory of the Oral Torah.

Likutei Moharan 12 "And Jacob kissed Rachel, and he raised his voice, and wept" (Gen. 29:11). Rashi interpreted that Jacob foresaw, by

Ruach HaKodesh, that she would not enter with him into the grave. "Rachel" refers to the Oral Torah, which is like a sheep/*rachel*; everyone "shears" it and issues rulings, which are like garments. Now, when a fit individual studies the teaching of a *tanna*, then the *tanna* kisses him, and he kisses the *tanna* and gives great pleasure to the *tanna*, as it is said, "His lips murmur in the grave" (Babylonian Talmud, *Y'vamot* 97a). "Jacob kissed"—this is the *tanna*. "Rachel"—this is the Oral Torah that the *tanna* taught. The *tanna* kissed and joined his soul to the *Ruach HaKodesh* that is in the *Shechinah*. "And he wept"—he foresaw by his own *Ruach HaKodesh*, which he brought forth out of his own mouth and sent into the Oral Torah, that in this exile most of the scholars would not be legitimate. That is, in their teachings, the *Ruach HaKodesh* of Rachel, of the Oral Torah, would not enter with him in the grave, and his lips would not murmur in the grave. This is why he wept.

Comment Nachman was quite clear about both his own legitimacy and the illegitimacy of most of his contemporaries. By what specific criteria, if any, can we distinguish between authentic and inauthentic Oral Torah?

Vayeitzei
Morrison Bial, 1999

"And he lighted on the place" (Gen. 28:11). What place? Sforno said it was where travelers spent the night. In the days before inns, good people would arrange rocks to form seats, a table, and a protective wall so that travelers would be comfortable. The fact that people cared for others made the spot "the place" and worthy of a site for blessing.

I prefer Sforno's humane interpretation to that of the sages who maintained that it was the spot where Adam, Abel, and Noah had sacrificed and was Moriah, the site of the *Akeidah*.

"Angels ascending and descending" (Gen. 28:12). Sorotzkin says that the angels were taking our prayers up to heaven and descending to take up new ones. I prefer my grandmother's explanation: that every time we perform a mitzvah, an angel is born and then it ascends to heaven through the merit of our deed. They descend to help us perform new mitzvot.

"Why did you steal my gods?" (Gen. 31:30). Why did Rachel steal the *t'rafim?* She knew that Laban depended on his gods for everything and especially in going to war. Without them he would feel deprived of all protection. There was no chance of his attacking Jacob.

Vayeitzei
Sheldon Marder, 2000

In *Vayetzei* Jacob, the indoorsman, discovers the great outdoors—sleeping under the stars on his stone pillow. It is, in fact, outside that Jacob begins to develop an interesting interior life. As K'li Yakar remarks in a comment on Gen. 28:10, נמצא שיציאה זו עשתה רושם גם בו בעצמו—this "leaving," or going outside his normal environment, makes an impression on Jacob himself. Is there some value in reading the story of Jacob—in the words of French philosopher Gaston Bachelard—as "a dialectic of outside and inside" (*The Poetics of Space*, Beacon, 1969)? Might we extend this to a dialectic of outsider and insider? And going a step further: is it fruitful to examine Jacob's relationships in terms of distance and intimacy?

Speaking of outside: The well-known passage in the Babylonian Talmud, *B'rachot* 26b cites the verse ויפגע במקום (*Vayifga bamakom*, "He came upon a certain place" [Gen. 28:11]) as proof that Jacob instituted the evening prayer (read: he came in contact with the Omnipresent). The same *sugya* credits Abraham ("looking down toward Sodom and Gomorrah" [Gen. 19:28]) and Isaac ("in the field" [Gen. 24:63]) with inventing the morning and afternoon prayers, respectively. How interesting that we indoor *shul* folk—spiritual tent-dwellers, as it were—trace the origins of our prayer-life to our ancestors' rugged, outdoor experiences.

Vayeitzei: It All Adds Up
Kenneth J. Weiss, 2001

"Jacob . . . put [a stone] under his head and lay down. . . . He had a dream . . . a *sulam* ['ladder']" (Gen. 28:11–12).

In our home are two artistic renderings of Jacob's dream. Together, they "paint a picture" of this Torah moment.

One—created by Ben Avram—is fanciful, Chagall-like. The entire scene is set into a sky-blue background. All the figures seem ethereal, not only the three angels (suspended near—not touching—the long, simple *sulam*), but also Jacob (one sees his serene face at rest, his long hair, his arms, then a flowing heavenly robe). The stone for his head is swathed in living greens. A stylized Jerusalem is in the background.

The other—a Shraga Weil serigraph—shows a real-life, fully human sleeping Jacob, resting under a striped multicolored blanket. The *sulam* seems to grow out of an *eitz chayim* of equal height. A new (dark) moon and a wheat sheaf accent the picture.

What of that *sulam* of which our patriarch dreamed? What was God showing him—and us? Gematria offers a midrashic suggestion: the word *sulam* has a numeric value of 130. So does *Sinai*—the place where Jacob's descendants would one day receive Torah. Perhaps God showed Jacob that mountain and said: One day we will meet at its peak. All that's necessary now is for you to begin the climb.

Vayeitzei
Kenneth J. Weiss, 2002

"Jacob left Beer-Sheba, and set out" (Gen. 28:10).

Alvin Fine, a gifted poet for our movement and our times, died recently. Consider his "Birth Is a Beginning" (*Mishkan T'filah: A Reform Siddur*, CCAR Press, 2007). I contend that it was inspired by Jacob's life story as found in *Vayeitzei*:

> Birth is a beginning
> and death a destination.
> And life is a journey:
> from childhood to maturity
> and youth to age;
> from innocence to awareness
> and ignorance to knowing;

from foolishness to discretion
and then, perhaps to wisdom;
from weakness to strength
or strength to weakness—
and often, back again.
From health to sickness
and back, we pray, to health again;
from offense to forgiveness,
from loneliness to love,
from joy to gratitude,
from pain to compassion,
and grief to understanding—
from fear to faith;
from defeat to defeat to defeat—
until, looking backward or ahead
we see that victory lies
not at some high place along the way,
but in having made the journey, stage by stage
a sacred pilgrimage.
Birth is a beginning
and death a destination.
But life is a journey,
from birth to death
to life everlasting.

Fine distills Torah's wisdom on "life as process." A modern midrash on *Vayeitzei*? I'd say so.

Vayeitzei
Kenneth J. Weiss, 2003

"*Adonai* is present in this place" (Gen. 28:16).
Recognizing divinity in the everyday:

- For Jacob, a place to lodge becomes much more: he awakens to the realization that, overnight, he had encountered God.

- Years later, it happens again. This time, a well-known face—Esau's—becomes much more: "To see your face is like seeing the face of God" (Gen. 33:10).

Life teaches Jacob well. Once callow and self-absorbed, he grows-evolves-deepens, so as to perceive "the Eternal One in the transitory now." Rabindranath Tagore captures it well: "Behold, I find You when dawn comes up golden. . . . In the current of life flowing" (Chaim Stern translation of a Hebrew translation of "Gitanjali").

Vayeitzei
Kenneth J. Weiss, 2004

"[Jacob] had a dream" (Gen. 28:12). So, Jacob stops for the night and sleeps where the Holy Temple would one day stand . . . and he dreams. Jacob—as we well know—envisions "a ladder . . . set on the ground and its top reached to heaven" (Gen. 28:12).

I love that vision, but I question it midrashically: why a ladder (or, in Plaut, a stairway)? If (part of) God's message was that this would be the site of the Holy Temple, why didn't Jacob picture that sort of grand and spiritual edifice . . . perhaps a nice multistory Temple complete with stairway?!

The ladder might well symbolize our people's spiritual evolution. Set firmly on the earth, its first rung(s) represent the desert Tabernacle. Subsequent rungs may translate as the Temple(s) destined to be constructed on Zion/Moriah. Higher rungs suggest the continuing evolution of Jewish spirituality: the synagogue, which enabled the dispersion of the Jewish people (as Jews!) to all earth's corners. As the ladder's top ascends to the heavens, so does our people's destiny: both reach to places and times beyond Jacob's vision or ken. The angels ascending and descending symbolize our people's ups and downs throughout history.

Then Jacob awakens and realizes what he's (fore)seen—**all** he's apprehended. He says, "Surely God is here [part of my present, part of my people's future] and I . . . I didn't realize . . . . How full of awe is this place. [It is] God's abode" (Gen. 28:16–17).

Vayeitzei
Alan Cook, 2005

In ויצא (*Vayeitzei*), Jacob gets a taste of his own medicine. The Talmud teaches that Jacob had been forewarned about Laban's penchant for treachery, and yet he had replied, "I am his equal in trickery" (Babylonian Talmud, *M'gilah* 13b).

So, Jacob worded his agreement with his uncle carefully, stating, "I will work seven years for **Rachel, your youngest daughter**" (Gen. 29:18). Nonetheless, a "wife swap" takes place.

Jacob is incensed that all night, he had called his bride Rachel, and Leah had never revealed her true identity. But he forgets that *he* had once masqueraded as his brother for his own personal gain.

Laban responds to Jacob by reminding him, "This is not done in our land: giving the youngest before the firstborn" (Gen. 29:26). The practice in Haran is thus different from what has been established throughout the Book of Genesis; Isaac displaced Ishmael, Jacob usurped Esau, and so forth.

The biblical author has fun with the text, painting a picture of deception and payback.

But Jacob is not unredeemable. In chapter 28 of our *sidrah*, Jacob has his famous dream, after which he proclaims, "Surely God was in this place and I, I did not know it" (v. 16). In his book on this subject, Rabbi Lawrence Kushner paraphrases the Kotzker Rabbi and notes that Jacob's ego is standing between him and true appreciation of God. But Jacob's transformation will not be complete until he grapples with the hard work of being ישראל (Yisrael), one who struggles to find his own identity in the presence of God.

Vayeitzei
Amy Scheinerman, 2006

Dreams, understood as communications from God, often mark a turning point: Joseph's dreams of sheaves of wheat and celestial luminaries, Pharaoh's dreams of cows and corn, and here, Jacob's dream of the סולם (*sulam*, "ladder").

On the other hand, Freud said that one of the three great humiliations in human history was the discovery that we are not in control of our own minds. He had in mind dreams that seep into our subconscious.

Deuteronomy 13:2–4 inveighs against dream interpreters. Our Sages were equally skeptical, promulgating their own textbook on dream interpretation in the Bablyonian Talmud, *B'rachot* 55–57. They vacillate between affirming that dreams are divine communications and considering them merely the "residue of the day" (as Freud put it). They agreed with Eric Fromm that "we are not only less reasonable and less decent in our dreams, but we are also wiser asleep than when we are awake . . ." if we interpret our dreams correctly (*The Forgotten Language: An Introduction to the Understanding of Dreams, Fairytales, and Myths*, Rinehart, Holt, 1951). They affirmed repeatedly, "All dreams follow the mouth," meaning that the interpretation the dreamer accepts is the meaning of the dream and will be determinative of the future. Thus they tell us how to interpret dreams, claiming that even horrendous images and acts betoken—for the most part—righteous behavior and blessings to come.

The Talmudic dreambook is an exercise in positive thinking. That alone can mark a valuable turning point in our lives.

Vayeitzei
Amy Scheinerman, 2007

"Avraham arose early in the morning [facing] the place where he stood before God" (Gen. 19:27). Our Rabbis understood from this פסוק (*pasuk*, "verse") that Avraham instituted שחרית (*Shacharit*). The Talmud (*B'rachot* 26b) assigns מנחה (*Minchah*) to Yitzchak on the basis of Gen. 24:63, and מעריב (*Maariv*) to Yaakov on the foundation of Gen. 28:11.

Rav Avraham Kook suggests that each set of prayers has its own nature, reflecting the character of the time of day and the spirit of the patriarch who instituted it, thereby revealing to us another dimension of תפילה (*t'filah*, "prayer").

Avraham's prayer reflects his determination to make a spiritual stand (בבקר . . . וישכם, *vayashkeim . . . baboker*, "he arose in the morning" [Gen. 19:27]), reminding us of the importance of cultivating in ourselves inner ethical fortitude. The quotidian conflicts and pressures of life can gnaw away at our resolve, but standing upright at day's inception helps us begin on an idealistic footing.

Yitzchak's afternoon prayer out in the field comes at a time when much of the day's work is accomplished and we can engage in evaluative meditation. It comes at a time when we would do well to remember that the world is far broader then our limited spheres. Yitzchak, who is associated with מדת הדין (*midat hadin*, the attribute of stern judgment) reminds us of the importance of staying the course we set in our morning prayer.

Yaakov's evening vision of the סלם (*sulam*, "ladder") and מלאכים (*malachim*, "angels") is accompanied by his subsequent revelatory realization that he is in a holy place, reminding us that chance meetings and unexpected events are an ever-present component of life offering us a myriad opportunities for growth and *chesed* (mercy).

Prayer, in its very nature and temporal frame, offers us a prescription for ethical fortitude, meditative evaluation, and delight and awe in all the opportunities life offers us.

Vayeitzei
Jeffrey Ballon, 2008

"He went out" (*vayeitzei* [Gen. 28:10]). How many occasions in your life has an action been as determinative as that? I remember at the age of ten leaving the culture of the "Old South," with its gentle post-war ways of raising ideal children, and moving to metropolitan New York City. Culture shock! The fall I left for college and moved two hundred miles from my little village still returns to me in my dreams. I had to square my shoulders to prevent my parents from knowing what I was feeling, fight back tears of anxiety, and walk through Wayland Arch into Wriston Quadrangle. My journey was not across the ford of Jabbok, but it was equally transformative. Walking through a simple arch and cutting away family was every bit as challenging as finding the right stone to sleep on. My life would never be the same, any more than Jacob would be the same after his adventure.

What do we need to survive these challenges? Jacob reveals his spiritual searching in his dreams. He shows concern for the physical environment by making sure even the flocks are watered. He may not have invented an alternative to fossil fuels, but he made sure he had the strength to water the flock efficiently. He did it alone and without a committee meeting. And mysteriously, he committed to a kiss and family. Were these places dangerous? I suggest to you they were at least adventurous, each an opportunity to find a place to prosper, a *Makom* to know, and intimacy that leads to the revelation of that which we did not know.

We are a people who have always had to move for our welfare and survival. Jacob is our father.

Vayeitzei
Amy Scheinerman, 2009

The enigmatic image of the *sulam*, Jacob's ladder or ramp, has inspired countless renderings in art, and even more commentaries.

Here is a troubling interpretation: Sforno (Ovadiah b. Yaakov, 1475–1550, Italy) sees the *sulam* as a reflection (from his historical perspective) or foreshadowing (from his theological perspective) of Jewish history. At precisely our lowest points we merit the blessing *ufaratzta yamah vakeidmah v'tzafonah vanegbah* ("You shall spread out to the west and to the east, to the north and to the south" [Gen. 28:14]). K'li Yakar (Sh'lomo Ephraim b. Aaron Luntschitz, 1550–1619) explains Sforno's claim: When Israel is doing well in the world, we trust in our own human power for security. However, when Israel is trapped in the depths of lowliness, we place our trust in God and rely on God's intervention. This inspires us to call out to God, our only hope, and God responds with salvation. Hence, both K'li Yakar and Sforno understand Gen. 25:14 this way: "Your descendants shall be as the dust of the earth," meaning when we have been reduced to mere dust, then we cry out to God and God responds so that we "spread out to the west and to the east, to the north and to the south."

I can appreciate the prescient warning in *Parashat Eikev* (Deut. 8:11–19) not to fall into the pattern of interpreting prosperity and security to mean, "My own power and the might of my own hand have won this wealth for me" (v. 17). However, to see all of Jewish history as an oscillating wave of success coupled with hubris, alternating with recognizing our powerlessness and being saved by God, suggests a chasm between God and humanity, and such an imbalance of power that intimacy with God is all but impossible.

וישלח *Vayishlach*

(Genesis 32:4–36:43)

Vayishlach
Lawrence S. Kushner, 1995

(Genesis 32) The midrash comments that Jacob prepares himself for his meeting with Esau with *milchamah* (dividing into camps), *t'filah* (prayer [v. 10]), and *minchah* (gift [vv. 19f.]). They, in fact, recommend this three-pronged approach as a model for all encounters with those about whose feelings toward us we are in the dark. What is a modern analogy—how do we "prepare for war" with such people? Should we? What is the content of our prayer? And what might be our gift—and how can such a gift be "honest," and not, as the Torah forbids, a bribe?

(Gen. 32:25–33) Hasn't Jacob suffered enough at Laban's hands for twenty years? Why should there be pain—the thigh wound—in his apotheosis, his encounter with a divine being and his assumption of his patriarchal name? Abraham's change of name is not marked by a wound—unless we consider his circumcision to be such. What is the role of suffering in individuals' fulfillment of their destiny—of a people's fulfillment? And why do the matriarchs seem not to suffer in their attainment of their destiny—or is childbirth (see Gen. 3:16) suffering enough?

Vayishlach
Lawrence S. Kushner, 1996

When Moses is called at the bush, the revealing of God's name is a major part of the story. Names also feature importantly in Gen. 32:23–33. Is Jacob's wrestle a kind of call as well? What has changed in Jacob's character to explain this change of name?

Vayishlach: Reconciliation?
Stephen E. Cohen, 1997

The enigmatic and tantalizing points over the letters in the Torah text serve to open the question: How wholehearted was Esau and Jacob's reconciliation?

B'reishit Rabbah "Esau ran toward him . . . and he kissed him" (Gen. 33:4). Rabbi Shimon ben Elazar said: The points above the word teach that Esau's compassion was aroused at that moment, and he kissed him with his whole heart. Rabbi Yannai said: If so, why are there points above the word? Rather, it teaches that he did not come to kiss him [*l'nashko*], but to bite him [*l'nashcho*]. And the neck of our father Jacob became like marble, and the teeth of that wicked one were blunted. And what about the phrase "And they wept"? This one wept for his neck and this one wept for his teeth. Rabbi Abahu in the name of Rabbi Yochanan cited here the verse: "Your neck is a tower of ivory" (Song of Songs 7:5).

Comment The two verbs *l'nasheik* and *l'nasheich* are clearly related etymologically—somewhere in the development of the language. Is the ambiguity of Esau's "love-bite" inherent in most, or all, kisses?

Vayishlach
Jim Ponet, 1998

How do you return to the re-promised (Gen. 31:3) land—and thus to history—after a protracted exile on the margins? Did Jacob intend to go through a truth and reconciliation process with Esau? Or was he drawn to a meeting with Esau only out of fear, as Ramban reads it?

Ramban cites *B'reishit Rabbah* 75:2: Esau was going on his merry way and you had to send messengers to him! *B'reishit Rabbah* applies Prov. 26:17 to Jacob, suggesting he acted foolishly, like a man who, seeing a robber asleep at a dangerous crossroads, awakens him and warns him, only to be mugged. Ramban discerns a paradigmatic failure in Jacob's return. Because Jacob appealed to Esau/Edom in his time, Judah Maccabee would in his day negotiate a friendship treaty with Rome (see I Macc. 1:8), and this in turn would seal the doom of Jerusalem by Rome. If only Jacob had not played politics but rather ignored Esau and relied on God.

In any event, the meeting of the brothers (Gen. 33:4) is the most important meeting in Jacob's life. The tradition is wonderfully ambivalent about this encounter, hence the dots pointed over the word *vayishakeihu*. Rashbi (*Sifrei B'haalot'cha* 69) explains while it is ironclad law that Esau hates Jacob, at this encounter Esau was really overcome with affection. But R. Yannai, at *B'reishit Rabbah* 88:12, instructs us not to read Esau as kissing but rather biting. This ambiguous moment, into which we still grow, out of which we still emerge, gives us our name into which we still grow.

Vayishlach
Morrison Bial, 1999

"A tribute to Esau" (Gen. 32:14). Amusing to see the ratio of males to females that Jacob sent. It is ten to one for sheep and goats, four to one for cattle, and only two to one for donkeys. He sends no males for the nursing camels. Is it the greater intelligence that reduces the ratio? But Jacob himself has four wives, and that would put him at the cow-bull ratio even worse than the donkeys.

"You have striven with God and with man and have prevailed" (Gen. 32:29). Jacob is wounded. We hear nothing of the angel's injuries. How did Jacob prevail? To withstand a midnight attack and emerge only slightly wounded, neither killing nor being killed, that is prevailing.

Vayishlach
Sheldon Marder, 2000

In his anxiety, Jacob prepares his servants for the inevitable encounter with Esau by instructing them how to answer Esau's queries: "Whose are you? Where are you going? And whose are these before you?" (Gen. 32:18).

Rabbi Yitzchak Meir of Ger (d. 1866) noticed that these questions bear a remarkable resemblance to the questions for self-examination suggested by Akavia ben Mahalalel in *Pirkei Avot* 3:1—"Whence have you come? Where are you going? Before whom will you ultimately give an accounting?" (Buber, *The Later Masters*). The humbling answers are, of course, a putrid drop; a place of dust, worms, and maggots; the Holy One.

In this episode Jacob has brought as a present for Esau 550 beasts, as Nahum Sarna says, "an extraordinarily lavish presentation" (*JPS Torah Commentary: Genesis,* ed. Nahum M. Sarna, Jewish Publication Society, 1991). What do the words "lavish presentation" make you think of? How do we encourage humility and modesty within a culture of hyper-materialism and narcissism? The rabbi of Ger discerns in Jacob's questions the seeds of something spiritual. How can we, too, reframe the questions in our communities in order to move those we lead from lives largely governed by material concerns to decision making grounded in Jewish spiritual values?

Vayishlach: What's in a Name?
Kenneth J. Weiss, 2001

"Your name shall no longer be Jacob, but Israel" (Gen. 32:29); (and yet) "Looking up, **Jacob** saw Esau coming" (Gen. 33:1); "God said to **Jacob**" (Gen. 35:1); etc.

In Gen. 32:29 Jacob's name became "Israel." Yet, through the rest of *B'reishit*, the name Jacob comes up again and again. Did his new name suggest that the young Jacob changed fundamentally as years and experiences impacted him? If so, why is he still called "Jacob" (even at his death—Gen. 49:33) rather than "Israel"?

After Gen. 32:29, "Jacob" meets and embraces Esau (chap. 33); chastises Simeon and Levi (34:30); goes up to Beth El (35:1); with Esau, buries their father (35:29); settles where his father had lived (37:1); blesses his sons on his deathbed (chapter 49); and on and on. "Israel" (culminating a scant list) blesses his grandsons Ephraim and Manasseh (48:8ff.).

Do we conclude that much of "Israel" was still (would always be) "Jacob-like"? Did he become "Israel" in some official document that was then filed away and forgotten? Was he still called "Jacob" because people knew him (only) by that name?

This we know: "Jacob" (despite the official name change!) remains at the center of the Genesis narratives until the moment of his death. "Israel" is rarely heard from—a shocking realization, belying the literal truth of Genesis 32:29. The best name is not the one we're given (even by God!), but the one we earn (*Tanchuma*).

Vayishlach
Kenneth J. Weiss, 2002

The Jabbok (*Yabok: yod-bet-kuf*) was—is—a Jordan River tributary: Jacob's place one restless (wrest-ful?) night (Gen. 32:23). An *ish* wrestles (*vayei-aveik: yod-**alef**-bet-kuf*) with Jacob there (Gen. 32:25). By adding the *alef*, Jabbok is transformed into a place where God is present, indeed integral.

Vayei-aveik is not unlike another word in our *parashah*. The Chatam Sofer explains: "[Many biblical commentators] explain the word *vayei-aveik*—wrestling—in two ways. On the one hand, it is derived from the word *avak*, 'dust'—that is, 'he stirred up the dust.' On the other hand, it is very similar to the word *vay'chabeik* [Gen. 33:4], which means 'he hugged.' This double meaning hints at the way [the *ish*] tries to defeat Jacob. First . . . Esau tries . . . to drag Jacob through the dust, to do violence to him . . . trample him underfoot. But he also welcomes him, connects with him, assimilates him . . . [thus] killing him with a kiss."

Torah's linguistic links: Coincidental? By design!

Vayishlach
Kenneth J. Weiss, 2003

In his temple bulletin five decades ago, Solomon Freehof reminded his readers that sibling rivalry is as old as siblings, starting with Cain versus Abel. But, Freehof notes, the shaky relationship between Jacob and Esau illustrates another possibility: sibling reconciliation.

For Freehof, three factors in their story made brotherly reconciliation possible:

Initiative—in sending messengers to Esau, Jacob took a first step.
Tact—the brothers, rather than taking the low road (dredging up old enmities), agree to start anew.
Time—Jacob appreciates life's brevity. (By the bye: mightn't an awareness of time's passage and our own mortality urge us to move beyond old antagonisms, find new ways to reconnect?)

Freehof's lesson: reconciliation—whether between family members, friends, or entire peoples—is doable! Israelis and Palestinians: are you listening?

. . . Thanks again—and always—Doctor!

Vayishlach
Kenneth J. Weiss, 2004

"גרתי [*Garti*, 'I stayed'] with Laban" (Gen. 32:5).

Abraham knew himself to be a גר (*ger*, "alien"; see *Chayei Sarah*). His grandson Jacob defines himself in the same way.

This self-assessment is at the core of Jacob's greeting to Esau: "I lived as an alien [גרתי, *garti*] with Laban." Yet, I survived those fear-filled years with my tradition and identity intact. How? Why? Because I (unlike you, my brother!) kept the mitzvot and lived within their framework. The mitzvot of our people (by which I lived and you did not!) protected me from the destructive atmosphere that surrounded me.*

Then as now, when we Jews live by the mitzvot, we know we are blessed by their structure and inner strength. Precisely because Jacob lived by, taught, and transmitted them, Laban's world could never destroy or even diminish him.

Jacob's message to his brother Esau is—patently, transparently—a message to us: Live a Jewish life and you will be impervious to the profane influences and seductions of the world that surround you.

---

*Rashi notes that the letters in the word גרתי, when transposed, read תרי״ג—the Hebrew number 613 (for the number of mitzvot).

Vayishlach
Alan Cook, 2005

In July of 1994, seventy-three-year-old Alvin Straight of Laurens, Iowa, decided to pay a visit to his eighty-year-old brother in Wisconsin. The siblings hadn't spoken in almost a decade, and Alvin decided that was long enough. However, he did not trust public transportation and was ineligible for a driver's license because of poor eyesight. So, he hitched a trailer to a 1966 John Deere mower and made the six-week, 240-mile journey to see his brother.

In this *sidrah*, Jacob prepares for a similar reunion. His odyssey is no less treacherous than Straight's, and he has no idea what sort of reception awaits him when he finally meets up with Esau.

The text is sprinkled with numerous references to a "face." Thirteen times, some variation of the root פ-נ-ה (*p-n-h*) is found. In Jacob's encounters (and, of course in our own), the face-to-face interaction is found to be the most preferable, the most powerful, and the most efficacious. As nerve-wracking as his encounter with Esau must have been, Jacob recognized that it had to take place before either of them could hope to move forward in life.

Similarly, when Jacob begins to wrestle—with himself, with God, with his past—he does so פנים אל פנים (*panim el panim*, "face-to-face"). He names the location of his fateful encounter Peniel, "for I have seen a divine being face-to-face, yet my life has been preserved."

May we all learn to face the world head-on and to encounter others face-to-face.

Vayishlach
Amy Scheinerman, 2006

Has sneaky, conniving Yaakov turned over a new leaf? Is his תשובה (*t'shuvah*, "repentance") complete? In the beginning of וישלח (*Vayishlach*) we find Yaakov maneuvering to his own advantage in preparation for his reunion with Esav. Yaakov propitiates Esav with gifts and separates his entourage in a posture of defense (as Rashi notes, "The further back, the more dear to Yaakov").

Is the brothers' reconciliation genuine? Rashi suggests not, that with good reason Yaakov continues to distrust Esav. Yet Yaakov goes through the motions of reconciliation.

Several midrashim criticize Yaakov for debasing himself before evil Esav (e.g., *B'reishit Rabbah* 75:2, 75:11). No doubt the Rabbis viewed the interchange through the prism of Israel's later relationship with Rome. Ramban adds to these midrashim, "Our fall at the hands of Edom was due to the fact that the kings of the Second Temple made advances to the Romans."

What of Esav? Rashi points out that the ניקוד (*nikud*, "vocalization") above the word וישקהו (*vayishakeihu*, "and he kissed him" [Gen. 33:4]) signals us that there are variant views: *Sifrei* holds that Esav's embrace was insincere; R. Shimon bar Yochai holds that despite his hatred for Yaakov, Esav's embrace at that moment was sincere.

Sforno praises Yaakov's measured behavior, contrasting it with that of the Zealots of the first century. His model is the parable of the reed that bends and survives (Babylonian Talmud, *Gittin* 56b and *Taanit* 20a).

We have barely left the season of repentance, and no doubt some relationships requiring extensive repair have received only the first "treatment" and require much more work. There is no quick fix, either for Yaakov and Esav, or for us. Small, slow steps, but the semblance of sincerity goes a long way.

Vayishlach
Amy Scheinerman, 2007

Why does Yaakov hold on so tenaciously to the מלאך (*malach*, "messenger, angel" [Gen. 32:27])? Where once he held his brother's heel for a free ride from womb to world, now he grasps the messenger and demands a blessing. One lesson we might draw from Yaakov is not to rely on miracles. The Talmud tells us, "One should never place oneself in a dangerous situation, saying, 'A miracle will come and save me.' Perhaps the miracle will not come. And even if a miracle does occur, one's merits are reduced" (*Shabbat* 32a). It is questionable if this is even a necessary lesson in our modern, science-saturated, skeptical age.

Perhaps the lesson to draw from Yaakov concerns the constructive balance between self-reliance and placing trust in God. (This is difficult enough in the twenty-first century.) Yaakov, the schemer, grows from the spoiled brat who considered only his own desires, to a man who, having encountered God in one place at one time, broadens his concerns to include the welfare of others. By the time he prepares to meet Esav again, he has come to realize that scheming alone—however clever—is insufficient. He needs God in his life—not only in Beth El, but everywhere he goes. He grasps the מלאך (*malach*) because he needs God's presence at all times and in all places.

Yaakov's life journey—from grasping the heel to grasping the מלאך (*malach*)—takes us from Beckett's *Waiting for Godot* to the Kotzker Rebbe, who taught, "Where is God's presence? Wherever we let God in."

Vayishlach
Amy Scheinerman, 2008

Yaakov, having purchased Esav's birthright through exploitation and received his blessing by deceit, fled to the hinterlands to escape Esav's righteous wrath. Two decades have passed, and Yaakov realizes that the "blessing" was more of a curse. He became a refugee from his homeland; was exploited, abused, and deceived by his own uncle; and still has no place to call his own.

Perhaps Yaakov is the sort of person who cannot understand the pain he has inflicted on others until the same pain is inflicted on him. Most importantly, in twenty-two years, he has not reclaimed his integrity. He must return and face Esav and risk everything to reconcile.

In the days before his encounter with his brother, Yaakov sends emissaries ahead of him to placate Esav with gifts. He refers to himself as Esav's servant and twice terms Esav *Adoni* (my lord). Is this newfound humility and self-effacement? Is this rank terror, as Ramban contends? Or is this evidence of *t'shuvah*? Ibn Ezra and Rashbam seem to believe the latter and, as evidence, point out that when Yitzchak dies, he is buried by "Esav and Yaakov, his sons" (Gen. 35:29); Esav has been restored to his position of firstborn.

How often does it take more than two decades to rectify the wrongs we have inflicted? Yaakov's example teaches us that it is never too late to reclaim our integrity. His example also teaches us that we should expect risk and be prepared to face loss. There is no quick fix or easy path to restoring our integrity when we have willingly abandoned it.

Vayishlach
Amy Scheinerman, 2009

"Dinah, Leah's daughter whom she had borne to Jacob, went out to see the women of the locality, and Shechem son of Hamor the Hivite, the local prince, saw her; he took her and lay her down and raped her" (Gen. 34:1–2).

What follows is a detailed, emotional, and gruesome description of the deceit and revenge inflicted by Dinah's brother on the entire population of Shechem for offending the clan of Jacob and tarnishing the family's honor. The entire remainder of chapter 34 chronicles the massacre, from planning through execution, to aftermath.

But where is Dinah after all this? We do not know because she is not mentioned again. What is her place in the family? What affect does the rape have on her? Is she healed? What happens to victims of violence and trauma once the scintillating details of the violence are no longer newsworthy items? Do we expect them to be silent and not bother anyone with their depressing memories? As Jews, we are sensitive to justice denied and justice delayed, but in the case of victims of abuse and trauma, we too often fail at justice by failing to listen, believe, and respond to those in our midst who are suffering. If we keep them silent, like Dinah, they are doubly victimized.

It is uncomfortable and indeed painful to acknowledge that abuse happens in our communities, and even that it is sometimes perpetuated by people with honorable titles. Yet our focus should be on those who have been hurt and who need healing.

וישב *Vayeishev*

(Genesis 37:1–40:23)

For additional commentary on *Vayeishev*, see "Chanukah."

Vayeishev
Lawrence S. Kushner, 1995

Poet Joel Rosenberg has wondered if the "apparent" confusion over the ownership of the caravan into which Joseph's brothers sold him—first by Ishmaelites (Gen. 37:25) and then, just three verses later, by Midianites (Gen. 37:28)—has any relationship to the descendants of Abraham's first marriage to Hagar (who bore Ishmael—Gen. 16:15) and Abraham's third marriage to Ketura (who bore Midian—Gen. 25:2).

We read in Gen. 39:20 that "Joseph's master took him and put him in the jail, a place where the prisoners of Pharaoh were incarcerated, and he was there in the jail." Where else would he be?

Vayeishev
Lawrence S. Kushner, 1996

Where was Reuven when Joseph needed him (Gen. 37:22, 37:29)? Did he so trust his brothers that, having persuaded them to throw Joseph into the pit rather than kill him, he believed that Joseph would be safe while he walked away? Where did he go?

We know from the dreams that Joseph is destined to rule over his family—somewhere. Had the brothers acted brotherly, this would still have happened—but they all would have been on good terms with each other. Similarly, in an earlier portion, Rebekah could surely have carried out the prophecy of Jacob's dominance without deceiving Isaac. Though the brothers tried to foil God's plan while Rebekah tried to carry it out, both enabled God's plan to be fulfilled in an unGodly fashion. Why did God refrain from showing all of them how to act morally?

Vayeishev: Joseph Astray
Stephen E. Cohen, 1997

After Jacob sends Joseph out to check on his brothers in Shechem, a man finds Joseph *to-eh basadeh,* usually translated "astray in the field" (Gen. 37:15). K'li Yakar follows an alternative—but entirely sound—understanding of the phrase.

K'li Yakar   Joseph went astray *regarding* the field referred to in the Cain and Abel story. For Joseph ought to have taken to heart what happened to Abel, that because of jealousy, a man killed his brother. But Joseph believed that in the case of Cain and Abel, in which it says explicitly "while they were in the field" (Gen. 4:8), that it was *about* the field that he said, "The field in which you are standing is mine!" Therefore, Joseph reasoned, "Cain had a motive, but my brothers would not kill me, for jealousy over a coat cannot compare to jealousy over a field." But in this Joseph "went astray" regarding the field. He did not understand the nature of jealousy: that over a small thing, a man will rise up and murder his neighbor.

Comment   Joseph's *"Hineini"* response to his father's request in Gen. 37:13 feels like an acknowledgment that he is in danger. Should Joseph have refused his father's request?

Vayeishev
Jim Ponet, 1998

Joseph/Yosef, the one who increases, is a Herzlian figure, a fiery, dream-driven life that utterly transforms the terms of Jewish history.

Can you not hear Joseph's narcissistic certainty in the words Herzl penned in his diary in 1897 after he had convened the first Zionist Congress in Basel? "At Basel I founded the Jewish state. If I were to say this today, I would be greeted by universal laughter. In five years, perhaps, and certainly in fifty, everyone will see it."

His brothers were right to call him a *baal chalomot* (dreamer [Gen. 37:19]). How much a master of dreams they did not know: a dreamer who interprets and who implements his dreams and who knows how to avoid being pulled into the dreams of others, such as Potiphar's wife (Gen. 39:11).

We always re-meet Joseph at Chanukah, the time when historical (and hemispherical) darkness is illuminated by a memory of what may yet be possible in history. Chanukah's strange mixture of the historical and the messianic is reflected in the Joseph narrative, where ambition and chutzpah combine with the miraculous to establish a career path.

Note that the Judah excursus at Gen. 38:26 serves to establish Judah as truth-teller. He had already shown himself a convincing orator at Gen. 37:26–27. Unlike Joseph and Reuben, Judah knows how to speak with his brothers so as to inspire affection.

Vayeishev
Stephen E. Cohen, 1999

Typically, in the midrashic literature, we find the Rabbinic sages defending and justifying the questionable behavior of the biblical protagonists. Here it is reversed. The passage begins with three sages imagining Joseph accusing his brothers of cruelty, or of promiscuity, or of arrogance. These sages, like the biblical text, offer no judgment as to the acceptability of Joseph's behavior. But then Rabbi Y'hudah bar Shimon weighs in with a ferocious assault on Joseph's ostensibly innocent report.

B'reishit Rabbah (84:7) "And Joseph brought their evil report to their father . . ." (Gen. 37:2). What did he say? Rabbi Meir, Rabbi Y'hudah, and Rabbi Shimon each expressed his opinion. Rabbi Meir: "Your sons are to be suspected regarding *eiver min hachai* [tearing a limb from a living animal]." Rabbi Shimon: "They are gazing at the local women." Rabbi Y'hudah: "They are insulting the sons of the concubines and referring to them as slaves." Rabbi Y'hudah bar Simon said: "For all three of these reports he was punished. The Holy One Blessed Be He said: 'You said, "Your sons are to be suspected regarding *eiver min hachai*." By your life! Even in the moment of their disgrace they were slaughtering properly *vayishchatu s'ir izim* [Gen. 37:31]. You said, "They are insulting the sons of the concubines and referring to them as slaves." Behold "Joseph was sold as a slave" (Ps. 105:17) [note that in this psalm the sale of Joseph is clearly rendered as God's plan—no mention is made of the brothers]. And you said, "They are gazing at the local women." By your life! I let the bear loose upon you! [referring to Potifar's wife].'"

Comment Why does Y'hudah bar Shimon blame the victim for his suffering?

Vayeishev
Sheldon Marder, 2000

"Hear this dream which I have dreamed. There we were binding sheaves [אלומים]" (Gen. 37:6–7). Rashi: "As the *Targum* translates it, 'tying bundles,' sheaves [עמרין]. And similarly, 'carrying his sheaves' [אלומותיו]; Ps. 126:6]." Wrote Martin Buber: "The Bible seeks to be read as One Book, so that no one of its parts remains self-contained; rather *every* part is held open to every other. The Bible seeks to be present as One Book for its readers so intensely that in reading or reciting an important passage they recall all the passages connected to it, and in particular those connected to it by linguistic identity, resemblance, or affinity; so intensely that all these passages illuminate and explain one another, so that they cohere into a unity of meaning . . ." (Martin Buber and Franz Rosenzweig, *Scripture and Translation*, trans. L. Rosenwald with Everett Fox, Indiana University Press, 1994, p. 91).

Vayeishev provides a rich, evocative illustration of Buber's teaching the sheaves in Joseph's dream and the sheaves in Psalm 126 are the only occurrences of אלומים/אלומות in the Bible, and both times the word appears in connection with dreaming! What "unity of meaning" is suggested by the Psalmist's use of this singular term from the Joseph narrative? Does Joseph's life story illuminate the psalm? Can the psalm be read as a commentary of sorts on Gen. 37:6–7? Is it possible that the framers of our liturgy utilized Psalm 126 in connection with *Birkat HaMazon* in order to have us reflect on "Joseph themes"—themes such as "abundance and scarcity" and "reversal of fortune"—as we sit around our Shabbat tables?

Vayeishev
Kenneth J. Weiss, 2001

NO! PERIOD!

"His master's wife said, 'Lie with me.' But he refused" (Gen. 39:7–8).

It's not what Potiphar's wife proposed, it's **why** and **how** Joseph refused her blandishments. Joseph, seventeen years old, hormones raging, said "No" to a beautiful woman, even though it would have been easy to share a "yes" moment with her that likely would never have been discovered by another soul.

Why was Joseph's response "No"? *B'reishit Rabbah* suggests that Joseph was about to succumb when he noticed that the woman had placed a sheet over the head of an idol engraved above her bed. Paraphrasing Joseph: You seem ashamed lest your idol see what we're about to do. How much more should I be ashamed before God, whose eyes see everything in the world? Rabbi Huna speculates that Joseph "saw his father's face, at which his blood cooled." Joseph felt watchful eyes, spying and recording.

The S'fat Emet puts a more positive spin on Joseph's refusal: he was raised well by his father, whose moral lessons he internalized. Adin Steinsaltz, indeed, speaks of Joseph's resistance to this temptation as the primary rationale for labeling him a tzaddik.

How was Joseph's refusal of Mrs. Potiphar's advances couched? The S'fat Emet notes that the answer to this key question affirms Joseph as a perennial positive role model. "**(First)** Joseph refused **(then)** said to his master's wife. . . ." His refusal was immediate and unequivocal. He allowed no possibility of being misunderstood: "No! Period!"

"Only **after** having made it clear that he refuses to sin may [a person] cite his reasons for refusing, as Joseph did" (see Gen. 28:8–9, as quoted in Alexander Zusia Freedman, *Wellsprings of Torah*, Judaica Press, 1974).

Vayeishev
Kenneth J. Weiss, 2004

Joseph's garments connote stages in his impactful life:

- His "ornamented tunic" (Gen. 37:3) attested to his father's singular love. Subsequently, Joseph and the כתנת פסים (*k'tonet pasim*) were forcibly separated.
- Potiphar's wife "caught [Joseph] by his coat/בבגדו [*bigdo*]" as he fled her seductive enticements (Gen. 39:12).
- Upon learning that Pharaoh had summoned him from the dungeon, Joseph "changed his clothes/שמלתיו [*simlotav*]" (Gen. 41:14).
- Later, Pharaoh gave Joseph "[official] robes of fine linen/בגדי שש [*bigdei sheish*]" (Gen. 41:42).
- Jacob surely carried Joseph's tunic with him when, decades later, he left for their improbable reunion: "So Israel set out with all/וכל [*v'chol*] that was his" (Gen. 46:1).

When father and son embraced in warm reunion, perhaps the old man (re)placed the bloodied tunic back where it belonged, around his beloved son's shoulders ... closing the circle.

Vayeishev
Alan Cook, 2005

"... וירד יהודה" (*Vayeired Y'hudah*, "Judah left" [Gen. 38:1]).

Rashi teaches that interrupting the story of Joseph being sold into slavery with the story of Judah and Tamar is not all that strange. He suggests that Judah was spurned by his brothers when they saw how their behavior toward Joseph had taken a toll on Jacob. For it was Judah who had suggested that they sell Joseph, and now the brothers feel they must distance themselves from Judah, given their father's distress.

Judah's actions to this point do not do much to recommend him as the one from whom we derive the name of our people and our faith. His interaction with Tamar is not exactly praiseworthy, either. So what positive is there that we can ascribe to Judah?

When confronted with the evidence, Judah admits to being the father of Tamar's child. He declares צדקה ממני (*tzad'kah mimeni*, "she is more right than I" [Gen. 38:26]). He recognizes his flaws in character that have brought them to this juncture, and he is finally ready to own up to who he has been (and tacitly vows to try to change).

Judah has come to terms with his identity. It took a departure from his brothers, from the family fold, for him to become a man and take responsibility for his actions.

In the epilogue of Arthur Miller's *Death of a Salesman*, Linda Loman stands by Willy's grave and laments, "He never knew who he was."

In contrast, Judah now knows what he is. He has determined that he will grow from this experience. And so, out of the bad, something positive springs forth, as Judah and Tamar's son Peretz becomes the progenitor of King David.

Vayeishev
Amy Scheinerman, 2006

In Gen. 37:25–27, Yosef's brothers sell him to a caravan of Ishmaelites coming from Gilead, but in Gen. 37:28, they haul him out of the pit and sell him to Midianites traders. If that isn't sufficiently confusing, in the very next verse, Reuven is surprised to find the pit that once confined Yosef empty.

Rashi's solution is to claim that the Ishmaelites sold Yosef to the Midianites, who in turn sold him to the Egyptians. Reuven, meanwhile, had not been present for the first transaction because he either had returned to serve his father (*B'reishit Rabbah* 84:15) or, alternatively, was engaged in כפרה (*kaparah*, "atonement") for his sin against his father (*B'reishit Rabbah* 84:19). Ibn Ezra, however, regards the Ishmaelites and Midianites as references to the same traders.

Rashbam, Rashi's grandson, attempts another solution: "The brothers threw Joseph into a pit . . . and then they sat down to eat. During their meal, they noticed an approaching caravan, which emboldened Judah to argue for selling Joseph into slavery. Meanwhile, Midianite merchants passed by, and they pulled him, and they took Joseph up out of the pit, and they sold Joseph to Ishmaelites for twenty weights of silver, and they brought Joseph into Egypt."

Many commentators trip over themselves in an attempt to suggest that the brothers merely discussed the possibility of selling Yosef when events overtook them and the Midianites surreptitiously stole him. Their guilty feelings (Gen. 44:16 and 45:5), however, suggest otherwise.

This story provides numerous avenues for discussing guilt and responsibility.

Vayeishev
Amy Scheinerman, 2007

Rav Avraham Kook pointed out a prescient connection between the conflict between Yosef and Y'hudah, and Chanukah, which begins next week. The brothers are emblematic of differing ideological schools of thought concerning the mission and meaning of Judaism. Yosef promoted the vision and mission of *Am Yisrael* as an אור גוים להיות ישועתי עד-קצה הארץ (*or goyim lih'yot y'shuati ad k'tzei haaretz*, "a light of nations, that My salvation may reach the ends of the earth" [Isa. 49:6]) and hence encouraged interaction between Jews and other peoples and nations to expose the latter to the teachings of Judaism. Y'hudah sought to protect the distinctiveness of the Jewish people and encouraged הן-עם לבדד ישכן ובגוים לא יתחשב (*hen am l'vadad yishkon uvagoyim lo yitchashav*, "them to be a people that dwells apart, not reckoned among the nations" [Num. 23:9]).

These ideologies arise in every generation, from the Hasmonean and the Hellenists to our own day. Do we seek openness, interaction, and assimilation, and to share our ways with others? Or do we seek distinctiveness and cultural intensity to preserve our values and traditions? Perhaps more realistically: how do we achieve a balance between two competing yet legitimate ideologies? Josef and Y'hudah, after all, were brothers. Just as they lived in the same family, these two ideologies coexist among one people. Y'hudah recognized this when he said, "What profit is there if we kill our brother?" (Gen. 37:26). And perhaps this is why Yaakov sends Y'hudah ahead of him to Yosef להורת לפניו גשנה (*l'horot l'fanav Goshnah*, "to point the way before him to Goshen" [Gen. 46:28]), to point out the way to him that Yaakov's clan would live among the Egyptians as well as separate from them in Goshen.

Vayeishev
Janice Garfunkel, 2008

Joseph gets in trouble in part because he is so clearly and outrageously his father's favorite and in part because of his own arrogance.

Rabbinic texts dwell a great deal on the virtue of humility, but "humility" is a theme I don't hear emphasized in modern, liberal Judaism. On the contrary, we in the twenty-first century focus much more on self-esteem, on positive thinking, on tooting our own horns. One rabbi, asked by a supervisor how she thought she was doing in her role, replied, "Well, that depends. Is this a job interview or Yom Kippur?" Meaning, except in the context of Yom Kippur, we are generally trained to emphasize our accomplishments and to downplay our weaknesses.

In job interviews, when asked to name our weaknesses, most of us talk about how, gosh darn, we are workaholics! Humility is not rewarded much.

The rabbis of old did not have to write resumes or college applications.

A lot of us are attracted to the rabbinate because we like to be the center of attention, because we like to be an authority. Many Jews come to be authorities—on law, medicine, mathematics—but rabbis are authorities on Torah, on how we ought to live our lives, even on the meaning of life! It is easy to fall into the trap of arrogance. It is easy for us to become prima donnas.

It is also easy for us to base all our feelings of self-worth on the approval of our congregants or those whom we lead. This is, of course, a form of arrogance. "Look at me! Look at what I can do! I dreamt that the sun and moon and eleven stars bowed down to me!"

Perhaps it isn't a bad idea for us to study some of those ancient texts on humility.

Vayeishev
Louis Reiser, 2009

Like the best novels, the opening line of the Joseph story tells it all. "Now Jacob settled in the land of his father's wandering, the land of Canaan" (Gen. 37:1). These words encompass the struggle of the past and the yearning for the future. The reader also knows of the uneasy balance between them.

"Jacob settled." Consider all the possible nuances:

- He came to rest in one place, no longer the wanderer.
- His life was quiet and orderly, past struggles resolved.
- Jacob could see the future he desired. The family business was in good hands.
- He had arrived at a good place in life. He had all that he needed: family, livelihood, status, and more.

Oh, the relief Jacob must feel. The struggle, the wandering, the uncertainty is past. Finally this family can be at ease. All is settled and established—*hakol sharir v'kayam*. Abraham's call to leave land and birthplace and father's house is resolved here where Jacob has it all.

This one brief, shining moment is soon shattered by Joseph's "death," the years of famine, and the eventual resettlement to Egypt. Still Jacob yearns for this one moment; his dying wish is to return to this place where "Abraham and his wife Sarah were buried; there

Isaac and his wife Rebekah were buried; and there I buried Leah—the field and the cave in it, bought from the Hittites" (Gen. 49:31–32).

Like Jacob, we and our congregants balance between past struggles and future uncertainties. May we recognize and acknowledge the blessing of our settled moments.

מקץ *Mikeitz*

(Genesis 41:1–44:17)

For additional commentary on *Mikeitz*, see "Chanukah."

Mikeitz
Lawrence S. Kushner, 1995

On the theory that the title of a *parashah* in some way summarizes the theme of the whole *parashah*, in what sense is *Mikeitz* ("at the end of") an appropriate title? Is something coming to an end, is it the end of something? (It is the end of Joseph's captivity—but how about the rest of the portion, and thereafter?)

"And he shaved himself and changed his garment" (Gen. 41:14); "and [Pharaoh] dressed him in linen garments" (41:42). At every juncture in his life, Joseph is changing his clothes—consider the "coat of many colors," the garment torn by Potiphar's wife, and these two verses. What does this image suggest? Are clothes the equivalent of name changes for Abraham, Sarah, and Jacob, suggesting a change in character? Which is the true Joseph—the boy/man inside or the clothes outside?

This *parashah* usually falls on Shabbat Chanukah. Is this merely an accident of the calendar or do you see some connection?

Mikeitz
Lawrence S. Kushner, 1996

Speaking of human action accomplishing or foiling God's plans—in which category did the butler's forgetting about Joseph fall?

Joseph and Pharaoh have two parallel dreams; the butler and baker each dream once. Why the difference?

In Gen. 39:5 (*Parashat Vayeishev*), God blesses Potiphar's house for Joseph's sake. We never read of God's hand in Joseph's administration of the land of Egypt. Is God present or absent in his actions as second to Pharaoh?

Mikeitz: Reunion and Intoxication
Stephen E. Cohen, 1997

Rashi injects a piece of new information into the story of Joseph's banquet with his brothers . . . before he sends them back, with the goblet planted in Benjamin's sack. The Maharal accepts Rashi's comment, but finds it requires further explanation.

Rashi "They drank and became drunk with him" (Gen. 43:34). From the day they had sold him, they had not drunk wine. Nor had he drunk any wine. And on that day, they drank.

Maharal (citing Rashi's comment) But this is difficult. Since they did not yet know it was Joseph, why would they drink now? Maybe they were wondering what this mighty and important minister wanted. "Yesterday he accused us of spying, and now he is drinking with us. It must be that he still thinks we are spies. And he wants to drink with us because 'wine goes in and the secret comes out.' So they said, 'If we **don't** drink, he will say, "You are not drinking because you are afraid of revealing your secret."' Therefore, let us drink with him, and become drunk and he will not hear anything from us, and we will clear ourselves from his suspicion."

Comment In Rashi's version of this story, what does the alcohol represent? Why would the brothers have abstained for all the years after selling Joseph? And why would Joseph have abstained after being sold? Finally, are there any interpretations beside the

Maharal's of why they would drink to intoxication at this particular moment?

Mikeitz
Jim Ponet, 1998

In this *parashah* we see that the dreamer is also a schemer, that the visionary interpreter has a political sense and, more importantly, an administrative and economic intuition. Is it Alan Greenspan at the Fed or George Soros advising the U.S. to shore up the IMF, or Robert Rubin at Treasury? The Jew rising to a position of responsibility in the established government, allied with the powerful, more Frankfurter than Brandeis.

Prime Minister Benjamin Netanyahu's father, Benzion, in his magisterial opus *The Origins of the Inquisition in Fifteenth Century Spain* (Random House, 1995), sees in this recurrent Jewish posture the historical origin of all anti-Semitism. He writes that it is "an ironclad rule in the history of group relations the majority's toleration of every minority lessens with the worsening of the majority's condition, especially when paralleled with a steady improvement of the minority's status. Any serious decline in the power of the rulers is then seen by the people as a suitable opportunity to strike at the minority with its entire force."

Not the Egypt of Joseph (arguably 1500 B.C.E.), but the Egypt under Persia in the sixth century B.C.E. and certainly the Egypt under Alexander and then Ptolemy in the fourth century B.C.E., was, as Peter Schafer puts it in *Judeophobia* (1997), "where it all started, where the major tensions and vectors which produced anti-Semitism were laid out."

Is Joseph out to save the Egyptians or to save himself by strengthening Pharaoh? The Egyptians end up enslaved to Pharaoh, alive but indentured. Is Joseph out to torment his brothers or to bring them to a demonstration of true penance? These questions hover unresolved over the Book of Genesis.

Mikeitz
Stephen E. Cohen, 1999

When Joseph's brothers first come down to Egypt for grain, he throws them in prison for three days. At that moment, for the first time, they remember and speak of Joseph in the pit. Ramban wonders about the fact that, in their remembering, we the reader are given a more detailed account of the assault than when the incident actually occurred.

Ramban   "Alas! We are guilty because of our brother, for we saw his suffering as he pleaded with us, but we did not hear" (Gen. 42:21). They considered their cruelty deserving of greater punishment than having sold him. For their brother, their own flesh, was pleading and prostrating before them; but they had no compassion. And the text did not detail this at the time. Perhaps because it is obvious and natural that a man will plead with his brothers when he comes into their power, to harm him, and he will swear to them by the life of their father, and do everything he can to save himself from death. Or perhaps the text sought to be brief about their disgrace. Or it may simply be the way that texts are sometimes brief in one place and lengthy in another place.

Comment   Ramban's question calls our attention to the genius of the Torah's use of flashback. It is not just the brothers who are forced to say *lo shamanu*, "we did not hear." We the reader had also not fully heard Joseph's cries. Only now, twenty years later, do we face the true cruelty of that moment.

Mikeitz
Sheldon Marder, 2000

Said Jacob to his sons, "Take some of the choice products of the land in your baggage, and carry them down as a gift for the man—some balm and some honey, gum, ladanum, pistachio nuts, and almonds" (Gen. 43:11). How is it that during the harsh seven-year famine Jacob has available this fine assortment of produce? "All these," writes Nogah Hareuveni, "produce crops even in drought years, since they require relatively small quantities of rain." In fact, Israel's wildflowers (which enable bees to produce honey) are *more* abundant in drought years "to ensure the next generations by hastening the flowering and seed-making process" (*Nature in Our Biblical Heritage,* Neot Kedumin, 1980). Israel's flowers respond to crisis in a quintessentially Jewish way—they do what it takes to ensure the next generations!

The phrase זמרת הארץ (*zimrat haaretz,* "choice products") occurs only once in the Bible, but three of these choice products (balm, gum, ladanum) occur strategically elsewhere. They were the very merchandise carried from Gilead to Egypt by the Ishmaelites who bought Joseph from his brothers. Now these products are brought to Egypt once again—this time as a gift for Joseph from his brothers! They are, says Rashi, "the reward of the righteous."

Reading *Mikeitz,* we citizens of the "world economy" might reflect on the ways in which choice products and merchandise still reflect and symbolize the comings and goings in our lives.

Mikeitz: Endings and Beginnings
Kenneth J. Weiss, 2001

"It was at the end of . . ." (Gen. 41:1).

Mikeitz is always read during or near Chanukah. Gematria suggests the link between the *parashah* and the Festival. *Mikeitz* has 2,025 words. The numerical value of *ner* (light) is 250. As Chanukah has 8 days, multiply 250 by 8 and add 25, since Chanukah begins on 25 Kislev. The total is 2,025, the exact number of words in *Mikeitz.*

In the year 2000, Chanukah fell very near the end of the year. It is always the last Jewish Festival of the secular year. The *parashah's* title and the Festival's timing move us to reflect on endings and transitions. December is a time to reflect and, if appropriate, to put loss and sadness (how much of these we've experienced recently!) behind us.

But consider: Are not endings also beginnings? Our *parashah* is called "at the end," yet it actually describes a beginning: the Israelite experience in Egypt, and Joseph's essential role.

Further: Is not life a series of endings that are also beginnings: weeks, years, life stages? How does this apply to the end of life? For those with faith, this end, too, marks a new beginning.

Mikeitz
Kenneth J. Weiss, 2004

Maurice Samuel wrote of Joseph's "unanalyzable and fatal gift of personal magnetism." Jacob/Israel acknowledged it. Joseph's brothers saw it too; fearful, they exiled him from their lives.

Potiphar's wife was drawn to Joseph (not just "any" slave). Pharaoh's cupbearer and baker experienced Joseph's gift, which Pharaoh himself learned of (and exploited). Joseph listened to—and (acknowledging God's help)—interpreted the monarch's dreams. Pharaoh—impressed and moved—appointed him to an office of supreme prominence and importance.

In every generation some are especially endowed. From presumptuous youth to powerful courtier, Joseph—throughout his life—influenced and shaped many, not least of all his own family.

Mikeitz
Alan Cook, 2005

"ופרעה חלם [*Ufaro choleim*, 'Pharaoh dreamed']" (Gen. 41:1).

Ordinarily, we would expect to see the grammatical construction of this phrase as ויחלם פרעה, *va'yachalam Paro*.

However, as the Malbim notes, this clues us in to the fact that Pharaoh's experience was different from ordinary dreaming. Joseph was able to interpret for Pharaoh, the Malbim writes, because he abandoned the assumptions that had bogged down the Egyptian courtiers: Joseph recognized that this was one dream, not two; that it concerned public welfare, not merely Pharaoh's personal affairs; and that it was not mystical and esoteric, but plain and straightforward.

Joseph had the perspective that Pharaoh's magicians lacked. Sometimes all it takes is for us to view a problem through a different lens, and then what once seemed to be an unsolvable puzzle or an unattainable goal suddenly comes into focus.

On חנוכה (Chanukah), we celebrate the ability and willingness of the Hasmoneans to respond in a courageous and forward-thinking manner to what might have appeared to many to be a daunting problem. Motivated by his love of Judaism, and his desire to preserve its traditions, Mattathias proclaimed, "Let everyone who is zealous for the law and supports the covenant come out with me!" (I Macc. 2:27).

He and his sons faced down a Syrian-Greek army that was more organized and better armed than they. But rather than go in with pessimism and see it as a losing battle, the Maccabees saw things from a different perspective, believed in the righteousness of their cause, and held out hope that victory was possible.

Mikeitz
Amy Scheinerman, 2007

Five Cities of Refuge: Weekly Reflections of Genesis, Exodus, Leviticus, Numbers, Deuteronomy, by Lawrence Kushner and David Mamet (Schocken, 2003), tells us that Yosef interprets three sets of double dreams. But does he? He interprets the dreams of the cupbearer and baker in prison, and Pharaoh's dreams of cows and corn once elevated from the dungeon, but his own dreams of sheaves of wheat and heavenly luminaries Yosef only recounts. It is his family that interprets the dreams and holds them against Yosef.

Wrestling with Angels: What Genesis Teaches Us About Our Spiritual Identity, Sexuality and Personal Relationships, by Naomi H. Rosenblatt and Joshua Horwitz (Delta, 1996), charges Yosef with "brash self-confidence" and "self-absorption." But is this accurate? Yosef ventures out to check on his brothers, a risky undertaking. He earns the trust of Potiphar, the prison warden, and Pharaoh; in each case he performs well beyond what is asked of him, exhibiting responsibility and integrity. Indeed, he saves the Egyptians and many others from starvation.

What is more, Yosef repeatedly and firmly rejects the advances of his master's wife (compare Reuven and Bilhah, or Y'hudah and Tamar).

Have we fallen into the trap of Yosef's family? Are we viewing Yosef through their jealous and suspicious eyes? Is this the modern tendency to convert every hero to an anti-hero? Another view suggests that Yosef is a צדיק (tzaddik) whose treatment of his brothers is both a test of their sincerity and תשובה (t'shuvah, "repentance") and an opportunity for them to atone and cleanse themselves of guilt. If we persist in seeing Yosef as self-absorbed and the interpreter of his early dreams, we fail to see the other side, not only of Yosef, but of ourselves. H. G. Wells wrote, "Moral indignation is jealousy with a halo."

Mikeitz
Amy Scheinerman, 2008

Yosef, once the poor lad tossed into a pit and sold into slavery, is now the prime minister of Egypt, and his own brothers, who once sought his demise, stand groveling before him. For one who would seek revenge, could anything be sweeter? If revenge was on Yosef's mind, we might expect that the sight of his brothers conjured up a vivid memory of that last day, when they threw him into the pit and then callously sat down to eat and drink.

But Yosef recalls something quite different: "For though Yosef recognized his brothers, they did not recognize him. Recalling the dreams that he had dreamed about them, Joseph said to them, 'You are spies, you have come to see the land in its nakedness'" (Gen. 42:8–9). Ramban claims that this demonstrates that Yosef wishes to be instrumental in the fulfillment of his divinely authored dreams. This suggests that Yosef must concoct a scheme to bring his father and youngest brother to Egypt. (No explanation is given for the missing "moon" of mother Rachel.) Hence when all is said and done, Yosef does not hold his brothers accountable for even their crime of selling him into slavery, for he sees everything that has transpired as part of God's plan (Gen. 45:5).

We are disinclined to see the events of our lives and the world around us as strictly providential. It seems to conflict with our notion of human free will. Yet Yosef both affirms human free will, by testing to see if his brothers have changed, and simultaneously affirms God's active involvement in the world.

Could we find such a balance?

Mikeitz
Amy Scheinerman, 2009

Parashat Mikeitz is almost always read during Chanukah and has come to be associated with the theme of the victory of the weak over the powerful. Even Pharaoh's dreams, in the opening *p'sukim* (verses) of the *parashah*, can be read through that lens: The ugly, gaunt cows overcome and consume the handsome, sturdy cows. The thin, scorched ears of grain swallow up the solid, full ears of grain. In this regard, it is significant that Pharaoh is standing by the Nile River in his dreams. The Nile, for Pharaoh, is a source of reliable power and abundance. For Jews, the Reed Sea is our site of redemption and reliance on God and the values of Torah: the waters part when God, Moses, and the people Israel act in concert.

In fact, *Mikeitz* turns the notion of who is powerful and who is weak on its head, just as Pharaoh's dreams suggest. Yosef, young and enslaved, possesses keen insight, self-control, and vision. In the long run, these are more powerful attributes than the throne of Egypt, and Pharaoh cannot survive without Yosef. We often mistake brute strength and propensity to coerce and control for genuine strength and meaningful power. *Mikeitz* therefore suits Chanukah well and is most often accompanied by Zechariah's words: *Lo v'chayil v'lo v'choach ki im b'ruchi*, "Not by might, nor by power, but by My spirit" (Zech. 4:6).

And thus Ben Zoma taught in *Pirkei Avot* 4:1, "Who is mighty? Those who conquer their evil impulse, as it is written [in Proverbs 16:32]: 'One who is slow to anger is better than the mighty, and one who rules over his spirit, than one who conquers a city.'" An apt description of Yosef. Does it describe us, as well? How do we conceive, cultivate, and use power and the powerful tug of the crowd?

ויגש *Vayigash*

(Genesis 44:18–47:27)

Vayigash
Lawrence S. Kushner, 1995

In this *parashah*, the root of the title word is repeated several times (see Gen. 44:18, 45:4). Judah approaches Joseph, as a result of which Joseph calls all the brothers to approach him. (Why doesn't he approach them?) One might even suggest that the place where the family will reside, Goshen, is an anagram of the root of *Vayigash*, n-g-sh. What are we to learn from all these approaches?

This *parashah* has become the paradigm for the test of *t'shuvah* (repentance)—whether, facing the same situation in which we originally sinned, we will this time act differently. Is Joseph therefore doing a favor to his brothers, helping them realize that they have done *t'shuvah*? Is he testing them to determine for himself if they have reformed? Is he just taking revenge by taunting them with power games? Can you think of other tests for true *t'shuvah*?

In Gen. 46:1–4 Jacob makes an offering to God before he enters Egypt, and God reassures him about his journey. Joseph, on the other hand, invites his family into Egypt without ever consulting God. Is Joseph, with all his insight into divinely sent dreams, as "religious" as his father? How would you compare the spirituality of Jacob and Joseph?

Vayigash
Lawrence S. Kushner, 1996

Judah is an intriguing foil for Joseph in these stories. From the callous brother willing to sell Joseph into slavery to the chastened father-in-law tricked into obeying the law of the *yibum* (levirate marriage), Judah appears in this *parashah* as the emblem of the brother who has done *t'shuvah* (repentance). Has Joseph himself grown? How would you compare the characters of the two brothers at this point in the story? Has Judah's sins helped him grow? Has Joseph been "cheated" of some maturation because he appears the innocent in these stories? Aren't we supposed to be innocents?

Indeed, in Gen. 46:33–34 Joseph seems to tell his brothers to lie about their occupation, which in Gen. 47:3 they refuse to do, acknowledging that they are shepherds. Do the brothers here show themselves more virtuous than Joseph, or are they engaging in a further betrayal of him, since he asked them to say something else? How important is truth-telling in the moral scheme of things?

Vayigash: Judah's Rope
Stephen E. Cohen, 1997

Joseph the prime minister is often pictured toying with his brothers, alternately accusing them and honoring them. In this midrash, however, Joseph is motionless, hidden, waiting for one of his brothers to come and find him.

B'reishit Rabbah **(93:4)** "Like deep water is counsel in the heart of man, but a man of understanding will draw it out" (Prov. 20:5) The image is of a deep well, whose waters are cold and clear, but no one is able to reach it to drink from it. Then a person comes and ties rope to rope, and cord to cord, and string to string, and draws forth the water and drinks from it, and then everyone comes and draws forth and drinks. Thus did Judah refuse to budge and continued to press Joseph, answering him word for word, until he stood right at Joseph's heart.

Comment Judah's speech does, somehow, force Joseph to reveal himself. Which are the crucial points in his speech, bringing him closer and closer to Joseph's heart?

Vayigash
Jim Ponet, 1998

Is Joseph caught up in a nightmare of vengeance, a perverse game of manipulation? Can he ever stop playing with his brothers this way? Not until something awakens him from the spell of the past (Gen. 42:9). Y'hudah/Judah, the *modeh*—the truth teller/confessor—turns the tide. He risks intimacy (*vayigash*), tells the truth, and so wins Joseph's heart, bringing the story to a conclusion that may not have been inevitable.

In "telling truth to power," Judah brings about the moment of *t'shuvah* (repentance), his confession both effecting Joseph's turn and confirming the turn in the brothers. Compare this to Yonah's confession to the sailors on board his ship of flight (Jon. 1:9). Yonah's true confessions are the key to the story.

Explore also the power of the verb *nigash* (to approach, draw near). See, for example, the first use of it in Genesis at 18:23 when it introduces Abraham's protest before God concerning Sodom and Gomorrah. At Gen. 27:21–22, the intimacy of *g'sha-nah* ("pray come near") does not preclude deceit. At Gen. 33:6–7 *nigash* is the verb used to describe Jacob's self-presentation to Esau. *Nigash* signals the danger of intimacy, the possibility of speech that may penetrate consciousness. It also signals war, as at II Samuel 10:13. (See *B'reishit Rabbah* 49:8.) Is there a connection between *nigash* and Goshen, that piece of Egypt where the children of Jacob/Israel dwell (Gen. 47:27)?

My hunch is that the ability to draw near, to achieve intimacy with gesture and language, is a Judaean character trait. Judah is expert at it, but Joseph, alas, fails. See Gen. 45:4, where he calls his brothers to *nigash*, approach him. Rashi, Ibn Ezra, and Hizkuni follow the midrash in maintaining that Joseph showed them that he was circumcised in an attempt to bridge the abyss between them and him.

Nigash, the verb of bridging gaps, always carries with it the risk of war. *Karov* (near) and *k'rav* (battle). *Lechem* (bread) and *milchamah* (war). See Lev. 10:3. Jews draw near—always at risk but out of necessity—to their host cultures, in language and gesture, as in Alexandria, in Spain, in Germany, in America.

Vayigash
Stephen E. Cohen, 1999

When Joseph finally reveals himself to his brothers, he orders the Egyptians out of the room. Ramban describes Joseph, in this moment, as still calculating and thinking clearly. Or HaChayim and Malbim are more interested in the emotional content of the phrase *lo yachol l'hitapeik* (could not control himself).

Ramban The reason for his removing all the Egyptians was so that they not hear about the sale [of Joseph by his brothers], for this would be a disgrace for them and also a stumbling block for him. For the servants of Pharaoh would say, "These men are deceivers; let them not dwell in our land nor walk in our palaces. They betrayed both their brother and their father. What are they likely to do to our king and his people?" And they would no longer believe in Joseph either.

Or HaChayim He had not the strength to wait until all those standing around would leave, and so he shouted, "Remove every person!"—that is, quickly—that they should not simply tell everyone to leave. Because if they all departed on their own, they would linger in going out. *Lo yachol l'hitapeik l'chol hanitzavim* means that he could not bear the length of time of the removal of all the crowd. And when the text says, "No one stood by Joseph," it means that no one delayed—they all departed immediately, together.

Malbim He could not prevent himself from weeping, so he gave his voice to weep. In other words, the voice with which he said, "Remove every person from me!" was weeping; he could not prevent himself from weeping.

Comment Is it conceivable that at this moment of dramatic climax Joseph was *both* shrewdly calculating *and* emotionally exploding?

Vayigash
Sheldon Marder, 2000

"Then Israel said to Joseph, 'Now I can die, having seen for myself that you are still alive'" (Gen. 46:30). In these poignant words Sforno hears a prayer: Jacob's plea that he die in his present state of "salvation"—rescued from years of grief over the loss of Joseph. Nahum Sarna hears Jacob saying, "I am ready for death now that my dearest wish has been fulfilled."

In Denise Levertov's poem "Death Psalm: O Lord of Mysteries" (*Poems 1972–1982*, New Directions Publishing Corporation, 2001), we meet an old woman who, like Jacob, is ready to die. "She accused herself / She forgave herself / . . . She abandoned certain angers / . . . She told her sons and daughters she was ready / . . . She did not die. / She did not die but lies half-speechless, incontinent, / aching in body, wandering in mind / in a hospital room. / . . . The black sores are parts of her that have died. / . . . She made ready to die, she prayed, she made her peace. . . . / But the hour has passed and she has not died."

S'forno says the message of Gen. 46:30 is this: Jacob wants death to come at *this* moment, while he is happy and feeling blessed, before additional troubles come upon him. But Levertov describes a different reality—a condition she calls "laggard death," death's defiance of our readiness for it. Incontinence, pain, black sores on the skin. Donald Capps (professor of pastoral theology at Princeton Theological Seminary) calls these signs of illness a "language of the body" to which pastoral care must be attentive. How can we help when death is "laggard"? How do we respond, in hospital or nursing home, to "sighs too deep for words"? How do we affirm life's goodness in the face of this all too common crisis, "laggard death"? (See Donald Capps, *The Poet's Gift toward the Renewal of Pastoral Care*, Westminister John Knox Press, 1993.)

Vayigash: "What's the Use to Complain: Nobody Would Listen"
Kenneth J. Weiss, 2001

"The days of the years of my life have been few and bad" (Gen. 47:9—R. E. Friedman).

My Grandma Weiss (*z"l*) never complained. For nearly all of her long life (she died at the age of one hundred years and six months!) she showed a happy disposition. But—with the words that comprise the theme of this *d'rash*—she let her family know that life was not always easy or good for her.

Grandma Weiss could have taught Jacob a thing or two, and—perhaps—added years to his life. When Pharaoh asked Jacob (upon the latter's arrival in Egypt) how old he was, Jacob couldn't help but "kvetch" a little. To paraphrase: I'm 130 years old and *oy vey* you should only know the troubles I've seen!

Notice that Gen. 47:8–9 has a total of thirty-three Hebrew words. Jacob lived to be 147: thirty-three years fewer than his father, Isaac. For every word of complaint, Jacob lost a year of life. If Jacob had only known (and followed the example of) my Grandma Weiss!

Vayigash
Kenneth J. Weiss, 2002

"The best of all the land of Egypt is yours" (Gen. 45:20).

Pharaoh grew to understand that reconciliation is at the very heart of meaningful living. To draw near, to break down barriers (or boundaries), to close the distance between estranged relatives, alienated friends—there is nothing more critical to living a life of meaning, happiness, and fulfillment.

Is not Egypt called *Mitzrayim* because it is a place characterized by *m'tzarim*—boundaries? There were political boundaries, spiritual boundaries, social boundaries (which, doubtless, are still in place).

It stands to reason that boundaries of this sort create a certain narrowness of perspective and relationship (*tzar* is defined as "narrow" or "adversary").

Remarkably, it was not this *Mitzrayim* that Pharaoh set aside for the Hebrew sojourners; through Joseph, Pharaoh learned that Jacob's people treasured reconciliation, relationship. So, Pharaoh offered to give them "the best of all the land of Egypt," that area whose very name—Goshen—embodies nearness.

Pharaoh gave to Joseph and his extended family a place (and a way, after twenty years of estrangement) to regenerate their familial bond.

Render Gen. 46:28 as follows: "And he [Jacob] sent Judah ahead of him to Joseph, to seek a way to reconcile [*Goshnah*]." In a place called "Reconciliation," our ancestors reconnected with one another, and our peoplehood was renewed.

Vayigash
Kenneth J. Weiss, 2003

"Enough. . . . My son Joseph . . ." (Gen. 45:28). Jacob—congenitally acquisitive, at the end of a lifetime pursuing "more"—had an unfillable, empty place.

Finally, life taught him (and Joseph, his son) a lesson that Torah preserves for us: neither wealth nor influence fills inner empty places; of rewards and possessions there is never "enough." So, what is enough? It's not about money; it's not about things. Jacob finally "got it": he learned that Joseph was his "enough."

"Enough," ultimately, is about sharing life with those whose lives give meaning to our own.

Vayigash
Kenneth J. Weiss, 2004

Rachel named her first son יוֹסֵף (Yosef). Why? Because after years of barrenness, Joseph's birth both "removed/אָסַף" (*asaf*) her disgrace and "added/יֹסֵף" (*yoseif*) a son to her life (Gen. 30:22–24).

Was Joseph mindful of all this when (in our *sidrah*) he revealed himself to his brothers? . . . I am he whom you "removed" from the family circle, your brother whom God will "add" once again to the Israelite peoplehood . . .

Pope John XXIII—baptized "Joseph"—once greeted a group of Jewish leaders as follows: "I am Joseph your brother." John—that lovable, ecumenical pope—may also have had both meanings in mind when he spoke: . . . Though my Church once "removed" you from among God's legitimate children. I vow to "add" you (once again) to those whom God will bless . . .

Vayigash
Alan Cook, 2005

"And Joseph gathered all of the כסף [*kesef*, 'money'] that was to be found in the land of Egypt and the land of Canaan" (Gen. 47:14).

A Chasidic commentary on this verse states that the כסף that Joseph gathered was not the money and riches of the land, as the פשט (*p'shat*) of the text suggests. Rather, Joseph gathered "sparks" (which shone like silver); he gathered the accumulated wisdom of Egypt and Canaan. He renewed his connection to his religion and to his God, and he recognized what learning could be gathered from the traditions of the surrounding cultures. In this way, Joseph provided for the future of בני ישראל (*B'nei Yisrael*, "the Children of Israel"). He assured that they would amass wealth so that they could become a גוי גדול עצום ורב (*goy gadol atzum varav*, "a great nation, vast and numerous"). But more than that, he ensured that they would have the wisdom to survive after his passing and the wherewithal to maintain faith and hope despite the coming years of Egyptian oppression.

When we educate our children and teach them how to make their way in the world, do we make similar provisions? We encourage them to pursue their goals, and society tells them that their success will be measured in financial terms. It is up to us to ensure that the riches our young people treasure are not merely the tangible signs of wealth, but also a strong sense of morality and spirituality.

We read, "וכל בניך למודי יי ורב שלום בניך" (*V'chol banayich limudei Adonai v'rav sh'lom banayich*, "And all your children shall be disciples of *Adonai*, and great shall be the happiness of your children" [Isa. 54:13]), and we are taught, "אל תקרי בניך אלא בוניך" (*Al tikri banayich aleh bonayich,* "Don't read it as 'your children', but rather 'your builders'" [Babylonian Talmud, *B'rachot* 64a]). But our children can be our builders only if they are given the proper tools.

Vayigash
Amy Scheinerman, 2006

The portion opens with a long and impassioned speech by Y'hudah to Yosef (Gen. 44:18–34). Throughout, Y'hudah remains polite and appropriate, but we sense that below the surface he is seething from the injustice of his and his brothers' predicament.

The midrash enlarges Y'hudah's speech into a two-way dialogue and allows Y'hudah full rein of his feelings. In *B'reishit Rabbah* 93:6 and *Tanchuma, Vayigash* 8, Y'hudah and Yosef spar, their verbal battle nearly boiling over into physical violence when Y'hudah threatens all Egypt.

Is the midrash giving Yosef fuller rein to test his brothers? punish his brothers? Is the midrash demonstrating how stressful situations incline people to unpack old baggage? Is Y'hudah's threat of violence a reminder to himself of his own complicity in selling Yosef into slavery, or is it a foreshadowing of the plagues to befall Egypt in the generation of Moses?

In our families and workplaces, we have all seen how stressful situations cause people to unpack "old baggage" that fuels fires rather than resolves conflicts. Alternatively, delivered appropriately, it can lead to healing.

In our פרשה (*parashah*), Y'hudah's speech inspires Yosef's self-revelation and the brothers' consequent reconciliation. In the midrash, Y'hudah's words light a conflagration that threatens to envelope far more than one family. The ideal and the real? How can we, in our families and workplaces, keep ourselves and others on the ideal track?

Vayigash
Amy Scheinerman, 2007

Yosef's life is a roller coaster. From favored son, he becomes hated brother, then slave to Potiphar, later elevated to head of Potiphar's household. In the next instant he is thrown into a dungeon whence he is elevated to prime minister. Twenty-two years after his brothers sell him into slavery, they appear before him and the tables have turned: Yosef holds the reins of power and authority. The brothers have come groveling for food. Yosef orchestrates an elaborate sequence of events that entrap the brothers, cause them extraordinary anxiety, and induce emotional suffering. What is his intent?

Does Yosef seek revenge? Abravanel and K'li Yakar say Yosef's scheme is designed to even the score, מדה כנגד מדה (*midah k'neged midah*, "measure for measure"). Is there a person alive who has never experienced the desire for revenge? Why wouldn't Yosef? Abravanel argues that the desire for revenge is a natural human urge. Alternatively, others suggest that Yosef sought to induce regret in his brothers, the beginning of תשובה (*t'shuvah*, "repentance").

S. R. Hirsch, however, offers a refreshing alternative: Yosef seeks to "bring about a double change. He must cause a change in his opinion of his brothers, but primarily in their opinion of him. Their opinions of one another must utterly change in order that they might enjoy a strong amicable relationship, for if not, if he were returned to his family only superficially, he would be lost to his family, and they to him."

Hirsch suggests that Yosef has risen above revenge. He seeks the personal growth prerequisite to authentic reconciliation.

Vayigash
Amy Scheinerman, 2008

Yosef reveals himself to his brothers and sends them back to Canaan laden with gifts for his father, Yaakov, who can hardly believe the good news that Yosef is alive. The brothers describe Yosef's exalted and powerful position in Egypt, and Yaakov sees the wagons that attest to his wealth, yet his response is, "Enough! My son Yosef is still alive. I must go to see him before I die" (Gen. 45:28).

Yaakov has been bereft of Yosef and emotionally starved for want of his son for many years. The riches that arrive by the wagonload have little value in the face of his reunion with Yosef.

The Babylonian Talmud, *Tamid* 32b, recounts that Alexander the Great reached the gates of *Gan Eden*, where he demanded entrance but was refused because he was not a tzaddik. Indignant at this treatment, he demanded a prize of great value, and the angel guarding the gate gave him a human eyeball. Alexander weighed the eyeball against all the gold and silver in his possession, but the eyeball exceeded it all. Yet when the angel covered the eyeball with dust (as we will all be when we die), the eyeball returned to its normal weight. The midrash explains that the human eye always covets more than it has so long as it lives.

Yaakov, through the devastating loss of his son, escaped the human curse of greed. In his loss, he came to understand what was truly important: his loved ones. Yosef, who has amassed riches beyond measure, also knows what is most important: being able to care for and protect his loved ones.

Vayigash
Amy Scheinerman, 2009

A change in perspective often makes all the difference.

When Y'hudah and his brothers are young, the realization that Yosef is loved more than the rest rankles beyond tolerance. They scheme to rid themselves of him. Y'hudah, whose idea it was to sell Yosef to an Ishmaelite caravan (Gen. 37:27), is the brother who pleads on Binyamin's behalf when the condemning goblet is found in his saddle pack (Gen. 44:18–22).

Y'hudah was once willing to risk breaking his father's heart by the presumed loss of Yosef. Now, a far more mature Y'hudah pleads, "The lad cannot leave his father; if he leaves his father, he will die!" (Gen. 44:22). Indeed, Y'hudah refers to his "father" no fewer than fourteen times within seventeen *p'sukim* ("verses"). Rebbe Y'hudah

Leib of Ger (the S'fat Emet) interprets *vayigash eilav* in Gen. 44:18 to mean that Y'hudah approached himself. Clearly, Yaakov has not changed. Where once his happiness depended upon one son, now it depends upon another, but in either case he still has his favorite. It is Y'hudah who has changed and grown. In realizing that his father will not change, he is able to change and view the family constellation from an adult, global perspective, rather than the narrow self-interested perspective of his childhood self.

The nineteenth-century painter John Constable wrote, "I never saw an ugly thing in my life: for let the form of an object be what it may—light, shade, and perspective will always make it beautiful." We might say that Y'hudah had reason to see ugliness in his family when he was young, but perhaps his maturity and wisdom are in coming to see the beauty of his family through the imperfect prism of his father's perspective, however troubling. Can we do the same?

ויחי Va-y'chi

(Genesis 47:28–50:26)

Va-y'chi
Ari Cartun, 1996

Does Genesis prefer primogeniture or prophetic election? The elevation of younger siblings over firstborns, such as Isaac, Jacob, Rachel, Judah, Peretz, and Ephraim, seems to be in direct contrast to the orderly primogeniture that led from Adam through Noah to Avram. So, unlike the creation of the world, which begins in chaos and ends in structure, our people begin in order and end in chaos. Given the chaos in the "orderly" generations from Adam to Noah and onward, is there something chaotic about structure?

Va-y'chi
Lawrence S. Kushner, 1996

What is this in Gen. 48:12—"And Joseph brought [the boys] out from his knees"—whether it is from Joseph's knees or, as the tradition has it, from Jacob's knees, do we have here an attempt on the part of a father or grandfather to give birth? Do we have a case of womb envy?

A good way of learning this *parashah* is to compare Jacob's blessings of his sons with Moses's blessings of the tribes in *V'zot Hab'rachah*. How do the sons compare with the tribes they founded?

Despite all the descriptions of burials and mourning, this is a portion called *Va-y'chi* ("and he lived"). What light does this *parashah* shed on the meanings of the lives of Jacob and Joseph?

Va-y'chi: Cursed Anger
Stephen E. Cohen, 1997

Jacob's deathbed rebuke of Levi and Shimon focuses on their anger.

Or HaChayim "Cursed is their anger for it was mighty" (Gen. 49:7). The meaning is: He cursed the excessive portion of their anger, the part that exceeded what is normal. But he allowed them the normal portion of anger found in every person, so that they might earn a portion in the world-to-come by harnessing it to the service of God.

Comment Levi's great-grandson kills an Egyptian in anger, smashes the tablets in anger, and strikes the rock in anger. Does Moses represent a step forward in this family's evolution from cursed anger to blessed rage?

Va-y'chi: Swear to Me
Stephen E. Cohen, 1998

In Jacob's deathbed request that Joseph return his body for burial in Canaan, we see father and son still struggling, right up to the end, to set the terms of their relationship. Both the Or HaChayim and the Malbim note Joseph's desire for moral autonomy, at odds with Jacob's inability to completely trust his most-loved son.

Or HaChayim The meaning of Joseph's reply is that he did not need to swear to him, that he was already prepared to do as Jacob asked—in fact, that he was obligated to do so, both because Jacob was his father and because it was his deathbed. When Jacob then responded, "*Hishavah li* / Swear to me," he meant that he accepted Joseph's words, but nevertheless asked him again to swear, emphasizing that it was for his own [Jacob's] sake: "*Hishavah li* / For me," meaning, "for *my* peace of mind."

Malbim Joseph meant, "It would be better if you *not* make me swear, and let me do it of my own accord, out of the mitzvah of *kibud* [respect]. For in this way the deed will be more whole than if you make me swear, thereby placing me under the compulsion of the oath. If you do so, the deed will not be a product of my own free will." Jacob's response was "Swear to me." Not, as with Eliezer, "*Ashbiacha / I will make you swear*" (Gen. 24:3), but rather "*Hishavah*/Swear"—of your own free will.

Comment Following either of these two readings, does the oath actually leave Joseph with any "free will" in fulfilling his father's wish?

Va-y'chi
Sheldon Marder, 2000

"But Israel stretched out his right hand and laid it on Ephraim's head, though he was younger, and his left hand on Manasseh's head—thus crossing his hands—although Manasseh was the firstborn" (Gen. 48:14). Rashi and the *Targum* agree that שכל את ידיו (*sikeil et yadav*, "thus crossing his hands") describes a cognitive act. According to their view, Jacob acted with understanding and wisdom—"he knowingly made his hands wise." S'forno differs: Jacob, he says, acted on the basis of physical touch, knew and understood through the touch of his hand without seeing—a phenomenon akin to what drummers call "muscle memory."

What sort of wisdom is conveyed in the phrase שכל את ידיו (*sikeil et yadav*)?

This question leads us back to the beginning of the Torah—to Gen. 3:6: "When the woman saw that the tree was good for eating and a delight to the eyes, and that the tree was desirable as a source of wisdom [להשכיל, *l'haskil*], she took of its fruit and ate." There is an artful symmetry between Gen. 3:5–7 and 48:10–14; these two sets of verses form an inclusion—a literary frame—around the Torah's tale of human moral development. The inclusion has two parts: the root ש-כ-ל (*s-k-l*), and the act of seeing—which appear in both places. The inclusion is a marker in the text to tell us that Jacob's final great moment of insight parallels or, more precisely, completes the "seeing" in the Garden of Eden. Adam's and Eve's eyes opened wide with wonder and delight and, finally, self-awareness; Jacob's eyes dim with age. Even the grammar has symbolic value: the wide-open potential of the infinitive (*l'hiskil* [Gen. 3:6]) is fulfilled in the conjugation of the verb in the perfect tense—להשכיל (*sikeil* [Gen. 48:14]). In their hunger for wisdom, the first humans consume the fruit of the forbidden tree; many narratives later, their naive wish comes to fruition in Jacob's experienced hands.

Va-y'chi
Kenneth J. Weiss, 2001

"You, O Judah, your brothers shall praise" (Gen. 49:8).

Was the *k'tonet pasim* (ornament tunic) given to the wrong son? Favoring one child over the rest is ill-advised. But—over the long term—perhaps Judah was more deserving of praise and recognition than his siblings:

- He may have saved Joseph's life: "What profit is there if we kill our brother?" (Gen. 37:26).
- Though he falls into Tamar's trap, Judah acknowledges his moral lapse: "She is more in the right than I" (Gen. 38:26).
- Judah guarantees Benjamin's safe return to their father: "I myself will be surety for him; you may hold me responsible" (Gen. 43:9).
- Judah offers himself in Benjamin's stead: "Please let your servant remain as a slave to my lord instead of the boy" (Gen. 44:33).

So—there was no *k'tonet pasim* for Judah. But, we Jews are an eternal people who will forever carry Judah's name: we are called "Jews," not "Joes" (Larry Kushner); our faith is called Judaism, not Josephism (David Wilfond). Which reward might have meant more then? Which means more now?

Va-y'chi
Kenneth J. Weiss, 2002

"Your two sons . . . shall be mine" (Gen. 48:5).

"Who is a Jew?" asks Pinchas Peli. He answers, "One who can speak with confidence about his Jewish grandchildren." I would modify: A Jew is one who can speak with confidence **to** his/her Jewish grandchildren!

In this *parashah*, Jacob spoke to his Jewish grandchildren (Joseph's sons); he blessed them as if they were his children. We, too, hope to live long enough to speak to—and bless—our own grandchildren, to share with them many of life's best moments. We can't know if we'll be around long enough to watch and help *our* grandchildren grow and mature. But—through an ethical will—we can better ensure that our impact survives us.

An ethical will (whether a written document or in video format) is a grandparent's ultimate gift to his/her grandchildren. Jacob could actually lay his hands on his grandsons' heads and ask God's blessing on them. Through an ethical will, we can (symbolically) do the same: we can record our values, our wishes, our formative events; we can transmit the lessons we learned along the way, our family stories, our Jewish beliefs, practices, traditions.

Let Jacob's words move us to tell our story for our progeny—including those we will never meet. Truly, a Jew is a person who can speak with confidence **to** his/her Jewish grandchildren.

Va-y'chi
Kenneth J. Weiss, 2003

In *The Five Books of Miriam: A Woman's Commentary on the Torah* (HarperOne, 1997), Ellen Frankel gives "Mother Rachel" a voice from the grave: "My poor beloved Jacob! [Out of love for me he adopted] our grandsons, Ephraim and Manasseh, as his own, and so gave our firstborn, Joseph, a double portion of the inheritance. . . . He never learned . . . never recognized that his playing favorites among the boys had once come close to destroying our family."

[KJW's *d'rash*:] Rachel becomes resigned: "I yearned to have Jacob lie near me forever. But, that wasn't to be: he instructed Joseph to bury him with his fathers at Machpelah, symbolizing his assent to a truth I could never teach him: the tradition passed from his ancestors through him belongs equally to ALL his sons—ALL the tribes of our people."

Va-y'chi
Kenneth J. Weiss, 2004

"[Jacob] blessed Joseph['s] . . . lads" (Gen. 48:15–16).

"The scepter shall not depart from Judah" (Gen. 49:10).

Jews yearn for Jewish descendants: we want to know that our cherished tradition will be transmitted to generations we'll never meet.

So, Jacob/Israel foretells what will be after he's gone: Joseph's sons will carry the tradition into the next generation; Judah's descendants will transmit it into the more distant future, becoming Israel's royal house—King David's birth-clan.

Jacob died, confident that his heirs would maintain and transmit his tradition into the future . . . Are we that confident?

Va-y'chi
Alan Cook, 2005

At the end of ויגש (*Yayigash*) we find the tearful reunion between Jacob and Joseph. The favored son meets his father after an absence of many years. Undoubtedly, as emotionally significant as that encounter was for both parties, there was still a great deal that went unsaid. There was still much for them to "catch up on."

So now, as Jacob lays on his sickbed, there is a great deal that he still has not said to Joseph. As Joseph approaches, Jacob proclaims, "ראה פניך לא פללתי" (*R'oh panecha lo filalti*, "I never expected to see you again" [Gen. 48:11]).

Gerson Rosenzweig, a newspaper editor and parodist who flourished at the beginning of the twentieth century, wrote a mock commentary on this phrase in "Tractate Disguise" of his *Talmud Yankee*. Though he meant his remarks to be satirical, they have resonance for us nonetheless. Rosenzweig writes, "Jacob heard that his son Joseph had been made wealthy in Egypt. He said, 'Perhaps he [Joseph] has adopted the habits of the rich and I will not see his face [because he will have disguised it].'"

Jacob never prayed that he would see Joseph's face because so much had transpired in both their lives since the last time they had met that he could not be certain they would encounter each other in the same manner that they had during Joseph's youth. Would there be the same affection passing between father and son, or would the passing of years have dulled that connection?

How often do we disguise ourselves from those whom we love? How often do we put barriers between ourselves and others?

Va-y'chi
Amy Scheinerman, 2006

The Yiddish proverb "Man plans, God laughs" comes to mind when reading the encounters between Joseph and his brothers. Joseph assures them twice that despite the brothers' best effort in Genesis 37 to rid themselves of him, God's plan prevailed (Gen. 45:5 and Gen. 50:20). Moreover, we know that the emotional reunion Joseph envisions as God's goal is not the end of the saga: Israel must endure four centuries of slavery in preparation for redemption and revelation.

The term we use for God's divine providence, השגחה (*hashgachah*), derives from Ps. 33:14: "From the place of God's habitation God looked intently [השגיח, *hishgiach*] upon all the inhabitants of the earth." Rabbi Chanina expresses the most extreme viewpoint in the Babylonian Talmud, *Chulin* 7b: "No one bruises his finger here on earth unless this was decreed against him from on high." Even Rambam speaks of השגחה כללית (*hashgachah k'lalit*, God's providential care of the world in general) and השגחה פרטית (*hashgachah p'ratit*, God's special oversight of individuals) in the *Guide of the Perplexed* 3:17–18, but he limits the latter to individuals who lead pious and scholarly lives.

In our day, we are more apt to look to the processes of nature combined with the results of human free will to explain why life and history unfold as they do. However, as science speaks increasingly of probabilities rather than certainties in describing the universe, will we revisit traditional formulations of השגחה (*hashgachah*), attributing to God the power behind the probabilities?

Va-y'chi
Amy Scheinerman, 2007

The scene with which this פרשה (*parashah*) opens, in which Yaakov bestows the blessing reserved for Yosef upon his sons, Ephraim and Menasheh, inspires many questions. Why do Ephraim and Menasheh alone among the grandchildren of Yaakov merit elevation to the status of sons, complete with land allocations in *Eretz Yisrael*? Is this Yaakov's clever way of doubling Yosef's inheritance? Why does Torah go to great length to describe Yaakov's crossed hands, Yosef's attempt to correct him, and Yaakov's refusal? Why do we bless our children by Ephraim and Menasheh rather than the patriarchs, Avraham, Yitzchak, and Yaakov?

One explanation is that Ephraim and Menasheh are the first pair of brothers we encounter in Torah who do not contend with one another and struggle for supremacy. Even when Yaakov crosses his hands, bestowing the primary blessing upon Ephraim, Menasheh does not object. This may explain the singular בך (*b'cha*, "by you") in Gen. 48:20; these brothers place their relationship and family unity above their individual egos.

Another explanation is that Ephraim and Menasheh did not grow up in *Eretz Yisrael* in the bosom of their extended family, but in Egypt. With all the dazzling temptations of Egypt, they nonetheless throw in their lot with their people and identify fully as Jews, staking their future on the covenant of Israel. This, too, is a model for contemporary Jews.

Both explanations paint a portrait of Ephraim and Menasheh as figures who exceed all expectations for them. This makes them excellent role models for our children and for ourselves.

Va-y'chi
Amy Scheinerman, 2008

Yosef's brothers know they are safe so long as their father Yaakov is alive. Once he dies, however, they panic. "What if Yosef still bears a grudge against us and pays us back for all the wrong that we did him!" (Gen. 50:15). So they sent a message to Yosef reminding him that their father Yaakov's most fervent wish had been that Yosef not exact revenge, but rather forgive his brothers. They also offer to become Yosef's slaves. "But Yosef said to them, 'Have no fear! Am I a substitute for God? Besides, although you intended me harm, God intended it for good, so as to bring about the present result—the survival of many people. And fear not. **I will sustain you and your children**'" (Gen. 50:19–21).

Yosef's pious response about God's divine providence in their lives seems undercut by his supposedly generous commitment to support them. Is this the ultimate fulfillment of the dreams? Or is this indeed Yosef's revenge?

In the Babylonian Talmud, *Beitzah* 32b, we find this teaching: "R. Natan ben Abba also said in the name of Rav: If someone is dependent upon another's table, the world looks dark to him, for it says, 'He wanders about for food—where is it?—he realizes that the day of darkness is ready, at hand' (Job 15:23). The Rabbis taught: one of three whose life is no life is a person who is dependent upon another for his meals."

Yosef's forgiveness seems incomplete. Are we the same way? It appears that he still seeks to punish his brothers. How often do we do the same thing, in the guise of kindness and generosity?

Va-y'chi
Amy Scheinerman, 2009

Yaakov lies on his deathbed. He must be imagining how the covenant passed down from his father, Yitzchak, and his grandfather, Avraham, will survive. Here he is in Egypt, surrounded by people who worship their pharaoh and a variety of animals. His entire family lives in this land, far from *Eretz Yisrael*, and a contentious clan they are. How will they be able to retain the insights of Avraham in this alien land, this idolatrous culture? Only the third generation, and already the enterprise seems threatened.

Yaakov summons his children for a final blessing, in particular calling Menasheh and Ephraim, sons of Yosef. In bestowing the blessing, Yaakov reverses the "natural" order of priority. We are not surprised; this happened in the two previous generations. But it happens differently here: Yaakov neither explicitly declares Ephraim superior nor asks the boys to switch places. Rather, he crosses his hands so that the right hand rests on the head of the younger brother, Ephraim.

Rabbi Chizkiyah ben Manoach Chizkuni (Provence, thirteenth century) explains that *sikeil et yadav* (Gen. 48:14) informs us that Yaakov acted with *seichel*—wisdom and insight. His manner of bestowing the blessing protected the dignity of each boy. Given the sibling relationships we have seen in the family line until this point, Yaakov's sensitivity and *seichel* were critically necessary.

There are times when we are called upon to choose between synagogue members, employees, or others. Yaakov's model reminds us that *how* is as important as *who*. In the case of Yaakov, it was critically necessary for preserving the unity of the family and hence ensuring their future.

Exodus

שמות Sh'mot

(Exodus 1:1–6:1)

Sh'mot
Ari Cartun, 1996

No detail is superfluous in the Torah, since so few are supplied. Thus, the beginning of this book is intriguing. It could have begun, "These are the *B'nei Yisrael* [Children of Israel] who went to Egypt and became a people there," since the rest of the chapter recounts our exponential growth from seventy people to six hundred thousand men over age twenty. But the text states, "These are **the names** of the Children of Israel." The names are emphasized. Why give such prominence to the names? And if names are so important, why are they totally absent from chapter 2 in the story of the birth of Moses? Why are no names mentioned until Moses is given his name?

Sh'mot
Lawrence S. Kushner, 1997

From Exod. 1:15 through 2:10 we are told primarily about heroic women who stood up to Pharaoh's decrees—the midwives Shiphrah and Puah, and three unnamed women, the baby's sister and mother, and Pharaoh's daughter. In a *parashah* whose title is "Names," to rephrase a question asked in this column last year by our colleague

Ari Cartun, why are these three women referred to only in terms of the men in their lives? Is this refusal to name, a sign of the modesty/anonymity of these heroic woman? Is it an attempt to universalize them—any woman, with any name, should feel herself capable of doing what they did?

In chapter 3, Moses looks at a burning bush and notes that it is not consumed. Our colleague Douglas Krantz, a volunteer firefighter, observed recently that if he had seen the bush burning, his first instinct would have been to put out the fire before he even noticed that it was not consuming the bush. Wouldn't we do the same thing? Why didn't Moses try to put out the fire? Are there fires we too should observe for a while before trying to extinguish them?

Sh'mot: Evil Genius
Stephen E. Cohen, 1997

Or HaChayim regards Pharaoh with deadly seriousness, inquiring relentlessly into the precise mechanics of the king's genocidal program.

Or HaChayim "And he said, 'Watch the birthstones'" (Exod. 1:16). What was the purpose of this "watching"? He could have simply said, "If it is a boy." Furthermore, why did he not decree against all babies? We cannot imagine that he was acting out of compassion. Behold, this wicked one schemed so that his plan would succeed. For who is the woman that would ever give herself to a midwife who might kill her child? Therefore he told them to follow exactly this procedure, and to do it all secretly, so that the women would not suspect. Before it became clear whether the baby was a boy or girl, the midwives were to look on the birthstones. If it was a boy, they were to kill him and to say that it was stillborn—not to wait until it came completely out into the world. His instruction to save the girls was for the same purpose, so that the birthing mothers would not suspect anything. They would see that sometimes their babies survived, and so they would not suspect the midwives. And they would not notice that the midwives were killing the boys and not the girls. It is even possible that he instructed them specifically not to announce that it had been a boy, but just to say that it was stillborn. For in this way they would prevent suspicion.

Comment If Pharaoh was as cruel as Or HaChayim suggests, how might we imagine his reaction to of the midwives' refusal to cooperate? Did he believe their excuse?

Sh'mot: Infanticide
Stephen E. Cohen, 1998

These two midrashim both reflect upon the Egyptian war against the Jewish babies, but they arise out of and describe two utterly different universes.

Shemot Rabbah **(1:12)** The Israelite women went out and gave birth in the field, under the apple tree, as it says, "Under the apple tree I roused you, / there your mother was in labor with you" (Song of Songs 8:5). When the Egyptians realized this, they rushed to kill them, but a miracle occurred and the babies were swallowed by the earth. Then the Egyptians brought oxen and plowed the ground over their backs, but after they left, the babies sprang forth again like the grass of the field, as it says, "I caused you to grow like the plant of the field" (Ezek. 16:7).

Pirkei D'Rabbi Eliezer The Israelite men would gather straw in the desert, and trample it with their donkeys, and so would their wives and daughters. And the straw of the desert would pierce the soles of their feet, and the blood would mix with the mortar. Now Rachel, granddaughter of Shetulach, was pregnant and trampling mortar with her husband, and the baby came out of her womb and was caught up in the brick mold. And her scream went up before God's Throne of Glory. The angel Michael descended and took the brick mold and carried it up before the Throne of Glory. In that night, the Holy One was revealed and slew the firstborn among the Egyptians.

Comment What would lead the author of one midrash to imagine vengeance for the death of a baby and another to imagine a miraculous rescue?

Sh'mot: Miriam's Prophecy
Stephen E. Cohen, December 1999

This midrash inquires unblinkingly into the family dynamics surrounding the birth and subsequent loss of the baby Moses. The verse "Miriam stood off at a distance" (Exod. 2:4) is reread to imply emotional distance from her mother.

***Midrash Sh'mot Rabbah* 1:25** Why did Miriam stand off at a distance? R. Amram said in the name of Rav: Because Miriam used to prophesy, saying, "My mother will one day bear a son who will deliver Israel." When Moses was born, the entire house was filled with light. Her father rose and kissed her on the head, saying, "My daughter, your prophecy is fulfilled!" And so she is called "Miriam the prophetess . . ." (Exod. 15:20). But then, when they cast him into the Nile, her mother rose and slapped her on the head, saying, "My daughter, what of your prophecy?" And so it is written, "His sister stood off at a distance . . ." to know what would be the conclusion of her prophecy.

Comment Is this a depiction of a **dysfunctional** family, or of a **normal** family suffering a heartbreaking tragedy?

Sh'mot
Sheldon Marder, 2000

"An angel of *Adonai* appeared to him in a blazing fire out of a bush. . . . And [God] said, '. . . Remove your sandals from your feet, for the place on which you stand is holy ground'" (Exod. 3:2, 3:5).

Writes the Malbim: As the shoe is to the foot, so the body is merely the outer garment of the human soul. Hence, in commanding Moses to remove his shoes, God meant to tell him: "If you wish to understand the ways of God and reach the level at which you will be able to behold the revelation of God, you must first cast off the forces and urges of the body that conceal the soul within. Only then will you be able to attain, to holiness."

"Remove your sandals" is read by some commentators as "remove materialism"—הרחקת הגשמיות, distance yourself from earthly concerns (K'li Yakar, Rabbeinu Bachya, et al.). So also, the S'fat Emet comments on this portion, "The real freedom that comes about by means of Torah is the freedom of the soul from its bodily prison." This is consistent with *Pirkei Avot* 6:4, "Sleep on the ground and live a life of deprivation," but not likely to be a path to holiness for many Jews today.

Yehuda Amichai, in one of his more despairing poems ("Time, #30," *The Early Books of Yehuda Amichai*, Sheep Meadow Press, 1979), reflects on the way human beings pile up material possessions as a way of fending off mortality:

> I can see you grasping
> desperately at all that surrounds you,
> books, children, a woman,
> musical instruments—
> but you don't know that this
> is nothing but pulling
> dry twigs and dead branches to your body
> for the big fire
> in which you'll burn.

Is the fire of the burning bush, the fire Amichai describes, a "bonfire of the vanities"—a corrosive fire that burns away the dross and leaves the essence? Can this be a useful metaphor for us as we, in the footsteps of Moses and the Malbim, probe the meaning of revelation?

Sh'mot: Custom-Designed Truths
Kenneth J. Weiss, 2001

"[Pharaoh] spoke to **the Hebrew midwives** . . ." (Exod. 1:15).

"Then Pharaoh charged **all his people** . . ." (Exod. 1:22).

Politicians have done it forever—telling their audiences what they want to hear. Yasser Arafat is a past master of the art; his statements to the Moslem world are radically different from what he wants the Western world to know. What he proclaims in English about Palestinian coexistence with Israel is diametrically different from what he says for attribution in Arabic. Arafat is hardly unique in customizing the "truths" he would like his audiences to believe.

The Pharaoh "who did not know Joseph" (Exod. 1:8) is an ancient model for this sort of behavior. In public, Pharaoh wishes to come across as even-handed, sensitive to the needs and concerns of all his people. Egypt, after all, is civilized and cultured—and the world should presume nothing less! So, he tells his people (and the world press hanging on every word), "Every boy that is born you shall throw into the Nile, but let every girl live" (Exod. l:22). But, prior to this nationwide broadcast, Pharaoh summons the Hebrew midwives, Shiphrah and Puah. In a safe and private corner, he takes off the gloves: "When you deliver the **Hebrew** women . . . if it is a boy, kill him" (Exod. 1:16).

Was anyone fooled then? Is anyone fooled today when modern "pharaohs" try the same trick? Not likely indeed. *Targum Onkelos* saw through the political double-speak, rendering Exod. 1:22 as "Every son that is born to **Jewish people** you shall throw into the river."

Oh great Pharaoh: how you underestimate us . . .

Sh'mot
Kenneth J. Weiss, 2002

"Remove your sandals from your feet" (Exod. 3:5).

Shoes, to me, suggest momentum—they enable us to walk, run, jump: to make our way in the world. We spend our days in them, going about our routines, our business. Shoes are about making a living . . .

Bare feet are about living a life: "Take off your shoes; stay awhile." "I can't wait to get home, take these shoes off, and put my feet up." There's something so elemental—might we add "spiritual"—about removing our shoes. It's the first thing many of us do at the end of the day, the first thing we want to do at the beach, in a park—whenever and wherever we're about to relax, to decompress.

God told Moses that—because he was standing on holy ground—he would have to remove his sandals. Why was that?

- As a symbol of humility in the presence of the sacred?
- To touch holiness more directly?

- To actually feel the earth as one of God's primary creations?
- To represent all humanity at this time and place, many of whom never wore sandals?

And another thing: how is it that Jewish practice encompasses both bare feet *and* covered heads? Over the centuries, scholars (including the Maharshal and the Vilna Gaon) have pointed out that the *kippah* has no basis in Jewish law. Nonetheless, covering one's head is a common (and comfortable) practice for many Jews.

So: bare feet and covered heads! Provocative juxtaposition! The Talmud (*Shabbat* 156b) recounts that astrologers told the mother of Nachman ben Yitzchak (fourth-century Babylonian scholar) that her son was destined to become a thief. To forestall this prediction, she insisted that he never leave the house bareheaded: "Cover your head that the fear of heaven will always be with you." I wonder: what would have happened had she told him instead, "Before you leave the house, take off your shoes"!

Sh'mot
Kenneth J. Weiss, 2003

The name "Moses" is derived from ancient Egyptian and means "child of" or "son of." Thus, Ramses means "son of Ra [the Egyptian sun god]." Moses is less a name than a generic designation.

My contention: Moses could have been "any man." He was whoever the people needed in a leader, a liberator. Predictably born of the tribe of Levi, he was (variously) shy and insecure, angrily righteous, defiantly obstinate, singleminded, commanding.

"Moses" was indispensable to the emancipation saga. If he didn't exist, the Torah "historians" would have to have invented him.

Sh'mot
Kenneth J. Weiss, 2004

"A bush all aflame . . ." (Exod. 3:2).
   For discussion:

- How long before Moses's time did God light the Burning Bush?
- Did God try—and fail—to engage others before Moses happened along? Or . . .
- Did God handpick Moses (perhaps) because he'd demonstrated character, having "struck down the Egyptian" (Exod. 2:12)?

A "bush all aflame yet . . . not consumed" symbolizes our immortal peoplehood: though despots can murder individual Jews, they cannot extinguish the flame of Jewishness.

That flame burns still: see it where Jews pray—feel it where Jews live.

Sh'mot
Alan Cook, 2005

"Joseph died, and all his brothers, and all that generation" (Exod. 1:6).

"But their God did not die" (*Sh'mot Rabbah* 1:8).

What a miracle it is that we have maintained Jewish continuity throughout the generations—sometimes in the face of seemingly insurmountable odds. Despite the oppression of numerous regimes, we have survived, while other empires have crumbled.

Despite the fact that Joseph's generation, the last one with any memory of Canaan, has perished, the people continue to flourish. The midrash, which states that "their God did not die," seems to suggest that those descendants of Jacob who remained maintained their national pride and continued to procreate so that their traditions could be passed on.

At the same time, we read, "A new king arose over Egypt who did not know Joseph" (Exod. 1:8). How could this have been the case? Would such a colorful figure have escaped notice in the Egyptian history books?

The commentators respond to this question, saying that it would not have been possible for the Pharaoh to be ignorant of Joseph's existence unless Joseph's own people had forgotten him. They had failed to tell the stories of his exploits that would have kept him alive in the hearts and minds of the Egyptians.

Our survival as a people and a civilization does not only require that we continue to have future generations to carry on our legacy. We must actively instruct these standard-bearers for our people, teaching them what our past was and about what we want our future to be.

Sh'mot
Amy Scheinerman, 2006

In Exod. 2:1, Yocheved observes Moshe's beauty and hides him from otherwise certain death. Ibn Ezra comments that "beautiful" should be understood as "good," but since it describes a baby, it can refer only to physical attributes. Nachmanides and Rashbam point out that every mother both thinks her child is incomparably beautiful and would hide her child under such circumstances. For Nachmanides, however, Torah includes these details to inform us that Yocheved recognizes in Moshe an unprecedented beauty that will inspire God to perform a miracle on his behalf.

What are the qualities that distinguish Moshe from birth? When do we first see Moshe's extraordinary qualities?

Certainly we do not see them in the execution of the taskmaster without trial, evidence, or judgment; this act of vigilantism is morally troubling.

Perhaps it is not until Moshe steps aside to view the Burning Bush (Exod. 3:1ff.) that we recognize in Moshe something unique. Lawrence Kushner in *Five Cities of Refuge* suggests that the Burning Bush is a "metaphor for the self, aflame with the presence of God that miraculously is not consumed" (p. 48). Moshe senses God's presence even in the emptiness of the מדבר (*midbar*, "wilderness"), his life in shambles, his future cloudy. Torah has mentioned others who did not see what was before them (Hagar, Gen. 21:19; and Avraham, Gen. 22:13). Moshe sees the bush and recognizes God's presence.

What can we do to maintain an open channel and awareness like Moshe?

Sh'mot
Amy Scheinerman, 2007

Abarbanel asks why the genealogy of Genesis 46 is repeated in the opening verses of שמות (Sh'mot). Nachmanides explains that Exodus begins with a recapitulation of the names of those who descended into Egypt because this hints at the overall themes of שמות (Sh'mot): exile and redemption. Egypt is the first exile, decreed in Gen. 15:13, where the Israelites labor as slaves until God redeems them. שמות (Sh'mot) ends with the completion of the משכן (Mishkan, "Tabernacle"), where the שכינה (Shechinah) abides among Israel.

We have become adroit at interpreting bondage and redemption on multiple levels (for individuals, groups, and nations) and in application to a multitude of situations (psychological, social, political, religious). Modern הגדות (Haggadot) are compendia of such interpretations. We say little, however, about the concept of exile, perhaps because of the long negative shadow it has historically cast on Jewish life in the Diaspora (for which we avoid the term גלות [galut, "exile"]).

Kabbalah offers a rich metaphorical vocabulary for exploring "exile" as a religious concept not necessarily tied with a political reality, or land, or the specifics of Jewish history (though of course it discusses that, as well). Alternatively, we might understand exile in the light of universal human experiences such as social alienation, spiritual loneliness, or modern (postmodern?) disaffection. In addition, it might be related to the Jungian concept of the Shadow (*Facing the Dragon* [Moore], *Why Good People Do Bad Things* [Hollis], and *Facing Evil* [Woodruff] provide ample food for thought).

Sh'mot
Michael Boyden, 2008

It was Rabbi Simcha Bunem of Pshis'cha who said that every person should have two pockets with a scrap of paper in each of them. On one should be written, "I am but dust and ashes," and on the other, "The world was created for me."

If anyone could have been full of himself, it was Moses. Having begun his life in a wicker basket cast into the river Nile, he brought the Israelites out of Egypt, faced God at Mount Sinai, and transformed a wretched bunch of slaves into a people fit to enter the Promised Land.

Moses could so easily have said, "The world was created for me," yet he remained modest. God called him to service with the words "Moses, Moses" (Exod. 3:4). Why was his name used twice? Was it, as our Sages suggest, "out of affection and in haste," or rather because Moses was frightened to respond? Indeed, the midrash adds, "Do not be afraid, because your righteousness goes before you."

One could superficially compare Moses's response to God's call to that of Jonah, but their motives were entirely different. Jonah tried to flee, but "Moses was more humble [*anav*] than anyone else on earth" (Num. 12:3). Nowhere else in the entire Bible is the term *anav* used to describe a human being.

What does *anav* mean? The midrash tells us that "he didn't boast about any of the attributes that people are generally proud to possess, such as his kingly status, his ability to prophesy, or his wisdom."

How, then, could a person who saw himself as "dust and ashes" nevertheless fulfill his calling? The answer lies in God's response to Moses: "For I shall be with you" (Exod. 3:12). Each of us, in times of uncertainty about our own worth, would do well to remember the final words of *Adon Olam*: "God is with me. I shall not fear."

Sh'mot
Amy Scheinerman, 2009

How do we identify God's influence and activity in the world?

"A long time after that, the king of Egypt died. The Israelites were groaning under the bondage and cried out; and their cry for help from the bondage rose up to God. God heard their moaning, and God remembered the covenant with Avraham and Yitzchak and Yaakov. God looked upon the Israelites, and God took notice of them" (Exodus 2:23–25).

Our Rabbis are sensitive to the suggestion in the text that God silently observed four centuries of Israelite suffering without intervention because the Israelites did not cry out or invoke God. *Shir HaShirim Rabbah* 2:15 offers this magnificent midrash of humans, angels, and the very earth working in concert to subvert Pharaoh's command to kill infant boys: "Every boy that is born you shall throw into the Nile" (Exod. 1:22).

R. Chanan said: What did the chaste and virtuous Israelite women do? They took their infants and hid them in holes [in their homes]. So the wicked Egyptians would take their own young children, bring them into the homes of the Israelites, and pinch their young until they cried. When the Israelite infants in their hiding places heard the Egyptian children cry, they cried with them. Then the Egyptians would seize the Israelite infants and cast them into the Nile. At that time the Holy One said to the ministering angels, "Descend from My Presence and look at the children of My beloved Avraham, Yitzchak, and Yaakov being thrown into the river." The ministering angels rushed headlong down from God's Presence and, standing up to their knees in the water, caught the children of Israel in their arms and set them upon rocks. Then out of each rock the Holy One brought forth nipples, which suckled the Israelite children.

וארא Va-eira

(Exodus 6:2–9:35)

Va-eira
Ari Cartun, 1996

The story of redemption is connected to the dichotomy between being swept away in water (the Israelite boys, baby Moses in the ark, the Nile turning to blood, the drowning of locusts and Egyptians in the Reed Sea, and the hail, which is frozen water) and the dryness of the wilderness desert, where the sweet springs of Elim and the bitter spring of Marah counterpoint each other. What has redemption to do with water?

Va-eira
Lawrence S. Kushner, 1997

Moses protests that he is *aral s'fatayim* ("a man of impeded speech"; literally, "uncircumcised lips" [Exod. 6:12]); in the previous *parashah* he says he is *k'vad peh* ("slow of speech" [Exod. 4:10]). Is there a difference between these two metaphors? Are they metaphors—what might the *orlah* (impediment/foreskin) on Moses's lips have been? And since *k'vad* is related to *k'vod*, might his heaviness have come from having been overwhelmed by seeing the *kavod* of the Holy One? In Exod. 4:11, God claims the responsibility for the condition of the human mouth or eyes or ears. Why does God create stuttering in people? Or deafness, or blindness? And if we deny God's role in these conditions, are we trivializing the role these conditions play in the life of a stuttering or deaf or blind person?

Ah, the hardening of Pharaoh's heart (Exod. 7:3). Does this minimize his free will? Or have his choices of evil behavior contributed to the hardening (the more evil one does, the harder it is to do *t'shuvah* [repentance] and start doing good)—but why does the Torah credit the hardening only to God?

Rabbinic commentaries suggest that each of the plagues reflected the defeat of an Egyptian deity (the Nile, the frog, the earth turned into lice, swarms of divine animals, the cow or bull, the sky where soot is thrown and hail descends on the grain). Was this serial Götterdämmerung for the sake of the Egyptians or the Israelites—or both? Was God trying to "convert" the Egyptians?

Va-eira: Human God
Stephen E. Cohen, 1997

When Moses asks how he can have any hope that Pharaoh will listen to him, God responds in startling language: "See, I have set you to be *Elohim* to Pharaoh, and Aaron your brother will be your prophet" (Exod. 7:1). Rashi and Ibn Ezra have different understandings of what it means for a human being to be *Elohim*.

Rashi Judge and ruler, to dominate him with plagues and sufferings.

Ibn Ezra The word "see" is significant: "I have given you a degree of grandeur, so that Pharaoh will **perceive** you at the level of angel." This is *Elohim*. And the angel speaks to the prophet, and the prophet to the people of his generation.

Comment According to Rashi, God empowers Moses with the ability to punish Pharaoh, but Ibn Ezra sees God imbuing Moses with an aura of majesty. Which would be more useful to Moses in confronting Pharaoh?

Va-eira: Pharaoh's Tears
Stephen E. Cohen, 1998

In Exod. 6:13, God commands Moses and Aaron regarding both the Israelites and Pharaoh, as it were, in a "single breath." By implication, according to this midrash, both the Israelites and Pharaoh were equally necessary to the divine plan.

***Shemot Rabbah* (7:4)** Rabbi Levi taught: A parable of a king who had an orchard and planted it with trees bearing no fruit, and also with trees bearing fruit. His servants said to him, "What benefit do you derive from these trees that bear no fruit?" He replied, "Just as I require fruit trees, so too do I need the others, for without the trees that bear no fruit, from what could I make baths and furnaces?" Thus it is said, "Regarding the Israelites and regarding Pharaoh" (Exod. 6:13). Just as the praise of the Holy One ascends from *Gan Eden* from the mouths of the righteous, so too does it ascend from *Geihinom* from the mouths of the wicked. As it is said, "Those who pass through the Valley of Bacha, they shall turn it into a water-spring" (Ps. 84:7). To what does this refer? The wicked shed tears like water-springs until they cool *Geihinom* with their tears.

Comment This midrash seems open to understanding Pharaoh as a human soul, albeit a wicked one in need of repentance. Are the tears of the wicked, in this midrash, tears of painful suffering or tears of remorse?

Va-eira: Wisdom Confounded
Stephen E. Cohen, 1999

The first verse of the *parashah* contains the two divine epithets—*Elohim* and *YHVH*—understood by the Rabbis as signifying the attributes of justice and of mercy, respectively. In addressing the shift in the verse, from *Elohim* to *YHVH*, this homily invokes a verse from *Kohelet*, producing a variety of caveats for rabbis, ancient and modern.

***Sh'mot Rabbah* 6:2** "And *Elohim* spoke to Moses, and said to him: 'I am *YHVH*'" (Exod. 6:2). Behold it is written: "For oppression [*oshek*] makes the sage foolish" (Eccles. 7:7). When a sage becomes involved [*mitasek*] in too many matters, his wisdom becomes confounded. Another interpretation: One who becomes involved [*mitasek*] in communal affairs forgets his learning. R. Y'hudah ben R. Shimon taught: "For oppression makes the sage foolish," this is Moses. *Oshek* refers to the criticisms with which Datan and Aviram attacked him. They accused him [after his first attempts with Pharaoh], saying, "*YHVH* will look upon you and judge!" (Exod. 5:21). Then Moses became angry and said to God, "From the moment that I came to Pharaoh he has done only evil to this people!" (Exod. 5:23). Then the Holy One replied, "I have described you as 'exceedingly humble' [Num. 12:3] and now you are angry with Me? By your life, you ought to know that 'the end of a matter is better than its beginning' [continuation of the *Kohelet* passage, Eccles. 7:8]." In that moment, the attribute of justice sought to strike Moses, as it says, "And *Elohim* spoke . . ." (Exod. 6:2). But then the Holy One thought, "Am I flesh and blood that I should have no mercy?" And so it says, "I am *YHVH*" (end of the verse).

Comment Does this midrash offer any consolation for those of us who choose a life of public service?

Va-eira
Sheldon Marder, 2000

"But Moses appealed to *Adonai*, saying, 'The Israelites would not listen to me. . . .' So *Adonai* spoke to both Moses and Aaron and gave them a charge to the Israelites" (Exod. 6:12–13).

S'fat Emet Even though the Israelites refused to listen, God commanded Moses and Aaron to continue speaking to them. For the words of God must leave a profound impression. They may not take effect all at once, but eventually they must accomplish their purpose, for holy words can never be lost on human beings.

Rashi, citing *Sh'mot Rabbah* God commanded Moses and Aaron to lead Israel gently (בנחת, *b'nachat*) and to be patient with them.

Comment Both commentaries see in these verses the need for patience on the part of leaders. How do we, as leaders, sustain our enthusiasm and optimism while waiting for holy words to take effect?

Leaders are respected for their strength; what does it mean to lead gently? In the Babylonian Talmud, *B'rachot* 56b, בנחת (*b'nachat*) means "walking gently"—the opposite of ברודף (*b'rodef*, "galloping"). From this we learn that gentleness is not the opposite of strength; it is the opposite of haste.

Va-eira: *Aveirah Goreret Aveirah*
Kenneth J. Weiss, 2001

"Pharaoh's heart stiffened" (Exod. 7:22, etc.); "The LORD stiffened the heart of Pharoah" (Exod. 9:12, etc.).

Why does God stiffen Pharaoh's heart, when Pharaoh ceases to do it himself? One midrash (*Sh'mot Rabbah* 11:6) suggests that God saw Pharaoh unwilling to relent, even after the first five plagues. So, God determined to stiffen his heart "in order to exact the whole punishment from him" (*Sh'mot Rabbah* 11:6).

But, just maybe, Pharaoh, over time, fell under the influence of his own inertia. Stiffening his heart the first time justified doing the same thing again, and yet again. After a time, his response might well have become, "The answer is No! Now, what is your question?" Pharaoh's heart stiffened even before "His Highness" realized it.

Perhaps Ben Azzai had this intractable ruler in mind when he said (in *Pirkei Avot* 4:2), "The reward of performing one mitzvah is [that you'll then do another] mitzvah, [**but**] the result of transgressing once is to transgress yet again [*mitzvah goreret mitzvah, aveirah goreret aveirah*]." Ben Azzai (or his spiritual antecedent) should have been hired as an advisor to Pharaoh: don't say "no" yet, for one "no" may well lead to another, indeed to a lifetime of "no's."

Va-eira
Kenneth J. Weiss, 2002

"The Pharaoh ... said, 'Plead with the LORD ...'" (Exod. 8:4).

Picture (no great stretch!) a swaggering, haughty, self-assured Pharaoh. He fears no one. Nothing awes him. His Egyptian subjects accept him as a god, but (their beliefs notwithstanding) . . . he is merely human.

Moses and Aaron are sent by *YHVH* to remind him of that incontrovertible fact: you may hold your people in thrall; but, by *God*, you're no god at all—just a man, fallible and phobic.

Perhaps, the plagues are a metaphorical MRI of the dark side of Pharaoh's psyche. His fears (blood, jumping and creeping things, threats to his people's well-being, darkness, the death of loved ones) draw us to posit that

- if Pharaoh has phobias, and
- if phobias are part of the human condition, then
- Pharaoh is (indeed) merely human.

Blood didn't unbalance him; he'd undoubtedly seen and shed much of it in his lifetime.

But frogs: that was something else entirely! To rid Egypt of them, Pharaoh (the Egyptian "god") summoned Moses and Aaron and—awestruck (for the first time?)—asked them to plead with *YHVH* (the *real* God) to remove the frogs. In fear, Pharaoh hunkered down and appealed for divine intervention.

Modern parlance has it that "there are no atheists in foxholes." A midrash (*Sh'mot Rabbah* 10:6) adds that the way of the wicked is to cry out to God when they are in trouble, but—when they have respite—they resume their wicked ways.

Did Pharaoh emerge from his foxhole a changed and deepened man? Awed by *YHVH*'s power to touch him in his most vulnerable places, did he renounce his wicked ways? And what of us: is our "phaith" merely phobia-driven?

Va-eira
Kenneth J. Weiss, 2003

If we Jews are to both "remember" and "observe" Shabbat, might we not expect God to both "remember" and "observe" the covenant into which He and we entered?

Yet, here in *Parashat Va-eira*, God (having heard the cry of the Israelite slaves) tells Moses, "I have *remembered* My covenant" (Exod. 6:5). Doesn't "remember" imply a prior forgetting? Whilst "Israel was in Egypt's land," might the covenant have slipped from God's mind?

ואזכר (*Va-ezkor*, "I have remembered"): strangely unsatisfying in this context. Why not ואשמר (*va-eshmor*): "I have kept/maintained My covenant with My people?"

Then again—maybe God remembers because we so easily forget...

Va-eira
Kenneth J. Weiss, 2004

Here's how to focus—then rivet—the attention of careful readers: just reverse verbs (even entire clauses) from commonsense sequence.

Consider:
Did Isaac (in Gen. 24:67) take Rebekah as his wife, then come to love her, as the text order implies?

Did God (in Exod. 3:9) hear the Israelites' cry and *only later* see the oppression under which they lived? Mightn't the text read, "I have seen how the Egyptians oppress the Israelites, whose cry has reached Me"?

In our *sidrah* (Exod. 6:6), God would have to free / והצלתי (*v'hitzalti*) our ancestors from their burdens, before bringing them out / והוצאתי (*v'hotzeiti*) from Egyptian bondage... hmmmmm...

Va-eira
Alan Cook, 2005

"See, I place you in the role of God to Pharaoh" (Exod. 7:1).

"They call me 'Wonderful' / So I am wonderful / In fact—it's so much who I am / It's part of my name" ("Wonderful," from the musical *Wicked*, by Stephen Schwartz and Winnie Holzman).

What is the difference between Moses and the "Wonderful" Wizard of Oz? Both seem to arrive at their positions by happenstance.

But whereas the wizard chooses to believe his own hype, Moses is humble enough to remain fairly resistant to it.

In the wizard's case, the figure behind the curtain is revealed to be nothing more than a humbug. But Moses accepts that God is guiding him. He knows that while he has been given the "role of God" to Pharaoh, that does not make him a god (כביכול! [*kivyachol*, "as if it were possible"]) or give him godlike powers. Rather, when Moses first encounters God at the Burning Bush, the voice that calls to him says, משה, משה! (Moshe, Moshe!). Moses remains the same after his encounter with the Divine as he was beforehand.

And in this humility, Moses actually comes closer to God. For God's name, as represented by the Tetragrammaton, also signifies a lack of change. God proclaims, אהיה אשר אהיה (*Ehyeh asher ehyeh* [Exod. 3:14]), "I am that which I am" (or, per Everett Fox in *The Five Books of Moses* (Schocken, 2000), "I will be-there howsoever I will be-there").

God does not change according to the needs of the hour. God does not hide behind shimmering emeralds that turn out to be all style and no substance.

Let us each strive to be equally "real" in our dealings with others. That would really be "wonderful."

Va-eira
Amy Scheinerman, 2006

Moshe encounters Pharaoh knowing full well that Pharaoh will not accede to God's demand. God had warned Moshe in Exod. 3:19–20 that Pharaoh would back down only in the face of superior power, but assured him that the plagues would persuade Pharaoh. Following the first five plagues, Torah tells us that Pharaoh hardens his heart (the root חזק is employed in Exod. 7:22 and 8:15; כבד, in 8:11, 8:28, and 9:7). Following the sixth plague, God is the direct agent who hardens Pharaoh's heart (Exod. 9:12): ויחזק יהוה את לב פרעה (*Va-y'chazeik Adonai et lev paroh*). The sense of God's stranglehold on Pharaoh's will and actions increases in Exod. 8:24–25 when Pharaoh admits his guilt and seeks to release the Israelites, but God reverses his thinking (Exod. 9:34–35).

Pharaoh hardens his own heart following the first five plagues, and God hardens Pharaoh's heart after each of the last five plagues. Nachmanides suggests that it was the magicians who hardened Pharaoh's heart following the first five plagues in an attempt to glorify themselves. Nahum Sarna, in *Exploring Exodus: The Origins of Biblical Israel* (Schocken, 1996), explains God's purpose: to forge a public, cosmic duel of acknowledged deities.

Torah itself elucidates another truth: What begins as an act of free choice (however obdurate) becomes a compulsion. How often do we follow a pattern of behavior we know to be wrong and destructive but cannot reverse course? How often do we blame it on our "nature" or "upbringing" or a myriad other excuses? Pharaoh knew by the end of our פרשה (*parashah*; Exod. 9:27ff.) that he stood guilty before God, yet his compulsion drove him forward.

Va-eira
Amy Scheinerman, 2007

In the opening פסוק (*pasuk*) of פרשת וארא (*Parashat Va-eira*), the redundancy of וידבר (*vay'dabeir*, "he spoke") and ויאמר (*vayomer*, "he said") provides an opening in *Midrash Rabbah Sh'mot* 4:1 to bring Eccles. 2:12 and ask: in what way did Sh'lomo and Moshe behold wisdom, yet engage in madness and folly?

The midrash informs us that although Sh'lomo understood the limits placed upon a king of Israel (Deut. 17:16–17), he took it upon himself to abrogate God's commandment because he believed he could violate the letter of the law without violating the intention behind the mitzvot. A clever *d'rash* ensues concerning the transfer of even the smallest letter, *yod*, followed by the admission that, in fact, late in life Sh'lomo was unable to withstand his wives' seducement to idolatry (I Kings 11:4). R. Shimon bar Yochai concludes, "It would have been preferable for Sh'lomo to have cleaned sewers." Sh'lomo beheld wisdom yet turned to madness and folly because, as the midrash has him say, "I tried to be wiser than Torah and persuaded myself that I knew the intention of Torah."

Is this midrash an attempt to squelch human interpretation of Torah in favor of a fundamentalist reading of, and adherence to, Torah—in direct contradiction to the famous *sugya* in the Babylonian Talmud, *Bava M'tzia* 59? Or is it a sober reminder that we sometimes make decisions not based on sound religious thinking, but due to an inflated ego or mere convenience, as Sh'lomo almost certainly did in this case?

The midrash next explains how Moshe fell into the Eccles. 2:12 trap. In Moshe's case, God's initial inclination to respond with justice (אלוהים, *Elohim*) is softened and converted to mercy (יהוה, *Adonai*) when God realizes that Moshe was concerned for Israel's suffering. It appears that the criterion of our intention in analyzing the **intention** behind the mitzvot matters greatly to the outcome.

Va-eira
Michael Boyden, 2008

At first sight, the plagues are a theological and a moral problem. How can God "harden Pharaoh's heart" and then punish him for his actions? Note, however, that it is only when we get to the sixth plague that we read, "But Adonai stiffened Pharaoh's heart" (Exod. 9:12). In other words, the initial instinct to ignore the Israelites' suffering was inherent in his nature. As the Rambam explains, "It was because he initially sinned out of choice and embittered the lives of the Israelites living in his land that *Adonai* stiffened his heart."

By contrast, the sixteenth-century Italian commentator Ovadiah Sforno suggests the opposite: If Pharaoh had freed the Israelites after the first five plagues, it would not have been done freely but rather on account of the plagues. Therefore, God hardened his heart to leave him free will!

Evil has two aspects—not only its effects upon the victim, but also what it does to the perpetrator. Pharaoh is a tragic figure who sinks deeper and deeper into a pit he digs for himself. Even his advisors remonstrate, "Don't you know that Egypt is lost?" But Pharaoh is no more able to hear common sense than were Hitler, Stalin, and all the other tyrants of our time. As R. Assi put it: "At first the evil impulse is like a spider's web, but later it becomes like cart ropes."

While Pharaoh, who was born free, becomes a slave to his impulses, the Israelites were born slaves but are led out to freedom. As Victor Frankl put it, "You cannot control what happens to you, but you can control your attitude towards what happens to you, and in that, you will be mastering change rather than allowing it to master you."

Va-eira

Amy Scheinerman, 2009

"Moshe was eighty years old and Aharon eighty-three when they made their demand on Pharaoh" (Exod. 7:7).

Pirkei Avot 5:23 provides a life-cycle schedule: "At five, one studies Tanach. At ten, Mishnah. At thirteen, the mitzvot. At fifteen, Talmud. At eighteen, marriage. At twenty, pursuit of a livelihood. At thirty, the peak of strength. At forty, understanding. At fifty, advisor. At sixty, old age. At seventy, the hoary head. At eighty, strength. At ninety, a bent back. At one hundred, it is as if one is already dead and passed out of this world."

If we examine various commentaries on this passage in *Pirkei Avot*, we find that some read *koach* (strength) at eighty as a sincere expression, but many read it as sardonic or a euphemism for weakness. But Torah suggests—through the model of Moshe—that eighty can be a time of remarkable capacity and strength. We have all known elders who retained their vitality because they had not only attained wisdom through learning and life's experiences, but chose to invest in others and thereby found great purpose to their latter years.

Sadly, there are many elders in our midst who do not feel that their lives have continuing meaning and value. Perhaps there is more we can do to integrate such people into the life of the community, pairing them with children who have no local grandparents so they can share their stories, wisdom, recipes, and love.

There is a message in this for each of us, as well. Age is, in large measure, attitude. We can be eighty with strength, or eighty with "strength."

בא Bo

(Exodus 10:1–13:16)

Bo
Ari Cartun, 1996

Inasmuch as the first and last plagues (Nile blood and death of sons) seem to be tit-for-tat retribution for the murder of Israelite boys by drowning in the Nile, what is the purpose of the middle eight plagues? Why have more than one plague anyway? And, considering that Psalms 78 and 105 list seven and eight plagues, respectively, why, *davka*, does Exodus enumerate ten?

Bo
Lawrence S. Kushner, 1997

Rashi suggests that one would think the whole Torah should begin with Exodus 12, the first mitzvah given to the Jewish people ("This month shall be to you the head of months" [v. 2]) Why does God wait till the announcement of the final plague before giving the mitzvah of Pesach observance? Might that mitzvah not have encouraged the people? Rashi's suggestion reminds us that the Torah is not just a book of laws. What is the relation between the Exodus narrative and the mitzvot that permeate it?

In Exod. 12:15 we are enjoined not to eat *chameitz*; in Exod. 12:39 we are told that the Israelites baked *matzot, ki lo chameitz* ("for it was not leavened"). Why are these passages not connected? We always give 12:39 as the reason why we eat no *chameitz* ("they could not tarry"). Are we mistaken in seeing this as the reason?

Bo: Into the Void
Stephen E. Cohen, 1997

According to Nachman of Bratzlav, "Pharaoh"/*paroh* refers to the Lurianic "Emptied Space" from which God withdrew, to make room for Creation. In that void, says Nachman, "unanswerable questions" arise concerning God. The mission of Moses is to go into that void, to rescue souls that have become trapped there.

Nachman of Bratzlav "Go in to *Paroh*, for I have hardened his heart" (Exod. 10:1). *Paroh* refers to the "Emptied Space [*chalal hapanui*]." There, in the Emptied Space, there is hard-heartedness. All of the wisdoms that come from there contain "hard-heartedness," because they remain in doubt regarding God. It is impossible to find God there, since God withdrew from there, as it were, to allow Creation to occur. Therefore, "the Eternal said to Moses, 'Go in to *Paroh*.'" Moses, specifically, should go in to *paroh*; it is forbidden for anyone else to enter there, only one who partakes of Moses, because it is impossible to find God there.

Comment With what words and what actions do we, contemporary rabbis, rescue souls trapped in the *chalal hapanui*? And are there forbidden regions, devoid of God, into which we should not venture?

Bo: The Darkness
Stephen E. Cohen, 1998

In *Sh'mot Rabbah*, we find the stunning assertion that the purpose of the plague of darkness was to conceal from the Egyptians the fact that God was causing those Israelites who were not inclined to leave Egypt to die! The Chasidic author of *Mei HaShiloach* grapples here with that midrash.

Mei HaShiloach The point of this midrash is that the Patriarchs had no extraneous thoughts. From all of their thoughts came forth souls—even several generations later. When Abraham went to rescue Lot, and to pursue and make war against the kings, he was uncertain whether or not to pursue, until the Holy One revealed to him that he had to pursue, for the sake of the "two fine doves" (Ruth and Naamah, who would be descended from Lot). So, from Abraham's thoughts not to pursue eventually issued the souls who, at the time of the Exodus, desired to "sit and not act." And they were inclined against doing battle against Egypt. These souls were rooted in Abraham's soul, and their characteristic was also from God. And they all died in the three days of darkness.

Comment *Mei HaShiloach* takes a stand against the thrust of the original midrash and holds that the Israelites who wanted to stay in Egypt were not really wicked, but were in fact rooted in Abraham's soul. Why, in either case, would it be necessary for these souls to "disappear" before the Exodus could occur?

Bo: The Blood Star
Stephen E. Cohen, 1999

In this *sidrah*, Pharaoh angrily rejects Moses's claim that the entire people need to go into the desert and employs a strangely worded exclamation: "See! Evil is opposite your faces . . ." (Exod. 10:10). Rashi notes that the *p'shat* is according to Onkelos's translation (i.e., "you intend evil") but then adds a lengthy and layered aggadic reading.

Rashi [As Onkelos translates it:] But I have seen an aggadic tradition that there is a star whose name is *Raah*. Pharaoh said to them, "I see by my astrology that the star *Raah* is rising toward you in the desert. And it represents blood and killing." Then, when the Israelites sinned with the Calf, and the Holy One sought to kill them, Moses referred to this prediction of Pharaoh's, "Let not the Egyptians say that with *Raah* he brought them forth" (Exod. 32:12). Immediately YHVH repented of the *Raah* and transformed the blood into the blood of circumcision that Joshua performed. And this is why it is written there: "Today I roll away the disgrace of Egypt from you"

(Josh. 5:9). That is, that the Egyptians would have been able to say, "We predicted your bloody fate in the desert."

Comment   In this passage, as in the mysterious passage of Zipporah's circumcision of her son, the blood of *milah* is explicitly to require to assuage God's blood-thirst. Is there any hint of this dimension in our own *b'rit milah* tradition?

Bo
Sheldon Marder, 2001

"Each of them shall take a lamb to a family" (Exod. 12:3).

"The whole community of Israel shall offer it" (Exod. 12:47).

What was the essence of *Pesach Mitzrayim*, the Passover in Egypt? Home ritual or a community gathering?

The phrase *beit avot* in Exod. 12:3 ("family" in JPS 1999; "parental home" in S. R. Hirsch's translation) conjures up the image of a traditional household with father at the head of the table. But verse 47 puts the proceedings in a different light. Here we find that, not families, but rather "the whole community" shall offer the lamb. The *M'chilta*, noting the difference between these two texts, almost seems to anticipate "Singles Seder" and the like. What, asks the midrash, is the intent of verse 47? "I might think that just as the Pesach lamb in Egypt was taken for each individual family, so too the Pesach lamb of all [future] generations [will be taken family by family], therefore, it is written: 'The whole community of Israel shall offer it.'" In other words, our Sages were aware that not everyone fits into a family configuration, and they stipulate that the ritual must include all members of the community.

Bo: Observe and Remember ... Pesach! A Midrashic Critique
Kenneth J. Weiss, 2001

"You shall **observe** [*ush'martem*] the [Feast of] Unleavened Bread" (Exod. 12:17).

"**Observe** this [blood on lintel and doorposts] as an institution for all time" (Exod. 12:24).

"This day shall be for you one of **remembrance** [*l'zikaron*]" (Exod. 12:14).

"**Remember** [*zachor*] this day, on which you went free" (Exod. 13:3).

(Preamble: The Decalogue in Exodus commands us to **remember** Shabbat. The version in Deuteronomy commands us to observe it.) Note that the verbs of the Shabbat mitzvah (mitzvot!) are right in front of us in *Parashat Bo*! In the verses dealing with Chag HaMatzot and Pesach in chapters 12 and 13 of Exodus, we are commanded to **observe** what were once two distinct Festivals and to **remember** them.

We're also commanded in these chapters to do something else of crucial importance. In addition to observing, in addition to remembering, we are told to **speak** of these rituals (*vaamartem* [Exod. 12:27, etc.]) and to **explain** them (*v'higadtah* [Exod. 13:8]) to our children.

Torah tells us to do Pesach, to remember Pesach, to speak of Pesach. And, is not Pesach—even in our own day—universally understood to be the most broadly observed holiday in the Jewish calendar? The Torah writers almost got it all when they committed the Shabbat mitzvot to writing. However, the message (and the impact?) was diluted (two Decalogues in two separate books). Additionally, though they commanded us to remember and observe, they never overtly commanded us to **speak** of Shabbat, to verbally transmit it, to explain it to our children!

Is that why we've struggled to promote the celebration of Shabbat ever since? Maybe so!

Bo

Kenneth J. Weiss, 2002

"You shall observe ה-מ-צ-ו-ת" (Exod. 12:17).

The Rabbis, when they see this verse, read *hamitzvot*, not *hamatzot*. Let's extend that thought. Suppose *mitzvot* was the original (and only!) word *ever* intended when, in these chapters, we come across the letters מ-צ-ו-ת.

Humor me here: Pesach is a time to observe commandments, indeed to "absorb" them fully (the verb *achal* means not only "to eat," but "to consume"; *Roget's Thesaurus* avers that a synonym for "consume" is "absorb"!). Might *matzot* be a misreading, an editor's misunderstanding? After all, the people really had *plenty* of time to let their dough rise while making ready for the Exodus journey: they knew of God's promise to rescue them well before the Holy One turned the Nile red. (Besides, Torah never explains *why* leaven should be avoided for the week.) Finally, wasn't the *primary* food symbolizing the Exodus a lamb (cf. Exod. 12:3ff.), "without blemish, a yearling male" (Exod. 12:5)?

So, perhaps the subject here is mitzvot, in which case חמץ (*chameitz*, its opposite) takes on a different meaning. Pesach is now understood to be a time to absorb—to internalize—the mitzvot (rather than consume the matzot!). God commands that one week each spring Jews reaffirm the undeniably central role of the mitzvot. Indeed, during Pesach, they are to avoid any *chimetz*, "delay," in internalizing the mitzvot; eschew the *chumtzah*, "acid," that results from a life devoid of them; in sum: never *hechemitz et hashaah*, "miss the opportunity" (to do mitzvot).

So, the Israelites may have been told, "You shall observe the mitzvot . . . throughout the ages. . . . You shall internalize the mitzvot . . ." (Exod. 12:17–18). And here's why: God, whom you will soon meet at Mount Sinai, will know you by them.

Bo
Kenneth J. Weiss, 2003

God is surely a better strategist than we sometimes realize: I see Pharaoh's servants as nothing less than God's "embedded assets," planted quietly, unobtrusively into Pharaoh's court years earlier.

Now—at the opportune moment—they come out of "left field" to deliver a stinging rebuke to their royal master. Who else but *YHVH* could have been behind their words: "Let the people go . . . ! Don't you know yet that Egypt has perished?" (Exod. 10:7). For just such a moment, God placed (His own) servants at the very foot of Pharaoh's throne.

Note the textual pun: Pharaoh's servants—עבדי פרעה (*avdei faroh*)—urge that the Israelites be freed "so they may serve"—ויעבדו (*v'yaavdu*)—their God.

Bo
Kenneth J. Weiss, 2004

Why was Moses—a Hebrew, an escaped felon—"esteemed in . . . Egypt, among Pharaoh's courtiers and . . . the people" (Exod. 11:3)? He'd become a "folk hero":

- Moses was connected to, indeed raised in, the royal household.
- Long after he'd fled to—perhaps died in—Midian, Moses reappeared, demanding that Pharaoh free the Israelites.
- Only Moses—commissioned by God—both brought about plagues (wreaking ten kinds of havoc) and interceded to halt them.

In sum, Moses spoke the language, reappeared from "nowhere," and (as God's emissary) confronted authority as he undertook his singular mission. Like many folk heroes, Moses was "bigger (even) than life"—Torah calls him גדול מאד (*gadol m'od* [Exod. 11:3]).

Bo
Alan Cook, 2006

"Hold out your arm toward the sky that there may be darkness upon the land of Egypt, a darkness that can be touched" (Exod. 10:21).

Much ink has been spilled over the question of whether all ten plagues visited upon Egypt were really necessary. Were it not for the stubbornness of Pharaoh, it seems likely that the average Egyptian would have been annoyed enough by the first few plagues to begin petitioning their rulers to take measures to alleviate their suffering. Then again, Egypt at the time was far from being a representative democracy!

But if we look at the plagues from a different angle, we find that each of them had an individual purpose in raising the awareness of the "Egyptian on the street" to the plight of the Israelites. The plague of darkness, for instance, affected not only the sight of those afflicted, but it was "a darkness that can be touched" (Exod. 10:21). In other words, it had a tangible, measurable impact on the Egyptians. It prevented them from even moving.

In contrast, "all the Israelites enjoyed light in their dwellings" (Exod. 10:23). So, while the Egyptians were beginning to appreciate what oppression felt like, the Jews were getting a foretaste of freedom.

This continues to be our mission: to engage in acts of *tikkun olam*, to bring brightness into the dark recesses of the world, and to always rise to the challenge of being a light unto the nations.

Bo

Amy Scheinerman, 2006

The ninth plague—darkness—is curiously different from the preceding plagues. The Egyptians are powerless to stop or reverse the first eight plagues. Can they not have dispelled the darkness by lighting lamps?

Sh'mot Rabbah 14:1–2 on Exod. 10:23 suggests that the thick darkness had substance, that it was the darkness of *Geihinom*, and that it was the darkness of evil and the primordial chaos out of which the universe emerged at Creation. In contrast, *Sh'mot Rabbah* 14:3 explains that "but all the Israelites enjoyed light in their dwellings" does not mean "in the land of Goshen" in general, but rather that each Israelite exuded light, a foreshadowing of the messianic age.

We can understand the darkness not as a physical phenomenon, but as a moral condition. *Sh'mot Rabbah* 14:3 supports this interpretation, telling us that the Israelites visit their Egyptian neighbors during the week of darkness, and could easily fleece them of silver and gold, but refrain from doing so. Hence the Egyptians donate their riches to the Israelites in gratitude after the plague lifts.

That same gold is used later both for the Golden Calf and the Ark and Tabernacle utensils, a reminder that every moment and event presents a moral choice. The darkness has not disappeared; we must continually light lamps to dispel its effects.

Bo

Amy Scheinerman, 2008

What is the nature of the plague of darkness? From astronomy comes the suggestion of an eclipse, but eclipses last minutes, not days. From psychology comes the suggestion of a deep depression that descended upon Egypt after suffering so many plagues, yet depression rarely lifts after a mere three days.

Traditional commentators focus on וימש חשך (*v'yameish choshech* [Exod. 10:21]). JPS translates, "a darkness that can be touched." Onkelos derives וימש (*v'yameish*) from מוש (*mush*), "to move away." Rashbam, following his grandfather Rashi, understands it as "to grow darker"—that is, the darkness grows increasingly gloomy. Ibn Ezra offers three alternatives: מוש (*mush*), "to touch or feel," as in Ps. 115:7; ממש (*misheish*), "to grope," as in Deut. 28:29; and מוש (*mush*), "to move away," as in Exod. 13:22. Sforno echoes Nachmanides that the darkness was like a thick fog that light could not penetrate.

Could the darkness be national moral blindness? The Egyptians abet in the enslavement of Israel and benefit from the injustice of slave labor without a hint of regret. Egypt lived in spiritual darkness, while in contrast ולכל־בני ישראל היה אור במושבתם (*ul'chol B'nei Yisrael hayah or b'moshvotam*), "but all the Israelites enjoyed light in their dwellings" (Exod. 10:23). *B'reishit Rabbah* 14:3 understands this verse to mean not "in the land of Goshen," but rather that Jews could see light wherever they were. Hence Israelites visited the homes of their Egyptian neighbors, noted where their valuables were, but took nothing. When the time for the Exodus arrived and the Egyptians denied they had anything to lend the Israelites, the Israelites recalled precisely both objects and their locations within Egyptian homes. Impressed that the Israelites had not taken advantage of the darkness to steal, the Egyptians willingly turned over their valuables.

Bo
Amy Scheinerman, 2008

Between Moshe's announcement to the Egyptians of the impending tenth plague and its actual execution, Torah diverts to a discussion of how the Pesach sacrifice is to be made on this momentous occasion, and in the future as a yearly observance for coming generations. Exodus 12:2 begins this passage by addressing Israel's new calendar: "This month shall mark for you the beginning of the months; it shall be the first of the months of the year for you."

How does a society inaugurate a new calendar? Historically, the calendar is set according to the ascension of the ruler to the throne. Our case is no different: the Exodus marked the moment when Israel coalesced into a nation ruled by God, not Pharaoh. Our religious calendar, going back to Creation, also affirms this, and further affirms the unity of all humanity. This *pasuk* reminds us that Pesach is not a celebration of freedom, but rather our redemption by God. This, in turn, reminds us that God is the source of all possibilities in our lives, as well as the strength to pursue them.

In our calendar, each new month is marked by the new moon, which waxes and wanes over the course of the month. The silver sliver of light at the beginning of each month promises renewal and rebirth. As Sfat Emet taught, the Jewish people goes through cycles of success and prosperity alternating with suffering and degradation, yet our calendar continually reminds us that brighter days lie ahead. Therefore, we can always hope for better times and another redemption.

Perhaps we would do well to teach more about the Jewish calendar and integrate it into the lives of our communities to reap the teachings and rewards of its inherent messages.

Bo
David Novak, 2009

Our Jewish calendar is born in *Parashat Bo*: "This month shall mark for you the beginning of the months; it shall be the first of the months of the year for you" (Exod. 12:2). It is here that the foundation for

Jewish time is born and with it the first of our Pilgrimage Festivals, Pesach (Passover). That the first month is not when we observe Rosh HaShanah (often translated as our new year) is an embedded confusion that prevails over the generations. What is so beautiful about our Jewish way of keeping time is that we keep time with freedom.

It is in our first month that we hold our commemoration each year of our miraculous trip from slavery to freedom facilitated by a "mighty hand and an outstretched arm" (Deut. 26:8). It is in the beginning of God's Creation where Genesis embarks; our unique Jewish narrative, cemented in this freedom story, begins here.

This should be considered an enduring contribution to humanity. Pharaoh's evil only meets its comeuppance through the supernatural intervention of God, who, through Moses's agency, is able to lead a broken people from oppression to a journey through the desert. This is a journey that finds both literal and metaphoric meaning, as the journey that began then is one we are still on.

We recommit ourselves to pursuing freedom for people who are oppressed, adding our hands, feet, and intellect to the task. Someday soon we all hope we will enter into a world of true freedom for all peoples.

בשלח B'shalach

(Exodus 13:17–17:16)

For additional commentary on *B'shalach*, see "Tu BiSh'vat."

B'shalach
Ari Cartun, 1996

The locusts of plague seven are drowned in the Reed Sea by an east wind, as are the Egyptians in this *parashah*, equating them. Chapter 1 uses verbs like ירבו *yirbu* (multiplied) and ישרצו *yishr'tzu* (were prolific) to describe Israel's explosive growth—but these verbs (ירבו *yirbu* = ארבה *arbeh* = locust) also describe locusts. What do locusts, Israelites, and Egyptians have in common?

B'shalach
Lawrence S. Kushner, 1997

Why does God give Pharaoh the credit for letting the people go (Exod. 13:17)? Moses tells the people, "Stand and see the victory of *Adonai*!" (Exod. 14:13). God seems to correct him: "Speak to the Israelites that they should move on!" (Exod. 14:15). Why does Moses want the people to appreciate God's work, while God seems to want the people to act? Which shows the greater faith—to admire the work of God or, as the Rabbis credit Nachshon ben Aminadav, to step forward into the Sea? What motivates Moses to say, "Stand and see"?

B'shalach: Standing Firm; Standing Still
Stephen E. Cohen, 1998

Most translators understand Moses's *Hityatzvu* (Exod. 14:13) as an encouragement to the trapped Israelites: "Stand firm." Ibn Ezra, however, renders it as "Stand still, do nothing, and watch God's deliverance."

Ibn Ezra   "Fear not, stand and see the deliverance of the Eternal" (Exod. 14:13). This means "**You** shall not do battle, but shall watch the deliverance of the Eternal." One might wonder how a huge camp of six hundred thousand men would fear those pursuing after them. And why would they not fight for their lives and for their children? The answer is that the Egyptians had been the Israelites' masters—and this generation that went forth from Egypt had learned from their youth to suffer the yoke of Egypt; their spirit was crushed. How, then, would they fight against their masters? And God caused that generation to perish, for they did not have the strength to battle against the Canaanites, until a new generation arose, the generation of the wilderness, who had never seen exile. And their spirit was exalted.

Comment   Does Ibn Ezra's comment have any bearing on the question of Jewish resistance to the Holocaust or not?

B'shalach: Crying Out
Stephen E. Cohen, 1998

Rashi's first comment on *Mah titzak eilai* ("Why do you cry out to Me?" [Exod. 14:15]) is well-known and loved by modern Jews, treasured for its emphasis on human self-reliance. His *Davar Acher*, however, radically undermines that message.

Rashi   We have learned that Moses was standing and praying, and the Blessed Holy One said, "This is not a time to expand in prayer; the Israelites are in danger!" But the *Davar Acher* is: "Why do you cry out? Upon Me . . . !" That is, "The thing depends upon Me, not upon you." This is similar to what God says [Isa. 45:11]: "Will you command Me regarding My children and the work of My hands?"

Comment   The *Davar Acher* leaves the human being utterly disempowered, impotent, and discouraged even from crying out. Why does Rashi include it?

B'shalach: God in the Waves
Stephen E. Cohen, 1999

A bit of fun in the midrash on "Horse and rider God has hurled into the sea [*ramah vayam*]" (Exod. 15:1).

Sh'mot Rabbah 23:14   "To a mare among Pharaoh's chariots I have compared thee my beloved" (Song of Songs 1:9). What is meant by "I have compared thee"? The waves of the sea appeared as mares, and the horses of the Egyptian chariots were lustful stallions. They ran after them until they sank into the sea. Then the Egyptian said to his stallion, "Yesterday when I led you to the water to drink, did you not follow me? And now you are going to drown me in the sea!" And the stallion replied to him, *Ramah vayam / R'eih mah bayam*, "Look what is in the sea!"

Comment   No comment!

B'shalach
Sheldon Marder, 2001

What is the nature of the miraculous? "A miracle," wrote Maimonides in *Guide of the Perplexed* (3:24), "cannot prove what is impossible; it is only useful to confirm what is possible." Writing in 1944, Muriel Rukeyser told us that the gift of being a Jew in the twentieth century was "daring to live for the impossible" (from "Letter to the Front" [#VII] in *Beast in View*, 1944).

We Jews have a history of doubting God's ability to perform miracles, even while we celebrate, commemorate, and pray for them. As the author of one of the "historical psalms" put it, "Our ancestors in Egypt did not understand Your miracles and they rebelled at the sea" (Ps. 106:7). Second Isaiah wonders whether God, after the first destruction, still had the ability to redeem: "Awake, awake . . . !" he shouts. "Awake as in days of old! It was You that dried up the Sea ... that made the abysses of the Sea a road the redeemed might walk. So let the ransomed of *Adonai* return, and come with shouting to Zion" (Isa. 51:9–11). It is a disturbing image of God "asleep at the wheel."

In *B'shalach* we read, "But the Israelites had marched through the sea on dry ground" (Exod. 14:29). Reflecting on this verse, Rabbi Elimelech of Lizensk (1717–87) wrote with frustration about the human tendency to sleepwalk through life: "People fail to realize that nature itself is a great miracle. Only when confronted by an event that is obviously supernatural do they understand that God's providence and miracles are present even in everyday nature, which we tend to take for granted" (*Noam Elimelech*).

In his poem "Miracles," Yehuda Amichai applied nearly photographic perspective to our perception of events great and small:

> From far away everything looks like a miracle,
> but up close even a miracle doesn't look like one.
> Even a crosser of the divided Red Sea
> saw only the sweating back
> of the walker in front of him
> and the movement of his large thighs....
> The real miracles occur at the next table
> in a restaurant in Albuquerque.... (translated by Karen Alkalay-Gut, from *Modern Poetry in Translation*, New Series, No. 4, Winter 1993–94, p. 16)

We think of historical events in terms of "what happened." But when thinking about miracles, is it perhaps more useful to think in terms of "what was experienced," "what is remembered," and "why it matters"?

B'shalach: What Is a Miracle Anyway?
Kenneth J. Weiss, 2001

"The LORD ... turned the sea into dry ground" (Exod. 14:21).
"The LORD hurled the Egyptians into the sea" (Exod. 14:27).

Torah teaches that God split the sea so our ancestors could walk through it to freedom, and then God turned the waters back and drowned the Egyptians—miracle upon miracle.

Yitta Halberstam and Judith Leventhal, in their book, *Small Miracles of Love and Friendship* (Adams Media, 2002), understand miracles to be everyday occurrences—random acts, perhaps coincidences—that are also totally consistent with natural law. The book's "Introduction" opens, "There are moments in life when we catch our breath and glimpse God's presence." One example from their book: While walking down a dark, unfamiliar street, a man hears muffled screams; a woman is being attacked. Frightened, meek by nature, he considers fleeing. Somehow emboldened, he enters the fray and chases the attacker away. He speaks softly, "It's OK—you're safe now." After a time, he hears "[the woman's] words, uttered in wonder, in amazement. 'Dad, is that you?'" And—out steps his youngest daughter (pp. 6–7). Coincidence? Miracle!? In this and in countless other moments like them, God participates in—impacts—our everyday world even now!

Martin Buber defines a miracle as "an abiding astonishment." Thus, the Exodus—which is almost synonymous with the word "miracle" to many people—is understood as an event in which the people believed they saw "the great hand of God." Then as now when wondrous things happen, we can see them as random coincidences or know them to be God's hand touching our lives.

Read *Small Miracles*—you may understand the Exodus and perceive everyday occurrences, as well, in an all-new way.

B'shalach
Kenneth J. Weiss, 2004

Pharaoh—having released the Israelites—regrets his decision. Soon, he and his army are in hot pursuit. The Israelites, encamped at the sea, witness their advance and, in despair, approach Moses.

Moses reassures his skittish, frightened community: "Have no fear! Stand by and witness *YHVH*'s salvation. . . . *YHVH* will battle for you; hold your peace" (Exod. 14:13–14).

Then—oddly—YHVH (sounding exasperated) chastises Moses! "Why do you cry out to Me? Tell the Israelites to get moving" (Exod. 14:15). Perhaps Moses complained in words that have been lost . . .

But, there's a deeper message here. God says to Moses (to us too!): in crises, when the time for talk ends, act! No more words; go—move forward—now!

Nachshon? . . . ah, there you are . . .

B'shalach
Alan Cook, 2006

The *sidrah* בשלח (*B'shalach*) is accompanied by a haftarah reading from the Book of Judges. Both the Song at the Sea and the Song of Deborah are said to be among our oldest biblical texts, perhaps even predating the stories that place them in their current context in our biblical canon.

But perhaps the two readings are paired not merely because they each contain the vivid poetry of a song or because they both speak of God's redemptive might. Perhaps they are paired because of a very significant lesson that they can teach us about responding in the face of a challenge.

B'midbar Rabbah teaches that as the Israelites approached the Sea of Reeds, arguments arose among the tribes as to who would be the first to enter the waters. In the midst of these disagreements, Nachshon ben Aminadav stepped bravely into the waters, whereupon they parted, and the Israelites marched on dry land.

Similarly, we find in the Book of Judges that Deborah's general, Barak, shows some reluctance to enter into battle against Sisera and his army. It is Deborah and Yael who ultimately step up to the challenge and take the actions that seal the Israelites' victory.

Sometimes it is not the trained generals and the charismatic leaders who drive the action. The qualities of leadership can be found within "little people" such as Nachshon, Deborah, or Yael: people who took action not for any hope of future glory, but because they believed that it was the right thing to do. It is not the Jewish way to sit back and wait for someone else to set things right. We are called to "jump in" ourselves.

B'shalach
Amy Scheinerman, 2007

The first steps of a forty-year journey—בשלח פרעה את-העם (*B'shalach paroh et haam*), "When Pharoah let the people go" (Exod. 13:17)—raise a question. Why doesn't Torah say, "When God sent Israel out of Egypt" or "When Israel left Egypt"? Is this a reflection of the Israelites' state of mind? They still consider Pharaoh the ultimate power and do not yet acknowledge God as Sovereign of the universe. The continuation of the *pasuk* supports this notion, for God leads them in a circuitous route, knowing that "the people may have a change of heart when they see war, and return to Egypt" (ibid.). Is the path through the Sea of Reeds a way to avoid warfare or an opportunity for God to enter their lives again by splitting the sea and drowning the Egyptians, as Abarbanel suggests and Rabbi Yosef b. Yitzchak Bechor Shor (twelfth-century tosafist) affirms?

The Israelites' journey is a model for our spiritual journeys through life. Many begin as unexpectedly. Like our ancestors, we often search for evidence of God's presence and participation in our lives but fail to recognize it. Like our ancestors, we often lose heart and seek to return to what is familiar.

Carol Ochs suggests an alternative metaphor befitting both our national story and our lives: the spiritual walk. "The length is indeterminate, the walk begins anytime, no preparation is called for, the way is not clearly defined, and we have little concern with distance traveled or landmarks passed because we have no clearly defined destination. In other words, on the journey we are moving *toward* something while on the walk we are strolling *with* someone" (*Women and Spirituality*, Rowman & Littlefield, 1997, p. 113). Had the Israelites recognized they were walking *with* God and *with* one another, might they have mustered the strength and courage to take the direct route?

B'shalach
Amy Scheinerman, 2008

פרשת בשלח (*Parashat B'shalach*) tells us that the menu for the first Shabbat following the Exodus was quail and manna, catered by God in response to Israel's grumbling and legitimate need for food.

מן (*man*, "manna") is mentioned in Numbers 11 as well, though here it is not described as לחם (*lechem*, "bread"), as it is in our פרשה (*parashah*). Rather it is likened to coriander, and the Israelites must grind, boil, and form it into cakes in order to eat it. In Exodus, God rains down מן (*man*) in response to general hunger; God does not express anger at the Israelites' grumblings, but Moshe and Aharon note it (Exod. 16:7). In contrast, the Numbers account accuses the אספסף (*asafsuf*, "riffraff" [Num. 11:4]) of inciting the people on account of their own gluttonous cravings, suggesting that the complainers are not inspired by legitimate hunger. In this account, God responds with anger (Num. 11:10).

Manna can be viewed as a test of the Israelites' ability to subsist on the same limited daily diet. But more to the point, the miracle of מן (*man*) brings into sharp focus questions about the nature and meaning of miracles. Many of these questions are raised in the Talmud, *Yoma* 75–76: Are miracles always fundamental abrogations of nature? Does the regularity of the arrival of מן (*man*) diminish its miraculous quality? (*Yoma* 76 suggests the opposite, reflected in the power of the morning blessings, ניסים בכל־יום (*Nisim B'chol Yom*). Is human participation (gathering, grinding, boiling, shaping) necessary for human appreciation? Is the element of human participation (as in Moshe's role in parting the ים סוף [*Yam Suf*, "Sea of Reeds"]) a model for us?

B'shalach
Michael Boyden, 2009

Imagine the situation. The children of Israel reach the banks of the Reed Sea. They look back and, seeing the advancing Egyptian forces with their horses and chariots, are gripped by fear.

They protest to Moses, "What have you done to us bringing us out of Egypt?" (Exod. 14:11). How easy it is to blame others and not to take responsibility for our actions! No one forced them to leave.

But even in their distress they fail to act, thinking, as we sometimes do, that someone else will solve their problems. But God's response to Moses is unambiguous: "Why do you cry to Me? Tell the Israelites to get moving!" (Exod. 14:15). Prayer has its place, but so does action.

When people are confused and frightened, it requires a very special person to take the initiative. As *Midrash M'chilta* relates, no one wanted to get his feet wet first by jumping into the sea, but "while they were standing there and telling each other what to do, Nachshon ben Aminadav jumped and fell into the water."

Even the great Moses is startled by his act, and according to the midrash, it takes God to intervene and exclaim, "My friend is drowning in the sea, the waters are covering him, the enemy is pursuing, and all you can do is offer lots of prayers!" Taken aback, Moses asks what he should do. "Lift up your rod" is God's simple reply.

In so many situations in life, we feel unable to cope or lack the inner strength to effect change. However, the obstacles are not always as great as they would seem, if we would only have the will to act and the courage to believe.

B'shalach: Shabbat Shirah
Amy Scheinerman, 2009

Shabbat Shirah offers us two ancient songs: *Shirat HaYam* sung by Moshe and the Israelites upon crossing the Reed Sea, and *Shirat D'vorah* sung by Deborah and Barak in the haftarah for this Shabbat. Both poems celebrate divine redemption and exalt God's military power and prowess. *Shirat HaYam* depicts God as a warrior who "triumphed gloriously; / horse and driver God has hurled into the sea. . . . / Pharaoh's chariots and his army / God has cast into the sea, / and the pick of his officers / are drowned in the Sea of Reeds" (Exod. 15:1, 15:4). Just as God "threw the Egyptian army into a panic" (Exod. 14:24), so too, "the Lord threw Sisera and all his chariots and army into a panic" (Judges 4:15).

The two songs end on very different notes. *Shirat HaYam* ends on a messianic note. The exultant closing verses imagine God ensconced in the Temple and Israel "planted in Your own mountain" (Exod. 15:17), from which God will eternally reign. In contrast, *Shirat D'vorah* ends with the heartbreaking image of Sisera's mother waiting in vain for the return of her son, while the Israelites divide the spoils of war; and we learn that this battle brought forty years of peace. The first paints for us a picture of the idealized future presumably stretching on without limit, while the latter describes the present and wrenching reality, which in the best circumstance brings peace for only two generations.

Setting aside the troubling view of God as our divine warrior, taken together these two songs deliver a sober message: it is well and good to contemplate and envision the ultimate outcome of a war, but at the same time we must realize and consider the immediate effects of war on those involved and the possibility of an outcome considerably short of the ideal. The decision to engage in war (when one has the freedom to make this decision) must entail both.

B'shalach
Stephen Wylen, 2009

Vay'hi—"It came to pass that when Pharaoh expelled the people, God did not lead them the way of the land of the Philistines, though it was near, for God said, "Lest the people change their minds when they see war and return to Egypt" (Exod. 13:17).

The Talmud, *M'gilah* 10, says that whenever a story begins with *vay'hi*, it stands for *vay hi*, "woe unto them." This indicates that trouble is coming for the Jews. What could be bad about leaving slavery and going to freedom?

According to Rabbi H. D. Urbach, the trouble that the Torah is predicting with the word *vay'hi* is the transformation from dream to reality. For four hundred years the Jews had dreamed of emancipation. Now that freedom has become a reality, the people have to deal with war, hunger, thirst, and an uncertain future. Says Urbach, "This is the fate of all utopian ideals; their realization cannot live up to the hopes of those who work to make them happen."

This was one reason many Jews opposed Zionism a century ago. They feared that the reality of Jewish statehood could never live up to our messianic dreams. The world is shaped by those who are not afraid to confront head-on the crushing forces of reality. This same principle applies to the utopian hopes of our time—for health care reform, for Israeli-Arab peace, etc. Once we start efforts at making a better future, things get messy. The only other choice is to refuse redemption and remain slaves forever.

יתרו *Yitro*

(Exodus 18:1–20:23)

For additional commentary on *Yitro*, see "Shavuot."

Yitro
Arnold Jacob Wolf, 1996

Who spoke at Sinai? Who heard? Why was Sinai chosen? Why is Exodus 19 so vague and undifferentiated in its description of revelation? Was Leo Baeck correct in asserting that out of mystery always comes commandment? Contrast the (purposeful) vagueness with the precision of chapter 20. Is prophecy a category of (better) understanding holy Scripture as the word of God? (See Arthur Green, *Seek My Face, Speak My Name: A Jewish Mystical Theology*, Jewish Lights Publishing, 2003, pp. 108–114.)

Yitro
Lawrence S. Kushner, 1997

Since Jethro comes to congratulate Moses on the victory over the Egyptians at the Reed Sea, chapter 18 might well have concluded the previous *parashah*, with Exodus 19 beginning a new portion describing the giving of the Torah. Why do you think the Rabbis wanted to herald the giving of the Torah by this story of Jethro and Moses (chap. 18)?

In Exod. 18:15–16, Moses notes that the people come to him when there is a problem so that he may *d'rosh Elohim* (inquire of

God); he then judges (*v'shafat'ti*) between the two individuals and makes known the *chukim* (laws) and *torot* (statutes) of God. "Makes known"—*v'hodati*—suggests that the *chukim* and *torot* have already been laid down, and the immediate case is merely an opportunity for Moses to tell them to the people. How does the giving of the whole Torah at Sinai improve on this system? If the laws and statutes have already been determined by God, why did God not reveal them all in a body earlier?

The *M'chilta* suggests that the Ten Commandments can be read across as well as vertically, reading the first ("I am Adonai . . .") together with the sixth ("You shall not murder"), the second ("You shall have no other gods") together with the seventh ("You shall not commit adultery"), and so forth. What do we learn from these connections? Why did God not give them in this form in the Written Torah?

Yitro: Do Not Covet
Stephen E. Cohen, 1998

Ibn Ezra and S'fat Emet offer conflicting responses to the Torah's uncharacteristic attempt, in the last of the Ten Commandments (Exod. 20:14), to legislate our inner life.

Ibn Ezra Many have wondered about this mitzvah. How can a man not covet a beautiful thing, when it is attractive to his eyes? I will give you a parable: A peasant with common sense who saw the daughter of the king would not covet her, even though she was extremely beautiful, to be with her. For he knows that it is impossible. The peasant is not like the madmen who desire wings, like a bird of the sky. It cannot be; likewise, no man desires to sleep with his mother, even though she is beautiful. For they have trained him from childhood to know that she is forbidden to him.

S'fat Emet Ibn Ezra gave his explanation. Look there. But in truth it appears there is desire for the things of this world, but man's desire must be to fulfill the word of God. And this pleasure should overcome the pleasures of the world.

Comment Ibn Ezra argues for moral education that will eliminate our forbidden desires. S'fat Emet, on the other hand, regards these desires as inevitable and wants them defeated by a more powerful, holy impulse. Which approach offers a better strategy for an ethical life?

Yitro: Bridging the Gap
Melanie Aron, 1999

It is not just with regard to the Ten Principles that the question of revelation has posed difficulties. The idea of communication between the Infinite and the finite has challenged Jews in every generation. Clearly the biblical author saw a difficulty, for we find both in Exodus (20:16) and in Deuteronomy (5:24) that the people ask Moses to act as their intermediary.

Shir HaShirim Rabbah 12:2 R. Y'hoshua b. Levi and the Rabbis joined the issue. R. Y'hoshua said Israel heard two utterances from the mouth of the Holy One, blessed be He, namely "I am" and "Thou shalt not have. . . ." The Rabbis, however, say that Israel heard all the commandments from the mouth of the Holy One, blessed be He.

S'forno on Exodus 19:8 *Kol asher diber Adonai naaseh* ["All that the Lord has spoken we will do"] explains that the people "were doubtful whether Moses's prophecy was [actually] the words of *HaShem* or [received] from an angel."

Babylonian Talmud, *Sukkah* **4b–5a** Rabbi Yosei stated, "Neither did the *Shechinah* ever descend to earth, nor did Moses or Elijah ever ascend to heaven, as it is written, 'The heavens are the heavens of the Lord, but the earth He hath given to the sons of men' (Ps. 115:16). But did not the *Shechinah* descend to earth? Is it not in fact written, 'And the Lord came down upon Mount Sinai' (Exod. 19:20)? That was ten handbreadths above [the summit]. In this regard, we know clearly that the ark was nine [handbreadths high], since it is written, 'And they shall make an ark of acacia wood a cubit and half high' (Exod. 25:10) [i.e., nine handbreadths—a cubit equals six handbreadths], but whence do we know that the ark cover was a handbreadth [high]?"

Comment Does the contemporary tabernacle, the synagogue, help us bridge this distance of ten handbreaths, as did the ancient Ark?

Yitro: Reader and Interpreter
Stephen E. Cohen, 1999

The public reading from the Torah has long been understood as a re-enactment of the revelation at Sinai. But at Sinai, who was the reader and who was giving the interpretation?

Babylonian Talmud, *B'rachot* 45a   R. Shimon b. Pazi said, "Whence do we learn that the interpreter is not permitted to raise his voice louder than the reader?" From what is said: "Moses spoke and God responded to him in a voice" (Exod. 19:19). What does it mean by "... in a voice"? In the voice of Moses [usually understood to mean "in the same volume as Moses's voice"].

Tosafot   You may ask: How does the verse prove anything about reader and interpreter? If that were the intent of the verse, then God should have spoken first, and then Moses responded . . . and Moses could not raise his voice louder than the Holy One.

Mei HaShiloach   In Tractate *B'rachot* we learn from this verse that the interpreter must not raise his voice louder than the reader. And this is puzzling; see the *Tosafot* and the Rif. And the point here is that in fact, **Moses** uttered the Ten Commandments to Israel. But the ultimate purpose was that the words of Torah be inscribed upon the hearts of the Children of Israel. And this was from God, who inscribed on the heart of each and every person, according to His will. And it was in this respect that God was, as it were, the Interpreter. After the Ten Commandments issued from the mouth of Moses, then the Holy One returned and inscribed them upon their hearts.

Comment   How close is *Mei HaShiloach*'s comment to a liberal understanding of the revelation?

Yitro
Sheldon Marder, 2001

What a relief to be finished with the tale of "two nations obsessed with each other" (as J. P. Fokkelman describes Egypt and Israel in *The Literary Guide to the Bible*, ed. Robert Alter and Frank Kermode,

Belknap Press of Harvard University Press, 1990) and arrive safe and sound at Mount Sinai!

"You shall not steal" (Exod. 20:13).

Iturei Torah relates the following story: Once a precious object disappeared from the home of the Kotzker Rebbe. The whole household thought it had been stolen. When word of this reached the Kotzker, he was outraged ("his heart roared"). "What? Stolen?" said the Rebbe. "Is it not written 'You shall not steal'?" The author of the S'fat Emet (Rabbi Y'hudah Aryeh Loeb Alter) would tell his own story of this event years later: "At that very time," wrote Alter, "I too was in Kotzk. I was a child when I heard these words of the Rebbe. And to this day the commandment 'You shall not steal' stands before my eyes like a wall of fire."

We might read this story in light of the adage that a person is known by three things: *kiso*, *koso*, and *kaaso*, or, his pocket, his hat, and his cup. What do we learn about the Kotzker Rebbe from his anger in this incident? And what are our children learning about us from the things that make us angry? The Rebbe's roaring heart warns us that adults have the power to create "walls of fire" that children will see for the rest of their lives.

Yitro: Moses's *Yeter*!
Kenneth J. Weiss, 2002

"Moses heeded his father-in-law and did just as he had said" (Exod. 18:24).

We meet Moses's father-in-law, Jethro (Yitro) early in *Sh'mot*. In the first chapter of our *parashah*, we learn more about him. Following the people's passage through the *Yam Suf* (Sea of Reeds), after the battle with Amalek, Yitro "brought Moses's sons and wife to him in the wilderness" (Exod. 18:5).

Yitro's indelible impact on Moses came the following day, when he witnessed Moses sitting as judge for the people. Yitro speaks to Moses, "Why do you act alone [as magistrate], while all the people stand about you from morning until evening" (Exod. 18:14)? Yitro listens as Moses responds, he then offers wise counsel, which Moses heeds.

Moses chooses "capable men out of all Israel" to assist him in judging between the people (Exod. 18:25).

One senses that Moses was, generally speaking, not open to advice from others; he did not seek it, he rarely valued it. The exception, Yitro's crystal-clear admonition regarding the then extant judicial "system": "The thing you are doing is not right . . ." (Exod. 18:17). How very much Yitro added, thereby, to Moses's life, how abundantly Yitro enhanced Moses's work. Moses and the people gained significantly, what an advantage it was for Moses to have had Yitro in his life. Therefore, he was known as Yitro—*Yeter Shelo*: for Moses, Jethro was "his abundance," "his gain," "his advantage." Is there not a *Yitro/Yitrai*(?) at the core of your life as there is at the core of mine?*

A name drawn from a person's singular contribution: it's not at all unique in Torah, clear back (at least!) to Avraham.

**M'chilta*, Tractate *Amalek*, chap. 3, contains a discussion of Jethro's seven names, among them *Yetro* and *Yeter*.

Yitro
Kenneth J. Weiss, 2004

Believe Me—I know how life fails; I've watched the human race self-destruct. So, I'm giving you Ten Commandments. They comprise a blueprint: *My* blueprint for the continuation of life. I give them to you directly: no intermediary.

Here's what I need you to know:

Firstly, my credentials: "I am יהוה אלהיך [*Adonai Elohecha*] who delivered you out of Egypt" (Exod. 20:2). I am unique, singular. You may neither replicate Me nor use My name falsely. To enhance both your humanity and our relationship, I'm establishing for you a day—Shabbat—whose dual purpose is sanctity and renewal.

Secondly, a few basic values to root and stabilize you. With these in place, you can (over time, you must!) refine and grow an inclusive, dynamic system of laws. Start with these: you must value others' lives, their relationships, their property. Value truth as well, while separating yourself from falseness.

Thirdly—climactically: the core commandment. You must live by this *mitzvat hamitzvot*. If you turn your back on it, My entire system—Creation itself—fails (again!). How can I possibly transmit to you the singular importance of this mitzvah? By playing to your humanness—may I say your weakness: only *this* mitzvah (of the Ten) offers a reward.

"Honor your father and your mother, that you may long endure on the land that *YHVH*, your God, is giving you" (Exod. 20:12).

(God continues)—Here's My thinking: parents are My generational emissaries. Responsible for the transmission of the tradition, they model the essential values at the core of life. And, as children become parents, there will remain an ever-renewable connection between Me and the dynamic unfolding of humanity.

The fifth commandment is inseparable from believing in Me!

... Want to live? Honor your parents!

Yitro

Kenneth J. Weiss, 2004

At Mount Sinai, God and Moses modeled for us a way to transmit mitzvot and meaning through the ages. First, "*YHVH* came down" (Exod. 19:20) onto Mount Sinai. Then, when God called him to ascend, "Moses went up" (ibid.). **Where they met, God taught and Moses learned.**

God's foundational act on Sinai was to come down and meet with Moses. Imitating *YHVH*, "Moses went down to the people..." (Exod. 19:25). **Where they met, Moses taught and the people learned.**

Moses's example lives in us: we, too, are charged with transmitting what we've learned to those whom we must teach.

Yitro

Alan Cook, 2006

According to *Time* magazine's list of the greatest inventions of 2005, the top innovation of the past year was a dog named Snuppy. Snuppy, an Afghan hound, is the first known cloned dog, the product of many years of South Korean research. Having succeeded in working with the unpredictable canine reproductive cycle, scientists feel that they are one step closer to cloning humans.

Although geneticists assure us that if human cloning is ever attempted, it will be used solely for therapeutic purposes, it is sometimes intriguing to imagine what we would do if the option to clone ourselves existed. After all, there are never enough hours in the day to accomplish all that we need to do. "For the task is too heavy for you; you cannot do it alone" (Exod. 18:18).

Yes, like Moses, we need to learn to delegate. We need to be willing to heed the advice of יתרו (Yitro).

Though our first instinct may be to proclaim, "Here I am, send me!" (Isa. 6:8) when we see a job to be done, the reality is that it takes teamwork to accomplish the big, important tasks in life.

As Moses realized, delegation of responsibility is not an admission of weakness; it is an expression of courage: the willingness to relinquish a bit of control and to embrace the wisdom and experience that others may bring to the table.

Yitro
Amy Scheinerman, 2007

We learn the value of adopting best practices from this *parashah*. Yitro says to Moshe, "What is this thing that you are doing **to the people**? . . . The thing you are doing is not right; you will surely wear yourself out, and these people as well" (Exod. 18:14, 18:17–18). He concludes, "If you do this—**and God so commands you**—you will be able to bear up; and all these people too will go home unwearied" (Exod. 18:23).

Yitro's primary concern is not Moshe's welfare (the needs, desires, and egos of leadership) but rather the needs of the community. The message is clear for both rabbis and synagogue lay leaders.

Yitro inserts a striking phrase: "and God **so commands you**." The simplest reading is problematic, for it suggests that God speaks to Moshe through Yitro. Ibn Ezra offers another reading: "should

God so command you." Rav Kook provides yet another explanation: The Babylonian Talmud, *Shabbat* 10a, relates that two judges working long hours, overcome by exhaustion, are advised by Rabbi Chiya to limit their court time. Chiya says, "It says that Moshe judged the people 'from morning to evening.' Could it be that Moshe sat and judged all day? When did he study Torah? Rather, Torah teaches us that a judge who judges with complete fairness, even for a single hour, is considered to be God's partner in creating the world. For the Torah uses a similar phrase to describe Creation: 'It was evening and morning, one day.'" Connecting leadership with Creation reminds us that even God shared power with the angels and rested, leaving room for others and ensuring renewal.

Yitro

Amy Scheinerman, 2008

The penultimate פסוק (*pasuk*) of יתרו (*Yitro*) concerns the מזבח אבנים (*mizbach avanim* [Exod. 20:22]). The altar is not to be built with גזית (*gazit*, "hewn stones") because wielding metal tools would be like a sword profaning them. Rashi remarks that an implement of violence should not be used to create an altar whose purpose is to forge peace between Israel and her God.

Rashbam, however, interprets hewn stones to mean that stonecutters carve pictures and images into the stones; this is what is forbidden. Ibn Ezra rejects this interpretation by stating somewhat sardonically, "Perhaps [those who raise this objection] can explain to us why the Tabernacle and the Temple—locations of greater holiness than the altar—were decorated with cherubim and other images." Nachmanides points out that the Talmud, *Sotah* 48b, permits the use of the שמיר (*shamir*), the miraculous stone-cutting worm. *P'sikta Rabbati* provides the most fanciful explanation of all: the stones flew into place of their own accord.

Does this apply to Solomon's Temple, as well? *M'chilta* quotes I Kings 6:7 to explain that the stones were cut at the quarry and hauled to הר-הבית (*Har HaBayit*, "the Temple Mount"), thereby emphasizing that the tools were "not heard" in its vicinity. Rambam, who counts this as mitzvah #426, follows *M'chilta* when he says in *Hilchot Beit HaB'chirah* 1:8 that the stones were not cut on the Temple Mount. (Hence, the שמיר [*shamir*] was not needed for this task and was reserved for cutting the stones of the breastplate.)

What is at stake in each interpretation? How do the commentators balance the desire of Torah to separate the מזבח (*mizbach*, "altar") from tools with the potential for violence, with the need to provide an explanation not only for the past, but for the future?

Yitro
Joshua Minkin, 2009

"Excuse me, Rabbi, I think things would go better around here if…"

How many times have we heard these words? How often do we hear them as a thinly veiled challenge to rabbinic authority, a response to a perceived slight, or an attempt by the speaker to elevate him/herself at the rabbi's expense? How often do we truly listen to what follows next? Despite the motivation behind the comment, can we absorb its content and focus on the suggestion being offered?

Certainly, it is easier when the person making the suggestion offers it privately, as does Jethro in this *parashah*. Furthermore, Jethro first asks why Moses operates as he does. Perhaps this is a special case; maybe there is a purpose not immediately evident. Only then does Jethro explain the problem with the situation he sees and how both the nation and Moses himself are adversely impacted, before proposing an alternative.

Moses is able to accept Jethro's sage advice without feeling his authority is being challenged or compromised. He could have thought: I am the one to whom God spoke; where does my father-in-law get off telling me how to run things? Where was he when the waters needed to be parted? Moses is able to set aside his ego and consider Jethro's idea on its merits. Recognizing its inherent wisdom and practicality, he implements it.

Are we able to do the same, and can we communicate openness to the people we serve? There are Jethros in every congregation and organization: people with business knowledge, fund-raising expertise, and interpersonal skills. We can view them as a threat or welcome their participation, approach them with suspicion and fear, or recognize the wisdom and blessing of their suggestion. Some suggestions are valuable, even in the most intensely politicized congregations, and even if introduced by, "Rabbi, I think things would go better around here if . . ."

משפטים *Mishpatim*

(Exodus 21:1–24:18)

For additional commentary on *Mishpatim*, see "Chol HaMo-eid Sukkot" and "Shavuot."

Mishpatim
Stephen M. Wylen, 1996

"The night burglar may be killed if caught in the act, but the housebreaker by day may not be killed, and if he is killed, the homeowner is guilty of murder" (Exod. 22:1–2).

Some sages say the night burglar is more dangerous because he has no fear of human beings. He breaks in, knowing that the homeowner is at home. The day burglar presumes that the house is empty. Other sages say the night burglar is worse because he has no fear of God. He thinks that because it is dark he is unseen, forgetting that God sees all. Which is the greater guarantor of lawfulness: for people to fear God, or for people to fear the judgment of women and men?

Mishpatim
Lawrence S. Kushner, 1997

Critical theory interprets these laws as deriving from actual precedents in which *shof'tim* made decisions based on the cases their litigants brought before them. But the traditional view holds that God gave these laws to Moses on Sinai along with all the others. Did God know in advance that cases like these would come before judges in the future? Did God choose this "casuistic" language ("if . . . then") rather than the apodictic tone of the Decalogue ("You shall . . .") to show judges how to adjust the apodictic laws to specific cases? Some people argue that to mention the actions described in the "if" clauses gives people the idea to do them—why might God have wanted to give Israelites the idea of acting according to some of the cases mentioned here (servants, burglars, fighters, etc.)? Might all these examples serve as tests of our self-restraint?

Chasidic interpretations of Torah urge us to internalize the details—as though the *eved ivri* ("Hebrew slave" [Exod. 21:2]) referred to us or our souls. What do we learn about our inner life with God if we see the laws here as describing spiritual struggles rather than interpersonal ones? And why do the servant passages lead all the rest?

This year *Parashat Mishpatim* falls on Rosh Chodesh Adar I. While Purim falls only in Adar II, the notion that *Nichnas Adar, nichnas simchah* ("when Adar enters, joy enters") may also apply to Adar I. How does this *parashah* increase our joy? (Is there a relation between lawfulness, the security of knowing what the law and the consequences for breaking it are, that increases our joy? To us they sometimes seem opposed to each other!)

Mishpatim: Choosing Slavery
Stephen E. Cohen, 1998

K'li Yakar, with most of the rabbis, harshly criticizes the Hebrew slave who chooses not to go free in the seventh year. He reads the ear-piercing ritual as an acting out, in the physical world, of an inner psychological drama.

K'li Yakar The reason for piercing him specifically at the door and the doorpost: Because after six years, the Torah opens a door for him, to go out from slavery to freedom. The door is swinging on its hinges, but this indolent one has no desire to go out. He is like one who sits in prison, and they open the door for him, saying, "Go, flee for your life!" But he chooses the superficially good things that he has, as the text says, "For it is good for him . . ." (Deut. 15:16) with regard to food and drink; thus he leaves the door open and does not want to go out. It is right that he be pierced at the door.

Comment How close do you imagine K'li Yakar's interpretation is to the original symbolic meaning of the ear-piercing ritual?

Mishpatim: Ripples in a Pond
Melanie Aron, 1999

Are we responsible for the unforeseen consequences of our actions?

"When a fire is started and spreads to thorns so that stacked, standing, or growing grain [i.e., a field] is consumed, he who started the fire must make resitution" (Exod. 22:5).

Rashi Although he lit the fire on his own soil and it extended by itself through the thorns that it came across, he has to make restitution because he did not guard his fire (burning coals) that it should not extend and cause damage.

Sh'mirat HaLashon If you unnecessarily told Reuven that Shimon spoke against him or wronged him and Reuven grew angry to the extent that Shimon's life is in danger, you have an even greater obligation than usual to remove the danger. If you are unable to do so yourself, you must ask others to help you.

Comment What fires might we have ignited in the hearts of other? How might we make restitution?

Mishpatim: They Saw God
Stephen E. Cohen, 2000

What are we to make of the vision of God glimpsed by the Israelite leadership in Exodus 24? The voice of the text seems strangely subdued, as though itself unsure what to think, and the episode is tucked away at the end of the portion, separated far off from the main body of the revelation narrative. The text's clearest expression of ambivalence is a negative statement "unto [or against] the nobles of the Children of Israel He did not stretch forth His hand"

(Exod. 24:11). Here are three widely differing understandings of this verse.

Rashi They looked and they stared and thereby incurred the death penalty. However, because the Holy One did not want to spoil the rejoicing of the Torah, He waited to execute Nadav and Avihu until the dedication of the Tabernacle. And the elders He waited to execute until "the people were complaining." "He did not stretch forth His hand . . ." indicating that they **deserved** to have the hand sent forth against them.

Sforno "He did not stretch forth His hand": To bring them out of their senses, so that they might prophesy, as was the case with the other prophets, of whom it says "the hand of *YHWH* was upon me."

Daat Z'keinim MiBaalei HaTosafot He did not stretch forth His hand to cover His face, preventing them from seeing Him as He did with Moses in the cleft in the rock: "I shall cover with my hand" (Exod. 33:22).

Comment Which of these three interpretations seems to be closest to the *p'shat* of the text?

Mishpatim
Sheldon Marder, 2001

"The choice first fruits of your soil you shall bring to the house of *Adonai* your God. You shall not boil a kid in its mother's milk" (Exod. 23:19).

"You shall not boil a kid" occurs three times in the Torah: Exod. 23:19, Exod. 34:26, and Deut. 14:21. Why in the two Exodus verses is "You shall not boil a kid" attached to the commandment to bring "choice first fruits" to the Temple? Ibn Ezra suggests that *g'di* shares a common root with the word *meged*, which means "delicacies"—especially fine fruit (as in Babylonian Talmud, *Shabbat* 127b). In "Writing a Commentary on the Torah" (1990) Nahum Sarna recalls that exegete Menachem ben Saruq (910–970) took *g'di* to mean "berries" and that the twelfth-century lexicographer Menachem ben Solomon similarly argued that "mother's milk" is the juice of the bud that contains the berry. Such an interpretation, according to Sarna, boils down to this: don't bring first fruits to the priest before they are ripe. But why rescue these little-known commentaries from their obscurity? To dramatize one important point: at one time in Jewish history there existed an exegetical open-mindedness and creativity that virtually disappeared after the Middle Ages—an open-mindedness that allowed commentators to reinterpret and, in effect, challenge a verse that is the cornerstone of kashrut.

In what areas of Jewish or institutional thinking has our creativity diminished? Has open-mindedness succumbed to the fear of challenging fundamental assumptions? Is it possible for a religious tradition to be "boiled in its mother's milk," as it were? To be so in thrall to its past that all the life—all the vital juices—have been cooked out of it?

Mishpatim: Wholly Holy!
Kenneth J. Weiss, 2002

"You shall be holy people to Me" (Exod. 22:30).

First, the profound, singular, life-turning experience at Mount Sinai (the transmission of the Ten Utterances), then God's command that an altar be built on which to sacrifice burnt offerings—elevating, godly, holy events, these.

But see what follows. We run headlong into a series of civil laws dealing with slaves, assault, injury, an ox that gores, falling into a pit, breaking and entering, money lending, blasphemy—an exhaustive (exhausting?) array of (call them what they are) mundane rulings: *mishpatim* that seem not to rise to the level of what immediately precedes them. If so, then, as Rashi asks, "why is this section dealing with civil law placed immediately after that commanding the arrangements for the altar? To tell you that you should seat the Sanhedrin near the Temple."

That's it, then! The *mishpatim* are linked to that which precedes them. You are in receipt of the profound, overarching mitzvot, hereafter popularized as the Ten Commandments; you will build an altar and offer sacrifices thereon. Now come civil laws, which—if you live by them—will sanctify your every act.

Yes, even civil ordinances are regarded as divine commandments. That must be Rashi's point: let the Sanhedrin remember its godly mandate. Is that also why Israel's Knesset members are seated in the shape of a menorah? Yes to symbolize that everyday *mishpatim*—the most secular of civil edicts—must, in Jewish life, be imbued with sanctity.

To be wholly Jewish is to be wholly holy in our everyday life, our language, our business, with our families, our friends, our competitors, too. "You shall be holy people. . . ." This precursor to the Holiness Code sums it up: be wholly holy.

Mishpatim
Kenneth J. Weiss, 2003

Here, Torah says, "You shall not wrong a stranger or oppress him. . . . You shall not ill-treat any widow or orphan" (Exod. 22:20–21).

There, Torah admonishes, "You shall not favor a weak person in his dispute. . . . You shall take no bribe" (Exod. 23:3, 23:8—R. E. Friedman).

So—is Torah instructing us to be compassionate or dispassionate, empathic or impartial? Don't we increase the chance of wronging society's weakest members if we don't tilt toward them in their disputes? Doesn't Judaism, on its face, urge us toward *rachmanut* (compassion) in their case?

Maimonides says: Yes! Be cognizant—particularly when interacting with widows and orphans—of "their souls [which] are exceedingly depressed. . . ." Speak "tenderly" with them; show them "unvarying courtesy." Speak sensitively to them; protect their property; try not to provoke or pain them; don't hit or (even) curse them. In sum, deal compassionately with those whose lives are especially difficult.

But—when such people come before the bar of justice (*din*), another set of values supercedes. Here, partiality has no place. We are told that a widow once approached Rabbi Y'hoshua of Kutno, tearfully complaining to him that a townsman had wronged her. She asked the rabbi to judge between them. Should the rabbi—weighing these countervailing verses from *Parashat Mishpatim*—lean toward the poor widow or seek to render impartial justice?

Rabbi Y'hoshua, we learn, recused himself from her case, noting that when Torah teaches, "You shall take no bribe," this includes not only money but also (especially?) tears. Tears—particularly those of a widow—could serve to unduly influence a judge, making a fair and appropriate judgment so much more difficult to reach. *Rachmanut*: yes. *Din*: also yes.

Mishpatim
Kenneth J. Weiss, 2004

How many mitzvot can fit on the head of a pin? This *sidrah* seems to attempt an answer to that conundrum. The laws that flow out of *Parashat Mishpatim* deal with life's daily concerns: respect for others, property rights, thievery, quarrels, personal injury, orphans' and widows' rights, blasphemy, false testimony, bribery.

Camouflaged herein is a clear, timeless message—simple yet elegant. It reaches to Judaism's moral core. In three sentences, we are commanded to be true to (and live by) a lesson forged in Egyptian slavery, renewed and reaffirmed at the seder table each and every springtime.

Precisely eighteen verses (!) separate the statement of this keystone directive and its reemphasis. Exodus 22:20 reads, "You shall not wrong a stranger or oppress him, for you were strangers in the land of Egypt." Exodus 23:9 restates, even deepens, "You shall not oppress a stranger, for you know the נפש [*nefesh,* "soul"] of the stranger, having yourselves been strangers in the land of Egypt."

Note now the pivotal demi-verse (Exod. 22:30a) found centered between these admonitions: "You shall be holy people to Me." God admonishes: You want Me to receive you as אנשי קדש (*anshei kodesh*, "holy people")? Then you must draw from your history—your centuries of persecution—the unshakable belief that even strangers are human beings, entitled to dignified treatment. S. R. Hirsch expresses it perfectly: "Show that you are a Jew—hold the stranger sacred."

In sum: You shall be holy. How? Start (and finish!) by affirming the holiness even of the stranger.

Mishpatim
Kenneth J. Weiss, 2005

"The people [could not] come up to Mount Sinai" (Exod. 19:23). "[There was] thunder and lightning, the blare of the horn and the mountain smoking, [such that] when the people saw [all this] they fell back" (Exod. 20:15). God, we are taught, transmitted the Ten Commandments as the people stood "at a distance" (Exod. 20:15, 20:18).

Soon thereafter, God seems to have tired of special effects. God's message: Let's talk *tachlis*. Here are the משפטים (*mishpatim*): My rules for everyday life. Moses: "you shall set these rules before them [לפניהם, *lifneihem*]" (Exod. 21:1). Straight talk here. No distancing. But, to whom or what does לפניהם (*lifneihem*) refer? Two possibilities:

- Perhaps, as Rashi suggests, God (through Moses) presented these rules "before them [= the Israelites]" and no other people. That is, though the Ten Commandments were created for everyone, these ordinances—targeted only to Israel—spell out, in practical terms, how God expects the people of Israel to live.
- Perhaps God's message is: if you have to make a choice, position the משפטים (*mishpatim*) "before them [i.e., the Ten Commandments"! God wants Israel to know that these ordinances have priority; they are immediate and practical, indispensable rules and standards by which the Israelites must live every single day.

Judaism is founded on universal values as symbolized by the Ten Commandments. But we Jews have always emphasized this life, the everyday world we know. Thus, our משפטים (*mishpatim*) are about caring for one another, dealing kindly with one another, doing *tikkun olam*—one deed and one person at a time.

Yes—cleave to the Ten Commandments, but live these משפטים (*mishpatim*); they inform, indeed shape, your (day-to-day) life . . .

Mishpatim
Alan Cook, 2006

In the 1979 film *Being There*, Peter Sellers portrays Chance the gardener, a simple man who is thrust into an alternate life when he is mistakenly believed to be Chauncey Gardner, a brilliant man of the world. Chance's oft-repeated refrain throughout the film is "I like to watch"; although this is misinterpreted by many to indicate a predilection for voyeurism, he is merely stating that his favorite pastime, besides gardening, is television viewing.

Chance rises to some prominence simply by "being there," but that is not enough for us.

At the conclusion of פרשת משפטים (*Parashat Mishpatim*), Moses is commanded to ascend the mountain, והיה שם (*vehyeih sham*, "and be there" [Exod. 24:12]). For Moses, "being there" is not a passive activity. He may not just stand on the sidelines and watch. The goal is not merely for him to arrive at a particular location, but to be acutely aware of what is going on once he arrives.

A covenant is being forged between God and the Jewish people, and it is a two-way street. The people (and Moses, their representative) must agree to carry out their end of the bargain. By attesting נעשה ונשמע (*naaseh v'nishma*, "we will do and obey" [Exod. 24:7]), they are declaring their intention to be active participants in a covenant with God, rather than simply "being there."

In order to truly be "doers" and "obeyers," we, like our Israelite ancestors, must always "be there" when called. We must be ready and willing to accept the challenges placed before us.

Mishpatim
Amy Scheinerman, 2007

Much of *Mishpatim* is a treasure trove of social laws gratifying modern sensibilities. Yet the *parashah* opens with laws of slavery that make us wince with embarrassment. Perhaps Torah begins here because our ancestors, newly released from bondage, are expected, in their approach to one another, to institute God's mitzvot with empathy.

So, too, are we to be open and empathetic in our interpretation of tradition.

Perhaps Torah begins here to remind us that even when the formal institutions of slavery are dismantled, the experience and reality of slavery remain, taking on new forms in human existence: working under abysmal conditions, entrapment in dangerous marriages, living in deadly political situations, suffering from debilitating mental anguish. Perhaps Torah wants us to understand that a broad array of human experiences can be understood as *avdut* (confinement in a *mitzrayim*, a narrow place) requiring *g'ulah* (redemption). Perhaps Torah begins with slavery to emphasize freedom and redemption as goals and guideposts for justice.

Perhaps *Mishpatim* begins with the laws of slavery because throughout our lives we struggle to move from *avdut* to *avodah*, from entrapment to freely given service to God. Although slavery was a recognized, legal institution in the ancient world, Torah seeks to mitigate it, limit it, dissolve it. If the owner merely knocks out a slave's tooth, he goes free. If the slave chooses to remain a slave, he is physically punished for that choice. Perhaps Torah wants us to ask in what ways we are enslaved while thinking ourselves free, and how we can redeem ourselves to better serve God.

Mishpatim
Amy Scheinerman, 2008

Nachmanides suggests that the laws in the beginning of משפטים (*Mishpatim*) are recorded in order of importance: murder, the most serious, followed by honoring parents, then the prohibition of theft. Yet all are preceded by the laws concerning slavery. Nachmanides suggests this is the case because the laws concerning slavery are connected with the structure of the cosmos itself through the number seven. The slave is freed in the seventh year, mirroring the seventh day of rest. Similarly, the Jubilee year comes after seven squared years. The secret behind them all, Nachmanides tells us, is found in his commentary on Genesis 1 (where he explained that each day of Creation corresponds to a millennium in the history of the world;

hence the Messiah would come after six thousand years of human history).

Nachmanides seems to be telling us that the laws concerning slavery take precedence because they allude to cosmogony that in turn reveals the date the Messiah will arrive.

This raises the issue of how we might set the priority of laws. Yet Rabbi Y'hudah HaNasi taught, "Be as attentive to a minor mitzvah as to a major one, for you do not know the reward for each of the mitzvot" (*Pirkei Avot* 2:1), and Ben Azzai taught, "Pursue even a minor mitzvah and flee from an *aveirah* "sin"; for one mitzvah generates another, and an *aveirah* generates another. Thus the reward for a mitzvah is another mitzvah, and the penalty for an *aveirah* is another *aveirah*" (*Pirkei Avot* 4:2).

In reality, we order the mitzvot. On what basis?

Mishpatim
Jeffrey Ballon and Amy Scheinerman, 2009

Sh'mot Rabbah 51:8 tells us: "As soon as Israel accepted the Torah, the Holy One invested them with some of the splendor of God's own majesty. With what precisely did God invest them? Crowns, according to R. Yochanan. Weapons, according to R. Shimon ben Yochai, upon which God's Holy Name was engraved. As long as this sword was in their hands, the angel of death had no power over them."

Parashat Mishpatim contains majestic crowns and the protective sword. There is majesty in entering into a covenant with the Holy One; Israel becomes the unique vessel for the gift of the crown of Torah to the world. In addition to the crowns, God supplies the sword of the warrior archetype so Israel can civilize and preserve its society through mitzvot inculcating justice and mercy and subduing human grandiosity.

The restrictions and requirements of the laws in *Parashat Mishpatim* control and contain human grandiosity that can, if uncontrolled, threaten everyone. The mitzvot redirect our energies toward constructive growth of the individual psyche as well as society. The sword engraved with God's Holy Name ensures it will be used redemptively, not violently. This suggests that there are occasions when it is in the community's best interest for a rabbi to act the part of the sword by saying no: to business conducted in the synagogue on Shabbat (however worthy the cause), "*Havdalah* b'nei mitzvah" that treat *Minchah* as a mere appetizer before the evening gala, or other attempts to degrade the quality of sacred time.

תרומה *T'rumah*

(Exodus 25:1–27:19)

T'rumah
Richard N. Levy, 1996

The menorah, with its branches and flowers, is clearly symbolic of a tree (the Tree of Life—hence, Torah?). The *k'ruvim* (cherubim [Exod. 25:18]) are also clearly symbolic, though in the Written Torah, the referends are less clear. How about the Ark? Is it symbolic (why the gold and the crown?) or purely utilitarian? Are the ten curtains symbolic? How about the other objects? And the recurring colors? In Exodus 31, the repetition of *m'lachah* (work) in the Shabbat and *Mishkan* (Tabernacle) paragraphs creates the Talmudic definition of prohibited Shabbat work and perhaps suggests that the *Mishkan* is a model of Creation. If so, how do the various parts of the *Mishkan* help us to relate to God's Creation?

T'rumah
Lawrence S. Kushner, 1997

The initial verse of the *parashah* is paradoxical: "Tell the Israelites to bring an offering to me; from every person whose heart is willing, take the offering" (Exod. 25:2). Is this a command or is it a free-will offering? How are command and free will, command and desire, related?

Exodus 25:22 ("There I will meet and speak with you") raises a question that the midrashic Moses and the biblical Solomon also ask: why would the God who fills all space want a particular place to meet with the Israelites, suggesting to them that God dwells only in that space? Why did God choose the specific place before the *aron* (Ark)? How can a particular space help us deal with an infinite God?

T'rumah: God's Chamber
Stephen E. Cohen, 1998

Sh'mot Rabbah (33:1)   A parable of a king who had an only daughter: One of the kings came and married her, then sought to return to his own land with his wife. The father replied: "I have given you my only daughter. I cannot part from her, nor can I tell you not to take her, for she is your wife. Grant me this favor wherever you go, make a small room for me, that I may live with you, for I cannot bear to leave my daughter. Thus did the Holy One say to Israel: "I have given you the Torah, but I cannot bear to part from her. Everywhere you go, 'Make for Me a Sanctuary' [Exod. 25:8]."

Comment   The emotional appeal of the fairy tale contained here is clear; any parent can appreciate the father's ambivalence about his daughter's marriage. But what is the theological content of this midrash? Does God struggle with an inability to separate from the Torah? Does this interfere with the Israel-Torah marriage?

T'rumah: Integrity and Wholeness
Melanie Aron, 1999

All the instructions in this *parashah* are given in the second person except that concerning the Ark, where we read, "They shall make an Ark of acacia wood" (Exod. 25:10).

The JPS Torah Commentary: Exodus by Nahum M. Sarna (Jewish Publication Society, 1991, p. 159) sees the uniqueness of this verse expressing the centrality of the Ark to the entire construction project.

The Ark, and not the animal sacrifices, is the true focus of the Tabernacle. Some commentators believe that the Israelites would have more difficulty understanding the role of the Ark than that of the altar or the laver. These were being used in pagan worship at that time as well. However, there is archeological evidence that it was a custom of the time to place important documents, treaties, etc., in beautifully made receptacles.

Babylonian Talmud, *Yoma* **72b**   "Within and without shalt thou overlay it" (Exod. 25:11). Rabbah said: Any scholar whose inside is not like his outside is not a scholar. Abayei, or as some say, Rabbah b. Ula said: He is called abominable. (Job 15:6 is read as concerning one who drinks the water of Torah and yet has iniquity in him.)

R. Yannai proclaimed: Woe unto him who has no court, but makes a gateway for his court. (The fear of the LORD is the court; learning should lead to it. Learning without reverence, the "gateway without the court," is sinful.)

Rabbah said to the Sages: I beseech you, do not inherit a double *Geihinom*. (One who engages in Torah study without possessing fear of heaven suffers in this world, wherein he denies himself pleasure for the sake of his study, as well as in the other world.)

Comment   When does our *yirah* (fear) lag behind our study? How is authenticity related to integrity and wholeness?

T'rumah: Family Heirlooms
Stephen E. Cohen, 2000

This midrash examines the passive form of the idiom "Every person with whom are to be found. . . ." According to the midrash, this phrase refers specifically to individuals who had received their contribution to the *Mishkan* (Tabernacle) as an inheritance from their ancestors.

***Sh'mot Rabbah* 33:10**   Rabbi Tavyomi said: When our father Jacob's time came to depart from the world, he called to his sons and said to them, "Be aware that the Holy One will one day tell your children to make a Tabernacle. Have all the materials already prepared." Some of them prepared themselves, and some of them forgot about it.

And when Moses came and said to their descendents that they should make a Tabernacle, some of them brought something of their own, and others brought something that had been passed down into their hands, as it is written: "Every person with whom are to be found blue thread and purple thread...." And also "Every one with whom acacia wood is to be found...."

Comment Which group are we and our congregants more like: those who brought a contribution to the *Mishkan* that had been faithfully passed down to them, or those who were forced to find or create a new contribution? Does the midrash consider one type of contribution preferable to the other?

T'rumah
Sheldon Marder, 2001

For a sermon in support of Jewish education, or to celebrate HUC-JIR's 125th anniversary:

"The poles shall remain in the rings of the Ark: they shall not be removed from it" (Exod. 25:15). Grounding his interpretation in the Rabbinic idea that the Ark is "the crown of the Torah," Alshech reads the verse metaphorically: "As the Ark required poles for transporting it from one place to another, so the students of Torah require supporters to provide them with sustenance. Thus the Torah states that the Ark's poles must remain in the rings at all times to teach, symbolically, that those who provide sustenance for students of Torah must never withdraw their support—not even for a moment, for, without their help, the studies could not go on."

T'rumah: God's Seamless Presence
Kenneth J. Weiss, 2002

At Mount Sinai, represented by the desert Sanctuary, the Temple, the synagogue, the Jewish home, God was and is ever-present. Thanks to Torah, we overhear *YHVH* speaking to Moses to accept *t'rumot* (gifts) "from every person whose heart so moves him.... And let them make Me a *Mikdash* [Sanctuary] that I may dwell among them" (Exod. 25:2, 25:8).

It seems as though God is telling Moses: This mountain is holy; it will always symbolize our encounter. When you leave here, draw from its holiness. Replicate it in the holy place (the *Mikdash*) you and they will build for Me, so that, as I sit with you now, I will dwell (*v'shachanti z'man atid!*) among them always.

Cassuto teaches that as the people left Mount Sinai after the life-turning events that occurred there, "it seemed to them as though the link had been broken. . . ." Thus, they needed a visible token, a reassurance that the bond they'd forged would not—could not—break. Thus, the *Mikdash*—so God could dwell among them. The spirit of Sinai, renewed in the *Mikdash*, was transferred to the Temple (*Beit HaMikdash*) and—over time and historical flow—to the synagogue. Each successive institution had the same underlying purpose: *v'shachanti b'tocham*, "that I may dwell among them" (Exod. 25:8). Indeed, the Jewish home (*mikdash m'at*) also carries forward—more personally—the message of God's presence.

V'shachanti b'tocham: these words were—and remain—reassurance to every generation of our people that God will ever dwell among us, be accessible to us, be present for us. For a people as numerous as the stars in the sky, scattered to the west, east, north, and south, God's seamless presence is vouchsafed by Torah in ageless words: *v'shachanti b'tocham*.

T'rumah
Kenneth J. Weiss, 2003

"Pure gold . . . inside and out" (Exod. 25:11).

As *Parashat T'rumah* opens, a single, consistent message emerges. In ingenious—nay, inspired—ways, that message is rendered clear, uncompromising. Stripped of nuance, the message is: God values **only** that which is given in the right spirit.

This point is driven home no less than three times in the first eleven verses of Exodus 25.

1. In commenting on Exod. 25:2, "accept gifts for Me from every person whose heart so moves him," *Torat Moshe* teaches that gold (as well as other precious substances) belongs to God in the first place. So, when a person gives these, "the gift . . . is not [in] the [material] wealth . . . but [in] the willingness of [the] heart"—the golden motivation. Indeed, *Torat Moshe* concludes, you should "not [even accept] anything from one whose heart does **not** make him [her] willing."
2. The Ark is to be overlaid with "pure gold." The purity—one might surmise—is at least as much a function of the giver's motivation as it is a description of the metal itself.
3. The *zahav tahor* (pure gold) is intended to overlay the Ark "inside and out." The gold covering the unseen surfaces of the Ark—the inner panels—represents the intangible (yet conclusive!) inner motivation of a sincere, "golden-hearted" benefactor.

Like the Holy Ark, may we be characterized by pure gold, both inside and out.

T'rumah
Kenneth J. Weiss, 2004

"You shall accept *t'rumah* [gifts] for Me" (Exod. 25:2).

A Lutheran pastor spoke to me of "snow," which, he suggested, could refer to a single snowflake, no one of which may be significant. But, add it to the millions, the billions of other snowflakes and the result is a beautiful, magical day.

Like "snow," *t'rumah* could refer to a single gift, no one of which is sufficient to create a desert Tabernacle. But, add it to the many gifts of various kinds to be accepted "from every person whose heart so moves him" (Exod. 25:2) and the result is a Sanctuary.

Collective nouns like "snow," like *t'rumah*, are common in our daily parlance. "Jewishness," "democracy," "humor," "marriage"—though singular in form, each of these represent countless verbalizations, deeds, manifestations.

Take "marriage": this word represents a lifetime of little and large deeds, thoughts, words. Marriage is a mutual giving and receiving of love and devotion, of faithful caring in bad times and good. Marriage is commitment: countless acts of giving and sharing life's gifts and challenges—a "pattern unbreakable."

Little snowflakes, small gifts, marriage's lifetime of little and large deeds: "countless" perhaps. But, added together, they each and all count—a lot!

T'rumah
Kenneth J. Weiss, 2005

"God Wants You!" That message links this *sidrah* to the two that precede it. פרשת יתרו (*Parashat Yitro*) presents the Ten Commandments—universal principles that reach to the heart and meaning of life. פרשת משפטים (*Parashat Mishpatim*) imparts rules that delineate an Israelite's relationship to people and property. Here, in פרשת תרומה (*Parashat T'rumah*), God asks for freewill gifts with which to build a Sanctuary—**the** symbol of God's constant presence.

Pinchas Peli teaches us that although "the immediate purpose of (asking people to contribute) was to collect materials for building a sanctuary, [there was also] an educational purpose: to convert the people *from passive participants* in their relationship with (God) . . . to *active partners*" (italics mine).

These three *sidrot* share a cohesive purpose and goal: to teach that God needs *everyone* as active partners. God says, become My partner on *your* terms. Do any combination of these:

- Observe—adhere to—the Ten Commandments: overarching, universal principles.
- Live your life by the משפטים (*mishpatim*): your everyday rules and ordinances.
- Bring Me gifts, give Me time: "Make Me a Sanctuary" (Exod. 25:8).

Thus, I appeal to all of you, each on your own level . . . join Me!

T'rumah
Alan Cook, 2006

Was the משכן (*Mishkan*, "Tabernacle"), which our *parashah* describes in such detail, ever actually built? If so, how were acacia trees, precious metals, fine fabrics, or *tachash* skins found in the midst of the desert?

While one could approach this question solely from the perspective of faith, proclaim, "היפלא מיהיה דבר?" (*hayipaleih mei'adonai davar*, "Is anything too hard for *Adonai*?") and accept that if God wanted such a structure built, God would provide the necessary raw materials, we can also view the blueprint of the משכן (*Mishkan*) as a rhetorical tool. The ultimate goal, perhaps, is not to construct an ornate portable Sanctuary. Rather, we are taught to strive for holiness, to create an environment that is fit for God to dwell within. This need not consist of a physical structure; it may be a space within the individual hearts, minds, and souls of the members of the Israelite community.

The problem with constructing that sort of sacred space is that no one can give us the technical specifications for doing so. The precise dimensions needed will differ for each individual.

Hence the משכן (*Mishkan*). Whether it is ever constructed or not, it gives us a tangible way of dealing with an incredibly intangible concept: the struggle to believe in a Deity who cannot be seen, touched, smelled, heard, or tasted directly.

The film *Field of Dreams* taught us, "If you build it, he will come." We may construct the most elaborate facilities that our endowments and building funds can pay for. But if we fail to build the spiritual sanctuaries within our hearts and souls, and within those of our congregants, God will not come.

I am indebted to John Schwartzberg, congregant at Temple Sinai of Denver, Colorado, for his insights into this *sidrah*.

T'rumah
Amy Scheinerman, 2007

Abarbanel exhorts us not to dismiss this section of Torah, thinking that the laws of the Tabernacle do not apply to those in the Diaspora and the laws of priestly purity are irrelevant in an age when there is no Temple. "The Torah is a tool to prepare the way for us to become 'like God, knowing good' [Gen. 3:5], to keep us alive in every place and at all times."

In this context, we see the תרומה (*t'rumah*, "gifts") of our ancestors as immediately relevant to our lives: they made the Tabernacle and service of God central to their lives, not an extracurricular activity for free time. In the wilderness, the *Mishkan* was geographically central to the nation; in the Diaspora, especially in a secular society, we must go out of our way to keep God central to our lives.

Professor Yeshayahu Leibowitz noted that, save one, the utensils of the Temple service were to be rooted in a particular place, "the place that the Lord your God will choose." Only the *aron* (Ark) containing the Torah had poles permanently fixed to it, precisely because it was not to be fixed to one place. Torah, by its nature, is transportable through time and space.

Promoting the notion that Torah is an ancient collection of myths, legends, and archaic institutions removes the poles and fixes Torah to one time and place. Teaching Torah as sacred text that speaks to each generation and every situation retains the poles and allows us to invite God's holiness into our midst.

T'rumah
Amy Scheinerman, 2008

In פרשת ויצא (*Parashat Vayeitzei*), Yaakov discovers God where he dreams of the סלם (*sulam*, "ladder"). He names the place בית-אל (Beit El). At Mount Sinai, Israel receives God's Torah with the instructions to build in the wilderness a בית-אל (*Beit El*, "House of God") that would travel with them from place to place. פרשת תרומה (*Parashat T'rumah*) opens the last third of שמות (*Sh'mot*), which concerns itself almost exclusively with the details of the Tabernacle. We have come from Yaakov's limited comprehension of God's domain to the Israelites' understanding of God's universality; from one spot called בית-אל (Beit El) to a בית-אל (*Beit El*) that goes everywhere with Israel because God is everywhere.

Have we assimilated that revelation in our lives? Do we seek and find God wherever we go: in the bedroom, boardroom, family room, and classroom? Do our priorities and behavior reflect the best Jewish values wherever we find ourselves?

Abravanel explains that the Tabernacle was built to contradict the ancient notion that gods lived exclusively in heaven, far from humanity. The Tabernacle draws God down to earth and invites God into the affairs of human lives. God lives in our midst when we live in God's presence.

Perhaps this is why the last third of Exodus—which deals almost exclusively with the משכן (*Mishkan*)—begins with an account of the gifts the Israelites bring to build the Tabernacle, rather than a description of its design and layout or the rites to be performed there. We feel God's presence most strongly when we behave in accordance with the values of Torah. If the actual physical משכן (*Mishkan*) cannot stand close by, our actions create a spiritual משכן (*Mishkan*) in which we feel God's presence.

T'rumah
Jeffrey Ballon and Amy Scheinerman, 2009

T'rumah provides a blueprint for creating sacred space. Having a sacred space—such as the Tabernacle, synagogue, or God's earth beneath the *rakiyah* (firmament)—permits us to create sacred time.

Regrettably, our postindustrial society promotes homogeneous time: a 24/7 news cycle, nonstop sports broadcasting, and round-the-clock Internet shopping permit no distinction between the holy and the mundane. Creating heterogeneity in space and time—which includes both the mundane *and* the sacred—is a challenge to us as rabbis. We see the contrast between sacred and mundane most starkly in

Havdalah, but where else do we find a clear boundary that permits us to enter sacred time and space?

T'rumah does not deal in generalities. It describes a myriad of details that convey in their specificity the sacred. This is how we might approach both time and space. It is with specificity and attention to detail that we can create sacred space and holy time.

Blessing the children at a Shabbat table set with a white cloth, special dishes, and gleaming candles creates holy time and sacred space, the heterogeneity we seek. There is a world of difference between a chuppah set before the *aron kodesh* (holy ark) and a chuppah erected under a chandelier in a catering hall. Is a young person's first *aliyah* part of a cumbersome ceremony necessary to earn him or her the "main event," an elaborate reception, or is the experience of becoming bar/bat mitzvah a genuine initiation into the sacred community of Israel that elevates the young person to full participant in creating sacred space and holy time? The answer is in the details.

תְּצַוֶּה *T'tzaveh*

(Exodus 27:20–30:10)

For additional commentary on T'tzaveh, see "Purim."

T'tzaveh
Steven Kushner, 1996

Why, after God had made it so clear that the *Mishkan* (Tabernacle) was to be constructed from gifts of the heart, does *Parashat T'zaveh* commence with the language of mitzvah? How is it that the oil for the lamps is *not* optional but obligatory? Is a distinction being made between ritual/worship (the offering of oil) and the place in which it is done? Might we make a similar distinction when it comes to our houses of worship and the mitzvot we perform in them?

Then, following the instructions for the building of the *Mishkan*, Torah turns to the design of the priestly garb. Specifically, the *choshen* (breastpiece) is to be held in place by a *p'til t'cheilet* (cord of blue [Exod. 28:28]). This cord of blue appears in only two other places: in Exod. 39:31, where it is to hang from the shining thing (צִיץ [*tzitz*, "frontlet"], upon which the name of God is inscribed) of the *neizer hakodesh* (holy diadem); and then in Numbers 15:38, with regard to the צִיצִת (*tzitzit*, "fringes"). Is there a connection between the צִיץ (*tzitz*) and the צִיצִת (*tzitzit*)? What might they share in common with the *choshen* that they all merit this unique blue string?

T'tzaveh
Lawrence S. Kushner, 1997

The descriptions of the *bigdei kodesh* (priestly vestments) sound very much like the descriptions of the furniture that clothe the *Mishkan* itself. Is the person of the *kohein* (priest) being compared to the Tabernacle? Is the *kohein* a *mikdash m'at*? And if we are all to be a *mamlechet kohanim* (kingdom of priests [Exod. 19:6]), is each of us a tabernacle as well? If so, do we need *bigdei kodesh*? Do suits or dresses or jeans have the potential to be *bigdei kodesh*?

In Exod. 28:32 a strange Hebrew expression is used for the hole in the ephod through which the *Kohein Gadol* (High Priest) shall put his head: *v'hayah pi rosho b'tocho*. It then says, *safah yihyeh l' fiv saviv*. Taken literally, it means that the *Kohein Gadol* is to put his head through the mouth of the ephod, with lips all around. We are used to thinking of prophets having God's word put into their mouths; here the suggestion is that the *Kohein* is in the mouth (of God?), and that he is surrounded by lips. Does this imply that the *Kohein* **is** the word of God—that the offerings as arranged by the *Kohein* (or in future times by the *Bat Kohein* as well) are the actualization of the word of God?

T'tzaveh: Vestments and Atonement
Stephen E. Cohen, 1998

Citing an old tradition regarding the atoning function of the priestly vestments, K'li Yakar offers a reassessment of the third of Hillel's famous proselytes in Tractate *Shabbat*.

K'li Yakar on Exodus 28: 39 The eight vestments atoned for eight sins: four of them for the most serious sins (idolatry, incest, murder, and gossip) and four for general categories that contain all other sins (perversion of justice, presumptuousness, sinful fantasies, and insolence). This may explain the story of the proselyte who thought, "I shall convert so that I may become High Priest and wear these vestments" (Babylonian Talmud, *Shabbat* 31a). Was he really such a fool that he desired to convert merely to wear these clothes? Rather, after hearing the voice of the scribe reading aloud, "These are the vestments that they shall make," he must have heard also their symbolic meanings, the sins for which the vestments atone. And the proselyte was aware that he had sinned all these sins and that he needed these atonements.

Comment The visceral response of many Jews in our own time to the clothing of the rabbi on the bimah suggests a priestly aspect of the contemporary rabbinate. Do the priest/rabbi's vestments effect atonement primarily for him/herself or for the members of the community?

T'tzaveh: To Everything There Is a Time
Melanie Aron, 1999

The Rabbis note a lack of proper sequence in the building of the Tabernacle while the Israelites are still in the desert. Doesn't a king first conquer his territory and then build his palace? Similarly, a groom first studies, then marries.

Babylonian Talmud, *K'tubot* **62b** Later, he [Rabbi] was engaged in preparation for the marriage of his son into the family of R. Yosei b. Zimra. It was agreed that he [the son] should spend twelve years at the academy [before the marriage]. When the girl was led before him, he said to them, "Let it be six years." When they made her pass before him a second time, he said, "I would rather marry [her first] and then proceed [to the academy]." He felt abashed before his father, but the latter said to him, "My son, you have the mind of your Creator," for in Scripture it is written first, "Thou bringest them in and plantest them" [Exod. 15:17—understood as only after the settlement in the Promised Land was the Sanctuary, symbol of the union between God and Israel, to be built], and later it is written, "And let them make Me a Sanctuary that I may dwell among them" [Exod. 25:8].

I believe that a clue to God's change of heart can be found in the culminating passage of this portion (Exod. 29:42–46): "For there I will meet with you, and there I will speak with you, and there I will meet the Israelites, and it shall be sanctified by My Presence. I will sanctify the Tent of Meeting and the altar, and I will consecrate Aaron and his sons to serve Me as priests. I will abide among the Israelites and I will be their God. And they shall know that I, the Lord, am their God who brought them out from the land of Egypt that I might abide among them, I the LORD am their God."

Comment Which of our goals require putting the cart before the horse?

T'tzaveh: Bells and Pomegranates
Stephen E. Cohen, 2000

Many Rabbinic commentators have linked the "voice" of the bells on the hem of the robe of the *Kohein Gadol* (High Priest) to the human voice. The Maharal extends the symbolism by relating the silence of the *rimonim*, the yarn "pomegranates," to human silence.

Maharal on Exodus 28:34 It may be said that the purpose of the *Kohein*'s robe was contained in both the bells and the pomegranates, as it is written, "a golden bell and a pomegranate, a golden bell and a pomegranate" (Exod. 28:34). But the pomegranate has no mouth, simply the pomegranate itself, like an egg, which is closed and has no mouth. This teaches us the way of God that a person should limit their speech, and keep their mouth shut, with regard to ordinary matters. This is why he had pomegranates. And he also made a sound [with the golden bells] for the purpose of *k'dushah* [holiness], because of course when speech is for a holy purpose, one should not be silent but should open their mouth. For this reason there were bells on his robe, as it says, "and his sound/voice would be heard when he entered the *kodesh* [Sanctuary]" (Exod. 28:35). And with this quality a person should garb themselves.

Comment Many traditional sources teach us to "say little and do much." But modern psychological wisdom urges us to "express ourselves"—freely and frequently. Is there a traditional balance between speaking and keeping quiet that we might recover?

T'tzaveh
Sheldon Marder, 2001

This portion challenges us to think about the geography of Jewish spirituality. For instance, professor of Bible Jon D. Levenson sees in the passage beginning "For there I will meet with you . . ." (Exod. 29:42–46) P's idea that "the goal of the exodus is not so much the promised land as it is the intimacy with *YHVH* made available to Israel in the Tabernacle. He rescued her so that He might set up Tent in her midst . . ." (*Jewish Spirituality: From the Sixteenth-Century Revival to the Present*, ed. Arthur Green, Crossroad Publishing Company, 1989, p. 37). In the words of Psalm 11:4, "The LORD is in His holy temple." Or, as R. Aha puts it in *Midrash T'hillim* 113, "The *Shechinah* will never depart from the Western Wall."

How do we reconcile such localized notions of God's presence with texts that suggest the omnipresence of the Divine? Pardes Yosef seems to suggest that it is up to us to carry God's light out of our institutionalized "holy places" into the world at large. Commenting on "Light the lamp outside the curtain" (Exod. 27:21), Yosef of Piavinitz states, "All Jews must light a *ner tamid* [eternal light] in their own hearts, and not just in the Holy Tabernacle—not just in the synagogue, in the house of study, in the house of prayer. You must light the lamp 'outside the curtain'—in the street and marketplace, in ordinary activities, in all your interactions with people."

T'tzaveh: V'ha-ikar
Kenneth J. Weiss, 2002

"I will be their God" (Exod. 29:45b).

The Tabernacle, its furnishings, its design and dimensions, the priestly garments and accoutrements, the ceremony of ordination—the details describing these fill the bulk of chapters 25–31 of Exodus. Details galore . . .

But, God reminds Moses (and us!): don't lose sight of My principle message! There **is** a path through all of this, a truth you must hold onto and transmit. Three texts—at the beginning, near the middle, and at the end—are your signposts, Moses. Heed the details, but here's the core of what I want you to know and transmit: tell the people

> "I shall dwell among them" (Exod. 25:8).
> "They shall know that I—*YHVH*—am their God, who brought them out from the land of Egypt" (Exod. 29:46).

They "must keep My Sabbaths, for this is a sign ... throughout the ages" (Exod. 31:13).

In sum I am with you; we are, were, and will always be bonded; the Sabbath will forever signify—and strengthen—our bond. God tells Moses *that's* the path, the truth, the *ikar*!

So (yet)—what immediately follows in the flow of Torah? God gives the tablets to Moses (Exod. 31:18) while (simultaneously?) the restless people at the foot of Sinai build a Golden Calf. *V'ha-ikar*...

And today ... ?

T'tzaveh
Kenneth J. Weiss, 2003

"*L'haalot ner tamid*"—for kindling lamps regularly (Exod. 27:20).

Each of us is a *ner* (light)—we're born that way. We are built so that, some day, we may kindle our own flames, shed our own unique light. Our parents teach us how they add to the light of the world by performing mitzvot that enhance and brighten other lives. We see that every mitzvah sheds light like a flame. As a candle is made to be lit, so every person is created to perform mitzvot. Yes: "the mitzvah **is** a light" (Prov. 6:23).

So—if every person is a *ner*, what is a *ner tamid*? It is both a reality and a vision. For now, it is that small flame that is found in every synagogue. Surely, it is also a source of motivation: we are to visit it regularly and return home inspired by it. It should move us to want to kindle our own lights through the mitzvot we do.

Rashi understands *ner tamid* to mean "every single light." When each of us, as a *ner*, lives a life replete with mitzvo*t*, the resulting flames and their collective illumination will brighten the world with a pervasive, everlasting light. With each mitzvah, we kindle a new flame, add to the light of the world—diminish the darkness.

"Elevating" the *ner tamid* beyond our sanctuaries, making of God's entire creation an enlightened, holy place—isn't that *the* Jewish aspiration: "*l'haalot ner tamid*"?

T'tzaveh
Kenneth J. Weiss, 2005

"Pomegranates . . . and . . . bells of gold . . . all around the hem" (Exod. 28:33–34).

The High Priest's robe, מעיל (*m'il*), had golden bells attached to its hem—perhaps to ward off evil spirits, or simply to "announce" Aaron's presence.

In *HaKetav v'HaKabalah*, Rabbi Jacob Zvi ben Gamliel Mecklenburg suggests that the bells had a more symbolic purpose: to be an "auditory counterpart" to ציצית (*tzitzit*). Let's speculate: as ritual fringes remind and motivate many modern Jews to live lives defined by the 613 mitzvot, so the bells on the hem of the High Priest's מעיל (*m'il*) reminded Aaron of his sacred responsibility: to be an exemplary role model of a life lived in consonance with the mitzvot.

Aaron's very robe bolsters this supposition:

1. Alternating between the bells on its hem were pomegranates, which tradition suggests each have 613 seeds, one for each of the mitzvot.
2. "The opening for the head shall be in the middle of it [בתוכן, *b'tocho*]" (Exod. 28:32), which can also mean in its center . . . at its core. Aaron: "get your head into" (mentally focus on) the mitzvot. Ensuring that they inform your people's lives is your central, your core responsibility.

T'tzaveh: Shabbat Zachor
Alan Cook, 2006

In תצוה (*T'tzaveh*) we find the command to construct an incense-burning altar. This furnishing of the משכן (*Mishkan*, "Tabernacle") is outlined in this *sidrah*, while the remainder of the משכן (*Mishkan*) was described in the previous portion.

Why is this altar set apart from everything else?

The incense burned on this altar wafted up to the heavens, creating a ריח-ניחוח (*rei-ach nichoach*) that was pleasing to God. Aaron and his sons facilitated this offering, bringing the lowly of the world—the "average Joes" among the Israelites—into a close relationship with the Divine.

Rabbi Avraham Schorr, in his work *HaLekach v'HaLebuv*, writes that this is why the Torah states "from evening to morning" (Exod. 27:21). Schorr writes, "Aaron's job was to elevate the lowly toward the heights of heaven, as the agent to the bride [i.e., God], he elevated the lowly from eveningtime until they were able to greet the day."

It is fitting that we read תצוה (*T'tzaveh*) in conjunction with שבת זכור (Shabbat Zachor), during which we recall the wickedness of Amalek. For Amalek sought to destroy our spirit. When our ancestors were getting their first taste of freedom, Amalek attacked the weak and the infirm at the back of the camp, in an effort to create fear and despair. On שבת זכור (Shabbat Zachor) we celebrate the fact that they did not succeed; though many tyrants have sought to destroy us, we are still here.

We are still here, due in part to the efforts of individuals like Aaron and his descendants, who knew how to love the Jewish people, to raise their spirits, and to bring them closer to one another and to God.

T'tzaveh
Amy Scheinerman, 2007

Although the *yahrzeit* of Moses (7 Adar) falls on the week when this portion is read, Moses's name is not mentioned in *T'tzaveh*, leaving room for Aaron and the priesthood to stand in the Torah's spotlight.

Modern discomfort with the sacrificial cult and rituals of the Tabernacle contribute to many misconceptions about ancient Jewish worship. For our ancestors, the Tabernacle was the nexus of heaven and earth: when Jews gather in community and sacrifice the best they have to God, the abyss between heaven and earth is closed. The hereditary priesthood does not guarantee that all *kohanim* will be religiously and morally worthy, but it ensures that children will be prepared for a life of service. In a society that places great emphasis on rights, privileges, and pleasures, this *parashah* provides a means to revisit the concepts of service and commitment that are implicit in the institutions of the Tabernacle.

The priestly garments illustrate this point. They constitute a uniform that marks the priest as an instrument both of God and the people Israel; indeed the headpiece of the *Kohein Gadol* (High Priest) declares he is sanctified to God. On many occasions, the *Kohein Gadol* dons colorful, highly adorned garb to minister in the Tabernacle, reflecting God's majesty. On Yom Kippur, he wears simple linen, reflecting Israel's contrition.

The Babylonian Talmud, *Shabbat* 31a, records that a gentile approached Shammai and Hillel requesting conversion in order to become the *Kohein Gadol*. Hillel converted him and taught him Torah, whereby he absorbed the concepts of service and commitment and no longer desired the glory of being *Kohein Gadol*.

T'tzaveh
Amy Scheinerman, 2008

פרשת תצוה (*Parashat T'tzaveh*) is the only פרשה (*parashah*) in the last four books of Torah in which Moses's name is not mentioned even once. What is more, the traditional date of Moses's death—7 Adar—always coincides with the week in which we read תצוה (*T'tzaveh*). Taken together, and in consideration of Torah's emphasis on how God buried Moses and no one to this day knows where his grave is located, we sense a concerted effort to prevent Moses from becoming an object of worship. When we consider how the graves of other sages (for example, in Tiberias and Tz'fat) have become locations of worship, with prayers even directed to these sages to intercede in heaven on behalf of the worshiper, we can appreciate this perspective. Imagine if we did know the location of Moses's grave. What might the scene there be like?

Nevertheless, every generation needs heroes and role models they can revere without worshiping. Whom do we hold up to our people as models worthy of reverence and emulation? In this age of debunking, and demonstrating that all beings are significantly flawed, have we surrendered the authority to choose our heroes to the secular subjects of reverence around us, athletes and rock stars of dubious integrity? Is it time to resurrect the prophets and sages who inspired previous generations and, through them, assert the importance of Jewish religious and moral values to sustain, inspire, and elevate Jews in every generation? Whom should we hold up as Jewish heroes?

T'tzaveh: Shabbat Zachor
Amy Scheinerman, 2009

Are the sons of Aharon priests by virtue of their lineage, or must they earn the status? Do they become priests by birth or merit?

In the beginning of the *parashah*, we are told that Aharon and his sons are to set up the lamps of the Tabernacle. Which sons? Ibn Ezra tells us that the subsequent verse (Exod. 28:10) stipulates Nadav, Avihu, Elazar, and Itamar because it is likely that Aharon had many other sons who were not ordained as priests (he cites Josh. 21:19, in which Aharon's family is assigned thirteen towns). Nachmanides tells us that these four sons of Aharon are named and anointed so that we should not think that anointing the father automatically conveyed priestly status on the sons as well. Elazar's son, Phineas, was excluded, as were other sons and grandsons alive at the time of the ordination; only progeny born after the ordination would be priests.

Abarbanel disagrees, but Ibn Ezra and Nachmanides bring up an important point about automatic status and succession.

Many of us work for organizations whose leaders are volunteers. Sometimes the leadership positions are considered desirable for the involvement and status they confer. Sometimes it is difficult to find people willing to do the work required. Yet, our communities need and deserve "the best and the brightest" in positions of authority and leadership. Raising the status of these positions and requiring leadership training and Jewish study to prepare for stepping into these roles can help us achieve that goal. At the same time, we should be open to recognizing those with innate talent who arise at the moment—both Mordecai and Esther were needed by our people.

כי תשא Ki Tisa

(Exodus 30:11–34:35)

For additional commentary on *Ki Tisa*, see "Chol HaMo-eid Sukkot" and "Pesach."

Ki Tisa
Lawrence S. Kushner, 1996

(Exod. 30:12) The heads had to be lifted up because they fell asleep from Moses's counting so slowly (*k'vad peh*).

(Exod. 31:2) Because he was a shadowy character basking in the light of his father.

(Exod. 31:6) Because he worked for a company that tented houses filled with termites, and his father, who was easily overcome by the fumes, was always leaning on his uncle.

(Exod. 31:1–11) Based on the Pittsburgh Platform, we may argue that because the Tabernacle was only "part of the system of training the Jewish people for its mission during its national life in Palestine," the connection of Shabbat and the *Mishkan* must mean that it is a mitzvah to work on the Sabbath as a sign that we reject the *Mishkan* as a model for the messianic future.

(Exod. 32:2) Aaron built the Golden Calf to discourage the wearing of earrings by young men.

Ki Tisa
Lawrence S. Kushner, 1997

Before the problem arises, the solution is arranged. The Rabbis chose not to begin this portion with the story of the Golden Calf, but rather with three other sections—the half-shekel offering (not a freewill offering) for Tabernacle upkeep, various details of the Tabernacle itself, and the *V'shamru* section of Shabbat injunctions. If the "problem" in this *parashah* is the people's desire for a visible evidence of God's presence, the *Kadosh Baruch Hu* provides two solutions—one in space—the Tabernacle—and other, more lasting, in time—Shabbat (which, as David Hartman has noted, has spatial implications as well). Since both the institutions of the *Mishkan* and Shabbat preceded the Golden Calf, why did Aaron not point these out to the people as they waited for Moses?

God fashions the writing on the tablets with the finger of God; Aaron fashions the molten calf with an engraving tool. What could have gone through his mind (we know the midrash suggesting that he was saving them from the punishment that would befall them were they to kill him as the Rabbis argue they had killed Hur)—did he think he was acting in *imitatio Dei*? Did he think this creature was a "visual representation" of the Decalogue?

Moses of course also wants a visual representation of God—Exod. 33:17–34:9—but God gives him instead of a calf (or Shabbat or the Tabernacle) the words of the thirteen attributes of God's mercy. Given the anger of so many of God's actions, and God's apparent sanctioning of Moses's anger at breaking the tablets, why does God decide to give Moses this tangible representation of the Divine?

Ki Tisa: God and Image
Stephen E. Cohen, 1998

Ibn Ezra and Ramban offer conflicting theories as to what the people asked of Aaron and what he meant the calf to be.

Ibn Ezra *Aseih lanu Elohim* ("make us a god" [Exod. 32:1]). The word *Elohim* refers to the Divine Glory encamped within a physical image. If you reflect upon the first journey [i.e., Exod. 13:20–22, the pillars of fire and cloud] you will understand this. Behold, the calf was done for the glory of God, and the "mixed multitude" led a small minority of Israel into idolatry.

Ramban (on Ibn Ezra's comment)   But this seems incorrect to me. For the calf was not constructed according to the science of astrology, so that its image would contain the Divine Glory. Rather, they made this image simply in order to focus, through its worship, upon its essential quality/*inyan*. As to the comparison with the first journey, Aaron would never have sought to imitate God. He intended simply to draw upon the calf, so that their journey would partake of that particular quality. And the *maskil* will understand.

Comment   What does Ramban see as the *inyan* of the calf? Why does he not make it explicit?

Ki Tisa: Does God Repent?
Janet and Sheldon Marder, 1999

In this portion God threatens to destroy the Israelites for building the Golden Calf. Then, when Moses intercedes through prayer, God changes His mind (*vayinachem* [Exod. 32:14]). Rashi (on Gen. 6:6) explains that "every instance of *nichum* in the Bible has the meaning of reconsidering what to do." Ibn Ezra finds problematic the notion of God reversing Himself. Alshech tries to understand God's reversal in terms of human psychology, basing himself on a literal reading of Exod. 32:14.

Ibn Ezra   Heaven forbid that God should reconsider [change His mind]. It is only that the Torah speaks in human language, as it says, "God regretted [*vayinachem*] having made the human being, and God's heart was saddened" (Gen. 6:6). For thus it is written, "The Glory of Israel does not deceive or change His mind, for He is not human that He should change His mind" (I Sam. 15:29).

Alshech   "*Adonai* renounced the evil which He spoke of doing to His people" (Exod. 32:14). Human nature is such that a person who represses his anger and keeps it within is crueler, and much more likely to take vengeance than a person who finds an outlet for his anger. Anger dissipates somewhat when one gives vent to it in harsh words. Thus, "Adonai renounced the evil." God did not take vengeance—"which He spoke of doing to His people"—because God's anger found expression in words. Thus it was possible for Moses to prevent the people's punishment.

Comment Is God's divinity compromised by the act of "reconsidering"? How do Ibn Ezra and Alshech understand Moses's "heroic" role as Israel's intercessor with God? Many modern Jews are attracted to the Rabbinic notion of *chutzpah k'lapei shamayim*—God's willingness to be questioned and challenged by human beings. Is petitionary prayer, by definition, a form of *chutzpah k'lapei shamayim*?

Ki Tisa: Cleansing but Not Cleansing
Stephen E. Cohen, 2000

When Moses calls out the thirteen attributes from the cleft in the rock, he uses the intensive form *v'nakeih lo y'nakeh*, meaning "he shall surely not cleanse." Both the grammar and the theology of this phrase, however, bothered our Sages. And the editor of the *machzor*, using his cutting tool, completely reversed the argument of the verse.

Exodus 34:7 "Granting mercy to the thousandth generation, forgiving iniquity, transgression and sin, and cleansing not cleansing, visiting the iniquity of the fathers upon the children."

Rashi "Cleansing not cleansing." The simple meaning is that God does not forgive sin completely, but rather exacts payment little by little. And our Sages interpreted that "cleansing" refers to those who repent, and "not cleansing" refers to those who do not repent.

High Holy Day and Festival *Machzor* "Granting mercy to the thousandth generation, forgiving iniquity, transgression and sin, and cleansing."

Comment Knowing the original, complete biblical version of this verse, what are we meant to be thinking as we sing this verse on the holy days? Are we repudiating the sentiment of the Torah text? Or are we allowing ourselves to silently wonder if complete cleansing is possible?

Ki Tisa

Sheldon Marder, 2001

"*Adonai* passed before him and proclaimed . . ." (Exod. 34:6). Professor Arnold Eisen asserts that Exodus 34 is "the theological high point of the Torah [because] it is the only place in Torah that God describes Himself" (*New Traditions*, Spring 1985). For Rabbi Yochanan, God's unique moment of self-description brought to mind an intimate scene. God as religious mentor, wrapped in a tallit, teaching Moses how to daven.

"Were it not written in the text," said R. Yochanan, "it would be impossible for us to say such a thing: this verse teaches us that the Holy One wrapped Himself like a *sh'liach tzibur* and showed Moses the order of prayer. God said to Moses: Whenever Israel sins, let them carry out this service [*k'seder hazeh*] before Me, and I will forgive them" (Babylonian Talmud, *Rosh HaShanah* 17b).

Iturei Torah notes the importance of the phrase *k'seder hazeh*: when Israel prays, they should begin with the first quality—"compassion"— and not with the last—"visits iniquity" (vol. 3, p. 268).

Moses's experience of God in Exodus 34 is the experience our tradition wants us to have every time we pray: an intimate experience with God who is, first and foremost, compassionate and merciful. Why, then, the term *El*, which is usually associated with God's attribute of justice? Rashi cites the *M'chilta*'s assertion that *El* too denotes mercy, as in Psalm 22: "*Eli, Eli* [my God, my God], why have you forsaken me?"

Ki Tisa

Kenneth J. Weiss, 2002

"As soon as Moses came near the camp and saw the calf and the dancing, he became enraged" (Exod. 32:19).

God told Moses—as they met on Sinai—about the molten calf: "Your people . . . have acted basely" (Exod. 32:7). So—the calf itself was no surprise to Moses. Indeed, Moses cooled *YHVH*'s blazing anger over the calf before descending from the mountain.

So, what caused Moses to lose his cool, such that he "became enraged and . . . hurled the tablets from his hands and shattered them at the foot of the mountain" (Exod. 32:19)?

Sforno postulates. Like a parent who—while away—learns that his children misbehaved in his absence, Moses believed (early on) that he would be able to redirect his wayward children upon his return home. He'd discipline and correct them. But, says Sforno, what Moses saw was much worse than even he could handle with equanimity: "When he actually beheld the Children of Israel **dancing** [my emphasis] around their idol, rejoicing in their sin, he despaired of ever being able to make them mend their ways." Torah suggests that it was their dancing—even more than the idol—that devastated Moses.

Misbehaving is one thing; reveling in it magnifies the offense. Parenting never was an easy job—back then . . . even now.

Ki Tisa
Kenneth J. Weiss, 2003

"The Sabbath . . . shall be a sign for all time between Me and the people of Israel" (Exod. 31:16–17).

Overusing a word like "sign" diminishes its meaning and impact. In Torah, the word "sign" (אות, *ot*) is appended to a scant handful of events and objects. Its purpose: to accentuate, to emphasize.

So—in Genesis—the lights of Creation's fourth day were "signs" (1:14); the rainbow was a "sign" (9:12, 9:17), as was circumcision (17:11). In Exodus, this word gave special emphasis to God's wonders and the plagues (4:8, 4:9, 8:19), to the blood on the Israelites' doorposts (12:13), and to *t'fillin* (13:9, 13:16). In our *parashah*, Shabbat is called a "sign"—a singular phenomenon emphasizing the special relationship between God and Israel.

Only special—noteworthy—events and objects are referred to as "signs." Only Shabbat among all Torah's holy days is called a "sign." Interesting: Shabbat alone, of all the *otot*, is reemphasized (twice, no less!) in the Holiness Code (Lev. 19:3, 19:30).

In Torah, Shabbat is no less than the *ot ha-otot*, the "sign of signs." But—it should not be just a **sign**; it should be the **sign**al reality of our lives as Jews, our **sign**ature! Do we today give Shabbat such stellar meaning? I have **sign**ificant doubts!

Ki Tisa
Kenneth J. Weiss, 2004

"Out came this calf!" (Exod. 32:24b).

After Aaron commanded the people to bring him gold jewelry, which he "molded and made . . . into a molten calf" (Exod. 32:4), he could tell Moses, "I [in all innocence!] hurled [their jewelry] into the fire and" (Exod. 32:24) the Golden Calf simply . . . emerged!

O, how some of our biblical "role models" could prevaricate! Torah suggests that this predilection to lie (so as to avoid consequences flowing from doing/saying the wrong thing), goes back to Adam. When God asks Adam, "Did you eat of the tree from which I had forbidden you to eat?" our hero (rootstock of humanity's genetic inclination to dissemble?) blames "the woman You put at my side—she gave me of the tree and I ate" (Gen. 3:11–12). Adam shamelessly projects partial blame on God: "You put [her] at my side." Eve responds in kind: "The serpent duped me, and I ate" (Gen. 3:13). Her unverbalized (but hardly subtle) message to God: "The serpent [whom You created!] duped me." Adam and Eve: role models for us all.

Whereas, times have changed—human nature has not: the "other guy" is still to blame! Example 1: **we're** not responsible for our children's educational shortcomings; parents accuse teachers who can't teach, teachers condemn parents who don't parent. Example 2: criminals blame their victims or their home environment for their criminal behavior.

I call it the "Adam syndrome": anything to evade the truth, elude the consequence.

Ki Tisa
Kenneth J. Weiss, 2005

"יהוה [*Adonai*] would speak to Moses face-to-face" (Exod. 33:11).

"You cannot see My face" (Exod. 33:20).

"Moses—whom יהוה [*Adonai*] singled out, face-to-face" (Deut. 34:10).

Although Moses came no closer to seeing God than any of us ever will, Torah texts affirm for us their intimate connection: they "spoke" face-to-face; God singled out Moses; Moses spent forty days and nights in God's presence, after which Moses's "face was radiant" (Exod. 34:29).

God's message to Moses—and through Moses to us—may be that we may well find God even though we will never see God. Moses finds God through the relationship they evolve, the time they spend together. Though destined never to see God's face, Moses's own face nonetheless radiates the reality of God in Moses's life.

Countless writers testify to the truth that even average human beings can find God. Though none saw God, they are each confident they found God through their own life experiences. God's message to them—to us: if you are receptive, if you seek and ask, you'll find Me.

So—Harold Kushner writes that he found God in the hands of the doctors who tried to save his son's life. Rabindranath Tagore finds God in "the ploughman" "the merry shouts of children" "when dawn comes up golden, bearing gifts" "in the current of life," "in the wealth of joys . . . in birth . . . and in death." Yitta Halberstam and Judith Leventhal find God when they recognize coincidence "for what it truly is—God's gentle tap on the shoulder or God's veritable shout: 'Hello from Heaven! . . .'" Ellen Frankel reminds us that we are each created בצלם אלהים (*b'tzelem Elohim*)—in God's likeness; if we could only "recognize God within our own features . . . we would recognize God . . . in each person we meet—and act accordingly."

Moses couldn't see God's face—clearly, no one ever will. I believe that God is surprised—and offended—that today so many diametrically opposed religious fundamentalists adamantly assert that they—alone—have found (and speak for!) God.

How sad for God—how tragic for us all.

Ki Tisa
Alan Cook, 2006

The *Chasidim* tell the story of a child who was playing hide-and-seek with a friend. After some time, he realized that his friend had abandoned the game, and he ran crying to his grandfather, "I hid, but my friend didn't look for me!" His grandfather lamented, "It is the same with God. God says, 'I hide, but nobody seeks me.'"

Much time has been spent debating what, if any, was the sin of the people who built the Golden Calf. Y'hudah HaLevi, in the *Kuzari*, suggests, "The people did not intend to commit idolatry but imagined that they were striving to worship the true God." Having no frame of reference other than their experiences in Egypt, they built a calf, reminiscent of Egyptian deities. HaLevi continues that the people, faced with a God they could not see, "were prompted to ask for a tangible object of worship *without* repudiating God who had brought them out of Egypt." The frustration of these Israelites is understandable. Even Moses longs to see concrete representation of who or what God is, despite the unprecedented intimacy that he enjoys with God, when he pleads, הראני נא את-כבודך (*Har'eini na et k'vodecha*), "Oh, let me behold Your Presence!" (Exod. 33:18).

What Moses and the Israelites come to realize, as we all must, is that each of us will encounter God in our own way. We don't need tangible representations to help us draw nearer to the Divine. We need only to seek, and God will be there to respond. As the Koretzer Rebbe said, "God accepts every invitation. You seek God? Extend an invitation."

Ki Tisa: Shabbat Parah
Amy Scheinerman, 2007

Parashat Ki Tisa and the *maftir* for Shabbat Parah combine to tell a tale of mothers and children, responsibility and purification. We speak much about rights these days, but the point here is responsibilities.

Torah is explicit: Aaron casts gold jewelry into a prepared mold ויעשהו עגל מסכה (*vayaaseihu eigel maseichah*), "and he made it into a molten calf" (Exod. 32:4). Yet only twenty verses later, Aaron dissembles to Moses: "They gave it to me and I hurled it into the fire and out came this calf!" (Exod. 32:24). Aaron has absolved himself of responsibility on three counts: (1) actively collecting the jewelry from the Israelites; (2) placing jewelry into a mold to produce a calf; (3) the intention of producing a golden calf.

Parashat Ki Tisa comes at the midpoint in the year—between one Rosh HaShanah and the next—a reminder that atonement is achieved not by denying our mistakes, but by accepting responsibility for, and correcting, them.

Of the פרה אדמה (*parah adumah*, "red heifer"), the subject of the *maftir* for Shabbat Parah, *B'midbar Rabbah* 19:8 says, "Let the mother come and repair the damage the offspring has caused," suggesting that the purification affected by the red heifer is an antidote to the sin of the Golden Calf.

A peculiar facet to the ritual of the red heifer: its ashes purify the impure but render impure those who are pure. Perhaps there is a lesson here about accepting responsibility: When we approach God knowing that we are impure and have done wrong, we accept responsibility for our actions and can thereby be purified. But when we approach God as Aaron approached Moses, denying responsibility, thinking we are already pure, we come away impure.

Ki Tisa
Amy Scheinerman, 2008

In פרשת כי תשא (*Parashat Ki Tisa*) God instructs Moses to fashion a laver and stand for the priests to wash; to produce sacred anointing oil from choice spices in order to anoint the ארון העדות, אהל מועד (*Aron HaEidut, Ohel Mo-eid,* "Ark of the Pact, Tent of Meeting") and the furnishings of the משכן (*Mishkan,* "Tabernacle"); and to produce incense to be offered on the altar. Imagine Moses's relief when God assigns Bezalel and Oholiav to craft the furnishings of the Tabernacle. Building the Tabernacle will not all depend on one person—nor should it.

Bezalel ben Uri is from the largest tribe, Judah. Oholiav ben Achisamach is from the smallest tribe, Dan. This alone demonstrates that exceptional talent and divine endowment are not restricted to any one group or persons of particular status. *Tanchuma Ki Tisa* 13 interprets God's choice of artisans as a message that all Israelite society is to be involved in the construction of the Tabernacle, a reminder to reach out to the fringes of our communities and draw people in toward the center. With so many demands on our time, it is easy to focus on those who contribute the most time, energy, and resources. Yet often there are Oholiavs on the periphery waiting to be noticed.

Exodus 30:34 specifies three herbs to be combined with frankincense to produce incense. The third, חלבנה (*chelbanah*), is identified as galbanum, an aromatic gum resin with a disagreeable bitter taste and a musky odor. Rashi tell us that galbanum reminds us that our communities include deliberate and unrepentant sinners who should be brought into the life of the community. We all too often draw an imaginary line shy of those who are "disagreeable" and "distasteful."

Torah's elevation of Oholiav and Rashi's interpretation of galbanum remind us to rethink our concept of community.

Ki Tisa
Amy Scheinerman, 2009

In Exod. 30:17ff., God instructs Moshe to make a copper laver so that Aharon and his sons can wash their hands and feet before entering the *Ohel Mo-eid* and approach the altar to serve.

Nachmanides explains that washing is a sign of respect for God because one would hardly approach the king's table or handle the king's food and wine with filthy hands. Moreover, since the priests normally served barefoot, we can presume that their feet are filthy as well. But then Nachmanides reveals what in his mind is the real purpose of the laver: the figure of a man with hands stretched upward symbolizes the ten *s'firot*. As *Sefer Y'tzirah* says of Avraham, "He made a covenant with God between the ten fingers of his hand [the covenant of the tongue] and the ten toes of his feet [*b'rit milah*]." Nachmanides concludes that washing is therefore an act of *k'dushah* and points out that Onkelos translates "sanctify" in place of "wash."

We need not be devotees of mysticism to appreciate the meaning behind Nachmanides' explanation: every ritual act is an act of *k'dushah*, reminding us that the intellectual and spiritual, physical and metaphysical, are integrally bound together in our service to God. Holiness derives from our ability to integrate all the ways in which we experience the world and can relate to God.

Nachmanides points out that the mitzvah here is washing with water; the laver is simply the means and venue for the washing. The priest could have washed elsewhere and fulfilled the mitzvah. Water evokes the image of Torah (*mayim chayim*), reminding us that mitzvot afford us opportunities to attain the *k'dushah* Nachmanides speaks about, in which every aspect of ourselves is combined in connecting with God.

ויקהל-פקודי Vayak'heil/P'kudei

(Exodus 35:1–38:20 and Exodus 38:21–40:38)

Vayak'heil/P'kudei
Lawrence S. Kushner, 1996

(Exod. 35:5) This is merely a fragment from a second millennium B.C.E. textbook teaching Israelite children their colors.

(Exod. 35:7–9) The original version is merely a shopping list by the author of the E document (Elisheva?) or the P document (Puah IP).

(Exod. 35:25) This verse proves conclusively that anyone who listens to *kol ishah* becomes wise in heart.

(Exod. 36:14) The first *m'chitzah* was clearly created to separate the sheep from the goats. For this reason, the early Reformers—favoring animal equality—eliminated it.

(Exod. 37:17) This verse indicates that the original menorah was intended to be used on Purim, since the *kaftor* (the fabled "knop") was large enough to drink from. *Al tikra "mikshah asah et hamenorah" ela "mashkeh"* (Don't read it as "a menorah made of hammered work" ... but rather as "drink").

Vayak'heil/P'kudei
Lawrence S. Kushner, 1997

The Sages suggest that *Vayak'heil* describes a convocation on the day after Yom Kippur, following Moses's second descent from Sinai.

If Moses wanted to inform the people after the interruption of the Golden Calf that the construction of the *Mishkan* could now proceed, we can understand how important was this announcement that their desire to see some physical manifestation of the presence of God in their midst was about to be fulfilled. But if the Torah was also for the ages, when God knew that both the *Mishkan* and the *Beit HaMikdash* would be destroyed, why does the Torah devote so much space to the Tabernacle's construction?

This *parashah* deals with the bringing of the materials for the *Mishkan* and the construction of its parts. Yet the Rabbis chose to begin it with a reminder of the injunction to observe Shabbat, on which no *m'lachah* (which also describes the work of the *Mishkan*) may be done. We find this coupling of Shabbat to the *Mishkan* in the previous week's *parashah* as well (Exod. 31:12ff.). How do you account for this continuing tension between Shabbat and the *m'lechet haMishkan*?

While elsewhere the *Mishkan* is connected to the Creation, here it is tied to the Exodus, in whose honor the month of Nisan is made the beginning of months. Why could not God have instructed the Israelites to build the **movable** *Mishkan* in Egypt—wouldn't that have made their slavery a bit easier to bear?

Vayak'heil/P'kudei: Wholeness
Stephen E. Cohen, 1998

The Ishbitzer, author of *Mei HaShiloach,* explicates the juxtaposition of Shabbat and the *Mishkan* with an emphasis on the quality of wholeness.

Mei HaShiloach   The key point is that Shabbat is mentioned just before the work of the *Mishkan*, because in the building of the *Mishkan*, all of Israel were united in their hearts, without any competition of one individual against another. At first, every skilled craftsperson worked on their own assignment and perceived that s/he had produced an extremely marvelous creation. But afterwards, when they saw the joining together of all the pieces—all the curtains and planks—they saw that each piece was connected to the others as though a single person had made them. And they understood that everything they had done had been not by their own intellect, but through the aid of God—resulting, ultimately, in the single harmonious form of the building. How then could any one craftsperson pride him/herself above anyone else?

Comment The Ishbitzer makes no reference to the roles of Moses or Betzalel in achieving the wholeness of the building. Must the human leader "vanish" in order for the people to experience the guiding hand of God?

Vayak'heil/P'kudei: The Spirit of Giving
Janet and Sheldon Marder, 1999

In the Babylonian Talmud (*Sh'kalim* 2b), R. Abba bar Acha says, "It is difficult to understand the nature of this people. When asked to contribute to making the [Golden] Calf, they give; when asked to contribute to building the Tabernacle, they give." The *Y'rushalmi* (Jerusalem Talmud, *Sh'kalim* 1:1) probes further: "Why does the Torah say that 'all the people' (Exod. 32:3) broke off their earrings to build the calf, but only 'those whose spirit moved them' (Exod. 35:21) gave to build the Tabernacle?" Rabbi Meir Shapira of Lublin (in *Iturei Torah*) bases his answer on the psychology of charitable giving.

Iturei Torah This is the explanation: Sometimes those who collect for charity assure the givers that the funds will be used for a holy purpose, but eventually it becomes clear that the money was collected under false pretenses, and the funds were wasted and used for unworthy purposes. This is what happened with the Golden Calf. Not all of the Israelites were aware that they were collecting to build a calf. They were promised, "This is your god, O Israel" (Exod. 32:4). That is, they thought the funds were being collected for a sacred purpose. That is why "all the people" donated their gold. When they realized later that the money had been collected deceitfully, they were sorely disillusioned. And when it came time to collect offerings for the Tabernacle, they no longer had faith. Thus, only "those whose spirit moved them" donated.

Comment Shapira's comments may lead us to reflect on what elements are crucial to effective fund-raising and how one's "giving history" shapes one's current philanthropic habits. How do we educate our children to become generous yet discerning givers? And what strategies are necessary today to deal with the cynicism and distrust that have taken root in our Jewish communities?

Vayak'heil/P'kudei: The Idea of Stopping
Stephen E. Cohen, 2000

In this *sidrah*, hundreds of verses describe the construction of the Tabernacle, all of which unfolds perfectly according to divine plan and without the slightest perturbation—with one exception. A single unforeseen event occurs when the workmen and Moses realize that the divine instruction never included a command to "stop."

Exodus 36:5–7 And they said to Moses: "The people have brought more than enough for the work of the Tabernacle." And Moses sent forth the herald in the camp, saying, "Let man and woman do no more...." And the people stopped.

K'li Yakar In order to make the building of the Tabernacle parallel in every respect to the building of the world, Moses commanded that it be proclaimed, "Let man and woman do no more work." But why not? Would it have been a sin for them to bring more than was needed? It was because Moses perceived that the design of the Tabernacle was modeled on the design of the entire world. And our Sages, in Tractate *Chagigah*, said that when the Holy One created the world, it went on expanding until the Holy One rebuked it, saying to the world, "Enough!" Thus when Moses saw the thing growing and expanding without end, he rebuked them saying, "Do no more work!" For this is what the Holy One had done in creating the world.

Comment Why is the command to "cease and desist" not built in at the beginning of the creation process—both that of the universe and of the Tabernacle?

Vayak'heil/P'kudei: Opulence and the Divine Presence
Stephen E. Cohen, 2000

The Rabbinic tradition usually emphasizes the continuities between the Tabernacle in the wilderness and the later sacred structures of the

First and Second Temples. Here, however, the sixteenth-century Italian commentator Ovadiah Sforno highlights the differences between the *Mishkan* and the two Temples, in order to deliver a powerful ethical message.

Exodus 38:24 All the gold that was prepared for the work, for all of the holy work, the gold of the waving, was 29 talents and 730 shekels.

Sforno The Torah records the exact amount of the gold and the silver and the copper that went into the work of the Tabernacle, which was of very small value compared to the wealth that went into the First Temple—which is described in the Book of Kings. And even more than that was the wealth that was in Herod's Temple [described in Tractate *Sotah, Perek HaNotel*]. And in spite of this, the Divine Glory appeared more constantly in Moses's Tabernacle than it did in the First Temple. And it never appeared at all in the Second Temple. And this teaches that neither the measure of wealth nor the size of the building causes the *Shechinah* to rest upon Israel. Rather, God desires those who revere Him and their actions, and dwells among them.

Comment Although Sforno does not say this, is it possible that the *Shechinah* simply cannot dwell in a place of opulence?

Vayak'heil/P'kudei
Sheldon Marder, 2001

The artistry and imagery of Temple and Tabernacle have inspired visions of society and human character. Two examples:

1. "And Moses said to the Israelites: 'See, Adonai has singled out by name Bezalel'" (Exod. 35:30). In his book *The Newly Built Jerusalem* (1924), Bezalel School founder Boris Schatz sees the Temple as the "dwelling place of the Jewish creative spirit" and envisions a "Third Temple" as cultural shrine museum, library, or archive. Israeli art historian Tamar Manor-Friedman writes, "One of the most recurrent themes in the works of the Bezalel artists is the First Temple and its sacred vessels." Through architecture, sculpture, and painting, these artists of the 1910s,

'20s, and '30s transformed the Temple from messianic symbol to icon of the modern Zionist spirit ("Renew Our Days as of Old," *The Jerusalem Review*, 1998/99).

2. "For over the Tabernacle a cloud of *Adonai* rested by day, and fire would appear in it by night" (Exod. 40:38). This alludes to the "whole person" (*haadam hashaleim*) whose nature is like that of the Tabernacle, as it is said, "They are the temple of God." In those times when life is good to him, when success shines like the sun across his path, he realizes that no one is invulnerable forever and keeps in mind the cloud that could come and eclipse his sun. But, "fire would appear in it by night." In his hour of misfortune, hemmed in by darkness and night, he will not lose the spark of holiness nor will he despair—for the sun will shine for him yet (*Yalkut Eliezer* in *Iturei Torah*, vol. 3, p. 299).

What qualities of Tabernacle and Temple might inspire or sustain our visions?

Vayak'heil/P'kudei
Kenneth J. Weiss, 2002

"These are the things that *YHVH* has commanded you to do: On six days work may be done, but on the seventh day you shall have a Sabbath of complete rest" (Exod. 35:1–2).

First, God commands: Do! Then, God commands: On Shabbat, do not do! The rest of *Vayak'heil* is all about doing: making, bringing, designing; producing Tabernacle and furnishings, cloth and planks, yarns and posts, screens, ark, altar and lampstand.

Here's the conundrum: To not do on Shabbat is one of Torah's principal mitzvot. We must defer everything on Shabbat, even the creation of sacred space. And yet, with the end of Shabbat, we must reengage in the world of space, perform the positive mitzvot that God commands of us if we are to function fully as God's partners.

So—are we valued for who we are or for what we do? Are we "human beings" or "human doings"? A Jewish response is "Yes!" Yes—we are both: we are valued for who we are, for our unique potential:

our "beingness." Yes—we are judged by the mitzvot we perform, model, transmit: our "doingness."

It's not "either-or"; it's "both-and." While "being" on Shabbat, we renew our ability to do. While "doing" on the weekdays, we must remain true to who we are. The goal: to merge our being with our doing, to bring *chol* (the mundane) ever closer to Shabbat.

Vayak'heil/P'kudei
Kenneth J. Weiss, 2003

Popular assumptions notwithstanding, the heart—in biblical psychology—is ever so much more than the seat of the intellect. In this *parashah*, the heart comes across as the generator of emotion and spirituality.

Parashat Vayak'heil describes the construction of the *Mishkan*. It does so in numbing detail. Why? Perhaps to accentuate, indeed to highlight—in clear, purposeful, intentional prose—the spirit of the people: their selflessness, their spontaneity and generosity, their pure joy. The primary point of this *parashah* is to record how utterly the people loved what they were doing—were enchanted by what they were building. They were—we must conclude—deeply, ardently moved, as the Hebrew text makes absolutely clear. Over and over, we are told that their hearts moved and motivated them:

- The gifts were from everyone *n'div libo* (Exod. 35:5), *n'div lev* (35:22), *nadav libam* (35:29), from the willingness of their hearts.
- Those who created, rendered, and/or fashioned the *Mishkan*'s furnishings did so with *chacham lev* or *chochmat lev*, literally wise hearts (Exod. 35:10, 35:25, 35:35, 36:1, 36:2, 36:8).

At God's direction (indeed, in God's shadow—*b'tzal'el*), our ancestors joyfully created a place of unique sanctity, rare beauty. Their hands built the *Mishkan*; but their **hearts** rendered it Israel's spiritual home: an edifice founded on love and *k'dushah*.

Vayak'heil/P'kudei
Kenneth J. Weiss, 2003

"The sockets of the sanctuary" (Exod. 38:27).

Students of Torah know that surface language often conceals deeper spiritual truths. Is *Parashat P'kudei* about accounting or (more deeply) about being accountable?

Our first impression is of record keeping: listed are the gifts that were given and used in the construction of the Tabernacle. The silver, as an example, was used primarily to cast both the sockets (one hundred of them) that secured the *Mishkan*'s foundation and the "hooks for the posts" (Exod. 38:28).

The Hebrew word for "socket" is *adon*. Rabbi Isaac Meir Alter points out in his *Chidushei HaRim* that the one hundred sockets needed to secure the Tabernacle are paralleled by the one hundred blessings every Jew is expected to recite daily. Additionally, the word for "socket"—*adon*—also translates as "master." As the one hundred sockets anchored the *Mishkan*, so our one hundred blessings anchor us in the world that God (**the** Master!) has given into our keeping.

Vayak'heil/P'kudei
Kenneth J. Weiss, 2004

The people thronged (literally, "gathered"—ויקהל, *vayikaheil*) against Aaron, bidding him to "make . . . a god who shall go before us" (Exod. 32:1). Aaron placated the mob, telling them to remove items of jewelry "and bring them to me" (Exod. 32:2).

To build the *Mishkan*, Moses first "convoked [ויקהל, *vayak'heil*] the whole Israelite community" (Exod. 35:1). After reminding them to keep Shabbat, Moses "said . . . to the whole community of Israelites" that God commands them to take gifts "from everyone whose heart so moves him . . . gifts for יהוה [*Adonai*]" (Exod. 35:4–5).

Obvious conclusion: whereas a throng of individuals can fashion an idol, it takes a community—every person's wholehearted, two-handed effort—to create something worthy (a holy place). True then, true now: when we Jews come together as a cohesive community, when every person feels invested, when hands and hearts join for the purpose of building something or helping someone, it's astonishing what we can—and do—create.

A midrash says that the *Mishkan* was strong enough to endure only because "the whole Israelite community" participated in its construction. Whereas the Golden Calf was utterly and immediately destroyed, the Tabernacle—as a Jewish worship place, a spiritual focal center—has endured through subsequent manifestations: the Temples on Zion, the synagogues that are omnipresent wherever our people settle.

Want to create for eternity? *Siftei Tzaddikim* tells us how: Pay heed, Israel, "gather together and always be united in heart and mind. Such is the will of God."

Vayak'heil/P'kudei
Kenneth J. Weiss, 2005

"On the seventh day, you shall have a Sabbath of complete rest . . . [after which] let all . . . who are skilled come and make . . . the Tabernacle" (Exod. 35:2, 35:10–11).

So, Abraham Joshua Heschel may have been reading this *sidrah* when the idea came, inspiration dawned.

Heschel intuited a core truth: that Shabbat is the prism through which the rest of Torah must be viewed. In our *sidrah*, Moses called together (ויקהל, *vayak'heil*) the entire community to reaffirm two ideas—Shabbat and Tabernacle—which (from God's perspective) were two halves of the same whole.

Moses's announcement in sum: Six days a week you will construct the Tabernacle—a structure symbolizing *YHVH*'s abiding presence. On the seventh day—Shabbat—you will fashion a different sort of "edifice."

As the Tabernacle was to be a physical place symbolic of God's presence, Shabbat was to be a spiritual "place." As the Tabernacle required an ark and poles, tables, lamps, and altar, Shabbat required rest, renewal, and refreshment of soul. As Tabernacle ceremonies were celebrated by priests in special vestments, Shabbat was celebrated by "every Jew" in his/her "finest": clothing befitting the singularity of the day.

Thus, Heschel taught us: as the goal of the weekday was "a Tabernacle in space," the goal of Shabbat was "a palace in time." The Tabernacle represented where God (symbolically) spent workdays, while the "Palace" epitomizes where God meets us each Shabbat.

"These . . . *YHVH* has commanded you to do" (Exod. 35:1): fashion that "Palace" and that Tabernacle.

Vayak'heil/P'kudei
Kenneth J. Weiss, 2005

To count is one thing. To record—to formalize an accounting—is something else, something more. In Exodus 32 God vows to "make an accounting" (v. 34) of those who sinned in the matter of the Golden Calf. In this *sidrah*, Moses supervises the careful accounting of the raw materials contributed to build the Tabernacle (Exod. 38:21).

These scriptural building projects—diametrically different in moral and spiritual tone—both spawn accountings that Torah insists are permanently (eternally!) valid. Thus the same verb פקד (*pakad*) is used in both instances, suggesting (in both contexts) "a mustering, a numbering," but more: a permanent record.

In addition, *Sh'mot Rabbah* 51:8 urges us to note that the word אלה (*eileh*, "these") introduces both the Golden Calf and the Tabernacle records:

- אלה אלהיך (*Eileh elohecha*)—"These [the gold bangles and baubles you offered to create a Golden Calf] have become your god . . ." (Exod. 32:4).
- אלה פקודי (*Eileh p'kudei*)—"These [the quantities of gold you contributed to the building of your praying place] are [quantified in] the records of the Tabernacle" (Exod. 38:21).

Furthermore, whereas Moses burned the אלה (*eileh*) that was the Golden Calf, "ground it to powder . . . strewed it upon the water and . . . made the Israelites drink it" (Exod. 32:20), the אלה (*eileh*) that was integrated into the Tabernacle accompanied our people "throughout their journeys" (Exod. 40:38). Surely it inspired—survived through?—future manifestations of our people's sanctuaries: in the Temples on Zion and in our synagogues in "earth's four corners" (Isaiah 11:12).

Vayak'heil/P'kudei
Alan Cook, 2006

Hollywood loves a formula, and one of the best-loved formulas of the motion picture industry is the so-called "buddy movie." In these films we find two characters, with completely opposite characteristics, drawn together by unusual circumstances. So, for instance, we have fastidious Felix Ungar paired with slovenly Oscar Madison.

Bezalel and Oholiab, charged with construction of the משכן (*Mishkan*, "Tabernacle"), seem similarly mismatched.

Bezalel was from the tribe of Judah, which went on to become very prosperous, while Oholiab was of the tribe of Dan, which ultimately disappeared. But neither of them would have been suited for the task had they attempted to tackle it singlehandedly. Just as the buddies depicted on the silver screen must learn to work together to overcome the obstacles that the screenwriters place before them, so too must these artisans learn to work with one another's strengths to build a place suitable for God to dwell within.

Arthur Green has noted that the concept of מלאכה (*m'lachah*, "work"), with but one exception, occurs in the Torah only in three contexts: God's creation of the world, the prohibition of work on the Sabbath and Festivals, and the construction and upkeep of the משכן (*Mishkan*). The completion of the work of the משכן (*Mishkan*) at the end of Exodus parallels the completion of God's work on Creation at the beginning of Genesis.

While only God could begin the work of Creation, humankind has the ability—and the responsibility—to work toward its completion. We can do so only by bridging differences, embracing unlikely partnerships, and learning to work together.

Thanks to Rabbi Joshua Garroway.

Vayak'heil/P'kudei
Amy Scheinerman, 2007

Moses singles out Bezalel ben Uri ben Hur to oversee the construction of the Tabernacle. Rashi suggests that Bezalel had *yichus*: he is Miriam's son. Ibn Ezra comments that the insertion of ראו (*r'u*, "see") in Exod. 35:30 indicates that Bezalel's inherent wisdom qualifies him for the task, but that Moses and the Israelites need to recognize this trait.

The Babylonian Talmud, *B'rachot 55a*, focuses on the mode of notification of the choice to teach us the importance of achieving consensus in making public appointments: God asks Moses if Bezalel is acceptable to him, and Moses responds that if Bezalel meets with God's approval, then Moses agrees. God then instructs Moses to ask the people, who respond that if Bezalel meets with Moses's approval, they find him acceptable. This approach is politically wise, for it brings everyone onboard.

Rav Kook notes in a commentary on ויקהל (*Vayak'heil*) that a great leader possesses three traits: (1) integrity and purity of soul; (2) wisdom to guide people; (3) charisma and eloquence. Bezalel is endowed with all three: רוח אלהים בחכמה בתבונה ובדעת ובכל-מלאכה (*ruach Elohim b'chochmah bitvunah uv'daat uv'chol m'lachah*, "a divine spirit of skill, ability, and knowledge in every kind of craft" [Exod. 35:31]). Their order matters: Rav Kook points out integrity and purity of soul are essential. Leaders who excel only in the superficial traits of charisma and eloquence often become corrupt. We might have thought wisdom the pinnacle, as Prov. 3:13–18 suggests, but Prov. 8:12–21 reminds us that wisdom applied leads to a life of integrity, and integrity is at the core of Torah, the blueprint of Creation.

Vayak'heil/P'kudei
Amy Scheinerman, 2008

ויקהל משה את-כל-עדת בני ישראל (*Vayak'heil Moshe et kol adat B'nei Yisrael*), "Moses then convoked the whole Israelite community" (Exod. 35:1). This is probably the first, and last, time all Jews have shown up at the same time for anything. Not even Yom Kippur draws us all in. Yet when Moshe has the entire Jewish people in the pews at one time, what is the first thing he tells them? To work for six days and rest on the seventh, keeping Shabbat holy to God. One is reminded of Achad Ha'am's adage, "More than Israel has kept the Sabbath, the Sabbath has kept Israel." God provided at least one day a week for the community to assemble and check in.

What are we to make of the seemingly harsh death sentence for one who works on Shabbat? Perhaps in conjunction with the teaching that God confers on us a נשמה יתרה (*n'shamah y'teirah*), an extra soul, on Shabbat, it seems less harsh and more enlightened: if we ignore Shabbat, then we do not receive the bonus spiritual experience of the holy day. This perspective personalizes Achad Ha'am's teaching, which was surely intended to be an observation about community.

Significantly, the commandment concerning Shabbat includes the exhortation to work for six days—to be productive and contribute to society. As much as we are to refrain from work to renew ourselves on Shabbat, we are to spend the remainder of the week—the bulk of our time—productively engaged, inspired by our Shabbat rest and renewal.

Vayak'heil/P'kudei
Amy Scheinerman, 2009

Parashiyot T'rumah and *T'tzaveh* lay out the construction of the *Mishkan* in an orderly manner. *T'rumah* delineates the *keilim* (utensils), their dimensions and attributes, and *T'tzaveh* describes the *bigdei kodesh* (holy garments) of the *kohanim* (priests). The logic is clear: first prepare the home where God's *Shechinah* would dwell, and then describe the individuals who would minister to God there.

Rambam points out that that *mizbei-ach hazahav*, the golden altar that used most of the gold employed in the *Mishkan*, comes at the very end of *T'tzaveh* (Exod. 30:1–10). Perhaps this is to remind us that the *Shechinah* rests among us only once we have prepared a venue and ourselves for that encounter to take place.

In *Parashat P'kudei*, Torah tells us that the gold used in the wilderness *Mishkan* came to 29 talents and 730 shekels. Sforno points out that far more gold was used in the First Temple. (For example, I Kings 10:14ff. records that Sh'lomo used 666 talents of gold in one year alone.) Sforno goes on to note that Herod used even more when rebuilding the Temple in his day. Yet, the *Shechinah* was a far greater and more constant presence in the *Mishkan* than in Solomon's Temple, and not present at all in the Second Temple, "for the Lord values those who fear God" (Ps. 147:11) and dwells among them because of their *yirah* (fear) and *maasim* (deeds).

We expend considerable resources preparing a "place" to serve God, but is our preparation aimed at service? And how do we—and might we—prepare ourselves for service to God?

Leviticus

ויקרא Vayikra
(Leviticus 1:1–5:26)

Vayikra
Lawrence S. Kushner, 1997

When the offerer places hands on the head of the animal to be offered (Lev. 1:4), what is being suggested? Is the animal a substitute for, or a symbol of, the offerer? Is it a sublimated self-sacrifice? If so, is prayer, which replaced the *korbanot* (offerings), also an offering of the self? How can we help our people give this kind of depth to their davening?

Reading the descriptions of the *minchah*, the meal offering, makes us think of making pancakes. They smell good, too, and it was the fragrance of the cooking that was the real offering to God—a *rei-ach nichoach*. How could we turn our cooking into the service of God?

Vayikra: Never Satisfied
Stephen E. Cohen, 1998

The following midrash seems to be reflecting upon the psychological reality that some part of us always feels we are falling short.

***Vayikra Rabbah* (4:2)** "All of a man's labor is for his mouth, and yet the *nefesh* [soul] is not filled" (Eccles. 6:7). Rabbi Sh'muel bar Ami said. No matter how many mitzvot and good deeds a man stores up, he still cannot satisfy the thread that issues from his mouth; "the *nefesh* is not filled." A parable of a commoner who married a princess: Even though he feeds her with every delicacy in the world, he never fulfills his obligation to her, since she is a princess. Likewise, no matter how much a man does for his *nefesh,* he never fulfills his obligation, since it comes from above.

Comment Is there any hint here of a possible "therapy" for this frustrating relationship between the self and the soul?

Vayikra: Approaching God
Janet and Sheldon Marder, 1999

On Shabbat, halachah forbids us from killing any living creature—even a fly or an ant. How then can it be *Shabbesdik* to immerse ourselves in the rules of ritual killing? The ancient sacrifices were "lifted up" to God; so also, several commentators interpret these sacrificial texts in ways that remain uplifting.

Martin Buber (adapted from *Ten Rungs*) In the Torah's first mention of sacrifice it says, "And Abel, he too brought an offering" (Gen. 4:4). The "he" is what Abel brought—he brought himself to God.

S'fat Emet "When a person among you brings a *korban* [offering] to God" (Lev. 1:2). The meaning is that a person must give his innermost strength and will to God. In other words, "Nullify your will before His will" (*Pirkei Avot* 2:4). The meaning of *korban* is to bring all your deeds near to the Holy One.

P'sikta Rabbati (*Piska* 25) "Honor *Adonai* with whatever excellence God has given you" (Prov. 3:9). This means: with whatever gifts God has bestowed upon you, bring honor to the Holy One. If you are a person with good looks, honor God with the beauty God has given you. And if your voice is pleasing, rise up and honor God with your voice.

Baal HaTanya (in *Iturei Torah*) Why does the text say *Adam ki yakriv mikem* instead of *Adam mikem ki yakriv* [*yakriv* can mean "to bring an offering" or "to draw near" to something or someone] (Lev. 1:2)? This is the explanation: *Adam ki yakriv*, when a person wants to get closer to the Holy One, he must make a sacrifice *mikem*—that is, from his very self. He must sacrifice the "animal" within himself, the evil and bestial elements of his personality.

Comment Ancient biblical sacrifice was an offering up of one's own substance, a gift of something precious and personal. Can we still give ourselves in this way, surrendering and subordinating some part of our ego? What would it actually mean today to offer oneself to God? How does our tradition help us to sacrifice the "beast" within ourselves—the part of ourselves that is capable of cruelty and brutality—so that we become human beings who cringe at the thought of giving pain to others?

Vayikra: Humility and Glory
Stephen E. Cohen, 2000

The opening verse of *Vayikra* speaks directly to the greatness of Moses; it was he that received the Word of God and brought it to the world. The midrash attempts to use the *verse* as an occasion to preach the virtues of humility and to suggest that greatness comes as humility's reward. But the Eitz Yosef supercommentary notes the absurdity of being humble in order to achieve greatness.

***Vayikra Rabbah* 1:5** "And [God] called to Moses" (Lev. 1:1). R. Akiva taught in the name of R. Shimon b. Azai: Move yourself two or three rows back from the place you deserve, and sit until they say, "Come up." Much better that they say to you, "Rise up! Rise up!" than that they should say to you, "Go down. Go down." Thus Hillel said, "In lowering myself I am elevated. And in elevating myself I am lowered." You will find that when the Holy One revealed Himself to Moses from within the bush, Moses hid his face. And the Holy One said to him, "It is you that I send to Pharoah. If you do not redeem them, no one will redeem them." And at the Sea, Moses stood off to the side. And the Holy One said, "And you; lift your staff . . . and split the sea. If you do not split it, no one will." At Sinai, Moses stood off to the side. The Holy One said, "Go up! If you do not go up, no one will go up." At the Tent of Meeting, he stood off to the side. The Holy One said, "How much longer will you humble yourself? The moment is waiting just for you!" Know that this is the case, for the Divine Utterance called specifically to Moses, *Vayikra el Moshe*.

Eitz Yosef   Hillel intended here a general lesson in humility. His intent was not that from humility will come fame and honor. For these things are meaningless. His intent was that humility brings spiritual greatness.

Comment   Do you picture Moses as a humble man? In what sense do you understand the text's assertion that Moses was *anav m'od mikol adam*, "more humble than any other man" (Num. 12:3)?

Vayikra
Sheldon Marder, 2001

"In case it is a chieftain who incurs guilt"—*Asher nasi yecheta* (Lev. 4:22).

Rashi wonders why *asher* is used in this context. And he says, "*L'shon ashrei* (read this rather as 'fortunate'): Fortunate is the generation whose leader directs his heart to make atonement for his sin committed in error, how much more so when the leader repents of his deliberate sins (*Sifra*)."

But Rabbi Menachem David of Amshinov wants to know, "What is the *osher*—what is the nature of this fortune—for the generation whose leader does *t'shuvah* [repentance]? Isn't it better for the generation if its leader does not sin in the first place? But, in fact," explains Menachem David, "this is not the case. For a leader who never tastes the taste of sin is unable to show compassion to another person who has sinned. Such a leader does not understand or empathize with the brokenness of the sinner, rather, he distances himself from these others who are not like him."

Vayikra
Kenneth J. Weiss, 2002

"When any of you presents an offering [*korban*] . . . to *YHVH*" (Lev. 1:2).

The Isaiahs cautioned early on: God does not want **offerings** presented by "hands stained with crime" (Isa. 1:15); God asks, "What need have I of all your sacrifices?" (Isa. 1:11). Nor does God want **fasts** engaged in by those who "strike with a wicked fist" (Isa. 58:4); God asks, "Do you call that a fast?" (Isa. 58:5).

Whether sacrifices then or fasts now: God demands not hypocritical ritual, but moral intent! We are to renew closeness (*k-r-b*) to God, to reaffirm what really matters, to reconnect to Judaism's basic values. We are to be God's partners: "Cease to do evil; learn to do good" (Isa. 1:16–17); "Let the oppressed go free . . . break off every yoke" (Isa. 58:6). In sum, God really wants people (us!) to turn from our evil, our greed, our callousness. God wants us to be just, compassionate, kind. God esteems the motive, not the act.

The Isaiahs warned us long ago: *korban*—as sacrifice or fast—affirms our partnership with God, or it is meaningless! Can our truly meaningful Yom Kippur fast in 2002/5763 be our *korban*?

Vayikra: Shabbat Zachor
Kenneth J. Weiss, 2003

"*Adonai* called . . ." (Lev. 1:1).

"Remember . . ." (Deut. 25:17).

Through Moses, God calls us to remember. God says, remember people who made a difference: those who sought to destroy you, those who stood by your side. Remember where you came from; recall why I created you and what I expect of you—how you must live so as to make the world (through mitzvot) a better place. Call to mind how you used to worship Me (with burnt offerings) and why. Remember (and reaffirm) our covenant: your role in maintaining it—and Mine as well.

Memory is at the core of every Jewish observance, virtually every Jewish text. Weekly we recall—through *k'riat haTorah* (reading of the Torah)—how our ancestors lived: their deeds, their thoughts, their relationships, their ambitions, their foibles. Annually our holidays and Festivals renew for us past events and their eternal meaning. Purim is of little consequence unless it moves us to psychodramatize—through fable and costume—that archetypal story. Through Purim's prism, we see our own times more honestly: every generation knows its own Esther, Mordecai, Haman.

Vayikra . . . zachor! God is calling to us: Remember! Let nothing of import slip into forgetfulness! Yes, memory is a subtext on this particular Shabbat; but, isn't it fundamental to everything we value as Jews? One who does not remember his/her past . . .

Vayikra
Kenneth J. Weiss, 2004

A core reason why our ancestors offered sacrifices in biblical days was to rebalance their lives. Ancient "psychoanalysts" knew (no less than today's Freudians and Jungians): when a person does (or believes he has done) the wrong thing—even unintentionally, even if no one else knows about it!—that person needs to mollify his/her guilty conscience.

Yes, the Aaronide priests commanded that there be certain, prescribed sacrifices: a burnt offering, a meal offering. But I surmise that the most meaningful sacrifices—the ones eliciting the most passion, the most fervor on the part of supplicants—were those designated, זבח שלמים (*zevach sh'lamim*), commonly translated as "thanksgiving" or "well-being offerings."

Return with me to that term's most basic meaning: the goal of offering a זבח שלמים (*zevach sh'lamim*) was to feel whole (שלם, *shaleim*) again, to renew one's sense of inner peace.

The חטאת (*chatat*, "purgation") offering (of Leviticus 4) is the זבח שלמים (*zevach sh'lamim*) only personalized! A person who seeks to ameliorate his/her sin—to "rebalance"—may offer a sacrifice for that purpose. So, if a priest sins (Lev. 4:3), or "the whole community" (4:13), or "a chieftain . . . incurs guilt . . . unwittingly" (4:22)—"if *any* person" sins unintentionally (4:27), let that person bring an appropriate sacrifice. Through this offering, one who feels as though he or she is falling "to pieces" can experience renewal, reaffirmation—be "at peace" once again.

. . . Step right up, folks! Feeling guilty? Burdened? Conflicted? Are you sincerely repentant? Bring your חטאת (*chatat*) offering here and feel שלם (*shaleim*) all over again. Wholeness and inner peace (virtually) guaranteed!

(PS—Just don't do it again!)

Vayikra
Kenneth J. Weiss, 2005

"*YHVH* called . . ." (Lev. 1:1).

From the very beginning, *YHVH*—through Moshe—called us to **do**—not just talk, to **act** rather than promise. As Exodus ends, Moses completes the building of the Tabernacle. As Leviticus opens, Moses transmits God's command: stay busy—offer sacrifices. There's **always** more to do.

The Tabernacle was more than a place representing *YHVH*'s presence; it was also God's way of teaching us a lesson: we best fulfill our role in the world by doing deeds, performing mitzvot. God wanted us—wants us still—to build, to use our hands, to create with them so as to make the world a better place. Deeds are the human language God demands that we speak.

From Torah times, *YHVH* has called us to concretize, to make actual our prayers, our good intentions. With the Tabernacle completed, the sacrifices offered therein constituted a further manifestation of God's command "to do": today, I accept your sacrifices (so long as they sincerely reflect your good intentions). Through sacrificing, you will grasp the concept of transforming words of prayer into deeds.

You've built a Tabernacle—good! But your work never ends! Keep your hands open and willing. Together—step-by-step—we'll perfect the world.

Written in the aftermath of—and to encourage our concrete support for—relief efforts following the Asian tsunami of December 2004.

Vayikra
Alan Cook, 2006

נפש כי תחטא (*Nefesh ki techeta*), "When a person incurs guilt" (Lev. 4:2).

אשר נשיא יחטא (*Asher nasi yecheta*), "In case it is a chieftain who incurs guilt" (Lev. 4:22).

Why does the Torah speak only of the possibility that an individual may sin, while in the case of a leader, it seems to assume that sin is inevitable? The commentators say that this teaches that ultimately, our leaders must admit their frailties and their fallibility. A good leader accepts responsibility for his or her failings and thus leads a community by example. If a leader can do so, certainly the average person on the street can admit to his or her failings.

On occasion, the Torah tells us, even the High Priest might make an error, impacting not only himself but the entire Israelite community. Such a sin was לאשמת העם (*l'ashmat haam*), "so that the blame falls upon the people" (Lev. 4:3), and thus the כהן (*kohein*, "priest") had to own up to the error, and take measures to correct it, before the people were adversely affected (a plague from an angry God, perhaps?) or were led astray ("If the כהן גדול [*Kohein Gadol*, 'High Priest'] can do things that way, why can't I?"). Would that all leaders could learn from this example.

The word "sacrifice" is derived from a Latin root that means "holiness." Our word קרבן (*korban*) is, of course, derived from the idea of "drawing close to God." Both of these terms indicate the forging of a special relationship with the Divine.

Though we no longer offer sacrifices, certainly we can engage in acts of holiness and strive to be closer to our God. And, as leaders, we can encourage others to do the same.

Vayikra
Amy Scheinerman, 2007

With ויקרא (*Vayikra*), we enter the vastly complex world of the sacrificial cult. It has been suggested that animal sacrifices in the Tabernacle came to replace the human sacrifices of the heathen world, a way of satisfying a primordial human need without committing murder. The prayer of the third-century *Amora* Rav Sheshet, recited when he undertook a fast, is recorded in the Babylonian Talmud, *B'rachot* 17a: "Master of the universe, you know that when the Temple stood, a person who sinned would bring a sacrifice. Although only the fats and blood would be offered on the altar, the person would be granted full atonement. Now I have fasted, and my fat and my blood have diminished. May it be Your will that the decrease in my fat and blood should be considered as if I offered them on the altar, and my offering was accepted."

Our discomfort with animal sacrifices and our preference for lofty moral and social ideals leads us to quote Isaiah 58 and Micah 6:6 as the true desire of God above animal sacrifices. Leviticus itself lends support: "You shall be holy, for I, the Lord your God, am holy" (Lev. 19:2).

Yet what of our need to sacrifice? Deeply embedded in the human psyche is the knowledge that when we sacrifice something of value, we bind ourselves to the one who receives our sacrifice. What is true for our human relationships is true for our relationship with God. Rav Sheshet felt it, quite literally, in his bones.

Vayikra
Janice Garfunkel, 2009

BILVAVI

Bilvavi mishkan evneh lahadar k'vodo,
Uv'mishkan mizbei-ach asim l'karnei hodo.
Ul'ner tamid ekach li et eish ha-akeidah,
Ul'korban akriv lo et nafshi,
Et nafshi hayechidah.
In my heart a sanctuary I shall build,
To the splendor of God's honor.
And in the sanctuary an altar I shall place,
To the rays of God's glory.

And for an eternal flame I shall take me
The fire of the *Akeidah*;
And for a sacrifice I shall offer to God my soul,
My one and only soul.

Many Reform Jews run lukewarm when it comes to the emphasis on Temple offerings in *Parashat Vayikra*. The first time I heard the *zemer* "*Bilvavi Mishkan Evneh*" at a *s'udah sh'lishit*, I was moved by both the haunting melody and the yearning, passionate words: it is the embodiment of *d'veikut*, the yearning to be close to the Holy One, to give all, even one's very soul, on the altar of a passionate love of God. I am moved by the idea of building a sanctuary in my heart, of burning with the flame of love and passion for the holy. Here *korban* (sacrifice) ceases to be distant, irrelevant, and ritualistic; it becomes the very meaning and driving force of our existence, drawing ever nearer to the Source of all.

(*Bilvavi* was written in the 1960s by Rabbi Yitzchak Hutner. A melody was composed by Shmuel Brazil. Hutner based his poem on a line written by Rabbi Eliezer Azikri, 1533–1600, author of *Y'did Nefesh*. More recently, a book series has been written titled *Bilvavi Mishkan Evneh* by Israeli Rabbi Itamar Schwarz; it is a practical manual for how to attain *d'veikut* to God.)

צו Tzav

(Leviticus 6:1–8:36)

For additional commentary on Tzav, see "Purim."

Tzav
Henry Bamberger, 1996

Five offerings (*KoRBanot*) that bring us near (*K-R-V*) to God are mentioned in this *parashah*: the *olah* (burnt offering [Lev. 6:1–6]), the *minchah* (meal offering [6:7–11]), the *chatat* (purgation offering [6:17–23]), the *asham* (reparation offering [7:1–10]), and the *sh'lamim* (well-being offering [7:11–21]). The *olah* goes up (*oleh*), mingling totally with the invisible realm of God; the *minchah*, the gift of grain, was the Rabbis' favorite, because everyone could afford to bring it; and the *sh'lamim*, wholly eaten by priests and people, was the forerunner of our sense of the meal as a holy celebration. What is our *olah*—what do we send totally into the realm of God? What is our *minchah*? What is the *minchah* of the poor today? And what do we offer up as a *chatat* to compensate for our sins? What do we offer up as an *asham*, to make good a debt?

Tzav
Lawrence S. Kushner, March 1997

Part of the *korbanot* (offerings) that the Israelites brought went to the *kohanim* (priests). This was, in a sense, their "salary"—so important was the bringing of the priests' due that the text calls it a *chok olam*, a law for all time (Lev. 6:11). Do people view the dues that go toward rabbinic salaries as a bringing of something holy? Why or why not? Should they?

Anointing (note Lev. 8:10ff.) is a mysterious process. On one level it appears to be a rite of ensuring fruitfulness, symbolized by the olive oil. But why pour it over the head? And why was fruitfulness so important in the consecrating of the *kohanim*?

Tzav: The Broken Heart
Stephen E. Cohen, 1998

When the sacrifices were replaced by prayer, the human heart became the new offering.

Vayikra Rabbah 7:2 Rabbi Abba bar Yudan said: Everything that the Holy Blessed One pronounced *pasul* (not kosher, or unfit) in animals is considered *kasher* (kosher or fit) in human beings. Animals are *pasul* if they are blind, or broken, or disfigured, or have warts. But a human being is *kasher* with a broken or crushed heart. Rabbi Alexandri said: If an ordinary person uses a broken vessel, it is a disgrace. But the vessels of the Holy Blessed One are broken, as it says, "The Eternal is near to the brokenhearted" (Ps. 34:19); "Who heals the brokenhearted . . ." (Ps. 147:3); "I am with the person of contrite and humble spirit" (Isa. 57:15); "The sacrifices of God are a broken spirit" (Ps. 51:19).

Comment Is the implication of these midrashic comments that God **rejects** the whole, unbroken heart—perhaps because it is too proud and self-sufficient? Or is it simply that both the unbroken and the broken heart are acceptable?

Tzav: Sin and Restoration
Janet and Sheldon Marder, 1998

This portion is rich in commentary about the act of *t'shuvah*—the spiritual experience of alienation and return.

Menachem Mendl of Kotzk   "This is the Torah of the burnt offering and the meal offering and the sin offering and the guilt offering" (Lev. 7:37). There are those who come to the Torah by way of burnt offerings and meal offerings, and there are those who come to the Torah only through sin offerings and guilt offerings.

Beit Yaakov   R. Yaakov of Ishbitza in *Iturei Torah*: "He shall carry the ashes out of the camp to a clean place" (Lev. 6:4). Even Israel's *p'solet* [rubbish], a Jew who seems to have no spark of holiness left within, even one who is completely "outside the camp," even such a person may be restored. For it is God's will that "none be banished from Him" (II Sam. 14:14). Thus, it is forbidden to despair of any Jew who has turned aside from the straight path, for there is still hope that he will return. And thus Scripture says that even the ashes in which no spark of holy fire remains should be carried "to a clean place."

Comment   What kinds of spiritual paths is Menachem Mendl describing? Beit Yaakov's reference to a sinful or alienated person as "rubbish" is repugnant; is there value, even so, in this text's teaching that God wants to find a way to bring everyone back? Should we engage actively in the mitzvah of "carrying the ashes to a clean place"—helping those who are "outside the camp" to return?

Tzav: God's Preferences
Stephen E. Cohen, 2000

Parashat Tzav deals with the sacrifices, and in chapter 4 of *Vayikra Rabbah*, the Sages ask quite honestly what, if anything, was unique about Israelite animal sacrifice? In the following excerpt, we see the Sages' characteristic confidence in the superiority of Jewish sacrifices—which is then quietly undermined by a comment from Rabbi.

***Vayikra Rabbah* 7:4**   Rabbi Azanah of Kfar Hittaya taught: A parable of a king who had two cooks. One cooked him a meal, and he ate it and enjoyed it. The second cooked him a meal, which he also ate and enjoyed. We would not know which he enjoyed more, except that he commands the second one, saying, "Make me another such meal."

From this, we know that he enjoyed the second meal more. Thus, Noah offered a sacrifice, which was pleasing to the Holy One, and Israel also offered a sacrifice. We would not know which was more pleasing, except that God commanded Israel, saying, "Be sure to offer Me My sweet savor . . ." (Num. 28:2). Israel's is more pleasing, as it is written, "Then shall the offering of Judah and Jerusalem be pleasant to the Eternal as in the days of old and in former years" (Mal. 3:4). "The days of old"—this is the time of Moses. "In former years"—the time of Solomon. But Rabbi says: "The days of old"—this is the time of Noah. In former years"—this is the time of Abel, for there was no idolatry in his time.

Comment What is Rabbi implying by reading Malachi's "Golden Age" as the times of Noah and of Abel? Is this not a rejection of the fundamental Jewish belief that our religion represented a giant leap forward for humanity?

Tzav
Zoe Klein and Jonathan Klein, 2001

"Command Aaron and his children, saying, 'This is the Torah of the elevation offering'" (Lev. 6:2).

R. Heschel of Kracow "Command" can only mean "urge on" (Rashi). If there is only "command," one needs extra urging. Since the Holy Blessed One commands something, the *yetzer* [refers to *yetzer hara*] steps in so that one will not fulfill it. This is the reason our Sages said, "One who is commanded to do something and then performs it is greater than one not commanded yet does it. One who is not commanded does not face the *yetzer* as much" (Babylonian Talmud, *Kiddushin* 31).

Comment Many of our congregants do not feel obligated to perform certain mitzvot, yet R. Heschel would argue that being commanded elevates the significance of actually performing mitzvot. Which is more valuable for our congregants to learn from us, the "how-to"s of performing mitzvot or the underlying concept of commandedness? Should we encourage the fulfillment of certain mitzvot that our congregants do not feel commanded to perform?

Tzav
Kenneth J. Weiss, 2002

"When any of you presents an offering [*korban*] . . . to *YHVH*" (Lev. 1:2).

The Isaiahs cautioned early on: God does not want **offerings** presented by "hands stained with crime" (Isa. 1:15); God asks, "What need have I of all your sacrifices?" (Isa. 1:11). Nor does God want **fasts** engaged in by those who "strike with a wicked fist" (Isa. 58:4); God asks, "Do you call that a fast?" (Isa. 58:5).

Whether sacrifices then or fasts now: God demands not hypocritical ritual, but moral intent! We are to renew closeness (*k-r-b*) to God, to reaffirm what really matters, to reconnect to Judaism's basic values. We are to be God's partners: "cease to do evil; learn to do good" (Isa. 1:16–17), "let the oppressed go free . . . break off every yoke" (Isa. 58:6). In sum, God really wants people (us!) to turn from our evil, our greed, our callousness. God wants us to be just, compassionate, kind. God esteems the motive, not the act.

The Isaiahs warned us long ago: *korban*—as sacrifice or fast—affirms our partnership with God, or it is meaningless! Can our truly meaningful Yom Kippur fast in 2002/5763 be our *korban*?

Tzav
Kenneth J. Weiss, 2003

"The bush was not consumed" (Exod. 3:2).

"A perpetual fire . . . not to go out" (Lev. 6:6).

Did "our" *eish* (fire) first appear in the Midianite *s'neh* (bush)? So it seems: this *eish* burned yet did not consume its host. Was it ever extinguished—that flaming fire in the unconsumed bush? Moses "went back to his father-in-law" (Exod. 4:18) as the bush (apparently) continued to burn. Perhaps Aaron, when he met Moses at "the mountain of God" (Exod. 4:27), carried the flame out of Midian on an indestructible branch of the unconsumed *s'neh*!? Perhaps he preserved it for the altar of the desert *Mishkan* (Tabernacle), from which it was transmitted to the Jerusalem Temples, to facilitate the sacrificial ritual.

Might not this *eish* be the "perpetual fire," mentioned in this *parashah*? The *eish* from Horeb burns still. It will blaze forever in Jewish people and places. Isn't every *ner tamid* (eternal light) kindled from that ancient, ageless *eish*? Isn't every Jew in every age commanded to keep that flame vital and alive—our *eish* within? This is the spark of God; it distinguishes humans from other forms of life. That spark, that inner flame, serves each of us as a gyroscope, offering balance and guidance. It started in an insignificant bush in the Midianite wilderness, burned on sacrificial altars, and today radiates in our sanctuaries and within us.

K'dushah (holiness) is its gift and its message.

Tzav: Shabbat HaGadol
Kenneth J. Weiss, 2004

Shabbat HaGadol (the Great Sabbath) is so designated because of what it "announces": Pesach is coming! Get ready, shift gears, move mentally from the everyday to Pesach's sacred message.

Parashat Tzav is an apt *sidrah* for the Shabbat preceding Pesach, because it intimates God's omnipresence. In Torah days, God designed a "communications bridge," linking God to the people. Through sacrifices—burnt and meal offerings, sin and guilt offerings, *sh'lamim* (well-being) offerings—God and people could (through Aaron and his sons – ordained priests) "commune."

Judaism affirms God's abiding nearness: in matters spiritual (as *Parashat Tzav* exemplifies), in everyday life, *and* when crisis comes (Pesach's message). Hearing our people's cry, responding to our people's pleas, God "dropped everything" so as to deliver us from slavery to freedom—from soul-death to renewed life.

Shabbat HaGadol and Pesach come together to deliver a crucial message: God is accessible and active at all times. And, this יהוה (*Adonai*) of ours—when the chips are down—is right there: leading us, comforting us, uplifting and (if necessary) rescuing us.

Tzav

Amy Scheinerman, 2009

In *Parashat Tzav* we are told that eating certain sacrifices in a state of *tumah* (impurity), eating banned fats, and consuming blood result in the punishment of *kareit*. The punishment of *kareit* applies as well to those who eat leaven during Pesach (Exod. 12:19) or fail to offer the paschal sacrifice (Babylonian Talmud, *Shabbat* 133), fail to be circumcised (Gen. 17:14; Babylonian Talmud, *Shabbat* 133), desecrate Shabbat, and commit incest (Lev. 20:17). *Mishnah K'ritot* 1:1 delineates thirty-six offenses in all for which *kareit* is the penalty.

While Josephus suggests that *kareit* was a form of capital punishment ("To those who were guilty of such insolent behavior, [Moses] ordered death for his punishment" [*Antiquities of the Jews* 3.12:1]), in fact *kareit* is a divine punishment of being cut off from one's people, either by a premature death or physical separation from the community. The Babylonian Talmud, *Mo-eid Katan* 28a (and Jerusalem Talmud, *Bikurim* 2:1) debates the precise age early death by *kareit* would occur and suggests that perhaps the manner of death is a factor as well. Dying childless was also considered a means of *kareit*, because without heirs, one is "cut off" from the people Israel in the future. Maimonides (*Mishneh Torah, Hilchot T'shuvah* 8:5) explains that the most egregious sinners will suffer a *kareit* that means annihilation of their souls in *olam haba*.

The one exception to this pattern is the case of siblings who marry; it appears that *kareit* is communal banishment (Lev. 20:17).

Torah appears to distinguish between punishments imposed by the community and those imposed by heaven on the basis of the effect on the community. Perhaps this is a first lesson in tempering our judgment of others, and leaving some judgments to heaven, while keeping our doors and hearts open to those in our midst.

שמיני Sh'mini
(Leviticus 9:1–11:47)

Sh'mini
Henry Bamberger, 1996

There are four sections to this portion: (1) the culmination of the *kohanim*'s (priest's) consecration (Lev. 9:1–24); (2) the death of Nadav and Avihu (10:1–11); (3) the failure of Aaron and his remaining sons to eat the proper offerings in a timely fashion, due to their grief (10:12–20); and (4) the list of permitted and forbidden animals (11:1–47). While the second and third sections are obviously connected, how do these connect with the first and fourth? Why do you think the nature of the sin of Nadav and Avihu is so obscure—why is *eish zarah* (alien fire [Lev. 10:1]) never explained?

The early Reformers saw chapter 11 and the other passages detailing the laws of kashrut as much a part of the ancient wilderness tales—and as irrelevant to modern religious life—as the laws of *korbanot* (offerings) in which they are embedded. Do you agree? Is God speaking only to the wilderness generation and not to us? If so, why did we not limit all the "ritual mitzvot" (including the laws of sukkah building, *lulav* and *etrog*, Shabbat) only to the wilderness?

Sh'mini
Stephen Wylen, 1997

Nadab and Abihu die when they present strange fire before Adonai. God tells Moses, "Through those near to Me I show Myself holy" (Lev. 10:3). Are pious people meant to suffer? If so, is this an incentive to be religious? Is *yisurin shel ahavah,* the sufferings of love, an incentive to be Jewish in today's world, or should this doctrine be suppressed? If good people are not meant to suffer, why does it happen so often?

Rabbi Y'hudah HaNasi explained the above principle of Torah with an example: "For me," he said, "being a day late paying the butcher would be a desecration of God's name" (Babylonian Talmud, *Yoma* 86a). Is that because he was rich, or a leader, because he was a Torah scholar? What behaviors should we demand of ourselves as contemporary American Reform rabbis so that God may be shown holy through our nearness? How can we harmonize our sanctified behavior with the call to be more intimate and personal in presenting Judaism? How should a Reform rabbi respond at a party when someone asks permission to tell an off-color joke in your presence?

Sh'mini: Fatal Fire
Stephen E. Cohen, 1998

The midrash offers a wide range of suggestions as to what exactly Nadav and Avihu did wrong. Some of these have little or no basis in the Torah text, but seem, rather, to emerge out of the Rabbis' own life experience.

Tanchuma, ***Acharei Mot*** **6** Rabbi Menachma in the name of Rabbi Y'hoshua ben N'chemyah said: Moses and Aaron would lead the march, and Nadav and Avihu would follow, and then the rest of the people Israel. And Nadav and Avihu would say, "When will these two old men die, so that we may lead the community in their place?" Rabbi Yudan in the name of Rabbi Ibo said, "They said this openly to each other, in front of Moses and Aaron." Rabbi Pinchas said, "They thought it in their hearts."

Comment If, as R. Pinchas suggests, Nadav and Avihu kept their ambitions completely private, were these thoughts normal, maybe forgivable?

Sh'mini
Herbert Bronstein, 1999

The most striking element in this portion is one we would also like to pass over: the "death by fire" of the newly ordained sons of Aaron. This seemingly demonic aspect of divinity, like the "strange fire" that young priests brought to the altar, is alien to a modern sensibility that seeks in Torah, if not a morally edifying core, at least some cogent rhyme and reason. Is it possible that in this story there is something that goes to the heart of religion? Reading this story I have often recalled how, as counselors at summer camp, in order to evoke the gratifying "oohs and aahs" of the campers and to cultivate our own popularity with them, we put various chemicals into the setup for the Saturday night *Havdalah* campfire, which then flared up with marvelous colors. We claimed credit for these marvels and "got points."

The *eish zarah*, the "strange" or "alien fire" that the priests brought while introducing themselves for the first time in their central role of public worship, reminds us of the phrase *avodah zarah*, "idolatry." If we agree with Erich Fromm that all idolatry is reduceable to the service of the ego-self, then we have a message to bring.

It is the purpose of the priest, of any religious leadership, those who are "brought near" and whose purpose is "to bring others near," to bring about a sense of holiness associated with the presence of God *bikrovai ekadeish*, "through those near to Me I show Myself holy" (Lev. 10:3). But what if the purpose of the priest becomes to draw attention to himself, to his own capabilities, to his own personality by introducing this gimmick or that which may seem to be for spiritual purposes but whose underlying goal is to make people feel, "Isn't he or she great"?

This may be the case with much latter-day Jewish guruism. It might be *eish zarah*, "not commanded." We do indeed have some basis for an explanation of our story along these lines in the interpretation of the words "They died before the LORD" (Lev. 10:2) to mean they died "spiritually."

Sh'mini: Grief and Faith
Stephen E. Cohen, 2000

Nearly all readings of Moses's words to his brother Aaron following the stunning deaths of Nadav and Avihu understand his comments as an attempt to comfort his brother in the moment of his devastating loss. Rashbam, however, sees Moses not offering words of comfort, but rather urging on Aaron the commandment set forth in Lev. 21:10–12, prohibiting the High Priest from performing the basic mourning rituals even for his closest family member.

Rashbam on Leviticus 10:3 Immediately when Aaron heard, he sought to stop the service and mourn his sons. *And Moses said to Aaron,* "Do not mourn and do not weep and do not cease from your service. For this thing that I am telling you, *this is what God spoke, saying, 'By those close to Me I will be sanctified.'* That is, by the High Priests, who are close to Me, to serve Me, I desire to be sanctified, so that My name and My service not be desecrated. For thus the Holy One has said to me, 'The *kohein* [priest] who is greatest of his brothers, his head he shall not leave wild and his garments he shall not tear' (Lev. 21:10). Do not leave off of the service, for you are *Kohein Gadol* [High Priest]; do not go out and do not desecrate. Rather let the Holy One and the service be sanctified by your hand."

Comment Why did the Torah instruct the *Kohein Gadol* to refrain from mourning? Does a leader's public display of grief shake the faith of a community?

Sh'mini
Zoe Klein and Jonathan Klein, 2001

"Rabbi Simeon said to [Elijah]: What does the Holy One, blessed be God, study in the firmament? He said to him: God studies the sacrificial offerings" (*Zohar*).

"You shall sanctify yourselves and be Holy, for I am Holy. You shall not make yourselves unclean through any swarming thing that moves upon the earth" (Lev. 11:44). There are very few biblical statutes that are connected with the demand for holiness, mostly concerning the priesthood and idolatry "and none of these have the demand with the same staccato emphasis and repetition [as the dietary laws]" (R. Jacob Milgrom). The prohibitions of blood and the slaughtering methods "teach the inviolability of all life, that animal life is conceded to man's lust and need only on the condition that a qualified few will actually do the killing, and that death must be effected in such a way that the slaughterer's sense of reverence for life may never be blunted" (Milgrom).

In what ways are we, in our profession, in danger of having our "reverence for life" blunted? Are there prohibitions we should impose upon ourselves to protect it?

Sh'mini
Kenneth J. Weiss, 2002

"You shall not eat . . . the swine—[for] although it has true hoofs . . . it does not chew the cud" (Lev. 11:4, 11:7).

The Talmud, *Chulin* 42a, tells us that Moses left nothing to chance or possible misinterpretation. Ever the consummate educator, Moses showed his people—one by one—the animals they could and could not eat.

So, he must have held up a pig, showed the people its (dis)qualifying characteristics, and concluded, "It is unclean for you." The midrash *(Vayikra Rabbah* 13:5) "fleshes out" the lesson: Why is the swine unfit? Because it is a dissembler: it extends its kosher (looking) forelegs for all to see (while, presumably, hiding its snout—the unclean part), as if to announce, "See: I am clean!" The pig is *t'reif* because it conceals its true nature.

Dissembling or hypocrisy is not limited to the *chazir*—hard to believe, I realize. Politicians are good at it. Enron's corporate officers raised (lowered?) the practice to an all-new level, with the endorsement of its accounting firm.

Eric Yoffie sees signs of this even in our synagogues: So often, our leaders speak of the importance of providing the best possible religious education to our young people. Yet—in this area—we are failing, and so "many of our synagogue leaders have removed themselves from involvement in [and responsibility for?—my judgmental query] the religious school." We publicly acknowledge that we must educate well. We say it is a top priority. But we don't do what we say. So, many Jews continue to characterize religious school as "the castor oil of Jewish life."

Just saying "I am clean" doesn't make me clean. Just saying, "Enron is in great shape" doesn't make it so. Just saying we care about religious education doesn't make it better—or even good. What we say must reflect what we do. As Moses might tell the *chazir*, "Chew on that for a while!"

Sh'mini
Kenneth J. Weiss, 2003

"Alien fire" (Lev. 10:1).

Nadav and Avihu were surely aware of the eternal *eish* described in *Parashat Tzav*. Through Moses, God instructed "Aaron and his sons, thus: 'This is the ritual of the burnt offering'" (Lev. 6:2). God commanded, "A perpetual fire shall be kept burning on the altar, not to go out" (Lev. 6:6).

But, Nadav and Avihu (rebellious youth!) must have thought: Fire is fire. What's the difference? They didn't get it: there is (and was!) only one **eternal** *eish*. Transmitted from the unconsumed *s'neh* (bush), it alone was pure in its creation, its purpose. It alone represented the constructive (not the destructive) aspects of fire, one of earth's fundamental elements. To bring their *eish zarah* (alien fire) to God's altar was to deny symbolically God's unique place and role, to deny the holy God's eternal existence. And—for Aaron's sons to do this so soon after being thoroughly instructed as to their duties: that's why "fire [born of that ancient, original, eternal *eish*?] came forth from the Lord and consumed them" (Lev. 10:2).

Sh'mini
Kenneth J. Weiss, 2004

Aaron's sons—Nadab and Abihu—die suddenly. Having displeased יהוה (*Adonai*), they suffer the harshest consequences. Aaron's reaction to their deaths is contained in the terse phrase וידם אהרן (*vayidom Aharon* [Lev. 10:3b]), commonly translated, "And Aaron was silent."

Perhaps that is the sum and substance of Aaron's reaction: silence, suggesting one or more of the following:

- He was dumbfounded in the aftermath of the deaths.
- He was mortified—beyond embarrassment—because of what his sons did.
- He was unutterably angry at Moses's harsh response, the absence of a single word of commiseration (see Lev. 10:3).
- He was unable to share the devastating news of the deaths with his wife and others in the family.

For any or all of these reasons, Aaron's silence is understandable. However, I believe that "silence" does not adequately convey Aaron's response. The verb וידם (*vayidom*) suggests more—infinitely more—as seen in other biblical settings. In the Book of Hosea, verbs from the same *shoresh* (root) have the connotation of something (or someone) who is "destroyed" (Hos. 4:5–6) or "cut off " (Hos. 10:7, 10:15). In Lamentations, the verb (in context) could justifiably be rendered "dumbfounded, devastated" (see Lam. 2:10 and 3:28; similarly, see Exod. 15:16 and Jer. 25:37).

Aaron may have been silent . . . but in his silence there was devastation: news of his sons' death nearly destroyed him. He felt cut off—from his dead sons, from his God. For (at least) those first moments, the forward momentum of his life ceased. He was dumbfounded into silence.

Probe a little. Draw a line between the verb וידם (*vayidom*) and the noun דם (*dam*, blood)*: Aaron "bled out"! He hemorrhaged! His sons' death wounded him—mortally. Aaron's response was anguish, mute despair: *Vayidom Aharon!*

What more could Torah say: *Vayidom haTorah!*

---

*Rivka Dori of Hebrew Union College–Jewish Institute of Religion, Los Angeles, verifies a "linguistic connection"!

Sh'mini
Kenneth J. Weiss, 2005

"You must distinguish" (Lev. 10:10).

When you were young, I wanted to spare you life's complexities. So I sheltered you. But, you're no longer children. It's time you learned to master crucial life skills, among them the ability to distinguish, to differentiate: day-by-day to choose well, wisely, sensitively.

Genesis and innocence are long past. Now, life's dilemmas impact you continually, life . . . choices are urgent . . . inevitable. My mitzvot will guide you toward the way you *should* live, but—day-in, day-out—*you* will have to choose which path you'll walk. Facing—then making—choices is a core responsibility of every person.

Our *sidrah* subtly illustrates this: I instructed Aaron and his progeny to practice sobriety when entering the Tent of Meeting, for no one (while inebriated) can "distinguish between the sacred and the profane . . . the unclean and the clean" (Lev. 10:10). I reminded everyday Israelites, as well: choice is at the heart of life. An example: you must distinguish between food that is fit ("the creatures . . . you may eat" [Lev. 11:2]) and food that is not.

So—augment (redouble!) your ability to distinguish, differentiate, choose—because that's what mature life's all about. Here's why: though you'll always be My sons and daughters, you are no longer children.

Sh'mini
Alan Cook, 2006

"Bar Kapara said in the name of Rabbi Jeremiah ben Eleazar, 'Aaron's sons died on account of four things: for drawing near to the holy place, for offering, for the strange fire, and for not having taken counsel from one another'" (*Vayikra Rabbah* 20:8).

In שמיני (*Sh'mini*), mere verses after the ordination of Aaron and his sons, we read of the deaths of נדב, Nadav, and אביהוא, Avihu (although little commentary on this event is found until אחרי מות, *Acharei Mot*). How do we avoid repeating the sins of these men?

Drawing near to the holy place. Every place where a person can go can be holy. We should ask whether we have taken the opportunity to make it so. That is, we bring holiness to others through our professional work, but have we made our time with our families special and sacred? Have we done so for our leisure activities?

Offering. Do we attempt to be martyrs? Do we sacrifice our well-being thinking that we are serving our constituencies, when in fact we may be burning ourselves out, making us ineffective and unable to assist anyone?

Strange fire. When counseling others, do we "meet them where they are" and offer them guidance that is sensible and helpful, or do we have difficulty connecting with them in a meaningful way?

Not having taken counsel from one another. Do we seek out colleagues who can assist us in professional growth, or do we try to operate in a vacuum and carry the future of Judaism on our own shoulders?

We can learn from the mistakes of נדב (Nadav) and אביהוא (Avihu) and make the offerings of our hands and our hearts pleasing to God.

Sh'mini
Amy Scheinerman, 2007

Mary Douglas, in *Leviticus as Literature* (Oxford University Press, 2001), described ויקרא (*Vayikra*) as a priestly pocket manual for officiating in the complex sacrificial cult, as well as a literary blueprint of the משכן (*Mishkan*, "Tabernacle"). The only two narratives are literary analogs to the curtains at the entrance of the Holy and the Holy of Holies. The first "curtain" is found in שמיני (*Sh'mini*): the deaths of Nadab and Abihu, who brought alien fire to the משכן (*Mishkan*).

The explanations of the shocking deaths of Aaron's sons are many. They were intoxicated, disrespectful of their elders, lacked faith in

God, or entered the sanctuary inappropriately attired. Alternatively, excessive piety brought them too close to the altar fire.

The account is followed by a curious *pasuk*: "Moshe spoke to Aharon and his **remaining** [נותרים, *notarim*] sons, Eleazar and Itamar: 'Take what **remains** [נותרת, *noteret*] of the grain offering of the Lord's gifts and eat it **unleavened beside the altar**, for it is most holy'" (Lev. 10:12). "Remain" describes both the sons of Aharon and the grain offering, suggesting an intimate connection.

Nadab and Abihu's abrogation to themselves of the authority to designate offerings was playing God, the first step toward promoting themselves as gods to be worshiped. Leaders in the ancient world were often considered gods; this "curtain" delineates that boundary for Israel. The *remaining* sons are equated with the *remaining* unleavened offerings, reminding us both that those in positions of leadership must strive for humility and that the purpose of leaders is to serve.

Sh'mini
Joshua Minkin, 2009

"And Aaron was silent" (Lev. 10:3). How could this be? A father watches his sons engulfed in flames and consumed before his eyes, yet he does not shout out, he does not protest, he does not cry out in anguish. Our Sages claim that Aaron is silent because he accepts God's judgment. What happened to the stages of grief, the bargaining, the denial, the anger? All the way to acceptance in a flash?

As a father who has lost his child, I cannot accept this understanding. Yet this passage still speaks to me. Our tradition affords us the opportunity to catch our breath after experiencing a death. We are excused from our job, at least through shivah, and when we do return, people are understanding if we need to stop in the midst of a sermon, take a few breaths, and wipe our eyes before continuing.

But the pain does not end when shivah concludes, it does not end when *sh'loshim* finishes. It is a constant companion, and we must learn to cope despite the pain. Sometimes, often at predictable occasions, the pain becomes overwhelming, even much later. We, like

Aaron, as leaders of our people, push ourselves to be there for them, no matter how much it hurts. We permit ourselves no time to "bare our heads and rend our clothes." We feel guilty taking time to grieve; we know we are only human, but also know how much people depend on us.

There are times we can predict the pain will be especially bad: Mother's Day and Father's Day; birthdays that will never be celebrated with additional candles; *yahrzeit*, when we remember their last moments on earth. This is when we might emulate Aaron and be silent—and allow someone else to give the sermon, lead the service, teach the class.

תזריע-מצרע   Tazria/M'tzora
(Leviticus 12:1–13:59 and Leviticus 14:1–15:33)

Tazria/M'tzora
Henry Bamberger, 1996

My *kashya* is Lev. 13:13ff. I have no problem with the idea that the least bit of *tzaraat* (scaly affection) renders one unclean. I cannot make sense, however, out of the idea that if one is completely covered with scales that cleanness returns, much less the idea that if one is in that condition of cleanness, the least bit of healing renders one unclean again. I have heard this compared to mixing plants in a field or linen and wool, the idea being that mixtures are disturbing. It doesn't ring true for me. Moreover, the *m'forshim* (commentators) don't seem perturbed by this. At least they hardly make mention of it. I suppose that it would be unreasonable to expect them to say, "My! Here is something strange! I haven't the least idea what it means." However . . .

Tazria/M'tzora
Stephen Wylen, 1997

The opening section of *Tazria* describes the ritual for a woman to overcome the impurity of childbirth. This section gives rise to one of our old, traditional *makshim*: how can one acquire impurity through the performance of a mitzvah, since Scripture says, *Yirat Adonai t'horah, omedet l'ad*, "The fear of *Adonai* is pure, abiding forever" (Ps. 19:10)? Bearing children is a mitzvah—*p'ru ur'vu* ("be fruitful and multiply" [Gen. 1:28])—yet the woman who does so must bring an atonement sacrifice. How do you explain this?

The woman must bring a sheep, but she may bring two doves instead "if her means do not suffice for a sheep" (Lev. 12:8). The same means test applies to all *t'horah* (purification) offerings in *Tazria* and *M'tzora*. But, the Torah does not say who applies the means test. Who do you think applied it? What direction does that give us for temple dues policy? What is the relative value of a sheep versus two doves? Do our modern Jewish institutions demonstrate the same range of demands for support, or more or less?

When a person has white spots on the skin, that person is *tamei*, "impure," but if the person becomes white all over then that person is *tahor*, "pure" (Lev. 13:12ff.). Can something be so bad it's good? What analogies can you find to this situation in modern religious life?

Tazria/M'tzora: Disease and Sin
Stephen E. Cohen, 1998

In their responses to the biblical disease *tzaraat* (scaly affection), the Rabbis of the midrash wrestle with the ancient problem of the spiritual dimension of disease. Their comments are sometimes compassionate, sometimes cruel—often both within a single commentary. The following excerpt is from the *nechemta* at the end of a discourse on *tzaraat* and sin.

Vayikra Rabbah 16:9 Why does the *kohein* [priest] slaughter one bird and set the other free? To teach that just as the slaughtered bird cannot return, so too the affliction cannot return. In that moment, the Holy One summons His legions, saying, "I did not smite him without cause. But now, 'I have seen his ways and I will heal him'" (Isa. 57:18)."

Comment Can the real hope and encouragement offered by this text be "disentangled" from the harsh blaming of the victim?

Tazria/M'tzora
Herbert Bronstein, 1999

Many would like to skip these readings. Our hearts go out to the bar or bat mitzvah assigned them. Some have given up and replaced them with other texts. Others rely on the old Rabbinic aural wordplay of *motzi ra* (one who spreads lies) and remind our people of the plague of gossip and gossip mongering, a salutory message especially in this age of commercial media sensationalism. Others explore the glory of our medical tradition.

I suggest only two other interpretative directions that may be worthwhile. One is to explore the significance for our time of the extreme care and attention given in these portions to individuals who are haplessly stricken with a disfigurement and, further, to their inner need for spiritual restoration as well as to their total reintegration into the community. In a time of a morally horrific exclusion of huge numbers of people, including children, from adequate medical care in the richest nation in the world, this seems to be a worthwhile topic in which to engage. Notice in Lev. 14:21 that special care is taken for those without means for a full ritual course of cleansing. Also, should we not extend the *nega* or "blow" of *tzaraat* to disfigurements of personality? There is the child, for example, in whom other children sense a weakness or find some weak personality trait and begin to pick on him, tear him down, as do adults in their own way. We can help our people understand that such personality disfigurements, perhaps unpleasant to us, result from an earlier serious blow or a series of blows or hurts to the person that often have damaged the person's self-esteem. To add to these further hurts by teasing, exclusion, or meanness is to extend the plague. What such sufferers need is personal care and social re-integration. We do not need priests for this. Rather, when we help in this way, we are engaging in a sacred priestly vocation.

Tazria/M'tzora: Never Again
Stephen E. Cohen, 2000

Like many modern readers, the author of *Midrash Tanchuma* wonders why a woman after childbirth is required to bring a "sin offering." Could the answer proposed here have been first suggested by a husband who had tried to serve as his wife's labor coach?

Tanchuma, Tazria **4**   Said our Rabbis of blessed memory: One hundred gasps the woman gasps, as it is said, "Behold, you come from nothingness, and your making is naught/*mei-afa*" (Isa. 41:24). What does *mei-afa* mean? *Mei-ah fo-ot*: One hundred gasps she gasps when she sits upon the birthstool, ninety-nine for death and one for life. And when the pain encompasses her, she vows that she will never again couple with her husband. Therefore she brings a sacrifice, as it says, "She shall bring a yearling lamb" (Lev. 12:6).

Chapter 16 of *Vayikra Rabbah* is an extended homily that returns repeatedly to the pun *motzi ra* (one who spreads lies) for the word *m'tzora* (leper). In the following excerpt, our attention is directed to the mouth itself, the "watery" setting from which issue the opposing fires of Torah, and *lashon hara* (gossip).

Vayikra Rabbah **16:4**   "This shall be the Torah of the *m'tzora*" (Lev. 14:2). Behold it is written, "And to the wicked God says, 'What are you doing telling of My laws, and taking My covenant into your mouth?'" (Ps. 50:16). Ben Azai was sitting and explicating, and fire was blazing around him. They said to him, "Are you engaged in the study of the *merkavah*?" He replied, "No, I am stringing together the words of Torah, the Prophets, and the Writings. And the words of Torah are rejoicing as on the day they were given at Sinai, when 'the mountain was ablaze' (Deut. 4:11)." Rabbi Elazar said in the name of R. Yosei ben Zimra, "There are 248 organs in a person; some of them are flat and some are erect. Now the tongue here it is, set between two cheeks, and a stream of water flows beneath it, and it is folded several times. Yet how many fires it ignites! What if it were standing erect?" This is why Moses warned Israel: This is the Torah of the *m'tzora / motzi ra*.

Comment   What common "chemistry" is shared by the fire of Torah and the fire of *lashon hara*? And in what do they differ?

Tazria/M'tzora
Zoe Klein and Jonathan Klein, 2001

"When a woman conceives and bears a male, she shall be impure for seven days" (Lev. 12:2).

Domimtz, in the Name of Rabbi Y. M. Harlap Despite the fact that we know that each birth causes impurity afterward, would we say as a result that women should not give birth? It is a decree, and birthing within the realm of impurity is still birthing, and many, many mitzvot accompany it, and joy and hope and [a personal sense of] strength and such is [the way of our future] Redemption.

Comment When offered money to build our institutions from "impure" people, are we permitted to accept it as a source for many future mitzvot? Where and when do we draw the line?

"He shall slaughter the lamb in a place where the sin offering and the elevation offering are slaughtered, in a holy place, for it is like the sin offering of guilt for the priest; it is the holiest" (Lev. 14:13).

R. Simchah Zisel of Kelm "Anyone who sacrifices [his or her] *yetzer* [refers to *yetzer hara*], and confesses through it, is as if [he or she] has honored the Holy Blessed One in both worlds" (Babylonian Talmud, *Sanhedrin* 43b). But, to be a slaughterer, one needs to know the symbols of slaughter, how to slaughter, and what to slaughter.

Comment Rabbi Simchah Zisel seems to be advocating a form of self-realization, a deeper consciousness of one's shortcomings. He also acknowledges the wisdom that is required to achieve expiation. As rabbis, we struggle with our own *yetzer*; how do we promote self-actualization while we struggle for the same?

Tazria/M'tzora
Kenneth J. Weiss, 2002

"This shall be the ritual for *ham'tzora* [= *hamotzi ra*]" (the leper = the one who spreads lies) (Lev. 14:2).

Minimize fat intake; don't eat after dinner; exercise often; keep far from stress—smoking, too; lower cholesterol levels. Many of us now live our lives in consonance with (some combination of) these suggestions. The goal: physical fitness and a longer life.

Did you know that "fitness"—today's word to describe the ageless desire to live longer and better—was originally a midrashic concept? The "proof" is in a parable:

> A peddler used to go around towns in the vicinity of Sepphoris, crying out, "Who wants to buy the elixir of life?" He'd draw huge crowds around him. Rabbi Yannai . . . [once] heard him . . . and said to him, "Come here and sell it to me." Said the peddler, "Neither you nor people like you require what I have to sell." The rabbi pressed him, and the peddler . . . brought out a Book of Psalms and showed him the verse that reads, "Who is the man who is eager for life, who desires years of good fortune?" (Ps. 34:13). The peddler continued, "Then do this: 'Guard your tongue from evil'" (Ps. 34:14). So Rabbi Yannai said, "All the days of my life I have read this verse and did not know how it was to be explained, until this peddler came and clarified it for me." (*Vayikra Rabbah* 16:2)

There you have it: for fitness, avoid fat, cholesterol, smoking—also, evil speech: don't be a *motzi ra*. For, gossip and its derivatives—worry, hatred, quarrels, anger—also jeopardize our fitness, indeed, our very life. We learn: fitness is about the entire body—not least of all the tongue!

Tazria/M'tzora
Kenneth J. Weiss, 2003

"She shall bring . . . a sin-offering" (Lev. 12:6).

Why were women, shortly after giving birth, commanded to bring a sin offering? What sin could a new mother have committed? Commentators stretch so as to justify: the sin offering was for "ritual decontamination" only (insensitive to our ears; unresponsive, too!).

A thought: might the sin offering have been God's way of precluding the commonplace—a warning to new parents? Be proud of who your child is, what she/he does. However, avoid the sin of *exaggerated* pride in his/her beauty, brilliance, ability!

God's message: Before you start promoting your child as the most beautiful, the smartest, the most accomplished—superior in every way—remember this: It was I who commanded you, "Be fruitful and multiply" (Gen. 1:28). Furthermore, be ever mindful of a related fact (to keep things in proper perspective): three are needed to create every new life—"neither man without woman nor woman without man, and neither without the Divine Spirit" (*B'reishit Rabbah* 8:9). Torah's take: "Let us make man in our image, after our likeness" (Gen. 1:26).

So—love, nurture, guide, and teach your child, but let your pride be leavened with humility. Reaffirm that every child (not just yours!) is endowed with My spark. Be proud, but keep false pride at bay.

Tazria/M'tzora: Shabbat HaGadol
Kenneth J. Weiss, 2003

"It appears like a *nega* to me" (Lev. 14:35—R. E. Friedman).

Plagues—a centerpiece of the Passover story—torment us still! In the Bronstein/Baskin Haggadah, we rehearse the plagues of our own times, those "that threaten everyone everywhere. . . . The making of war, the teaching of hate and violence, despoliation of the earth, perversion . . . , fomenting . . . , neglect . . . , oppression . . . , corruption . . . , subjugation. . . ." In this way, Bronstein introduces the Ten Plagues of Exodus, the *makot* that God brought upon Pharaoh and his people.

Of all the plagues that tormented Egypt, only the tenth is referred to in Torah as a *nega* (which I'd translate as "a blow"). The first nine plagues wrought devastation upon devastation. But the tenth plague—the death of the firstborn—is singularly referred to as "a blow," for it touched real individuals in their very deepest places. In our *parashah*, this word, *nega*, reemerges; here, it refers to an affliction on a house.* Linking this *nega* to the one in the Pesach story creates a platform for a timeless Shabbat HaGadol sermon.

(Very briefly,) we note the context in *Parashat M'tzorah*, transitioning quickly to the one in Exodus (11:1ff.). At any time, whether in ancient Egypt or in 2003, the most painful, most personal blow—the deepest hurt—was/is/always will be—the loss of a child (firstborn or otherwise). The death of a child is an unspeakable tragedy: truly a *nega*, a blow—a singular loss of a unique and precious soul.

So—the message this Pesach is: Treasure every young life, for no two children have ever been born alike! Speak and listen to them. Nurture, treasure, and guide them. Discuss life's risks and their own vulnerability and mortality.

For—we can live through the misfortunes depicted in the first nine plagues. But the death of a child is a blow, a wound, a *nega* from which there is no recovery.

---

*In *Parashat Tazria*, we see *nega* referring to a leprous affliction on a person.

Tazria/M'tzora
Kenneth J. Weiss, 2004

"A צרעת [*tazraat*, 'eruptive'] plague upon a house" (Lev. 14:34).

A plague on a house—**sounds** biblical, Levitical! Perhaps, Torah is speaking of a fungus, a mold—some sort of infestation, infection, contagion.

But even in 2004, this verse speaks to us. Hillel Silverman refreshes its meaning: "In our own time, there is ample evidence of . . . the contemporary plagues of delinquency, corruption, rebellion, and violence" (*From Week To Week*, Hartmore House, 1975, pp. 105–6).

These are ubiquitous: preoccupied parents; children who can't trust; spouses who—living together—allow their lives to grow apart. Anger—hot or frigidly silent. Putting self before family, materialism before morality, possessions before people: today's plagues dwarf the molds and viruses alluded to in our *sidrah*.

(Indeed, in Torah days, the concern was for plagues on **houses**; today, we rue our modern plagues, which infest, disrupt, even threaten to destroy our **homes**, our lives!)

What to do? Larry Hoffman offers a timely remedy: an annual "moral house-cleaning" as part of *b'dikat chameitz* (the search for *chameitz*) on the eve of each Pesach. We must admit our destructive behaviors and perverted values, then discard them as we do our leavened crumbs.

צרעת (tzaraat): conceivably built from three little, yet weighty words:

צר = distress, trouble
רע = evil, bad
עת = a time, a period

צרעת (tzaraat)—at all times, at all costs, shun it . . . if necessary discard it!

Tazria/M'tzora: Shabbat HaChodesh
Kenneth J. Weiss, 2005

"A woman at childbirth" (Lev. 12:2).

Torah's poets and wordsmiths threw us a curveball: to many readers, the word תזריע (*tazria*) carries a negative connotation. תזריע (*tazria*) actually means "bring forth seed," coming as it does from the root זרע (*zara*), meaning "to sow."

But, consider the greater Levitical context into which this word falls. In Leviticus 10, we read of the "זרה [*zarah*, 'alien, unauthorized, strange'] fire" offered by Nadav and Avihu and their punishment.

In Leviticus 13–14, we learn about צרעת (*tzaraat*), a leprous disease afflicting persons and houses, and מצרע (*m'tzora*), one who suffers from this disease.

These words—מצרע (*m'tzorah*), צרעת (*tzaraat*), תזריע (*tazria*), זרה (*zarah*)—sound similar. Acknowledging the oral culture of Torah times, they thus share (even today) a negative cast.

And yet, תזריע (*tazria*) suggests new life, new growth. In human terms, תזריע (*tazria*) literally refers to a woman who is about to give birth. Childbirth—while inspiring awe and mystery—is neither "alien" nor "strange," nor is it an afflictive disease.

פרשת תזריע (*Parashat Tazria*) coincides this year with פרשת החודש (*Parashat HaChodesh*), which introduces the Hebrew month of Nisan—the spring month: harbinger of life renewed.

So . . . "*Tazria*" is all good!

Tazria/M'tzora
Kenneth J. Weiss, 2005

It just wouldn't stop. The lies . . . the gossip . . . the slander: my reputation was besmirched. Because of him, no one knew the real me; he stole my identity.

He's a "word-leper," one who defiles with his mouth. He does this by maligning others, disparaging others, ruining their lives. Such a person even corrupts words of Torah and prayer by allowing them to cross his lips, to issue from his filthy mouth.

Tradition describes the "word-leper." But what of his/her victim? Where am **I** in Torah—I who lived my life, strove to be honest, sought to make the world a better place? Has Torah overlooked me and all the word-leper's victims . . . we who daily bear the distrust, the skepticism, the silence of those who once knew and loved us?

No, in truth . . . Torah has not forgotten us: when you read of the birds and the lambs sacrificed for the word-leper's guilt, you'll envision us as well. We are acknowledged through them: all of us are the "word-leper's" innocent victims.

Tazria/M'tzora
Alan Cook, 2006

"If the eruption spreads out over the skin so that it covers all the skin of the affected person from head to foot, wherever the priest can see—if the priest sees that the eruption has covered the whole body—he shall pronounce the affected person clean; he is clean, for he has turned all white" (Lev. 13:12–13).

This command seems incongruous in the context of the remainder of תזריע (*Tazria*) and מצורע (*M'tzora*). How can a person be "clean" (טהור, *tahor*) if he is covered in a skin eruption of some sort? And if the prevailing concern throughout the *sidrot* is isolation of an infected person, does not pronouncing the above individual "clean" (and allowing him to remain in the camp) negate the effectiveness of such quarantines?

Of course, being pronounced טהור (*tahor*) or טמא (*tamei*) was not a medical diagnosis, but rather a spiritual one. The afflicted individual is examined not by a physician but by a priest. By the time that צרעת (tzaraat, "eruption") covers the entire body, the condition cannot be hidden. If we accept the traditional view that a person with צרעת (tzaraat) had been guilty of לשון הרע (lashon hara, "gossip") or some other transgression, then certainly one whose entire body has been covered with an eruption would have his guilt exposed to the entire community.

We do not wish to suffer the pain and indignity of צרעת (tzaraat), yet we would do well to heed the example of the infected individual. When we are willing to expose our human frailties to others, we may find the inspiration to work to overcome them. Thus we come closer to טהרה (tahorah, "purity").

Tazria/M'tzora
Amy Scheinerman, 2007

There are two general approaches modern commentaries take to interpreting צרעת (tzaraat). The first is to follow the classic midrash that identifies the מצרע (m'tzora, "leper") as one who מוציא שם רע (motzi shem ra, spreads lies), suggesting that צרעת (tzaraat) results from the spiritual and moral failing of slander and gossip; in other words, צרעת (tzaraat) is moral malaise expressed physically (Vayikra Rabbah 16:1). This explains why the afflicted person must be separated from the community for a time and reintroduced only after the symptoms disappear: לשון הרע (lashon hara, "gossip and slander") and רכילות (r'chilut, "rumors") are highly contagious and pollute a community.

The second approach is to note that the functions of physician and cleric are both fulfilled by the כהן (kohein), affirming the contemporary sensitivity to the relationship between physical and spiritual aspects of illness. We have come to appreciate the importance of pursuing mental health and seeking the emotional care and well-being of those who suffer physically.

Perhaps the two approaches might be considered in conjunction. The מצרע (m'tzora) who is guilty of being מוציא שם רע (motzi shem ra) carries the very real burden of his/her guilt. It weighs him/her down. Not surprisingly, guilt turned inward attacks the body just as it attacks the soul. For this, a two-pronged approach is needed that reflects the dual role of the כהן (*kohein*) as physician and cleric. The "cure" is, of course, תשובה (*t'shuvah*, "repentance"), which requires both a tangible change in the behavior of the מצרע (*m'tzora*) as well as atonement where possible to rectify the damage done—the spiritual and the physical.

Tazria/M'tzora
Amy Scheinerman, 2008

It is difficult for modern people to comprehend the concept of טמאה (*tumah*). The various translations—"unclean," "impure," and even worse, "polluted"—compound our incomprehension. Hence the notion that childbirth, contact with a corpse, or skin afflictions convey טמאה (*tumah*) is troubling.

Our ancestors understood their human bodies as the creation and gift of God, and from that idea flowed others that we struggle to understand and appreciate. For them, as for us, life was filled with frightening and threatening events, including childbirth, the death of a loved one, and bodily afflictions. Each, in its own way, threatens to separate one from God and the community—for physical reasons, emotional reasons, or a combination of the two. The state of טמאה (*tumah*) recognizes that separation and seeks to remedy it. The very fact of טמאה (*tumah*) engages the services of a כהן (*kohein*) to intervene, inspect, visit regularly, and draw the טמא (*tamei*, "purified") person back into the embrace of the community, healed and whole.

Perhaps a new term is in order to reflect how טמאה (*tumah*) functioned in ancient Israel. The state of טמאה (*tumah*) reflects the acknowledgment of a threatening disruption to life and its consequent potential separation from God and the community. The rituals of טמאה (*tumah*) can give rise to a path back to God and community when events in life intervene. טמאה (*tumah*) always culminates in bringing a קרבן (*korban*, "offering")—that quintessential ritual of "drawing close" to God in ancient Israel. We would benefit from a communal mechanism for healing and wholeness.

Tazria/M'tzora
Amy Scheinerman, 2008

The Rabbis famously explained צרעת (*tzaraat*, scaly affection) as a punishment for the ethical violation of לשון הרע (*lashon hara*, "gossip and slander"), an interpretation that appeals to modern liberal Jews who are often uncomfortable with the physicality of the purity laws.

What is the nature of the plague that afflicts a house, and why is it that if the occupants remove all their possessions before the כהן (*kohein*) inspects, only the house and not the possessions are declared טמא (*tamei*, "pure")? The Babylonian Talmud, *Yoma* 11b, tells us that the plague is caused by the owner's selfishness. One who says, "The house and everything in it are mine, and I do not have to share it with anyone else," brings the plague upon his house. *Vayikra Rabbah* 17:3 lists ten sins that bring צרעת (*tzaraat*) upon a house; the tenth is greed. The midrash learns this from reading Lev. 14:35, ובא אשר-לו בית (*uva asher lo habayit*), as "that keeps his house to himself." *Vayikra Rabbah* 17:2 explains that if people refuse to share what they have with their neighbors, the plague comes to force them to empty their houses and reveal their possessions for all to see.

The Rabbis' proclivity to view צרעת (*tzaraat*) as a punishment for ethical violations reinforces the ritual for purification from צרעת (*tzaraat*) described in Lev. 14:14. The blood of the reparation sacrifice and the oil brought as a reparation offering are daubed on the ridge of the right ear, thumb of the right hand, and big toe of the right foot, and finally the oil is drizzled on the head. All the extremities on the right side are anointed, reminding us that our entire bodies must be brought into line with God's ethical requirements.

Tazria/M'tzora
Amy Scheinerman, 2009

The laws of *tumah* and *tahorah* are beyond recondite: what relevance do they have for us in the twenty-first century? While for some they are metaphorical, for others they are meaningless.

Rav Avraham Kook, in his book *Orot*, teaches that the more encompassing of life a spiritual framework is, the greater the level of purity it requires. He cites the *Mikdash* (Temple) as his prime example. "The Temple projected an ethical and holy influence on a wide range of life's aspects—from the noble heights of divine inspiration and prophecy, through the powers of imagination and the emotions . . . all the way down to the physical level of flesh and blood. . . . Because its impact reached even the lowest levels of physical existence . . . the Temple and its service required an exact and precise purity" (*Gold from the Land of Israel: A New Light on the Weekly Torah Portions from the Writings of Rabbi Abraham Isaac HaKohen Kook*, by Chanan Morrison, Urim Publications, 2007, p. 192).

Could an analogy be made to our synagogues, schools, and communal institutions? To the extent that we offer a Judaism that speaks to every aspect of life, Judaism will encompass more facets of our people's lives—religiously, spiritually, intellectually, socially—and elicit a correspondingly strong commitment. This is by no means a call to the traditional categories and stringencies of *tumah* and *tahorah*, nor a call to any form of orthodoxy. But it is a call to increase the intensity of the Jewish culture we offer and teach. We must respond to the way people live, the moral challenges they face, the spiritual needs they feel. At the same time, we would be wise to wed modern technology to ancient and emerging wisdom in new and creative ways.

אחרי מות-קדשים *Acharei Mot / K'doshim*

(Leviticus 16:1–18:30 and Leviticus 19:1–20:27)

For additional commentary on *Acharei Mot*, see "Yom Kippur."

Acharei Mot / K'doshim
Henry Bamberger, 1996

The Bible is convinced that "clothes make the person"—or at least reveal a person's inner nature (cf. Adam and Eve, Joseph's many changes, the prophet's symbolic garb, Mordechai's royal robes). What do Aaron's Yom Kippur clothes (Lev. 16:4) reveal about him? How are they *kodesh* (holy)—that is, how do they manifest *k'dushah* (holiness)?

Once more Aaron and the *m'tzora* (leper) engage in similar rites—this time, offering up one creature and letting its double go off with its burden (cf. Lev. 14:4–7) What does the experience of the *m'tzora* teach us about the atonement of all the people? Which goat or bird is the more blessed—the one offered up or the one sent away with the burden?

What significance do you see in the order of topics in Leviticus 19? How does each topic connect with the one before and after it?

Acharei Mot / K'doshim
Lawrence S. Kushner, 1997

The description of Aaron's atonement rites informs important parts of the traditional Yom Kippur service: the morning Torah reading and the afternoon *Avodah* service. Reform has chosen an alternative Torah reading—*Atem N'tzavim*—and the priestly rites play but a small part in the afternoon service of *Gates of Repentance*. Is there any value in helping our people recall Aaron's practices on Yom Kippur? Are there sustaining lessons to be found in any of these metaphors in Leviticus 16: changing into the "holy linen clothing" (v. 4); making atonement for himself and his family first, before the congregation (vv. 5, 11, 15); casting lots over the two goats (v. 8); the fate of the sacrificed goat compared to the scapegoat (vv. 9–10, 21–22); sprinkling the blood of the bullocks on the altar and the *kaporet*, the Ark cover (vv. 14–15, 18–19; what relation is there between *kaporet* and *kippur* [atonement]?); Aaron's making atonement in the holy place all alone (v. 17); the bathing of Aaron and the person who escorted the goat to Azazel (vv. 24, 26)?

We often note that part of the problem with the Torah's attack on homosexuality in Leviticus 18 results from its time-bound connection to polytheistic practices in ancient Egypt and Canaan. Does this argument also suggest that, if they are consensual, the other forbidden sexual relationships in this chapter are also objectionable only because of their ties to ancient polytheistic practices? What other values differentiate these relationships?

When Korach tells Moses that all the congregation are holy (Num. 16:3), Rashi notes that he is contradicting the opening verses of *K'doshim*, which proclaim *k'doshim tih'yu* ("you shall be holy" [Lev. 19:2])—holiness is a developing condition, not a completed one. Only God is *kadosh* (holy) now. If we obey all the mitzvot in this portion, will we be holy then? Are those who obey more mitzvot more holy than those who obey fewer? Is holiness a quality we feel in ourselves when we do a mitzvah, or is it recognized only by God, or by other people?

This *parashah* is surely the most powerful, sustained treatment of social justice in the Torah. It is also the proof text of the prophets' insistence that devotion to God be accompanied by devotion to human welfare. But this *parashah* also includes concerns about the welfare of the earth (*kil'ayim*) and the nature of our clothing (*shaatneiz*), injunctions that we usually deride as outmoded. On what basis do we turn the prophets' sermons on their head and say that we must act justly toward each other but need not bother about mixed seeds and mixed threads (Lev. 19:19)? Do we thereby undermine the authority of the entire social message of this portion?

Acharei Mot / K'doshim: Why Rebuke?
Stephen E. Cohen, 1998

The Hebrew of Lev. 19:17 is notoriously ambiguous. The phrase *Lo tisa alav cheit*, in particular, is unclear—understood by some commentators as "Do not lay sin upon him" and by others as "Do not bear sin because of him." Ramban agrees with Onkelos in accepting the latter reading, but disagrees as to the actual benefit derived from rebuking.

Ramban Onkelos's interpretation is "Rebuke him, for **you** will be guilty if he sins and you have not rebuked him." In my opinion, however, the correct reading is: If he has done something to you not to your liking, rebuke him, saying, "Why have you done this to me?" And *do not bear sin because of him*, by concealing the hatred in your heart. For when you have rebuked him, either he will win you over, or he will repent and you can forgive him.

Comment For Onkelos the original problem being addressed by *hochei-ach tochiach* is sin, whereas for Ramban the original problem is hatred. In what different ways does rebuke address these two problems?

Acharei Mot / K'doshim
Herbert Bronstein, 1999

Rabbis today are unlikely to follow Akiva in utilizing every extra letter or sign as an interpretive strategy, nor would our people be willing to go for that. Akiva needed radically to expand Torah in order to keep Judaism alive. Our task—for the same purpose—is to try to make Torah significant. But is it possible that one lowly word, understandably overlooked amidst the towering peaks of that scriptural sacred mountain—the "Holiness Code"—might still be, both for us and for our people, quite significant?

I am thinking of the word "all" in our text, read as if it were (as indeed it might very well be) underlined, emphasized: "Speak to **all** of the congregation of the Children of Israel" (Lev. 19:2).

Throughout the Book of Leviticus there are all kinds of addressees —"speak to Aaron" or to "Aaron and his sons" or to the "Levites"— but "speak to all of the congregation" is never in this particular locution otherwise found in the entire Book of Leviticus!

The emphasis on gathering the entire congregation did not go unnoticed as early as *Sifra*, *Vayikra Rabbah*, and then down through Rashi and Ramban. In their view, the entire congregation had to be present because all the essentials (*gufei*) of Torah depend on this section.

In ancient times religion was identified with the cult (sometimes extremely complex) and therefore with a "professional" priesthood or religious elite. In this book—called *Torat HaKohanim*—the "priestly book" par excellence, here of all places all the congregation is involved. That was a religious revolution at the time. In our time we have devolved back from being a "kingdom of priests and a holy people" (Exod. 19:6) to the configuration of rabbis not only as priests but as vicarious Jews for the congregation, as if the text said, "Speak to rabbis. . . ."

Also we are struggling with the conflict between personal autonomy (central to the faith of modernity) and mitzvah. The word for congregation, *eidah*, refers to the Israelite community as a religious community united not only by shared principles or values but also by shared observances and religious institutions. The word *mo-eid*—set season—is related to *eidah* and to *Ohel Mo-eid* as a place for set meetings created not by convention but rooted in divine commandment incumbent on all the congregation.

Acharei Mot / K'doshim: One of Ibn Ezra's Secrets
Stephen E. Cohen, 2000

Our Sages wondered and wondered about Azazel, the mysterious place or entity toward which the scapegoat of Yom Kippur was sent.

Ibn Ezra on Leviticus 16:8 Rav Sh'muel said that even though the text says of the goat for the *chatat* [purgation offering] that it was "for God," nevertheless, the scapegoat also was for God. But this is unnecessary, for it was not a *korban* (offering), since it was not slaughtered. And if you are able to understand the secret that follows the word *"Azazel,"* then you shall know its secret, and the secret of its name, for there are similar occurrences in the Bible. And I will reveal to you a bit of the secret, in a hint: *When you are thirty-three, you shall know it.*

Ramban Rabbi Abraham ibn Ezra is of faithful spirit, and he conceals the thing. But I, the gossip, shall reveal his secret! For our Rabbis have already revealed it in many places, and this is the secret matter: they served other gods, that is, the angels, and they brought them *korbanot*, and bread for a sweet savor, as it is said, "My oil and My incense you set before them! My bread that I gave to you—I had fed you fine flour and oil and honey, and you set it before them for a sweet savor" (Ezek. 16:18–19). Now if you look carefully throughout the Scripture and the tradition, the Torah completely forbids accepting their divinity, and any worship of them. However, on Yom Kippur, the Holy One commanded that the goat be sent out into the wilderness, to the Prince who rules the desolate places. And it is appropriate for him, for he is its master, and from his power comes destruction and desolation, for he operates at the level of the stars of the sword, and blood, and wars, and quarrels, and injuries, and plagues, disintegration and destruction. In astrology, it is the sign of Mars, and among the nations, it is Esau; among the animals, it is goats, and in its domain are also demons, called *mazikin* by the Rabbis and *s'irim* by the Scripture.

Comment If this is, in fact, Ibn Ezra's secret, we can easily understand his decision to leave Azazel's identity undisclosed. Why does Ramban feel compelled to reveal it?

Acharei Mot / K'doshim: The Great Principle of the Torah
Stephen E. Cohen, 2000

K'li Yakar begins his comment with the assertion that "Love your neighbor as yourself" is equivalent to Hillel's famous negative formulation. Turning to the Gemara's story of the *ger* (convert) and his question, K'li Yakar proposes to imagine that question not as an insolent provocation, but as a sincere and important request.

K'li Yakar Our Sages said that this is the great principle of the Torah. And in Tractate *Shabbat* there is the story of the convert who said, "Teach me the entire Torah while I stand upon one foot," and Hillel taught him the verse, "Love your neighbor as yourself—that which is hateful to you do not do to your fellow. The rest is commentary; go and learn." Apparently, he was a *ger tzedek* [righteous convert], not one of those who provoke teachers by asking mockingly that they teach them the whole Torah while he actually stands on one foot. Rather, he asked Hillel to set the entire Torah for him upon a single foundation, that is, a single "footing" upon which he could rest all of the mitzvot. And in this way, he would not fall prey to the forgetfulness that is common with converts, who have not learned the mitzvot from childhood. This is why he asked him for a single principle that incorporates the entire Torah.

Comment When Hillel needed to encapsulate the entire Torah in a single sentence, why did he not choose a *pasuk* from Scripture? Was his decision somehow related to the problems inherent in reducing Torah to a single principle?

Acharei Mot / K'doshim
Sheldon Marder, 2001

"Speak to the whole Israelite community" (Lev. 19:2). "This *parashah*," writes Rashi, "was stated in an assembly." With that as his point of departure, the S'fat Emet asserts that "a person can attain holiness only by negating his own self, putting the whole of Israel before himself; holiness can be present only when there is oneness" (3:158). Holiness, in other words flows from self-sacrifice for the sake of the common good.

"You shall love [the stranger] as yourself for you were strangers in the land of Egypt" (Lev. 19:34). Not only does holiness flow from acts of self-sacrifice, in this instance holiness is grounded in Israel's experience of alienation and degradation: verse 34 commands Israel to build a society based on empathy, based on "oneness."

The *Sifra* tells us that most of the Torah's essential elements occur in *K'doshim*, which is why these laws, according to Rashi, were stated in an assembly. Holiness is not private affair; it is not a one-to-one encounter with divinity. Rather, holiness describes a society in which relationships are grounded in eternal values.

In her book *Cosmopolitan Culture*—a study of Babylon, Constantinople, Vienna, and New York—sociologist Bonnie Menes Kahn argues that the mark of a great society, the distinguishing trait of a truly cosmopolitan city, is how it treats the stranger.

What constitute, for us, the distinguishing marks of a holy society?

Acharei Mot / K'doshim
Kenneth J. Weiss, 2002

"You shall not take vengeance or bear a grudge [*lo tikom v'lo tikor*].... Love your neighbor as yourself [*v'ahavta l'rei-acha kamocha*]: I am the LORD" (Lev. 19:18).

This verse takes mitzvah to an intensely new level. With some exceptions, Torah's negative commands prohibit inappropriate deeds: idolatry, stealing, lying, swearing falsely, cursing the deaf, taking bribes, gossiping, using false measures. When one performs a prohibited deed, witnesses and/or testimony can verify that a line has been crossed, a sin committed.

Here, however, we find mitzvot that address thought patterns, something that cannot be externally verified. Being vengeful, bearing a grudge: God prohibits these even though they are sins of attitude, not of deed. How can—why should—a mitzvah address something as amorphous as an attitude? Modern psychologists affirm Rabbinic insight: if vengeance and grudge-bearing dictated our daily life pattern, then spite and bitterness would be at the heart of human relationships. So—for your own sake and *mipnei darchei shalom* (for the sake of peace)—don't go there!

We choose to be vengeful, to bear grudges—or not. That's why God can command, *Lo tikom v'lo titor* . . . God knows (and so do we!): the decision to feel positively toward others is also ours alone. And—that's the message of Lev. 19:18b, *V'ahavta l'rei-acha kamocha*: more than a feeling, love, too, is our choice, our decision! Thus, God says: I prohibit you from bearing animus toward others; indeed, I command you to love them as yourself. Choose your attitudes well; like your deeds, they are addressed by My mitzvot.

Acharei Mot / K'doshim
Kenneth J. Weiss, 2003

(Written during shivah following the deaths of the seven Columbia astronauts.)

"After the death" (Lev. 16:1).

In the aftermath of a death, life itself feels different. Things that had always seemed consequential—acquisitiveness, power, influence—fade into insignificance "after the death."

Aaron's two sons lose their lives (Leviticus 10). Through Moses, God subtly acknowledges Aaron's changed circumstances: you have to move on, Aaron. In the days immediately following his loss, God enjoined what Aaron needed: tasks and rituals—procedures, prohibitions, prescribed garments, etc. We, too—following a loss—need, look to, and appreciate the rituals enjoined by our tradition: the funeral, the meal of consolation, the structure of the shivah period—these enduring customs and rituals comfort mourners in the first days.

The simple white tunic Aaron was instructed to wear is deeply symbolic in this context: fancy vestments (fancy anything!) mean nothing in the aftermath of horrendous loss. Simple things—love, connection, health, gratitude, faith (all symbolized by the simple tunic)—these (and these alone) matter.

Simple, sincere words of comfort matter, too. The president sought to comfort us "after the death" of the astronauts: "We remember not only one moment of tragedy, but seven lives of great purpose and achievement."

Right after the seven deaths, life felt different for most of us . . .

Acharei Mot / K'doshim
Kenneth J. Weiss, 2003

"You shall not . . . place a stumbling block before the blind. You shall fear your God" (Lev. 19:14).

Language enhances our perception. Deceitfully used, language can also become a stumbling block, designed to cloak, even obscure. Politicians who make mutually exclusive promises to different constituencies regularly employ such stumbling blocks. Enron and World Com execs resorted to them, as did the folks running Phillip Morris and Lorillard! Now, let's add pharmaceutical maker Bayer, "some of [whose] senior executives knew its anti-cholesterol drug 'Baycol' was causing illness and death long before Bayer pulled it off the market."

"Verbal veiling" is commonplace:

- Saying whatever's necessary to whomever's listening to get elected
- Knowing of financial misconduct, yet hiding it
- Being cognizant of real dangers to health and life, yet not disclosing
- Misrepresenting a product so as to falsely enhance its value in the marketplace

These are very real stumbling blocks, one and all.

Torah wouldn't bother to prohibit stumbling blocks if human beings did not so readily resort to them! Torah warns: You mustn't exploit people's naivete. You who use stumbling blocks to blindside the gullible will learn—to your chagrin—that God (who sees all—always!) will be a stumbling block to you! "You [had better!] fear your God."

Acharei Mot / K'doshim
Kenneth J. Weiss, 2004

I wonder: what if **every** mitzvah in the Holiness Code were phrased in the affirmative?

Leviticus 19:4 (rather than reading "Do not turn to idols or make molten gods") could be rendered, "I (alone!) am your God!" Leviticus 19:9–10 might instruct, "Leave the edges of your fields and that which falls of your vineyard for the poor and the stranger." What if 19:11 read, "You shall respect others' property; you shall deal forthrightly and honestly with one another"?

Leviticus 19:13b might say, "You shall pay a laborer his wages at the end of each day"; 19:15 would teach, "You shall render only fair and just decisions"; 19:17–18 could be reduced to the authoritative "Love your neighbor as yourself"; 19:35 would be subsumed into verse 36: "God expects an honest balance, honest weights."

God's message here is: (try your best to) emulate Me; "be holy, for I, the LORD your God, am holy" (Lev. 19:2).

Negative phrasing, I believe, diminishes the impact of the Holiness Code's ultimately positive message! Surely, the "Holiness Code" should teach us more about how to live holy lives and less about what "unholy" practices to avoid?

Acharei Mot / K'doshim: Shabbat HaGadol
Kenneth J. Weiss, 2005

"You shall keep My laws . . . My rules . . . My charge" (Lev. 18:5, 18:30).

Although our ancestors left Egypt, God was concerned that they hadn't really left Egypt behind . . . would they one day wish to "return"?

So, at the beginning of פרשת בשלח (*Parashat B'shalach*), we read that God led "the people roundabout" lest they "have a change of heart . . . and return to Egypt" (Exod. 13:17–18). Paraphrasing God's concern: Yes, you've walked out of Egypt, but have you sufficiently distanced yourselves from her corrupting influence? You need to turn away from your slave past and toward Me—My values, My mitzvot, for they are your future!

In Leviticus 18 we read of the sex offenses that (though common in Egypt) the Israelites were commanded to reject. Using these as an example, Moses—speaking God's words—says, ושמרתם (*Ush'martem*),

"You shall watch" yourselves, so as "not to engage in any of the abhorrent practices" that you witnessed; "you shall not defile yourselves through them" (Lev. 18:30).

The message: every Pesach, retell and relive your deliverance from Egypt. God charges you each Passover: ושמרתם (Ush'martem), "You shall watch" (and keep!) God's laws and rules (Lev. 18:5); live by, teach, and transmit Torah. ושמרתם (Ush'martem), "You shall watch" (and keep!) your distance from Egypt and her ways: leave everything Egyptian behind you!

Acharei Mot / K'doshim
Kenneth J. Weiss, 2005

קדושים תהיו (K'doshim tih'yu), "You shall be holy" (Lev. 19:2).

Each individual Jew can—is expected to—live by Torah's laws, edicts, and rules. Note that the Ten Commandments and the משפטים (mishpatim, "rules") that follow (Exodus 19–24) are (virtually all) addressed to individuals—every Jew is commanded to live by these regulations and is responsible for doing so.

But, it is the community of Jews—the collective Jewish people—who are told to be holy; to imitate God by becoming קדושים (k'doshim), "holy."

Only when individuals live up to the best that Judaism teaches—only if all of us strive together—can we as a people aspire to (let alone achieve) holiness. Presumably, if any single "miscreant"—any one among us—does not live by God's commandments, all of us are held back from the ideal of "communal holiness."

On the other hand, consider what we as a people can do—have at times done—when we unite, reinforce one another, reach jointly to achieve a holy purpose. Israel is—at its best—individual Jews striving together for a common (yes holy!) goal: consider campaigns including (but not limited to) Operation Magic Carpet and Operation Solomon, efforts that saved endangered Jewish populations.

The S'fat Emet reaffirms Rashi: "Only in full assembly can we be holy." Thus, we read קדושים תהיו (K'doshim tih'yu): "(All of) you shall be holy." Talmud teaches, "All Jews are responsible for one another."

Rabbi Mayer Twersky deepens the lesson by rendering this phrase, "All Jews are bound up with one another."

That's where holiness can be achieved . . . found . . . lived.

Acharei Mot / K'doshim
Alan Cook, 2006

"The stranger who resides with you shall be to you as one of your citizens; you shall love him as yourself, for you were strangers in the land of Egypt: I the LORD am your God" (Lev. 19:34).

The concept of the גר (*ger*, "stranger") is significant to the Jewish experience. Many times in the Torah we are reminded of our past as גרים (*gerim*) and urged not to mistreat the גר (*ger*) in our own midst. This teaching is a key component of the "Holiness Code" found in קדושים (*K'doshim*). But do we ever consider how we play the part of the stranger in our encounters with others?

We become strangers when our public identity is different from our private one—when we act differently toward our congregants than we do toward our friends and family. Our congregants become strangers when they do not take the time to play an active part in the worship, programming, and educational opportunities that our Jewish institutions offer. And all Jews risk becoming strangers when they fail to heed לא תעמד על-דם רעך (*Lo taamod al dam rei-echa*, "Do not profit by the blood of your fellow" [Lev. 19:16]) and turn a blind eye to the suffering of others.

Being a גר (*ger*) is not an easy way to shirk one's responsibility to the community. In fact, the גר (*ger*) is expected to fulfill many of the mitzvot that are incumbent upon a native-born member of the Israelite community: keeping Shabbat, refraining from eating leavened foods during Passover, and so forth. We are repeatedly told, "There shall be one law for citizen and stranger."

So let us cease to be strangers and remove the masks that distance us from one another. Then can we rightly aspire to holiness.

Acharei Mot / K'doshim
Amy Scheinerman, 2007

We read אחרי מות-קדושים (*Acharei Mot / K'doshim*) during *S'firat Ha-Omer* (the counting of the Omer), the period that marks our ancestors' ascendance from the tarpits of Egypt to the heights of Sinai, from little connection with God, to the momentous revelation and commitment to God's covenant. How did they accomplish this in only forty-nine days? Tradition holds that the forty-nine days of the Omer should be spent in pursuit of character improvement to cultivate in ourselves the מידות (*midot*, "virtues") needed to fully live the values of Torah. As R. Akiva taught: דרך ארץ קדמה לתורה (*derech eretz kadmah laTorah*, "upstanding behavior takes precedent over the Torah").

Akiva also taught that "You shall love your neighbor as yourself" (Lev. 19:18) is a great principle of Torah. Hillel taught that the essence lies in avoiding treating people hatefully and that our own sensitivities can tell us where that subjective boundary lies. Our Torah portion is more prescriptive: Lev. 19:9 requires us to reserve a portion of our produce (and by extension income) for those in need. It's a matter of both what we do and what we refrain from doing.

Leviticus 19:18 explicitly seeks to instill a sense of peoplehood among Israel: "You shall not take revenge and you shall not bear a grudge against the members of your people; you shall love your neighbor as yourself." In Lev. 19:9 the mitzvah of פאה (*pei-ah*, "corner of the field") commands a wider concern: all those in need. This week we commemorate Yom HaZikaron and celebrate Yom HaAtzama-ut, strengthening our ties with our people in Israel and around the world. Our Torah portion reminds us to balance that with a concern for all those in need.

Acharei Mot / K'doshim
Amy Scheinerman, 2008

Leviticus 17:3 tells us that sheep or goats slaughtered either within or outside the camp must be brought to the entrance of the אהל מועד

(*Ohel Mo-eid*, "Tent of Meeting") and offered as a קרבן (*korban*, "sacrifice") before God. The penalty for violation is כרת (*kareit*, "being cut off"). For some scholars this is understood to preclude eating meat unless the animal is a prescribed sacrifice. Minimally, it suggests that the slaughter of an animal should never be a casual act.

We know that God's initial dietary blueprint for humanity (Gen. 1:29) prescribed a vegetarian diet, as affirmed by Rashi, Ibn Ezra, Rambam, Nachmanides, and Joseph Albo, among others. Deuteronomy 12:20 tells us כי־תאוה נפשך לאכל בשר (*ki t'aveh nafsh'cha le-echol basar*, "because you have the urge to eat meat"), eating meat is permitted. This has come to be known as בשר תאוה (*b'sar taavah*), "lust meat," permitted due to craving, though the Babylonian Talmud, *Chulin* 84a, adjures us to partake sparingly. Between Genesis and Deuteronomy may be a stage reflected in Lev. 17:3 in which consumption of meat was permitted only if it was a sacrifice.

Our Sages taught us to concern ourselves with צער בעלי חיים (*tzaar baalei chayim*, kindness to animals), and today that issue looms larger than ever, as we cannot ignore factory farms imposing cramped confined spaces on animals and often imposing drugs and mutilation before they are painfully slaughtered. In addition, the principle of בל תשחית (*bal tashchit*, "do not destroy") requires us to consider the exhorbitant use of land, grain, water, and energy in animal agriculture.

The efforts of the eco-kashrut movement, which considers sustainable agriculture and organic farming practices, and the הכשר צדק (Hekhsher Tzedek) certification of the Conservative Movement, which incorporates social justice concerns into dietary concerns, are worth our attention.

Acharei Mot / K'doshim
Amy Scheinerman, 2008

We still struggle to understand what ואהבת לרעך כמוך (*v'ahavta l'rei-acha kamocha*, "love your fellow as yourself" [Lev. 19:18]) means. Perhaps the differing approaches of R. Akiva and Ben Azai are instructive. Akiva taught זה כלל גדול בתורה (*zeh klal gadol b'Torah*), this is the great organizing or motivating principle of Torah. But Ben

Azai held with Gen. 5:1, that God creating humanity in the divine likeness is the foundation of Torah. Do we see ourselves reflected in the visages of others, as Akiva taught? Or do we see God's countenance reflected in the faces of our neighbors, as Ben Azai taught?

We might worry that R. Akiva's teaching promotes narcissism because it suggests that we are the center and arbiter of reality. Yet perhaps Akiva meant to convey that we are merely the center of our own experience and from that can understand and appreciate the experiences of others; in other words, it is not enlightened self-interest, but rather compassion that paves the road to קדושה (*k'dushah*, "holiness"). Ben Azai's approach might be seen as excessively abstract, yet it conveys an ideal that reminds us that all behavior should be aimed at קדושה (*k'dushah*).

In 1621, Robert Burton wrote in *The Anatomy of Melancholy*, considered by some the first major work in Western cognitive science, "Conquer thyself. Till thou hast done this, thou art but slave for it is almost as well to be subjected to another's appetite as to thine own." Burton's insight bridges the teachings of Akiva and Ben Azai and makes clear that self-governance is the key to reflecting the divine image and viewing others with compassion.

Acharei Mot / K'doshim
Janice Garfunkel, 2009

When I was a child, a woman came to our house to help with the cleaning once a week. My mother once instructed me to put my wallet in a drawer before she came (it had been sitting on top of my dresser) because the Torah tells us not to "put a stumbling block before the blind" (Lev. 19:14). That means, explained my mom, that we do not tempt people to do the wrong thing; we do not set them up to fail.

It was an interesting lesson. On the one hand, I am responsible for my own behavior, not the behavior of others. On the other hand, of course, what I do affects others, and I can choose to strew stumbling blocks wherever I go, or I can try to be more careful about the temptations I might throw down in the paths of others.

As rabbis, we have plenty of opportunity to put down, or pick up, stumbling blocks. It is so easy to say the wrong thing, inadvertently insult someone, and out the door they go, never to return. Ultimately, we cannot take responsibility for the decisions others make.

But we can try to notice the stumbling blocks we or our communities are putting in the paths of others. Is it hard for someone without children to feel comfortable at our Purim service? Can Jews without a college degree or much money find a place in our community? Can someone coming to our building for the first time even figure out by which door they are supposed to enter?

אמר *Emor*

(Leviticus 21:1–24:23)

For additional commentary on *Emor*, see "Sukkot," "Chol HaMo-eid Sukkot," and "Pesach."

Emor
Lawrence S. Kushner, 1996

(Lev. 21:1–8) These special restrictions on the *kohanim* (priests) inhibit their descendants to this day—except in the Reform Movement. We barely recognize *kohanim*, let alone impose the Torah's restrictions on them. This was done in the nineteenth century in the name of equality, but nowadays with the emphasis on Jews deepening their identities, does it still make sense to encourage people of *kohein* families to ignore their distinctiveness? Why should we encourage Jewish women to explore their uniqueness as Jews, but not *kohanim*?

(Lev. 21:16–23) This section usually disturbs us—why should *kohanim* with physical disfigurements be prohibited from assisting others in making their offerings? They are permitted to remain in the Tabernacle courts and eat the food reserved for the priests, so that Israelites bringing their offerings could see them. Are they to learn that disfigured human beings are also created in the image of God—does God have disabilities, too? If Moses was a stutterer, is God?

Emor
Lawrence S. Kushner, 1997

This portion returns us to the conduct of the *kohanim* (priests). The Reform Movement eliminated priestly distinctions for its members over a century ago, though this portion shows another side of their distinctiveness—the extra restrictions placed on them regarding marriage and attendance upon the dead. How do we view members of priestly families today who *wish* to take these restrictions on themselves, who wish to be called to the Torah, not necessarily first but at least by their title *hakohein* (or *bat kohein*)?

The most troubling parts of this *parashah* are the restrictions on *kohanim* who have a physical disfigurement (Lev. 21:16–23). If we believe that we should not reject mitzvot out of hand, but should respond even to those we feel contradict the equality advocated by other mitzvot (though "equality" may be inappropriate in referring to the *kohanim*), what would we say to God about these restrictions on disfigured *kohanim*?

Leviticus 22:7 is a verse that shapes the opening chapter of *Masechet B'rachot* in the Mishnah, and in a way the Mishnah (and hence, the Talmud) itself. The time when sunset allows *kohanim* who are temporarily *tamei* (impure) to eat of their *t'rumah* (offering) introduces the Mishnah's treatment of the *Sh'ma*, and prayer in general. What might Y'hudah HaNasi have seen in this verse, tying human actions to the rhythms of the natural world that caused him to give it such prominence?

Emor: Kiddush HaShem
Stephen E. Cohen, 1998

"You shall not profane My holy name, but I shall be sanctified among the Children of Israel" (Lev. 22:32). The tradition understands this verse as containing the commandment, in both negative and positive forms, to offer ourselves under certain circumstances to martyrdom.

Maharal of Prague The human being has three components: intellect, soul, and body. And in them occur, respectively, the three fundamental sins of *avodah zarah* [idolatry], murder, and *gilui arayot* [sexual sin]. For this reason, these three sins are always grouped together, and about them the Sages said, "Be killed rather than transgress them" (Babylonian Talmud, *Sanhedrin* 74a). This is because each of these three sins destroys one of the essential components of a person. Therefore if a person seeks to save himself by committing one of them, behold, he destroys himself by the transgression . . . and so accomplishes nothing.

Comment   Would a person faced with the choice of martyrdom go through the "cost-benefit analysis" proposed by the Maharal?

Emor: The Blasphemer
Stephen E. Cohen, 1999

Here occurs one of the **few** narrative passages in Leviticus: the episode of the blasphemer (Lev. 24:10–23). Rashi transmits three Rabbinic explications of the opening verb of the passage, *vayeitzei*. Each offers a different perspective on the "going out" that leads to this man's sin and ultimately to his death by stoning.

Rashi   Whence did he go out? Rabbi Levi says: He went out from this world. Rabbi Berechyah says: He departed from the preceding passage. He mocked, saying: "The *kohein* will arrange the shewbread each Shabbat . . . but a king eats a hot meal every day. This cold nine-day-old bread? I wonder!" And one tannaitic source says: He emerged from Moses's court, defeated. He had gone to set up his tent within the camp of Dan, and they said to him, "By what right are you here?" He replied, "I am of the sons of Dan." They said to him, "Every man by his banner, according to the sign of the house of their **fathers** [Num. 2:2]." [Note: this man's mother was Israelite, but his father was Egyptian.] He went to Moses's court and emerged, defeated. Then he stood and blasphemed.

Comment   What motivates the individual who mocks the sacred text? Compare R. Berechyah's sarcast with the blasphemer in Rashi's third source, who was personally defeated by the Israelite judicial system.

Emor: Building the Temple
Stephen E. Cohen, 2000

Rashi invokes the image of the Festival cycle as a "Temple in time" in order to address the surprising insertion of the mitzvot of *pei-ah* and *leket* in the middle of the Festivals in this week's portion. Maharal then picks up Rashi's theme and weaves it with a clever anti-reading of Prov. 19:17. The total effect is a beautiful and inspiring meditation on the mitzvot of feeding the poor.

Rashi on Leviticus 23:22 Why did the Scripture choose to locate this mitzvah in the middle of the Festivals, with Pesach and Shavuot on one side and Rosh HaShanah, Yom Kippur, and Sukkot on the other? To teach you that anyone who gives *leket*, *shich'chah*, and *pei-ah* to the poor in the proper way, they are considered to have rebuilt the Temple and to have offered their sacrifices within it.

Maharal Rashi does not categorize these contributions as "charity," which, although the Torah does urge it upon us, ultimately one gives it because of feeling sorry and taking pity on the poor person. But these contributions [i.e., *pie-ah*, *shich'cha*, and *leket*] that Scripture requires and commands us to give, without a doubt they are of greater importance. As the Sages said, "Greater is one who is commanded and performs, than one who is not commanded, and performs" (Babylonian Talmud, *Kiddushin* 31a). And, as it is written, "one who has compassion on the poor makes a loan to God" (Prov. 19:17). That is, one who gives out of compassion, and not out of obligation, this is one who "makes a loan," and this is not the same as giving outright. But one who gives to the poor out of obligation has given completely to God. And this is what is compared to offering a sacrifice in the Temple.

Comment Do you distinguish in your own giving between "obligatory" giving and "compassionate" giving? Is this a useful distinction, and if so, would you agree with Maharal that "obligatory" giving is somehow more "complete"?

Emor
Sheldon Marder 2001

What is the purpose of religious activity?

Bayom hash'mini mikra kodesh yih'yeh lachem (Lev. 23:36]): Is the day of assembly "for you" (*lachem*)—that is, a day devoted to human concerns? Or is it a day of devotion to God—*atzeret l'Adonai*, as Deut. 16:8 describes it? Y'hudah HaNasi takes a close look at these two verses:

> "On the seventh day [of Passover] you shall hold a day of assembly for *Adonai* your God" [Deut. 16:8]. Rabbi says: Could it be that a person should be restricted to the house of study the whole day? Scripture teaches [elsewhere, concerning the "day of assembly"— *atzeret*], "for you" [Lev. 23:36; Num. 29:35]. Could it be that a person should eat and drink the whole day? Scripture teaches, "a day of assembly for *Adonai* your God." How is it possible [to reconcile these two texts]? Devote part [of the day] to the house of study and part to eating and drinking. (*Sifrei* to Deuteronomy 135)

For many modern Jews, the purpose of religious activity is self-actualization; others take the more traditional view of religion that its purpose is devotion to God. Y'hudah HaNasi teaches us not to reduce our religious lives to a choice between *lachem* and *l'Adonai*, between self-satisfaction and selfless devotion—but to embrace both.

Emor
Kenneth J. Weiss, 2002

"*Ach*, the tenth day" (Lev. 23:27); "*Ach*, on the fifteenth day" (Lev. 23:39).

Some forty times in Torah—and dozens more times throughout *Tanach*—the word *ach* (or *ak*) occurs in the text. In *Parashat Emor*, this word introduces Yom Kippur (Lev. 23:27) and Sukkot (23:39). Elsewhere in *Vayikra*, the word is followed by important points relating to kashrut (11:4), clean water (11:36), priestly conduct (21:23), consecrating "a firstling of animals" (27:26), and—lastly—a prohibition against selling or redeeming possessions "proscribed for the Lord" (27:28).

If the schools of Torah writers had had modern computer tools available to them (bolding, underlining, other methods to suggest emphasis and special focus), perhaps the word *ach* would not have been necessary. In the context of Holy Scripture, *ach* appears to convey a significant message to the reader: OK wake up, refocus now. Though we all agree that every word of Scripture is of infinite value, what follows is the salient, crucial, central, irreducible point in this entire discussion/section/context. Note it well. Remember it always.

Emor
Kenneth J. Weiss, 2003

"You shall not profane My holy name" (Lev. 22:32).

Parashat K'doshim defines righteous living from a Torah perspective: "You shall be holy, for I, the Lord your God, am holy" (Lev. 19:2). When we live a holy life we sanctify God's name (*kiddush HaShem*), thus enhancing "the dignity and honor of Judaism" (Plaut, p. 892).

In *Parashat Emor*, God reinforces the message: profaning God's name is a "behavior that brings public disgrace on Jews and Judaism" (Plaut, ibid.)—in Hebrew, *chilul HaShem*.

As this *parashah* ends, Torah dramatizes the difference between sanctifying and profaning God's name. Here we find the famous (and famously misunderstood) concept called *lex talionis*: "If anyone maims his fellow, as he has done so shall it be done to him" (Lev. 24:19)

Jewish tradition understands that to literally exact an eye for an eye or a limb for a limb would constitute mere brute retaliation: a form of *chilul HaShem*. *Kiddush HaShem* demands a higher—an ethical, a "godly"—response, entailing both an appreciation for the severity of maiming another person and suitable monetary compensation.

The message: your victim—no less than you—was created in God's image, after God's likeness. So, you will appropriately compensate your victim. God commands—and Jewish values demand—no less.

Emor
Kenneth J. Weiss, 2004

"On six days work may be done" (Lev. 23:3).

God instructs Moses to tell the people, "You shall proclaim . . . sacred occasions" (Lev. 23:2b).

Yet . . . the very next sentence mentions the six days of work and Shabbat. Hmm!

The Gaon of Vilna stretches to justify this apparent non sequitur: the "six days," he writes, refers not to the workweek, but to the six Festivals of the Jewish year during which work required in conjunction with each Festival (i.e., food preparation) may be done. Could be . . .

But why not accept this verse within its literal context: among God's "fixed times" ("sacred occasions") **are** the six days of work each week, followed by "a Sabbath of the Lord" on which we are to "do no work." Judaism teaches that in the messianic age, all days will be Sabbaths—days of rest, renewal, worship, family. In our real world, however—utterly pre-messianic as it is—workdays, too, can be deemed "sacred."

It is a mitzvah to keep consecrated days. It is no less a mitzvah to support one's family, to be productive. God fixes times for celebration **and** for work: "sacred occasions" one and all.

Emor
Kenneth J. Weiss, 2005

Each individual Jew is responsible for constructing her/his life by the mitzvot. Among these mitzvot (as detailed in *Sidrah K'doshim*) are revering your parents, keeping Shabbat, sharing your bounty with the poor, respecting the property and personhood of others, acting morally in all matters . . .

To the degree that we so live our lives, we contribute to the holiness of the community: collectively, we can "be holy, as I, יהוה אלהיכם [*Adonai Eloheichem*, '*Adonai* your God'], am holy" (Lev. 19:2).

Now, in *Parashat Emor*, we find the "seal"—the liturgical affirmation—of holiness as it was understood and practiced in Torah days. Here, יהוה (*Adonai*)—through Moses—addresses the community (in the plural): "You shall faithfully observe My commandments.... You shall not profane My holy name, that I may be sanctified in the midst of the Israelite people" (Lev. 22:31–32).

Torah speaks to each Jew (thus to all Jews):

- You have a responsibility—live by the mitzvot. To do less is to profane God's name.
- By precept and example, inspire your fellow Jews to live as you live. Together, you will sanctify God's name . . . in deed . . .
- . . . but also (symbolically) in word: so, pray the קדושה (*K'dushah*) only when a minyan is present (Babylonian Talmud, *B'rachot* 21b). For, Torah teaches that God will "be sanctified in the midst of the Israelite people." Individuals can perform acts of קדושה (*k'dushah*, "holiness"). Only a community can aspire to and affirm a state of קדושה (*k'dushah*).

And when do we join together for communal worship (complete with קדושה [*K'dushah*])? Glad you asked! Refer, please, to the Festival calendar (for such gatherings) immediately following: "These are My fixed times, the fixed times of יהוה [*Adonai*]" (Lev. 23:2ff.).

In sum, as an individual, live rightly; as a community, strive toward and affirm the holiness of the One whose holiness we all emulate.

Emor
Alan Cook, 2006

Throughout the Torah, we are reminded of our indebtedness to God because God chose us and freed us from Egyptian bondage. The concept is mentioned twice in פרשת אמר (*Parashat Emor*).

As the wicked child of the Passover הגדה (Haggadah) might say, "So what?" We were slaves once, but now we're not. Why not celebrate our freedom and get on with things?

The *Zohar* provides a story to explain. Rabbi Yosei asked his teacher Rabbi Shimon bar Yochai about the constant repetition of this trope. He asked why God felt it necessary to continually remind the Israelites about the circumstances regarding their freedom, particularly when God had gone so far as to tell Abraham before the fact that this was part of the divine plan for the world. Rabbi Shimon replied that God's promise referred only to freeing the Israelites from their physical subjugation. It would take much more time for them to overcome their spiritual subjugation.

Spiritual freedom could come only with God's gentle instruction. The establishment of Festivals—the ritual calendar outlined in אמר (*Emor*)—gave them fixed times at which to show their gratitude. And if these celebrations served to remind them of both their physical and spiritual emancipation, so much the better! Ultimately, religious freedom can be fully appreciated only if political freedom has also been granted; only a person who is truly free has it in his power to mark a regular day of rest.

Emor
Amy Scheinerman, 2007

The portion opens with a delineation of the rules of the priesthood, including prohibitions against contact with the dead, and restrictions concerning whom *kohanim* (priests) may marry. Leviticus 21:16–24 articulates the disturbing rule that a *kohein* with a *mum* (defect) may not officiate at a sacrifice, but may benefit from the emoluments.

We might understand banning profligate priests, but barring physically impaired *kohanim* from officiating offends our moral sensibilities. Torah offers no explanation. This passage raises many questions: Is human imperfection offensive to God? Is a *kohein*'s physical perfection in some way a reflection of God's perfection?

Equally disturbing is the seeming equation between people and animals suggested by Lev. 22:21–22, where we read that the animal offerings are subject to restrictions similar to those of the *kohanim*; many of the same physical imperfections are listed.

Rashi on Lev. 22:17 quotes Malachi (1:8), who suggests God would be offended by an imperfect offering. Yet Malachi speaks of the officiant, not the offering. Is Rashi suggesting that the officiant is part of the offering and the two cannot be separated? Understood metaphorically, this would suggest that our intent and attitude matter when we seek to fulfill mitzvot.

The Rabbis equivocate on the matter of intent, at times claiming intent is crucial to the fulfillment of a mitzvah, other times arguing that the act alone suffices. Perhaps Rashi is suggesting that we should aim to bring our whole selves to acts of service to God.

Emor
Amy Scheinerman, 2008

Leviticus 23:10–21 describes the wave offering of sheaves of barley in the spring. The priests would elevate them on מחרת השבת (*machorat hashabbat*, "the day after shabbat"). This passage is the source of the tradition of ספירת העמר (*S'firat HaOmer*, "counting of the Omer"). Hence it is important to understand precisely what מחרת השבת (*machorat hashabbat*) connotes, since the initiation of the counting determines what day Shavuot begins.

The Babylonian Talmud, *M'nachot* 65–66, records two disagreements between the Sages and the Boethusians, a Second Temple group of ten identified with the Sadducees.

The first disagreement concerns מחרת השבת (*machorat hashabbat*). While the Sages understood שבת (*shabbat*) to refer to the first day of Pesach on which labor was forbidden, the Boethusians claimed שבת (*shabbat*) should be understood literally as the שבת (Shabbat) during Pesach. According to the Sages' understanding, Shavuot falls fifty days after Pesach begins, on whatever day of the week that might be. According to the Boethusians' interpretation, Shavuot always falls conveniently on Sunday.

The second disagreement concerns the purchasing of the daily תמיד (*tamid*). The Sages held that because the תמיד (*tamid*) belongs to everyone, it is purchased with public funds. The Boethusians held that individuals may donate the תמיד (*tamid*) offering on behalf of the nation.

These differences reflect differing conceptions of nationhood. For the Boethusians, Israel is a collective of individuals, a nation like other nations. The calendar could be arranged for convenience, and wealthy individuals could save the treasury money by offering sacrifices made on behalf of everyone. For the Sages, however, Israel is a גוי קדוש (*goy kadosh*), a holy entity with sacred responsibilities that can only be met when the people acts in concert as one organism in response to God's command. We see echoes of these disagreements today in conflicts between personal spirituality and communal religiosity.

Emor
Amy Scheinerman, 2009

"*Adonai* spoke to Moses saying: Command the Israelite people to bring you clear oil [*shemen zach*] of beaten olives for lighting, for kindling lamps regularly. Aaron shall set them up in the Tent of Meeting outside the curtain of testimony to burn from evening to morning before *Adonai* regularly; it is a law for all time throughout the ages. He shall set up the lamps on the pure lampstand before *Adonai* to burn regularly [*tamid*]" (Lev. 24:1–4).

In *Vayikra Rabbah* 31:4, Ben Kapara expounds: "For You light my lamp" (Ps. 18:29). Thus God says to humankind, "Your lamp is in My hand, and shall My lamp be in your hand?" That "your lamp is in My hand" we know from "The human spirit is *Adonai*'s lamp" (Prov. 20:27). "My lamp in your hand" we know from "To cause a lamp to burn continually" (Lev. 24:2f.). The inference is that God says, "If you light My lamp, I shall light yours."

Ben Kapara speaks about the divine-human relationship as mutuality and reciprocity. God sustains our souls, and we sustain God through Torah. Ben Kaparah is attuned to God within (our souls) and God without (Torah).

Two fundamental instructions pertaining to the *ner tamid* (eternal light): to bring the best oil possible (*shemen zach*) and to kindle the lights regularly (*tamid*) so that the lampstand will be lit at all times. The first reminds us to operate from the best we have—the spark of the Divine within us. The second reminds us that doing so requires persistence and vigilance; for the *ner tamid* to remain lit, the lampstand must be cleaned, refilled, and relit daily. Excellent reminders for us to be *nerot Adonai*.

בהר-בחקתי B'har/B'chukotai

(Leviticus 25:1–26:2 and Leviticus 26:3–27:34)

B'har/B'chukotai
Lawrence S. Kushner, 1996

(Lev. 25:23) If "the land is Mine," and we are but settlers, what is the meaning of the eighth commandment, "Thou shalt not steal"? If human beings do not own anything, why should stealing from other humans be so serious a crime?

The element of rest associated with the cycle of seven (here seven times seven) connects a "ritual" observance, the *Yoveil* (Jubilee), with social justice, assistance to the poor. What is the connection of the redemption of the land to the redemption of impoverished human beings? Is there an echo of the creation of *adam* (man) from the *adamah* (earth)? Or does it suggest the special connection between the Israelite and the Land of Israel?

The beginning of *B'chukotai* reminds us of the second paragraph of the *Sh'ma*, Deut. 11:13–21, which the Reform Movement long ago excised from the prayer book, seemingly because it suggests that human misdeeds (*aveirot*) affect the course of nature. Doesn't a spiritual approach to the world require that sense of connection between our acts and the physical world? Or are the early verses in this *parashah* merely a subjective statement of how the world feels when we do wrong?

B'har/B'chukotai
Lawrence S. Kushner, 1997

Some of the most powerful statements about the poor (Lev. 25:25–28, 25:35–43) are found interwoven with the laws of redemption of property in the Jubilee year. Why should assistance to the poor be tied to redemption of the land? Is the obligation to assist the poor lessened—or increased—outside of *Eretz Yisrael*, where land redemption does not apply?

The Rabbis probably appended Lev. 26:1–2 to this *parashah* so that the next portion could begin with the topic words *Im b'chukotai* ("If . . . My laws"). By appending this coda about idolatry, Shabbat, and reverence for the *Mikdash*, what dimension do they add to the topic of the Jubilee and the treatment of servants and the poor?

Having compared prophetic admonitions to verses from the Torah in *K'doshim*, we would be remiss not to do so here (Lev. 26:30–39), where the prophecies of exile as punishment for disobedience to the mitzvot are first enunciated, as well as the prophecies of return (Lev. 26:40–45). If God has already announced this fate for Israel, why did God need the prophets?

B'har/B'chukotai: Streching Forth the Hand
Stephen E. Cohen, 1998

The Eitz Yosef supercommentary to *Vayikrah Rabbah* transmits a lovely teaching about *tzedakah*, which reads the word *v'hayah* in Isa. 32:17 as a pictogram.

Vayikra Rabbah 34:13 More than the wealthy one does for the poor, the poor one does for the wealthy.

Eitz Yosef This relates to a teaching on *V'hayah maaseih hatzedakah shalom*, "For the work of the righteous shall be peace" (Isa. 32:17). In the word *v'hayah* the outstretched arm of the giver of *tzedakah* is the *vav*. The hand of the giver is the *hei*. The coin being given to the poor is the *yod*. And the final *hei* is the hand of the poor. This is why the significance of the act for the giver is greater than what the giver does for the poor. But this is **only** true when the giver bestirs himself, of his own goodwill, stretching forth his hand to the poor. In **this** case, the *vav* is his arm, and his arm and hand and coin together compose the greater part of the Tetragrammaton. If, however, he does not give until the poor person stretches out his hand and begs from him, then his act is reduced to only two letters of the Name.

Comment Maimonides' famous eight rungs of *tzedakah* also teaches the superiority of giving willingly, before being asked. Does the Eitz Yosef teaching add substantively to Maimonides' doctrine, or does it simply provide poetic color?

B'har/B'chukotai: The Power in the Mouth
Stephen E. Cohen, 1999

Midrash Vayikra Rabbah argues that the prohibition against "oppression" in business specifically means oppression with words and offers two striking poetic images to convey the creative/destructive power of speech. The S'fat Emet "spiritualizes" one of the images of the midrash.

Vayikra Rabbah 33:1 "If you sell to your kinsman or buy from your kinsman, do not oppress one another" (Lev. 25:14). As it is written, "Death and life are in the power of the tongue" (Prov. 18:21). Aquila translates this verse using the image of a spoon-knife, death at one end and life at the other. Ben Sira said: A glowing coal is before him. He blows upon it and it burns; he spits upon it and it goes out.

S'fat Emet The vitality of the Blessed Name is in everything in the world, for the Holy One created the world with Torah, and the Torah is called "Fire." And so the power of Torah is in everything, but it is concealed within the "coal." And we must search for and find the light of Torah that is in everything. And this depends upon the "tongue," that is, the life force of a person, which is their *ruach*. Through a person's *ruach*, the vitality that is in everything is awakened and revealed. This is "he blows upon it." Conversely, materialism is referred to in the midrash by "he spits upon it"—for without *ruach*, the mouth simply extinguishes the innerness [*p'nimiyut*] of a thing.

Comment S'fat Emet's reworking of the image of the "glowing coal" is ingenious, but hasn't he removed (or at least watered down) the potent ethical message of both the Torah verse and the midrashic commentary?

B'har/B'chukotai: War of Words
Stephen E. Cohen, 2000

The midrash on *al tonu*, "do not oppress" (Lev. 25:14), moves far afield from the narrow concern of the original Torah text, which deals exclusively with buying and selling land. The Sages understand *al tonu* as prohibiting verbal abuse in general. In this excerpt from *Vayikra Rabbah*, they select Abijah's impassioned public accusation of Jeroboam, in II Chronicles, as a paradigm of verbal aggression.

Vayikra Rabbah **33:5** R. Sh'muel bar Nachmani said: You have stated that Jeroboam was afflicted, but actually it was Abijah who was afflicted. And why was he afflicted? R. Yochanan and Resh Lakish and the Sages each held an opinion. R. Yochanan said: Because he jeered at them in public, as it is written, "You are a great mob, and you have golden calves with you, which Jeroboam made as gods for you!" (II Chron. 13:8). Resh Lakish said: Because he insulted Ahijah the Shiloni and called him "worthless," as it is written, "Empty, worthless men have gathered around [Jeroboam]" (II Chron. 13:7). And the Sages said: Because idolatry came under his control and he did not burn it out, as it is written, "Abijah pursued Jeroboam and captured cities from him—Beit El . . ." (II Chron. 13:19), and it is written that Jeroboam had set up one of the golden calves in Beit El. And behold, these things are *kal vachomer* if a king who insults another king, like himself, is punished by the text, then an ordinary person who insults his fellow, how much the more so? Therefore did Moses warn Israel, "When you sell to your neighbor, or buy from your neighbor, do not oppress him" (Lev. 25:14).

Comment The three opinions transmitted in the midrash reflect dissension among the Rabbis as to who was to blame for the civil war between Jeroboam and Rehoboam. Compare and contrast them.

B'har/B'chukotai: The Right Reward
Stephen E. Cohen, 2000

The rabbis of the Middle Ages puzzled over the blatantly material rewards and punishments promised in this portion. K'li Yakar, in his commentary, presents a survey of the great explanations for why the Torah speaks of material rewards rather than the theologically more meaningful spiritual reward of *olam haba* (the world-to-come). The following, one of the approaches selected and summarized by K'li Yakar, seems uncannily attuned to our modern times.

Rabbeinu Nissim and the Kuzari, according to K'li Yakar   In those days, all the world denied divine providence and believed that all events occurred by necessity, rather than by God's will. So the Holy One sought to bolster the "corner of providence" with these benefits, which could be seen by everyone—that everyone who did God's will was safeguarded, in all these ways. For if He had promised them spiritual rewards, the people would have remained in their repudiation. For one who seeks to lie will find a way.

Comment   In general, do you think that you, your friends, and your congregants are motivated to perform mitzvot more by some version of the material rewards promised by *B'chukotai* or by a spiritual reward?

B'har/B'chukotai
Sheldon Marder, 2001

"If you follow My laws" (Lev. 26:3). What is the meaning of Jewish observance?

The verses that come next in the *parashah* (Lev. 26:4–13) focus on the tangible "here and now" rewards of observance of the law. But commentators, responding to the concerns of their own day, shift the focus. For instance, *Minchah B'lulah*, cited in *Iturei Torah* (vol. 4, p. 154), sees in this text a link between observance of mitzvot and all of Israel's past and future redemptions. How so? The word *im* alludes to Egypt because it is an acronym for Aaron and Moses; as an acronym for Esther and Mordechai, it alludes to Persia; and, likewise, *im* alludes to Elijah and the Messiah. Thus, the little word *im* teaches that Israel's redemption is always achieved by human beings who walk the path of the mitzvot.

The modern Jew's "primary difficulty," wrote Heschel, "is not in his inability to comprehend the divine origin of the law; his essential difficulty is in his inability to sense the presence of divine meaning in the fulfillment of the law" ("Toward an Understanding of Halachah," *CCAR Yearbook*, 1953).

What do we believe will happen "if you follow My laws"? Is our movement's greater emphasis on mitzvot leading to a greater ability to experience "divine meaning"? What do we believe about redemption? Is it a meaningful basis for Jewish observance in our communities?

B'har/B'chukotai
Kenneth J. Weiss, 2002

"Do not exact . . . advance or accrued interest" (Lev. 25:36).

Our daughter Jennifer gave birth to a fine baby boy. As he grew and developed, she began reflecting on how quickly time was passing. "Look at him, Dad. He's changing so quickly; he's not a baby anymore: he's already becoming a little boy."

I understood Jennifer's words: having barely met her baby, she saw him evolving through life's early stages more quickly than she ever could have imagined.

Rabbi Zalman Sorotkin would have understood her, too. He teaches that the most important resource we have in life is time: every moment that passes is one less moment to live; it is the loss of an irreducible, irreplaceable resource. Time is what puts everything else into perspective.

Not everyone values time in this way. In *Parashat B'har* we are taught, "Do not exact . . . advance or accrued interest" (Lev. 25:36) from your brother. For one who lends money at interest, time is primarily an opportunity to grow his own wealth. As the lender charges accrued interest (*marbit*) on a loan, time's passage becomes a money-making opportunity: with every passing hour, every passing day, the *marbit* increases.

I agree with Rabbi Sorotkin's understanding: time seems to cascade as it carries us and our children too quickly from one of life's stages to the next, moving us to wonder at its breathless passage.

When Jennifer told us that her son was growing up too quickly, that his babyhood was already a thing of the past even as she was still getting used to it, I empathized. In my heart, I responded, "Have another child, Jen. Maybe that will help. Start time's clock again." So—she did!

B'har/B'chukotai
Kenneth J. Weiss, 2003

One day late last February, Fred Rogers died. For more than thirty years, Mr. Rogers taught generations of children that they could share and express love, while feeling secure about themselves and their place in the world. Jay, one of my temple kids (now twenty-one), e-mailed me when he heard of Mr. Rogers' death: "[His life's] lesson has never been more important: go out and do something good for the world!"

The physician's credo is "Do no harm." A core Jewish value is *bal tashchit*, "do not destroy." In our *parashah* we read, "Do not wrong one another" (Lev. 25:17).

But there's more: as human beings, we are to go out and do some good, preserve and sanctify life, do what is right in our relationships with one another. Gently, lovingly, Mr. Rogers modeled these life-affirming guidelines.

Jay's note concluded, "Mr. Rogers simply put these guidelines into words that we could comprehend when we were little kids. So go out and do some good. . . . Mr. Rogers: thanks for the lessons . . . rest in peace!"

B'har/B'chukotai
Kenneth J. Weiss, 2003

"If you follow My laws and faithfully observe My commandments" (Lev. 26:3).

Shalom—derived from the Hebrew root שלם (*sh-l-m*)—suggests a sense of wholeness, completeness: feeling at-one within. The opposite of *shalom* is to feel scattered, in pieces: troubled.

Leviticus 26 is a poetic sermon with this core message: that peace—first and foremost—is a state of mind. The text above (26:3) begins with "if"; we each can choose to live life by God's edicts, the rewards of which are immeasurable, nothing less than a peacefulness within: "I will grant peace **in** the land, and you shall lie down untroubled by anyone" (Lev. 26:6). (Note: God will grant peace **in** the land, not to the land: you will feel inner peacefulness in your land, and no one will torment you.)

If, on the other hand, you spurn the way of life God commands, you will know unremitting restlessness and fear. Peacefulness (serenity) will elude you. Indeed, "The sound of a driven leaf shall put them to flight. Fleeing as though from the sword, they shall fall though none pursues" (Lev. 26:36). (Note that this verse is in the third person: those who detach from God's laws and mitzvot will experience remoteness or disconnection—even from God Himself.)

Peaceful or in pieces: it's our choice.

B'har/B'chukotai
Kenneth J. Weiss, 2004

"You are . . . strangers [גרים, *gerim*] and settlers with Me" (Lev. 25:23—Hertz).

The Dubner Magid makes the case (as rendered in *Wellsprings of Torah*): God says, you and I relate "'as strangers and settlers.' If you . . . [remember] that you are here [on the land] but temporarily, then I will be a settler in your midst. . . . My Presence will dwell with you permanently. But, if you [think of] yourselves as settlers, as permanent owners of the land . . . which . . . is actually . . . Mine, [I] will be a stranger [and] will not dwell in your midst."

In *K'doshim* (Lev. 19:34) and elsewhere, God reminds us that "[we] were strangers [גרים, *gerim*] in the land of Egypt." In Leviticus 25, we learn (through the Magid) that God settles permanently among us only when we are mindful that we are always strangers, that is, "here but temporarily." In Lev. 26:11–12, God assures the people: If you do as I say, "I will establish My abode in your midst and . . . will be ever present."

To sum up:

- In Egypt you were strangers.
- Indeed, My permanent presence among you hinges on your understanding that you will ever (and everywhere!) be strangers.
- "The earth is the Lord's" (Ps. 24:1)—not yours!

B'har/B'chukotai
Kenneth J. Weiss, 2005

Wouldn't בהר (B'har)—"On the Mountain"—have been a more apt name for the *sidrah* in Exodus when God transmitted the Ten Commandments on Mount Sinai?

Perhaps not . . . I suggest that this *parashah* called בהר (B'har) comes here and now precisely to make a point: that the revelation on Sinai—far from being a single episode or experience—is perpetual and ever renewable.

Much transpires between the time when Moses receives the commandments (in Exodus 20) and here/now, near the end of Leviticus. In the interim: the rules of daily life are explicated, the desert Tabernacle described and built, a census taken, a golden calf celebrated . . . then pulverized, the priests' garb—and the sacrificial ritual—numbingly detailed. Nadav and Avihu err and pay the price; kashrut is introduced. Other topics—including (but not limited to) the Holiness Code and annual days of obligation—are developed.

Now, our attention turns once again to Sinai, the mountain where God once spoke the Ten Commandments. On the mountain, God speaks yet again, this time about a Sabbath (then a Sabbatical and a Jubilee) for the land. We read also of the moral sensitivities buttressing these idealized observances.

This *sidrah*'s undying message: If God can speak at the mountain a second time, God can speak from there often, continually (even to us . . . even now!). We, too, can hear God's voice, summoning and challenging us . . . if we are willing to listen.

B'har/B'chukotai
Kenneth J. Weiss, 2005

"If you follow My laws and faithfully observe My commandments... I will establish My abode in your midst" (Lev. 26:3, 26:11).

"But if you... do not observe all these commandments... I will spurn you" (Lev. 26:14, 26:30b)

"I will remember My covenant with Jacob... Isaac, and... Abraham" (Lev. 26:42).

Reward and punishment in a nutshell... succinct, unmistakable: how much clearer can Torah be? God tells the people both how they should live and the consequences of their actions.

God sums up: Live as I have prescribed and I will be ever present to you; available, accessible—close enough to hear even your whispered prayer, even your heart's unverbalized meditations.

God continues: Turn your back on Me and I will turn away from you. You will be all alone—bereft.*

God concludes: You come from good stock—the best! You're blessed with generations of good exemplars—the best. Jacob, and before him Isaac, and even before him Abraham taught you to live by these mitzvot.

I hold you to their highest standard. I expect nothing less. Shape up!

---

*It is noteworthy that Lev. 26:39b–46 no longer addresses "**you**, the Israelite people"; rather, "**they**" are addressed: "**they** shall confess... **they** trespassed... **they** shall atone." Torah's language seems to suggest distancing... perhaps disaffection?

B'har/B'chukotai
Alan Cook, 2006

In בחקתי (*B'chukotai*), the Israelites are told not only of the wondrous blessings that await them if they follow God's commandments (Lev. 26:3–13), but also of the severe punishments that may befall them if they fail to follow the mitzvot (Lev. 26:15–43).

The consequences for failing to obey God are very harsh; they include plagues, poor crops, and cannibalism of the perpetrators' own children. Do we really wish to subscribe to such a seemingly vengeful God?

Perhaps the warning and reproof are both merited. The Israelites, after all, would be residing in the midst of other nations who might be partaking of the very practices that God has previously labeled as abhorrent. It would take such a scolding to dissuade the people from their natural predilection to "keep up with the Joneses" by adopting the practices of neighboring people. Thus God resorts to the lengthy תוכחה (*tocheichah*, "rebuke").

But Reform Jews find some of the mitzvot to be inapplicable to modern life; some we have abandoned, while others have been adapted to fit twenty-first-century sensibilities. Do we believe that tremendous calamities will befall us if we fail to adhere to God's laws?

The first part of the chapter deals with this question. God desires to show us נחמה (*nechamah*, "consolation") rather than תוכחה (*tocheichah*). If we are good and moral people and attempt to follow the spirit of the mitzvot even when we cannot or do not follow them to the letter, then God will bestow kindness upon us.

And as we wish God to treat us with נחמה (*nechamah*), so may we be inclined to treat others in that manner.

B'har/B'chukotai
Amy Scheinerman, 2007

"Proclaim liberty throughout the land to all its inhabitants" (וקראתם דרור בארץ לכל ישביה, *Uk'ratem d'ror baaretz l'chol yoshveha* [Lev. 25:10]) is inscribed on the Liberty Bell in Philadelphia, the "City of Brotherly Love." How fitting.

The *Yoveil* (Jubilee) year follows seven cycles of the *Sh'mitah* (Sabbatical year). The mystical, cosmological seven of Creation is squared, and the year following is proclaimed a Jubilee year of release. Yet while the *Yoveil* begins on the first of Tishrei, the announcement of the *Yoveil*, heralded by the blowing of the shofar, comes at the close of Yom Kippur, ten days later. Why?

The Babylonian Talmud, *Rosh HaShanah* 8b, tells us that during the ten days from Rosh HaShanah until Yom Kippur, former slaves were neither sent home nor compelled to work. Rather, they spent this time in the homes of their former masters transitioning from servitude to freedom. They feasted in celebration of their impending freedom together with their former masters, and then, after Yom Kippur, their former masters sent them off with generous gifts that enabled them to begin their lives anew, their lives re-created.

Perhaps the ten-day delay was intended to permit those who had been masters and those who had been slaves to do far more than take their leave of one another: they interacted as equals and friends, razing the old social hierarchy and raising a new banner of friendship and camaraderie. These ten days permitted the former master and servant to heal whatever rifts—psychological, social, economic—existed. After all, Yom Kippur is about spiritual healing and reconciliation. What fitting words to display in the City of Brotherly Love.

B'har/B'chukotai
Amy Scheinerman, 2008

The שמיטה (*sh'mitah*) is an example of values-driven economics. This ancient code of land tenure directs us to provide the land a Sabbath for rest and renewal, teaching us that human welfare and the ecology of the environment are inextricably bound up with one another.

We might note that the remission of debts associated with שמיטה (*sh'mitah*) is found not here, but in Deuteronomy 15 in the context of how Israel must respond to poverty in its midst. Similarly, the release from indentured servitude associated with בהר (*B'har*) is found in Exodus 21, among the first mitzvot commanded the newly liberated slaves at Sinai, but is not mentioned in Leviticus 25. In בהר (*B'har*) the focus is on the land itself, God's possession, which it is our obligation to redeem: גאלה תתנו לארץ (*g'ulah titnu laaretz* [Lev. 25:24]).

Rashi points out that the פרשה (*parashah*) opens with the words וידבר יהוה אל משה בהר סיני (*Vay'dabeir Adonai el Moshe b'har sinai*, "Adonai spoke to Moses on Mount Sinai" [Lev. 25:1]) and asks: Why are the words בהר סיני (*b'har sinai*) added? To remind us that the welfare of the land itself is no less important than remission of debt and freedom from servitude.

Through the ages, we have come to see earth's resources as God's gifts to us, but בהר (*B'har*) teaches otherwise. The land has rights of its own and is in need of redemption just as people are. The Babylonian Talmud, *K'tubot* 11b, provides a vision of the messianic age when, figuratively, money will grow from trees: cakes and fine clothing will sprout directly from the ground without any human endeavor. Rav Kook understood this פרשה (*parashah*), in conjunction with the passage in *K'tubot*, to be a hint of *Gan Eden* (Garden of Eden), where the primordial humans enjoyed produce without labor. *Gan Eden* was a paradise not only for the people, but for the land, as well.

B'har/B'chukotai
Amy Scheinerman, 2008

Parashat B'chukotai opens אם בחקתי תלכו ואת מצותי תשמרו ועשיתם אתם (*Im b'chukotai teileichu v'et mitzvotai tishm'ru vaasitem otam*, "If you follow my laws and keep my commandments and do them" [Lev. 26:3]). The three verbs—"follow," "keep," and "do"—appear redundant. Drawing on *Sifra*, Rashi explains that since תשמרו (*tishm'ru*) and ועשיתם (*vaasitem*) mean to observe and fulfill the mitzvot, תלכו (*teileichu*) means we should "labor in Torah." He compares this troika of verbs with Deut. 5:1, ולמדתם אתם ושמרתם לעשתם (*ulmadtem otam ush'martem laasotam*, "study them, keep them, and do them"). Why isn't it sufficient to "observe and fulfill" the mitzvot? What does it mean to "labor in Torah"?

Gur Aryeh (Rabbi Judah Loew ben Bezalel) explains that תלכו (*teileichu*) connotes movement from place to place, suggesting that in our Torah study we should strive to move to ever more sophisticated levels of understanding and meaning.

Pirkei Avot 6:4 prescribes the lifestyle of the תלמיד חכם (*talmid chacham*) who seeks the happiness described in Ps. 128:2: ascetic living to make room to labor in Torah. We can certainly take this as hyperbole, since Judaism generally frowns on asceticism. *Pirkei Avot* reminds us that we have limited energy, time, and resources and therefore must consider what we will forego to make room for Torah study. In a world where we are encouraged to do it all and have it all, Torah teaches in Lev. 26:5 that if Israel keeps God's mitzvot, we will be able to eat bread to satiety. Rashi comments, "He will eat little yet be blessed in his innards." Torah fills our souls as food fills our bellies; a little Torah goes a long way. Rabbi Loew's תלכו (*teileichu*) takes us even further.

Leviticus 26:10, "You shall have to clear out the old to make room for the new," assures us that when we labor in Torah, new understandings will come to fill and sustain us.

B'har/B'chukotai
David Novak, 2009

Often overshadowed by the *tocheichah* (rebuke) at its conclusion is the instruction at the outset of *B'har/B'chukotai* concerning the need for economic compassion in our transactional relationships with people and the land. That this is a Jewish value is not surprising. What is stunning is how our text recognizes that economic irresponsibility then, as now, can undermine fundamental life-sustaining relationships.

If there is any comfort to be had from the economic prescriptions of *B'har/B'chukotai* it is this: we live in relationships with one another that often involve the exchange of goods, money, and property. The key word is "relationship." The economy is, at its core, about people. Losing sight of this reduces our troubles to numbers and randomized anxiety.

Our communal praxis requires that even in the throes of economic anxiety, we remind ourselves and others of the need for economic compassion in the treatment of laborers, kinsmen, the land, and slaves. We must not permit economic needs to overtake our humanity, even when we feel threatened by loss of job or income, a collapsing stock market, and the undermining of assumptions that long sustained us. Just as importantly, Torah reminds us to make sure that those around us are housed, fed, clothed, and cared for.

This is little comfort to those who suffer economically. In affirming our responsibility toward each other—individually and communally—we can lessen the fear and loneliness that economic distress engenders. That we were slaves to Pharaoh in Egypt reminds us of our responsibility to approach with compassion and respect the humanity of those in economic distress.

Numbers

במדבר *B'midbar*

(Numbers 1:1–4:20)

B'midbar
Lawrence S. Kushner, 1996

The name of this *parashah* and of the book it introduces means "In the wilderness"—actually, "In the wilderness of." The haftarah from Hosea suggests two meanings for wilderness: a negative one (Hosea 2:5) and a positive one (Hosea 2:16). If this first *parashah* in the Book of *B'midbar* presents the positive ideal, why do all the tribes arranged in order around the *Mishkan* (Tabernacle) suggest a positive image? Is everyone marching in lockstep with the Tabernacle in the center the ideal? Is this a little like Eden—too perfect to be human?

B'midbar
Lawrence S. Kushner, 1997

"But you shall not enumerate the tribe of Levi ... you shall enumerate their tasks over the *Mishkan* [Tabernacle]" (Num. 1:49–50).

The tribe of Levi is not numbered, seemingly because they are not going to war. Thus, the census number of 603,550 (Num. 1:46) excluded not only women, men under twenty, and men over the age at which they were not able to fight, but also the entire tribe of Levi, which has a different role in the community We might wish that the other uncounted groups were also singled out for their special responsibilities. If we were to add a section describing those responsibilities, how might it read?

"Each person with their own standard" (Num. 2:2).

The word "standard" in English, meaning "an approved model" (1980 *Random House College Dictionary*) derives from the idea of "standard" as a banner. The old JPS translation quoted above suggests that each person has his/her own standard (*diglo*)—but the meaning seems to be that the *degel* is common to every ancestral house—but perhaps not. The Bible elsewhere frowns on individuals each doing what is right in their own eyes (e.g., Deut. 12:8), but here it suggests that individuals might each have their own flag. If many flags are all right but many standards are not, what is the difference? What might it mean for us to urge some common standards, but individualistic flags?

B'midbar: Flags
Stephen E. Cohen, 1998

In an interesting parallel to the biblical institution of kingship, this midrash depicts God granting banners to the people—not as a means of divine service, but in response to their nationalistic desires.

Midrash Tanchuma, Parashat B'midbar 10   "Every man by his banner, by the emblem of the house of their fathers" (Num. 2:2); "He brought me into the house of wine, and His banner over me was love" (Song of Songs 2:4). "He brought me into the house of wine"—this is the moment when the Holy One revealed Himself upon Mount Sinai—twenty-two thousand chariots of angels descended with Him, with banners flying. When the Israelites saw this, they began craving banners of their own, saying, "Oh, that we might have banners like those!" The Blessed Holy One said, "You crave banners, behold, I grant you your wish," and immediately showed His love for Israel, saying to Moses, "Go make banners such as they crave." This is "His banner over me was love."

Comment   What gives flags and banners the intense emotional appeal acknowledged in this midrash?

B'midbar: His Banner over Me
Stephen E. Cohen, 1999

The word *degel* (banner) occurs only in this week's portion and in one other biblical book: the Song of Songs (*Shir HaShirim*). *Midrash Tanchuma* draws heavily upon the passionate language of *Shir HaShirim* to uncover the symbolic meaning of the *d'galim* (banners) of *B'midbar*.

Tanchuma, Parashat B'midbar 10   "He brought me into the house of wine, and his banner over me was love" (Song of Songs 2:4). Rabbi Chananya taught: It used to be that every person who pointed at the face of the king would be immediately executed. But little children go to school [the "house of wine / Torah"] and point to the Tetragrammaton with their fingers. And the Holy One says, "His *degel* [punning on *agudal*/thumb] over Me was love."

Comment   This midrash alludes to both of the twin religious emotions of love and fear. Is the experience of "fear and trembling" a necessary precursor to the love of God?

B'midbar: Signs of Separation
Stephen E. Cohen, 2000

The banners of the tribes, mentioned here for the first time, are of ambiguous significance. They are not, in themselves, objects of mitzvah or *k'dushah* (holiness). The symbolic and emotional power of banners however, is well-known. The early Rabbinic midrashim depict the Israelites seeing the banners of the angelic hosts at Sinai and craving them for themselves. *B'midbar Rabbah* describes each banner bearing a design that tells of that tribe's "personality." The medieval commentators, on the other hand, sought to mitigate the popular enthusiasm for these banners, in particular, perhaps, their tendency to divide Jew from Jew. Rashi imagines them as simple colored cloths, and Ibn Ezra retains the tradition of the tribal designs but finds them significant only as an assembled collection.

Rashi on Numbers 2:2   Each banner had a distinctive sign—a colored cloth hanging from it. And the color of each was different from the colors of the others. The color of each was like that of the stone set in the breastplate of the High Priest. And in this way, everyone would recognize their own banner.

Ibn Ezra   There were symobols on each banner. And our early Sages said that on the banner of Reuben was the image of a man. And on the banner of Judah was the image of a lion. And on the banner of Ephraim, the image of a bull. And on the banner of Dan, the image of an eagle. Thus, the signs of the four primary tribes combined to represent the appearance of the *k'ruvim* [angels] seen by the prophet.

Comment   What might be the consequences of presenting the Israeli flag and/or the American flag in a synagogue? Do either of these flags serve the functions identified by Rashi or Ibn Ezra?

B'midbar
Sheldon Marder, 2001

Much is made in Jewish tradition of names, from the name changes of Avram, Sarai, and Yaakov, signifying spiritual growth, to Zelda's poem about the multiplicity of names life gives us.

"These were the names of Aaron's sons. These were the names of Aaron's sons, the anointed priests who were ordained for priesthood" (Num. 3:2–3).

Why the double iteration of "these were the names" in consecutive verses? In his commentary on the laws of Shabbat, *Eglei Tal*, the Sochatchover Rebbe (Abraham Bornstein) teaches that the phrase occurs twice, "first in the naming of the sons, and then in the characterization of the son as priests, in order to show that even after their anointment to the priesthood, the sons of Aaron did not receive new names but were still considered the same human beings as before."

Jews do not change their names upon ordination, according to Bornstein, because scholars and rabbis remain fallible human beings, no holier than others and made of the same clay.

B'midbar
Kenneth J. Weiss, 2002

"Take a census" (Num. 1:2).

Near the end of Leviticus, God tells the Israelites: If you live by My laws and observe My mitzvot you will pursue and defeat your enemies. How many of you there are isn't crucial: "Five of you shall give chase to a hundred, and a hundred of you shall give chase to ten thousand" (Lev. 26:8).

But that doesn't compute: if five can chase off a hundred, then a hundred can do the same to two thousand, not ten thousand. So, Torah must be teaching us that simple math isn't always the whole answer. We learn that when people come together, when they work as an integrated team, they symbiotically draw strength from one another, amplify one another; they become greater than the sum of their parts.

Yet here—at the beginning of *B'midbar*—God tells Moses that he is to take a census of the people. Interesting! Rashi says that God counted the people "every hour" out of love. Sforno believes that numbering the people dramatizes each person's individuality. But aren't we Jews more than a total of all the individuals who are counted at a given time? We have never been blessed with great numbers, but we have made a disproportionate difference in the world. We are greater than the sum of our parts.

Perhaps God ordered a census in order to tell each person so numbered that—more than being counted—he or she must be someone God can count on, count in. Census taking in Torah must be a spiritual endeavor: not just "count me," but "you can count on me." And that's how Jews should be counted.

B'midbar
Kenneth J. Weiss, 2003

"The Lord spoke . . . in the wilderness of Sinai. . . . Take a census" (Num. 1:1–2).

We know Torah's fourth book by two names:

- The Hebrew name (*B'midbar*) provides locale. The book is set in the Sinai wilderness—a place that is harsh, unforgiving, trackless. Food is scarce, water virtually nonexistent. A *midbar* (wilderness) is "nature unrefined," characterized by endless potential and ceaseless danger.
- The English name (Numbers) suggests God's (and our ancestors') earliest efforts to tame (or at least to moderate) that overwhelming wilderness. How? By requiring and completing a census of the Israelite community, tribe-by-tribe (Num. 1:2ff.), by numbering and assigning ritual duties to each of the Levitical clans (Lev. 3:1ff.): these (and subsequent) measures enabled the people to grasp—to quantify (e.g., to "get a handle on")—their situation, despite their unbounded, chaotic surroundings.

Consider this parallel:

- In Genesis 1, at the beginning of Creation, our new world was a wilderness ("formless and void"); God brought shape and order by speaking: "Let there be light."
- In Numbers 1, at the beginning of the second month following the Exodus from Egypt, our people's new world was the Sinai wilderness; once again, God brought shape and order by speaking: "Take a census."

B'midbar
Kenneth J. Weiss, 2004

"They camped . . . they marched" (Num. 2:34).

The setting, of course, is the Sinai wilderness. A census is taken; then the tribal groups are assigned specific sites "around the Tent of Meeting" (Num. 2:2).

Lots of activity. Lots of organizing. Thereupon (in the last verse of chap. 2), a subtle restatement of a core truth: even here in the מדבר (*midbar*, "wilderness")—whether encamped or on the move—all of you compose a covenanted people, a fact you must not forget.

When you are encamped, your tribal banner—symbolic of the principles by which you live—will fly close by. It's a physical reminder of who you are, what you stand for: "so they camped by their standards" (Num. 2:34).

When you are on the march, you will remain within your family circle. Walking in community with those whose lineage you share will reaffirm your covenant, your peoplehood: "they marched, each with his clan according to his ancestral house" (ibid.).

Doesn't all this evoke the message of *Sh'ma*: "When you sit in your house and when you walk on the way: ואהבת את יהיה אלהיך [*V'ahavta et Adonai Elohecha*]"?

B'midbar
Kenneth J. Weiss, 2005

"The wilderness of Sinai" (Num. 1:1)

B'midar Rabbah 1:7 teaches: "Through three things—fire, water, and wilderness—Torah was given." God tested our forebears by recourse to these three fundamentals and thus determined that Israel was fit to receive Torah. To wit:

- **Fire:** Moses turned aside to view a burning bush, but he did **not** turn aside from the mission given him: to free his people from Egyptian slavery.
- **Water:** Our people's Exodus could have been terminated at the Sea of Reeds, but inspired by Nachshon's example and Moses's words, they crossed through to freedom.
- **Wilderness:** The מדבר (*midbar*, "wilderness") was a forty-year-long test. Could our people grow away from Egyptian influence and into a renewed nation? They could and did!

Over the centuries of our existence—ever since Torah days—our fitness, our resolve, has continuously been at issue. Yes, God tests even us, to wit:

- **Fire:** Does the flame from the Burning Bush still glow in us, or is it diminished now to a mere symbol: the נר תמיד (*ner tamid*, "eternal light") we visit in synagogue, yet refuse to internalize?

Water: Despite our centuries-long dispersion, having crossed waters not unlike the ים סוף (*Yam Suf*, Sea of Reeds), do we still treasure and nurture our connection to Israel and Jewish values?
Wilderness: Are we "giving in" to *galut* (diaspora)? Has our dispersion fostered disconnection?

Midrash Rabbah teaches us that God tested our ancestors' fitness to receive Torah. But we cannot rest on their laurels. Perhaps God's test consists now of a single question: Are we resolved to preserve and transmit Torah to future generations?*

---

*Inspired by Rabbi Meir Shapiro of Lublin.

B'midbar
Alan Cook, 2006

When we think of the wilderness, we usually think of a desolate, barren space. Hollywood set decorators would depict a desert wilderness as being covered with sand as far as the eye can see, with no water or vegetation, save for a tumbleweed rolling by every now and then. Perhaps an animal or human skeleton might be thrown into the scene to further drive home the point: this is truly a God-forsaken place.

But the wilderness in which the Israelites find themselves in the midst of במדבר (*B'midbar*) is far from God-forsaken. In fact, the locale that provides the backdrop for forty years of our people's wandering and is the setting for the vast majority of the Torah's narrative is a place in which God's presence is deeply felt. In essence, God says to the Israelites, "This place of emptiness, full of the unknown, need not be scary to you. It is a place of promise and opportunity."

Indeed, the revelation at Sinai and other seminal moments in the lives of the Israelites would likely not have been as powerful had God caused them to take place in the midst of civilization, with numerous distractions assaulting the senses. Just as Jacob had to let go of everything and just pause to appreciate God's grandeur before he could proclaim, אכן יש יהוה במקום הזה ואנכי לא ידעתי (*Achein yeish Adonai bamakom hazeh v'anochi lo yadati*, "Surely *Adonai* is present in this place, and I did not know it!" [Gen. 28:16]), so too did our ancestors need this open space, to clear their minds of the slave mentality that they had known for so many generations and give themselves over to the possibility of being part of a chosen people.

B'midbar
Amy Scheinerman, 2007

Numbers 2 describes how the Israelites set up camp in the wilderness. Each tribe was assigned a position with respect to the *Ohel Mo-eid* (Tent of Meeting), and each tribe camped under the banner of its ancestral house. What were these banners and whence this arrangement of tribes?

B'midbar Rabbah 2:8 tells us that the arrangement of tribes reflects the arrangement of Yaakov's twelve sons when they brought his bier out of Egypt for burial in *Maarat HaMachpelah* (the Cave of Machpelah) in Hebron. Their positions around the coffin, designated by Yaakov, were the "banners of their ancestral houses." The banners, midrash tells us, are not objects or tangible symbols, but rather positions vis-à-vis *K'lal Yisrael*. It is about relationships and the overall unity of *Am Yisrael*.

Perhaps each generation worries about the degree to which the Jewish community is splintered and in need of unity and healing. For each generation, the issues are different. Today, we are beset by divisions between the movements, concern about our people's attachment to Israel, and worries about the shrinking numbers of Jews seriously engaged in Jewish study and observance. The recent National Jewish Population Study noted a decline in "ethnic cohesiveness." Steven Cohen's recent report concludes, "It is now clear that a sense of commitment to a particular people—the Jewish People—is in decline." The price of assimilation? universalizing our message? insularity within our movements? other factors?

The image of the Israelites encamped around the *Ohel Mo-eid* is inspiring, each tribe in its position making of itself the banner of its ancestral house.

B'midbar

Amy Scheinerman, 2008

במדבר (*B'midbar*) opens with a consultation between God and Moshe in the אהל מועד (*Ohel Mo-eid*, "Tent of Meeting"). *B'midbar Rabbah* 1:3 points out that previously God spoke to Moses in very public venues: at the Burning Bush (Exod. 3:4), in Egypt (Exod. 12:1), in Midian (Exod. 4:19), and at Sinai (Lev. 25:1). Now that the משכן (*Mishkan*, "Tabernacle") has been built, God reflects, "Modesty is a beautiful thing, as Micah said, והצנע לכת עם אלהיך [v'*hatzneia lechet im Elohecha*, 'to walk modestly with your God' (Micah 6:8)]." Henceforth God speaks to Moshe only in the privacy of the אהל מועד (*Ohel Mo-eid*). The midrash continues with a paean to Moshe's modesty.

The מדה (*midah*, "attribute") of ענוה (*anavah*, "modesty") is treated beautifully in Rabbi Mendel of Satanov's *Cheshbon HaNefesh*:

> Man's self-adoration is the strongest love that God implanted within the animal spirit. . . . It is from this self-adoration that honor stems. . . . [Self-adoration] was primarily placed within him to fulfill a specific purpose desired by God. When taken to the extreme, however, it becomes a tempest that is antagonistic to the regimen of the intellectual spirit. The end result is that it subjugates the precious soul and makes it subservient to its acquired desire. This is the prime enterprise of the *yetzer hara* [evil inclination]: to have the desire for real honor degenerate into the pursuit of honor.

The comment on God's preference for modesty (*B'midbar Rabbah* 3:1) inspires R. Y'hoshua ben Levi to comment that had the nations of the world realized what a boon the Temple could be to them, they would have built fortifications around it to protect it. He then articulates the traditional doctrine of Israel's chosenness but with an aspect we often forget: selection of Israel does not mean that God will indulge Israel more or forgive her more readily. Quite to the contrary: the standards of behavior for Israel are higher because Israel enjoys the privilege of having received Torah. We see here the modesty inherent in the traditional doctrine of chosenness.

B'midbar
Amy Scheinerman, 2009

The census at the beginning of *Sefer B'midbar* supplies neither spine-tingling suspense nor riveting reading. Indeed, it is rather dull—a long list of names and numbers running the length of two columns.

Rashi comments that because the Israelites are so precious to God, God counts them at regular intervals: when they left Egypt, following the Golden Calf (to determine how many remained), when the *Shechinah* came to dwell among them, on the first of Nisan when the *Mishkan* (Tabernacle) was erected, and on the first of Iyar that followed. Rashi is teaching us that counting can be an act of love. When we name each person individually and keep track of him/her, we express deep caring and commitment.

We count what is important to us. As a child, I counted candy solicited on Halloween and pennies saved in a jar. As a young mother, I would continually count my children and their friends at the playground or in a museum to ensure they were all present and safe.

Do we count the people in our lives, as God repeatedly counted the Israelites? Do we go through the rosters of our synagogues and organizations regularly and periodically check on those we have not had contact with in some time? Do we do the same with friends and family? Or are we unable to find the time, given the weight of other responsibilities pressing on us? And if we cannot find the time, is it possible that such a counting might be more important than some of the other weighty matters on our desks?

נשא *Naso*
(Numbers 4:21–7:89)

Naso
Lawrence S. Kushner, 1996

The root נשא (*nun-sin-alef*) recurs several times in this *parashah*, suggesting that the Rabbis had that in mind when they arranged for this portion to begin where it does. Is there a connection between the נשא (*naso*) of the census ("Lift up the head of the Gershonites" [Num. 4:22]); the families' burdens (משא, *masa* [Num. 4:24, 4:31–32]); the *Birkat Kohanim*, "Priestly Benediction" (ישא, *yisa*, "raise" [Num. 6:26]); and the gifts of the נשיאים (*n'si-im*, "chieftains" [Numbers 7])?

Some commentators think that the test of the *sotah* is more to reprimand the husband's jealousy than the wife's unfaithfulness. Do you agree? If, as in the third commandment, it is God's prerogative to be jealous, is marital jealousy a kind of blasphemy?

Naso
Paul J. Citrin, 1996

The *parashah* raises seven topics, including the numbering of the Levites and assigning to them *Mishkan* (Tabernacle)–related tasks; reiteration of who is unclean and must remain outside the camp; confession and restitution for misappropriation of property; law of the *sotah*; the Nazirite vow; the Priestly Blessing; the gifts of the princes for the *Mishkan*. Initially, these topics may seem disconnected, yet links may be found if we answer these questions: What is the message behind the persistent use of the root נשא—*naso, yisa,* and *n'si-im,* "to count," "to lift up," "to be exalted"? What is the common concern reflected in specifically assigning tasks to each priestly family, the law of the *sotah,* and the enumeration of the identical gifts of the princes? Recall the narrative of Cain: in what ways is the Gen. 4:7 phrase הלוא אם־תיטיב שאת (*Halo im teitiv s'eit,* "Surely if you do right, there is uplift") echoed in the *parashah*? How does the portion understand and respond to psychological reality versus "objective" reality?

Naso
Lawrence S. Kushner, 1997

In the Ten Commandments, God is called *El kana*—a God, some say, whose vocation is *kinah,* "jealousy/zealousness" (in Hebrew and Greek they are the same word). Does this suggest that a jealous husband is acting in the image of God? Yes, you may say—God is jealous lest Israel be theologically unfaithful. Yet the jealous husband in the *sotah* passage has no proof. Is jealousy an admirable virtue? Is zeal? (Pinchas, after all, will be rewarded for his zeal only by having a covenant of peacefulness imposed upon him).

Vows (*n'darim*) have a poor press in the Torah, Written and Oral. The midrash suggests that the *Nazir* is to bring a *chatat* because of the sin of excess deprivation. But don't vows encourage us to improve our lives? If we keep them, they can be helpful; why should we refrain from them out of fear of the human weakness of not keeping them? The Christian men's group Promise Keepers is aware of how hard vows are to keep and has set up a whole organization to assist their members to be faithful to what they vow. Should we look again at the tradition's wariness of *n'darim*?

Naso: Lifting the Hands
Stephen E. Cohen, 1998

According to K'li Yakar, the blessings flow from the *kohein*'s (priest's) ten fingers. But the *Kitzur Shulchan Aruch* finds the Holy One in the spaces "between" the *kohein*'s fingers.

K'li Yakar Each of the three blessings in *Birkat Kohanim* (Priestly Benediction) begins with the letter *yod*, whose hidden components [i.e., *vav* and *dalet*] add up to ten, and whose revealed aspect [i.e., the *yod* itself] also has the value ten. This alludes to the double nature of each blessing—they each flow to the visible body and to the hidden soul. And our Sages have taught: "Three share in the creation of a person. The father provides five white elements—the ligaments, the bones, the brain, the nails, and the whites of the eyes. The mother provides five red elements—the skin, the muscle, the blood, the hair, and the black of the eye. And the Holy One contributes the ten spiritual components—*ruach* [spirit] *n'shamah* [soul], facial expression, sight, hearing, speech, walk, *dei-ah* [knowledge], *binah* [wisdom], and *haskeil* [enlightenment]." These components, totaling twenty, are all blessed when the *kohein* lifts his ten fingers, and from each finger flows a double blessing—to the physical body and to the spiritual.

Kitzur Shulchan Aruch When the *kohein* lifts his hands, there should be a total of five spaces between his fingers. This must be done, because it is written, "He is watching through the windows, peering through the lattices" (Song of Songs 2:9). Instead of "*hacharakim* / the lattices" read "*hei*/five *charakim*/lattices." And he must be very careful that the tips of his thumbs not touch each other, lest that window be spoiled.

Comment What are the different understandings of the role and function of the *kohein* reflected in these two commentaries?

Naso: The *Nazir*
Stephen E. Cohen, 1998

While discussing the case of a *Nazir* who accidentally makes contact with a dead body, the Torah refers to him as having "sinned." The sin, according to R. Elazar, was the decision to become a *Nazir* in the first place! K'li Yakar seeks to understand this surprising opinion.

K'li Yakar   "He shall provide him atonement for having sinned" (Num. 6:11). Rabbi Elazar says: Because he deprived himself of wine. And his comment is bizarre, because the text calls the *Nazir* "*kadosh*" [holy], how then can R. Elazar say that he is called a sinner? I would interpret R. Elazar's words thus: A simple, honest man feels no need to take upon himself ascetic practices and to abstain from permitted behavior. The *Nazir* shows that he knows his own spirit to be uncontrolled, and for this reason he leaps and vows against the evil inclination (*yetzer hara*). And in this he causes himself grief, for regarding every sworn thing his *yetzer* grows stronger. And this is why the oath taker is called a sinner: his *yetzer* is incited within him, and they say to him, "It is enough for you that which the Torah forbids; there is no need to add to it." And one who adds to the prohibitions of the Torah adds to the incitement of his *yetzer hara*, and the Torah may not give him the additional strength to resist.

Comment   Should we regard Samson an example of *Nazir* overcome by his own *yetzer*?

Naso: Leadership and Peace
Stephen E. Cohen, 2000

In the ancient Priestly Blessing, with its expanding threefold structure, the Torah uses the subconscious power of rhythm to carry us on a swelling wave of poetry before finally delivering us on the shore of *shalom*. But "peace" has many meanings, and the Maharal of Prague finds one specific dimension revealed in the juxtaposition with the offerings of the chieftains/*n'si-im*.

Maharal on "May he give you peace" (Num. 6:26) and "The chieftains of Israel offered" (Num. 7:2)   The fundamental peace for Israel was brought about through the chieftains. For the chieftain establishes peace within his tribe, between one individual and another. And moreover, when there is among these twelve chieftains a bond and a connection with each other, then there is a complete and ideal peace/wholeness. And I have heard from my teachers that this is why the section of the chieftains is juxtaposed to the Priestly Blessing [which ends with "peace"]—to teach that the peace that God gives will be achieved through the chieftains, when they achieve a single unity. And do not wonder what is the benefit of internal peace if there is no peace with our enemies, because it is about this that the midrash speaks: "Great is peace; even if Israel worships idols—if there is peace among them, then Satan cannot rule over them" (*B'midbar Rabbah* 11:7).

Comment Is there an element of the function of *nasi* (chieftain) in our role as rabbi? Does the peace of the Jewish people depend on our ability to cooperate and establish bonds with each other and with non-Reform colleagues?

Naso
Sheldon Marder, 2001

"*Adonai* bestow favor upon you and grant you peace!" (Num. 6:26).

What is the source of a text's power? Often the power of a Rabbinic text lies in the *machloket* that sharpens different approaches or ideologies. Sometimes the power resides in a text's ability to make us feel closer to God. The midrash on Num. 6:26 in *B'midbar Rabbah* (*Naso* 11:7)—an extended meditation on the many facets and ramifications of peace—points to another source of power, beyond the intellectual and spiritual excitement of *kitvei kodesh* (holy texts). A few excerpts from the midrash:

"Great is peace, for it outweighs everything else. We say in our morning prayers: 'He makes peace and creates everything.' Thus, if there is no peace, there is, as it were, nothing left in creation."

"Great is peace. . . . In the Priestly Benediction, God concludes with peace, 'And give you peace.' This teaches that other blessings in themselves are useless unless peace goes with them."

"Great is peace, for even the angels in heaven need peace, as it is said, 'He makes peace in high places' [Job 25:2]. Now can we not reason from the less important to the more important? If peace is needed in heaven—a place where there is no hatred or rancor—how much more is it needed on earth, a place where all kinds of conflict exist."

The scope and diversity of the entire passage teach that a text's power resides, most of all, in its moral urgency and in its belief that human beings have the power to transform themselves and their society.

Naso
Kenneth J. Weiss, 2002

"May *YHVH* bless you and watch over you" (Num. 6:24—R. E. Friedman).

If only I'd known: Years ago a woman in our congregation, a "friend," announced that she and her family had just moved into their new home. "Rabbi," she said, "we'd like you to come over and bless our house." "You mean affix a mezuzah," I responded. "I'd be honored to do that. But I cannot bless your new home—only God can bless."

I explained that I'd be pleased to recite appropriate prayers and ask God's blessing on her home and family. No: that was not what she wanted. She needed me to bless; nothing else would do. Her husband, overhearing the conversation, affirmed and sought to explain my position to his wife, without success.

I understand *Birkat Kohanim* as a petition to God, asking that God bless the people of Israel, that God protect, deal kindly and graciously, bestow favor and grant peace.

Rabbis have all been asked to bless babies, places, events. This rabbi knows in his heart that he can only pray that God extend blessing to those who need or wish it.

Did my "friend" and I ever move on, put this misunderstanding behind us? No—unequivocally no!

An indelible lesson, and an abiding sadness for me.

Naso
Kenneth J. Weiss, 2003

"The Nazirite . . . shall present . . . a sin offering" (Num. 6:13–14); "The Lord bless you" (Num. 6:24).

Among other things, a Nazirite vowed to "abstain from wine and any other intoxicant" (Num. 6:3). But, Maimonides warns us, don't emulate the Nazirite. One who practices self-denial, abstaining from anything (or everything!) adjudged to be evil, enters "an evil path [on which it is] forbidden to walk" (*Mishneh Torah* 3:1).

Life's comforts and luxuries—including the joys and companionship of marriage, the gladness enhanced by wine, the pleasure of good food—are among God's gifts. Gifts, by definition, are given for people to enjoy. One must not "inflict on [her- or] himself vows of abstinence from things permitted" (ibid.).

Numbers 6 delivers this unmistakable message; it comes in three parts:

1. Here's what a Nazirite does.
2. Here's how a Nazirite sins (by his vow of abstinence) and is penalized for it (for why would Torah prescribe a sin offering if he had not sinned?!).
3. *L'heifech*: here's how God would have us live. As encapsulated in the few verses of the *Birkat Kohanim* we are taught to enjoy life and its pleasures. The first sentence begins, "The LORD bless you." Abarbanel teaches that these words refer to material goods: God offers these to us for enjoyment, not for self-denial.

Of course, we are to keep "things/stuff" in perspective: the final words—"grant you peace"—suggest a sense of harmony and balance. Hillel Silverman (among others) puts it this way: as God blesses us with possessions, so may God protect us from being possessed by them.

Naso
Kenneth J. Weiss, 2004

The *Birkat Kohanim* (Priestly Benediction) has, for millenia, elicited spirituality, admiration—and curiosity. Who composed it? Who first verbalized it? To whom was it initially addressed? Does it contain any hidden message/code (Dan Brown: ready! set! delve!)? When Aaron or David or Solomon blessed the people, did they know (and/or utilize) these exact words?

The mathematics of the formula have been scrutinized. In Plaut's "Gleanings," Bachya is referenced: the three sentences have three, five, and seven words respectively (three for the Patriarchs, five for books of Torah, seven for the number of heavens). Cassuto is also cited: there are fifteen, twenty, and twenty-five letters respectively in the three blessings, a total of sixty letters, "the basis of the sexagesimal system of ancient Babylon."

Yet another take: a student of gematria notes that the fifteenth and final word of *Birkat Kohanim* is שלום (*shalom*)—peace. Fourteen, the number of words preceding שלום (*shalom*), is the numerical equivalent of the Hebrew word יד (*yad*), meaning "hand." This explains why—upon greeting someone—it is appropriate to extend your hand and say שלום (*Shalom*)! (The handshake, I learned, goes back to at least 2800 B.C.E.: one always shook with the right hand, because that is the "weapon-bearing" hand. The message: I'll wage no war.)

When a Jew shakes another's hand, he/she says: I bear no rancor; indeed I wish you peace.

Naso
Kenneth J. Weiss, 2005

Moses completes the construction of the desert Tabernacle. After he anoints it and its furnishings, the leaders of the Israelites (נשיאי ישראל, *n'si-ei Yisrael*) bring forward their offerings for the dedication of the altar. Chapter 7 of Numbers details the identical gifts offered by each of the chieftains on behalf of each tribal family. Challenged to find meaning in the repetition of these gifts in twelve identical paragraphs, one might wonder why Torah preserved this episode—verse after numbing verse.

Richard Elliot Friedman asks, "What is the function of this lengthy, repetitive list of . . . donations . . . ?" He suggests it "establishes the importance of donations for maintaining the religious establishment." Further, it "conveys that [everyone has] a share in what goes on ... the altar. No tribe is favored ... or fails to contribute." The Rabbi of Przysucha posits that the repetition actually accords uniqueness to each gift, since each chieftain contributed "solely of his own free will."

May I add:

- Each tribe is given a different day—its own "moment in the sun"—to offer gifts for the altar's dedication (Num. 7:11). Picture each clan planning their own "presentation day": a tribal holiday, a time for celebration and festivity. From this perspective, why shouldn't each tribe's heartfelt gifts be noted ... affirmed?
- This extended chapter suggests a "God's-eye view" of the twelve days of tribal celebrations. After each tribe's gifts are noted, all of them are acknowledged together: "silver bowls, 12; silver basins, 12; gold ladles, 12" (Num. 7:84ff.).

Each tribe contributed from its own personal resources, with its own unique ceremony. Though identical, each tribe's gift was worthy of being singled out for special mention.

Naso
Alan Cook, 2006

פרשת נשא (*Parashat Naso*) is meant to be an "uplifting" portion. It begins with a census of the Kohathites—literally, a lifting of their heads.

But there is much more to this *sidrah*, the longest in the entire Torah, than the delineation of the Kohathites responsibilities. We have the juxtaposition of two significant ideas in the lives of the biblical Israelites: the oath of the נזיר (*Nazir*, "Nazirite") and the test of the סוטה (*sotah*).

What do these elements have in common with one another? Like the census taking that opens the *sidrah*, they each provide the Israelites with opportunities to be lifted up—to rise above the rest of the crowd.

As disturbing as the סוטה (*sotah*) ritual may appear, particularly given our modern sensibilities that ascribe to both partners equal responsibility for the success or failure of a relationship, it is an undeniably powerful practice. It asks both parties to exercise control over their appetites: by refraining from illicit sexual relations, and by not succumbing to anger and jealousy.

Similarly, one who takes an oath as a נזיר (*Nazir*) is controlling his appetite by abstaining from alcoholic beverages and by focusing all of his attention on service to God.

We need our appetites—what some would call our יצר הרע (*yetzer hara*, "evil inclination")—to give us ambition. Without such instincts, cities would not be built and future generations would never be born. The trick is to achieve balance between יצר הטוב (*yetzer hatov*, "good inclination") and יצר הרע (*yetzer hara*) within ourselves, so that we are worthy of receiving God's blessing, the threefold benediction of the כהנים (*kohanim*, "priests"), which concludes our *sidrah*.

Naso
Amy Scheinerman, 2007

The Babylonian Talmud, *Masechet M'gilah* 23a, tells us that there are three *aliyot* on Shabbat *minchah* (afternoon), Monday, and Thursday because *Birkat Kohanim* (Priestly Benediction) consists of three *pasukim* (verses). Our blessing God before and after reading Torah is a reflection of the *kohanim* (priests) invoking God's blessing on the people. *Midrash Tanchuma* suggests that when the people bless one another in this way, God affirms their sentiment and participates in the blessing. Thus we have a network of blessings: we bless God, God blesses the *kohanim*, the *kohanim* bless the people, and God blesses the people.

No wonder *duchenen* is an awe-inspiring ritual for so many. The *kohanim* remove their shoes, wash their hands, and ascend the bimah. Facing the people, they pray that God will turn the divine countenance toward them. Face to face, face to Face.

The Babylonian Talmud, *Sotah* 39a, teaches us the blessing that the *kohanim* recited prior to *duchenen*. Rabbi Zeira in the name of Rav Chisda recounts: "Blessed are You, LORD our God, Sovereign of the universe, who sanctifies us with the holiness of Aharon and commands us to bless God's people with love." The mention of love here is most unusual.

Love connotes connection, caring, commitment. It precludes arrogance, superiority, and distance. The pre-*duchenen* blessing suggests that blessing another is a matter of love, of actively extending ourselves for that person. *Birkat Kohanim*, with the special blessing of the *kohanim*, and the commentaries of our midrash suggest that we have the power to bless others and invoke God's blessing through the act of love. What is more, without genuine love for others, our words are devoid of blessing.

Naso
Amy Scheinerman, 2008

Marital harmony is subject to jealousy in every age. A man overcome with suspicion and jealousy had a religious option: the ritual of the *sotah*. We are apt to view the trial by ordeal as humiliating, barbaric, and primitive, but perhaps in an age lacking in counseling on the one hand and restraining orders on the other, it was the least destructive option.

Consuming water with a little dirt and ink is not likely to make a woman sick. The higher probability is that the ordeal will exonerate her of the charge of adultery. And more: Torah assures that acquittal comes with the blessing of fertility. If the woman is subsequently discovered to be pregnant, the ritual of the ordeal permits only one conclusion: the husband is the father, regardless of biological reality. Hence the wife returns to her husband justified, he is exceedingly remorseful, and any child born will be cherished as special recompense from God.

Rabban Yochanan ben Zakkai effectively legislated the ordeal out of existence due to the hypocrisy of subjecting women alone to the ordeal. *Mishnah Sotah* 9:9 informs us, "When adulterers became numerous, the bitter waters ceased, and Rabban Yochanan ben Zakkai abolished them, as it is written, 'I will not punish your daughters when they commit harlotry, nor your brides when they commit adultery; for they themselves go aside with harlots, and they sacrifice with cult prostitutes; therefore the people who do not understand shall fall' (Hosea 4:14)."

The Rabbis ruled that no man could bring his wife before the priest and accuse her of adultery unless he had warned her—in the earshot of reliable witnesses—not to be seen with precisely the man with whom he now accused her of dallying. Shades of *ben soreir u'moreh* (the wayward and rebellious son).

Naso
Amy Scheinerman, 2009

"The LORD spoke to Moses saying: Instruct the Israelites to remove from camp anyone with an eruption or a discharge and anyone defiled by a corpse . . . so that they do not defile the camp of those in whose midst I dwell" (Num. 5:1–3).

We understand the purity concerns at the heart of this instruction, but we might be disturbed that physical differences and disease are a source of *tumah* (impurity) as much as contact with a corpse. What does this teach in our day about those who do not fit comfortably into our communities by reason of physical disabilities, sexual orientation, or even political and philosophical perspectives? In a society that finds differences alarming and too often shuns those different "outside the camp," we have good reason to be concerned.

Commenting on these *p'sukim*, *Midrash B'midbar Rabbah* 7:1 provides guidance: "When Israel came out of Egypt, the vast majority of them were afflicted with some blemish. Why? Because they had been working in clay and bricks and climbing to the tops of buildings. . . . When they came to the wilderness of Sinai, God said, 'Is it consonant with the dignity of the Torah that I should give it to a generation of cripples? If, on the other hand, I wait until others take their place, I shall be delaying the revelation.' What, then, did God do? God bade the angels come down to Israel and heal them."

Who is "unblemished"? The midrash reminds us that just as God sent healing angels, so too can we heal one another. Are we doing that?

בהעלתך *B'haalot'cha*

(Numbers 8:1–12:16)

B'haalot'cha
Paul J. Citrin, 1996

Visual aids to community and spirituality characterize this portion. The light of the menorah shining forward, the divine cloud over the *Mishkan* (Tabernacle), and reference to Jethro/Hobab as the eyes of the people all point to vision. Why does Jethro fail to respond to Moses's plea to "be to us instead of eyes" (Num. 10:31)? Why is the Torah silent about his decision?

The silver trumpets sounded for war, assembly, and to announce Festivals appeal to the ear. With regard to the trumpets as a war alarm, the text says, "When you go to war, blow trumpets, and you shall **be remembered** before the LORD your God and shall be saved from your enemies" (Num. 10:9). Why does the text use the passive/reflexive *vanizkartem*?

The sense of touch is invoked when the people validate the Levites by placing hands upon them. Why is it necessary for the people to legitimize whom God has chosen? What are the sources of authority for communal leadership? How is the report of Eldad and Medad a mirror image of the story of Miriam and Aaron attacking Moses?

B'haalot'cha
Lawrence S. Kushner, 1997

The first person to kindle light in the Torah was not a woman blessing candles, but Aaron "raising up" light before the menorah. The first being to kindle light, of course, was God—but the first human being was the *Kohein Gadol* (High Priest). As this rite devolved upon women, did some of the priestly aura devolve on women as well? If Aaron was kindling light to illumine the menorah as the Hebrew implies, what does the woman illumine when she lights candles?

One somewhat misogynistic midrash suggests that women have the mitzvah of lighting candles to compensate for Eve's having denied the light of immortality to humanity. Leaving aside Adam's equal complicity in this act, is there an affirmation of immortality in the lighting of Shabbat candles? If so, why is it a mitzvah to light candles only on Shabbat and Festivals? (To light *yahrzeit* candles, of course, is but a *minhag* [custom].)

B'haalot'cha: Moses's Marriage
Stephen E. Cohen, 1998

In contrast to the intense family dramas of Genesis, the Torah is virtually silent regarding the personal life of Moses. A brief and enigmatic exception is the conversation between Miriam and Aaron regarding Moses's Cushite wife. Nearly all the midrashic sources share an understanding regarding the content of their conversation, which is completely absent from the Torah text itself—to wit, that Moses had separated from his wife.

Yalkut Shimoni, Parashat B'haalot'cha, 247:737   When the seventy elders were appointed, all the Israelites lit candles and rejoiced. Miriam said, "How happy their wives must be, to see their husbands attaining such high office." Tziporah replied, "Woe is them. From now on their husbands will not sleep with them. From now on they will be barren." Miriam asked, "How do you know?" Tziporah replied, "From your brother. From the moment he was consecrated for divine revelation, he has not recognized his own bed." When Miriam heard this, she went and told Aaron.

Comment Is this midrashic tradition concerned with a universal problem of the impact of public office upon a person's marriage, or is it responding to some specific feature of Moses's situation or personality?

B'haalot'cha: The *Ger* Departing
Stephen E. Cohen, 1999

Moses's father-in-law, referred to in this portion as Hovav, is generally regarded in the tradition as the *ger* ("convert") par excellence. So the Rabbis share Moses's anxiety regarding Hovav's choice to depart from the Israelites and to return to his own land and birthplace.

Numbers 10:31 And [Moses] said: "Please, do not leave us, for you have known our encampments in the wilderness, and you have been as eyes for us."

K'li Yakar Moses meant: "I am afraid that the leaving will be from us, that is, because of what you know of our encampments" (as Rashi interprets *al kein yadata chanoteinu*). For all of the encampments were full of arguing and strife against the *Shechinah*. So I worry that you will not return to us, and that even if you do go with us, your thoughts will be for your own land, saying, "Would that I had wings like a dove to fly away and dwell elsewhere in peace." And so I beg you, "Do not depart, *even* from us . . . and if you stay, all Israel will be inspired by your example."

Comment In K'li Yakar's expansion of Moses's plea, why does Moses confess to Hovav that he will continue to worry even if Hovav decides to stay with them?

B'haalot'cha: The Syncopated Journey
Stephen E. Cohen, 2000

The Torah, in the *sidrah*, goes far beyond stating the general rule that "when the cloud lifted, they would travel" and "when the cloud rested, they would halt." We are made to consider, one by one, all of the different experiences of encamping and of striking camp faced by our people in the wilderness. Ramban offers a sensitive analysis of each of these experiences.

Ramban on Numbers 9:19–23 The reason for this section is to say that even if the cloud stayed upon the *Mishkan* [Tabernacle] for many days (Num. 9:19), and that place happened to be undesirable, and they wanted desperately to depart from there, nonetheless they would not disobey the divine will. And likewise, "if the cloud stayed only a number of days" (Num. 9:20), that is, just two or three days, and the people were exhausted, and their strength depleted by the journey, they would do God's will and walk on after the cloud. And it further relates that there were occasions when they halted only for one night and had to set out again in the morning (Num. 9:21), after they had walked all night and arrived there in the morning—and the cloud stopped for one full day and one night, and then departed in the second morning, and they would begin again. And this was even more difficult than the previous case, because the people had come to think that they would stay there, and they unpacked the wagons and set down their burdens as is the way of those who finish a journey. But then the cloud would lift on the second morning, and they would have to pick up their burdens again, without having a chance to prepare for the journey.

Comment We typically think of the mitzvot providing structure and order for our lives, a set of disciplines and rhythms that help us live a life of harmony and holiness. Which aspects of Jewish life correspond to Ramban's depictions of our experience in the wilderness, characterized by unpredictability and arrhythmia?

B'haalot'cha
Sheldon Marder, 2001

"Why have You dealt ill with Your servant? . . . Let me see no more of my wretchedness!" (Num. 11:11, 11:15).

Recognizing the "deep tension" here between Moses and God, Walter Brueggemann calls these verses "a rather shocking prayer." In fact, he wonders whether this is prayer or ploy—and indeed the "ploy" works: God's hand is forced, and God responds immediately to Moses's self-pity and his plea for death by making pragmatic, structural changes (in verse 16) ("Prayer as an Act of Daring Dance," in *The Psalms and the Life of Faith*, Fortress Press, 1995).

Brueggemann uses the metaphor of dance to explore the covenantal partnership in all its variety—its elements of intimacy and freedom, responsibility and initiative, surprise and improvisation. Still, how is dance possible when the partners are angry, close to estrangement, and in a state of "deep tension"?

Heschel helps answer the question. He reflects on Israel's murmuring, rebellion, and stubbornness and asks, "*Ribono Shel Olam*, why do you bother with us?" And he concludes, "The only way to understand the paradox is that God takes [us] very seriously ("Jewish Theology"—a 1968 speech in the anthology *Moral Grandeur and Spiritual Audacity: Essays*, Farrar, Straus and Giroux, 1996).

However, the theological quandary in many of our communities today is this: How serious are **we** about God? And, if we decide to get serious, where does someone with "two left feet" begin?

B'haalot'cha
Kenneth J. Weiss, 2002

"Now Moses was a very humble man" (Num. 12:3).

Moses was reared in Pharaoh's household. In that setting, humility was likely not one of the primary virtues impressed upon him. Furthermore, God spoke with Moses "mouth to mouth, plainly . . . and he [beheld] the likeness of *YHVH*" (Num. 12:8). Still and all, Torah characterizes him as "a humble man."

Humility is ascribed to Aaron, as well. *Sifrei* on Num. 8:3 suggests that Aaron—despite privilege and opportunity—never changed. The Rabbi of Przysucha adds that, honored and respected though he was, he never became "conceited or arrogant, but remained as humble and meek as he had been before."

And what of their sister Miriam, who was prominent in her own right? When stricken with "snow-white scales" (Num. 12:10), even she had to be isolated outside the camp for seven days—just like any other Israelite. We understand Miriam, too, to have been humbly human.

Three siblings: all humble by coincidence? I think not! What then? Nature? Perhaps nurture? One thing seems clear: the role of parents in modeling and instilling good qualities in their children cannot be overstated.

B'haalot'cha
Kenneth J. Weiss, 2003

"We remember the fish that we used to eat free in Egypt" (Num. 11:5).

Reminiscence is refracted memory (indeed, is not memory often refracted—even diminished—if only somewhat?), an imprecise recollection of events past.

When the "riffraff" among the Israelites "took to complaining bitterly before the Lord" (Num. 11:1), they justified their complaints and their "gluttonous craving" by recalling (through their own emotional prism) how much better life was in Egypt, what with free fish along with cucumbers, melons, leeks, onions, and garlic. Our ancestors were reminiscing about a past that—human nature suggests—they did not (could not?) recall objectively.

How universally human is the penchant to romanticize the past. In reminiscence, every single one of my HUC days was meaningful, stress-free, rewarding. In reminiscence, my days as a Navy chaplain were invariably ordered and predictable, our worship services uniformly (!) meaningful and moving, my clergy colleagues ever kind and understanding.

The "good old days"—objectively speaking we realize that they were probably never as good as we lovingly remember them to have been.

The second verse of *Parashat B'haalot'cha* "sheds light" on this inclination to idealize the past. The lamps of the menorah are to be mounted so as "to give light at the front of the lampstand" (Num. 8:2). This symbol makes the point: we envision our future, suffused with light; but our reminiscences of events past, are—like the back of the lampstand—left in shadow: imprecise... diminished.

B'haalot'cha
Kenneth J. Weiss, 2004

From Moses's daily log: I feel confounded—undone! I try my best to meet their every need. But—they're never satisfied.

Yesterday, they demanded meat. "Where am I to get meat?" (Num. 11:13a), I asked יהוה (*Adonai*) in my distress; "I cannot carry all this people by myself" (Num. 11:14). יהוה (*Adonai*) responded helpfully: "Gather for Me seventy of Israel's elders... and bring them to the Tent of Meeting.... I will come down and... draw upon the spirit that is on you and put it on them [so that] they [will] share the burden of the people with you" (Num. 11:16–17).

Of those elders, most weren't really helpful; they "spoke in ecstasy, but did not continue" (Num. 11:25b). But two of them—Eldad and Medad by name—were men of a different sort. Though they never entered the Tent of Meeting, they were infused with the same spirit: they prophesied in the camp (מתנבאים במחנה, *mitnab'im bamachaneh* [Num. 11:27]).

Joshua urged me to restrain them. But I refused; these boys seemed the "genuine article." I sensed something special in them: a true prophetic spirit. They reminded me of my own youthful reluctance to accept the mantle of leadership (Exod. 4:13, etc.; *B'midbar Rabbah* 15:19).*

Joshua, I sensed, might have mistaken Eldad and Medad as competitors to his own successorship. Trust me Josh: the sixth book of תנ״ך (*Tanach*) will never be named the Book of Eldad and Medad. Still, I did appreciate those two: "Would that all יהוה's [*Adonai*'s] people were prophets" (Num. 11:29).

---

*"The prophet... is not moved by a will to experience prophecy. What he achieves comes against his will.... He does not call for it; he is called upon" (Abraham Joshua Heschel).

B'haalot'cha
Kenneth J. Weiss, 2005

"The people were like grumblers" (Num. 11:1—R. E. Friedman)

Torah neither judges nor condemns people who complain in the face of real difficulties (and Israel suffered many during the wilderness journey!). Indeed, God responded with plenteous food and abundant sweet water after learning of their hunger and thirst.

Here, however, things are different. "The people are not complaining about some specific problem. They actually have everything they need and [seem to be grumbling merely] for the sake of grumbling" (Pinchas H. Peli, *Torah Today: A Renewed Encounter with Scripture*, 2nd ed., University of Texas Press, 2004).

So, who actually grumbled? Numbers 11:4 tells us it was "the riff-raff . . . and the children of Israel [בני ישראל]." Restless, disaffected, they cried out their longing for the free fish and plenteous vegetables of Egypt.

יהוה (*Adonai*) tells Moses, "Gather for me seventy of Israel's elders" (Num. 11:16). Incensed by the "grumblers," God and Moses act to marshal the voices of experience, reason, and balance—the quiet, thoughtful voices of the people's elders. They'll calm the waters. They'll speak sense to the rebels and teach the children that grumbling—complaining—is nonproductive; it brings no positive results. (Torah reminds us here of the crucial role of elders.)

. . . One of my friends recently passed away. Charlie was a resident of Seacrest Village Retirement Communities of San Diego County, where I am "consulting rabbi." "How are you doing, Charlie?" I'd ask whenever I'd see him. Tired, frail, barely able to walk, Charlie would invariably respond with a smile, "No complaints."

"No complaints" did not mean he had nothing to complain about—he had lots of issues: the degradation of his eighty-seven-year-old body, the loss of his vitality, his ever-failing health. But Charlie ascertained something over the years: there's no benefit—no point—to complaining. Grumbling doesn't change things.

. . . Moses could have used someone like Charlie among the seventy elders; he'd have made a real contribution. Charlie would have cautioned the "riffraff" and the children: this is **not** how to act!

Stop your gratuitous grumbling. When asked, respond . . . No complaints!

B'haalot'cha
Alan Cook, 2006

The job of leadership isn't easy. Moses faces many trials from the Israelites throughout his career, several of which occur in this *sidrah*. Having faced ongoing complaints about food and having vented his frustration to God, Moses is just about ready to throw in the towel. Is it any wonder, then, that when he is told that Eldad and Medad have taken to prophesying in the camp, Moses does not react with concern or consternation, but rather seems to endorse their endeavor. "Would that all the Lord's people were prophets, that the Lord put His spirit upon them!" (Num. 11:29).

Later, when his own siblings begin to speak against him, it is not Moses who castigates them, but God. Moses does not call attention to the fact that God speaks with him "mouth to mouth, plainly and not in riddles" (Num. 12:8).

Moses has a special relationship with God, but he frequently finds it to be a tremendous burden, rather than a blessing. At several junctures, including in בהעלתך (*B'haalot'cha*), he seems to be on the verge of career burnout. Perhaps this is why he welcomes new "franchisees" Eldad and Medad to join the prophetic field, and why he doesn't brag to Miriam and Aaron about his relationship with God.

Jewish leaders of today have things a bit easier. We can delegate. We can empower those whom we lead to find their own connections with the Divine. We can give the Jews in our communities the opportunity to be prophets of their own destinies and help them to recognize God's spirit that resides within each of them.

B'haalot'cha: Pesach Sheini
Amy Scheinerman, 2007

R. Levi comments (*Yalkut, Pinchas*, 782) that God originally intended that every summer month be replete with a חג (*Chag*, "Festival") for Israel to celebrate. The incident of the Golden Calf caused God to revoke the Festivals intended for Tammuz, Av, and Elul, but God made up for these three months in Tishrei with Rosh HaShanah, Yom Kippur, and Sukkot. The Festival assigned to *Iyar* is פסח שני (Pesach Sheini), provided for in Num. 9:6–12.

בהעלותך (*B'haalot'cha*) tells us that those who, on the fourteenth of Nisan following the Exodus, were טמא (*tamei*, "unclean") by reason of contact with a corpse, came to Moses seeking a remedy. Moses inquired of God, who established a second chance one month later: those who are impure or traveling far from the cultic center on the fourteenth of Nisan may offer the פסח (*pesach*) sacrifice and eat it with matzah and *maror* one month later.

פסח שני (Pesach Sheini) is a second chance that teaches us that it's never too late. This is the message of the High Holy Days, as well. We say prayers of repentance and ask for forgiveness thrice daily, yet Rosh HaShanah comes yearly to facilitate our repentance in the midst of our people, lest we missed those opportunities—another chance for spiritual renewal and reconciliation with God. Six months later comes פסח שני (Pesach Sheini), affording the opportunity to reconnect with communal ritual. Today, without the Temple sacrifice, פסח שני (Pesach Sheini) has no practical import. Perhaps we still need it—or something analogous—to provide entrée back to the community for those who have strayed.

B'haalot'cha
Alan Cook, 2008

The first modern skyscrapers were built in the mid-1880s. The first was either the Home Insurance Building in Chicago, which was ten stories tall, or the twenty-story New York World Building, in New

York City. As architectural know-how has developed, the quest has been for bigger, grander, and taller buildings.

What is this thirst to touch the sky? What makes us gaze heavenward and dream of an office or apartment in the clouds?

For some, perhaps, the drive is for power. But many are driven by a basic human instinct to strive to be the best.

Such ambition is not necessarily frowned upon. In the beginning of *B'haalot'cha*, Aaron is told to aim high. The text states "when you ascend" or "when you lift up the lights" (Num. 8:2).

Lighting the lights of the menorah is a fairly mundane task. And yet, it is granted great importance. We do not know whether Aaron would have had to strain, or stand on a ladder, or take other measures to reach the various branches. Yet in some way, this task required one to ascend—perhaps physically, perhaps spiritually—to another level. A simple task, elevated to great importance.

We learn from this that we should strive to make our lives equally meaningful, approaching every task with *kavanah*. We should always be aiming higher—and holding ourselves to high standards.

What can one person do? Well, if as individuals we speak out against injustices, decry excesses, and demand excellence from all, then perhaps others will catch on.

If we lead our lives according to the principles preached by the prophets, holding ourselves and others to high moral and ethical standards, perhaps we can help to make this world a better place.

It doesn't hurt to aim high.

B'haalot'cha
Amy Scheinerman, 2009

B'haalot'cha has an unusual feature in the *sefer Torah* (Torah scroll). An inverted *nun* appears twice, bracketing Num. 10:35–36, the *p'sukim* we read as we rise to open the ark prior to reading Torah publicly: "Whenever the Ark was carried forward, Moshe would say, 'Arise, *Adonai*! May Your enemies be scattered and Your foes flee before You.' And when it halted, he would say, 'Return, *Adonai*, You who are Israel's myriads of thousands!'"

Talmud records in *Shabbat* 116a that Rav Sh'muel bar Nachmani taught in the name of R. Yonatan: "The Book of Numbers is divided into three books, and the books of Torah total seven, as it is written, 'Wisdom has built her house; she has hewn her seven pillars' (Prov. 9:1])."

This allows us to see Torah—when composed of seven books rather than five—as a reflection of the cosmology of the universe. Seven books mirror the seven days of Creation. More to the point, five books of Torah place Leviticus at the center, with command and obedience the core of the divine-human relationship. With seven books, the pinnacle shifts from Leviticus to these two *p'sukim* that speak to a relationship of mutuality with God: God encourages and leads Israel, and Israel seeks God's guidance and direction. Israel and God move together through the wilderness, through life and history, and Torah is an important point where they interface.

With the *Mishkan* (Tabernacle) and *Mikdash* (Temple) gone, Torah, the record of the covenant, is Israel's home (Prov. 9:1) and a meeting for God and Israel.

שְׁלַח-לְךָ Sh'lach L'cha

(Numbers 13:1–15:41)

Sh'lach L'cha
Paul J. Citrin, 1996

Eating and consuming are recurring images of stormy emotion in this *parashah:* Ten spies claim the land "**eats up** its inhabitants" (Num. 13:32); Joshua and Caleb, conversely, say that Canaan's populace is "**bread** for us" (Num. 14:9). God's response to the people's faithlessness is to state, "Your carcasses shall be **consumed** in the wilderness" (Num. 14:29). Next comes the law of *challah*, separation of the dough offering. Why is there such extensive imagery of eating in this portion?

Chapter 15 also includes a listing of the offerings the people are to bring for their sins once they enter the land. Such a list is encouraging after the divine decree of a forty-year detour in the wilderness. The Torah tells us that the stranger is also obligated to bring such offerings, that the same law applies to him. Thus, can we assume that the law of *tzitzit* (fringes), which is next to the section on offerings, also applies equally to the stranger? Should a non-Jew who wishes to affix a mezuzah to her door be so encouraged?

Sh'lach L'cha
Lawrence S. Kushner, 1997

Sober-sided people of today might well applaud the careful, balanced presentation made by the majority of the scouts returning from their visit to Canaan. They might even applaud the response of the people—upon weighing the fruitfulness of the land against the perceived strength of the inhabitants, the cost-benefit analysis would clearly seem to argue against taking the land. But God is furious at the scouts' report and punishes the people who agree with them. What was missing from their report, of course, was trust in the word of God. And trust is a hard commodity to find these days too. Weighing faith in God's promise as stated in the Torah against our own experience, where would we come out in this story? Can this story be used to sway those who look at the world only from a cost-benefit viewpoint?

The Rabbis chose to provide a remedy for the seeing problems of the scouts by ordering the wearing of *tzitzit* (fringes) as a reminder of the mitzvot that are to guide the way in which we understand the world. This passage also includes a reminder that God brought us out of Egypt. The Reform Movement eliminated the reading of the *tzitzit* passage from the liturgy but retained the reminder of the Exodus. Is *zeicher litziat Mitzrayim* (the memory of being brought out of Egypt) sufficient to keep us from viewing the world only through our own eyes and hearts?

Sh'lach L'cha: The Land That Eats
Stephen E. Cohen, 1998

Nachman of Bratzlav accepts the observation of the spies regarding the Promised Land, that "it is a land that devours its inhabitants" (Num. 13:32).

Likutei Moharan The nature of eating is that food is transformed into the eater. For example, when an animal eats vegetation such as grass, the grass is transformed into the animal, when it enters its belly. So, too, when a human eats the animal, the animal is transformed into the human. And into every place that the food reaches, as it is distributed among the organs, it is transformed into the organ itself. For example, the part of the food that reaches the brain becomes the brain. And the part that enters the heart becomes the heart, and so with the other organs. This is the meaning of "a land that eats its inhabitants." For the Land is of the aspect of faith/*emunah*, as it is written, "Dwell in the land, and feed on faith" (Ps. 37:3). So the meaning of "It eats its inhabitants" is that when one enters the Land, which is of the aspect of faith, one is "eaten" by that Land, that is, transformed into the Land itself, which is faith.

Comment   Nachman here seems to describe faith/*emunah* as a state into which we are "absorbed," once we enter a new host environment. Is it more helpful to speak of faith as a state of being or, rather, as a movement—for example, making a leap or taking a stance?

Sh'lach L'cha: Spies and *Tzitzit*
Stephen E. Cohen, 1999

Reading the commandment of *tzitzit* (fringes) at the end of this week's portion, we are struck by the recurrence of the verb *latur*, which had featured so prominently in the narrative of the spies. S'fat Emet highlights this repetition as he seeks to understand the text's disparaging of our own hearts and eyes.

S'fat Emet on *Sh'lach L'cha* (5659)   Regarding the fact that the mitzvah of *tzitzit* follows on the episode of the spies, Rashi comments, "The heart and the eyes are the *m'raglim* [spies] of the body, and they lead it to sin."

Behold, they are spies to scout out/*latur* the land of the material world, in order to repair and to bring forth the holy sparks that are found in the world. For the strength of the body spreads out through the eye and the heart, in all the places of physicality and of matter; therefore they are in a place of danger. Thus, too, the spies. They were great men, but they were sent into a place of danger. They were called *m'raglim* because they went to the bottom-most rung, which is called *regel*. And it is written *vayavo ad Chevron* (Num. 13:22), in the singular, because until then they remained unified. But afterwards, *vayavo-u ad nachal Eshkol* (Num. 13:23), in the plural, because that was a place of danger, and they could not maintain their unity.

Comment Rashi's full statement on *v'lo taturu acharei l'vavchem v'acharei eineichem* ("so that you do not follow your heart and eyes" [Num. 15:39]) is "The eye sees, the heart desires, and the body sins." Is S'fat Emet more trusting that the "scouts" of our soul can be safely sent out into the dangerous land of the material world?

Sh'lach L'cha
Yossi Feintuch, June 2000

Avraham Arazi in *Mi Maayan HaAggadah* addresses the severity of the *lashon hara* (slander) iniquity perpetrated by the ten spies. In general, their reporting was correct and they did not fail to tell of the land's bounty. "We came unto the land and surely it floweth with milk and honey" (Num. 13:27). Nonetheless, these very words snarled the whole nation. By beginning their report with words of glory and praise, the spies were able consequently to gain the people's faith also in their words that slandered the land. "For this is the way of those engaging in *lashon hara*: they commence with favorable [words] and conclude with unfavorable [words]." Moreover, for reporting, "And we were in our sight as grasshoppers" [after seeing the Nephilim; Num. 13:33], *HaKadosh Baruch Hu* forgave the spies. But for saying, "And so we were in their sight" (Num. 13:33), *HaKadosh Baruch Hu* took the spies to task, saying, "How is it that you presume to know how I made them to perceive you? Who is to say that you were not perceived as angels in their eyes?" Haz"al sought further to alert us to the fact that while the spies slandered only trees and stones, how much more careful we should be with slandering our own fellows.

Sh'lach L'cha
Sheldon Marder, 2001

"Once, when the Israelites were in the wilderness, they came upon a man gathering wood on the Sabbath day" (Num. 15:32–36). In the

Babylonian Talmud, *Shabbat* 96a, R. Akiva identifies the wood gatherer as Zelophechad (derived from the use of the word *bamidbar*, "in the wilderness," in Num. 15:32 and again in Num. 27:3 with reference to Zelophechad—*Avinu meit bamidbar*, "Our father died in the wilderness"). But Akiva's detective work disturbs R. Y'hudah b. Bafyra: "Akiva, you will have to render judgment in either case. If you are right [about the identity of the wood gatherer], the Bible has hidden this, yet you reveal it! And if [it was] not [Zelophechad], then you have slandered a righteous man!" (*Shabbat* 96b). Akiva, what were you thinking? Y'hudah's sharp rebuke reminds us that decisions about the sharing of information are invariably as thorny as Zelophechad's namesake—the caper (*tzalaf*) tree.

Sh'lach L'cha
Kenneth J. Weiss, 2002

"Send men to scout the land of Canaan" (Num. 13:2); "Is [it] good or bad?" (13:19); "Is the soil rich or poor?" (13:20).

Moses knew what he was doing . . . and the timing was no accident, either: it was "the season of the first ripe grapes" (Num. 13:20). Moses's message to the scouts: go in, peruse, look beneath surface appearances; then return to us with (the best and biggest) fruits; their size and beauty should convince everyone to enter and possess Canaan—our promised inheritance—now!

Sefer HaZehut quotes Moses as telling the spies, "Even if the land should seem bad to you, it is good. Though it may be hidden, the sanctity of the land is always there . . . once you have entered the Land, all this sanctity that was hitherto concealed will be revealed to you." A former Chief Rabbi of Jerusalem—Joseph Hayyim Sonnenfeld—applies this message to his (to our!) beloved city. On the text, "And seek the good of Jerusalem," he teaches that this means we must always try to see only the goodness of Jerusalem.

Now, in this bloody spring of 2002, we must work harder than ever to see, and to preserve, the sanctity and goodness of Jerusalem. It is still *Ir Shalom* (City of Peace) even as the encouragement of terror and the death of innocents exacerbate the enmity and the hatred.

May Jerusalem's sanctity and goodness one day be renewed and universally shared: a new *shalom* emanating from *Ir Shalom. Kein y'hi ratzon*—may it be God's will!

Sh'lach L'cha
Kenneth J. Weiss, 2003

"Send men . . . each one a chieftain" (Num. 13:2).
"Joshua . . . sent two spies" (haftarah, Joshua 2:1).

Those whom Moses designates to go into Canaan, reconnoiter the land, and return with word of what they see are never referred to in Torah as "spies" (*m'raglim*). Rather, they are tribal leaders, commissioned to peruse (*latur*) the land on behalf of the people.

God—through Moses—seeks to probe the mind-set of our newly liberated ancestors. God could have instructed Moses to select twelve observant individuals gifted with the ability to absorb, assess, and report what they found. However, God commands that people of influence—"**heads** of the Children of Israel" (Num. 13:3)—be sent into Canaan. Their report to the community would carry significant weight. Free to draw their own conclusions, these leaders possessed the stature to inspire the people to follow them into the land. They could also (as ten of the twelve actually did!) dishearten the people and convince them that any incursion would result in certain defeat—utter destruction. God's plan: **precisely** to send in the leaders. If **they** proved faithless, their entire generation would be doomed!

Some forty years later, Joshua—in this week's haftarah—has taken over the reins of leadership. At the end of the desert sojourn, he sends in two spies (*m'raglim*)—not leaders or chieftains!—to explore Jericho. In Moses's time, faithlessness and fear permeated the people—reaching even to its leaders. Now—a generation later—the people (even the *m'raglim*!) trust God and God's promise: "The Eternal has put the whole country in our hands" (Josh. 2:24).

Under Moses, the Israelites were removed from Egypt. Only in Joshua's time was Egypt removed (exorcised) from them.

Sh'lach L'cha
Kenneth J. Weiss, 2004

"We looked like grasshoppers to ourselves" (Num. 13:33).

Julius Lester teaches us something important about self-perception: "How we see ourselves determines how we see others. If I am a grasshopper to myself, then others will appear as giants to me."

Too often we encounter people who exhibit the "grasshopper syndrome"—a sense of low self-esteem and a concomitant belief in "the other's" exaggerated size and influence:

- "When my co-worker is away, 'they' expect me to do both his work and my own."
- "'They' don't pay me anything like what others receive."
- "'They' scheduled me straight through the day without a break."
- "My new office is small and isolated: 'they' didn't consult me when they built it."

A friend of long standing—a Jewish professional—shared these allegations with me as I began to contemplate this *sidrah*. I spoke to him of his self-worth, his gifts, his invaluable contribution to his community and our people—to no avail. My dear friend couldn't see it; he looked like a grasshopper to himself.

Of the twelve who scouted the land, ten suffered from the "grasshopper syndrome." Their fear and doubt sprang not from what they saw and heard in Canaan, but from a failed spirit. Only two—Joshua and Caleb—believed. Only they could affirm: "יהוה [*Adonai*] is with us. Have no fear" (Num. 14:9).

The "grasshopper syndrome" infects biblical scouts **and** (regrettably) modern (Jewish) professionals as well.

Sh'lach L'cha
Kenneth J. Weiss, 2005

"[Knotted] fringe[s]...recall all the commandments of יהוה [*Adonai*] [to] observe them" (Num. 15:39).

Our rationalist Reform ancestors discarded numerous mitzvot, dismissing them as "dated," "irrelevant," or just "irrational." Over the decades—as a movement and as spiritual individuals—we've re-evaluated much of that which our forebears summarily discarded. The mitzvah to wear ציצית (*tzitzit*, "fringes"), once universally ignored (even condemned!) has, in liberal Jewish circles, received new life and purpose.

Though few among us wear knotted fringes on the corners of our clothing, growing numbers of non-Orthodox Jews pray enwrapped in טליתות (tallitot) with ציצית (*tzitzit*). We've come to appreciate the verses in this *sidrah* (Num. 15:37–41) that speak of them. Our conscious awareness of the ציצית (*tzitzit*) will remind us not to pursue our vain, emotional, greedy desires. Seeing the fringes, we'll instead call to mind God's commandments and—in doing them—extend God's holy purpose in the world. Living within the context of the mitzvot **is** doing God's work in the world.

> Looking at the knotted fringes,
> You will remember as a knot around your finger
> That everything you see and whatever you desire
> Can be seen and done as one of My mitzvot. (Author unknown)

Sh'lach L'cha
Alan Cook, 2006

שלח לך (*Sh'lach L'cha*) contains two key ideas: the sending of the spies to Canaan and their subsequent report to the people, and the mitzvah of ציצית (*tzitzit*, "fringes"). What connection can be found in the juxtaposition of these two concepts?

Perhaps the answer can be found in the passage about ציצית (*tzitzit*), where the text states, וראיתם אותו (*ur'item oto*, "look at it" [Num. 15:39]). It seems that this *sidrah* is all about seeing—what we choose to see, and what we ignore.

Caleb and Joshua saw the beauty of the land. The remaining spies could see only obstacles that stood in the way of the Israelites taking possession of the land. And the Israelites themselves, who heard the spies' reports, were blinded by their fear of the unknown, rather than being open to the opportunities that would be afforded to them as they enjoyed freedom in the land that had been promised to their ancestors.

By contrast, the ציצית (*tzitzit*) require us to have our eyes open to appreciate them, and in so doing we are reminded of God's mitzvot and of the kindness that God showed to us in redeeming us from Egypt.

We can go through our lives with blinders before our eyes, refusing to bear witness to God's graciousness toward us. Or, we can open eyes that have previously been blind and proclaim, אשרינו (*Ashreinu*), "How greatly have we been blessed!"

Sh'lach L'cha
Amy Scheinerman, 2007

Long ago, a good friend laughingly explained to me that her house was a perpetual chaotic mess not because she was a working mother of two autistic children but because she was performing a public service for her friends: when they saw the disastrous condition of her house, they felt righteous in comparison. I marveled at her lack of self-consciousness, and her unusual perspective.

The spies return to Moses and report, "We were as grasshoppers in our own eyes, and so were we in their eyes" (Num. 13:33). The Babylonian Talmud, *Sotah* 35a, and *Tanchuma* (*Sh'lach*, 7) envision God responding to the spies, "You do not know what you have just let your mouths utter. I am ready to put up with your saying, 'We were as grasshoppers in our own eyes,' but I take offense at your asserting, 'and so we were in their eyes.' Could you possibly know how I made you appear in their eyes? How do you know but that in their eyes you were like angels?"

Short of a social anxiety, many people presume to know how others view them but are wrong. The cost can be enormous for both parties. For the Israelites, the cost was forty additional years in the wilderness. For individuals, the cost can be the loss of a potentially valuable relationship for both parties due to a false sense of disease and distrust. In communities (our congregations and institutions and their boards and committees), these inaccurate presumptions can wreak havoc and disrupt the conduct of business and progress of the community.

Sh'lach L'cha
Amy Scheinerman, 2008

"God spoke to Moshe, saying, 'Send men for yourself to explore the land of Canaan, which I am giving to the Israelites. Send one man from each ancestral tribe, each one a chieftain among them'" (Num. 13:1–2).

Rashi notices the seemingly extraneous *l'cha* in the name of this week's *parashah* and imagines God saying, "Moshe, you send them in accordance with your own assessment of the situation. As for Me, I would not recommend sending spies." God thinks the timing is poor but allows Moshe freedom to exercise his judgment as leader. For Rashi, the people as a whole are not sufficiently prepared for what lies ahead.

K'li Yakar (Rabbi Sh'lomo Efraim of Luntchitz, 1550–1619) imagines a different conversation, in which God says, "Moshe, if you want you can send men, but if you ask for My opinion, I think you should send women, not men. After all, the men despise *Eretz Yisrael*. Didn't they say, 'Why is God bringing us to this land to die by the sword? Our wives and children will be taken captive! It would be better for us to return to Egypt!' (Num. 14:3). But the women have a great love for *Eretz Yisrael*. [The daughters of Zelphehad] said, 'Give us a portion' in the Land (Num. 27:4). If you listen to Me, Moshe, I know what the future holds. It is better to send the women who love *Eretz Yisrael*. They will not come back with a negative report. But if you feel that the men have enough integrity and enough love for the Land, go ahead and send them. It's your responsibility. As for Me, I would send the women." For K'li Yakar, the people are divided among those who are prepared and those who are not.

Six weeks ago we celebrated the sixtieth anniversary of the State of Israel. The questions and perspectives raised by Rashi and K'li Yakar can apply to the *M'dinat Yisrael* in our day as they applied to *Eretz Yisrael* in their days. We understand the strength of unity, but there is strength as well in diversity of opinion. But where are the limits?

Sh'lach L'cha
Jeffrey Ballon, 2009

After Moses assigned a mission to the princes of Israel to scout out the land that lay before them, several realities emerged.

The majority report was not positive: "So they spread evil report of the land" (Num. 14:36). A dozen men are selected. A ten-man majority reports back that the cities are fortified—filled with giants—and that it would be best for the people of Israel to proceed no further. Abort the mission of moving Israel into the land of Canaan, they advise. The risk is too great. No wonder a fuss ensues. We should have stayed in Egypt.

Readers of Walt Whitman might be reminded of these lines from his poem "Once I Pass'd through a Populous City":

> Once I pass'd through a populous city, imprinting my brain,
>   for future use, with its shows, architecture, customs, and
>   traditions;
> Yet now, of all that city, I remember only a woman I casually
>   met there, who detain'd me for love of me;
> Day by day and night by night we were together,—All else has
>   long been forgotten by me; . . .

The *sidrah* then establishes the bravery of Caleb and Joshua, who, upon their return, bring a huge stave of grapes from the valley of Eshkol. The imagination permits the reader to infer the loyalty these two men had to one another just to curry the strength to carry such a burden back to their camp. Perhaps it also infers that people who are in positions of power, like the ten princes, see things differently from the ordinary persons who make up their polis.

Our modern political situations may reflect some of this same situation. It is our modern challenge.

קרח *Korach*

(Numbers 16:1–18:32)

Korach
Paul J. Citrin, 1996

Immediately following the destruction of Korach and company, God commands Aaron and Eleazar, through Moses, to make an altar covering out of the fire pans of the rebels, explaining that the fire pans "have become holy because they were offered before the Lord" (Num. 17:3). The fire pans are intended to be a reminder of Korach's rebellion. How is it possible, despite Korach's faction using the pans for an offering, that instruments of rebellion and sin could still be considered holy?

Twice more after the destruction of Korach, there are reports of further rebellion by those who had sympathized with Korach. It makes one wonder: does the mentality of rebellion and rejection of legitimate authority take on a life and momentum of its own that defies both reason and the threat of horrible punishment?

Once the duties and perquisites of the Levites are reestablished, the Torah tells us that the Levites themselves must give a tithe of their tithe to God. That tenth of a tenth is to be "the best thereof." Why does God *not* define what constitutes "the best"?

Korach: Swallowed Alive
Stephen E. Cohen, 1998

The author of K'li Yakar shines a startling new light on the story of Korach, using a familiar old dictum from *Pirkei Avot*.

K'li Yakar   On "The earth opened its mouth and swallowed them up and their homes" (Num. 16:32): Why did this specific miracle occur? Because of what our Sages have taught: "Pray for the welfare of the government, for were it not for the fear of it, men would swallow each other alive" (*Pirkei Avot* 3:2). Korach and his followers wanted no leader at all, saying, "The entire congregation all of them are holy, and the Eternal is in their midst, why then do you raise yourself up over the congregation?" (Num. 16:3). And if their inflammatory advice were heeded, then men would swallow each other alive.

Comment   K'li Yakar seems to suggest that Korach's challenge to Moses was based upon a sincere (albeit naive and destructive) dispute about human nature and the need for hierarchy. Was it then, contrary to the assertion of *Pirkei Avot* 5:20, a dispute for the sake of heaven?

Korach: The Roots of Rebellion
Stephen E. Cohen, 1999

Ibn Ezra and Nachmanides offer conflicting accounts of the events leading up to Korach's rebellion. Both commentators are particularly troubled, not simply by Korach's challenge, but especially by the apparent popularity of this movement against the man of God.

Ibn Ezra   This incident occurred in the wilderness of Sinai, when the firstborns were replaced as priests by the tribe of Levi (see Num. 3:11–13). For the Israelites suspected that Moses did this of his own accord, to give power to his brother, and to his relatives the sons of Kehat, and to the entire tribe of Levi, who were his family. And the proof of all this is the concluding miracle of the story, the staff that sprouted almond blossoms, so that all the Israelites could see that God had chosen the tribe of Levi in place of the firstborns.

Ramban Rabbi Abraham says that the incident occurred in the Sinai wilderness after the firstborns were replaced as priests, and R. Abraham states in many places, "There is no before or after in the Torah," whenever he wishes. But I have expressed my opinion that the entire Torah proceeds chronologically, except where the text explicitly states otherwise, and then only for good reason. This particular incident occurred in the wilderness of Paran, at Kadesh Barnea, after the incident of the spies. For while Israel was in the Sinai Wilderness, no evil happened to them. Even with the Calf, though the sin was very great, those that died were very few, and Moses had prayed on the people's behalf and had saved them from destruction. The people at that time loved Moses and obeyed him, and if anyone had rebelled against him, the people would have stoned the rebel to death. All that time, Korach endured Aaron's appointment, and the firstborns endured the ordination of the Levites. But when they entered the Wilderness of Paran, many were burnt to death at Taveira, and many more died at Kivrot HaTaava. And when the people sinned and heeded the spies, Moses did not pray on their behalf and the princes of the tribes died in the plague, and it was decreed that the entire generation would die in the wilderness, then the spirit of the people became bitter, and they thought that Moses was leading them to disaster. Then Korach saw his opportunity.

Comment Does Ramban disagree with Ibn Ezra about the causes of the rebellion, or simply about the time and place? What different assumptions about the Torah text lead Ramban to reject Ibn Ezra's use of the principle *Ein mukdam um'uchar baTorah* ("There is no before or after in the Torah")?

Korach
Yossi Feintuch, 2000

Korach ben Itzhar and his cohorts "combined against Moses and Aaron and said to them, '. . . For all the community are holy'" (Num. 16:3). Yeshayahu Leibowitz in *Emunah, Histona va'Arakhim* (Jerusalem: Akadamon, 5742, p. 117) comments that Korach was the first one to seek and undermine Moses's conception of Israel's holiness; we find this concept only three verses before Korach's own statement on Israel's holiness. At the end of *Parashat Sh'lach L'cha*, Moses says, "Thus you shall be reminded to observe all My commandments and to be holy to your God" (Num. 15:40). What it means is that the people of Israel is not holy but is rather required to attain holiness. Israel's holiness is not a reality but a purpose and goal that Israel aspires perpetually to achieve. Israel's holiness is contingent upon *vaasitem et kol mitzvotai*, "to observe all My commandments"—a stipulation that clashes with human nature. While Korach sees Israel's holiness as inherent, a given fact, Moses demands that the people seek it continuously without the guarantee that they will attain it.

Y. Leibowitz thus comments that Moses's Judaism is difficult; it means knowing that we are not a holy people. Conversely, Korach's Judaism is very convenient, by which every Jew may pride himself of belonging to a chosen people that is intrinsically holy. Such a person is not required to do anything. In contrast to Korach, Israel's holiness is not a fact but a mission. It is not a reality but a task.

Korach
Sheldon Marder, 2001

This *parashah* begins and ends with "taking" in Num. 16:1: *vayikach Korach*—Korach threatens to take over; and in 18:26 and 18:28, *tikchu mei-eit b'nei Yisrael*—the Levites take tithes from the Israelites. The verb *lakach* frames the movement from rebellion and violence to a final portrait of the Levitical social order. Indeed, the verb is like a musical note running through these three chapters—eleven occurrences in all, each resonating against the others to remind us that a dynamic and meaningful process is unfolding.

Can attention to this sort of pattern in a *parashah* help make us more attentive to the patterns in everyday speech and conversation—and, thus, better listeners?

Korach
Kenneth J. Weiss, 2002

"Now Korach . . . betook himself" (Num. 16:1).

In the weeks and months following 9/11, politics in America took a back seat to national unity. For a while, at least, political debate, partisan rhetoric—even crime rates—declined dramatically. We found common ground and we shared it. National crisis brought out the best in us.

Not so at a time of crisis described in *Sefer B'midbar*. Twelve scouts entered Canaan, only two of whom afterwards affirmed their belief in God's promise that the land would, indeed, be theirs: "Let's roll," said Caleb and Joshua. "Let's not," responded the rest. The people, letting despair overwhelm their faith, refused to move.

Exploiting their vulnerability, Korach—a Levite, yet!—sought to foment rebellion. Far from uniting behind Moses, Korach and his followers became, as it were, biblical Libertarians: We're all holy, Moses! How can you presume superior holiness? We're all leaders! How is it that you present yourself as our leader?

Rabbi Tzvi Kollisher notes that the singular verb *vayikach* affirms that Korach betook himself (alone!), as did his followers (each and separately) to challenge Moses's position. The rebels shared no common ideal for the future. Their goal: self-promotion through agitation.

At a time of national crisis, Korach traded on the despair of the people. Americans—for a time, at least—united so as to overcome it.

Korach
Kenneth J. Weiss, 2003

"The next day, the whole Israelite community complained" (Num. 17:6).

"I take exception": might not a Jew have invented and perfected this phrase and the meaning it conveys? An unmistakable pattern of behavior emerges as we read of the wilderness experience: how common (I'm tempted to say "natural!") is their (our!) penchant for k'vetching.

It is not news that our people were not "happy wanderers." From biblical days to our own, this pattern has been engraved into every facet of our history and culture—even into Jewish folk humor (two Jews—three synagogues...). It manifests itself as a social divisiveness (ever been to a Jewish Federation board meeting?) and as skepticism—dare I say cynicism—directed at virtually all leaders (elected, self-appointed, Jewish or not).

We are—and have ever been—a fractious people, and I am convinced that this quality is (and always has been) a rationale for anti-Semitism. Other religious cultures taught obedience to authority: when the Pope issued orders, the Christian community responded, "Yes, Sir!" But, not the Jews! Upon hearing the same words from the same source—ever ready to argue, doubt, question, challenge—the Jews (called "querulous" by Abba Eban, "quarrelsome" by Jack Riemer!) answered, "Why?"

Textual "proof" you seek? The word *vayilonu* in the verse cited above is based on the Hebrew verb *l-y-n* (לין) meaning "to lodge," "to stay overnight." Here, however, it translates as "complain" or "rail" (JPS). Complainers: omnipresent, they "lodge where we lodge," the word "Why?" on the tip of their tongues!

Korach
Kenneth J. Weiss, 2004

Moses's passionate concern was to maintain the unity of the people, to see them through the numerous ordeals inherent in their wilderness journey, to bring them—with center intact—to the land (and the destiny) that God had promised them. His challenge, after all, was not merely to move them from the place they'd fled (Egypt) to the place they'd been promised; it was to grow them from an enslaved people, subjugated and fearful, into a free people: proud, blessed, possessing an eternal destiny—and a promise.

On (more than) one occasion, the community experienced disaffections, disgruntlements: a fraying. For one reason or many, there were individuals who were not happy. Among them: Korach. He "betook himself" to oppose Moses. So did Datan. So did Abiram. As did On, as did each of the 250 others who challenged Moses. There wasn't one rebellion; there were (at least) 253 separate rebellions. The singular verb in Num. 16:1 confirms it: "Korach . . . betook himself [ויקח, *vayikach*—third person singular!] . . . to rise up against Moses" (Num. 6:1–2). The conjunction "and" preceding the names of each of the other malcontents ודתן ואבירם . . . ואון ("and Datan and Abiram . . . and On") must be "Torah shorthand" for the same verb ויקח (*vayikach*), suggesting that these dissenters were not unified: each rebelled in his own way, for his own purpose.

By contrast, Moses knew that his purpose was to preserve our peoplehood, to safely convey our ancestors (= us!) through all of life's challenges to the Promised Land. On the fringes, some mutinied. But, Moses "betook himself" to hold the center and bring us home.

Korach
Alan Cook, 2005

Korach is not the first rebel of the *Tanach*. He's not the most dangerous rebel, necessarily, nor is he even the only one to voice his particular gripe. But he is the one who receives perhaps the greatest degree of focus.

Korach's chutzpah in lodging his complaint so exacerbates Moses that he finds himself provoked enough to enter into a verbal quarrel with the insurgents. Moses proclaims, רב לכם (*rav lachem*), "You guys are too much!" (Num. 16:7), after which he states, המעט (*ham'at*), "Is it too little for you?" (16:9). What are we to make of this language of contrasts?

We might be tempted to attribute Moses's consternation to a wounded ego; after all, it seems to be **his** leadership that is being called into question. But if we carefully analyze Korach's complaint, we can see why it would disturb Moses, and why he might choose to respond in such an unusual manner.

Korach asserts, כל העדה כלם קדשים (*chol ha-eidah kulam k'doshim*), "All of the congregation is holy, each and every one of them" (Num. 16:3). Nechama Leibowitz and other commentators suggest that this is Korach's sin: he diminishes the importance of community, and a common goal, in placing emphasis on the desires and ambitions of individuals.

The Torah (and later tradition), with its emphasis on כלל ישראל (*K'lal Yisrael*), understands that occasionally individual freedoms must be abrogated for the sake of the larger community. For Korach, the demands of participating in society are רב (*rav*), too great. In sparking such a pointless quarrel, he and his followers show themselves to be מעט (*m'at*), far too small-minded and petty.

Korach
Alan Cook, 2006

What was the true complaint of Korach and his fellow rebels? All of the men who protested against the leadership of Moses and Aaron were leaders of the community, אנשי שם (*anshei shem*, "men of repute" [Num. 16:2]). All of them had important responsibilities in serving the Israelites.

Yet in a camp of over six hundred thousand, there must be some centralized leadership. Korach and his friends were jealous because they had not been selected to be the political or spiritual leader of the community. In their vanity, they believed that the only way for them to make a name for themselves was to ascend to the highest positions of leadership. They failed to comprehend how each of them contributed to the welfare of the community. They imagined that they were relegated to being "nobodies," without an inheritance among their people.

But the words of God to Aaron (in Num. 18:20) may be applied to all of the people of Israel, then and now: "I am your portion and your share among the Israelites."

As Reb Zusya taught, in the world-to-come we will not be asked why we were not more like Moses, or Aaron, or any other well-known figure in our people's history. Rather, we will be asked why we were not the best "us" we could be.

Korach and his followers should not have been concerned about how they fared in comparison to Moses and Aaron. They should simply have been grateful that God had made them part of a treasured people.

Korach
Amy Scheinerman, 2007

Korach's rebellion is presented as the attempt of second-tier authority to grab the political power and authority of those at the top by appealing to the disgruntled masses. The aggadic explanations in the Babylonian Talmud, *Sanhedrin* 109–110, support this view, supplying a detailed description of how Korach stirred up unrest.

In contrast, *B'midbar Rabbah* 18:3 (and additionally *Tanchuma, Korach*, 2) takes a different and more courageous direction, raising an issue that is still with us. In this midrash Korach challenges Moses's interpretation of halachah: If a garment is blue, is it exempt from the mitzvah of fringes? If a house is filled with Torah scrolls, is it exempt from the mitzvah of mezuzah? Korach concludes that what Moses teaches as God's will is merely Moses's creation. Even Moses must have experienced the same sense when he visited Rabbi Akiva's academy. Rambam and Ibn Ezra hinted at the same question.

Today, the question is repeatedly asked openly, and the challenge is in many ways the opposite one: to respond in a way that affirms the sanctity of text while acknowledging the human component of Scripture. "Debunking" the divine nature of Torah was the exercise of previous generations that sought to establish a historical basis to at least some of the narratives in order to prove "authenticity." Today the challenge is to teach the religious meaning and divine value of studying Torah and living a life of Torah, through whatever interpretation and stream one chooses.

Korach
Alan Cook, 2008

Eric Moussambani is not exactly a household name. He is from Equatorial Guinea, and in the 2000 Olympic games he competed in the

100-meter freestyle race. Eric had learned to swim just nine months prior to the race. He had never before seen a swimming pool, having trained in rivers near his home. Because he was admitted in a "wild card" slot, he never had to swim a qualifying round. Several times during the event, he struggled, believing that he was drowning.

Eric did not win. In fact, he had the slowest recorded time in an Olympic heat, one minute and fifty-two seconds. But the fact that he completed the race is itself a victory. It shows us that miracles still do occur, though it may be difficult for us to recognize them.

Korach is full of miraculous occurrences: the ground opens and swallows the rebels alive; their followers are consumed in a sudden firestorm; and Aaron's staff produces flowers, while the others remain unchanged.

These miracles are bold. They disrupt the natural order, grabbing the attention of those who witness them. Yet, in the postbiblical world, we do not see evidence of such earth-shattering events. We might even ask whether miracles of this scope do—or ever did—occur.

Just as we struggle with this question, so did our Sages. The Talmud notes that "miracles do not take place on the hour." Years later, philosopher Franz Rosenzweig took a different approach: "Every miracle can be explained—after the event. Every miracle is possible, even the most absurd. . . . In fact nothing is miraculous about a miracle except that it comes when it does."

God, we pray that You will open our eyes so that we may recognize the miracles that You perform on our behalf every day.

Korach
David Novak, 2009

Korach appears in the Torah right after the devastation wrought by the false report brought by the *m'raglim* (spies) concerning the Promised Land. The report itself was frightening enough, but even more astounding was how well it undermined the people's confidence in God and their own ability to persevere with God's protection.

On the heels of the *m'raglim*, Korach challenges Moses and Aaron for the power to lead: "You have gone too far. All the people in the community are holy, and God is with them. Why are you setting yourselves above God's congregation?" (Num. 16:3).

Yet who is Korach challenging if not God? What does this say about Korach? Is Korach's desire for power so all-consuming that it doesn't allow him to experience what happened with the *m'raglim,* even to the extent that he is willing to risk further undermining the God-people relationship? Is he only thinking of the short-term outcome and not the long-term effect?

This story is terribly frustrating because power struggles still consume us, especially in our communities where we work so hard to create sacred connections among people. These power struggles undermine us, and they undermine what we are trying to teach, learn, and practice from our tradition.

Korach's action led others to join him in undermining God, Moses, and this inchoate people. Korach and his band lost their lives and were swallowed by the earth. Today the earth is not going to swallow all of the megalomaniac Korachs that roam its surface—but we must be vigilant in not allowing their warped sense of reality to take hold.

חקת-בלק *Chukat/Balak*

(Numbers 19:1–22:1 and Numbers 22:2–25:9)

Chukat/Balak
Paul J. Citrin, 1996

These two *parashiyot* are so rich and full, I will directly plunge into a few *kashiyot*.

Among the mysteries surrounding the red heifer is the omission of calling it a *chukat olam* (eternal law). Is use of the ashes of the red heifer only for the desert period? May fresh *parot adumot* (red heifers) be killed and burned as needed? Do we need to develop in our times ways to purify ourselves from contact with those who are spiritually and morally dead—abusers of all stripes who degrade, those who exploit, those who slander?

Why is Aaron punished along with Moses, since it was Moses who smote the rock and berated the people? Could it be the case that Aaron's real sin was his failure to calm Moses, knowing well the explosive temper of Moses?

God gives permission to Balaam to go with Balak's men to speak only the divine word. Why, then, when Balaam sets out, are we told "God's anger was kindled because he went" (Num. 22:22)? Was this a divine mixed message or was God concerned that Balaam might forget his role as a *nav*—a spokesman? How do we maintain a balance between the goals of our vocation and our ego needs?

Chukat/Balak: Striking the Rock
Stephen E. Cohen, 1998

Rabbi Moshe HaKohein and the Maharal have subtly but significantly different understandings of the role of anger in Moses's failure at the Waters of Merivah.

Rabbi Moshe HaKohein HaSepharadi (quoted by Ibn Ezra) Because the Israelites had enraged him, he said, "From this rock shall we draw for you water?" (Num. 20:10), by which he meant, "We do not have the ability to draw water from the rock; it is only in the power of God." But he was not sufficiently clear in his expression, and the people thought he meant that God could not bring forth water from the rock. And this is the meaning of "For you did not sanctify Me" (Num. 20:12) [then Rabbi Moshe brings as textual support]: "They angered him at the Waters of Merivah, and it went ill with Moses because of them. For they angered his spirit, and he spoke with his lips" (Ps. 106:32–33). Behold, the sin was in his mode of expression, not in the striking.

Maharal The sin of Moses and Aaron is as stated in the text: "Because you did not have faith in Me, to sanctify Me" (Num. 20:12). And this was in their striking the rock twice, when a miracle was performed for them. For this was a departure from faith—that they did this thing in anger. And anyone who performs a mitzvah in anger, especially when a miracle is being performed for them, as they did in saying, "Listen rebels," and in striking the rock, this is not faith. For faith is that one who trusts in God must always be glad—anger never accompanies faith.

Comment For Rabbi Moshe HaKohein, Moses's essential failure was miscommunication; for the Maharal, the failure was an emotional lapse. Does the Maharal understand anger as a sign of fear? Or arrogance? Or is it anger itself that is incompatible with faith?

Chukat/Balak: Moses's Match
Stephen E. Cohen, 1998

Rabbi Nachman of Bratzlav epitomizes the extreme ambivalence with which Jewish tradition has regarded Bilaam. Bilaam emerges in this text as Moses's doppelganger, his "match" in the negative realm of reality—equal to him in prophetic power, but trapped by desire and wickedness.

Likutei Moharan Bilaam was Moses's "match" within the *k'lipah* ["shell" or negative side of reality]. About him it says, "who knows the knowledge of the Most High" (Num. 24:16). Also, the letters of Bilaam [*bet, lamed, ayin, mem*] indicate that he was, within *k'lipah*, equal to the Torah. For *bet* is the first letter of the Torah, *lamed* is the last letter, *ayin* [= 70] corresponds to the seventy faces of Torah, and *mem* [= 40] corresponds to the forty days in which the Torah was given. And because he was in the realm of *k'lipah*, he was trapped most deeply in sexual desire, as it says, *hahaskein hiskanti*, "Have I been in the habit of doing this?" (Num. 22:30). [This phrase is taken in the Gemara Tractate *Sanhedrin* as indicating sexual perversions with his donkey.]

Comment In what way does Nachman see Bilaam "matching" Moses and the Torah? What is the "knowledge of the Most High" if not an understanding of God's sovereignty and the truth of the Torah?

Chukat/Balak: In the Book of the Wars of *YHVH*
Stephen E. Cohen, 1999

To modern eyes, a fragment quoted verbatim from the lost Book of the Wars of *YHVH* testifies powerfully to the human authorship of the Torah text. The Sages, however, read this fragment through a different lens.

Numbers 21:14 As it is written in the Book of the Wars of *YHVH, et vaheiv b'sufah.*

Babylonian Talmud, *Kiddushin* **30a** "They shall not be put to shame when they speak with their enemies in the gate" (Ps. 127:5). R. Chiya bar Abba said: Even a father and son, a teacher and student, who study Torah in a certain "gate" [i.e., subject matter] they become enemies to each other. But Rava said: They do not budge from there until they become beloved of each other, as it is written, *b'sefer milchamot HaShem*, "the wars of God are in/over/about the Book" (Num. 21:14). And the verse continues, *et vaheiv b'sufah*, which can be read *ahavah basof*, "In the end, there is love."

Comment   Does the enmity that R. Chiya bar Abba perceives arising in Torah study occur primarily between individuals of differing status (i.e., father and son, teacher and son), or does it arise also within a *chevruta*? What causes it?

Chukat/Balak
Yossi Feintuch, 2000

The *Yalkut* wonders, why was it that Aaron was punished together with Moses—"You shall not lead this congregation into the land" (Num. 20:12)—when it was Moses alone who struck the rock instead of ordering it to yield its water? This episode teaches, then, that the one who joins or attaches himself to transgressors, it is reckoned to him as though he himself was a transgressor. *Zayit Raanan* adds that Aaron's culpability lies in failing to exhort Moses not to strike the rock and particularly after the first strike. In so doing Aaron seemed to have consented to Moses's actions, hence, he too was punished.

Chafeitz Chayim points out that in this *parashah* there is not even one single break, neither *p'tuchah* nor *s'tumah* to distinguish between one matter and another. Admittedly, Bilaam was a prophet who received his prophecy from divine inspiration, but he lacked the lofty singularities and the good virtues of Israel's prophets. His own prophecies left no impression on him; he neither observed them nor learned a thing from them. *Haz"al* note that Moses used the divisions in the text for pausing, thus allowing him to explore their meaning. Bilaam, by contrast, was carried away by the sweeping flow of his words of prophecy without knowing or discerning their meaning. Hence, the entire *parashah* has no divisions.

Chukat/Balak
Sheldon Marder, May 2001

"And Moses raised his hand and struck the rock twice with his rod. Out came copious water" (Num. 20:11). In Gabriel Preil's poem

"Biographical Note" (translation by Howard Schwartz in *Modern Poems on the Bible: An Anthology,* ed. David Curzon, Jewish Publication Society, 1994), the image of water from the rock is the poet's metaphor for the creative process:

> It has been many years
> since I was imprisoned
> in the hothouse.
> My bread is sour
> and in my bones there grows
> the rust of time.
> Every desire turns to snow.
>
> But when I beat my head
> against the rock
> of a poem
> the fountain that springs forth
> is sweet.
>
> Had it not been for this
> I could have been a knight
> flickering and dying
> in a forest of loves,
> or one whose wrath
> sets cities and villages
> on fire.
>
> Praise to the rock.

Preil's poem reminds us that metaphor is a good tool for reflecting on our own creative process—especially when we choose a metaphor as complex as this one central to biblical narrative and fraught with moral ambiguity.

We're accustomed to viewing Moses's striking the rock as a sin, an act of defiance for which Moses is ultimately punished. Preil "rehabilitates" the image of striking the rock by using it as a metaphor for the fruitful agony of the creative process. This could also be a metaphor for the process of Jewish study—particularly the encounter with difficult texts against which we "beat our heads" in order to bring forth fountains of insight. What are the "rocks" in our lives that deserve our praise?

Chukat/Balak
Sheldon Marder, 2001

Mah tovu ohalecha Yaakov, mishk'notecha Yisrael ("How fair are your tents, O Jacob, your dwellings, O Israel" [Num. 24:5]).

"How beautiful are thy tents, Jacob / Even now," mused Yehuda Amichai, "when there are neither tents nor Jacob's / tribes, I say, how beautiful . . ." ("Time," *The Early Books of Yehuda Amichai*, Sheep Meadow Press, 1979).

How do we Jews—believers in Heschel's "cathedrals in time"—think about our "tents and dwelling places"? In other words, what role does "a sense of place" have in Jewish thought and culture? Robert Friend's poem "Arabic Lesson" (*The Next Room*, Menard Press, 1995) shows us one way to reflect on these kinds of questions through language:

> "Ahel," Arabic for "family,"
> cognate of "ohel," the Hebrew word for "tent"—
> for desert dwellers a home:
> grandfather, grandmother, father, mother, kids—
> a family,
> all under one roof—
>
> their floor sand
> covered by mats, their roof and walls skin
> flapping in the wind.
>
> A Bedouin living in our kind of house
> solid against the weather
> complains,
> "I can't sleep. The walls don't move."

In what ways do our homes, shuls, and workplaces shape our worldview and our relationships? Do we, in some subtle way, take on certain characteristics of the places we live in, work in, and pray in? What does "a sense of place" mean to us as Jews? What might a poem called "Hebrew Lesson" look like?

Chukat/Balak
Kenneth J. Weiss, 2002

"How goodly are your tents . . . [and] your dwellings" (Num. 24:5).

Balaam saw our people encamped below the mountain on which he stood. His word-picture of the scene, say the Rabbis, hints at a key—and lasting—Jewish value.

Balaam speaks of "tents" and "dwellings," which—our Rabbis teach—are distinct from one another. "Tents," suggests *Targum Yonatan*, are schools; "dwellings" are homes. Balaam, seeing them all, exclaims, *Mah Tovu*—"How goodly." *Malbim* seems to infer that it is not the structures Balaam calls "goodly"; he is, rather, alluding to the goodness being inculcated and modeled within them. *Malbim* concludes that Balaam waxed poetic over Israel's moral—rather than aesthetic—beauty. When schools teach and homes model goodness, that value can be effectively transmitted to our children.

A final word on tents as schools: "This is the law [*haTorah*]: when a person dies in a tent . . ." (Num. 19:14). The *Chafeitz Chayim* sees a warning here: study Torah now (= always); don't postpone, lest death overtake you.

How goodly are our tents and dwellings?

Chukat/Balak
Kenneth J. Weiss, 2003

"I can only utter the word that God puts into my mouth" (Num. 22:38b).

I call my enterprise "Balaam's Momentous Words" (BMW, for short!): when I bless someone, they stay blessed; when I curse someone, they know they are cursed.

Once Balak—the king of Moab—needed my services. He ordered me to place one of my patented curses on Israel. But I was doomed to fail. Though the king commanded (and even bribed) me to do it, God would not allow it. I could not curse God's blessed people.

My talking donkey totally baffled me. I couldn't fathom why this animal, whom I knew and trusted, suddenly refused to move. But then he spoke to me, directly after which I saw God's angel. Then, I knew! I knew what God wanted. The king of Moab **was** a force to reckon with. But the King of kings: He gave me the gift of language, implanted in me a conscience—a moral gyroscope: a spark of Himself. I could not **but** say what God wished me to say.

And so (King Balak's fury notwithstanding) I praised Israel. Though Balak ordered a curse, God commanded me to bless with words that could only be true: "How fair are your tents, O Jacob, your dwellings, O Israel!" (Num. 24:5).

Chukat/Balak
Kenneth J. Weiss, 2004

There was this perfect time, place, and setting: a garden of surpassing beauty; a man and a woman—innocent, naïve; four rivers offering limitless water, endless sustenance: life in all its loveliness, with all it possibilities...

From בראשית (*B'reishit*) to the מדבר (*midbar*), time and events degraded that beautiful, perfect vision. In subtle (and transparent) ways, the world changed, became... coarser. Life carried us far away from Eden.

And... it is in this week's *sidrah* that the idyllic vision is dispatched once and for all. We confront new realities, a whole different (a diametrically different!) world:

- Not a garden in Eden, but an unrelenting, unforgiving wilderness
- Not a land of plenty, but a daily battle for survival
- Not the idealistic Adam, but the driven, anxious Moses

- Not childlike Eve, but worldly-wise Miriam
- Not endless ease, but ceaseless struggle . . .

Rudely, brusquely, *Parashat Chukat* commands, "Wake up!" Look around you; no one is spared, not even Israel's consummate leaders:

- Moses "loses it" and is punished.
- Miriam (Moses's strength, a staff for her people) dies.
- Aaron (pursuer of peace) dies as well.

In reality, life is harsh, no (longer a) beautiful, perfect garden.

Of course, we return to the fanciful stories of בראשית (*B'reishit*) yearly; they renew our sense that the world (though not redeemed) is redeemable. There was this perfect time, place, and setting . . . we pray to know it again.

Chukat/Balak
Kenneth J. Weiss, 2004

Balaam—though speaking to King Balak—conveys critical intelligence to Israel. God has a message to deliver to the people: "[There is] no harm . . . in sight for Jacob, no woe in view for Israel" (Num. 23:21). God's message: Israel's future is bright and promising. Her tents are fair, her roots are planted deep into fertile soil; Israel can overcome all enemies! Balaam relays this message to an errant king even though it was intended for Israel, God's chosen (and errant?) people.

Leave it to Israel to squander a blessing: immediately after receiving God's optimistic projection, "the people profaned themselves by whoring with the Moabite women. . . . They also worshiped . . . Baal-peor" (Num. 25:1–3). What a waste!

Micah—pained still by the errors of that earlier time—teaches his contemporaries (and us!) how to hold onto blessing. In *Haftarat Balak*, he makes the case in perfect phrases: all that יהוה (*Adonai*) requires of you is "to do justice and to love goodness and to walk modestly with your God" (Micah 6:8).

Some day we'll "get it."

Chukat/Balak
Alan Cook, 2005

The חוק (*chok*, "law") that חקת (*Chukat*) describes is the ritual of the red heifer, a procedure that seems to defy our understanding. Although the mixture described therein is meant for purification, at least three people become unclean while preparing it!

The whole point of a חוק (*chok*), however, is that we observe it without seeking a rational basis for it. Rabbi Yochanan ben Zakkai taught that because it appears in the Torah as a divine law, we are duty-bound to observe it (*P'sikta D'Rav Kahana* 4:7). Rabbi Joshua of Siknin stated that the ritual of the red heifer is one of four laws in the Torah that have no rational explanation (*B'midbar Rabbah* 19:5).

So, God tells us to follow the ritual of פרה אדומה (*parah adumah*, "red heifer") "because I said so!" We all know that this rarely is a satisfying explanation when we tell children to do something; can we accept it as a rationale for a religious ritual? Certainly the founders of our movement didn't; they chose to "maintain only such ceremonies as elevate and sanctify our lives, but reject all such as are not adapted to the views and habits of modern civilization" (*Pittsburgh Platform*, 1885).

Nonetheless, there are certain ideas that even the most rational Reform Jew should accept on faith. Following the Shoah, a brief poem was found in a cellar in Cologne, France: "I believe in the sun even when it is not shining. I believe in love, even when I do not feel it. I believe in God, even when God is silent."

Sometimes we can make do without logical explanations. Sometimes we can just **believe.**

Chukat/Balak
Alan Cook, 2005

בלק (*Balak*) is one of five *sidrot* (six, if we count חיי שרה, *Chayei Sarah*) named for an individual. No patriarchs are so honored. Even Moses, to whom God said, "Take two tablets and call me in the morning" (with apologies to Red Buttons), never got his own portion!

What the individuals gifted with eponymous Torah portions have in common is that during their lifetimes they make extremely pivotal decisions. These choices have the potential to change the world as it has been known up to that point. We can see this in the stories of Noah, Sarah, Yitro, and Korach.

If we consider the actions of two characters who appear in this *sidrah*, Balak and Pinchas, we find that they each act in much the same way, with markedly different results. Balak is convinced that cursing the Israelites will enable him to defeat them in battle. Pinchas is convinced that only by slaying Zimri and Cozbi can he stem the plague and restore God's favor upon the Israelites. Both seek to maintain the world order as they understand it; both act with great zeal for their cause (Pinchas's zeal is described as קנאה [*kinah*], perhaps the only instance of this term appearing in a positive light).

Since only one worldview can prosper, only one individual is judged to have used his zeal in an appropriate fashion. In hiring Bilaam, Balak seeks to wreak havoc on the entire Israelite community. Pinchas, however, is rewarded for keeping his zeal in check, smiting only those who had done wrong (and who should have known better).

Zealotry is not necessarily a bad thing. As with any emotion, however, we must take care to keep it under control.

Chukat/Balak
Alan Cook, 2006

Water plays a role in three ways in חקת (*Chukat*): the waters of נדה (*nidah*, "lustration") made from the ashes of the red heifer, the waters of Meribah, and the water provided by God at Be'er. All of these instances show water's significance in human life.

The מי נדה (*mei nidah*), or so-called "waters of lustration," are used to cleanse people or objects that have come into contact with a dead body. This shows us water's power for purification.

The rules for concocting the מי נדה (*mei nidah*) are juxtaposed with the narrative that informs us of Miriam's passing. Since this immediately leads to a crisis when the Israelites find themselves without water, the midrash concludes that Miriam was capable of locating water in any setting or circumstance. Once she died, the people were forced to find other means of hydration.

In frustration, Moses strikes the rock that he has been told will provide water for the people, rather than speaking to it as he has been commanded. Here, water takes on a somewhat negative connotation, as this incident is what prevents Moses from entering Israel.

Yet at Be'er, just one chapter later, the people respond to their need for water by singing, and water is provided.

Perhaps the lesson is that, like anything in life, water must not be taken for granted. Water has the power to heal, and water has the power to destroy. It is an essential part of our human existence, and we should learn to celebrate it, as the Israelites finally learn to do at Be'er.

Chukat/Balak
Amy Scheinerman, 2007

In פרשת חקת (*Parashat Chukat*), Aaron dies atop Mount Hor. His vestments are placed on his son Eleazar, the second High Priest, and the Israelites mourn for thirty days. We presume that Moses buried his brother, but Torah does not tell us this. The transition has been smoothly managed, and while the people miss Aaron, they do not deify him. When Moses dies on Mount Nebo, פרשת וזאת הברכה (*Parashat V'zot Hab'rachah*) tells us that God buries him and keeps his burial place a secret, presumably lest the people treat it as a sacred site and worship there. Such could easily become idolatry.

Shortly after Aaron's death, the Israelites become restive and complain to Moses about the paucity of food and water in the wilderness. Torah recounts (Num. 21:6ff.) that God sent *seraph* serpents to attack the people in punishment. When they appealed to Moses, he interceded with God, who instructed him to construct a *seraph* of his own and mount it on a pole; those who gazed at it would be healed from the bite of the *seraph*.

When King Hezekiah undertook massive reforms to sweep idolatry away, he ground to dust Moses's bronze *seraph* because it had become the object of worship (II Kings 18:4). Although it had been made at the behest of God and had effected healing, in time it became an idol.

This reminds us that religious practices separated from their purpose and moral grounding run the risk of becoming idols in time.

Chukat/Balak
Amy Scheinerman, 2007

A donkey who demonstrates insight and wisdom and speaks words of truth while his master proves himself the true ass provides abundant food for thought.

Was Bilaam truly a prophet? Some commentators see Bilaam as a genuine prophet to the gentiles. This explains why God is concerned about his utterances and must convert his curses to blessings. Others see Bilaam as alternatively arrogant and greedy, or pathetic and foolish, in either case perpetuating fraud for economic gain. *Tanchuma* passes this moral judgment: "When the gift of prophecy was given to the gentile nations, many of them misused it, seeking to destroy rather than to bless."

What does it mean to be truly human? If the donkey can sense the impropriety and immortality of Bilaam's venture, but the prophet himself cannot, who is created בצלם אלהים (*b'tzelem Elohim*, "in the image of God") and who is the animal?

When significant financial gain is dangled in front of our face, how do we hold fast to principle? Does it always take a divine roadblock to keep us on the right path? How do we avoid distracting temptations that threaten to waylay us?

Are we instruments of blessing?

We are never far from the account told in פרשת בלק (*Parashat Balak*) because we begin morning minyan with the words of Bilaam: מה־טבו אהליך יעקב (*Mah tovu ohalecha Yaakov*, "How fair are your tents, O Jacob" [Num. 24:5]). This reminds us both that our lives as Jews are inextricably bound up with those of the rest of the world and that the questions raised by the conduct of Bilaam in פרשת בלק (*Parashat Balak*) are questions with which we should continually wrestle.

Chukat
Janice Garfunkel, 2008

Parashat Chukat seems to revolve around issues of leadership and power, dependence and independence, a timely theme for American Independence Day weekend.

Miriam dies, there is no water, and the people congregate against Moses and Aaron. Moses was supposed to have set up a system of shared leadership back in *Parashat Yitro* and again in *B'haalotcha*. But there is no evidence of shared leadership here. The whole community turns in anger only to Moses and Aaron, and one can only imagine that as the rabble demands from them water, these two men are not feeling all that personally powerful. Moses and Aaron are completely objectified: they seem to exist solely to meet the incessant demands of their children—oops—I mean people (we can see why, in Num. 11:12 Moses felt like a nursing mother).

A theme of Torah is the movement from the intimacy and dependence of infancy to greater independence and ultimately, we hope, a return to intimacy but with the independence of adulthood rather than the dependence of an infant. Perhaps the "sin" of Moses is when he cried out, "Listen, rebels! From this rock shall we bring forth for you water?" (Num. 20:10). God realized that after all these years in the wilderness, Moses and Aaron had lost even the desire to empower the people, to train them in independence. The Israelites cannot possibly enter the Promised Land still expecting these two men to take responsibility for everything. Why, for example, didn't Moses and Aaron suggest that the whole people pray for the water together? Any lessons in this for us as rabbis and parents?

Balak
Jeffrey Ballon, 2008

As a television viewer of the "Golden Age," I remember the signature phrase "Have Gun Will Travel." Paladin's business card demonstrated the gunslinger's readiness to accept a task without regard for context. The dramatic test of Balaam, the spell-casting magician archetype of this *sidrah*, shows similar moral impairment. When society enables opportunists to make themselves available to bless or to curse based on who pays the fee, there can be no claim to morality.

Poor leaders ultimately cede responsibility to those with questionable ethical grounding for the sake of convenience. It is unnecessary to identify by name the members of Congress or clergy who exemplify this principle in order to understand the lesson. Nor would I exclude myself in the practice of a rabbinate where some decisions I have made too often have been based on no higher standard than it's the easier thing to do.

A donkey is known for being unpredictably independent. Knocking Balaam off his feet represents the escape of unbridled energy. Francis or Mr. Ed aside, the mule represents the uncontrolled life, the intrusion of raw spirit from the shadows. We think we can manage everything until reality kicks us up against a wall and we get hurt a bit. But that is when we learn. The challenging trials associated with all transformative experience allow us to contemplate the resolution of such energies: redemption. The insight penetrates; there is motivation for saying, *Mah tovu ohalecha Yaakov* ("How fair are your tents, O Jacob" [Num. 24:5]). Tomorrow's promise lives with the secure dweller.

Chukat/Balak
Louis Rieser, 2009

The journey toward death follows parallel tracks. The one dying travels a different path from the one who offers comfort and care. The account in this *parashah* of the death of Aaron offers an opportunity to highlight these different paths. An extended description of Aaron's death is included in the *Midrash Petirat Aaron*, found in *Otzar Midrashim* and translated by our colleague Rabbi Bernard Mehlman in the *Journal of Reform Judaism* 27, no. 3 (1980): 49–58.

A beautiful passage in this midrash captures the difficulty Moses has in telling his brother Aaron, the one who has accompanied him since the days of the Burning Bush, that he is facing imminent death. At first Moses objects, "Master of the universe, it is unfitting for me to go to my brother to say to him, ascend to Mount Hor and prepare to die there." God reassures Moses and teaches him to "tell him with sweet and gentle words, so that he understands the matter." One feels, along with Moses, the anguish and the sorrow.

This midrash expresses the anger Aaron feels when he reaches his burial place and realizes he will not have an opportunity to commune with his family before death. Similarly we hear the anger of the Israelites when they discover that their beloved Aaron has left them. Accusations against Moses fly until God intervenes and "opens the entrance of the cave so all Israel could see Aaron lying on his bier."

Many different discussions of death and the dying process flow from this rich midrash.

פינחס *Pinchas*

(Numbers 25:10–30:1)

Pinchas: Succession
Stephen E. Cohen, 1998

According to the *p'shat* of Num. 27:17, Moses urged God to designate for him a worthy successor, who would "go out before them and go in before them." This midrash from *Yalkut Shimoni* reads a bitter complaint between the lines.

Yalkut Shimoni A parable of a king, who saw an orphan girl and sought to marry her. He sent for and proposed to her, but she replied, "I am not worthy to marry the king." He proposed to her seven times and she declined. Finally, with many requests, he took her. After a time, the king grew angry with her and decided to divorce her. Then she said, "I did not want to marry you; it was you who sought me. Now that you have decreed to divorce me, and to marry another, do not do to her as you have done to me." So too did the Holy One pursue Moses, and Moses replied, "I am not a man of words" (Exod. 4:10). After a while, God convinced him, and he went on his mission. After all the miracles had been worked through him, the Holy One then said to him, "You shall not bring this congregation into the land" (Num. 20:12). And Moses said, "Master of the universe, I did not seek the leadership. Since You have decreed that I will not enter, do not do to the next one as You have done to me—appoint one who will go out before them and who will go in before them."

Comment In this powerful midrash, Moses directs a stinging rebuke toward God. What response, if any, could God offer to Moses?

Pinchas: God's Lottery
Stephen E. Cohen, 1999

The Torah resorts in two instances to a lottery to determine a course of action: in the Yom Kippur ritual of the scapegoat, and in this week's *sidrah* to allocate the portions of the land among the twelve tribes. The actual lottery, as described in the Book of Joshua, involved drawing out small scrolls containing written descriptions of the boundaries of the various parcels of land. But the Sages of the Talmud and midrash were uneasy about allowing such an enormous matter to be guided by "chance."

Midrash Tanchuma Even before the lot came up, Elazar the High Priest foretold by the Holy Spirit, "Let the lot of Tribe *P'loni* arise, so that he may take Portion *P'loni*.'" And Joshua stretched out his hand and it came up. But even this sign was unnecessary, because the lot itself cried out as it came up, "I am the lot of Tribe *P'loni*, and I have arisen in Location *P'loni*!'" How do we know that the lot spoke? It is said, *al pi hagoral* ("assigned by lot," but *al pi* can also mean "from the mouth of").

Comment Does the Torah itself consider the lottery to be God's way of revealing the divine will? The author of the midrash clearly regards a simple lottery as an **insufficient** indication of God's will and therefore adds the "miraculous" divine signals to the lottery. What makes a sign from God sufficient?

Pinchas
Yossi Feintuch, 2000

Rav Y. Iger notes the significance of the fact that the two *parashiyot* preceding *Pinchas* (i.e., *Chukat/Balak* and the two *parashiyot* that follow it (i.e., *Matot/Mas'ei*) are usually joined together. *Parashat Pinchas*, by contrast, is always by itself. This is to teach us that Pinchas was a zealot and that every zealot is alone. Even when there are many zealots, each one walks his own way. Woe to the generation that sees its zealots unite. Pinchas as the Torah has it was rewarded with God's "covenant of peace" (Num. 25:12); indeed he was given "a pact of priesthood for all time because he took impassioned action for his God" (Num. 25:13). Adm'or Yehezkel wonders, why does Scripture say "for his God" rather than "for God"?

The significance of the added "his" is telling us that Pinchas did what he did out of his perception of God that was not shared by others. Rav B. Y. Nathan assumes that the significance of Pinchas's reward with God's covenant of peace lies in the belief that the road to peace is always better and more impressive than the road of fanaticism and war. *Yalkut Margaliot* adds that a leader in Israel should possess both attributes: jealousy against fence breakers (*portzei gadeir*) who endanger in their actions the nation's existence, and the attribute of peace and moderation—not always should one act only out of jealousy.

Pinchas
Sheldon Marder, 2001

"Take Joshua the son of Nun, a man in whom there is spirit" (Num. 27:18). What was God really saying to Moses? According to the Seer of Lublin (R. Yaakov Hurwitz), God told Moses to "take a man in whom there is spirit" because only one who knows his or her own spirit can have knowledge also of the spirit of others. One West Coast program to train clergy to become spiritual directors requires that each candidate spend a year under the guidance of another spiritual director before beginning the course of study. Given that many prospective Jews-by-choice and others now come to rabbis seeking spiritual guidance, how do we develop the resources to meet this challenge? Is there a spiritual dimension to leadership development programs in our synagogues and Jewish organizations?

Pinchas
Kenneth J. Weiss, 2002

"Let *YHVH* . . . appoint someone" (Num. 27:16).

I didn't forget, Moses. At the waters of Meribath-kadesh "you disobeyed My command to uphold My sanctity in their sight" (Num. 27:14). So, you'll die here on Abarim.

Moses, looking beyond his death sentence, voices his concern: Someone must succeed me. This people can't be set adrift; they need an *ish*—a human being (neither a super-being nor a miracle worker) who is capable, honest, inspired. (He might have continued: Now I understand—I, too, am [just] an *ish*: fallible and . . . mortal!)

God assents: "Single out Joshua . . . an inspired man" (Num. 27:18). "Invest him with some of your authority [*meihod'cha*]" (Num. 27:20). So, Moses commissions this *ish* publicly, ensuring an orderly transition.

In gematria, the numerical value of *meihod'cha* is seventy-five—the same as for the word *hasod*, "the secret." While commissioning Joshua, Moses perhaps shared the secret a leader must understand: you will know reward but only much later on (Rashi); meanwhile, you will experience self-doubt, loneliness, slander, envy, and incessant criticism. Now Joshua: lead them in. *Atah ha-ish*—you are the man!

Pinchas
Kenneth J. Weiss, 2003

"The sons of Korach . . . did not die" (Num. 26:11).

We've all known (perhaps even been victimized by) such a person. She or he is the one who makes a practice of publicly criticizing the rabbi, harassing synagogue leadership with endless negative feedback, passing along *lashon hara* even in social settings, even while attending services. Every community seems to have people who engage regularly in destructive behaviors like (but not necessarily limited to) these. I suggest that in *every* generation from the beginning of our peoplehood, there have been troublemakers like these on the scene (and/or making a scene!).

Care to speculate on where such people come from, how they came to be? The answer might well lie in one of the verses of our *parashah*, *Pinchas*, where we read, "The children of Korach . . . did not die" (Num. 26:11). R. E. Friedman demonstrates that Korach's descendants actually flourished and "later [became] the composers or singers of psalms" (see Pss. 42, 44, 45, etc.). By contrast, the children of Dathan and Abiram did die after partaking in "the direct rejection of Moses' and God's authority."

Lamentably, Korach's descendants live still. Rabbi Mordecai Ha-Cohen suggests, indeed, that they are reborn in every generation. We see them stirring up controversy, fomenting discontent, criticizing endlessly, by their attitudes and actions keeping harmony and shalom ever just beyond our reach.

Pinchas
Kenneth J. Weiss, 2004

We know a little about Zelophechad:

- He was Joseph's great-great-great grandson, through Joseph's son, Manasseh.
- He died in the wilderness "for his own sin" (Num. 27:3).
- He sired five daughters and no sons.

After his death, Zelophechad's daughters approached Moses, Eleazar, and others, insisting that their father was **not** among Korach's rebellious followers (ibid.).

Confidently—ably—these women also advocate for their own rights of inheritance. God upholds their claim: "The plea of Zelophechad's daughters is just [R. E. Friedman's translation: 'Zelophechad's daughters speak right']: . . . give them a hereditary holding among their father's kinsmen" (Num. 27:7).

צלפחד (Zelophechad): what a provocative name! When reduced to its basic components צל (*tzeil*, "shadow") and פחד (*pachad*, "fear"), the name suggests a person who is afraid of shadows, implying something imaginary or foreboding—a specter perhaps, or darkness. Let's hypothesize:

- Either: Zelophechad, a contemporary of Korach (whose rebellion epitomized a dark time), was anxious to distance himself from that event and fearful of being mistaken as one of the insurgents.
- Or: he was apprehensive because his progeny (absent a son) could be deprived of their rightful inheritance.

In hindsight, Zelophechad had nothing to fear. Thanks to his capable daughters, his reputation and his family inheritance were safe. His fear was itself a shadow, nothing more.

Pinchas
Alan Cook, 2005

As the Book of *B'midbar* draws to a conclusion, Moses is informed of his impending death. His first reaction is to inquire about his successor. God responds by instructing Moses, "Lay your hand [ידך, *yad'cha*]" (Num. 27:18) on Joshua ben Nun and instill in him "some of your authority" (JPS translation of מהודך, *meihod'cha* [Num. 27:20]).

Yet Moses instead lays his **hands** (ידיו, *yadav* [Num. 27:23]) upon Joshua. He goes above and beyond God's command, in the presence of the community, so that the people will accept Joshua as a fitting successor and not view him as a "pretender to the throne."

Moses might have had reason to be disappointed with this turn of events: it confirms that he will not be guiding the Israelites to the culmination of their journey; it signifies the conclusion of his unique relationship with God; and in passing over Gershom or Eliezer as potential successors, it ends any hope Moses might have had in establishing a dynasty. Nevertheless, Moses is able to rise above his disappointment and recognize what is in the people's best interest.

In Exod. 3:4, when Moses encounters the Burning Bush, God calls to him, "Moses! Moses!" The midrash suggests that this refers to Moses's humility: he was the same Moses before his encounter with the Divine as he was after it (*B'midbar Rabbah* 14:21). This same modesty allows Moses to accept the transfer of leadership to Joshua.

Perhaps this is a standard that we should strive to emulate. When presented with opportunities to lead, teach, judge, or otherwise make use of our expertise, let us not allow our egos to drive our actions. Instead, like Moses, let us emerge from such situations the same as when we entered into them.

Pinchas
Alan Cook, 2006

The daughters of Zelophechad are calm in presenting their case to Moses, arguing that they, too, should be entitled to land in Israel even though their father died without any male offspring. They do not rant and rave but present their case in a rational manner. What a relief this must have been for Moses, who has had to deal with loud complaints and rebellions throughout his career (indeed, Zelophechad's daughters take pains to distance their father from the events surrounding Korach's protest).

Moses consults with God for an answer to the women's plea, rather than suggesting an answer himself. Resh Lakish suggests that the word ותקרבנה (*vatikravnah*, "came near") in this passage (Num. 27:1) suggests that the daughters had gone through all the proper channels. First they drew near to one another, then they consulted with their tribal chiefs, and so on up the appropriate chain of command until they reached Moses. To show appreciation of the respect that they had shown him, Moses honored them by bringing their case before God.

The daughters do not make their request out of greed. Rather, they express concern about their father's name being lost to history, and they express a desire to inherit land in Israel.

Perhaps the actions of the daughters of Zelophechad can serve as a metaphor for our interactions with the Divine. When we approach God with the motive of serving our own interests, our petitions may not be heard. But when we express concern for the world and seek to bring healing to the sick, freedom to the captive, and so forth, then our prayers, like the request of Zelophechad's daughters, are deemed worthy.

Pinchas
Amy Scheinerman, 2007

פנחס (*Pinchas*) is among the few פרשיות (*parashiyot*) named for biblical personages. The incident most closely associated with his name is recounted in the last four *p'sukim* of פרשת בלק (*Parashat Balak*): following the idolatry committed by the Israelites at Baal-peor, God commands Moses to publicly impale the ringleaders, but before the punishment is carried out, Zimri brings his Midianite lover Cozbi for a tryst in the Tabernacle, inspiring Pinchas, imbued with zeal for God and Torah, to run them both through with a spear in one stroke.

Parashat Pinchas opens with God's declaration of approbation concerning Pinchas's act: "I grant [Pinchas] My pact of friendship. It shall be for him and his descendants after him a pact of priesthood for all time, because he took impassioned action for his God, thus making expiation for the Israelites" (Num. 25:10).

We rightly look askance at vigilanteeism, whether committed by Moses (who killed the taskmaster in Egypt) or Pinchas, who acted with fanatical zeal. God's approval makes this passage all the more difficult. We struggle with the balance between human ethics derived through reason, and divine ethics derived through revelation.

The account of Pinchas is a stark reminder that Judaism has developed a thoughtful process for arriving at decisions concerning human behavior. The very process of halachah, however we employ it, requires study, deliberation, debate, and thoughtfulness, not a rush to fulfill inner zeal. It is revelation and reason in harmony.

The business of doing Torah propels us to wrestle with God, struggle with our traditions, and ultimately arrive at religious imperatives in which we can have ethical confidence.

Pinchas
Amy Scheinerman, 2008

Parashat Pinchas follows three troubling accounts: the rebellion of Korach and his minions, the episode of Bilaam, and the violence of

Pinchas. Korach's rebellion is corrupt politics, Bilaam is corrupted prophecy (though God corrects it in time), and Pinchas is both gone awry and in the extreme. The wilderness experience seems to confirm that while you can take the people out of Egypt, it is an entirely different matter to take Egypt out of the people.

Yet in the annals of troubling Torah passages, the opening of *Parashat Pinchas* nears the top of the list. The gushing praise for the crude and merciless vigilantism exhibited by Pinchas (detailed in last week's *parashah*) is disturbing in and of itself, but here we find it exalted by God, whose wrath is calmed only by Pinchas's brutality.

Yet much in the *parashah* serves to restore our sense of equilibrium. The petition of the daughters of Zelophechad to inherit from their father who died without leaving a male heir inspires Moses to bring their case before God. As a result, the law of succession as it had heretofore been practiced and understood is amended and made more compassionate. With God's appointment of Yehoshua bin Nun to lead the people after Moses, we have a resounded affirmation that the demagoguery of Korach, false prophecy of Bilaam, and violence of Pinchas are not the Jewish way; peaceful adjudication of complaints and a peaceful transition of power are.

What a striking contrast to Pinchas's vigilantism. We are still in the process of leaving the corruption of Egypt behind us.

Pinchas
David Novak, 2009

Parashat Pinchas is an oft-visited *parashah* because it provides the exceptional recipe for drawing close to God that is *B'midbar*, chapter 28.

Through marking time with our Festivals, our season of *t'shuvah* (repentance), Shabbat, and Rosh Chodesh, we are given instruction on what to bring as an additional offering: animals, oil, flour, liquid. For many of us who listen to this chapter, we are hearing instructions for a time long ago and far away. As the additional *maftir* reading (when it is done), it is usually an afterthought.

This is a missed opportunity.

Our system of communal (and individual) prayer replaces sacrifice. That does not obviate the desire of contemporary Jews—and yes, even liberal Jews—to experience a closeness to the Holy One. We have an opportunity to remind contemporary Jews that the desire to experience God, to draw close, is not unique in our time; it is inherent in every age. It is embedded in our sacred texts, though in a ritual idiom that may make it inaccessible for many. Our job is to unlock the potential of a ritual for drawing close to God by reinterpreting it and and inviting people to share their ideas for how we can bring God closer to our experience.

מטות-מסעי Matot/Mas'ei
(Numbers 30:2–32:42 and Numbers 33:1–36:13)

Matot/Mas'ei: Cities of Refuge
Stephen E. Cohen, 1998

Rashi takes the uneven distribution of the cities of refuge as an indication of a "high-crime" region. *Siftei Chachamim* catches an important weakness in Rashi's analysis, and proposes an elegant solution.

Rashi Even though nine tribes settled in Canaan, and east of the Jordan only two and a half, they each had three cities of refuge because in Gil'ad murderers were common, as it is said, "Gil'ad is a city of evildoers, steeped in blood" (Hosea 6:8).

Siftei Chachamim If you say since the cities of refuge took in only accidental manslayers, and not murderers, why does Rashi say that in Gil'ad "murderers were common"? And if the reference is to accidental manslayers, how could it be that accidental manslayers were common [any more than anywhere else]? The response is that Rashi clearly means that intentional murder was widespread in Gil'ad but that these were murders without witnesses, and the murderers claimed, "We killed accidentally." This was widespread in Gil'ad and required three cities of refuge.

Comment Is it ironic, or mere coincidence, that the name Gil'ad—meaning "Mound of Witness"—is taken by *Siftei Chachamim* as a place of "unwitnessed" crime?

Matot/Mas'ei: Genocide
Stephen E. Cohen, 1999

The Gemara explains that Elazar was forced to teach the laws of purification of vessels after the war against Midian because Moses's wisdom departed in the heat of his anger.

Babylonian Talmud, *P'sachim* 66B   Resh Lakish said: Any man who is angry, if he is wise, then his wisdom departs from him . . . we know this from Moses, as it is written, "And Moses was enraged with the officers of the army" (Num. 31:14), and then it is written, "Then Elazar spoke to the men of the army that went to the battle. This is the law of the Torah that God commanded Moses" (Num. 31:21). Because from Moses it had departed.

Comment   Could we extend Resh Lakish's argument and suggest that Moses's lapse of wisdom included his demand that his army destroy all the Midianite women and male children? Why do none of our traditional commentaries even contemplate this possibility? Are we the first generation of Jews to have difficulty with Moses's genocidal order?

Matot/Mas'ei
Yossi Feintuch, 2000

Midrash Tanchuma and other commentators note the textual change between God's instruction to Moses in *B'midbar* (Numbers) 31:2 and Moses's own instruction to the Israelites in the following verse. While *Adonai* commands, "Seek vengeance, the vengeance of the Children of Israel from the Midianites; afterwards you will be gathered to your kinspeople," Moses commands the Israelites to "exact vengeance of *Adonai* upon Midian." Why did Moses change the divine text? The *Tanchuma* has Moses explaining to God, "Master of the universe, if we had been uncircumcised or idolaters, or reneging on mitzvot, the Midianites would not have hated us nor would they chase us; they do so, however, because of the Torah that you gave us. Hence, this vengeance is yours."

K'li Yakar understands the change differently: it ties it to Moses's impending death. Hence Moses thinks to himself: If I tell them

(Israel) the whole truth, that is, Israel should go to war with Midian for their own honor and right afterwards I'll die, they would not go to war. They might say: If this vengeance was for the sake of our honor, we would rather give it up lest Moses die. A. Arazi's *Mi-Maayan HaAggadah* notes that Moses could have postponed the war with Midian, thus prolonging his own life; what a grave dilemma! The love of Israel triumphed in him over the mightiest force in any human soul—the love of life. Moses would rather die himself as long as Israel fulfills God's command to go war against Midian.

Matot/Mas'ei
Sheldon Marder, 2001

"The towns that you assign to the Levites shall comprise the six cities of refuge . . . to which you shall add forty-two towns" (Num. 35:6).

R. Abraham Joshua Heschel of Opatov wrote in his *Ohev Yisrael* that the six cities correspond to the six words *Sh'ma Yisrael Adonai Eloheinu Adonai Echad*, and the forty-two towns correspond to the passage that concludes "and upon your gates" (Deut. 6:9). Thus, according to R. Heschel, these forty-eight words are a "place" of refuge: no matter one's sin, a person of faith can find shelter and protection there by loving God and accepting *ol malchut shamayim* ("the yoke of the kingdom of Heaven").

"Sometimes," wrote Etty Hillesum—in her diary from the Holocaust years—"I want to flee with everything I possess into a few words, seek refuge in them. But there are still no words to shelter me. I am in search of a haven, yet I must first build it for myself, stone by stone. Everyone seeks a home, a refuge. And I am always in search of a few words" (from *An Interrupted Life: The Diaries, 1941–1943 and Letters from Westbork*, Picador, 1996).

Worlds apart theologically, yet Hillesum and Heschel are joined in spirit by the idea that words have real substance and, thus, can become a home or haven, a "city of refuge," as it were. Why does this idea strike us as so quintessentially Jewish? Is there a way to build this idea into the prayer life of our communities today?

Matot/Mas'ei
Kenneth J. Weiss, 2002

"Six cities of refuge . . . [and] forty-two [additional] towns" (Num. 35:6).

Cities of refuge—words of refuge: one of the great Chasidim, A. J. Heschel of Opatov, noted that "the six cities of refuge correspond to the six [Hebrew] words of *Sh'ma*." A coincidence? By design?

Either way, the midrashic embellishments are rich and suggestive: as our ancestors found safe harbor in these cities, so we find spiritual refuge in our watchword. As God instructed Moses to establish havens for the unintentional "manslayer," so we know that *Sh'ma* is a haven for every Jew longing for at-one-ment with the Divine. Sanctuary can be a protected place or a deeply-held belief—or both. Refuge—whether physical or spiritual—is an ancient and universal human need.

Coincidentally (or by design!), the ancient Hawaiians established cities of refuge. How did they function—and when? The answer resides with "the big Kahuna" (we'd know him as the *Kohein Gadol*)! One of those ten lost tribes really got lost . . . but what a paradise they found(ed)!

P.S. (Not) coincidentally: forty-two additional towns parallel the forty-two words of V'ahavta . . .

Matot/Mas'ei
Kenneth J. Weiss, 2003

"He shall not break his pledge; he must carry out all that has crossed his lips" (Num. 30:3).

Believing that God actually placed words in his mouth, Balaam asks Balak this definitive, rhetorical question: "Have I the power to speak freely?" (Num. 22:38). No, he concludes: I am not free to speak; "I can utter only the word that God puts into my mouth" (ibid.).

Moses offers a contrasting message with respect to the power of speech; he teaches Israel through their tribal leaders: you are free to speak, indeed to vow, to take an oath, to make a promise. However, your word is your bond! Freedom does not imply irresponsibility: you must intend to live up to any pledge even as you verbalize it; you "must carry out all that has crossed [your] lips" (Num. 30:3).

Lo yacheil d'varo, "he shall not break his word" (Num. 30:3): Hillel Silverman sees a link between the words *yacheil* (to break, profane) and *chol* (something ordinary, profane—literally, "sand"). Jews distinguish between the holy and the *chol*. Whereas words based on sincere intent are holy, words intended to deceive are an affront to God—they are common, profane, just so much sand.

God intends that people be truthful, that words be true: for only true words possess holiness. Indeed, a midrash suggests that when a righteous person speaks righteously, God will assure that "all that proceeds from . . . [his] mouth . . . will come true" (*Avodat Yisrael*).

Matot/Mas'ei
Kenneth J. Weiss, 2004

Life is a process, a series of interconnected episodes. Each episode is part of life's unfolding: toddlers become children who become young adults, then spouses, then parents. Each stage of life tells its own story, even as it is one of a flow of stories: "a journey, a going—a growing."

Since 2002, Sue and I have learned that retirement, too, is a series of stages. Retirement in one's sixties is as different from retirement in one's nineties as starting out on one's career path is different from reaching a professional pinnacle.

Life—all of life—is lived stage by stage.

Richard Elliot Friedman suggests that the Book of Numbers—concluding with *Parashat Mas'ei*—models this universal truth. מסעי (*mas'ei*) can be translated as "marches," "travels," "stages." Like the interconnected stories in Genesis, like the flow of stages in our own lives, these stories should be understood as interrelated episodes from Israel's wilderness journey. "The journey," he writes, "is the unifying element" (*Commentary on the Torah*, HarperOne, 2003).

In Torah as in our lives, "life is a journey, a sacred pilgrimage" (Alvin Fine, "Birth is a Beginning," *Mishkan T'filah: A Reform Siddur*, CCAR Press, 2007, p. 575).

Matot/Mas'ei
Alan Cook, 2005

Malcolm Gladwell's *Blink* (Little Brown & Co., 2005) speaks of the benefits and the disadvantages of making decisions based on "gut instincts." Good use of such instincts allows, for instance, improvisational comedy troupes to create coherent and funny scenes without a script. Improper attention to such reactions leads to disasters like "New Coke" (because people prefer a *sip* of sweeter-tasting Pepsi, with which New Coke sought to compete, but they prefer to *drink* Classic Coca-Cola).

In *Matot*, we find instances of such "gut reactions." The Reubenites and Gadites (later to be joined by half of Manasseh) seek to remain on the east side of the Jordan, despite never having seen firsthand what sort of land awaits them in Canaan. Having experienced the good pasture where they are currently camped, they jump to the conclusion that it won't get any better than that. So, they approach Moses with their request to settle where they are.

Moses himself can't help but act instinctively. He presumes that the tribes' request is predicated on a desire to avoid battle and speaks harshly to them, essentially accusing them of treason.

The hasty reaction from both sides may or may not have been justified. Some commentators agree with Moses's dismay that the leaders of the tribes put the needs of their flocks before the needs of their kinsmen (see Num. 32:16). Others chastise Moses for not seeing the bigger picture: settlements east of the Jordan would increase the territorial holdings of the Israelites.

This seems to be largely a case of misunderstood intentions due to a poor use of semantics. Both parties' "gut instincts" have failed them.

Sometimes we have to *think* before we *blink*.

Matot/Mas'ei
Alan Cook, 2005

As the Israelites prepare to enter the land, the people are told to establish cities of refuge so that one who unintentionally murders another may flee there. This instruction comes after the cataloging of the Israelites' travels up to this point. Yet, surprisingly, the revelation of the Torah is omitted from this listing of journeys. Mordecai Ha-Cohen, in *Al HaTorah*, suggests that this omission comes to teach us that the Torah, once given, is timeless; it is relevant in all places and at all times.

But if this is true, then how are we to understand these cities of refuge? The commandment providing for the ערי מקלט (*arei miklat*) shows compassion but appears to flout the Torah's injunction against murder. Is the Torah contradicting itself? Is it "going soft"?

In *The Merchant of Venice*, Portia declares, "The quality of mercy is not strain'd. . . . It is an attribute to God Himself; and earthly power doth then show likest God's when mercy seasons justice."

It may seem ironic to cite a work considered by many to be anti-Semitic in order to explore our *sidrah*. But Portia does have a point. The ערי מקלט (*arei miklat*) are not intended to condone the actions of the murderer; indeed, one who murders intentionally is not eligible to take refuge in such a city. But the cities of refuge do serve to remind us that accidents do happen, and in such cases, mercy should indeed "season justice." Even in the case of a brutal act such as murder, the facts are not always black and white. The ערי מקלט (*arei miklat*) allow for mercy in those cases where shades of gray creep in.

Matot/Mas'ei
Alan Cook, 2006

It seems curious that while there is a *sidrah* named מטות (*Matot*, "Tribes"), there is none with a name like בני ישראל (*B'nei Yisrael*, "Children of Israel"). The individual identity of the tribes is celebrated, but not the collective identity of the nation.

The idea of the whole nation coming together כל ישראל (*kol Yisrael*, "all of Israel") does not appear until the beginning of Deuteronomy (1:1). The tribes all fight for their own best interests and only rarely seem to come together in a loose conglomeration, usually in order to fend off attacks by neighboring armies.

Yet Moses knows that things will have to change when the people enter Canaan, and this is why he is taken aback when representatives of Reuben, Gad, and Manasseh wish to claim their tribal stakes on the "other side of the Jordan." He tells them that they must not shirk their responsibility to their kinsmen and must work for the greater good of the whole Israelite community, rather than focus solely on their own self-interests.

We see the people beginning to comprehend what it means to be a nation as the Book of במדבר (*B'midbar*) concludes. In מסעי (*Mas'ei*) we read, אלה מסעי בני-ישראל (*Eileh mas'ei V'nei Yisrael*, "These were the marches of the Children of Israel" [Num. 33:1]), suggesting that the people have now realized that each of their fates is intertwined with those of the men and women marching alongside them. When they arrive in Canaan, they will have to look out for each other and provide for the landless Levites. They will have to make the final transition from the slave mentality of "every person for himself" to a comprehension of the value of כלל-ישראל (*K'lal Yisrael*, "the community of Israel").

Matot/Mas'ei
Amy Scheinerman, 2007

מטות (*Matot*) opens with an exhortation concerning vows: If a man makes a vow, it stands and he is held accountable. If a woman under the guardianship of her father or husband makes a vow, however, the father or husband has the option of annulling the vow on the day he learns of it; only a widow's or divorcee's vow is binding to the last.

In *Mishnah N'darim* 9:1–2, R. Eliezer expresses a different criterion for reversing a vow. Here he—and the חכמים (*chachamim*, "Sages") agree—releases one from a vow if the nature of the vow dishonors one's parents. R. Eliezer further releases one from a vow made on a contingency that changes in the course of time, but חכמים (*chachamim*) prohibit this.

Both Torah and Mishnah approach human vows with an understanding that there are times when people make mistakes, perhaps acting out of uncontrolled emotion. However, while Torah couches annulment in the context of men as free agents and as those who control the females in their purview, Mishnah raises the discussion to a level of the criteria appropriate for releasing people from their inappropriate vows. The mitzvah of כבוד אב ואם (*k'vod av v'eim*, "honoring father and mother") takes precedence over a vow, on the one hand, but the world is always changing, and if we claim unforeseen change in our surroundings to legitimate release from a vow, then what commitment will ever stand?

In a day and age where words are bandied about glibly, promises often forgotten, and many fail to assume responsibility for what they have said, the subject of vows reminds us of the importance of our words and commitments.

Matot/Mas'ei
Micky Boyden, 2008

There are some Torah portions whose values differ widely from our own. One such *parashah* is *Matot*.

Matot, which deals largely with vows, imposes considerable limits upon the right of women to take commitments upon themselves. Should a father object to his daughter's vows, then "none of her vows or self-imposed obligations shall stand."

Whereas one could argue, as the Torah does, that she is young and needs protection from her own folly (what about sons!), this argument falls down when she marries and a similar right of veto transfers to her husband.

Interestingly, Rabbi Issachar Eilenburg, who lived in Posen in the sixteenth century, argued that the right of veto only extended to the husband in the event that the vow that his wife had taken upon herself caused her emotional distress.

However, even more problematic is the *parashah*'s description of the vengeance taken upon the Midianites: "They took the field against Midian, as *Adonai* had commanded Moses, and slew every male. . . . The Israelites took the women and the children of the Midianites captive, and seized as booty all their beasts, all their herds, and all their wealth" (Num. 31:7, 31:9).

Perhaps it is comforting to know that this may have just been wishful thinking, since the Midianites appear later in the Book of Judges.

Nevertheless, how should we as Reform Jews relate to such material? Our thinking and values have moved on. Clearly, not everything that was acceptable or prescribed in Torah times meets our moral approval today.

Our challenge, in the words of Rabbi Avraham Isaac Kook, first Ashkenazi chief rabbi in British mandate Palestine, is "to renew the old and sanctify the new." Precisely because we do not believe that everything old is necessarily holy, we are duty-bound to search for what is sacred in our modern world.

Matot/Mas'ei
Amy Scheinerman, 2008

Parashat Mas'ei opens with forty-nine *p'sukim* (verses) recounting the forty-two stops in the Israelites' forty-year wilderness wandering. Numbers 33:2 tells us, *Vayichtov Moshe et motza-eihem l'mas'eihem al pi Adonai* ("Moses recorded the starting points of their various marches as directed by *Adonai*"). Ibn Ezra applies *al pi Adonai* ("as directed by *Adonai*") to *motza-eihem l'ma'seihim* ("the starting points of their various marches") and concludes that God planned Israel's extensive and exhausting itinerary through the wilderness, step-by-step, in stages. Nachmanides applies *al pi Adonai* instead to *vayichtov* ("recorded") and holds that it was the recording that God here commands; the Israelites were already encamping and journeying according to God's instructions. Rashi, citing R. Moshe HaDarshan, anticipates this issue and sides with Nachmanides. He addresses the question "Why record each stop along the route?" and suggests two reasons for the recounting. The first is to publicize God's loving deeds: although God had the Israelites move about for four decades, they were permitted rest at intervals, suggesting that even when the journey is tough, we don't go it alone. Perhaps his point is that even amidst God's disappointment in and anger at the Israelites' spiritual immaturity and inappropriate behavior, God nonetheless loves and supports them in their much-needed growth trek. Rashi attributes the second reason to R. Tanchuma via a *mashal l'melech,* a parable of a king who recounts every step in a journey with his son that includes discomfort and illness, suggesting that God journeys with Israel every step of the way, experiencing what they experience. However alone we may feel at times, we are never truly alone. Harold Kushner makes that point eloquently in his commentary on Psalm 23, *The Lord Is My Shepherd* (Knopf, 2003).

Matot/Mas'ei
Amy Scheinerman, 2009

Most of *B'midbar* is the story of Moshe's struggle to keep the Israelites together and moving forward—physically and spiritually—through the wilderness.

The tribes of Reuven and Gad ask Moshe for permission to remain in trans-Jordan and not accompany the other tribes to settle in *Eretz Yisrael*: "The land that the LORD has conquered for the community of Israel is cattle country, and your servants have cattle. . . . Do not move us across the Jordan" (Num. 32:4–5). Moshe expresses anger at their selfishness—"Are your brethren to go to war while you stay here?" (32:6)—to which they respond, "We will build here sheepfolds for our flocks and towns for our children" (32:16). Their words betray their priorities: affluence precedes family and community in their value system. *Midrash HaGadol* tells us that the tribes of Reuven and Gad owned no more cattle than did their brethren; they merely spent more time concerned with their possessions.

Is this not what we face today? We often bemoan misplaced priorities: Jews who value wealth above all else, soccer above religious education, secular pleasures above communal celebrations. Americans in general live increasingly disconnected and scattered lives; community and connection elude far too many, as amply documented and discussed by Robert Putnam in *Bowling Alone*, as well as Robert Bellah, who wrote in *Habits of the Heart: Individualism and Commitment in American Life* (University of California Press, 2007, p. 6), "American cultural traditions define personality, achievement, and the purpose of human life in ways that leave the individual suspended in glorious, but terrifying, isolation."

The need for connection remains, and many are searching for a spiritual home. What more can we do to make our synagogues and institutions inviting, enriching, and nourishing and facilitate the mitzvah *al tifros min hatzibbur* (not separating from the community)?

Deuteronomy

דברים *D'varim*

(Deuteronomy 1:1–3:22)

D'varim
Lawrence S. Kushner, 1996

In Deut. 1:9–10, Moses bemoans the fact that "today you have become like the stars of heaven in multitude," suggesting that God's promise to Abraham (Gen. 15:5) has already come true. Was he right? Was God promising Abraham only a people of the size that was ready to enter the Land, or was it a promise for the ages? What are we to make of the fact that if God's promise has come true in Moses's day, Moses isn't so happy about it? Do we always want God's promises to come true?

D'varim: The Long Journey
Stephen E. Cohen, 1999

The Ishbitzer Rebbe, author of the *Mei HaShiloach*, cites the tradition from *Sifrei* that upon leaving Sinai, the Israelites made the eleven-day journey to Kadesh, miraculously, in only three days. Counter to the earlier sages, however, *Mei HaShiloach* casts this rapid journey in a negative light.

Mei HaShiloach   At the receiving of the Torah, the heart of Israel was not yet completely purified, to be drawn after the divine will. They only knew intellectually that it would benefit them to fulfill the will of God, but their hearts were not purified. This is referred to in the verse "Moses spoke [to them] . . . it is eleven days journey from Horeb to Kadesh-barnea" (Deut. 1:1–2). That is: When you were at Horeb, and you received the Torah, you thought that your hearts were purified, and you traveled [to Kadesh] in only three days. But in truth, it could not be, for it is a journey of eleven days. And the words of Torah were not yet fixed in your hearts until the passage of forty years, by means of all the stumblings and the trials. By means of this your hearts were purified. As it is said, "A man cannot understand the words of Torah until he has stumbled/*nichshal* regarding them" (Babylonian Talmud, *Gittin* 63a).

Comment   We can surely appreciate the Ishbitzer's insistence on the requirements of time, experience, and the lessons that come from failure for the attainment of complete purity of heart. But what advice is implied here for a young person who is seeking? Are all paths more or less equal, as long as they take time, involve stumbling, and lead to "experience"?

D'varim
Sheldon Marder, 2001

"Pick from each of your tribes men who are wise, discerning, and experienced [*chachamim un'vonim viduim*], and I will appoint them as your heads" (Deut. 1:13).

Is Moses looking for individuals with all three traits, or is he asking for three different kinds of people? What distinguishes wisdom from discernment? The *chacham* from the *navon*? These are among the questions that excited the *chachamim* (sages) who wrote the *Sifrei* commentary on this verse:

> With regard to this [verse] Arios asked R. Yosei, "Who is a *chacham*?" He replied to him, "Whoever maintains [*m'kayeim*] his learning." "But," [asked Arios], "is this not a *navon*?" He replied to him, "*Navon* has already been mentioned [separately]." What is the difference [then] between a wise person and a discerning person? A wise person resembles a rich money changer. When someone brings him [money] to examine, he examines it,

and when no one brings him [money] to examine, he takes out his own and examines it. A discerning person resembles a poor money changer. When someone brings him [money] to examine, he examines it, and when no one brings him [money], he sits waiting anxiously.

The *Sifrei* sees *chacham* and *navon* not as intellectual qualities that coexist in one individual, but as two entirely different people. Both are "money changers"—both deal with an object of supreme value (Torah). The *navon*, however, is dependent upon outside stimulation to pursue his studies, while the *chacham* posseses the internal resources and rich inner life for fruitful learning on his own. As Professor Steven Fraade has pointed out, the *navon* may be a source of sacred wisdom, but the *chacham* is its very embodiment (*From Tradition to Commentary: Torah and Its Interpretation in the Midrash Sifrei to Deuteronomy*, SUNY Series in Judaica, 1991). What kinds of rabbis are we? And how does one move from being a *navon* to being a *chacham* who "maintains" one's learning?

D'varim
Kenneth J. Weiss, 2002

"These are the words" (Deut. 1:1). Do our words affirm or deny God?

"These are *had'varim*." Let's translate midrashically: "These are the *d'varim* of God" (of *Hei*, that being one of God's appellations). On God's behalf, Moses retells the wilderness experience.

Early on, Moses recalls when the people urged him to "send men [into Canaan] to reconnoiter the land" (Deut. 1:22); the twelve return to report that "it is a good land that the LORD our God is giving to us" (1:25b). Moses tells everyone that they needn't fear, that God would see to their successful conquest. Turning their backs on God, however, the people refuse to cross over. Torah continues, "And YHVH heard the sound of your words [*et kol divreichem*] and was angry" (1:34).

The people, by their words, spurn God, ignore the *b'rit* (covenant). In contrast, when Moses spoke, he spoke for God. Need "proof"?

Had'varim is preceded by the word *eileh*, an anagram of which is *HaEl*. Moses surely spoke God's words...

Do *we*?

D'varim
Kenneth J. Weiss, 2003

"The words that Moses addressed" (Deut. 1:1).

Growth is a process—steps forward, steps backward—rarely a straight line. As he matured, Moses developed into a self-confident and capable orator—from "I'm not a man of words...I'm...heavy of tongue" (Exod. 4:10) to "Moses addressed...all Israel" (Deut. 1:1). Over time, Moses evolved, able to relay—and even clarify—God's commandments (see the verb באר, *bei-eir* [Deut. 1:5]).

Like Moses, every person is capable of growth.

Peoples can grow, too. Israel grew over the forty years it needed to complete the journey from Horeb (Mount Sinai) to the eastern bank of the Jordan.

Growth is not about moving from here to there. Growth is about moving through stages, some lengthy and difficult.

D'varim
Kenneth J. Weiss, 2004

Step back a moment. View the life of Moses in its entirety: born a Levite, rescued then raised as Pharaoh's grandson, defender of human rights, fugitive, shepherd, reluctant messenger, inspirational and influential leader, father figure, grand patriarch...

Moses's life was replete with experiences, lessons and perspectives, wisdom and warnings. Thus, in his "December" years, Moses had much to say: a life story to teach and transmit. ספר דברים (*Sefer D'varim*, Book of Deuteronomy) is, in a sense, Moses's "ethical will."

I work in a senior residence—Jewish, kosher—the only one of its kind and quality in the San Diego area. The average age of residents is upper eighties. People in their nineties and above are my daily companions. Like Moses, these people have exquisite stories to tell—experiences, perspectives, wisdom. Zalman Schachter-Shalomi speaks of "eldering": elders are "agent[s] of evolution [who] herald . . . the next phase of human development"; they bring a "seasoned" approach to living life; they leave behind treasures that will enrich a new generation. "Eldering" affirms the enormous potential and process that can be a part of growing older.

Moses modeled "eldering" millennia ago: he left us Deuteronomy—a treasure that continues to enrich each new generation of readers.

D'varim: Shabbat Chazon
Alan Cook, 2005

"These are the words that Moses addressed to *all* Israel" (Deut. 1:1).

"Though you pray at length, I will not listen" (Isa. 1:15).

Moses begins his book-length valedictory address with "words." But these are not just any words; Moses knows that this will be his final opportunity to address the multitude that he has led, and struggled with, for the past forty years. So he chooses his words very carefully.

No word in the Torah is extraneous. So what is the purpose of the word כל (*kol*, "all") in the first verse of Deuteronomy? Our commentators say that it indicates that Moses was able to address each of the Israelites individually, according to their needs. He told them what they wanted, or needed, to hear.

This careful choice of words stands in marked contrast to what we are told about Israelite behavior in the days prior to the destruction of the Temple in Jerusalem. The *sinat chinam* (groundless hatred) that prevailed left everyone unwilling, or unable, to speak a kind word to their neighbors.

In the haftarah for Shabbat Chazon, selected to help put us in the proper mind-set for observing Tishah B'Av, Isaiah preaches that God will not listen to prayer that is devoid of any true meaning. He exhorts the Israelites to devote themselves to justice, rather than merely paying it lip service.

We must choose our words carefully, as we seek to imbue them with meaning, love, and justice.

D'varim
Alan Cook, 2006

"Give me a word, any word, and I show you that the root of that word is Greek."

This is one of the running gags in the film *My Big Fat Greek Wedding*. Gus Portokalos, the patriarch of the family depicted in the film, is convinced that every word in the English language has Greek origins.

In the case of "Deuteronomy," Gus would be correct; the term, of course, derives from *deuteronomos*, "a second telling of the law." But Gus didn't care about the veracity of his word etymologies. His peculiar habit was just a manner of asserting his ethnic pride.

In a sense, that is what Moses is doing in דברים (*D'varim*). He knows all of the events he is retelling. And even though the generation that left Egypt has all died off in the forty years of wandering, undoubtedly those Israelites who now stand before Moses among the hills of Moab to hear his valedictory address are well aware of the details of the adventures of their forebears as well.

No, well before George Santayana said it, Moses understood that those who do not remember the past are condemned to repeat it. Moses does not make the speeches that compose Deuteronomy only because he likes to hear himself speak. Nor does he do so to tell the people anything new. Rather, he speaks so that all those assembled will understand the importance of what they have experienced and so that they will continue to appreciate the blessings that God has bestowed upon them.

Let us continue the retelling, lest we become complacent about our past.

D'varim: Shabbat Chazon
Amy Scheinerman, 2007

Moshe's initial sermon of recapitulation is brimming with explanation for events in the lives of the Israelites throughout their four-decade wilderness wandering. Torah presumes that events can be fully understood in the light of God's reasoning and Moshe's explications.

Yet this is שבת חזון (Shabbat Chazon), and with Tishah B'Av a few days away, we are reminded that when tragedy strikes, not all explanations are complete or satisfying or helpful. Isaiah's explanation in this week's haftarah and explanations of the destructions of the Jerusalem Temples by our חכמים (*chachamim*) are both true and incomplete. Surely idolatry and insensitivity, disunity and שינת חינם (*sinat chinam*, "groundless hatred") were factors in both cases, but the devastation wrought by the destruction of the First and Second Temples can hardly be conflated into two sins, however pervasive and severe. But perhaps it's enough.

A story is told about the Chatam Sofer, who encountered a very elderly man and asked the secret of his longevity. The man replied that when calamity struck, rather than asking God why he had been visited with such sorrow, he accepted what happened. He followed the philosophy of Jeremiah: "Of what shall a living man complain? A man for his sins! Let us search and examine our ways and return to *Adonai*. Let us lift our hearts with our hands to God in heaven" (Lamentations 3:39–41).

Viktor Frankl taught much the same lesson in his writings and through logotherapy. We cannot always understand suffering, but we can find meaning in our existence, even amidst suffering. May this Tishah B'Av provide us each with the opportunity for a meaningful fast.

D'varim
Amy Scheinerman, 2008

Torah sets a high standard for its judicial system. Moses reviews how he appointed magistrates to hear disputes among the Israelites and instructed them: "You shall not be partial in judgment: hear out low and high alike. Fear no man, for judgment is God's. And any matter that is too difficult for you, you shall bring to me and I will hear it" (Deut. 1:17).

Rashi interprets this *pasuk* at length drawing on *Sifrei* 17 and Babylonian Talmud, *Sanhedrin* 8a. He makes four points. First, judges should be appointed without consideration of their personal appeal or family connections; only their individual qualifications should secure a position for them. Second, judges should not take it upon themselves to decide the relative importance of cases: whether concerning a *p'rutah* or one hundred *maneh*, each case should receive a judge's full attention. On the basis of *Targum Onkelos*, Rashi adds that rendering decisions to protect the assets of the poor or the dignity of the wealthy violate Torah's standard for justice. Third, judges should not allow fear to influence their decisions, for the decisions reflect God and reflect upon God. Fourth, concerning *ki hamishpat leilohim hu* ("for judgment is God's"), Moses reminds the magistrates that when they make a fair and fearless decision, they do so as an extension of God, but when they fail to judge fairly and fearlessly, they turn the judgment against God. *Takrivun eilai* ("you shall bring it to me") reinforces this point. Rashi provides the example of Moses's upsurge of ego (*eilai*) that rendered him unable to decide in the case of the daughters of Zelophechad.

We engage in less *p'sak din* (legal rulings) than we do communal leadership, often influencing who rises to positions of power and authority and how they operate in those positions. Deuteronomy 1:17 and Rashi's commentary provide sage advice.

D'varim
Joshua Minkin, 2009

We all dream of living a long life well spent and then bequeathing to our children the benefit of our experiences: advice that will hold them in good stead over the course of their lives. It is the rare individual who accomplishes this goal. Most of us are so busy with our lives that we barely take time to reflect, let alone write down our reflections for posterity.

Moses, given the gift of prescience concerning his own death, writes the Book of Deuteronomy.

What would **we** say if given such an opportunity? Would we impart to our progeny rules to live by learned through bitter experience? Recall our mistakes for them to avoid? Remind them of those now gone in the hope their memory will continue? Deuteronomy contains all this and more.

Recently America lost a leader who was given such a gift. Rep. Jack Kemp ז״ל, after being diagnosed with cancer, published a letter to his grandchildren in the aftermath of the presidential election. In it he echoes the Jewish view that the world and humankind are unfinished works waiting to be perfected. He recalls "Lincoln's view of our nation as an 'unfinished work,'" saying, "Isn't that equally true of all of us?" He reminds us that "unity doesn't require uniformity or unanimity; it does require putting the good of our people ahead of what's good for mere political or personal advantage." Words that could have been written by Moses.

ואתחנן Va-et'chanan

(Deuteronomy 3:23–7:11)

Va-et'chanan
Lawrence S. Kushner, 1996

(Deut. 4:2) As Reform Jews, we are often charged with violating this prohibition against adding to or subtracting from the Torah. In such matters as confirmation, ecological issues, and opposition to certain wars, have we added to the mitzvot? And in our historic opposition to kashrut, *nidah*, and other mitzvot, have we subtracted?

Va-et'chanan: SH'MA YISRAEL
Stephen E. Cohen, 1999

The declaration of the *Sh'ma* is so central to Jewish life that we would expect a single "mainstream" understanding of its content. But a survey of the traditional commentaries reveals a vast range of meanings derived by Jews reflecting upon the "watchword of our faith." Here are two examples: Rashi sees the *Sh'ma* pointing forward to the messianic future. The Malbim, on the other hand, finds in the *Sh'ma* a reference to the pivotal turning point in the past history of religion.

Rashi Read the verse with the following insertions: *YHVH*, [who is at this time] *Eloheinu*/our God, [but not the God of the idolatrous nations, will in the future be] *YHVH ECHAD*. As it is said, "Then I will grant the nations a clear speech, and they will all proclaim the name *YHVH*" (Zeph. 3:9). And it is said, "In that day, *YHVH* will be *Echad*, and His name will be *Echad*" (Zech. 14:9).

Malbim   All earlier peoples imagined that there were gods who caused good and other gods who caused evil, for they could not imagine that the good and the evil that exist in the world sprang from the same source. And they feared the evil cause and they loved the good cause. But we unify fear and love in the One God, when we say "*YHVH* our *Elohim YHVH ECHAD*." For *YHVH* refers to the quality of mercy, which causes "good," and *Elohim* refers to the quality of justice, which causes judgment and punishment. And because it is all one, and all for the good, the name *YHVH* occurs twice.

Comment   What is the functional significance of the recitation of the *Sh'ma* for you? Is it a theological affirmation or a cultural performance? Is it a moment of feeling, of intellection, of will? Is it all of these or none of these?

Va-et'chanan
Kenneth J. Weiss, 2002

"You shall love" (Deut. 6:5).

The first words of *V'ahavta* reveal a fundamental fact about love: we are told to love God because the choice to love or not is **ours**. More than an emotion, love is a decision.

Couples speak of "falling" in love. No, I tell them: love is not about falling; it's about deciding. You must **decide** to love, and do so daily. If you do that, you'll stay married forever, no matter what. Whether it's God or our spouse or a child or parent: to love is our choice.

But—then, there's the fifth commandment: it says, "Honor your father and your mother" (Deut. 5:16). Why not "love," if the decision to love is ours to make? Perhaps . . . the verb hints at the complexity of that relationship above all others. Perhaps . . . the word "love" was used in the first set of tablets that Moses destroyed. Perhaps . . . honoring parents is the surest way to learn to love them. Perhaps . . .

Va-et'chanan
Kenneth J. Weiss, 2003

"You shall love . . . God" (Deut. 6:5); "You shall not try . . . God" (Deut. 6:16).

We recite the *V'ahavta* weekly, or even more often: "You shall love *Adonai* your God. . . ." To love God, say the Rabbis, is to live by God's mitzvot, to embrace God's creation, to improve God's world. More than a feeling, to love God is to act.

"You shall not try . . . God" is the opposite side of the same coin: even (especially!) in the Promised Land where it may be easy to forget, to lose perspective. Moses warns: upon entering the land, avoid foreign temptations, foreign gods!

In sum, there are do's and don'ts to loving God!

Va-et'chanan
Kenneth J. Weiss, 2004

Moses could plead (ואתחנן, *va-et'chanan*, "I pleaded") with יהוה (*Adonai*) precisely because they were "near neighbors." Thus, our *sidrah*'s very name points us to one of its significant themes: God's immanence. God **is** near enough to hear our pleas, our whispers . . . our silent prayers.

Phrases in these chapters buttress the crucial affirmation that God is close enough to sense, to feel . . . to love.

1. Moses not only pleads with God; he addresses God in the (personal) singular: "**You**," אתה (Deut. 3:24).
2. Other nations have "gods," but no other "great nation . . . has a god so close . . . as is יהוה [*Adonai*] our God whenever we call on Him" (Deut. 4:7). Just think: our great Creator-God, this deity above all worlds, nevertheless cares about **me** and **my** distress, listens to **my** prayer.
3. At Mount Sinai, "יהוה [*Adonai*] made [a] covenant . . . with us, the living, every one of us"—doing so "face to face" (Deut.

5:3–4). Consider: what other god could/would relay transcendent laws in so intimate a way?
4. שמע (*Sh'ma*), "Listen!" is commanded of Israel in the singular. As a parent to a child, God talks and teaches. ואהבת (*V'ahavta*) represents God's accessibility: You shall **love** יהוה (*Adonai*). Isn't "love" about bonding, about caring for, about relating to? One can't love a transcendent being; one can only love—and share love with—a being who is near . . . available . . . close enough to feel.

Va-et'chanan
Alan Cook, 2005

In the year 325 c.e., the Council of Nicea adopted the Nicene Creed. It laid out the central tenets of Catholicism; ostensibly any Catholic who does not believe or follow this creed is damned. The Apostles' Creed, from circa 700, carries equal weight for Episcopalians. For Presbyterians, it's the Westminster Confession of 1646. Muslims have a credal profession of faith, known as the *Kalimat-as-Shahadat*.

But while many have tried, no Jewish figure has succeeded in formulating articles of faith that are universally accepted by all Jews.

If one were to approach the "Jew on the street" and ask him what is the central belief of Judaism, he would be likely to respond, "The שמע [*Sh'ma*]." This formula is indeed integral to our faith; it is usually the first prayer we learn and the last we forget.

The unspoken power of the שמע (*Sh'ma*) is that it reminds us that God is with us, even during our darkest moments. Perhaps this is why its words have been on the lips of those who died for קדוש השם (*kiddush HaShem*). Its message comforts us, just as Isaiah's reminder that "the word of our God is always fulfilled" provides comfort on שבת נחמו (Shabbat Nachamu).

So if the שמע (*Sh'ma*) bears such weight and power, why not consider it our Jewish creed? Because those religions that adhere to creeds emphasize belief as the path to salvation. Judaism, while endorsing the power of belief, focuses on the deeds that stem from those beliefs. We must heed both parts of the exhortation of our *sidrah*: ושמרתם ועשיתם (*Ush'martem vaasitem*), "Observe them faithfully" (Deut. 4:6). Our beliefs, our creeds, have no meaning unless we put them into action.

Va-et'chanan
Alan Cook, 2006

The *sidrah* ואתחנן (*Va-et'chanan*) is one of only two that takes its name from a first-person verbal form. In the other, וארא (*Va-eira*), the speaker is God, making our *sidrah* the sole *sidrah* in the entire Torah predicated on the statement of one individual.

Moses is renowned in our tradition for his humility. He did not choose his role in life; it was chosen for him. Yet as we come to the homilies in דברים (*D'varim*, "Deuteronomy"), and the conclusion of the Torah, we find that that characteristic self-effacement has been set aside. Moses is a man who realizes that his days are coming to an end. He has much that he still wishes to accomplish. And so, his concern shifts. Surely, he is still engaged with the leadership of the Israelites whom he has brought to this juncture on the banks of the Jordan. Yet, now he also speaks for himself, in the language of "I." "I pleaded," he says. "Let me cross over and see the good land" (Deut. 3:23–25).

Of course, Moses is not permitted to cross, and so his life becomes a chronicle of a dream unfulfilled. Having worked to lead the people to the Promised Land, he will be denied the opportunity to enter.

We can learn from Moses to be passionate about those things that matter to us. Like Moses, we may not always get our way. But there is a time to be silent and go along with the crowd. And there is a time to step forward, make our voices heard, and say, "What about me?"

Va-et'chanan: Shabbat Nachamu
Amy Scheinerman, 2007

With ואתחנן (*Va-et'chanan*) and its accompanying haftarah נחמו (*Nachamu*), we cross the bridge from admonition to consolation. How appropriate that our פרשה (*parashah*) should include Moshe's review of the revelation at Sinai, complete with the עשרת הדברות (*Aseret HaDib'rot*, "Ten Commandments") material begging to be studied by every generation.

Despite the day's theme of consolation, our פרשה (*parashah*) opens with an account of God's wrath toward Moshe and the edict that Moshe would end his life east of the Jordan River. God commands Moshe to ascend Mount Pisgah and gaze 360 degrees around, to see whence he came and where he will not be permitted to venture. In fact, "seeing" is mentioned repeatedly throughout the פרשה (*parashah*). Yet when Moshe describes the revelation and the flaming spectacle, it is not the sight of it, but the sound of God that touches the soul: "The mountain was ablaze with flames to the very skies, dark with densest clouds. The Lord spoke to you out of the fire; you heard the sound of words but perceived no shape—nothing but a voice" (Deut. 4:11–12).

Torah offers us a steadfast formula for keeping God's presence in our lives: Torah study. Talmud asserts that since the destruction of the Temple, God's only domain in this world is four cubits of halachah (*B'rachot* 8a), an enterprise requiring copious study. As ואתחנן (*Va-et'chanan*) describes it, "You heard the sound of words but perceived no shape—nothing but a voice." Thus, Rabbi Chananyah ben Teradyon assures us in *Pirkei Avot* 3:3, when two people meet and exchange words of Torah, the *Shechinah* hovers over them. What powerful consolation there is in this.

Va-et'chanan
Micky Boyden, 2008

Parashat Va-et'chanan deals with the period preceding Moses's death. Having brought his people this far, there is nothing that he would have liked more than to have been the leader who brought them into the Promised Land. This would have been the crowning glory of his life; but God had other plans. *Der Mensch tracht und Gott lacht* (loosely translated, "Man proposes but God disposes").

The word *va-etchanan* comes from the root *CHaNaN*, which is related to the word *chein* ("grace" or "favor"). It reminds us of the occurrence of the same word in an entirely different context. When Moses meets God on Mount Sinai, he pleads, "Show me Your way that I may know that I have found favor [*chein*] in Your sight" (Exod. 33:13).

While Moses may have been the greatest of the prophets and Israel's foremost leader, he is still uncertain of himself. The Torah describes him as being "more humble than anyone on the face of the earth" (Num. 12:3).

Only a person able to accept his limitations is able to turn to his people at the end of his life and declare, "I shall not cross over the Jordan, but you shall cross over and inherit this land" (Deut. 4:22).

Moses could have easily preoccupied himself before his death with writing his funeral oration or trying to hold onto power, but his thoughts and concerns are elsewhere. He turns to his people and warns them, "Beware lest you forget your covenant with God" (Deut. 4:23). Moses's supreme characteristics are his humility and his ability to place his people's needs above his own. Both religious and political leaders have much to learn from him.

Va-et'chanan
Janice Garfunkel, 2009

In this *parashah*, we are commanded to "love *Adonai* your God with all your heart" (Deut. 6:5). Elsewhere, we are commanded to love our fellow human beings. Both Christianity as expressed today, and secular American culture seem to place a great deal of emphasis on the power of love. "God is love," they say. The underlying meaning of many movies can be summed up with the words "Love conquers all." All you need is love.

Having grown up in the Reform Movement, I must say I heard very little about "love." The emphasis was on justice and on our obligations to our fellow human beings, on doing mitzvot (good deeds) living worthy lives, figuring out what is the most moral path to follow . . . all very good things to emphasize. But I do wonder if we have perhaps given the topic of love to the "other team." If so, we ought to reclaim it! Certainly it is important to tell our people that God loves them, especially for those who believe in a personal God. (Since many do not, is that why we don't talk about it so much?)

Loving God, loving our neighbor, loving the stranger, these are all mitzvot we ought to talk about more. *Ahavah rabbah ahavtanu, Adonai* ("How deeply You have loved us, *Adonai*"). Let us feel embraced and supported by a loving God and a loving Jewish community, and let us return that love in abundance! Love is not all we need, but we most definitely do need love.

עֵקֶב *Eikev*

(Deuteronomy 7:12–11:25)

Eikev
Lawrence S. Kushner, 1996

(Deut. 8:10) This proof text for *Birkat HaMazon* suggests that all three ("you shall eat, you shall be satisfied, you shall bless") are mitzvot. Do you agree that eating is a mitzvah (i.e., that abstaining from food is a sin)? That being satisfied is a mitzvah (i.e., that the inability to find satisfaction is a sin)? That blessing is a mitzvah (and being able only to curse one's life is a sin)?

Eikev: Old and New
Stephen E. Cohen, 1999

Rashi chooses the passage *V'hayah im shamoa* (Deut. 11:13ff.) as his opportunity to assert the connection between old teaching and new understandings in Torah.

Deuteronomy 11:13 If you hearken, yes, hearken—*Im shamoa tishm'u.*

Rashi *Im shamoa*—If you listen to the old . . . *tishm'u*—you will hear the new.

Comment Have we deleted from the Reform siddur the very passage that warns us against such a deletion?

Eikev
Kenneth J. Weiss, 2002

"*V'hayah eikev...*" (Deut. 7:12).

Here's the deal: love God, live by the mitzvot, destroy the seven nations, remain consecrated to *YHVH*.

JPS translates the first words of the *parashah*, "And if you obey these rules and observe them faithfully." R. E. Friedman renders it, "And it will be because you'll listen to these judgments and observe and do them." The reward: God will maintain the covenant.

So, which is it? What is the meaning of the word *eikev*? "If" implies reward conditional upon proof of appropriate behavior. "Because" affirms behavior that will lead to reward. Is Torah here beseeching the people to live a certain way, or is it expressing certainty that they will do so? *Pilpul* for the ages...

Eikev
Kenneth J. Weiss, 2003

"Give thanks to *Adonai* your God" (Deut. 8:10).

Gratitude has forever been a fundamental Jewish value. During both trying **and** favorable times, we are commanded to acknowledge God's blessings.

Even in the Sinai wilderness—the ageless venue of deprivation—despite trials of all kinds, we were commanded to remember and be thankful.

By contrast, Deut. 8:3–9 reads like "*Dayeinu*." God "gave you manna to eat... [your] clothes did not wear out, nor did your feet swell...." God will bring "you into a good land ... where you may eat ... without stint, where you will lack nothing." ("*Da-Da-yeinu...!*")

In times of affliction—in *dayeinu* times too—acknowledge and thank God, who delivers, nourishes, and guides you.

Eikev
Kenneth J. Weiss, 2004

"[God] chose you ... from among all peoples" (Deut. 10:15).

Detractors say, "**Chosen** for privilege," "**Chosen** for special status." We respond, "No! Chosen for responsibility," "Chosen to exemplify Torah—to live by the mitzvot ... to repair our broken world."

The phrase "chosen people" is widely misunderstood by many (non-Jews, Jews too!). Let's recall: God chose us in Torah days as a parent "chooses" to challenge his/her responsible—precocious—child: I know you'll grow up to be a mensch, to make a difference ... I know you'll make me proud!

We're chosen, perhaps. More to the point, we're expected to live up to God's highest standard ... and that is a privilege!

Eikev
Alan Cook, 2005

In *Jewish Meditation: A Practical Guide* (Schocken, 1995), Rabbi Aryeh Kaplan writes, "The most important discipline of Judaism involves the blessing. When a blessing is recited before eating, then the act itself becomes a spiritual undertaking. Through the blessing, the act of eating becomes a contemplative exercise. Just as one can contemplate a flower or a melody, one can contemplate the act of eating."

The problem with Rabbi Kaplan's assertion is that עקב (*Eikev*) does not command us to bless our food *before* consuming it. In providing the context for ברכת המזון (*Birkat HaMazon*, "Blessing after Meals"), our *sidrah* proclaims, ואכלת ושבעת וברכת (*v'achalta, v'savata, uveirachta,* when you have eaten and been sated, bless [Deut. 8:10]) in precisely that order! We are expected to bless only after we have eaten and are satisfied. Is the blessing an afterthought?

In most instances, the blessing precedes the act (with Shabbat candles, of course, being one notable exception). How can eating become a spiritual undertaking if we are not even contemplating the spiritual element of our meal until after our bellies are completely full?

The practice of reciting המוציא (*HaMotzi*) or another appropriate prayer prior to consuming food does alleviate some of these concerns. But does the recitation of ברכת המזון (*Birkat HaMazon*) then become a ברכה לבטלה (*b'rachah l'vatalah,* a wasted blessing)?

Perhaps ברכת המזון (*Birkat HaMazon*) is not about our individual dining experience. Perhaps it is not about the here and now. Perhaps, instead, it looks forward to a future day, a messianic age, when all will live in harmony with God and with the earth. On that day, all will understand what it means to eat and be satisfied.

Eikev
Alan Cook, 2006

"Because I said so!" may be a classic rebuttal from a parent to a child when a household rule is challenged, but most parents soon come to see that such an argument is ineffective. Youngsters want a rational answer to their query of "Why should I?" and not a vague parental fiat.

This is true for most of us. In our efforts to understand **how** the world works and to figure out the social norms expected by the culture in which we live, we generally want to have some comprehension of the **why**, as well.

עקב (*Eikev*) represents one of the Torah's attempts to explain the whys. It speaks of the rewards that will follow if the Israelites follow the laws set before them, and it also delineates the consequences. The people are told that if they faithfully observe the commandments, God "will grant the rain for your land in season. . . . You shall gather in your new grain and wine and oil" (Deut. 11:14).

Such a promise was undoubtedly inspiring to our ancestors, who enjoyed an agrarian lifestyle and needed such blessings. Does it resonate with us in quite the same way?

Most of us don't perform mitzvot in a quest for a particular reward. On the other hand, we don't do things just because God said so and live only according to blind faith. Rather, we find that these mitzvot work for us because they help us lead lives that are morally and ethically sound.

Eikev
Amy Scheinerman, 2007

Our פרשה (*parashah*), from which the second paragraph of שמע (*Sh'ma*) is excerpted, reads like an extended version on that theme, far more graphic and detailed. Loyalty to God's covenant, in addition to being rewarded with new grain, wine and oil, fertile flocks and herds, health and well-being for people and animals alike, will bring military victories and secure borders. Amidst the promises and warning, Moses reminds the Israelites that God subjected them to privation in the wilderness and then nourished them with manna to teach them כי לא על-הלחם לבדו יחיה האדם כי על-כל-מוצא פי-יהוה יחיה האדם (*ki lo al halechem l'vado yich'yeh haadam ki al kol motza pi Adonai yich'yeh haadam*), "that a human being does not live on bread alone, but that one may live on anything that *Adonai* decrees" (Deut. 8:3).

Many are troubled by Deuteronomic theology's assertion of God's rewards and punishments in the face of increasing scientific knowledge of the processes of nature. Moreover, the image of a micromanaging God troubles many. But this is not the only way to interpret עקב (*Eikev*). עקב (*Eikev*) emphasizes the importance of community in pursuing Jewish life; it is addressed to an entire nation and serves as a warning that disunity and internal dissension will compromise their mission.

Many are apt to interpret Deut. 8:3 as promoting the notion that people need **more** than bread to live productive lives, perhaps along the lines of R. Elazar ben Azariah's teaching in *Pirkei Avot* 3:21: אם אין קמח, אין תורה (*Im ein kemach, ein Torah*, "If there is no flour, there is no Torah"). But R. Elazar also taught: אם אין תורה, אין קמח (*Im ein Torah, ein kemach*, "If there is no Torah, there is no flour"). In the context of פרשת עקב (*Parashat Eikev*), "man cannot live by bread alone" suggests that a Jew can live without bread, with only the manna from heaven, and if he or she possesses the right attitude toward that manna, it will nourish and sustain. This supplies an interesting twist to our view of materialism.

Eikev
Jeffrey Ballon, 2008

The uplifting speeches attributed to Moses in this *sidrah* contrast sharply with his behavior as God's neophyte messenger in Exodus. Here Moses reflects a mature "warrior persona" as defined by Dr. Robert L. Moore, professor of psychoanalysis, culture, and spirituality at the University of Chicago Theological Seminary and author of *Facing the Dragon* and *The Archetype of Initiation*. A true warrior willingly stands in service of a "Majestic Being or King" (i.e., *Adonai Elohecha*, "*Adonai* your God") providing the protection necessary for the community to prosper. The energy of the "warrior" emerges from the same source as *yetzer hara* (evil inclination). Each reflects archetypical forces that when held in balance properly channel activity to the maintenance of society.

Now accepting the role of sacred elder, Moses reviews his career and shapes the narrative of his communal experience into a legacy so Israel can survive its next challenge. With great oratory, he morphs into Moshe Rabbeinu, replacement for the stuttering foundling. His acquisition of sophisticated speech changes the way *Am Yisrael* (the people Israel) responds to his leadership. Now they (we) can grow beyond him, listen, and succeed. Moses had to grow past the heated anger of his youth that pushed him to strike taskmasters and rocks. His mature tongue healed, inspiration comes easily. Moses will die, and Israel, dying to its old ways, can move on. Transformed, both learn to bless. The indulgent warrior, like cattle feeding on grass (Deut. 11:15), is associated with mere consumption with no notion of blessing. The balanced warrior in the proper service of Majesty will take in, evaluate, and bless. As it says, *V'achalta v'savata u'veirachta et Adonai Elohecha*, "You shall eat, be satisfied, and bless *Adonai* your God" (Deut. 8:10).

Eikev
Louis Rieser, 2009

Deuteronomy 11:13–17, the problematic second paragraph of the *Sh'ma*, poses an existential threat. Disobedience leads to exile. For the traditionally minded, the twice daily recitation of these verses stands as a harsh reminder of our life as exiles.

The midrash (*Sifrei, Parashat Eikev*) seeks an understanding that justifies our continued attention to these verses. The focus shifts from God's gift of rain, or its denial, to a reinterpretation of the opening words, "If you carefully listen to my commandments," asking implicitly why one should continue to obey the mitzvot once the exile has occurred. Two parables are offered.

One parable (*piskei* 9) views the mitzvot as a balm, a salve to ease the wounds of exile. The wounds, however, are permanent, impervious to any enduring cure. The mitzvot serve as a protective bandage, but if the bandage is removed, the sores will return and produce ulcers. A second parable (*piskei* 7) takes a more hopeful view. Israel is an exiled queen, and the mitzvot are the signs of royalty she once wore. The queen's father advises her to retain her royal ways so she will be prepared to reclaim her proper place when the time comes.

These parables reflect a debate over the enduring value of the mitzvot. Are they a treatment for our chronic wounds? Or are they a measure of character that we cultivate? Do we perform mitzvot for today or for the future? The midrash provides a platform for a far-reaching discussion on why we persist in the observance of the Torah's commandments.

ראה   R'eih

(Deuteronomy 11:26–16:17)

For additional commentary on *R'eih*, see "Sukkot."

R'eih
Lawrence S. Kushner, 1996

Perhaps the only time the Torah recognizes the reality of human limitations is in Deut. 15, verses 4 and 11. In the former we are commanded that there shall be no poor among us, and the following verses tell us how to ensure that. But verse 11 acknowledges that human greed is too strong to alleviate poverty forever. Why does God choose to tell us how we will respond to this command—won't this foreknowledge dampen any will we might have to wipe out poverty?

R'eih
Kenneth J. Weiss, 2003

"See . . . I set before you blessing and curse" (Deut. 11:26).

You can't be "mostly law-abiding." A person is considered a criminal even if he rigorously observes every law except one (a murderer who has never committed fraud or burgled a home is still a criminal!).

Basically, life is about stark choices, about black and white; gray is remarkably rare. Sforno interprets Deut. 11:26 well: "Behold, I have put before you two extreme opposites. . . . If you do not choose the path that leads to blessing, you have [by default!] chosen the path that leads to curse. There is no middle ground." You can't be "somewhat blessed"!

The path of blessing—though a "narrow bridge"—is the right choice. Rejecting that, you've chosen (by default!) the accursed path: broader, ever downhill—starkly, diametrically, opposite.

R'eih
Kenneth J. Weiss, 2004

An article in the *Baltimore Times* features Rabbi Simcha Avrohom Halevi Ashlag, who finds and corrects *ketubah* errors, thereby (?!?) reversing the fortunes of couples who seek him out.

A couple married fourteen years couldn't have children. Rabbi Ashlag found a major error in their *ketubah*, invalidated it, and wrote a new one. He then "gave the woman a second Jewish name. Since then, the couple has had two daughters."

Kayn aynhoreh!

Redo your *ketubah*, change your luck!

Here's a (possible) Torah source for warding off the evil eye: Deut. 15:10 exhorts people to give to the needy, "for [when you do] . . . God will bless you." Ellen Frankel in *The Five Books of Miriam* affirms through one of her many voices that "tithes protect wealth." She retells this story: a pious farmer always tithed and was prosperous; his son rejects dad's example and loses his wealth. The son reinstitutes the tithe, and . . . prosperity returns . . .

Pooh-pooh-pooh!

R'eih
Alan Cook, 2005

"I used to think I was poor. Then they told me I wasn't poor, I was needy. Then they told me it was self-defeating to think of myself as needy. I was deprived. Then they told me deprived was a bad image. I was underprivileged. Then they told me underprivileged was overused. I was disadvantaged. I still don't have a dime, but I have a great vocabulary" (Jules Feiffer).

"There shall be no needy among you" (Deut. 15:4).

Poverty is epidemic. It was recognized by the Torah, and it continues to afflict our world. We can try to ignore it, or imagine it away using the creative semantics that Feiffer mocks, but the fact remains that poverty kills nearly eight million people annually. And the Jewish community is not immune.

Why would the Torah make the promise that poverty would be eradicated if that was not to be the case? Even in Israel, the immediate context with which our *sidrah* concerns itself, there is an impoverished class. How do we reconcile the facts with the Torah's overt promise?

We cannot remove this single *pasuk* (verse) from its context. ראה (*R'eih*) presents us with concrete examples of how we work in partnership with God to improve our world. The text admits, "There will never cease to be needy ones in your land," but continues, "open your hand to the poor and needy kinsman in your land" (Deut. 15:11). The earlier verse explores a possibility; the latter explains the actions needed to make it reality.

By taking concrete actions, giving voice to the poor, and promoting sustainable development, the day can come when the words of Deut. 15:4 will be fact, and not fantasy.

R'eih
Alan Cook, 2006

ראה (*R'eih*) demonstrates the differences between individual responsibility and group responsibility when it proclaims, "See, I set before you this day blessing and curse" (Deut. 11:26). The grammar is awkward. The word ראה (*r'eih*, "see") is addressed to the individual. But לפניכם (*lifneichem*, "before you") is plural; Moses is now speaking to the entire group of Israelites.

What can we learn from this unusual grammatical construction? Perhaps the verse is striving to make us less egocentric. The word "see" awakens each of us as individuals. But then we are addressed as a group, as if to say, "This is not all about you. You must not be content just to stay out of trouble and keep your own nose clean. Rather, you as an individual must work to help others understand the paths set before them. You, working in harmony with your neighbors, will determine whether you take a path toward blessing or steer down the road that leads to curse." We are each instructed to examine our individual character and to ensure that we live up to high moral standards, and we are urged to demand similar standards from those who lead our communities.

The prophet Isaiah proclaims, "All your children shall be taught of the Lord, and great shall be the peace of your children" (Isa. 54:13). The midrash suggests that we should not read בניך (*banayich*, "your children") but rather בוניך (*bonaiyich*, "your builders"). When those who have been charged with building our Jewish future come to understand that the choice between blessing and curse is not an individual decision, but a group one, then will we all come to know peace.

R'eih

Amy Scheinerman, 2007

"See, I have set before you today blessing and curse" (Deut. 11:26). The mention of curse inspires *Midrash Rabbah* on ראה (*R'eih*) to ponder the tradition of reading the תוכחה (*tocheichah*, the curses of Deut. 28:15–69) quickly and in an undertone.

Midrash Rabbah D'varim 4:1 asks: May we divide up the curses among several readers? The answer is no, for as R. Chiya b. Gamda taught: Because of what is written in Prov. 3:11, "My son, do not despise the discipline of the Lord and do not spurn God's chastening [ואל תקץ בתוכחתו] *v'al takotz b'tochachto*." This means: do not allow the rebukes of the תוכחה (*tocheichah*) to appear cut in pieces [קוצין].

Yet another explanation assures us that the curses are not meant to inflict pain, but rather to remind us that, endowed with free will, we can choose blessing rather than curse. The opening verse of our פרשה (*parashah*) is the proof text: "See, I have set before you today blessing and curse."

Many today argue that human free will is an illusion—Paul Breer, Owen Flanagan, Michael Silberstein, and Daniel Wegner, among others—and that we are no more than animals operating according to instinct and responding to environment. Janet Radcliffe Richards, in *Human Nature after Darwin*, writes, "If we understand that there are good evolutionary reasons for our wanting people to suffer when they have done direct or indirect harm to us, then we can account for our strong feelings about the appropriateness of retribution without presuming they are a guide to moral truth" (Routledge, 2000, p. 210).

Torah asserts not only that we have choice, but that the very meaning of being human and alive is to assert our free will and make appropriate choices. When we do not, we must be prepared for rebuke, and the measure of our humanity is our ability to understand the rebuke as a loving gift.

R'eih
Amy Scheinerman 2008

Ki yarchiv Adonai Elohecha et g'vul'cha kaasher diber lach (Deut. 12:20): Torah tells us that God will reward the Israelites by enlarging their territorial acquisition. Midrash explains this boon as a reward for *tzedakah*, though Torah says nothing of charity. Quoting Prov. 18:16, "A person's gift makes room for him and brings him before great people," *D'varim Rabbah* 4:8 recounts the travels of R. Eliezer and R. Y'hoshua to collect *tzedakah*. A certain Abba Yudan goes to great lengths to avoid them so he will not have to contribute to their fund, but his wife insists that he make a substantial contribution: the proceeds of half his field. Abba Yudan asks the rabbis to pray for him, and they pray, "May God fulfill your needs." As a result, when Abba Yudan plows the remaining half of his field, he unearths a valuable treasure, which he shares with the rabbis on their return trip through town, saying, "Your prayer has borne fruit."

The midrash continues with the examples of R. Chiya and Resh Lakish, who each gave generous donors seats of honor on the basis of "A person's gift makes room for him and brings him before great people."

This midrash opens up questions concerning the purpose and intent of giving *tzedakah*, the rewards of generosity, and the manner in which we respond to donors based on the size of their donation. In the world of synagogues and Jewish institutions, these are increasingly important questions to address as we seek to involve people in Jewish life who do not all possess exceptional means.

R'eih
Janice Garfunkel, 2009

Many people tithe, though most do not. A babysitter I knew earned $900 each month and gave $90 each month to her church.

While we are no longer bound by the biblical injunction to tithe, our tradition teaches that giving 10 percent of our income to *tzedakah* is "average," 5 percent is considered miserly, and 20 percent is desirable.

Current societal norms demand that we be non-intrusive concerning one another's personal finances. But certainly we rabbis can raise this topic more emphatically and with more specifics than others can. I, personally, do not annually set aside 10 percent of my income for *tzedakah*. I have many good reasons (or excuses), and I am sure I am far from alone among rabbis. But I think I would be more generous if doing so were the norm and the expectation. We leaders, myself included, should be shaping what is the "norm."

In a society where there is so much encouragement to spend lavishly on luxury cars, expensive homes, interior decorating and remodeling, fine clothing and restaurants, and the latest electronic gizmo, there ought to be a way to make *tzedakah* a higher and more admired form of spending.

שפטים   Shof'tim

(Deuteronomy 16:18–21:9)

Shof'tim
Lawrence S. Kushner, 1996

The famous phrase *Tzedek tzedek tirdof* ("Justice, justice shall you pursue" [Deut. 16:20], which Nelson Glueck is reputed to have once called the essence of Reform Judaism) is given here as the *sine qua non* of both aspects of the covenant—the life of the people and the right to the land. But not until Deut. 17:5 do we receive instructions regarding the kind of justice that we should pursue. The immediate example of *tzedek* (beginning in Deut. 16:21) is the eradication of various idolatrous practices. What is the connection between doing *tzedek* and wiping out idolatry?

For those of us who counseled conscientious objectors during the Vietnam War, Deuteronomy 20 and its Talmudic commentary were a prime source for a Jewish view of opposition to participation in war. Since R. Akiva argued that any person could be "fearful and fainthearted" (Deut. 20:8), the "draft exemptions" in this chapter become universal, with the Rabbis ruling that they applied only in the case of a war of expansion (*milchemet mitzvah*) and not a war of self-defense (*milchemet chovah*). Twenty-five years and more after that harrowing time, how do these laws and their Rabbinic expansion read now?

Shof'tim: Divine Law, Human Judge
Stephen E. Cohen, 1997

Even the most traditional Jewish viewpoint recognizes that divine law requires interpretation and application by a human judge. A verse in this *sidrah* calls for strict obedience to the decision of the human court: "Do not depart from the thing that they tell you, right or left" (Deut. 17:11). The commentaries on this verse speak to moments when we would question our human judiciary.

Sifrei: Even if he tells you that what seems to you to be right is left, or what seems to you to be left is right, obey him.

Rashi: Even if he tells you that what is right is left, or that what is left is right.

Comment: Note the difference in the language—Rashi makes just a small change in *Sifrei*'s wording, but with enormous consequences. In *Sifrei*'s scenario, the citizen and the judge disagree—but the judge's superior learning and wisdom prevail, intact. In Rashi's formulation, the judge is actually wrong, but his status and authority prevail. *Sifrei* asks the citizen to be **convinced**, reassuring him, "Trust your judge." Rashi grants the citizen the real possibility that he is right and the judge is wrong—and then asks the citizen to be silent. What room do either of these commentaries leave, if any, for individual conscience?

Shof'tim: Who Speaks for God?
Stephen E. Cohen, 2000

The great debate between Liberal and Orthodox Judaism turns on one question: Does the Commanding Voice of God speak through the decision of the communally appointed judge or in the personal conscience of each individual? With stunning clarity, רמבן (Ramban) spells out the worst case facing the Orthodox Jew: he or she may believe that the appointed judge is instructing them to kill an innocent man. רמבן (Ramban) then proceeds to make the case against personal autonomy: "Do not depart from the thing that they tell you—right or left" (Deut. 17:11).

רמב״ן (**Ramban**) Even when you believe they are wrong, and it seems as obvious to you as the difference between your right and your left, do as they command. And do not say, "How can I eat this forbidden חלב [*cheilev*, 'fat']?" or "How can I execute this innocent man?" Rather, you should say, "I have been commanded by God to perform His commandments as I have been instructed by those who stand before Him, for it is by means of their reasoning that He has given me the Torah, even though they may be in error." And the need for this commandment is extremely great, for we have the Torah in writing, and it is obvious that not all opinions will be alike regarding new situations. And disagreements will increase, and the Torah will become many *Torot*. . . . The spirit of God is upon those who serve in His sanctuary. "God loves justice and will not leave His pious ones. They are protected forever" (Ps. 37:28) from error and from stumbling.

Comment We may, with good reason, doubt the assertion that God always protects a pious judge from error. But how do we, as Reform rabbis, respond to Ramban's warning that in a Judaism of personal autonomy, "the Torah will become many *Torot*"?

Shof'tim
Kenneth J. Weiss, 2003

Stories, legends, laws; sacrifices, Festivals; rewards and punishments; blessings and curses; heroes and anti-heroes: Torah, though divinely inspired, is variegated, its textual impact upon readers uneven from one *parashah* to the next.

Parashat Shof'tim is characterized by some of the most sensitive, most ennobling, most godly, moving, and spiritual ideas to be found anywhere.

Vibrant sermonic seeds—elevating and inspirational for any reader—these exemplify

Torah at its best:

- "Justice, justice shall you pursue" (Deut. 16:20).
- Requiring at least two witnesses to convict in any capital case (17:6).

- Establishing cities of refuge (19:2ff.).
- Urging a soldier to leave the battlefield if he hadn't yet dedicated his home, harvested his vineyard, or married his beloved (20:5ff.).
- Offering terms of peace before any attack (20:10).
- Prohibiting deforestation, wastefulness (20:19).

Inspired Scripture that truly inspires . . .

Shof'tim
Kenneth J. Weiss, 2004

צדק צדק (*Tzedek, tzedek,* "Justice, justice" [Deut. 16:20]) may be a redundancy, justified by any one (or more) of the rationales we've heard.*

I believe these words reflect—and complete—a number of dualities that are mentioned (or are implicit) in our *sidrah*. Taken together, one is drawn to conclude that there is no redundancy here at all:

- "A person shall be put to death only on the testimony of **two** (or more) **witnesses**" (Deut. 17:6).
- (At least) **two levels of judiciary** are proposed here ("magistrates and officials," in 16:18; and a court of appeals "if a case is too baffling for you to decide," in 17:8ff.).
- Justice and punishment are **equally** (= impartially) meted out for "**man or woman** who has affronted . . . God" (17:2).
- Justice is **both demanded by God and essential for society to survive.**

Might not one of the two (ostensibly) identical words represent justice as a legal concept and ideal, while the other stands for צדקה (*tzedakah*)—justice in tangible form? צדק/*Tzedek* (and צדקה/*tzedakah*) "shall you pursue" (Deut. 16:20).

---

*To show that justice is equal for Jew or gentile, accused and accuser, etc.

Shof'tim
Alan Cook, 2005

"Great principles don't get lost once they come to light. They're right here; you just have to see them again!" (Jimmy Stewart as Jefferson Smith in *Mr. Smith Goes to Washington*).

Until recently, most Americans were probably only familiar with the filibuster if they had watched the climactic scene in Frank Capra's classic film. But then came the showdown in the Senate over the use of the filibuster to block judicial nominees, and suddenly the term became prevalent on the front pages of newspapers throughout the country.

A compromise seems to have been achieved, prior to the introduction of a "nuclear option" that might have brought an end to the filibuster. No matter what one thinks of the merits or deficits of the president's current slate of nominees to the bench, hopefully we can agree that the preservation of the filibuster was important.

For though Rashi exhorts us to follow "the magistrates who will be in charge at the time" (see Rashi on Deut. 17:9), we cannot do so without paying heed to the command צדק, צדק תרדף (*Tzedek, tzedek tirdof*, "Justice, justice shall you pursue" [Deut. 16:20]). We (or our duly-elected representatives) are duty-bound to give careful consideration to those who would seek to hold positions of authority within our judicial system.

They should be chosen not on the basis of partisan allegiances, but because of their commitment to the diligent pursuit of justice.

The world rests on three pillars: on justice, on truth, and on peace. If one of those pillars begins to falter, we had best beware.

Shof'tim
Alan Cook, 2006

"And should you ask yourselves, 'How can we know that the oracle was not spoken by the Lord?'—if the prophet speaks in the name of the Lord and the oracle does not come true, that oracle was not spoken by the Lord; the prophet has uttered it presumptuously: do not stand in dread of him" (Deut. 18:21–22).

We are often asked by those who are awestruck by the events described in the תנ״ך (*Tanach*) whether miracles still occur and whether prophecy has ceased. The question of miracles is perhaps easier to answer, for we need only open our eyes to appreciate the miracles of our modern world.

The question of prophets, on the other hand, proves a bit more complex. Certainly there are those who claim to know what God's plan is—not only fundamentalist religious leaders, but also athletes who claim that God is steering them to victory, and politicians worldwide who base their platforms on their interpretation of God's will. But do these individuals really speak for God? Are they the inheritors of the legacy of Isaiah and Jeremiah, of Amos and Micah?

Not when they use God in a self-serving manner and mock and demean the lives and values of others. How will we recognize a true prophet in our midst today? Such a prophet will not seek the limelight. Such a prophet will be content to do justice, love mercy, and walk humbly with his God.

Shof'tim
Amy Scheinerman, 2007

ספר דברים (*Sefer D'varim*) contrasts with ויקרא (*Vayikra*) and במדבר (*B'midbar*) on the subject of priestly emoluments. Leviticus 7:28ff. and Num. 18:9 designate parts of the sacrifices for Aaron and his sons and their descendants. Deuteronomy 18:1–5, however, expands the right of משפט הכהנים (*mishpat hakohanim*, the portion due to the priests) to encompass the entire Levitical tribe, or at least those Levites who serve as priests.

In Deut. 18:3–4 we learn that the priests' due includes the shoulder, cheeks, and stomach of sheep and oxen, as well as first fruits of the new grain, wine, and oil, and the first shearing of the sheep.

The Babylonian Talmud, *Shabbat* 10b, records that the fourth-century Babylonian *Amora* Rav Chisda, who was a כהן (*kohein*), still received emoluments—gifts of meat—although the Temple had not stood for several centuries. He would hold up two portions of meat and announce publicly, "I will give this meat to whoever teaches me a new saying of Rav." The student who nabbed the prize was Rava bar Mahsia; the teaching of Rav he recounted was that one should inform his neighbor when giving him a gift.

Rav's teaching concerns the dilemma of deciding whether to perform an act of גמילות חסדים (g'milut chasadim) privately and altruistically or in a more public manner. In the former case, the spiritual development of the one doing the חסד (chesed) is elevated; in the latter case, the doer of חסד (chesed) becomes a model to others, benefiting the world. Rav taught that the overall good to the world takes priority over the individual.

We often struggle with the dilemma of whether or not to recognize generosity publicly and if so, how. Rav Chisda's example provides guidance, as well as an insight into the meaning of public—as opposed to private—sacrifice and worship.

Shof'tim
Amy Scheinerman, 2008

The issue of *k'vod harav* (treating the rabbi with honor) has received ample attention of late and deservedly so. The strength and vibrancy of our communities depend upon it in larger measure than perhaps we are comfortable acknowledging, because to do so would seem self-serving.

Deuteronomy 19:15–21 outlines how justice is to be delivered in a court of law. Two witnesses are required to provide evidence, a thorough investigation must be conducted, and a scrupulous effort must be made to preserve not only the substance but also the appearance of impartial justice. In verse 17 we find a peculiar phrase: "the two parties to the dispute shall appear before the LORD, before the priests or magistrates in authority at the time." Why does Torah add "in authority at that time"? Could anyone possibly stand before a judge from a previous generation?

Rashi comments, "Even though he is not of equal stature to judges who existed in previous generations, one must listen to him, for one only has the judges available in his own time." Rashi seems to acknowledge that we are mere shadows of our predecessors, and so we might often feel. Our predecessors, in turn, no doubt felt much the same way.

While some were truly great, in many cases there is a tendency to idealize the past. The strength and vibrancy of our communities depend upon respect for God and Torah and, by extension, those who teach Torah. I offer the modest view of a true genius, Isaac Newton, who in a letter to the natural philosopher Robert Hooke wrote, "If I have seen further, it is by standing on the shoulders of giants."

Shof'tim
Jeffrey Ballon, 2009

"You shall appoint magistrates and officials for your tribes, in all the settlements that the Lord your God is giving you, and they shall govern the people with due justice" (Deut. 16:18).

President Obama is using this summer to nominate his first candidate for the Supreme Court. His criteria, according to one news report, are much like those of a rabbi: "an intellectual heavyweight with a common touch, someone whose brand of justice means seeing life from the perspective of the powerless." This year in particular, the economic realignment of many institutions, secular and religious, has made this challenge truer.

In *Shof'tim*, Moses reviews his career by offering a review of Israel's history and religious obligations. What a transformation has taken place in the last part of his life! He began life an abandoned child, a rebellious teen capable of manslaughter, forced into exile. His return resulted in the Exodus accompanied by a reactive attitude of the people that combined resentment and gratitude. Complaints ranged from "Where are you?" to "Where are our leeks and onions?" Reactions of the masses in the absence of their leader led to the construction of the idolatrous Golden Calf.

This Mosaic era of transition brought with it some of the same characteristics that we currently face in the secular world. The world of Moses is still our contemporary challenge. In the end Moses concludes with a blessing for Joshua, his candidate for leadership of *Am Yisrael* (the people Israel).

Yesterday or today, any *shofet* who is appointed to help us fulfill the covenant of Sinai has to make sure that justice remains the priority.

כי תצא Ki Teitzei

(Deuteronomy 21:10–25:19)

Ki Teitzei
Lawrence S. Kushner, 1995

(Deut. 21:10–14) If, like the Chasidim, you take this section as an allegory about warring against internal enemies like the *yetzer hara*, who are the captives, the enemies you take home from battle?

(Deut. 21:18–21) If you allegorize the *ben soreir umoreh*, what might he represent? Who is the "stubborn and rebellious son" in each of us? Why is this part of us represented as a **son**? What would we be like if we destroyed that part of us? The Rabbis believed this sentence was never earned out, but was only intended as a warning. Why might they have wanted to keep the internal *ben soreir umoreh* alive?

Ki Teitzei
Lawrence S. Kushner, 1996

Several parts of this *parashah* deal with men's treatment of women: as war captives (Deut. 21:10–14), competing wives (21:15–17), mothers of stubborn and rebellious sons (21:18–21), wearers of men's garments (22:5), partners of men in various kinds of relationships (22:13–23:1), prostitutes (23:18–19), divorcees (24:1–4), enablers of a new husband's exemption from civic responsibilities (24:5), levirate marriage partners (25:5–10), assaulters of their husband's enemies (25:11–12)—and metaphorically through the law of letting the mother bird go before taking the chicks (22:6–7). Many of these relationships are not what Genesis seemed to have in mind with its romantic picture of *eizer k'negdo* and man and woman returning to the Eden state of being one flesh. While many of the Deuteronomic passages try to protect the women involved, they suggest that in a restrictive patriarchal society, women's abilities to direct their own lives are quite limited. How might we deal with these situations in a way that would give women the greater authority over their own personal and familial lives that God seems to desire, for example, in the case of the daughters of Zelophechad (Num. 27:1–11)?

Ki Teitzei: The Captive Woman
Stephen E. Cohen, 1997

Rashi and Ramban present two diametrically opposed explanations of the Torah's instructions for the treatment of the captive woman (Deut. 21:10–14).

Rashi "She shall do her nails"—she shall let her fingernails grow long, so that she will be repulsive. "She shall remove the dress"—because it is attractive. "She shall sit in your house"—the house he uses regularly. He enters, and he meets her; he leaves, and he meets her, and sees her weeping, sees her degradation, so she becomes repulsive to him.

Ramban She is given one month's time to weep—the traditional period of mourning—to quiet her grief and her longing, for every sadness is followed by some relief and comfort. During this time, she will consider conversion; and her idolatry, her people, and her homeland will be in part rooted out from her heart. And she will be comforted for them and will cleave to this man.

Comment During the thirty-day waiting period, Rashi is willing to see the captive woman degraded and humiliated, so that in the end, the man will not want her; she will be set free and allowed to go home. Ramban is much more sensitive to her grief and suffering and seeks her consolation—with the ultimate aim that she never return home. Whose approach is more compassionate?

Ki Teitzei: The Rebellious Child
Stephen E. Cohen, 1998

In asserting that the *ben soreir umoreh* (Deut. 21:18) "never was and never will be" (Babylonian Talmud, *Sanhedrin* 71a), the Sages of the Talmud solved the problem of the Torah's harsh death sentence, but they created a new problem for future generations; to wit, why would the Torah describe and address a nonexistent reality?

K'li Yakar   Our Sages said: The stubborn and rebellious child never was and never will be. Why then is it mentioned in the Torah? It contains a wonderful instruction for all Israel, who are called "Children of the Living God." For they might perhaps rely upon this, saying, "Since we are His children, even if we are rebellious He will see no iniquity in Jacob (Num. 23:21) and will have mercy upon us, as a father has mercy on his children, and will not deliver us over to the quality of justice." But when they hear this passage, "All Israel will hear and will fear" (Deut. 21:21), and they will not rely upon being called "Children of God." For if in the earthly court, a father must hand over his child to die, so too in the heavenly court.

Comment   Is the spiritual pitfall of which K'li Yakar speaks, that is, an over-reliance on God's mercy, a real danger for modern Jews?

Ki Teitzei: The Meaning of Burial
Stephen E. Cohen, 2000

Ramban   A verse in this week's *sidrah* specifies the importance of burying the corpse of an executed criminal. Later, this verse came to be identified as the basis for the universal Jewish practice of burial of our dead. The Maharal offers an evocative, albeit pre-modern, rationale for burial (Deut. 21:23). Bury, yes, bury him on that day. Burial does not apply to animals, but only applies to humans. This is because the principle behind burial is of "storing away" something for the future. And because the human being has the potential to be alive in the future, he or she is buried in the earth. Burial, which is a "storing away," teaches of the potential for the future, when the dead will live again. A thing that is openly visible is "actual," whereas a thing that is stored away is "potential."

Comment Among our congregants, cremation has become a widely accepted alternative to burial. Do you consider cremation a legitimate alternative for Jews? If not, on the basis of what rationale do you insist on burial? Do you consider the Maharal's suggestion helpful?

Ki Teitzei: Now, I'm Going to Say This Just Once!
Kenneth J. Weiss, 2001

"You must not remain indifferent" (Deut. 22:3b). In the Holiness Code (Leviticus 19), God was training us, raising us, shaping us:

- Revere your parents and keep Shabbat; "I am, *Adonai*, your God."
- Don't make idols; "I am *Adonai*, your God."
- Don't steal or be false; don't profane.
- Etc.

Fifteen times in the Holiness Code, God's commandments end with (virtually) the same justification. That generation needed the repetition, the reinforcement: live a holy life because *Adonai*, your God, is holy. Not so the next generation, those to whom Moses is commanded to speak in the eleventh month of the fortieth year after Egypt. Moses's message this time: the mitzvot, including the seventy-two I'm about to share with you (in *Ki Teitzei*), must be at the core of how you treat one another!

"Why?" you ask. I'll tell you why, but I'm going to say this just once. Remember it, place it at the very foundation of the society you're about to build, the values you'll one day pass on. You will live by the mitzvot I'm teaching you because you may not do otherwise: *Lo tuchal l'hitaleim*, "You must not remain indifferent."

Ki Teitzei: Arch-Villains
Kenneth J. Weiss, 2003

Amalek is mentioned in the final verses of *Ki Teitzei* (Deut. 25:17–19). In gematria, I discovered, Amalek and *safeik* (doubt) carry the same numerical value.

I ask you (and myself): since these words **are** numerically equivalent, can't we substitute one for the other? The message: in the wilderness our people repeatedly questioned the Holy One, challenged God's resolve in delivering them from the Egyptians.

"Remember what [doubt] did to you on the way ... out of Egypt ... how [doubt] fell upon you ... and cut off all the weak ones at your rear" (Deut. 25:17–18 — R. E. Friedman).

Torah (through gematria) admonishes: **Doubt is our Amalek within!** It destroyed an entire generation!

Now: in your new home, you can—you must!—reject doubt, reaffirm your faith.

Ki Teitzei
Kenneth J. Weiss, 2004

It's יום תרועה (Yom T'ruah) in the Sinai. Reb Moshe's sermon is a masterpiece in three parts:

1. Premise: "כי [*Ki*, 'If'] תצא [*teitzei*, 'you (ever thought to) leave']" (Deut. 21:10a) Torah and the way of life it prescribes and preserves ... don't!
2. Body: You know how inclusive Torah is—it strengthens and protects us. It defines individual rights, personal status, property rights, gender and marital issues, money and lending laws, vows, *tzedakah*, levirate responsibilities, commercial ethics, etc.
3. Conclusion/punchline: You must not depart from all of this! Why? "Remember what Amalek did to you ... after you left [בצאתכם, *b'tzeitchem*] Egypt: ... he cut down all the stragglers [= the defenseless, the 'Torah-less!']" (Deut. 25:17–18).

כי תצא (*Ki Teitzei*) was Moses's sermon on that יום תרועה (Yom T'ruah): Stay "Torah true." "Do not forget!" (Deut. 25:19).

Ki Teitzei
Alan Cook, 2005

Seventy-two. That, of course, is the number of mitzvot contained in כי תצא (*Ki Teitzei*), according to tradition, a larger number than in any other *sidrah*. At first glance, these mitzvot seem to burst forth out of Moses's consciousness, with only tenuous links connecting the various themes of these commandments.

But, as many commentators both classical and modern have noted, the key to understanding the conglomeration of ideas presented in this sidrah seems to come in Deut. 22:3: "You shall not remain indifferent."

This call to action is a significant message of the Torah; perhaps it even goes hand in hand with Hillel's Golden Rule as one of the central themes upon which the Torah is based. For in fulfilling our Jewish mission as a light to the nations, we must not be indifferent toward others. This is why we are commanded, for instance, to construct a parapet for our roofs or to allow a mother bird to care for her young. We, who know what it means to be oppressed, must not allow others—humans or animals—to be overlooked and mistreated.

And this idea is given even more focus when we consider the final words of the *sidrah*, which remind us to always remember the enemy Amalek. Amalek is particularly scorned because of the manner in which they attacked, striking the unarmed women, children, elderly, and infirm at the rear of the camp. By remaining ever conscious of Amalek's crimes, we may be inspired to keep our eyes open, to find a place for the seventy-two mitzvot of כי תצא (*Ki Teitzei*) in our lives, and to speak up when others are being treated unjustly.

Ki Teitzei
Alan Cook, 2006

"Remember what Amalek did to you on your journey" (Deut. 25:17).

"Do not forget!" (Deut. 25:19).

What is the distinction to be made between the two injunctions that we are given regarding Amalek? What is the difference between זכור (*zachor*, "remember") and לא תשכח (*lo tishkach*, "do not forget")?

זכור (*zachor*) implies that it is up to the individual who reads (or hears) the words of כי תצא (*Ki Teitzei*) to personally take to heart the tale of the Amalekites and ensure that the enemies of the Jewish people do not prevail in his or her generation. Yet we have also been taught in our Haggadah, שלא אחד בלבד עמד עלינו לכלותינו (*Shelo echad bilvad amad Aleinu l'chaloteinu*, "for more than one enemy has risen again us to destroy us"). Because our people has faced adversaries in every generation, we are called upon to ensure that the lessons of our ancestors' encounter with Amalek are not lost. This is the message of לא תשכח (*lo tishkach*): that we must teach our children about this episode.

We do not wish to wallow in self-pity and constantly cast ourselves as victims or martyrs. We simply want to be aware of the troubling moments of our past so that they are not repeated.

The *sidrah* begins with instructions about the proper way to prepare for war. Surely, one of the best ways to ready oneself for battle is to remain ever vigilant, in times of peace as well as in times of conflict. Never again will we allow Amalek to surprise and ambush us.

Ki Teitzei
Amy Scheinerman, 2007

Deuteronomy 22:1–3 introduces the subject of *hilchot hashavat aveidah*, the laws concerning returning lost property. Secular society distinguishes between what is legal and what is ethical, recognizing that there is a gap between enforceable legislation and desirable ethical behavior. Indeed, the great jurist Oliver Wendell Holmes held that laws should guide acceptable legal conduct, not the broader realm of ethical behavior. He wrote, "If you want to know the law and nothing else, you must look at it as a bad man, who cares only for the material consequences which such knowledge enables him to predict, and not as a good one, who finds his reasons for conduct, whether inside the law or outside of it, in the vaguer sanctions of conscience." Torah goes much further and indeed attempts to bridge the gap between legal behavior and moral conduct. In the Babylonian Talmud, *Bava M'tzia* 25 and 28 discuss the lengths to which one must go to return lost articles.

Deuteronomy 6:18 says, ועשית הישר והטוב בעיני יהוה (*V'asita hayashar v'hatov b'einei Adonai*, "Do what is right and good in the sight of *Adonai*"), inspiring Nachmanides to comment, "It is impossible to mention in the Torah all human conduct with neighbors and friends, all business transactions, all the institutions of community and all of the nations. Rather, after having mentioned a number of them, such as 'Do not go about as a talebearer' (Lev. 19:16), 'Do not take vengeance or bear a grudge' (Lev. 19:18), 'Do not stand idly by your neighbor's blood' (Lev. 19:16), 'Do not curse the deaf' (Lev. 19:14), 'Stand before the aged' (Lev. 19:32), and others like them, [Torah] goes back to say in a general way that one should do the good and the straight in all matters."

Torah's goal is not merely to inculcate a law-abiding citizen, but to train a God-inspired soul. It is not surprising then that we find this mitzvah, which would make little sense in the world of Justice Holmes: "If you come across your enemy's ox or donkey going astray, bring it back to him" (Exod. 23:4).

Ki Teitzei
Micky Boyden, 2008

This week's *parashah* contains more mitzvot than any other portion in the entire Torah.

On the one hand, the Torah tells us that when we see our fellow human being's animal fallen on the road "do not ignore it; you must help him raise it" (Deut. 22:1). We are also taught not to abuse a needy and destitute laborer, irrespective of whether he is a fellow countryman or a foreign worker. "You must pay him his wages on the same day before the sun sets, for he is needy and urgently depends on it" (Deut. 24:15).

It is such injunctions that make us proud of being Jewish and of the rich heritage that we have shared with the world and that forms the basis of the values of Western civilization.

At the same time, *Ki Teitzei* also contains material of which we can be less proud. A bride found not to be a virgin is to be stoned to death for "committing fornication while under her father's authority" (Deut. 22:21). Likewise, an illegitimate child is not to be admitted into the congregation of God "even in the tenth generation" (Deut. 23:3). A husband could divorce his wife simply because "he finds something obnoxious about her" (Deut. 24:1).

Reform Judaism empowers us to be selective about our observance of mitzvot and to recognize that not everything in Jewish tradition is sacrosanct. At a time when Chabad attracts many Jews by its folksy approach and claim to love all Jews, we would do well to remember that its beliefs are not always in line with what we would view as prerequisites of an ethical society in the twenty-first century.

Ki Teitzei
Michael Boyden, 2009

When one looks at factory farming methods today and the manner in which animals are led to the slaughter, including those intended for *sh'chitah*, one wonders to what degree these practices are in line with the ethical demands of Judaism.

This week's *parashah* tells us that "if you see your fellow's ass or ox fallen on the road, do not ignore it; you must help him raise it" (Deut. 22:4).

Not only humans suffer. Animals feel pain as well, and we are commanded to come to their help. They should be fed before we feed ourselves.

This view is based upon the verse in the *Sh'ma* where we read: "And I shall put grass in your field for your cattle; and only afterwards does it continue, and you shall eat and be satisfied" (Deut. 11:15).

There is also the well-known mitzvah relating to the bird's nest: "If . . . you chance upon a bird's nest . . . with chicks or eggs and the mother is brooding over the chicks or the eggs, do not take the mother together with her young" (Deut. 22:6). Rashi's grandson, the Rashbam, sees a parallel between this mitzvah and the command against cooking a kid in its mother's milk, regarding both of these prohibitions as intending to prevent us from acting cruelly.

The Ramban, who lived in twelfth-century Spain, argues that these prohibitions "have a purpose and a use and serve to correct [*tikkun*] human beings."

In a world of kosher, *glatt* kosher, and a host of other *hechshers* (see http://www.hechshers.info/kashauth/index.htm), one wonders to what degree anyone spares a thought for the poor animals.

כי תבוא Ki Tavo

(Deuteronomy 26:1–29:8)

Ki Tavo
Lawrence S. Kushner, 1995

(Deut. 26:1–11) While the heart of this statement is quoted in the traditional *Magid* section of the Haggadah, the reading of this concise history of the Israelite people in the weekly cycle falls in the week preceding Rosh HaShanah. How does this reminder of our **communal** enslavement, redemption, and entry into the Land relate to the intensely **personal** aspect of Yom HaZikaron and Yom HaDin?

The curses with which this *parashah* abounds are disturbing to us. Why should the blessings not disturb us, but only the curses? If the rewards of good actions come from God, why should we fight the idea that God should punish wrong actions? Is it only the extreme nature of these curses that bothers us? Are we concerned whether God punishes the wicked at all? How are the wicked punished?

Ki Tavo
Lawrence S. Kushner, 1996

The rabbis who divided the *parashiyot and* gave them names clearly acted intentionally when they named last week's section *Ki Teitzei* and this week's *Ki Tavo.* Does last week's portion suggest lessons to be learned from the stay in Egypt and the deliverance from it (*ki teitzei,* "when you go out" [Deut. 21:10]), while this week's suggests different lessons that entering the Land (*ki tavo*, "when you enter" [Deut. 26:1]) will offer? If so, the curses that will fall upon us if we do not behave properly in the Land are unsettling. Does it suggest that now that we shall be in control of the Land we shall be liable to the same—or worse—plagues than the Egyptians who were in control of their land? We all know the "plagues" that befell us in the centuries when others were in control of our destinies—which plagues are worse?

Ki Tavo: First Fruits
Stephen E. Cohen, 1997

K'li Yakar notices that the description of the *bikurim* / first fruits offering begins with an uncommon phrase: "You shall possess [the land] and dwell in it" (Deut. 26:1), which he argues implies a particular mentality of **possession**. The purpose of the *bikurim* was to act as a corrective.

K'li Yakar We only find this phrase, "You shall possess it and dwell in it," in two places—here, and in the section discussing appointing a king (Deut. 17:14). Because after settling and possessing the land, Israel will grow fat, and kick, and desire for themselves the trappings of sovereignty, like all the other nations. So the intention in this offering of the first fruits is to subdue the arrogance following on conquest and settlement, in which their hearts will bring them to say that the land is theirs, that by their swords they possessed it, and they will forget God. For this reason, the text says, "When you come into the land that the Eternal your God gives you" (Deut. 36:1).

Comment In our own day, we often see religious feeling exacerbating, rather than controlling extreme nationalism. Does it in reality ever serve the corrective function that K'li Yakar suggests?

Ki Tavo: Inherit the Land
Stephen E. Cohen, 1998

Whereas the Torah *sidrah* anticipates the initial entry into the land, the haftarah from Isaiah envisions a return from later exile. In the

Rabbinic reading of Isaiah's prophecy, "the land" comes to be understood as the world-to-come.

Deuteronomy 26:1 And when you come into the land that the Eternal your God is giving to you as an inheritance, and you inherit it and settle in it....

Haftarah Ki Tavo, **Isaiah 60:21** And your people, all of them righteous, they shall inherit the land forever; a shoot from My own vineyard, the work of My hands, to be glorified.

Mishnah Sanhedrin **10:1** All Israel have a share in the world-to-come, as it is said: "And your people, all of them righteous, they shall inherit the land forever [*l'olam*]; a shoot from My own vineyard, the work of My hands, to be glorified."

Comment Is the mishnah understanding Isaiah's verse according to the *p'shat*, that is, that the people will one day in the future all be righteous; or is it saying that the people are **already** all righteous and therefore have a share in the *olam haba* (world-to-come)? Why is this mishnah used to introduce each chapter in *Pirkei Avot*?

Ki Tavo: Which Father? Which Aramean?
Stephen E. Cohen, 2000

In this *sidrah*, the declaration of the pilgrim to Jerusalem begins with the famous words *Arami oveid avi*, "My father was a fugitive Aramean" (Deut. 26:5). The Pesach Haggadah, the *Targum* of Onkelos, and Rashi all translate this phrase "An Aramean destroyed my father." But the great medieval proponents of the *p'shat* all agree that this cannot be the simple meaning of the text (*Targum Onkelos* on Deut. 26:5: "Laban the Aramean sought to destroy my father").

Rashi Laban sought to uproot everything, when he pursued Jacob. And since he intended to destroy Jacob, God considered him to have done it.

Rashbam Abraham was an Aramean, wandering and in exile from the land of Aram, as it is written "Go forth from your land..." (Gen. 12:1).

Ibn Ezra The word *oveid* is an intransitive verb. And if it had meant Laban, the text would have said *ma'abid* or *m'abeid* (destroy).

Furthermore, why would it say, "Laban sought to destroy my father and he went down to Egypt..." since Laban did not cause the descent into Egypt? The most likely meaning is that the Aramean is Jacob, and the text is saying, "When my father was in Aram, he was *oveid*," which in this case means "poor."

Comment What impelled Rashi and his predecessors to deny the *p'shat* of the verse? Was the characterization of Abraham/Jacob as an Aramean too objectionable? Or was the reminder of the hatred of Laban irresistible?

Ki Tavo: Tip the Scale!
Kenneth J. Weiss, 2001

"Cursed be one who will not uphold the words of this instruction, to do them" (Deut. 27:26—R. E. Friedman translation).

Remember Shabbat and keep it, speak of Shabbat and observe it: our tradition urges us both to think of Shabbat and to live it.

True! However, in our *parashah* (and so often throughout the literature), the spotlight is definitely more on what we do than on what we say. The K'tav Sofer tells us that "the curse [see text above] applies to those who say that it is not necessary to observe the commandments of the LORD in practice, claiming that the important thing is that one must understand their meaning and be good 'in one's heart.'"

Amen, says Rabbi Abraham Joshua Heschel. He asks, "What does God want of me?" His answer (in *God in Search of Man*) is that God wants deeds. God wants mitzvot. "The deed is the text, the trial and the risk. The sun goes down, but the deed goes on. God depends on us, awaits our deeds." So perform the deed! Do the mitzvah. Tip the scale and know blessing.

Ki Tavo
Kenneth J. Weiss, 2003

"When you enter the land..." (Deut. 26:1)

... recall that you doubted—even rebelled—during the past forty years. Then, turn your back on these regrettable behaviors.

Upon crossing the Jordan, you shall:

1. Offer first fruits: they epitomize your new land, your renewed connection to God who vouchsafed it to you (Deut. 26:2).
2. Recite: "My father was a fugitive Aramean" who lived and suffered in Egypt. God heard, freed us, then "brought us to this place and gave us this land" (Deut. 26:5–9).
3. Affirm: "I have neither transgressed nor forgotten any of Your commandments" (Deut. 26:13).

Taken together, these connote renewal in a new land: God's *am s'gulah* (treasured people [Deut. 26:18]) will refresh its faith, live out its promise.

Ki Tavo
Kenneth J. Weiss, 2004

Every rabbi is privileged, from time to time, to share in a couple's golden wedding anniversary. To celebrate fifty years of marriage is to gratefully acknowledge all that has happened over a half century: health and family . . . hardship and pain. Couples don't say, "Thank You, God, for the good years: 2–10, 18, 26–34, 48." Rather they say, "Thank You, God, for **all** our years, for **everything** we've gone through, for enabling us to reach this moment."

Understand Deut. 26:1–10 as a biblical paradigm for saying, "Thank You." Through gifts (first fruits) and a prescribed liturgical formula, Israelites acknowledge and affirm that life is downs ("The Egyptians dealt harshly with us" [Deut. 26:6]) and ups ("יהוה [*Adonai*] freed us . . . and . . . brought us to this place and gave us this land" [Deut. 26:8–9]).

In marriage . . . in all of life: Torah teaches us to appreciate the **full** scope of experiences that strengthen and enrich us.

Ki Tavo
Alan Cook, 2005

"My father was a fugitive Aramean. He went down to Egypt with meager numbers and sojourned there. . . . [God] brought us to this place and gave us . . . a land flowing with milk and honey" (Deut. 26:5–9).

Most Jews are probably familiar with this formula from the Passover seder. The story that it recounts seems well-suited for that holiday. But due to its place in the lectionary cycle, we find ourselves reading it during the month of Elul. As we engage in חשבון הנפש (*cheshbon hanefesh*) it is appropriate that we examine not only our individual past, but also the past of our people.

Remember the "Trip-Tik" from AAA? When using one to guide our journey, we have a choice. We could tear off and discard each individual page of the map as we complete each leg of the trip. Instead, most of us would choose to keep the map intact, so that we could look back at the places from which we've come. Life works in much the same way.

Abraham Joshua Heschel noted, "It was the glory of Greece to have discovered the idea of *cosmos*, the world of space; it was the achievement of Israel to have experienced history, the world of time."

We did not arrive at this moment on our own. God redeemed us, brought us to Israel, and enabled us to become what we are today. As we reflect on the past, and look forward to the future, let us remember God's place in it all.

Ki Tavo
Alan Cook, 2006

כי תבוא (*Ki Tavo*) begins with Moses instructing the Israelites to have a pageant of sorts when they arrive in ארץ ישראל (*Eretz Yisrael*). This expectation is understandable; since Moses himself will not be present to guide them and make sure that they are "doing the right thing," he feels compelled to orchestrate a lesson that will hopefully resonate with the people long after he has gone.

So he carefully scripts (with God's help) the message that the Levites will share with the people. In so doing, he outlines the blessings that the people may receive if they are faithful to God's laws (see Deuteronomy 28). Yet the blessings are to be bookended by some pretty severe curses—significant consequences that the Israelites will suffer if they fail to follow the mitzvot, including the need to cannibalize their own children for sustenance.

Are such graphic and drastic measures really called for? Could Moses not have chosen merely to "accentuate the positive"?

We need consequences in our lives. We need to know what we have to lose and what we have to gain. The severity of the potential punishments that Moses sets out highlights the desirability of earning the blessings and living life in such a manner that we are deserving of enjoying those blessings.

The structure of blessing surrounded on both sides by curses also serves as a metaphor for how we should lead our lives. We hew closely to the path established by Torah. We do not stray to the left or to the right but remain squarely in the middle.

Ki Tavo
Amy Scheinerman, 2007

כי תבוא (*Ki Tavo*) features a well-known תוכחה (*tocheichah*), a string of curses that will befall Israel should she fail to keep her covenant with God. Yet embedded in the midst of this frightening litany we read, "Because you would not serve the Lord your God in joy and gladness over the abundance of everything, you shall have to serve—in hunger and thirst, naked and lacking everything—the enemies whom the Lord will let loose against you" (Deut. 28:47–48). Can it be that the crux of the matter is approaching mitzvot with a sense of joy and gladness? Isn't it enough to observe them, to do what is right?

Two observations: First, a psychological comment. Torah is aware of the importance of cultivating what might be called "an attitude of gratitude," that is, a sense of appreciation for all our blessings. Those who do not approach life and their activities in this world from the perspective of counting their blessings experience much of life as a curse. Those with a keenly developed sense of appreciation can often see in curses partial blessings.

Second, serving God is not an anachronistic concept. I recently saw a church sign that read, "Most people want to serve God—but only in an advisory capacity." We live in a secular society that exalts a form of narcissism, lauding that which makes **us** happy, rather than encouraging us to make **others** happy. Torah reminds us that if we serve God (and this includes others) with genuine joy and gladness, we will be truly blessed.

Ki Tavo
Micky Boyden, 2008

This week's Torah portion is about historical sensitivity. Remember your narrative. Remember where you came from, and offer thanks for what you have. The Israelites are enjoined to bring their first fruits to the Temple in thanksgiving and make a public declaration with which we are familiar from the Passover Haggadah: "My father was a fugitive Aramean. . . . The Egyptians dealt harshly with us. . . . We cried to *Adonai* . . . [who] brought us to this place and gave us this land. . . . Therefore, I now bring the first fruits" (Deut. 26:5–10).

Note that the declaration is phrased in the singular: "My father was a fugitive Aramean."

Each and every person has a responsibility to fulfill this obligation. We can't be sensitive and appreciative for other people.

However, it isn't quite that simple. The Mishnah in Tractate *Sotah* states that the declaration has to be made in Hebrew. So what about those who are illiterate?

A beautiful solution is found in *Mishnah Bikurim* 3:7: "At first, anyone who knew how to read would read and someone would read for those who did not know how to read. They refrained from bringing [the first fruits]. It was decided that someone would read both for those who knew how to read and for those who didn't."

This desire to make everyone feel welcome and involved gains expression in our own time when Reform prayer books contain not only translations but also transliterations. Only when we make everyone feel at home can we expect them to feel equally part of our narrative.

Ki Tavo
Michael Boyden, 2009

Parashat Ki Tavo begins with memory, consciousness, and thanksgiving. After all, it is only when we remember our past and are sensitive to the blessings that we so often take for granted that we are likely to appreciate our world.

The Torah tells us of the obligation to bring the first fruits to Shiloh and later to the Temple in Jerusalem. The mitzvah is related in the singular, in order to emphasize that the obligation to appreciate cannot be transferred. Thanks must be personal.

Bringing the first fruits, however, is but the first phase in what is known as the *vidui maaseir*—the tithe confession, for it is not enough just to bring, but *how* we bring is important too.

The *vidui* contains three elements: "I have entered the land...." How easy it is to take Israel for granted! Nachmanides reminds us, "God has fulfilled His word, and I thank and praise Him."

The second element, which we recognize from the Pesach Haggadah, is about historical consciousness: "My father was a fugitive Aramean...." This element is vital, for it is only when we recall our past and what we have endured that we are likely to be sufficiently sensitive to the needs of others in order to proclaim the third element of the *vidui*: "I have cleared out the consecrated portion from the house and have given it to the Levite, the stranger, the orphan, and the widow."

It is that memory of our suffering that continues to inspire us to struggle for the rights of the disadvantaged in an all-too-often callous world even when we ourselves have been privileged to enter the land.

נצבים-וילך *Nitzavim/Vayeilech*

(Deuteronomy 29:9–30:20 and Deuteronomy 31:1–30)

Nitzavim/Vayeilech
Lawrence S. Kushner, 1995

(Deut. 29:16) "You have seen their detestable things [*shikutzeihem*]." Why are idolatry and polytheism so detestable to God? Why are they not just **misguided**? Is contemporary idolatry (ascribing power to money or possessions) so detestable? Is Deut. 29:25 helpful here? Is 30:17? (What does **"serving** other gods" mean? Note the *M'chilta* to Exod. 20:3, where *elohim acheirim* is seen as *elohim m'acheirim*—gods that alienate their worshipers.) And what do we say about non-Jews when we call them *shiksa* or *sheigitz*, derivatives of *shikutz*?

(Deut. 30:14) "The word is very near to you, in your mouth and your heart, to do it." How is the word "very near" to people who don't know Hebrew or very much Torah? This language sounds a lot like descriptions of prophecy—God putting the word into the prophet's mouth. We are to be a prophet people—how do we do that? Have you ever felt that God's word was in your mouth—that words and insights were flowing through you, as though you were a passive vessel for teachings you were not aware you knew? How might you explain that feeling?

The name of this *parashah*, which includes one of Moses's final speeches to his people, bears the same root as the portion *Lech L'cha*—the portion that introduces us to Abraham, the "father" of the Jewish people. How would you compare Abraham as he left Haran to Moses as he was about to leave his people, and life itself?

(Deut. 31:9–11) Moses did four things to ensure transmission of Torah: he wrote it down, he gave a copy each to the priests and the elders, and he commanded that it be read in public every *Sh'mitah* year. Why did he choose these specific things—and why did he do only these (e.g., not giving the Torah to more groups of people, not ordering more frequent public readings)? Have we improved on Moses by our three-times-a-week public reading, or does our custom reflect a lessened spiritual capacity that requires more frequent reading and more widespread access to text?

Nitzavim/Vayeilech
Lawrence S. Kushner, 1996

Maimonides urges us to show anger only when it will have a pedagogical purpose. God, it seems, gets angry a great deal—but the Israelites do not seem to learn from it. Why does God permit Godself to become angry so often? What can humans learn from this?

(Deut. 30:11–14) In what sense is the mitzvah that God commands us (or the "word" in v. 14) "in our mouth"? Jeremiah (31:33) says that only in days to come will it be on our heart—the language "in our mouth" suggests that we are all prophets, on whose tongue God has put the word to speak. In what sense can this be true?

(Deut. 31:6) "Be strong and of good courage"—God and Moses urge this on the people often. Was this a "time-bound" command, intended only for the rigors of conquering the Land—or was it intended as a mitzvah for all time, despite the fact that it escaped both Maimonides' and Nachmanides' enumeration? As Reform Jews, not averse to adding and subtracting mitzvot, would we see this as a mitzvah to be urged on our people at all times? What are some contemporary applications?

If Moses could write one copy of the Torah, surely God could have made it possible for him or others to write enough so that more people could read and study it. Why do you suppose God chose to have the Torah read aloud to the people—why was "hearing" the text preferred to seeing it?

Nitzavim/Vayeilech
Stephen E. Cohen, 1997

In his commentary on Deuteronomy 30, K'li Yakar **distinguishes** between two types of exile: one of which is imposed upon us, and another that we choose and live with, convinced that we really have no choice at all.

K'li Yakar At first the text says, "Among all the nations into which *YHVH* your God has driven you" (Deut 30:1), and then later, "Among all the nations into which *YHVH* your God has scattered you" (Deut. 30:3). There is a difference between "driven"— הדיחך [*hidichacha*] and "scattered"—הפיצך [*hefitz'cha*]. "Scattered" refers to the dispersion itself, whereas "driven" implies from the mitzvot—when Israel is among the nations, they can be, as a consequence, exiled from the mitzvot. Now, because of being driven from the mitzvot, the Jews may easily fall into error, saying that the Holy One no longer cares at all about their actions, and in this way, they may despair completely of ever being redeemed, thinking that the Holy One intentionally drove them away from the mitzvot, but this was not God's intention, for God eternally desires your performance of the mitzvot.

Comment K'li Yakar describes here a significant feature of the psychology of American Jewish assimilation. Many of our people do feel "in exile from the mitzvot" and regard it as an imposed condition—arising inexorably out of their historical circumstances. ("If God wanted me to observe the mitzvot, S/He would not have placed me in late-twentieth-century California.")

Nitzavim/Vayeilech: God in Exile
Stephen E. Cohen, 1998

In Rashi's skillful hands, a grammatical peculiarity in the Torah text gives rise to three startling theological assertions.

Deuteronomy 30:3   And the Eternal will return [*v'shav*] your captivity.

Rashi   It ought to have said *v'heshiv*, "will cause to return." Our Sages learned from this that, as it were, the Divine Presence is entrapped with Israel in the sorrow of their exile, and when they are redeemed, the Torah writes of God's own redemption—that God will return with them. And we may also say that the day of the ingathering of the exiles is so extremely difficult that it is as though God personally must take every single person by the hand, one at a time, each from their place, as it is said, "You shall be gathered one by one, Children of Israel" (Isa. 27:12). And even regarding the exiles of the other nations, we find the same thing, as in *v'shavti et sh'vut Mitzrayim* ["I will resore the fortunes of the Egyptians"] (Ezek. 29:14).

Comment   Is Rashi's final comment hinting at a unique, covenantal relationship between God and every nation in exile?

Nitzavim/Vayeilech: Model of Leadership
Stephen E. Cohen, 1998

In Deut. 31:7, Moses encourages Joshua with the expression *ki atah tavo et haam*, using the *kal* form of the verb when we would expect the *hifil*. In this case, Onkelos translates, "You shall go with this people [*at tei'ol im ama hadein*]." When, in verse 23, the text does use the *hifil* (*ki atah tavi*), Onkelos notes the distinction and translates, "You shall bring the Children of Israel [*at ta'eil yat B'nei Yisrael*]." Rashi (following the Babylonian Talmud, *Sanhedrin* 8a) elaborates on the difference between these two expressions, in which he perceives two different models of leadership.

Rashi on Deuteronomy 31:7 (quoting Onkelos)   "Behold you shall go with this people." Moses said to Joshua, "The elders of the generation will be with you, each with their opinion and with their advice." But the Holy One said to Joshua, "'You shall bring [*ki atah tavi*] the Children of Israel to the land that I promised to them' (Deut. 31:23). That is, bring them even against their will. Everything depends on you. Take a staff and strike their skulls. There can only be one leader for each generation, never two leaders for a generation."

Comment If we accept Rashi's attribution of views to Moses and God, what might motivate Moses to advocate a model of "shared leadership," and why would God be the voice for a more authoritarian form of leadership?

Nitzavim/Vayeilech: While Our Students Live
Elaine Rose Glickman, 1999

At the end of *Parashat Vayeilech,* Moses warns that he will call heaven and earth to witness against the Israelites . . . for he knows that after his death, the people will forsake the teachings of God. Yet we remain loyal to God as long as Moses's disciple Joshua lives, according to the Book of Judges; we serve God all the days of Joshua's life. In reconciling these apparently contradictory passages, Rashi beautifully demonstrates how teachers live on through their beloved students.

Rashi "After my death you shall surely act corruptly" (Deut. 31:29). But for all the days of Joshua, the Israelites did not act corruptly, as Scripture says, "And the people served *Adonai* all of Joshua's days" (Judges 2:7). From this we learn that a teacher cherishes a student as he cherishes his own life and that all the time Joshua would live, it would appear to Moses that he himself lived.

Comment As we contemplate our deeds this year and acknowledge our own mortality, what inspiration can we find in Rashi's interpretation? What sort of legacy will our teachings and our actions leave to our students, our colleagues, and our loved ones? How can we be certain that what we struggle to teach and achieve during our lifetime will endure after we have died?

Nitzavim/Vayeilech: What *T'shuvah* Requires?
Stephen E. Cohen, 2000

Moses's marvelous word of encouragement regarding the accessibility of the מצוה (mitzvah) remains as alive and inspiring as the day he uttered it. But what is the מצוה (mitzvah) of which he speaks? One possibility, explains K'li Yakar, is that Moses is referring to תשובה (*t'shuvah*, "repentance")—the subject of the preceding passage (Deut. 30:11): "For this מצוה [mitzvah] which I am commanding you this day is not too wondrous for you, nor too remote. . . ."

K'li Yakar Our Sages taught, "Who is one who does תשובה [*t'shuvah*]? It is, for example, an adulterer who has the opportunity to repeat the same sin, and he resists under the very same circumstances, in the same place, and with the same woman." But if this is so, then one who sinned with a woman across the sea might say that he cannot repair it until he has traveled for days and days, to the same place and the same woman with whom he sinned. And so he would be prevented from doing תשובה [*t'shuvah*]. Therefore the verse says that this is not the case. The thing/word is very close to you, in your mouth—this is confession, and in your heart—this is trembling. And this will be sufficient, for your mouth and your heart are the place of the sin, and also the place of תשובה [*t'shuvah*]. This is the meaning of "in the same place." And as to the requirement "with the same woman," they only said this for emphasis; the essence of תשובה [*t'shuvah*] does not require this.

Comment Has כלי יקר (K'li Yakar) diluted the Sages' rigorous standard for complete תשובה (*t'shuvah*)?

Nitzavim/Vayeilech: To Repent Is to Change!
Kenneth J. Weiss, 2001

"When you'll come back to *YHVH*, your God, with all your heart and with all your soul" (Deut. 30:10—R. E. Friedman).

Now **is** the time! Our tradition encourages—even enables—real change. *T'shuvah* suggests the human need to look within, to take stock honestly, and to "turn over a new leaf." Mordecai Kaplan teaches that *t'shuvah* means "nothing less than the continual remaking of human nature."

Deuteronomy 30:1–10 are among the verses we do not read on Yom Kippur, located as they are between the two segments that compose our Holy Day *parashah*. Yet, these verses reach to the very essence of the High Holy Day message: our need to rethink, reevaluate, return, renew. Moses tells his listeners (us included) that when the people return to God, God will be ready, receptive. God will restore the people to their fortunes and to their land.

To turn, to change is not easy for human beings, but "the gates of repentance are always open." Joseph Albo teaches that "repentance means a change of heart and mind and behavior." To rethink can lead to reevaluation. To reevaluate can lead to return. To return is to repent; to repent, to renew. And isn't renewal a core message of our Holy Days? Let this message from *Nitzavim* move us to begin if we have not done so. Yes: "choose life that you may live, love God, listen to His voice, and cling to Him" (Deut. 30:19–20).

Nitzavim/Vayeilech: First Take a Stand, Then Make Your Move
Kenneth J. Weiss, 2001

"Moses went and spoke these things to all Israel" (Deut. 31:1).

In last week's *parashah* (*Nitzavim*), the people of Israel are standing before God. But—more than standing, they are presenting themselves before God, ready and willing to enter into a covenant that will define a special and unique status. *Nitzav* is more than *omed*; the former implies being actively present, involved. *Nitzav*—the verb—indicates that there is a readiness to stand up . . . to stand for . . . to take a stand about something of importance. Thus, three men stand before Abraham at the door of his tent, just before making a startling announcement (Gen. 18:2). The Israelites stand (*vayityatzvu*) to meet God at the foot of Mount Sinai (Exod. 19:17). Later, Moses is told to present (*v'nitzavta* [Exod. 34:2]) himself before God on Mount Sinai, and God stands (*vayityatzeiv* [Exod. 34:5]) with Moses there. Last Shabbat, we read, *Atem nitzavim*, "You are standing."

This week's *parashah* begins with the words *Vayeilech Moshe*, "Moses went forth." The linkage between these two portions is provocative: one cannot really "go forth" until one knows what he or she is willing to stand up for. Moses went forth only after he and his followers took their stand.

Where did Moses go? *Tol'dot Yitzchak* suggests that he went wherever he could teach and model God's mitzvot. Early Rabbinic sources suggest that Moses went into the heart of every Jew who stood with him in the wilderness, and his spark was transmitted to every generation thereafter. Deuteronomy 31:1 offers textual "proof": "**Moses went** and spoke these things **to all Israel**."

Nitzavim/Vayeilech
Kenneth J. Weiss, 2003

God makes a covenant "with those who are standing here . . . this day . . . and with those who are not . . . here this day" (Deut. 29:14). To whom does "not . . . here" refer? Perhaps to:

- Past generations, including those who died en route to the land (whom God hasn't forgotten).
- Future generations, including our own: Jews born into the covenant.
- Those who, though within "earshot" that day, "tuned out," were mentally absent, lacked requisite *kavanah* (**not** unlike modern Jews who come to synagogue yet remain stubbornly, spiritually detached).

Many Jews weren't (totally) there. Some opted out—others (in every successive generation) still do! For those who do want in, the gate remains open: Torah's "not too baffling . . . nor is it beyond reach" (Deut. 30:11).

Nitzavim/Vayeilech
Kenneth J. Weiss, 2004

These linked *parashiyot* portray life:

- נצבים (*Nitzavim*): For awhile, we stand firm. We grow familiar with where we are, our stage in life: at school, later a profes-

sion; in our childhood, later as adults. We feel stable, durable, constant.
- וילך (*Vayeilech*): Invariably (episodically), we move on, things change; the past passes; transition is in the wind.

In Deuteronomy 31, Moses prepares his people for a transition: It's time for me to leave and for Joshua to step in.

Repeatedly, Moses encourages the people and Joshua, "Be strong and resolute"—especially at times of transition. He reassures them: you'll stand firm once again, even without me.

וילך משה (*Vayeilech Moshe*), "A life change overcame Moses," וידבר (*vay'dabeir*) "so he spoke [to his people]" (Deut. 31:1).

Nitzavim/Vayeilech
Alan Cook, 2005

This *sidrah* is packed with important ideas; the concept לא בשמים הוא (*Lo vashamayim hi*, "It is not in the heavens" [Deut. 30:12]) is practically our Reform mantra, heard echoing throughout the halls of HUC-JIR.

But perhaps the most intriguing statement is found in chapter 29, verse 28. Here we enter into a sort of covenant of justice with God, as we determine what we may be held responsible for and what is left in God's hands.

Dr. J. H. Hertz noted that most translations of this verse tend to break it at the אתנחתא (*etnachta*, the cantillation mark indicating the middle of a verse [at *Eloheinu*, "our God"]). This has the effect of giving God purview over concealed acts, while holding humanity liable for adjudicating overt acts. However, Hertz argues that the גרשיים (*geirshayim*, another cantillation mark) over the word והנגלת (*v'haniglot*, "but/and with overt acts") actually serves as a conjunctive, so that it is God who has power over both hidden and revealed acts. If we follow the latter reading, then what remains is for humanity to continue the transmission of Torah throughout the generations. But can we carry forth our tradition if we close our eyes to the "revealed acts" and leave it to God to deal with them? Teaching Torah faithfully to our children would seem to include devising a system to ensure that transgressions against its precepts are duly punished.

The Masoretes included *n'kudot* (vocalization) above the phrase לנו ולבנינו (*lanu ul'vaneinu*, "it is for us and our children"). Rashi feels that these serve to limit the scope of the preceding phrase. Punishment will be meted out to sinners at the appropriate time.

God balances the quality of דין (*din*, "judgment") with the quality of רחמים (*rachamim*, "compassion"); we should strive to do the same. לא בשמים הוא (*Lo vashamayim hi*)—justice rests not only in the heavens. We too must work to set and maintain moral standards for our community.

Nitzavim/Vayeilech
Alan Cook, 2005

"I can no more go out and come in" (Deut. 31:2—1917 JPS).

"Return, O Israel, to *Adonai* your God" (Hosea 14:2).

As the Israelites were approaching Canaan, Moses realized that he was approaching his final days on earth. For a man of 120 years, he was still in remarkable shape; "his eyes were undimmed and his vigor unabated" (Deut. 34:7). Nonetheless, he recognized that certain functions no longer came easily to him. He was unable to come and go as he once did. Some translations treat לצאת ולבוא (*latzeit v'lavo*, "to go out and come in" [Deut. 31:2]) as a hendiadys meaning "to be active," "to move around," or "to lead you." But the Rabbis focus not so much on **what** Moses could not do; rather they draw our attention to **why** he could not do it.

A discussion in the Babylonian Talmud, *Sotah* 13b, teaches that Moses could no longer engage in these activities because he was not permitted to do so. In order that the people might accept and show deference to Joshua's leadership, Moses's authority and ability to express the wisdom of Torah to others was gradually curtailed. Moses could no longer go out to and come in from the Divine Presence in the manner he had in his youth.

We are not saddled with this same difficulty; through the words of Hosea, God is urging us to draw ever closer. We need not rely upon a Moses to do our coming and going for us; we each can build (or repair) our own relationships with God. In this month of Elul, let us not drag our feet. Let us be swift to return to God.

Nitzavim/Vayeilech
Alan Cook, 2006

Imagine giving a teenager a standardized test on which all the answers had already been filled in. They would simply need to fill in their name in order to achieve a perfect score. What high-schooler, facing the daunting task of preparing for college entrance exams, would not leap at such an opportunity?

נצבים (*Nitzavim*) offers a similar scenario, with even higher stakes. The text tells us, "See, I set before you this day life and prosperity, death and adversity" (Deut. 30:15). As if further prompting was necessary, the Torah then adjures us, ובחרת בחיים (*Uvacharta bachayim*, "Choose life" [Deut. 30:19]).

Why must we be told to choose life? Isn't it basic human instinct to want to live, to fight for survival, to try to succeed?

It is, of course. But it's not always easy to do so. Life throws us curveballs and challenges. It sometimes seems easier just to follow the crowds and succumb to temptation, rather than walk on the proper path that God wishes for us to follow.

Thus, God gives us the answer: ובחרת בחיים (*Uvacharta bachayim*). And this is not a one-time choice, but a constant commitment that we reassess and renew on a daily basis. For life is as much about the journey as it is about the destination. Though the road may be difficult to traverse at times, God has promised us that the end result will be worthwhile.

Nitzavim/Vayeilech
Amy Scheinerman, 2007

Each year we read נצבים (*Nitzavim*) the Shabbat prior to Rosh HaShanah. How fitting that it speaks of Israel's return to God. In particular,

Deut. 30:1–10 employs a form of the term שוב (*shuv*, "return") no fewer than seven times.

When we examine each occurrence closely, a pattern emerges. Three occurrences speak of Israel's turning toward God: in Deut. 30:2 we find ושבת עד־יהוה אלהיך (*v'shavta ad Adonai Elohecha*, "and you return to *Adonai* your God"); in Deut. 30:8 we find ואתה תשוב (*v'atah tashuv*, "you shall return"); and in Deut. 30:10 we find כי תשוב אל־יהוה אלהיך בכל־לבבך ובכל־נפשך (*ki tashuv el Adonai Elohecha b'chol l'vav'cha uv'chol nafshecha*, "once you return to *Adonai* your God with all your heart and soul"). Interspersed with these three expressions of Israel's return to God are two in which God returns to Israel: Deut. 30:3, ושב יהוה אלהיך את־שבותך (*v'shav Adonai Elohecha et sh'vut'cha*, "and *Adonai* your God will return you from captivity"); and Deut. 30:9, כי ישוב יהוה לשוש עליך (*ki yashuv Adonai lasus alecha*, "for *Adonai* your God will return to rejoicing over you").

We might ask: What is the significance of the עד־יהוה (*ad Adonai*) in verse 2 and אל־יהוה (*el Adonai*) in verse 10? What is the significance of שב . . . את (*shav . . . et*) in verse 3 and ישוב . . . ל (*yashuv . . . l'*) in verse 9? Do they connote different types or levels of repentance and return? Do they suggest that תשובה (*t'shuvah*, "repentance") is not an all-or-nothing proposition, as classical treatises on repentance often seem to suggest?

Or perhaps the alternation of Israel's return and God's return suggests that תשובה (*t'shuvah*) is a spiritual dance of two partners who must both turn to face one another and come closer and closer until they meet in the middle? After all, how often is the rupture in a relationship black and white, with one party wholly righteous and the other party wholly wrong? The Chasidic parable of the king who offered to meet his estranged son halfway comes to mind.

Nitzavim/Vayeilech
Janice Garfunkel, 2008

Central to traditional Judaism, the Judaism of our ancestors for many centuries, is the notion of a covenant that is binding on us and our descendants for eternity.

Moderns are not so comfortable with the idea of something being "binding," especially a covenant entered into by one's ancestors, not oneself. We're all about choice, about what is meaningful and fulfilling to me now, today. Yeah, I'll do it if it adds meaning to my life. If not, then no thanks, I'll take a pass.

In fact, we even have something of a slogan in Reform Judaism: "We are **all** Jews by choice." Our *parashah* says, I don't think so. Our *parashah* says, Sorry, but your great-great-great-grandparents signed you up (or you signed yourself up), and like the Hotel California, you can check in any time you like, but you can never leave!

Of course, Jews do successfully leave. They abandon their Jewish identity, alas, in large numbers. Rashi said, *Yisrael af al pi she'choteh Yisrael hu*, "A Jew, even though he [or she] sins, is still a Jew." Which is to say, we feel one way about a Catholic with Catholic parents, but quite differently about a Catholic with Jewish parents.

I think that it behooves us Reform rabbis at least to wrestle together with our congregants about these ideas of a covenant that is binding across generations and of the place in Reform Judaism for notions of obligation, duty, commitment, and permanence. Were you and I, in fact, there at Sinai? Only if we feel like it?

Nitzavim/Vayeilech
Michael Boyden, 2008

Most people reach a stage in life when they realize that it is time to retire and leave the field to others. The question is: What do we leave behind?

In this week's *parashah*, Moses turns to the Children of Israel and says, "I am now 120 years old. I can no longer come and go" (Deut. 31:2). Would that all our leaders knew when it was time to step down!

That having been said, Moses nevertheless feels the need to convey two further messages to his people. God instructs him, "Write down this poem and teach it to the Children of Israel" (Deut. 31:19), and Moses does so (Deut 31: 22).

Maimonides explains this to mean that "every Jew is commanded to write a *sefer Torah* himself." He continues, "Even though his forefathers may have left him a Torah, he is nevertheless commanded to write his own. If he writes it himself, it is as though he had received it on Mount Sinai. If he does not know how to write, others should write one for him . . . and even if he writes just one letter, it is as though he had written all of it."

Moses's other final command to the people is the mitzvah of *hak'heil*, which enjoined them to assemble at the Temple every seventh year on the Feast of Sukkot to hear Torah. Everyone was required to be present—"men, women and children and the stranger in your camp" (Deut. 31:12).

Why were the children commanded to undertake the tiring journey to Jerusalem? The commentator Nachmanides responds, "Because they will hear and ask questions, and their parents will accustom them to learning."

What both of these mitzvot have in common is recognition of our duty to renew Torah and pass it on to our children. Already three thousand years ago, long before buzzwords such as "continuity," Moses understood that education was the key to the future of the Jewish people.

Everyone has the right to retire, including surely Moses, who had borne the burden of leadership for so long. However, he understood that the real test of leadership is not what we have done, but what we bequeath to those who come after us.

Nitzavim/Vayeilech
Janice Garfunkel, 2009

"Then the LORD thy God will turn thy captivity, and have compassion upon thee" (Deut. 30:3—1917 JPS).

In Deut. 30:3 we come across a strange grammatical construction. Rashi comments on it, saying we expect a *hifil* verb (*heishiv*), but find a *kal* (*shav*). He offers the midrash that God follows Israel into captivity (*sheivut*) and returns (*shav*) along with the people to the land. The 1917 JPS translation follows Rashi, defining *sheivut* as "captivity," from the root *shin-bet-yod* (or *hei*). But it seems just as possible to use the root *shin-bet-tav*—a cessation from work (hence *shabbat* or *sh'vitah*, "strike").

There are times when God's hiddenness overwhelms us and we find ourselves empty of belief; times when being a moral example, personally or collectively, feels too onerous. At such times we want a *sheivut* from our job of being holy. Let someone else carry the torch, some other group be a light unto the nations. We feel our actions are insincere, that we are just going through the motions. Our passage tells us that God is with us even then. Just by going through the motions, God turns our *sheivut* into *maasim tovim* (good works), and our prayers into *Avodat Adonai* (the service of the Eternal).

הַאֲזִינוּ *Haazinu*

(Deuteronomy 32:1–52)

Haazinu: Shabbat Shuvah
Lawrence S. Kushner, 1995

(Hosea 14:2) "Take with you words and return to God"—If God is everywhere, why do we need to "return" to God? How can our offering of words be equivalent to our ancestors' offering of animals?

(Hosea 14:4–6) What leads God to forgive us? Why should God forgive **us**?

Haazinu
Lawrence S. Kushner, 1996

While Deut. 32:8 is ambiguous, it appears that a relationship is being established between the establishment of the nations in Genesis 10 and the "number of the Israelites." Particularly given the midrashic interpretation of Deut. 33:2, that God offered the Torah to the nations, what is your understanding of why the Torah speaks so much about other nations—how we are to relate to the nations? Are we "responsible" for them? Are they responsible for us? What are we to learn from each other?

Haazinu: Rains Watering the Human Heart
Stephen E. Cohen, 1997

There is a striking parallel between the comments of Ibn Ezra and of S'fat Emet on the second verse of Moses's final song: "Let my teaching fall as the rain; let my speech distill as the dew" (Deut. 32:2).

Ibn Ezra Moses prayed that his words would be like the dew and the rain—that they would "water the earth," meaning, that his words should enter the hearts of those who hear him, with the effect of the rain upon the earth, causing it to give birth and to sprout with growth.

S'fat Emet For within every Jew there is a vital spark, and this spark must be awakened by Torah—like the earth, which contains the power to bring forth fruits and vegetables, and the rain awakens this power. For this reason the human/אדם [*adam*] is named after the earth/אדמה [*adamah*].

Comment As close as they are to each other, these two commentaries have different concerns. Ibn Ezra is thinking primarily of Moses and his poetic task, whereas S'fat Emet is more interested in the power of Torah generally. To what extent is the power of words—either poetry or Torah—bound up with the personalities of the speaker and the listener?

Haazinu: The Eye
Stephen E. Cohen, 1998

In one of the most memorable phrases of his farewell song, Moses describes God guarding Israel "like the *ishon* of His eye" (Deut. 32:10)—evoking the extreme delicacy, the sensitivity, and the mystery of the organ of sight. The word *ishon* itself, however, is of uncertain meaning and the *m'forshim* (commentators) debate the exact significance of Moses's image.

Rashi The *ishon* is the black of the eye, from which light comes forth.

***Siftei Chachamim* (on Rashi)** And why is it called *ishon*? Because in it can be seen the image of a tiny man/*ish*, just as can be seen in a mirror.

Rashbam The Holy One protects Israel as the *ishon* protects the eye. The *ishon* is the skin that folds over the eye.

Comment Rashi and I translate *ishon* as "pupil" and place the emphasis of the verse on the eye's unique involvement with the two divine elements of light and the human image. Rashbam translates *ishon* as "eyelid," emphasizing the eye's fragility. How do these two elements of our collective self-understanding relate to each other?

Haazinu: The Power of God's Land
Elaine Rose Glickman, 1999

The Song of Moses concludes with a glorious promise: God will take vengeance on Israel's enemies, causing God's holy nation to rejoice in God's holy land. Yet a variant reading of Deut. 32:43 suggests that the Land of Israel is itself imbued with enough holiness to make expiation for those who seek it.

***P'sikta Rabbati* 16** Once R. Berekiah and R. Elazar b. Pedat were wandering along the road outside Tiberias. They noticed coffins that had arrived from outside the Land of Israel that were being brought into the Land of Israel. R. Berechiah said to R. Elazar, "How can this benefit them? In life they left the Land—but in death they return to it?" R. Elazar said to him, "When they are buried in the Land of Israel, and a sprinkling of dust from the Land of Israel is placed upon them, it shall make atonement for them, as Scripture says 'And God's land shall make atonement for God's people' [a variant reading of Deut 32:43]."

Comment Often, when we speak of the Land of Israel, we speak of its turbulent politics, its awesome beauty, its magnificent history. Do we believe that the Jewish people has made the Land holy or that it has always contained an inherent holiness? What place does the Land of Israel hold not only in our ethnic consciousness, but also in our religious consciousness?

Haazinu
Sheldon Marder, 2000

"Give ear, O heavens, let me speak; / Let the earth hear the words I utter! / May my discourse come down as the rain, / My speech distill as the dew, / Like showers on young growth, / Like droplets on the grass" (Deut. 32:1–2).

Alerting us to the power of this poem, Ibn Ezra calls the series of four metaphors in verse 2 "the prophetic style that aims at intensity." Indeed, as we read the first verse of this portion—"Give ear, O heavens, let me speak; / Let the earth hear the words I utter!" we immediately think of the intense opening of Isaiah's prophecy: "Hear, O heavens, and give ear, O earth" (Isa. 1:2). "The talmudic rabbis," writes literary critic Harold Fisch, "had already noted [*Midrash Tanchuma*, section 2] the echoing of the verbs . . . האזיני . . . שמעו [*shimu . . . haazini*, in Isa. 1:2] but in a reverse order from the Song of Moses. The reason, they said, is that Moses was nearer to heaven than Isaiah and therefore applied the more intimate האזינו [*haazinu*], 'give ear,' to the heavens, while Isaiah, who was farther away from heaven, employed the more distant *shimu*, 'hear,' when speaking of heaven and the more intimate [האזיני] *haazini* when speaking of the earth" (*Poetry with a Purpose*, Indiana University Press, 1988, p. 65). As R. Akiva puts it in the midrash, "Moses spoke with heaven as a person speaks with a friend."

Parashat Haazinu then, provides a good backdrop for reflecting on the nature of religious language. How does our perceived distance from or closeness to God affect our prayer language? How can reflection on the kind of language we use in prayer lead us to insights about our experience of the Holy One?

Haazinu: Not Secretly, but in Broad Daylight
Lawrence Bach, 2001

"God spoke to Moses in the middle of that very day [*b'etzem hayom hazeh*], saying . . ." (Deut. 32:48).

In his comment on this verse, Rashi notes that three events in Torah happened *b'etzem hayom hazeh*. They are Noah's entering the ark (Gen. 7:13), God bringing forth Israel from Egypt (Exod. 12:51), and the speech in our *parashah* in which Moses is commanded to ascend Mount Nebo and die. For Rashi, all three moments provide God with an opportunity to show power "by the light of the day." Despite the efforts of those who would oppose God's will (Noah's contemporaries, the Egyptians, and the Israelites, respectively), God wins the day in broad daylight.

What else unites these three events? In what ways are they different from each other? How does (or doesn't) God continue to act *b'etzem hayom hazeh*?

Haazinu: Shabbat Shuvah
Kenneth J. Weiss, 2002

This week, we observe the first *yahrzeit* of the terrorist acts of 9/11/2001. On that tragic day, some three thousand people lost their lives in coordinated attacks that devastated all of us. The first anniversary of 9/11 falls precisely on the fulcrum of our Days of Awe, the fifth of Tishrei.

How do we deal with 9/11, one year later? What have we learned? What do we say? On this particular Shabbat Shuvah, what might *t'shuvah* mean? A year ago, Larry Hoffman—in *The Jewish Week*—excerpted from Amos, Job, and Nehemiah, urging us to lift ourselves, to rebuild life. A year ago, Mayer Perelmuter—in *Torat Hayim* (http://urj.org/learning/torah/)—called upon us to not only hear (*haazinu*) but to "hear with understanding . . . God's presence in our lives" (*tishma*). In his *d'rash* on *Haazinu* in 1999, Scott Sperling—also in *Torat Hayim*—recalled how "Moses struggled with the end of life"; he asked if Moses's struggle "will be ours."

Our colleagues' perspectives move us—especially this year—to raise and wrestle with some profound *t'shuvah* questions: Have we begun to rebuild in the year gone by? Do we "hear God's presence" better now than we did a year ago? Facing our own mortality, have we—since 9/11—reassessed the meaning of life and its inevitable end?

In sum: What—within us—has changed in the past year?

This Shabbat, let's memorialize the victims of 9/11, then dedicate ourselves to true *t'shuvah*. May 9/11 ever touch and deepen us. *Yitgadal v'yitkadash sh'mei raba* . . .

Haazinu: Shabbat Shuvah
Kenneth J. Weiss, 2003

"התורה הזאת [*HaTorah hazot*, 'This teaching'] . . . is your very life" (Deut. 32:46–47).

Moses was a born communicator:

- He recalled and cajoled.
- He taught and scolded.
- He challenged . . . promised . . . warned.

Perhaps *Parashat Haazinu* was history's first Shabbat Shuvah sermon. Moses sealed his poem by emphasizing Judaism's oldest, deepest, and most vital directives:

Take Torah to heart!
Teach Torah to your children!

What a great pedagogue Moses was:

- First, he told 'em what he'd teach 'em.
- Then, he taught 'em.
- Then, he told 'em what he'd taught 'em.

At the beginning, middle and end, "Reb" Moshe never let his listeners, his students forget his central, basic message: Torah is your life's core. If you know it, live it. Having lived it, transmit it. Moses's final dictate and warning (implicit but obvious): if you've veered from Torah, return now!

. . . Can there be any better, more apt, message for Shabbat Shuvah than that?

Haazinu: Shabbat Shuvah
Kenneth J. Weiss, 2004

In this corner—God: "The Rock!—whose deeds are perfect" (Deut. 32:4). And in this corner—history, the flow of time: "Remember the days of old . . . the years of ages past" (Deut. 32:7).

Agelessness versus change, the eternal versus the temporal . . . how often do we contemplate all this? Once a year (at least), we "return" to them, turn away from our pursuit of money . . . position . . . *koved*.

On שבת שובה (Shabbat Shuvah) we ponder both that which changes and ages and that which is perpetual.

ראש השנה (Rosh HaShanah) celebrates change; יום כיפור (Yom Kippur) epitomizes the eternal. On שבת שובה (Shabbat Shuvah) we're to "give ear," האזינו (*haazinu*), to both, focusing on who we are, where we've been, where we're heading, what will change, and what will remain ever the same.

Our *sidrah*'s poem carries us through these awesome days: we consider both "The Rock" and "the years of ages past," present, and future!

Haazinu
Alan Cook, 2005

We have been spending the last eight months or so reading in our Torah about Moses. Now, as we reach the end of our year, we prepare to bid him farewell.

It is not mere coincidence that Moses occupies our thoughts for so much of the year. The Torah understands that those people with whom we live can determine our lives. We have a tendency to imitate them and to adopt their standards as our own.

Moses is portrayed in very human terms. We do not make a god of him; he is only mortal and is subject to the same weaknesses that plague us all. Still, he accomplished great things during his career and enjoyed a unique relationship with God that we might all aspire to emulate.

In living with Moses these eight months, we may be inspired by his life to imbue our own lives with faith and meaning. Reb Zusya taught us that we will not be asked why we were not like Moses; we **may**, however, be asked why we failed to learn from Moses's example in seeking our full potential. Indeed, at the end of his valedictory address, Moses proclaims, "This is not a trifling thing for you: it is your very life" (Deut. 32:47).

For eight months of the year, we live with one of the greats of our people. The apocryphal book of Ben Sira teaches that "whoever touches pitch will be defiled." In the same manner, the one who touches light, warmth, and beauty may come away carrying these qualities.

Inspired by a sermon outline by Rabbi Milton Steinberg ז״ל.

Haazinu
Alan Cook, 2006

ושמרתם את-חקתי ואת-משפטי, אשר יעשה אתם האדם וחי בהם (*Ush'martem et chukotai v'et mishpatai asher yaaseh otam haadam vachai bahem*), "You shall keep My laws and My rules, by the pursuit of which human beings shall live" (Lev. 18:5).

"This is not a trifling thing for you: it is your very life" (Deut. 32:47).

Moses's final address to the Israelite people is certainly a powerful one. With the heavens and the earth bearing witness to his words, the man who once demured from leadership because he was slow of speech finds it within himself to deliver a fire-and-brimstone sermon.

But the purpose of the poem delivered in האזינו (*Haazinu*) is not to show off his oratorical skills or have a "last hurrah" with a captive audience. Rather, it is to pass the mantle of leadership on to Joshua while attempting to ensure that the people, after forty years of wandering and the passing of a generation, finally have abandoned their slave mentality. Moses's words reach an audience of free people—free at last to enjoy the land promised to their ancestors and free to worship in the manner of their forebears. But these same people, once they enter the land, will also be free to spurn all the laws of the Torah and to abandon all of the precepts that Moses has attempted to instill within them during their journey through the wilderness.

For this reason, Moses must emphasize the gravity of their situation. Their very life depends on their continuing to follow God's ways. Each Israelite must now choose to take the מצוות (mitzvot) to heart, וחי בהם (*vachai bahem*, "live by them" [Lev. 18:5]).

Haazinu: Shabbat Shuvah
Amy Scheinerman, 2007

On שבת שובה (Shabbat Shuvah) we are reminded that time is running out for repentance. How can this be? The gates of repentance are always open (*Eichah Rabbah* 3:43 and others*). The opportunity to repent and atone together with the global Jewish community is running out. The theme of running out of time brings out our awareness of both our human mortality and the pressing need for repentance. Those two realities permeate this season, are inextricably bound to one another, and are reinforced by our פרשה (*parashah*).

At the end of פרשת וילך (*Parashat Vayeilech*), God informs Moses of his impending death and instructs him to pen the poem that constitutes most of פרשת האזינו (*Parashat Haazinu*). Without a word of protest, Moses complies. האזינו (*Haazinu*) captures the mood of God and of a human leader whose four decades of frustration and pent up rage are tinged with sadness due to the expectation that Israel will quickly fall into sin.

Midrash, however, provides another dimension. In *D'varim Rabbah*, *Tanchuma*, and *Yalkut*, we find Moses protesting against his death prior to seeing the Land of Israel, appealing to God and then the angels and oceans to entreat God on his behalf. Finally, when Moses surrenders to his impending death, God cries out, "Who will rise up for Me against evildoers?" (Ps. 94:16). God cannot envision the world without Moses to stand in the breach and protect Israel from God's wrath. The angels (except Samael) cannot bring themselves to collect Moses's soul, and his soul itself pleads to remain with his body. Moses, no long complacent, begs God for more time, but God does not relent and, kissing Moses, takes his soul.

---

*"As the sea is always open for everyone who wishes to cleanse himself, so are the gates of repentance always open to the sinner" (*P'sikta*, ed. Buber, xxv, 157; *Midrash D'varim Rabbah* ii; *Midrash T'hillim* 63).

Haazinu
Jeffrey Ballon, 2008

Facts, even though they are true, won't be relevant or accepted unless a prior context has been established. Galileo's astronomy is a perfect example. Whether institutions accepted the sun as the center of the solar system made no difference to the sun, only to the institutions. I was having lunch with a retired lieutenant general whose civilian activities were noteworthy. A second civic leader arrived carrying a citation plaque for the general. In jest, but based on my military career, I announced, "Attention to Orders!" The general, understanding the language frame of the military, immediately stood up. The plaque was ceremoniously presented and everyone smiled. It became effective ritual because everyone knew his part in the behavioral frame.

Parashat Haazinu demonstrates the requirement of context in teaching, as well. Moses teaches us that rabbis should create an environment in which our learning can be transferred as easily as the plaque. When Moses created his frame for his final discourse, he began with the words *Haazinu hashamayim*, "Even the heavens shall give ear." He followed in the next half verse with *v'tishma haaretz*, "and the earth shall listen" (Deut. 32:1). In the creation of this grand metaphor, Moses presents his version of "Attention to Orders!" Educators call it "the inductive moment." Moses, the sacred elder, knew his exhortation to keep the covenant would resonate only if it reinforced a grander metaphor. In his Human Relations classes at HUC-JIR, Paul Steinberg ז״ל encapsulated this teaching: "Tell 'em how much you love 'em before you tell 'em how much you know!"

Haazinu
Amy Scheinerman, 2008

Pirkei Avot 5:4 asserts, "Avraham Avinu was tested with ten trials and withstood them all. This demonstrates Avraham Avinu's great love for God." The general opinion among commentators is that *Akeidat Yitzchak* (the Binding of Isaac) is the climactic tenth trial.

However, Rabbeinu Yonah holds that Avraham's purchase of the Cave of Machpelah to bury Sarah is the final trial. He supports his contention from the Babylonian Talmud, *Bava Batra* 15b, where Satan addresses God as follows: "Sovereign of the universe, I have traversed the world and found none so faithful as Your servant Avraham. For You said to him, 'Arise, walk through the land to the length and the breadth of it, for to you I will give it,' and even so, when he was unable to find any place in which to bury Sarah until he bought one for 400 shekels of silver, he did not complain against Your ways."

We might be surprised by Rabbeinu Yonah's contention that being forced to buy a plot of land that he had already been promised is a greater test than being asked to sacrifice his son. But perhaps the message is that there are times when mundane events that smack of injustice, corruption, and indecency are the greatest test of our integrity, patience, and trust in God. In the extraordinary situation, filled with drama, our hearts pounding and adrenaline flowing, we are more likely to rise to the occasion. In the mundane breaches of the everyday, we must draw from the deepest well of our souls for the qualities that matter most.

Haazinu: Shabbat Shuvah
David Novak, 2009

Moses is not a man of words: "Please, O Eternal One, I have never been a man of words, either in times past or now that You have spoken to Your servant; I am slow of speech and slow of tongue" (Exod. 4:10). How times change! Moses is fairly shouting: "Give ear, O heavens, let me speak; / Let the earth hear the words I utter!" (Deut. 32:1).

Here (hear) as Moses is preparing to take his leave of his singular life he is fairly screaming, ensuring that his words—prophetic in tenor—reach the generation before him about to enter the Promised Land. Yet like a voice ricocheting among the mountains, Moses's voice is projected beyond the people standing before him, far beyond his natural life. They are projected to us, in this moment.

The one who could not speak has found his voice. His message is emphatic. Do not forsake Torah. Torah as it is understood from Sinai. Torah as it is understood from our rabbis. Torah as it is understood by the commentators throughout the generations. Torah that we create with our lives and our lived experiences today. To forsake Torah is to forsake our very birthright as Jews, as people who count Moses's experience as integral to our narrative.

Moses speaks and his message is clear: "For it is not a futile thing for you, for it is your life; and by this matter will you live long on the land that you are crossing the Yardein there to inherit" (Deut. 32:47).

V'zot Hab'rachah

Deuteronomy 33:1–34:12

For additional commentary on *V'zot Hab'rachach*, see "Sh'mini Atzeret / Simchat Torah."

V'zot Hab'rachah
Amy Scheinerman, 2009

Moshe's final blessing, recorded in *Parashat V'zot Hab'rachah*, addresses these words to his own tribe, the Levites: "Let Your Thummim and Urim be with Your faithful one, whom You tested at Massah, challenged at the waters of Meribah" (Deut. 33:8). Why are the Levites mentioned in the singular (*chasidecha*)? Why does Moshe mention the Urim and Thummim in reverse of the usual order? Why are the events at Massah and the waters of Meribah (Exodus 17 and Numbers 20) mentioned here, and why does Moshe say that the "faithful one" was tested, when Torah describes the people testing Moshe?

K'li Yakar (R. Sh'lomo Ephraim b. Aharon of Luntshitz, d. 1619) offers an interpretation that, in consonance with Rambam's view, presumes that the sin at the waters of Meribah was not striking the rock, but lapsing into anger. K'li Yakar connects this incident to Yaakov's curse of Shimon and Levi for their failure to control their anger: "Cursed be their anger so fierce, and their wrath so relentless. I will divide them in Jacob, scatter them in Israel" (Gen. 49:7). Yaakov refers to the entire tribe of Levi; in contrast, K'li Yakar suggests Moshe refers to himself alone because he is taking on the curse of anger and its consequent punishment solo, making himself *kaparah* for his entire tribe.

Anger is a monumental challenge for many. Will the curse of anger bring punishment in its wake (disruption and damage to relationships, pain and suffering to victims of anger)? Will anger reverse the nature of decisions that should be made in consultation with our conscience, with God? Will expression of anger have long-term ramifications for our "tribe"? Moshe here exhibits the finest traits of humanity and leadership, accepting danger and responsibility in order to protect others.

Additional Readings

Rosh HaShanah

For additional related commentary, see *"B'reishit"* and *"Vayeira."*

Rosh HaShanah
Kenneth J. Weiss, 2002

Bear Bryant, the late football coach at the University of Alabama, was once contracted to film a television commercial for Southern Bell Telephone. The coach's speaking part was to be a single line, which would come at the very end of the spot. He was to say, as though barking orders to his players, "Call your Momma!" As Rabbi Vernon Kurtz retells the story, the filming didn't go as planned. As Coach Bryant turned toward the camera, his eyes welled up with tears; what he actually said was, "Call your Momma. I sure wish I could."

Genesis is replete with stories of missed and lost opportunities, fractured families, estrangements and, yes, remorse. The *Akeidah* (Gen. 22:1–19) is just such a story, one of intergenerational disconnection: Abraham and Isaac grew more remote after that day on Mount Moriah; Sarah died and never saw her son again.

As rabbis, we can affirm that family feuds are hardly a phenomenon solely of the biblical past. A core message embedded in the Rosh HaShanah Torah portion is that our High Holy Days offer time to renew and refresh relationships with our parents and/or our children and other family members. Each year's passage sharpens the message: Reconnect with a loved one! Call your Momma—now!

In messianic times, Judaism teaches, parents and children will renew their communication and reconcile with one another, even as the human race will (re)turn to God. Let it begin—in this new year, and with us!

Rosh HaShanah
Alan Cook, 2006

Time magazine recently published an issue that contained its staff's picks for the one hundred most influential people of the year. Those selected ran the gamut from politicians such as Bill Clinton and George H. W. Bush to humanitarians like Bill and Melinda Gates to entertainers such as Oprah Winfrey. Some of those selected are already household names; others are slowly climbing the ladder towards ubiquity.

Not to be outdone, *Time* essayist Joel Stein wrote a satirical piece in response to his colleagues' selections. He noted that few (if any) of these 100 individuals had had any significant influence on his life during the past year. So, he determined that he would compose the "Joel 100" as a way of recognizing those who had impacted his life in 2005–2006.

Stein's list was meant to be humorous and is largely self-serving. He names employees and proprietors of many of the businesses he frequents, in an effort to acquire free goods and services. Nevertheless, his concept does have some merit.

In this High Holy Day season, in addition to undergoing the חשבון נפש (*cheshbon nefesh*) for which our tradition calls, it would behoove us to spend some time looking outside ourselves. Who are the people who have mattered in our lives during the past year? How have we honored them? How have we acknowledged their contributions? Let us take time to give thanks for those "heroes"—many of them unsung—who help to give meaning to our days.

Rosh HaShanah

Amy Scheinerman, 2009

In his introduction to *The Personhood of God: Biblical Theology, Human Faith and the Divine Image* (Jewish Lights Publishing, 2009), Yochanan Muffs writes, "The anthropomorphic depiction of God in the Bible has been a delight to midrashists and mystics on the one hand, and an outrage to philosophers and theologians on the other . . . neither philosophy nor myth has had its way: in fact, both have had their wings clipped. Philosophy has lost its radical doubt (God is still affirmed as a person), while myth has lost its fire (God is not much of a person)."

In contrast to pagan traditions, in which gods cannot control their own fates and are enslaved by their physical needs, the God of Israel is liberated from such concerns and focuses instead on the moral growth of humanity, God's offspring and loving partners. Hence our Torah is consumed with the ever-urgent questions of how to establish moral relationships with God and with other human beings. The accounts of Genesis 21 and 22, the traditional scriptural readings for Rosh HaShanah, bring these issues into sharp focus and, mostly particularly, the dilemma of perceiving our relationship with God as conflicting with our relationship with the people we love. Avraham's all-consuming desire to do God's will at the expense of the welfare of those he loves most (Sarah, Hagar, Yishmael, Yitzchak) points to areas for moral growth and development in all of us. When we see God as wholly other and divorced from the immediate world of our relationships with human beings, we fail to recognize the God within us and the divine spark within others. God becomes splintered and deformed, and our moral lives do as well.

Yom Kippur

For additional related commentary, see *"Acharei Mot / K'doshim"* and *"Nitzavim / Vayeilech."*

Yom Kippur: Scapegoat
Stephen E. Cohen, 1997

Leviticus 16 and *Mishnah Yoma* describe two different rituals for casting off sin.

Leviticus 16:22   The goat shall bear upon himself all the sins to an uninhabited land; and [the designated man] shall send the goat into the wilderness.

Mishnah Yoma **6:6**   What would he do? . . . He pushed [the goat] from behind [off a cliff]. It rolled over and over as it fell. Before reaching halfway down the mountain, it would be [torn into] limbs and pieces.

Comment   In the Leviticus ritual, human sins are transferred and then set loose, sent "alive" out into the limitless, all-dissolving wilderness. In the Second Temple ritual of the *Mishnah*, the sins are sent out but not allowed out of the sight of the watchers—who follow and bear witness to the complete destruction of the living sin-goat. What psychologies of sin and atonement underpin these two versions of the scapegoat ritual?

Yom Kippur
Amy Scheinerman, 2007

A brief word concerning the traditional afternoon Torah reading for Yom Kippur, Leviticus 18: As on Rosh HaShanah when the traditional Torah reading for the second day is the chapter following that reading on the first day, I might have thought that on the afternoon of Yom Kippur we read the chapter following the morning's reading from אחרי מות (*Acharei Mot*). Leviticus 17 concerns sacrifices made for expiation and atonement in the pursuit of holiness, and the prohibition against consuming blood because it is the life force of the animal. These are themes in consonance with Yom Kippur: sacrifice, atonement, expiation, life and death. Yet our Sages assigned chapter 18, a catalogue of forbidden sexual relationships.

On Yom Kippur we have an altered relationship with our bodies. On this day alone: we rehearse our death, we purposefully cause our own suffering, we engage in extended contemplation of our nonexistence in the physical world. Sexual relations, a gift from God and encouraged on holy days, are specifically proscribed on Yom Kippur, even when it falls on Shabbat. The confluence of Yom Kippur and this afternoon's Torah reading delivers a powerful message: our instinctual urges and our physical longings can and must be tamed and sanctified. Relationships—especially intimate ones—should not be about satisfying ourselves alone; they ought to be raised to a higher level by considering the other person and the effect on family and community. God cares deeply about all this. Yom Kippur helps us train ourselves to be people who recognize and act on what is right, not merely what feels good.

Yom Kippur
Amy Scheinerman, 2008

Consider two autobiographies: Sherwin Nuland (*Lost in America: A Journey with My Father*, Vintage, 2004) and Russell Baker (*Growing Up*, Signet, 1992) tell difficult stories of troubled parents and complex relationships.

Nuland excoriates his father for outbursts of anger, frequent and severe for many years. Equally clear but not fully articulated is another side that Nuland—now in his seventies—has only partially come to acknowledge: a father who suffered a debilitating, painful, and degenerative illness throughout his adulthood, yet who went to work daily, came home faithfully every afternoon, never drank, was never physically abusive, and supported his family, even taking in relatives he despised because their presence in the home benefited his children.

In contrast, although Baker's diabetic father drank himself into an early grave, leaving his wife with three preschool-age children, Baker expresses no criticism. And while Baker's mother was demanding and cold, Baker saw a woman struggling valiantly to shepherd her children through the Depression and ensure that they had the opportunity to succeed in a harsh world. Rather than criticism, Baker employs humor to digest and express his relationship with his parents.

In the final analysis, while Nuland could see only the worst, Baker chose to see the best. Nuland could have seen his father as a tragic figure: an immigrant who never quite acquires the language, and suffers pain and impairment every day of his life, yet never veers from the path of raising two sons who will have opportunities he never had. Baker could have condemned his father for a self-absorbed lifestyle that resulted in his early demise and abandonment of his family; he could have condemned his mother for not being warm and nurturing. Each of us must choose how to tell ourselves the stories of those we memorialize through *Yizkor*.

Yom Kippur
Amy Scheinerman, 2008

God sends Jonah out of *Eretz Yisrael* to Nineveh, the capital of Assyria, not far from present-day Baghdad, to preach repentance. For Jonah to walk into Nineveh and counsel *t'shuvah* is for one of us to walk into Baghdad and counsel the same. The stakes were as high, and the danger was as great. In the ancient world, Assyria was unquestionably the most brutal nation on the planet.

It should not surprise us that Jonah does not initially accept his commission with grace and enthusiasm. He responds to God's call by turning tail and running in the opposite direction. Jonah is armed only with trust in God, which appears shaky. Moreover, Jonah is not resolved to God's viewpoint. Jonah appears to prefer that the Ninevites be annihilated rather than forgiven.

Also at play is the question of the depth of the Ninevites' repentance. They go through the actions of donning sackcloth and ashes, but does their behavior truly change? Perhaps this concerns Jonah; it certainly concerned biblical commentators who defended Jonah by asserting that he perceptively recognizes that the Ninevites' repentance is skin deep and does not penetrate to the heart.

It would be easy to read this book as a treatise on forgiving one's enemies, but that was the last thing on the minds of either the author or our Rabbis, who understood that if God forgives people as evil as the Ninevites, whose repentance is measurable only in outward signs, then God will surely forgive us, especially if our repentance is genuine.

Yom Kippur
Amy Scheinerman, 2009

The Baal Shem Tov taught that there are three ways to mourn: to cry, to be silent, and to sing.

Novelist Isabel Allende was born in Peru and raised in Chile. She fled to Venezuela with her husband and children when her uncle, Chilean president Salvador Allende was assassinated in 1973. Allende writes that she lived her life "with passion and in a hurry" until her twenty-eight-year-old daughter fell into a coma for a year and died. "During that year of agony and the following year of my grieving, everything stopped for me. There was nothing to do—just cry and remember. However, that year also gave me an opportunity to reflect upon my journey and the principles that hold me together" (*This I Believe: The Personal Philosophies of Remarkable Men and Women*, ed. Jay Allison and Dan Geidman, Henry Holt & Co., 2006, p. 13).

Yizkor at each Festival, but particularly on Yom Kippur, brings us again to moments of agony. What are we to do with the feelings of regret, disappointment, loss, and pain it can evoke? We can use them as a prism for the larger task of the High Holy Days: reviewing and redirecting our very lives and being. These emotions can be purifying and refining.

Allende writes that in her grief, "I discovered that there is consistency in my beliefs, my writing and the way I lead my life" (p. 13). Perhaps not all of us will find such confirmation. Perhaps we will find a new and better direction. I suspect that in truth Allende did, too, because she also writes, "Paralyzed and silent in her bed, my daughter Paula taught me a lesson that is now my mantra: You only have what you give. It's by spending yourself that you become rich" (p. 14).

If we can arrive at the place Allende arrived at—a place of generosity of spirit and love—then we will have transformed our sorrow into song.

Sukkot

For additional related commentary, see "*Emor.*"

Sukkot: *YHVH* of Hosts
Stephen E. Cohen, 1997

The editor of the *Mateh Levi* Festival *machzor* (Shmiras Shabes Publishing, 1966) discusses the spiritual significance of the general principle that the stars should be visible through the *s'chach* of the *sukkah*.

Mateh Levi   For in this the manifest works of God are revealed, as in the words of the poet: "When I see Your heavens, the work of Your fingers, the moon and stars that You have established" (Ps. 8:4).

Comment   We often regard the darkness of night as the dropping of a curtain, concealing the work of Creation. But *Mateh Levi*'s comment and his choice of Ps. 8:4 reminds us that the more awesome revelation of the Creation occurs at night, when the blanket of daylight is removed, laying bare the heart-stopping vastness of God's universe.

Sukkot: Fighting over *Lulavim*
Stephen E. Cohen, 1998

The Mishnah offers this humorous and superbly realistic depiction of Jewish communal life in the time of the Second Temple.

Mishnah Sukkah **44**   If the first day of the Festival falls on Shabbat, they bring their *lulav*s to the Temple Mount on the day before.

The *chazanim* receive them and arrange them on a shelf. The elders placed theirs in a compartment. And they taught the people to say, "Anyone who happens to get my *lulav*, behold it is theirs as a gift." The next day they would rise early and come, and the *chazanim* would throw the *lulav*s to them. And the people would grab at them, and they would hit each other. When the court saw that they were endangering themselves, they ruled that on Shabbat each individual should perform the mitzvah of taking the *lulav* in their own home.

Comment Did the inspiring ideal described in the first part of this mishnah fall apart because the *chazanim* were lazy and disorganized, or was the vision simple too lofty for a "flesh and blood" community to sustain?

Sukkot: We Wanted for Nothing
Elaine Rose Glickman, 1999

In the Torah reading for the first day of Sukkot, God reveals the meaning of this strange and beautiful Festival: that our generations may remember that God caused us to dwell in sukkot—booths—when God brought us out of Egypt. Like many commentators, Ramban ponders the significance of this remembrance. What is the deeper meaning of the sukkot? And why does God want us to recall dwelling in them?

Ramban "So that your generations may know that I made the Israelites dwell in sukkot" (Lev. 23:43). In sukkot—that is, in clouds of the Divine Glory. This is Rashi's interpretation, and I believe it correct according to the *p'shat*. This remembrance is in order that [your generations] will know that when they were in the wilderness, they came to no homes and they found no settled cities for forty years. Yet God was with them, so they wanted for nothing.

Comment Surrounded only by clouds of God's Glory, Ramban teaches, our ancestors in the wilderness wanted for nothing. Surrounded by the fruits of our modern age—big houses, sporty cars, top-of-the-line computers—we often feel that we want more. Are we still able to feel God's presence around us? As we enjoy our plenty, how can we remain focused on what is truly essential?

Sukkot
Sheldon Marder, 2000

The *Chafeitz Chayim* (quoted in *Iturei Torah*, vol. 7, p. 96) asks why Eccles. 3:2 reads "a time for being born and a time for dying" rather than "a time for living and a time for dying"? "Because," he explains, "human beings are so preoccupied and busy, and life is so very short, that, in truth, there is no time for living."

"You shall live in booths seven days" (Lev. 23:42). The Babylonian Talmud, *Sukkah* 28b, takes תשבו (*teishvu*, "you shall live") to mean that, for seven days, the sukkah is your permanent dwelling and your house is temporary: you eat and drink, exercise and study in the sukkah; you take your most beautiful belongings into the sukkah to adorn it.

Can this reversal of the temporary and the permanent dwelling places—what amounts to a rebellion against the normal pattern of life—teach us to rebel against the busyness and preoccupation that prevent us from living?

Sukkot
Kenneth J. Weiss, 2002

Sukkot reminds us yearly of the numerous natural forces that God controls and that we cannot. These recall to us life's fragility, its uncertainty—and its preciousness.

But: this year is different! Were there still a Sanhedrin, the Sages composing it might well issue an edict: on the fifteenth of Tishrei 5763, Jews living in Israel need not build sukkot, for the State of Israel is herself a sukkah! Powerful elements surround the Jewish state and threaten—daily, hourly—to demolish her. This past year she has been attacked by homicide bombers. Her people daily face sudden death. Palpable hatred buffets her. The sukkah, representing life's risks and transience, is a symbol of everyday life in the Israel of 2002.

Nowadays, Israel's implacable foes stand in place of nature's implacable forces. Israel's citizens—like a family sitting in its own sukkah—continue to be exposed, vulnerable: not to the unpredictable forces of an autumn day, but to unrelenting violent and murderous attacks. While eight days in a sukkah are a joy, a sacred mitzvah, eight months must be unbearable.

Let's conclude with *lulav* and *etrog*. Most years, we hold these in our hands and ask God's blessings. This year, the *arbaah minim* (four species), held together, symbolize our unity with Israel's people. The Jewish state has been pummeled all year; may we, the Jewish people, stand with her (if not within her): *am echad* (one people)! May God hold us, lift us, and bless us all.

Sukkot
Kenneth J. Weiss, 2003

We also know it as זמן שמחתנו (Z'man Simchateinu, "Season of Our Thanksgiving"). It's easy to suggest why: Sukkot comes in autumn, that mellow season.

Sukkot celebrates the ingathering of food: God has again provided sustenance for the immediate future. The booths of the Festival—symbolizing life's fragility—emphasize one of Judaism's most powerful messages: celebrate now, for who knows how long we'll be here?

On Sukkot we know the gratification of building, of creating something new (if also simple). The sukkah recalls our people's desert journey; it represents the enjoyment of nature; it welcomes with *koved* and joy our loved ones—both historical and contemporaneous: זמן שמחתנו (Z'man Simchateinu) indeed!

A prior gleaning on Sukkot reflected on modern-day Israel, likening her to a sukkah. No, says Rabbi Yitz Greenberg, consider the Diaspora: "The sukkah . . . instructs Jews not to become overly rooted, particularly not in the exile. For thousands of years Jews built homes in the Diaspora. Civilizations of extraordinary richness . . . were created. But, outside of Israel, all such Jewish homes and civilizations have proven . . . to be temporary ones, blown away when a turn of the wheel brought new forces to power."

Sukkot
Alan Cook, 2006

"Just as one cannot fulfill the obligation of Sukkot unless all four species are bound together, so Israel can only be redeemed when all Israelites hold together" (*Yalkut Shimoni* 188a).

The ארבע מינים (*arbaah minim*, "four species") are a significant element of the celebration of Sukkot. They appeal to our vision, our sense of touch, our sense of smell, and—if one shakes hard enough—our sense of hearing. If we follow the commentary of *P'skita Rabbati*, which compares the four species to four types of individuals, we learn that some of the species can appeal to our sense of taste, as well.

Just as we might wish that all plant life in our world be as pleasing as the *etrog*, which has both taste and smell, so might we wish that each individual in the household of Israel would devote his or her life to the study of Torah and the performance of mitzvot. Yet we know that this is not the case, and perhaps, ultimately, that is OK.

Would an *etrog* smell as sweet if everything in the world were similarly scented? Would it taste nearly as good if all species were just as flavorful?

The world needs all kinds of fruits and vegetables, just as we need all kinds of people. We give thanks for all of God's bounty on this חג האסיף (Chag HaAsif, "Festival of Ingathering") as we praise God, the One who is בורא עצי בשמים (*borei atzei b'samim*, "Creator of the fragrant trees") and the one שחלק מחכמתו ליראיו (*shechalak meichachmato l'rei-av*, "who deals portions from the divine knowledge to all who revere God."

Sukkot
Michael Boyden, 2008

By the time Sukkot comes around after the heavy rabbinic duties of the Yamim Noraim (Days of Awe), we are all looking for a bit of light relief. Sukkot is a time for celebration. In Israel it is Chag HaAsif—the Festival of the Ingathering of the Harvest.

The Torah teaches us, "At the time of the ingathering from your threshing floor and vat, you shall hold the Feast of Sukkot for seven days. And you shall rejoice on your feast, you, your son, your daughter, your male and female slaves, the Levite, the stranger, the orphan and the widow who are in your gates. . . . You shall have nothing but joy" (Deut. 16:13–15).

The repetition of the command to rejoice emphasizes the unique character of this Festival. Sukkot gives us an opportunity to have fun with our children as we build the sukkah and welcome our family and friends to celebrate with us. This is also traditionally the time when we invite the seven *ushpizin* to be our guests.

However, we would do well to remember that the slave, the Levite, the stranger, the orphan, and the widow also have a place at our table. These are the weakest members of society, who are unable to support themselves and are dependent upon our goodwill for their very survival.

Maimonides warns us, "When you eat and drink, you should feed the stranger, the orphan, and the widow together with all of the other wretched poor. However, whoever locks his door . . . and eats and drinks with his children and wife and does not give food and drink to the poor and the bitter of heart is not celebrating a mitzvah but simply gratifying his stomach" (*Mishneh Torah, Hilchot Yom Tov* 6).

Such an admonition is particularly apposite at Sukkot, because the sukkah is not only a temporary shelter erected by farmers, but primarily a reminder of the refugee huts built by the Children of Israel when they fled Egypt.

Sukkot, then, is the Festival of the refugee and the homeless, "for you were strangers in the land of Egypt."

Sukkot
Amy Scheinerman, 2009

Once the *Shalosh R'galim* (Three Pilgrimage Festivals) were integrally tied to the environment. Perhaps when we were separated from our Land, that connection was supplanted with a historical overlay that could be transported and transplanted to the countries of exile. It is time to reclaim the environmental connection, especially considering the crises looming: global climate change, air and water pollution, defoliation of the world's forests, and the disappearance of wetlands.

Following World War II, the American government sought to fuel a revitalization of the American economy. "The Story of Stuff" (http://storyofstuff.com/) quotes a post–World War II retail analyst named Victor LeBeau as saying, "Our enormously productive economy demands that we make consumption our way of life, that we convert the buying and use of goods into rituals, that we seek our spiritual satisfaction, our ego satisfaction, in consumption. We need things consumed, burned up, replaced and discarded at an ever accelerating rate." Whether or not this quote is historically accurate (I have been unable to confirm it), it has most certainly come frighteningly to fruition.

Sukkot can be the quintessential Jewish model of respect for the environment, sustainability, and recycling. Once sukkot were constructed of recycled materials and afforded us the opportunity to live much more closely in connection with the world, outside our hermetically sealed, energy-guzzling homes. These days, we are more likely to buy high-tech kits and decorate them with plastic decorations made with fossil fuels. The food our ancestors ate in their sukkot was the quail and manna of the wilderness—sufficient, but not excessive—while ours comes from the vast global agricultural industry.

Sukkot affords an opportunity to teach and live values that counteract our society's worship of consumption and waste.

Chol HaMo-eid Sukkot

For additional related commentary, see *"Ki Tisa"* and *"Eikev."*

Chol HaMo-eid Sukkot: Fortified by Blessings in Our Frail Booth
Kenneth J. Weiss, 2001

"You shall observe . . . the Feast of Ingathering at the turn of the year" (Exod. 34:22).

In our portion, Sukkot is referred to as Chag HaAsif, a name also found in Exod. 23:16. JPS translates Chag HaAsif as "the Feast of Ingathering," while Richard Elliott Friedman renders it "the Festival of Gathering."

When thought of as Sukkot, this Pilgrimage Festival effectively reminds us of life's fragility and delicacy and of nature's unpredictable yet determinative role in our everyday lives. Our lives are like Sukkot—frail, insubstantial, temporary. So are the lives of our loved ones. So is our health; so are our possessions.

This year, let us refer to the Festival beginning on the fifteenth of Tishrei as Chag HaAsif, during which we may focus—instead—on all that fortifies and stabilizes us. As Chag HaAsif, this Festival—grounded in an agricultural past—reminds us to be grateful for what we've gathered and continue to gather, beginning with the food that gives us and others sustenance. But, we've gathered ever so much more that we must acknowledge with gratitude on this Festival of Gathering:

- The many blessings with which God has blessed us—family and friends, health and prosperity, learning, love and fulfillment, joys beyond measure—in which we do rejoice through *Hallel*
- Nature's beauty and bounty, for which we thank God through the symbol of the Four Species
- Guests (*ushpizin*) from our rich past, whose yearly welcome suggests their eternal message and impact

All of this (and more) we affirm with gratitude on our Festival of Gathering. Taken together, they represent every Jew's immeasurable wealth. In our frail, fragile, tenuous sukkah, let us thank and praise God for all that we've been blessed to gather. Mindful, then, of all we've received, we need not feel all that frail after all.

Tenuousness and grandeur . . .

Fragility and strength . . .

Frail booth and blessings that fortify . . . together these do fuller justice to our annual celebration.

Chol HaMo-eid Sukkot
Kenneth J. Weiss, 2004

We're commanded to build a sukkah, symbolizing gratitude to God for food and life, for home and loved ones. After decorating our sukkah, we take up myrtle, willow, and palm and—with the *etrog*—shake them enthusiastically. We listen to the sounds they make and smell their lovely, subtle fragrance.

Reading Ecclesiastes reaffirms the lesson that everything we have and are is transitory . . . passing . . . delicate . . . infinitely sweet and precious.

The presence of *ushpizin*, symbolic guests—the great men and women from Judaism's history and from our own family's past—enhance our Sukkot observance.

A thought for Sukkot 5765: though we build the sukkah, it's the *ushpizin* who receive us there. We reconnect—briefly, annually—with those who influenced us or touched our lives while they lived. They come to reaffirm for us that—even across millennia—people "are all connected . . . that all lives intersect" (Albom). The sukkah thus evokes the undying bond between life's endless generations. Our sukkah shares in the divine; it bespeaks "heaven on earth."

Inspired by Mitch Albom's *The Five People You Meet in Heaven* (Hyperion, 2006).

Chol HaMo-eid Sukkot
Alan Cook, 2005

"So Moses declared to the Israelites the set times of *Adonai*" (Lev. 23:44).

The Three Pilgrimage Festivals are described in our tradition as מועדים (*mo-adim*), which is variously translated as "festivals," "set times," "seasons," or "sacred occasions." The Festival קידוש (*Kiddush*) thanks God for blessing our people with "seasons of joy; holidays and set times of gladness."

How do we celebrate such "set times"? Judaism is a very experiential, hands-on religion. We commemorate our Festivals by attempting to re-create our ancestors' experiences when they first observed these holidays. On Shavuot, we engage in study to recall the giving of the Torah; on Pesach, we hold סדרים (*s'darim*) that are meant to be imitative of the meal eaten prior to the Exodus. And on Sukkot, we dwell in booths that are reminiscent of those the Israelites lived in during their sojourn in the desert.

In short, during these Festivals we are testifying, before God and before all who may observe us in our rituals, that we have not forgotten our past. It takes only a minor shift in vowels to read *mo-adim* (seasons/times) as *me'idim* (from witnesses). We bear witness before God that our illustrious history is cause for celebration. We are מועדים לשמחה (*mo-adim l'simchah*), witnesses to the joy that can arise out of commemorating these "set times."

"'You are my witnesses—says *Adonai*—and I am God.' (Isa. 43:12). When you are my witnesses, I am God. But when you are not my witnesses, I, כביכול, [*kivyachol*, 'as it were'] am not God" (*P'sikta D'Rav*

Kahana 12:6). If we fail to bear witness to, and celebrate, the traditions of our Festivals, we do a disservice not only to ourselves and our heritage, but also to God.

Chol HaMo-eid Sukkot
Amy Scheinerman, 2007

On the Shabbat during Sukkot, as on the Shabbat during Pesach, we read Exod. 33:12–34:26 from כי תשא (*Ki Tisa*), a portion that recounts the second set of tablets Moses carved on Mount Sinai. The passage records God's thirteen attributes, although ironically these verses are omitted from the Torah service liturgy when on Shabbat. Coming shortly after Yom Kippur, during which we recited a modified version of Exod. 34:6–7 numerous times, it forms a beautiful bridge back to the High Holy Days.

Three question arise: (1) Why does this passage present God's compassion and kindness before mentioning God's judgment, given that Exod. 20:5–6 (the first set of tablets) presents God's judgment prior to God's compassion and kindness? (2) Why are the first three attributes names of God (אל יהיה, יהיה, *Adonai, Adonai, El*)? (3) Why is Torah here so strangely and dangerously anthropomorphic, describing God's descent in a cloud and telling us that God stands beside Moses and proclaims the attributes aloud?

Perhaps the answers to all three are intertwined: Lest the High Holy Days inspire in us the tendency to be judgmental and harsh, Torah teaches us that God's mercy and magnanimity are paramount and a model for how we should live our lives. The reiteration of יי (*Adonai*) bespeaks God's proclivity to forgive before we commit sin, and afterward, as well. God is described in graphic human terms because we, created on the divine model, aspire to live up to God's standards.

Chol HaMo-eid Sukkot
Amy Scheinerman, 2008

On Chol HaMo-eid Sukkot we read Exod. 33:12–34:26, which begins with an enigmatic passage. Moses and God engage in an intimate dialogue in which Moses requests to know God's essence and God responds, "I will make all My goodness pass before you, and I will proclaim before you the name Lord, and the grace that I grant and the compassion that I show" (Exod. 33:19). Moses then stands beside a cleft in the rock and God's Presence passes by. Moses glimpses God's "back" but cannot see God's "face."

The desire to see God, to experience God's presence, to know God's essence is the core of many religious experiences and related to the mitzvah of living in the sukkah.

Our Rabbis taught that a sukkah may not exceed twenty cubits in height because "the shade doesn't reach the ground" (*Mishnah Sukkot* 1:2–3). The mitzvah of sitting in the sukkah is produced not by the walls, but by sitting in the shade of the *s'chach*. In midrash *Sifra Emor* 17:11, R. Akiva explains this: "The sukkot were the clouds of Glory." For R. Akiva, who had Exod. 12:5 and 13:20–21 in mind, Sukkot was not a place, but rather the special providential clouds provided by God to guide the Israelites through the wilderness. The *s'chach* of our sukkot symbolizes the cloud of Glory that covered the Tabernacle throughout the wilderness wanderings, protecting and guiding our people. When we sit in the sukkah, the *s'chach* that shades us from the sun symbolizes God's protective power in our lives.

Sh'mini Atzeret / Simchat Torah

For additional related commentary, see *"Vayeira"* and *"Emor."*

Sh'mini Atzeret / Simchat Torah
Mordecai Finley, 1999

Perhaps you, too, remember the day when you learned that Shavuot is also called Atzeret and your first attempts at a homiletical-calendrical *binyan av m'shnei k'tuvim* (inference from two biblical verses). What must "Atzeret" really mean beyond "holiday of cessation"? Is there a Shavuot meaning redolent in the Atzeret ending Sukkot, and vice versa? In other words, do we call Shavuot "Atzeret" in order to teach us something about Sh'mini Atzeret, and does this in turn teach us something about Shavuot?

Here was my answer as a second-year rabbinical student: The *matan Torah* (giving of the Torah) at Shavuot-Atzeret precipitated our breakdown and God's bereavement. The *Sh'nei Luchot HaB'rit* (two tablets of the Covenant) crumbled in hurt and shame when they saw the haughty smirk on the face of the Molten Calf. The first *matan Torah* was like receiving a precious gift that we didn't understand and didn't know where to put. It told us something but made us uneasy, like premature advice. The Molten Calf was familiar.

Those months of *t'shuvah* until Moshe brought back the second tablets on Yom Kippur did their work, though. And the holiday of Sukkot was there to show us how to build the inner chamber where Torah could be kept and nourished. Sh'mini Atzeret was the day we move, cautiously, wordlessly, out of the sukkah and into a life of Torah—and the next day we celebrate it, sans Molten Calf. (That, by the way, is the secret meaning of Simchat Torah: all the joy, none of the *maseichah,* the "molten statue.")

But it wasn't until I learned some Aramaic and began to study *Zohar* that I saw deeper into Sh'mini Atzeret and the idea of revelation. *Atzra* (עצרא) in Aramaic is a press, like a wine press. The Aramaic word for "fruit" is *iba* (איבא), also seen as *inba* (אנבא), revealing clearly its root נבי \ נבא, which means in Aramaic "burst forth" and "to prophesy." Discovering this gave me a wonderful image of prophecy—the fruit swelling on the tree (of life), ripening in the heart of the human soul. The revelation at Shavuot, then, was God giving the fruit that we did not know yet how to assimilate for our consumption. We do the summer work of *Bein HaMeitzarim,* the Seven Weeks of Consolation, the *S'lichot* of Elul, the *t'shuvah* of Yamim Noraim (Days of Awe), and then the joy of Sukkot—by the time we get to Sh'mini Atzeret, we have pressed the fruit of prophecy into a wine we can drink. We drink the wine with joy on Simchat Torah.

Sh'mini Atzeret / Simchat Torah: Yizkor
Sheldon Marder, 2000

Another verse in Ecclesiastes—"A time for mourning and a time for dancing" (3:4)—links Sh'mini Atzeret, Sukkot, and Simchat Torah. The "time for mourning" is the eighth day of Sukkot (when *Yizkor* is said), and the "time for dancing" is, of course, Simchat Torah. Is it problematic that the Reform Movement creates a day of "mixed emotions," as it were—a hyphenated day of "mourning and dancing"—by joining Sh'mini Atzeret and Simchat Torah?

Pardes Yosef (quoted in *Iturei Torah,* vol. 7, p. 97) offers an interesting perspective on this blending of joy and sorrow, based on a grammatical inconsistency in Ecclesiastes 3. Why are all of the parallel verb structures in the infinitive, but one pair "ספוד רקוד"—(*s'fod-r'kod,* "mourning-dancing")—is different (lacking the letter למד [*lamed*])? Pardes Yosef answers that all of the other linked activities cannot be done simultaneously: at the time of being born, we are not dying; at the time of planting, we are not uprooting. However, it is possible for mourning and dancing to coexist. When a righteous person dies, says *Midrash Eichah*, God is filled with grief for the sake of humanity's loss, yet God rejoices when the soul of a righteous person enters eternity.

As the midrash teaches us to broaden our perspective—to see, as it were, through God's eyes as well as our own—can the juxtaposition of *Yizkor* and Simchat Torah lead to a similar broadening of perspective? Is there something to be gained from "mourning and dancing" on the same day?

"So Moses the servant of the LORD died there" (Deut. 34:5).

Of all the possible characterizations of Moses, why is he called "servant of God" at the very moment of his death? Ibn Ezra explains, "Even at his death he did what he was commanded to do, like a servant." However, we know from Deut. 3:25 (and elsewhere) that Moses, in fact, protested God's decree. In one midrash Moses argues, "Why should I die? Is it not better that people say, 'Here is Moses, the one who took us out of Egypt and split the sea for us,' rather than their saying, 'Moses was such and such'" (*Sifrei* to Deut. 3:39). And, according to another, Moses, hardly resigned and docile, "departed from [the Israelites] with great weeping" (*Petirat Moshe*—Jelinek, *Beit HaMidrash,* 1938, 1:126–27). Do Ibn Ezra's comment and the opposing evidence of Moses's refusal to "go gentle into that good night" have implications for end-of-life decision making in our own day?

Sh'mini Atzeret / Simchat Torah
Kenneth J. Weiss, 2002

El Paso is blessed in many ways. At least one of our blessings has a name. Hal Marcus is a marvelous, inspiring—and truly inspired—local artist, a Jew of Syrian decent. Three of his major pieces grace our synagogue—his synagogue. His magnum opus is called "Torah in Glass": four windows that measure some 160 square feet. It tells the story of the Five Books of Moses—from Creation on—in brilliantly colored stained glass.

Hal's work is actually a Simchat Torah midrash, as Rabbi Larry Bach writes, "The Written Torah ends with Moses, ascending Mount

Nebo and dying—according to a midrash—by a 'divine kiss.' In his 'midrash in glass,' Marcus has chosen not to portray Moses' death, but rather to allude to the way in which Moses lives through the lessons that he taught us. And so it is that the bottom of the fourth panel pictures a bar mitzvah reading from Torah. With his immediate family surrounding him he takes his place alongside the generations who have read and transmitted *torat mosheh*—The Torah of Moses. The timeless story still lives.

"Jews never finish reading Torah. . . . Marcus's windows don't really end either. As we arrive at the bottom of the fourth panel, our eyes are drawn along a ribbon of text that sits over a rainbow. The Hebrew is translated: 'So now write down this song and teach it to the children of Israel' (Deut. 31:19). The verse takes us back to the story of the Creation. Light bursts forth and we begin again."

Let us begin again.

Sh'mini Atzeret / Simchat Torah
Kenneth J. Weiss, 2003

Think of the seven (or eight) days of Sukkot as metaphor for a human life span: each day represents a decade.

In the beginning, everything is fresh and new, vibrant, alive in so many ways. The sukkah is beautiful—full of color . . . spirit . . . energy. The *lulav* and *etrog* are bright, newly harvested. The first meals taste better because of the "spice" of the outdoors, the spiritual ambiance. The weather (usually—not always!) is energizing, bracing: cool and comfortable, the first breath of autumn—the golden season.

The middle days represent our middle years: we're comfortable in our sukkot, at ease with Festival routines: prayers, meals, relaxation in our leafy, familiar venue. We've grown accustomed to spending time in spiritual activity, sharing hours with family and friends. Our daily pace seems somehow enhanced by the evenings we spend in our sukkot. We are rapt in our festive routine: Sukkot has become our "world view." Thoughts of the pre- (and post-)Sukkot world do not distract us.

Our (Festival's) last days are illustrated in Sukkot's faded symbols: the *etrog* is soft now and spongy, numerous hands having caressed it. The palm—backbone of the *lulav*—shows signs of folding in on itself from days of shaking and waving. The myrtle's small leaves—green still—are drier now and more brittle; the willow has become fetid. The sukkah appears withered; its dried-out fronds crackle with every passing breeze. Much of its fruit, now fallen to the ground, is decaying. The paper chains, the *ushpizin* pictures—even the chairs and tables (neither clean nor kempt as at the beginning): all show signs of age, the weight (if you will) of time's passage.

Sukkot is an annual celebration with a perennial relevance:

- Its days connote our years, our decades.
- Its spirit represents our spirit: that part of us that need **not** age though we age: a spark, a message, a suggestion of what can live on—be renewed—year after year.

Sh'mini Atzeret / Simchat Torah
Alan Cook, 2006

The late Jacob Cohen, more popularly known by his stage name, Rodney Dangerfield, built a career out of his frequent lament that he received "no respect."

Were we to anthropomorphize the *sidrot* of the Torah, we might hear a similar lament from פרשת וזאת הברכה (*Parashat V'zot Hab'rachah*). After all, of the fifty-four *sidrot* in the Torah, it does not merit its own Shabbat. In most Reform congregations, this selection is heard only amidst the hubbub of Simchat Torah celebrations.

The forty-one short verses of this *sidrah* are surely deserving of more respect than that; they delineate the passing and burial of our people's greatest leader. But the midrash suggests that it is perhaps because of Moses's stature that focus has been shifted away from this reading.

"No one knows his burial place to this day" (Deut. 34:6). This reminds us that although Moses was a wonderful figure, in the end he was merely a conduit for God, carrying out God's will. He is not deified or worshiped. He is, ultimately, merely a mortal.

That is not to say that Moses should get "no respect." He is deserving of great respect—but so are all humans, created in the divine image.

As we complete the annual cycle of reading and return once again to בראשית (*B'reishit*), we are reminded that the final letter of the Torah is ל (*lamed*) and the first letter is ב (*bet*). Torah cannot exist without לב (*lev*, "heart"). Let the message of Moses's seeming lack of respect teach us to open our hearts to all creatures big and small.

חזק, חזק ונתחזק (*Chazak, chazak v'nitchazeik*, "Be strong, be strong, let us find strength in each other").

Sh'mini Atzeret / Simchat Torah
Janice Garfunkel, 2008

Simchat Torah is, of course, a celebration of Torah and of *talmud Torah*. Learning is highly valued in Judaism, and we express this often. I have noticed, however, that *amcha* has transferred the Jewish love of learning from Torah to secular studies, and more specifically to studies that enhance career opportunities, sometimes with a focus on income-earning potential, other times with a focus on being prepared for a constantly changing world.

There is a tad of irony in the fact that the current expression of our love of learning has become in some ways a focus on income and class. I have often heard people (both Jews and non-Jews) warn children that if they don't study, they'd better be prepared to say, "Do you want fries with that?"—the message being, "Study now, or be humiliated by a low-income job in the future." What a contrast to the Talmudic stories of people who chose poverty, even extreme poverty, so that they could pursue *talmud Torah lishmah* (study for its own sake). One didn't study to become rich; rather, the purpose of wealth was to enable one to study.

Some liberal arts colleges similarly exalt learning for its own sake. My alma mater had a somewhat negative view of what they called "vocational education," focused only on acquiring marketable skills such as law or medicine, versus embracing education for the love of knowledge, for the purpose of becoming an educated, well-rounded, thoughtful, and thinking person.

One of our challenges as rabbis is to remind our people, as the Yiddish saying has it, that "Torah is the best *s'chorah*—merchandise."

Sh'mini Atzeret / Simchat Torah
Amy Scheinerman, 2009

Simchat Torah comes at a peculiar time. Why do we begin the cycle of Torah reading at the end of Sukkot? Why does it not coincide with Rosh HaShanah or Pesach, two starting points that we can experience spiritually, emotionally, and even viscerally? And why hold this joyous, boisterous celebration at the end of a long and intense season that begins with preparation for *t'shuvah* in Elul and continues through Rosh HaShanah, the *Aseret Y'mei T'shuvah* (Ten Days of Repentance), Yom Kippur, and a week of Sukkot? Isn't this a recipe for Simchat Torah to be anticlimactic? Yet it never is.

It is as if Simchat Torah comes when it does because God, who has enjoyed our close company for several weeks, has arranged one last celebration before the intensity of the season ends, the spiritual glow fades, and everyone returns to their warm, insulated homes and conventional routines. It is as if God anticipates missing our elevated attention, enhanced spiritual attunement, not to mention the joyous sounds and happy buzz of our gatherings (chanting of prayers, delivery of *d'rashot*, exchange of greetings, and excited social reconnection).

God, who rejoices in relationship with us, rejoices also in our relationships with one another, our communities and our communal celebrations. So God provides one last hurrah for us to celebrate. This one focuses on Torah, the divine gift that has made and kept us a community through the ages and in every place we wandered; Torah, which has kept us bound in loving relationship to God and one another.

Chanukah

For additional related commentary, see *"Vayeishev"* and *"Mikeitz."*

Chanukah
Stephen E. Cohen, 1999

Psalm 30 begins with the enigmatic words "a song for *chanukat habayit* [dedication of the house]," provoking the questions "Which house?" and "Which dedication?" S'fat Emet uncovers in the second verse of the psalm a profound link with the Festival of Chanukah, in the word *dilitani*.

S'fat Emet "I will exalt You, YHVH, for You have *dilitani* [usually translated 'lifted me up']" (Ps. 30:2). Radak wrote that *dilitani* connotes both lowering and raising up. And the idea here is that every descent of the Children of Israel is for the purpose of ascent. And every exile is in order to raise up the holy sparks that were scattered in those places. And this is really like a *d'li*/bucket that descends into the depths of the well and lifts up the water. Thus did the Holy One lower the souls of the Children of Israel that they might bring up the water from the deep wells. And so when we emerge from the foreign powers, and the holy sparks are lifted up from there, there is renewal [*hitchad'shut*] and great rejoicing. And in fact, this raising up of the sparks occurs every day. And so we recite *mizmor shir chanukat habayit* [a song for dedication of the house] every day.

Comment   The implication is that we praise God for bringing us down and for raising us up. If we could choose, though, would we not rather simply be allowed to lead a more "level" existence?

Chanukah
Kenneth J. Weiss, 2002

In big trouble, imprisoned in a strange land, Joseph never gave up, never lost faith. God was—and would ever remain—at his core. Joseph's spiritual flame never dimmed or weakened during his decades in Egypt.

When a foreign power occupied Jerusalem, Judah never gave up, never lost faith. He rallied the Maccabees and saw to the rededication of the Temple to God. Judah's spiritual flame never dimmed or weakened as he faced the Syrian-Greeks.

This year, let Chanukah's first candle honor both Joseph and Judah Maccabee. In their different eras, they tended Judaism's singular flame, thus transmitting our faith and peoplehood to new generations.

Chanukah
Kenneth J. Weiss, 2002

"Pharaoh dreamed . . ." (Gen. 41:1); "Jacob saw . . ." (Gen. 42:1).

Picture Wrigley Field in Chicago: classic in its simple beauty! The view—from almost any seat—is perfect! Now, imagine that the place is sold out and you find that your seat is just behind one of the support pillars that are characteristic of older sports facilities. Bummer!

Pharaoh's dreams represent just such an obstructed view: he could envision the pillar but couldn't imagine what was beyond it, around it. "In my . . . dream, I saw seven ears of grain . . ." (Gen. 41:22).

Pharaoh beheld an apparition—a mere specter, a glimmer, a clue. Jacob (*l'havdil*) perceived reality: "Jacob saw that there was grain in Egypt" (Gen. 42:1—R. E. Friedman). Might not Pharaoh and Jacob have envisioned the same grain (*shibalim/shever*) in two diametrically different ways? For the former the meaning of the grain was a mystery, for the latter it was the key to saving lives in a time of famine (a mystery solved!). Whereas Jacob saw "grain" (*shever* as collective noun), Pharaoh dreamt of only "seven ears of grain"; even his subconscious imagination was limited.

On this final day of Chanukah, let our Feast of Lights celebrate Jacob's enlightened perception. O mighty Pharaoh: talk to Joseph; he'll find you a seat with a better view.

Chanukah
Kenneth J. Weiss, 2003

"Now Jacob was settled" (Gen. 37:1).

Only when we feel "at home" in a place are we comfortable celebrating our Judaism publicly. Each Kislev, as an example, the Jews of Israel engage in the "old custom [of placing] the *Chanukiah* where its lights will be visible from the outside . . . [as] a demonstration of . . . pride and identity" (*Gates of the Seasons*, ed. Peter Knobel, CCAR Press, 1983, p. 3).

L'heifech: A number of Latin Americans of converso backgrounds have shared with me childhood memories of Chanukah celebrations in basements or behind closed doors. Our "Festival of Lights" has often been celebrated in dark, secret places when our people felt less than "at home."

Jacob, we are told, refused to live in that way. Upon moving into Canaan, he made it his home. Today, in modern Israel, Jacob's descendants (in their millions) proudly display their *chanukiyot*: they are "at home," settled in their land.

Chanukah
Kenneth J. Weiss, 2003

Yet another thematic interconnection linking *Parashat Mikeitz* and our Festival of Lights: in this week's *parashah*, seven years of abundance are followed by seven years of famine (Gen. 41:53–54); in the Chanukah story, a single cruse of consecrated oil fuels the eternal light for eight days.

Torah's lesson: "Plenty" is not a permanent fact of life. Everything has limits (even that miraculous cruse of oil).

Fortunes do turn—on a dime! Together, *Parashat Mikeitz* and Chanukah teach us to conserve resources wisely, to use them judiciously, to prepare for the inevitable rainy day.

Chanukah
Amy Scheinerman, 2006

Pharaoh's dreams of cows and corn in מקץ (*Mikeitz*) come on the tail of Yosef's dreams about sheaves of wheat and celestial luminaries in וישב (*Vayeishev*). While the interpretation of Yosef's dreams is transparent to the reader, and the meaning of Pharaoh's dreams is transparent to Yosef, what does this say about our dreams?

Eric Fromm, in *The Forgotten Language: An Introduction to the Understanding of Dreams, Fairy Tales, and Myths* (Henry Holt & Co., 1976, p. 101), wrote, "We are not only less reasonable and less decent in our dreams, but we are also wiser asleep than when we are awake." Our Sages would concur. In the Talmudic "Dreambook" in *B'rachot* 55a–57b, we find a virtual manual for dream interpretation whose guiding principle is, "All dreams follow the mouth." This means that any interpretation accepted by the dreamer is, in fact, the meaning of the dream. A concession to reality? Perhaps. The Rabbis proceed accordingly and delineate a remarkable list of dream elements, many of which include violence and immorality, and find positive meanings for almost every one. Perhaps it is the power of positive thinking, perhaps it is a religious mode for directing behavior.

In the case of Pharaoh, Yosef's interpretation leads him to appoint Yosef steward of Egypt, resulting in the saving of many lives during the ensuing famine, not to mention the saving of Yosef's family when his brothers come to Egypt in search of food. Chanukah teaches a tale of the power of ideas, words, and swords. Our פרשה (*parashah*) emphasizes the power of ideas to influence behavior.

Chanukah
Janice Garfunkel, 2008

As a child, I always felt a little uneasy and slightly embarrassed about Chanukah gelt. Anti-Semites always emphasized Jews and money, and here, a symbol of Chanukah was . . . coins! Chanukah gelt fed into all those anti-Semitic stereotypes about the Jewish love of gold, the Jewish miser gloating over his stack of coins.

So I was greatly relieved when finally, as an adult, I found a probable origin for the giving of gelt to children on Chanukah. One of the first things that the Maccabees did after regaining sovereignty was to mint coins. The coins minted by Antiochus were imprinted with images of idols. Imagine how difficult it was for Jews to handle these idolatrous images each time they made a purchase, and what a source of pride it was after the defeat of the Assyrians to show off Hasmonean coins (whose ancient designs serve as a model for modern Israel's *agurot*).

So, surprisingly, Chanukah gelt is not a symbol of money, materialism, purchasing power, or what we can acquire, but of self-rule and throwing off the yoke of religious persecution and foreign imperialism. Our children, too, can learn about the joys of a more personal sort of self-rule, the kind that means we proudly stick to our own values and culture and are not ruled by the persuasive song of the marketplace, the commercials, and the powerful tug of the crowd.

Chanukah
David Novak, 2009

Chanukah is not just eight days—it is every day. The word *chanukah* is part of the superscription to Psalm 30, "A psalm of David, a song for the dedication of the Temple."

Psalm 30 is part of daily worship throughout the year. In beginning our prayers each day we rededicate ourselves and our sanctuaries to our relationship with God. In it we ask that God continue to be present for us, to be, in a word, "dedicated" to hearing our voice, listening to our plea, feeling present.

This is not any different from the feeling of those on the ground during the reconsecration of the Temple at the time of the Hasmoneans. In feeling oppressed by outside forces, the people wanted to know that God did, in fact, hear them and respond to them. Whether it was God making the miracle or the people's dedication to God and the Jewish people that brought about the miracle of Chanukah, we are reminded in their voices and in their actions that we, too, struggle to make our voices heard by God and, in turn, experience God's response.

There is another aspect of Chanukah that is particularly appealing to moderns: the expansion of light at a time (in the Northern Hemisphere) when natural light is most limited. For eight consecutive nights, we light our *chanukiyah*, expanding the brightness cast.

In this light we see ourselves, we remind ourselves of the dedication of our ancestors, and we revel that, like those who came before us, we are here to celebrate miracles both ancient and modern.

Tu BiSh'vat

Tu BiSh'vat
Kenneth J. Weiss, 2002

"Greatly frightened, the Israelites cried out" (Exod. 14:10b).

Tu BiSh'vat is Judaism's faithful rebuttal to our ancestors' faithless behavior as reflected in *Parashat B'shalach*.

In these chapters, the Israelites demonstrate how short their memory is, how shallow their faith. Despite God's promise to bring them to Canaan, despite their recent deliverance from slavery, Pharaoh's last-minute pursuit traumatizes them. Later, the people—finding no fresh water at Marah (or at Rephidim) and no food in the wilderness—"grumbled" (Exod. 15:24 and 16:2) and "quarreled" (Exod. 17:2). These former slaves showed themselves to be both oblivious and faithless.

Tu BiSh'vat stands as a counterbalance to our ancestors' unfortunate (habitual?) loss of confidence in God's promise, God's presence. Tu BiSh'vat speaks to us: when the nights are long and the days brief; in the most frightening times of your life; when you feel like giving up—**don't**! When spring seems most distant, reaffirm spring's warmth and beauty: the gardens you love, the trees and their perennial gifts.

Tu BiSh'vat exhorts us: even at the edge of the darkest darkness, shed light. When enemies pursue you, when thirst or hunger or fear threatens you, keep your faith. When death seems closest, reaffirm life. In sum: when the ground is frozen, the sky still leaden, don't cry out or grumble or quarrel: instead, plant a tree. Is there any symbolic act more distinctively Jewish than that?

Tu BiSh'vat
Kenneth J. Weiss, 2004

"Who is like You, *YHVH* . . . ?" (Exod. 15:11).

The "Song at the Sea" commemorates our people's deliverance from the bitterness of Egyptian enslavement. *Mi Chamochah* is Moses's soaring salute to that deliverance: **only** *YHVH* could have freed us, then driven the pursuing enemy into the sea.

Since Tu BiSh'vat nearly always occurs when *Parashat B'shalach* is read, I deduce a broader message within *Mi Chamochah*. *YHVH*: You who delivered us from Egyptian bondage eons ago, continue (even now) to be our Deliverer from life's many deprivations.

Mi Chamochah—"Who **is** like you, O God," whose miracles—far from ending with deliverance—continue to our own day? You freed our ancestors, then supported them in the wilderness (*dayeinu!*). You renew nature continually. In history's darkest epochs, in each year's darkest, coldest months, You enjoin upon us the renewal of life, commanding us (on 15 *Sh'vat*) to plant trees in anticipation of spring.

Achad Ha'am writes that Moses sang this song, blithely ignorant that his challenge as Israel's leader was just beginning. I disagree: Moses, sensing the overwhelming difficulties of life in the wilderness, celebrates a God who will **always** be there—a God whose support is steadfast.

No god is like God, who liberates His people, then sees to the continuing well-being of the natural world. That's why we still sing Moses's ever-new song: "*YHVH* will reign [over the entire world] forever and ever."

This year, let's chant as we plant: *Mi Chamochah* should be the anthem of Tu BiSh'vat!

Tu BiSh'vat
Janice Garfunkel, 2009

There is a custom that we eat fifteen different kinds of fruit on Tu BiSh'vat. Living in Ohio, I never, ever see a fresh date, and fresh figs are rare. It is always a challenge to find carob pods. I love to include the fruits of Israel, as well as some exotic fruits from other lands.

"In the world-to-come, we will be held accountable for every (permissible) good thing our eyes saw, but which we did not eat" (Jerusalem Talmud, *Kiddushin* 4:12). Judaism is certainly not a hedonistic religion, but neither is it ascetic.

It is said that Samson Raphael Hirsch, in his later years, insisted on traveling to Switzerland. Why? In the world-to-come, the Holy One will ask us questions. Hirsch wanted to have an answer should God ask, "Did you see my Alps?"

The world that God has made is so full of blessings, of tastes, of life-changing experiences to be sought out and embraced. Many of us get used to living in our comfort zone. We eat the same breakfast every day. As we get older, we settle into our habits. We know what we like and what we don't.

It is always good to be reminded to stretch a little, to try new things: to marvel at the diversity of God's universe, new fruits to taste, new places to see, different kinds of people to get to know, new ways of building a better world. May you find much pleasure, and something new, in your Tu BiSh'vat celebration this year!

Tu BiSh'vat
Amy Scheinerman, 2009

Thanks to the kabbalists, the delightful celebration of Tu BiSh'vat is a staple in Jewish communities around the world.

For many, it has become a celebration of our connection to the earth, a reminder of our responsibility to a sustainable environment. This is all to the good. For others, Tu BiSh'vat is a celebration of mystical teachings: "for the tree of the fields is a person's life" (Deut. 20:19) and thus consuming the *sheva minim* mentioned in Deut. 8:8

with *kavanah* would allow the holy sparks in the fruit to be released from their shells, arise, and return to their divine source.

These are not separate ideas. Deuteronomy 8:3 tells us, "For not by bread alone does a person live, but rather by the word of the Lord." Yet the "word of God" is precisely what created this physical universe and the wonderful, nutritious, sustaining foods with which we both sustain life and celebrate Tu BiSh'vat. The line between physical and spiritual does not exist in the mind of the kabbalists—it is all one reality separated only by perception. What we do here in this world is mirrored—and therefore has divine ramifications—in heaven above. When we effect *tikkun* here, heaven itself is repaired, thus the importance of eating the *sheva minim* to release the sparks.

If we have learned anything from recent research into environmental change, sustainability, and biodiversity, it is the lesson of Tu BiSh'vat: heaven and earth are one tethered, mirrored reality, and what we do here has cosmic significance.

Purim

For additional related commentary, see "*T'tzaveh*."

Purim
Eric Wisnia, 1996

Abraham begat Isaac; Isaac begat Jacob; Jacob, also known as Israel, became the father of twelve sons. Now Jacob loved Joseph more than his other sons and gave him a coat of many colors. Joseph dreamed dreams and related them to his brothers. The brothers hated Joseph and sold him as a slave to Egypt.

Many years passed and famine struck the land of Canaan. The eleven brothers who had remained in Canaan now came to Egypt to buy food. They were taken before Joseph, who appeared to them as a great Egyptian lord. Joseph immediately recognized the ten older brothers, but not the youngest brother, Benjamin, who was but a lad when Joseph left and now had become an adult with a large beard. Joseph demanded that they identify themselves by name. The ten older brothers stated their names and stood forward to face their punishment. However, they counseled the youngest brother, Benjamin, not to reveal himself but to say instead that he was only their servant, lest he suffer the same fate as the older ten.

After their declarations, Joseph revealed himself to his brothers. He readily forgave the older ten their past sins against him, and he eagerly asked about the welfare of his beloved youngest brother. Benjamin, now taking heart at Joseph's kindness, revealed himself.

Joseph looked at him but did not recognize him through the beard. Joseph ordered the Lord High Barber to shave Benjamin and reveal the youthful face that Joseph remembered so well. Overcome with joy, Joseph fell on Benjamin's neck, and there was much joy and weeping as befitted the occasion. But then Joseph grew angry at Benjamin's deception and picked up the urn of water that the Lord High Barber had used in shaving Benjamin and threw it at Benjamin.

From this story our Sages of blessed memory derived the ancient maxim "A Benny shaved is a Benny urned."

Purim
Kenneth J. Weiss, 2004

Each Purim, we relive the story of Esther and Mordecai, Haman and Ahashverosh. The *M'gilah* is the script; we're the actors. Once a year, we step—figuratively—into the shoes of the queen who saved her people, the wise councilor, the paranoid egomaniacal villain, or the simpleminded monarch.

"The play's the thing"—but only because it reflects ever-fresh, ever-poignant truths. Celebrating Purim's story is a key childhood memory for many Jews—because of the costumes and the personalities they bring to life. We've all seen little girls actually "become" Queen Esther: regal, wise, and (befitting their queenly costumes) touchingly beautiful.

Of course, costumes predate Purim: the *kohanim* donned them routinely. *Sidrah T'tzaveh* designates them *bigdei kodesh*!—holy garb: breastpiece, ephod, robe, tunic, headdress, sash. These items, worn by the *kohein*, were an essential part of the Temple ritual.

Years ago, one of my bar mitzvah kids—Joe Amstater—referred to these priestly vestments as Aaron's "tools of the trade." Only when clothed in them, could Aaron "carry out his [religious duties]."

Joe affirmed that as a bar mitzvah he too (like the ancient priests) had his "tools of the trade." Thus referring to his tradition (Hebrew, Torah, synagogue) and his family, Joe promised that these "will grow with me" and enable "me to carry on my heritage."

Among Judaism's (and his own) "tools of the trade," Joe might have included the costumes of Purim; in their unique way, they keep alive memories, personalities, and values to which we return joyfully, year after year.

Purim
Kenneth J. Weiss, 2005

"This is the ritual of the sacrifice of well-being" (Lev. 7:11).

M'gilat Esther is a stylized midrash … the (maybe not-so-dimwitted) monarch, the beautiful queen, the arch-villain, and our hero who helps avert danger in the nick of time. The evil one—"the adversary and enemy … this wicked Haman" was "hanged … on the gallows which he had prepared for Mordecai" (Esther 7:6, 7:10).

Thereafter, Mordecai assumed (the late, unlamented) Haman's duties and was gifted with his worldly goods. Thereafter, "the Jews had light and gladness, joy and honor. And in every province and … city, there was … a feast day and a good day. [Verily] many of the people of the land became Jews" (Esther 8:16–17). So, our people undertook to observe the fourteenth and fifteenth days of Adar—that they "be remembered and kept throughout every generation, every family, every province and every city; and **these days of Purim should never fail among the Jews**" (Esther 9:28).

Purim, may I suggest, is a postbiblical expression of the זבח שלמים (*zevach sh'lamim*, "sacrifice of well-being") described in our *sidrah* and earlier in the Book of Leviticus. To wit:

- The word זבח (*zevach*) means "slaughter." Lest you think this refers only to an animal on the Temple altar, read Esther, chapters 7–9, wherein the slaughter of Haman, his sons, and all the enemies of the Jews is graphically described.
- The word שלום (*shalom*) describes, better than any other, the state of our people in Shushan once their enemies were defeated: the Jews finally knew what שלמים (*sh'lamim*), "well-being," really meant.

- Purim frequently occurs during the week when *Parashat Tzav* is read (four times in the last ten years!); is that because the "sacrifice of well-being" is detailed here?

Happy *Zevach Sh'lamim* Day—2005/5765!

Purim
Jeffrey Ballon, 2009

Purim cannot be fully understood until the element of disguise is explored. Congregants do not expect to hear a sermon about *M'gilat Esther*. They do, however, indulge in Purim parties and dressing their children in costumes with little or no self-examination.

In past generations, it was not unusual to change one's name, a disguise in the form of an alias to thwart the *malach hamavet* (angel of death). My grandmother was eighty-five years old before anyone in the family realized that the woman we called Ida was at one time named Rachel. As a child, Ida was disguised with the name Rachel after two of her siblings died.

In rabbinic school (at JIR) one year, mentioning the name "Mordecai" inspired us to drink wine; hearing "Haman" provoked us to stomp and howl. By the end of the *M'gilah*, we stomped at "Mordecai" and drank at "Haman." Dr. Atlas ז״ל predicted that in the messianic age we will not be able to distinguish between these two men: both will have been given the ability to create peace rather than enmity. Therefore Purim, the holiday of disguises, will enable Mordecai and Haman to shed the excess part of their egos so that neither will feel the need to triumph over the other but can join together in the era of peace. In the messianic age, putative enemies will meet without rancor, and the new way of standing before them will bring us all to an era of peace.

Shabbat HaGadol

For additional related commentary, see *"Tazria/M'tzora"* and *"Tzav."*

Shabbat HaGadol
Kenneth J. Weiss, 2005

"You shall keep My laws . . . My rules . . . My charge" (Lev. 18:5, 18:30).

Although our ancestors left Egypt, God was concerned that they hadn't really left Egypt behind . . . would they one day wish to "return"?

So, at the beginning of פרשת בשלח (*Parashat B'shalach*), we read that God led "the people roundabout" lest they "have a change of heart . . . and return to Egypt" (Exod. 13:17–18). Paraphrasing God's concern: Yes, you've walked out of Egypt, but have you sufficiently distanced yourselves from her corrupting influence? You need to turn away from your slave past and toward Me—My values, My mitzvot, for **they** are your future!

In Leviticus 18 we read of the sex offenses that (though common in Egypt) the Israelites were commanded to reject. Using these as an example, Moses—speaking God's words—says ושמרתם (*Ush'martem*), "You shall watch" yourselves, so as "not to engage in any of the abhorrent practices" that you witnessed, "you shall not defile yourselves through them" (Lev. 18:30).

The message: every Pesach, retell and relive your deliverance from Egypt. God charges you each Passover: ושמרתם (*Ush'martem*), "You shall watch" (and keep!) God's laws and rules (Lev. 18:5); live by, teach, and transmit Torah. ושמרתם (Ush'martem), "You shall watch" (and keep!) your distance from Egypt and her ways: leave everything Egyptian behind you!

Shabbat HaGadol
Alan Cook, 2006

What makes the Shabbat preceding פסח (Pesach) so "big" or "grand"? The name of this Shabbat is not found in the תנ״ך (Tanach) or in Rabbinic literature, so its origin is unclear.

Some commentators note that it was on a Shabbat that the Israelite families in Egypt took their lamb in anticipation of the first פסח (Pesach). This advance preparation was necessary to ensure that the lamb was without blemish, but it also enabled the people to get in a proper frame of mind. For the first time, the fledgling nation shook off the commands of their oppressors and reveled in the freedom that comes with a day of rest. Humans joined God in celebration of God's holy day.

Our tradition tells us that if everyone were to observe just two Shabbatot according to all of the relevant laws and customs, Israel would immediately be redeemed (Babylonian Talmud, *Shabbat* 118b). If the "first" Shabbat observed in Egypt prior to the Exodus met that criteria, then we have but one more to go. That Shabbat will certainly be a "big" and "grand" Shabbat. That Shabbat will inspire "the hearts of parents to be turned to their children, and the hearts of children to their parents" (Mal. 3:24).

But let us not worry about how our neighbors are observing Shabbat. Let us focus on our own celebrations. Let us call the Sabbath a delight. Let us put ourselves in the shoes of our ancestors in Egypt and strive to make each Shabbat as rich and meaningful as that very first one.

Pesach

For additional related commentary, see *"Bo," "Tzav,"* and *"Emor."*

Pesach: Reply to the *Chacham*
Stephen E. Cohen, 1998

S'fat Emet, like many other Chasidic sources, subverts the traditional valuing of the four sons of the Pesach seder. In this commentary on the Haggadah, he argues that each of the four questions of the four sons represents a kind of "exile" and that all four questions are to be found in every Jew. In addressing the question of the *chacham*, he plays on the double meaning of the word *taam*.

S'fat Emet The question of the *chacham* stands for the probings of the intellect, by means of which the *yetzer hara* raises doubts concerning the *chukim*. To this question, the response must always be ready that in performing the will of God, there is more meaning [*taam*] and joy than in understanding the meaning [*taam*] of the mitzvah. And this answer is implied in *Ein maftirin achar haPesach afikoman* [no food is eaten after the *afikoman*], that is, that the meaning [*taam*] of the mitzvah of matzah, although it has no taste [*taam*], is sweeter than any dessert.

Comment Does liberal Judaism retain, anywhere, the traditional category of the *chukim*?

Pesach

Amy Scheinerman, 2009

Pesach provides us with an overarching mythical narrative ("myth" here as used by Neil Gillman, drawing on Paul Tillich). The story of *y'tziat Mitzrayim* (the Exodus from Egypt) tells us what we are about: where we came from, where we are headed, and what values should fuel our journey—our purpose is all about redemption.

The pageantry of the Pesach seder is legion. It is always delightful and deeply meaningful to see the parade of symbols anew through the eyes of non-Jewish guests at our table experiencing a seder for the first time. They immediately make connections to the world we all inhabit. *Maror* and salt water bespeak the pain and agony of servitude—physically, politically, emotionally—of so many in a world still in need of redemption on every level. *Charoset* embodies the promise that bitterness and pain can give way to sweetness and freedom—it is thus a symbol of hope. Four cups of wine bespeak God's promises of redemption that we can make real for others through our commitments and actions when we are God's hands in the world.

Leil Pesach is a night of spectacle that can, and should, extend its reach throughout the year. One way to do this is to keep its symbols alive and vibrant. By bringing the symbols of Pesach into our teaching and preaching throughout the year, we teach and enable people to "see the world through Jewish eyes" continually. Even more, we keep alive the meaning of *y'tziat Mitzrayim*—the divine goal of redemption—and give it the vibrancy to inspire us all the more.

S'firat HaOmer

For additional related commentary, see *"Acharei Mot / K'doshim"* and *"Emor."*

S'firat HaOmer
David Novak, 2009

"The days of counting of the Omer are days of partial mourning and sadness. On these days, weddings, parties, haircuts, and dinners with dancing are not conducted, in memory of a plague during the lifetime of Rabbi Akiva. It was said that twelve thousand pairs of students died in one short period, because they did not respect one another! And all of them died between Pesach and Shavuot" (Babylonian Talmud, *Y'vamot* 62b).

The time has come to cease mourning Rabbi Akiva's students—or perhaps the military defeats at the time of the Bar Kochba rebellion against Roman rule in 132 C.E. Whether the legend concerning Rabbi Akiva's students (whose historicity is not established) or the defeats against the imperious Romans led to this period of semi-mourning, two thousand years of mourning is enough.

The period of time from Pesach to Shavuot, from redemption to revelation, should be a period of increasing anticipation and elevated receptivity to revelation, of renewed growth in the land and in our spiritual lives. To distract ourselves with this legend diminishes our focus during this period and hence the potential of this time to inspire religious insight.

This is about perspective. As a people, we devote two formal days during the *S'firah* to mourning the dead of the Shoah and the fallen of Israel; a third day is excessive. Let us reclaim the rest of the *S'firah* to revel in *Am Yisrael chai*, the living Jewish people, and our covenant with God.

S'firat HaOmer
Amy Scheinerman, 2009

Many years ago, Mark Hurvitz approached me to discuss his idea of creating a graphic representation of an Omer calendar. Mark's concept was to begin the journey through *S'firah* in the "bright red of rebellion" and gradually, over the course of seven weeks, arrive at the "brilliant violet of royalty" of Mount Sinai, prepared for covenant rather than rebellion. He wanted to help Jews not only count the Omer, but as they did, go through a spiritual process of embracing the covenant of Torah in preparation for Shavuot. Mark sent me a sketch he had made with colored pencils of a seven-by-seven grid to indicate what he had in mind. I loved his idea but decided to hand this one off to an expert: my father, Andrew Ross ז״ל, a graphic artist. My father rendered Mark's seven-by-seven grid with rich colors but then arranged Mark's stepping stones to Sinai in a spiral, as if one were ascending the mountain, step-by-step, from Pesach through Shavuot. Unfortunately, graphic applications and operating systems have changed drastically in the intervening years, and the spiral is lost. But with my far more limited artistic abilities, I produced a compromise: a spiral arranged as a seven-by-seven grid. I share it here. Mark and I then discussed appending short study texts for each day to facilitate spiritual movement and growth. We never completed this project but invite you to join in and help us complete it.

To view the Omer calendar in color go to: *scheinerman.net/judaism/shavuot/omer4.html*.

S'firat HaOmer

7	6	5	4	3	2	1
8	29	28	27	26	25	24
9	30	43	42	41	40	23
10	31	44	49	48	39	22
11	32	45	46	47	38	21
12	33	34	35	36	37	20
13	14	15	16	17	18	19

Chol HaMo-eid Pesach

For additional related commentary, see *"Ki Tisa."*

Chol HaMo-eid Pesach
Henry Bamberger, 1996

Having returned to Mount Sinai after witnessing the Golden Calf, Moses seems to want just what the people did—physical evidence of the presence of God. When he says, "Show me Your Glory" (Exod. 33:18), what do you think he wanted to see? What would satisfy you that you had seen God's Glory? Why do we read this part of the passage on the Shabbat in Pesach?

Is it Moses or God who proclaims the thirteen attributes (Exod. 34:6)? What would have been the effect if God had proclaimed them? Was hearing God proclaiming the word the same as experiencing the attribute? What is the connection of the thirteen attributes to Pesach?

There is a theory that this "Ritual Decalogue" (Exod. 34:10–26) is different from what Moses wrote on the old tablets and that the new tablets therefore contain different laws than the old. (Some early church fathers were fond of this view, since it convinced them that Israel only received the "ritual" laws and not the "moral" laws of the Ten Commandments.) Others maintain that the Ritual Decalogue is but an expansion of the words on the first tablets. What do you think? If you choose the second interpretation, how do the words in Exodus 34 modify some of the Ten Commandments? How does this controversy affect Pesach, which is not mentioned in the Ten Commandments?

Chol HaMo-eid Pesach
Stephen Wylen, 1997

God says to Moses, "Then I will take My hand away and you will see My back, but my face shall not be seen" (Exod. 33:23). What is meant here, symbolically, by "God's back" and "God's face"? Why can we see God's back but not God's face, and live?

Can we find God in our lives only retroactively, looking backwards, or can we project and see God's presence in our future, making life decisions accordingly? Compare this to Maimonides versus apocalyptic thinkers on the coming of the *Mashiach*—is the messianic age of classical Reform Jewish thinking prospective, à la the apocalyptics, or retrospective, à la Maimonides?

In his comment on the first chapter of Genesis, Abraham ibn Ezra cryptically refers us to this portion, *Ki Tisa*, if we want to know what is significant about God as Creator. What did Ibn Ezra mean by this? Why did he disguise his meaning and not tell us outright?

Why did the Sages pick this selection from *Ki Tisa* as the portion to be read on the intermediate Shabbat of the *Chagim*? Is it because of the Festival calendar in Exod. 34:18–26 or for some message in the broader context of Exodus 33–34?

Chol HaMo-eid Pesach
Herbert Bronstein, 1999

Today there is a great interest in mysticism or "spirituality." Some associate a focus on the mystic "high" or "sense of being filled" with a narcissistic focus on the self that seeks the "spiritual experience" as an end in itself. Moses yearns for the Presence, an experience of the *Kavod*. Such an experience does happen, twice, if not in a way that Moses may have expected. Neither one of them is the end in itself. In each case, a task for life, a regular responsibility for everyday engagement was laid upon Moses and through him upon the people. After the first experience Moses was told, "Carve two tablets of stone like the first" (Exod. 34:1). After the second experience of the Presence (Exod. 34:5–7), the covenant is extended, tasks are outlined, and again the commandment for the observance of Passover repeated (Exod. 34:18). Indeed, in certain mysticisms the end goal is the sheer experience of the transcendent. It is a characteristic of Judaism that the experience of the Presence is not ultimate but penultimate. Isaiah's experience of the seraphic chorus and the hem of the garment of God filling the sanctuary is capped by a mission, a *sh'lichut*. "Whom shall I send, and who will go for me?" (Isa. 6:8). So was the experience of Ezekiel foundational to our own mystical tradition. Tasks are assigned, commandments given, responsibilities undertaken. The implications for our people could be quite important these days.

Chol HaMo-eid Pesach: Freedom and Singing
Stephen E. Cohen, 2000

S'fat Emet teaches here that singing is itself a profound form of freedom. His comment speaks to the ultimate significance of the spirituals of the African-American slaves and of the Jewish songs of the ghettos and concentration camps.

S'fat Emet on *Shir HaShirim* (Song of Songs) The midrash says of the phrase *shir hashirim*, "Let us sing to the One who made us *sarim*/princes in the world." And this is related to that which I heard from my teacher and master, my grandfather, that the reason that *P'sukei D'zimrah* precede the blessings of the *Sh'ma* and the *T'filah* is to give song and praise for the privilege of singing praise. This is the meaning of *shir hashirim*—"the song of songs": To the extent to which a man masters his behavior, and aligns it with the Holy One, he awakens the aspect of Song, which resides within all creation. And this is the reason for reciting *Perek Shirah* every day. For all the songs derive from it, and the song of humanity is called "the song of songs." And therefore it is recited during Pesach, the time of our freedom.

Comment How do you think S'fat Emet understands the connection between "mastering our behavior" and song? What might be some other explanations for the liberating power of song?

Chol HaMo-eid Pesach
Zoe Klein and Jonathan Klein, 2001

> "My beloved answered and said to me, 'Rise up to yourself [*kumi lach*]'" (Song of Songs 2:10). "Truth shall grow from the land [*eretz*]" (Ps. 85:12). One needs to draw oneself to the source of his/her soul, each one according to his/her personal level. This is why it states, "Go to yourself [*lech l'cha*]" (Gen. 12:1), which is to say [go] to your source, "from your land [*mei-artz'cha*]" (ibid.), meaning that from all your materiality (*artziyut*), you should come to the source of your soul. This is the meaning of "My beloved answered and said to me, 'Rise up to yourself,'" meaning raise yourself up in order to draw yourself to your source, with all the sweet pleasantries that are "my friend my fair one," "and go to yourself [*ul'chi lach*]," to the source of your soul, which is the meaning of "truth shall grow from *eretz*." (Reb Baruch of Medzibezh, grandson of the Baal Shem Tov, Botzina DiN'hora)

In our daily lives, we are engrossed in the rhythm of routines. Baruch of Medzibezh argues, contrary to most spiritual traditions, that our corporeal existence is the starting point for reaching our highest potential, which is no longer material but rather spiritual. How does one discover what Reb Baruch calls the "soul source" when surrounded by materiality? Does physicality blind us to self-realization? Or does it allow us to embrace it?

On the last day of Passover, we pray for the morning dew to sustain us over the dry summer months. The mystics understand *T'filat Tal* and the corresponding *T'filat Geshem* for rain, recited during Sh'mini Atzeret, as having a spiritual significance far beyond the physical need for dew and rain. *Geshem* is linked to *gashmiyut*, or "corporeality." When we pray for rain, we are praying for the physical ability to survive, well aware that our holiday cycle is most rich during the rainy season, allowing us to reflect on who we are and offering us a greater God-consciousness during those months. *T'filat Geshem* becomes a prayer for *gashmiyut*, a knowledge that we are secure in our spirituality but unsure of our physical abundance. *T'filat Tal*, by contrast, is a prayer for the less-tangible, less-physical sustenance, a sustenance in spirituality. During the summer months, when physical pleasures and leisure are readily available, yet only Shavuot and Tishah B'Av link us to spiritual contemplation, we pray for the strength to survive the difficult season, culminating in Tishah B'Av, when connection to God is most challenged. *T'filat Tal* reminds us that, just as the morning moisture miraculously sustains us throughout the driest time of year, our connection to the far-less-tangible spiritual world is necessary for our lives to feel fulfilled. We, without hesitation, plan to transvalue *T'filat Tal* this year, from prayer for morning moisture into a plea for spiritual help through the summer months.

Should we, as a movement, reclaim *T'filat Tal* and *T'filat Geshem* on a spiritual level?

Chol HaMo-eid Pesach
Kenneth J. Weiss, 2002

"Then I will take *kapi* [My hand] away and you will see *achorai* [My back]; but *panai* [My face] must not be seen" (Exod. 33:23).

At seder we eat special foods, we see cherished faces, we renew and retell an old but ever-new story. In honor of Pesach, in recognition of Chag HaMatzot (when these were separate occasions), we avoid leavened foods for a week.

Just maybe, Exod. 33:23 is more than—on its surface—it appears to be. Might not the verse be an abstruse restatement of the mitzvah to observe Passover: return every year to the seder table, eat the special foods, observe the special rites, retell the story of the Exodus.

As you share the story among you, *vahasiroti et kapi* ("then I will take My hand away"): I will, year after year, enable you to uncover new meanings and understandings. So, every person around every table can, potentially, see *achorai* (My impact, My aftereffect) differently every year, especially those who grow sufficiently to ask the wise child's questions. However: don't attempt to prefigure My role (*panai*) before the annual retelling, for each retelling may lead to new perspective.

The story does not change from year to year; but—with God's help—we do!

Chol HaMo-eid Pesach
Kenneth J. Weiss, 2003

"A sacred occasion: you shall not work" (Lev. 23:7).

The additional Torah portion assigned for the Shabbat during Chol HaMo-eid Pesach delivers a clear and unmistakable message: the days of matzah consumption are to each year what Shabbat is to each week!

The first eight verses are separated from the rest of the Festival calendar contained in Leviticus 23 by a virtual barrier: a paragraph (six full verses!) detailing sheaves and waving, burnt offerings, meal offerings, and libations to God. Only after this "interruption" does the calendar continue with the Omer period, Shavuot, etc.

Let's look at the text. God tells Moses, "These are My fixed times, the fixed times of the LORD" (Lev. 23:2). Shabbat is noted first: a day of "complete rest, a sacred occasion. You shall do no work" (23:3). Then comes *Pesach l'Adonai*: a day for God (featuring a Passover sacrifice) followed by Chag HaMatzot. The first and seventh days are—like Shabbat—sacred occasions on which "you shall not work at your occupations" (23:7–8). Other Festivals are commanded with similar/identical words, but only later and only beyond the "word barrier" noted above.

Shabbat: every seventh day, a time of complete rest after seven days of work, a sacred occasion.

Pesach / Chag HaMatzot: following the first day ("a sacred occasion") come "seven days [on which] you shall make offerings by fire to the LORD," then another day that "shall be a sacred occasion: you shall not work" (Lev. 23:7–8). Might Pesach be the Sabbath "writ large"? Relish your unleavened challah.

Chol HaMo-eid Pesach
Kenneth J. Weiss, 2004

On Pesach, we are prohibited from eating any leavened food (*chameitz*) made from the five grains specified by the Rabbis. Over time, the word *chameitz* has been expanded and enhanced by subsequent midrashic interpretations. According to Yitz Greenberg (in *The Jewish Way*, Simon and Schuster, 1988, p. 41), when we discard *chameitz*, we are turning our backs on "the old slave existence [in Egypt] and entering the new condition of living as a free person."

Matzah—Passover's staple—therefore suggests far more than a lack of yeast and time for rising. Matzah is the hard bread that represents our hurried departure from the hard times we suffered in Egypt. It is the bread of freedom; to desist from *chameitz* each year is to reaffirm our rejection of Egypt (the place where, according to *World Book Encyclopedia*, leavened bread was invented!).

Larry Hoffman deepens the concept of *b'dikat chameitz*: as Pesach approaches, he teaches, let us search not only the darkest, least accessible corners of our pantry; let us also examine the secret, most painful corners of our lives, our relationships. Hoffman teaches that the month of Nisan is a time for "moral house cleaning": are there destructive bad habits, ongoing hard feelings, cold silences, angry words? Why not acknowledge these, and then, as Hoffman teaches, burn them as spiritual *chameitz* this Passover?

When at seder we hold up the matzah plate and welcome others to share it with us, we are declaring: we reject the *chameitz* in our lives.

Matzah—the bread of liberation—represents our resolve to move "beyond *chameitz*": from where we are to where we wish to be, from who we've been to who we know we can be, from how we've lived to the way we know we should live.

Chol HaMo-eid Pesach
Alan Cook, 2006

Each year at our *sedarim,* we sing דיינו (*Dayeinu*), showing our gratitude to God for all of the wonders performed for our ancestors as they went free from Egypt. Though the popular melody fits only about three or four of the verses, we know that the traditional formula encompasses over a dozen items for which we give thanks.

Of course, the list is not exhaustive. We have many things to be thankful for, and so we should regularly recount our many blessings. Yet occasionally we feel that God has ceased to perform miracles or that our prayers are falling on deaf ears (כביכול [*kivyachol*, "so to speak"]).

An anonymous poet has written, "I asked for strength, and God gave me difficulties to make me strong. / I asked for wisdom, and God gave me problems to solve. / I asked for prosperity, and God gave me brawn and brains to work. / I asked for courage, and God gave me dangers to overcome. / I asked for love, and God gave me troubled people to help. / I asked for favors, and God gave me opportunities. / I received nothing I wanted. I received everything I needed. / My prayers were answered."

We need not feel like the people in Ezekiel's vision, who proclaim, "Our bones are dried up, our hope is gone; we are doomed" (Ezek. 37:11, from the haftarah for Shabbat Chol HaMo-eid Pesach). We simply need to change our perspective, to bear witness to the miracles in the world and in our life, and to recognize that we will never sufficiently be able to thank God for all that has been done for us.

Chol HaMo-eid Pesach
Amy Scheinerman, 2007

The Torah portion designated for Chol HaMo-eid Pesach, Exod. 33:12–34:36, mentions Pesach in the context of an ancient Festival calendar, but it does not focus on the Exodus as we might have expected. Instead, it opens with Moses expressly asking God, in Exod. 33:13, אם-נא מצאתי חן בעיניך הודיעני נא את-דרכך ואדעך (*Im na matzati chein b'einecha hodi-eini na et d'rachecha v'eidaacha*, "If I have truly gained Your favor, pray let me know Your ways, that I may know You"), followed by God's admonition that no one can see God's face and live. Yet Moses will be privileged to glimpse God's back. Immediately following, God commands Moses to carve the second set of stone tablets and reiterates the covenant.

Reading this portion in the midst of Pesach reminds us that the liberation from Egypt, as redemptive as it is, is not an end in itself, nor is it complete without the covenant at Sinai. Israel's freedom has a larger goal: to free her to become God's people in action, as well as heritage. It is through fulfillment of religious obligation, by binding ourselves to the covenant, that we glimpse God. Torah, which provides our glimpse of God, is the goal.

Seventh Day of Pesach

For additional related commentary, see "*B'shalach*."

Seventh Day of Pesach
Kenneth J. Weiss, 2005

What is **the** most essential message of Pesach? Is it deliverance? The end of tyranny? The renewal of hope? God's intercession on behalf of our ancestors (and us!)?

I am convinced that Passover's most basic, most fundamental message embraces all of these. It is this: "You shall not oppress a stranger, for you know the feelings of the stranger, having yourselves been strangers in the land of Egypt" (Exod. 23:9).

Annually we (retell and) relive our Exodus story. We taste the bitterness of slavery; we read God's promises of liberation; we drink in the sweetness of freedom. Leaving the seder table, we reaffirm Judaism's ageless and universal lesson: that we cannot behave toward others the way the Egyptians behaved toward us! We are commanded to make Pesach ever new by seeking to make a difference in the lives of others, because we "know [their] feelings . . . having [ourselves] been strangers in the land of Egypt."

That is the nectar . . . the essence, the core and marrow: our prophetic mandate; that is the **lifeblood** of Pesach.

Our daughter Jennifer's father-in-law asked her, "What would you like your epitaph to be?" She responded, without hesitation: "She tried to make a difference." Jennifer knows—and so do we: our lives matter more when we reach out, see others, know their humanity, and try to make a difference in their lives.

Seventh Day of Pesach
Amy Scheinerman, 2008

Some have expressed concern about the militant tone of the שירה (Shirah). God is pictured as Israel's warrior general, and the destruction of the Egyptian charioteers is celebrated.

Rabbi Tzaddok HaKohein of Lublin, in *Sefer P'ri Tzaddik*, noted, "The intent of the Haggadah is not just the story itself . . . one is obliged to tell the story in such a way that he himself feels, and makes others feel, that they are indeed in the process of leaving Egypt and getting ready to go through the Sea. One must feel the joy and the freedom in his soul as if he is really leaving Egypt for good." Deuteronomy 16:14–15 commands joy not once, but twice: "You shall rejoice in your festival . . . and you shall be exceedingly happy."

אז ישיר משה (*Az yashir Moshe*, "Then Moses sang" [Exod. 15:1]). From the day God created the world, until the day Israel stood at the Sea, no one sang שירה (*shirah*, "a song") to God except Israel. God created Adam, but he never sang שירה (*shirah*). God saved Avraham from the fiery furnace and the kings, but he did not sing שירה (*shirah*). God saved Yitzchak from the knife, but he did not sing שירה (*shirah*). Yaakov escaped from [Esav's] angel, from Esav, and from the men of Shechem, but he did not sing שירה (*shirah*). When Israel came to the Sea and it split for them, they immediately sang שירה (*shirah*) to God, as it is written, אז ישיר משה ובני ישראל את־השירה הזאת ליהוה (*Az yashir Moshe uv'nei Yisrael et hashirah hazot l'Adonai*, "Then Moses and the Israelites sang this song to *Adonai*" [Exod. 15:1]). God said, "I have waited for this!" The word אז (*az*) denotes only joy, as it is written, "Then [אז, *az*] our mouths will be filled with laughter [Ps. 126:2]" (*Sh'mot Rabbah* 23:4).

שירת הים (*Shirat HaYam*) is an expression of pure, unbridled joy and relief in redemption. It is an image reflecting how the Israelites experienced God at that moment in time.

Eighth Day of Pesach

Eighth Day of Pesach: *Lechem Oni*
Stephen E. Cohen, 1998

The traditional Torah reading for the eighth day of Pesach includes the sole reference to matzah as *lechem oni*, which in the Aramaic of the Haggadah becomes *lachma anya*. With a play on words, S'fat Emet transforms the "bread of affliction" into the "bread of telling."

S'fat Emet on *Lechem Oni* (Deut. 16:3) Bread upon which we pronounce [*onin*] many words. For it is a mitzvah to tell of the Exodus. And it heals the mouth and the tongue. It is written, "The Ark carried those who carried it" [Babylonian Talmud, *Sotah* 35a], and every mitzvah gives strength and vitality to the part of the body that performs it. So the mitzvah of eating the *pesach* and matzah heals eating, and telling the story heals speech—this is why the Festival is called *Pesach Peh Sach* [the mouth speaking]. It is expressed in the comment "In the house the meal was the size of an olive, but the *Hallel* singing lifted the roof" [Babylonian Talmud, *P'sachim* 85b]. For the mouths of Israel are opened by means of the *pesach* and matzah. And this is the essence of the Exodus. This is why the matzah is referred to as *lechem oni*—"bread upon which we pronounce many words."

Comment S'fat Emet, here and elsewhere, asserts that the "essence of the Exodus" is for a Jew to be able to open their mouth and speak the truth. Do you consider this an adequate distillation of the themes of Passover?

Yom HaShoah

Yom HaShoah
Janice Garfunkel, 2009

Astounded at the number of people who seem to be "self-hating" Jews, I wondered if there were Jews in the 1930s who supported the Nazis. The answer is yes, there were.

Why? My theory is that for some people, it is unbearable to feel *sinat chinam*, to know one is hated for no reason. If the hate is our fault, some Jews reasoned, then we can do something about it, rather than feel powerless and impotent in the face of an irrational hatred. The problem, therefore, must be the evil deeds of fellow Jews. If only we can distance ourselves from them by excoriating them (or change them), we will be safe!

When my daughter was in preschool, a classmate told her she hated her because of an almost imperceptible black dot (a mole) on my daughter's face (irony: the girl was African American). *Sinat chinam* is not a figment of our imagination.

A wonderful song from *South Pacific* tells us that children must be taught to hate. I don't think this is true. They will hate another for being pretty. Or ugly. Or for being rich. Or poor. Or for having a mole, or for not having a mole. Most of all, for being different, or being vulnerable. We don't have to do anything wrong to be hated. Groundless, reasonless hatred oozes up around us, from within us.

Not to hate is what must be carefully taught. We must be the teachers.

Yom HaAtzma-ut

For additional related commentary, see "*Acharei Mot / K'doshim*."

Yom HaAtzma-ut
Amy Scheinerman, 2009

Among the many views of *olam haba* (the world-to-come), we find that of Sh'muel in the Babylonian Talmud, *B'rachot* 34b: "There is no difference between our time and the messianic age except that in the future time, *Am Yisrael* [the people Israel] will be free from subservience to other nations." This is, of course, in keeping with his perspective on slavery, as expressed in Talmud and encapsulated in the Pesach Haggadah, where Sh'muel pinpoints the beginning of slavery in *Avadim Hayinu*, as opposed to Rav, who sees slavery as a spiritual state of mind and finds the beginning of slavery in idolatry. Rambam agrees with Sh'muel: redemption is a matter of physical and political freedom.

Many of us use, or are familiar with, the prayer for the State of Israel that refers to her as *reishit tz'michat g'ulateinu*, "the first flowering of our redemption," suggesting not that the modern state is the fulfillment of the ancient dream, but rather is a step in that direction. Over and against this view is the opinion that Israel came into being through sweat, blood, and good fortune but is not a sign of the ultimate redemption.

In other segments of the Jewish community, the tension is between the mitzvah of establishing a sovereign Jewish state and the promise that God would establish it.

For us, the tension is more as stated above: is the meaning of Israel tinged with messianic value, or is it purely a practical political matter? Perhaps it is time to ask: why must we choose between the two? For liberal Jews who affirm human agency in *tikkun olam*, the combination is a natural *shiduch*.

Shavuot

For additional related commentary, see "*Yitro.*"

Shavuot
Stephen E. Cohen, 1999

Since ancient times, the Festival of Shavuot has merged agricultural imagery with a celebration of text. Here, Nachman of Bratzlav offers a new blending of the two worlds of nature and the word.

Likutei Moharan "Then Boaz said to Ruth, 'Listen well my daughter, do not go to glean in another field, and do not leave here'" (Ruth 2:8). When a person rises to pray and utters the words of prayer, he is gathering beautiful flowers. Like one walking in a field, picking beautiful blossoms one by one, until he has a bouquet. Then he continues picking, one at a time, making another bouquet, and joins them together. Thus he walks through the prayer, from letter to letter, until several letters are joined together into a sound. And so he forms complete words, and then two words are joined together. And then he walks on, gathering until he completes one blessing. How beautiful are the gleanings and gatherings of a person's prayer? But when the speech goes forth from the *nefesh*, it begs and pleads not to be separated from it, saying, "How can you separate from me, seeing the great bond and love that exists between us? True, you do have to walk further, in order to gather other treasures, but as you do, wherever you go, do not forget me, do not separate from me!" Boaz is the intellect, speaking to Ruth, the *nefesh*, saying, "Listen well my daughter, do not go to glean in another field!" That is, "Do not go on to pick other flowers/words/prayers!" "And do not leave here—but if you do have to go on to another word, do not depart completely from the first word."

Comment Is it even remotely possible to become aware of every letter of prayer, and yet to "hold them all together" in one's mind? Of what practical value might this teaching be?

Shavuot
Sheldon Marder, 2001

A poem called "Gleanings" by David Shimoni, translated by Ruth Finer Mintz (*Modern Hebrew Poetry: A Bilingual Anthology,* University of California Press, 1982, p. 86):

> Silence and aura. An ancient Yemenite woman gathers dry
> > branches for a bonfire,
> Her bent back between the green of grapevines darkens and
> > gleams in harvest sheens.
> Her dusky grandson with curly earlocks caught in mid-air in
> > the branches of fig.
> A slice of black bread between his teeth and his nimble fingers
> > pick the last of the fruit.
> A bird has burst out of the fig thicket, chirped suddenly in
> > the quiet world,
> Dropped to warm earth and pecked the bread crumbs fallen below.
> I too have joined the gleaners, silently as I lie on the
> > vineyard hill:
> I will furtively glean myself remnants of summer, sheens of
> > harvest: delicate, serene . . .

This question is raised in the Jerusalem Talmud, *Sh'vi-it* 8:6 concerning the sabbatical year: What is the intent of "you shall not reap, you shall not glean" in Lev. 25:5? The intent we are told, is this: You shall not reap as the reapers do, and you shall not glean as the gleaners do, but you may do so through some variation.

Shimoni's poem encourages us to find our own "variation"—to engage in a non-literal "gleaning" of experience. In what ways might we "join the gleaners"? By being more attentive to the details of our daily life?

Shavuot
Kenneth J. Weiss, 2002

"Wherever you go, I will go" (Ruth 1:16). Naomi's impact on Ruth was deep, meaningful, lasting. Yet, Naomi realized that Ruth, like Orpah, needed to live her own life, move on.

Three times she told them, "Turn back!" I've trained you and modeled a way of life for you. I've loved you as a mother loves her own children. But now, my life—what's left of it—will carry me back to my people, my homeland, my spiritual tradition. Your lives—still full of promise—must carry each of you to a people, a place, a spiritual tradition of your own choosing. "Turn back!" "Turn back!" Orpah "kissed her mother-in-law farewell"—she flew off to begin the next stage in her life. Ruth, however, knew that her life was interwoven with Naomi's . . .

In our kitchen hangs a small tapestry. Pictured is a springtime tree; a bird is flying above it through a blue sky. These words complete the tapestry: "There are two lasting things we can leave our children . . . one is roots . . . the other is wings. . . ."

Aren't Orpah and Ruth emblematic of the flight paths our own children might well follow? Some fly off—seeking a new place to take root and grow. Others fly away only to return: their wings carry them freely back to that which stabilizes and nourishes them still.

Lovingly, we pray for them.

Shavuot
Kenneth J. Weiss, 2003

"Thus shall you say to the house of Jacob . . ." (Exod. 19:3).

Our venue: the Sinai wilderness, "in front of the mountain" (Exod. 19:2).

The date: "the third new moon after the Israelites had [left] . . . Egypt" (Exod. 19:1).

The event: the (very) first Shavuot.

The people were in need of (and were about to receive) words from "on high": initial mitzvot, a code of conduct—a "constitution." God told Moses to address "the house of Jacob and . . . the Children of Israel" (Exod. 19:3). A midrash asks and answers the obvious question: why the redundancy? Aren't "the house of Jacob" and "the Children of Israel" one and the same? No, say the Rabbis: the former refers to the women of the community (Rashi later concurs), the latter to the men. Notably, God focuses Moses's attention on the women first, giving them precedence, since they bear, raise, and train the children. Thus, the women have **primary** responsibility for transmitting the lessons and mitzvot learned at Sinai.

Witness: the biblical Ruth, one of Jacob's (latter-day) daughters. Whereas our Torah portion annually recalls the code of conduct that forms the basis of our peoplehood, *M'gilat Ruth* exemplifies how one Jewish woman passed Judaism on to her progeny.

Shavuot's message: we **must** transmit Judaism. Transmit what? See Exodus 19–20. Transmit how? For inspiration, read *M'gilat Ruth*.

Shavuot
Alan Cook, 2006

Rabbi Zeira said, "This scroll tells us nothing either of ritual purity or impurity, either of things prohibited or permitted. Why then was it written? To teach how great is the reward of those who perform acts of kindness" (*Ruth Rabbah* 2:14).

Shavuot is probably the most ignored of the שלש רגלים (*Shalosh R'galim*, Three Pilgrimage Festivals). It usually occurs as the school year is ending, and it lacks the sensory associations, such as *lulav* and *etrog*, or *pesach*, matzah, and *maror*, that help us to make a visceral connection with the other Pilgrimage Festivals. Certainly the practice of holding confirmation ceremonies on Shavuot has brought new energy and enthusiasm to this holiday, but it is a shame that many of our congregants are unaware of, or unenthused by, Shavuot's importance as זמן מתן תורתנו (Z'man Matan Torateinu, "Season of the Giving of Our Torah").

Perhaps a reading of the Book of Ruth would benefit those who are uninformed about this Festival. Ruth's enthusiastic embrace of Jewish beliefs might inspire them to reconnect with their heritage. Albert Einstein is said to have remarked that his only regret about being born Jewish is that he never had the opportunity to **choose** to be Jewish. Similarly, some may find that being born into Judaism has made them complacent about the richness of their traditions. Ruth might help them to put everything into perspective.

The book also gives us a wonderful role model in Boaz, who shows kindness to Ruth before he ever becomes aware of who she truly is. In this way he embodies the principle ואהבת לרעך כמוך (*v'ahavta l'rei-acha kamocha*, "love your fellow as yourself" [Lev. 19:18]), identified by Hillel as the central tenet of the Torah.

Thus Ruth and Boaz can teach us to reexamine our own relationships with our Torah and with our faith.

Shavuot
Amy Scheinerman, 2008

Torah records that when he descended *Har Sinai* "Moshe went and repeated to the people all the commands of the Lord and all the rules; and all the people answered with one voice, saying, 'All the things that the Lord has commanded we will do!'" (Exod. 24:3). The *b'rit* was complete when the people accepted God's Torah and committed themselves to its instructions.

Moshe then set up an altar at the foot of the mountain, erected twelve pillars, and performed sacrifices of well-being. Moshe read the Torah aloud to the assembled throng, and then Torah tells us in Exod. 24:7, "[The people] said, 'All that the Lord has spoken we will faithfully do!'"

Were the Israelites accepting another Torah? For the Rabbis, of course, this marked the acceptance of both *Torah Shebichtav* (Written Torah) and *Torah Shebal Peh* (Oral Torah). Is there another way to understand this?

Perhaps the meaning is that Torah lives in our hearts and souls in two ways. We accept Torah as the tradition handed down by our parents and ancestors. It is an inheritance from the generations that came before. We study their commentaries, explore the meaning they ascribe to Torah, and participate in the life of the people that calls Torah its core: "All the things that the LORD has commanded we will do!"

But there is another way that Torah must live in our hearts and souls in order to be truly alive: we must discover our own interpretations and meaning. Revelation is ongoing. Those assembled at *Har Sinai* were the first generation, but in order to link ourselves to the chain we must allow Torah to percolate through our lives and bring meaning to our experiences in, and of, the world. That is why the Torah had to pass through *oznei haam* ("the ears of the people" [Exod. 24:7]) and they responded *Naaseh v'nishmah* ("We will do and we will hear"): they internalized Torah and made it their own—not only as a people, a generation, but each individually, as well, and not only to **do** but also to **hear** meaning, to take it into their hearts and allow it to beget meaning in their unique lives.

Shavuot
Amy Scheinerman, 2009

"Moshe came and summoned the elders of the people and put before them all that *Adonai* had commanded him. All the people answered as one, saying, 'All that *Adonai* has spoken we will do!' And Moshe brought back the people's words to *Adonai*. And *Adonai* said to Moshe, 'I will come to you in a thick cloud, in order that the people may hear when I speak with you and so trust you ever after'" (Exod. 19:7–9).

Why do the people accede to a contract whose conditions they do not yet know? Can this be a legitimate contract if the conditions are not stipulated at the time it is "signed"? Why does God feel it necessary for the people to hear God's voice in order for them to trust Moshe ever after? And how will the *av he-anan* ("a thick cloud") help? Torah describes *matan Torah* (revelation) as a dramatic and public spectacle. All there are participants, not mere witnesses. How else can they truly commit? They commit to entering a relationship with God (*Kol asher diber Adonai naaseh*, "All that *Adonai* has spoken we will do!" [Exod. 19:8]), and the particulars will arise from the living relationship they establish. God understands that Torah cannot be imparted only to Moshe, who in turn will teach *Am Yisrael*; it must enter each heart explicitly through a direct relationship. That is why each person must "hear when I speak with you" (Exod. 19:9).

But how will that help them trust Moshe, and why is that essential? Because Torah will be transmitted *l'dor vador* and to retain the sense of revelation anew in each generation, both components are necessary: the sense that one receives Torah directly from God, and the knowledge that one's teachers of Torah are trustworthy conveyers of Torah.

Rambam wrote, "*Am Yisrael* believed in Moshe, not because of the miracles he performed, but because it was our own eyes, and not those of others, that witnessed the revelation at Sinai, and our own ears, and not those of others, that heard the fire, thunder, and lightning" (*Mishneh Torah, Hilchot Y'sodei HaTorah* 8:1).

Each Jew must have a personal stake in Torah and in those who teach Torah.

Tishah B'Av

Tishah B'Av
Kenneth J. Weiss, 2002

Lamentations consists of five chapters. Tishah B'Av commemorates four major tragedies in our history and motivates us to pray that there'll never be a fifth. Excerpts from each of the first four chapters reflect past destructions, while words from the fifth can renew our own flickering hope in the future.

The first destruction occurred in 586 B.C.E. The Babylonians destroyed Solomon's Temple and with it the remnant of David's state. The people were carried into exile, the beautiful city rendered uninhabitable: "Zion spreads out her hands, / She has no one to comfort her; / The LORD has summoned against Jacob / His enemies . . . / Jerusalem has become . . . / A thing unclean" (Lam. 1:17).

Josephus records—in vivid language—the second destruction, dated 70 C.E. That Temple, too, was demolished; the ground on which the "holy house" stood did "no where appear visible, for the dead bodies that lay on it" (*The Life and Works of Flavius Josephus, Part 2*, John C. Winston, 2006, p. 823). The red of the blood was greater than the red in the destructive fire. "All your enemies / Jeer at you; / They hiss and gnash their teeth, / And cry: 'We've ruined her! / Ah, this is the day we hoped for'" (Lam. 2:16).

The third destruction was that of Spanish Jewry. Ferdinand and Isabella, the Inquisitors' court, the edict that Jews convert, leave, or die: 1492 has a whole other meaning for Jews than it does for most post-Columbian Americans. "All our enemies loudly / Rail against us. / Panic and pitfall are our lot, / Death and destruction" (Lam. 3:46–47).

Many still live who remember—with anguish—the fourth destruction: the Shoah. In Hitler's day, many believed they had only two choices: prolonged dying or sudden death: "Better off were the slain of the sword / than those slain by famine. . . . / Our days are done— / Alas, our doom has come!" (Lam. 4:9a, 4:18b).

The fifth destruction, should it ever come, may sweep us away, but not only us. Let the fifth chapter of *Eichah*—whose first word is *z'chor* (remember)—inspire us (God as well) to remember, to never forget. May our past destructions serve as old and valuable lessons. "Take us back, O Lord, to Yourself . . . / Renew our days as of old!" (Lam. 5:21). It's time for renewal now, and prayer too: no more destructions—ever! *Kein y'hi ratzon*—may it be God's will!

Tishah B'Av
Janice Garfunkel, 2008

A source of exasperation and confusion to me are two persistent errors made by Jews—including some rabbis and other experts—and therefore also by non-Jews: (1) the Western Wall is the holiest site in Judaism (actually, the Holy of Holies on the Temple Mount is our holiest site); and (2) the Western Wall is the last remaining remnant of the Temple. If you have been there yourself, you no doubt noticed it is not the only remaining wall; the southern, eastern, and northern walls are also still functioning nicely, else the Temple Mount platform would have collapsed. But printed even on the box of my "Jerusalem matzah meal," proudly made in Israel, are the words "Background photo: The last surviving wall of the Temple, the *Kotel Hamaaravi* (Western Wall), represents Judaism's holiest site."

So why is one little part of a larger western wall of the Temple Mount platform considered more holy than the rest? Why is that the one spot where we pray? The best explanation I have heard is that it is believed that that particular spot was the closest to the Holy of

Holies. According to the *Encyclopaedia Judaica* article on the "Western Wall," today's site seems to have developed its special status only around 1520. Earlier references to the western wall from which the Divine Presence never departed apparently referred to the western wall of the Holy of Holies, not the retaining wall. Tishah B'Av is a great time of year for Reform Jews to reconnect with the many fascinating themes associated with the Temple, including the unifying force of all Jews in the world oriented toward one spot on the earth when we pray.

Tishah B'Av
David Novak, 2009

In the brightest time of the year in the Northern Hemisphere, we dip into the darkness of our lived Jewish experience to mourn. We mourn what our tradition tells us befell our people on this day—and what modern historiography confirms in our time. It is not melodramatic to assert that the Jewish people, now numbering only 13.3 million, has had more than its fair share of tragedy rooted in the baseless hatred of others, religious and secular. Our people have been maimed, tortured, and killed.

This is what could be termed in modern business parlance as a "roll-up," that is, one day where all of the suffering in Jewish history (outside of the Shoah) is commemorated. This speaks to the idea that there is much to mourn while ironically we are still here. Tradition "stuffs" it all into one day, a fast day on which *Eichah* is read and a mournful tone is evident. By afternoon, however, that tone becomes diminished as, in the light of day, we see that the tragedies of our past do not mire us. They are part of our memory, and as Jews, memory is what we mine to inform our present experience.

In remembering the tragedies of the Jewish experience, we find an inverse message: that while our *y'rushah*, "inheritance," is this unbearable pain, we only dip into the darkness and move quickly toward the light. We look at the re-creation that occurs each day and continue to build and to plant, and in memory of those who died *al kiddush HaShem*, we live.

Glossary

Abarbanel—See Abravanel.

Abravanel—Rabbi Isaac ben Judah Abravanel (1437–1508). Portuguese rabbi, biblical commentator, philosopher and political stateman.

Akeidah—Lit. "binding." Refers to Genesis 22, the story of the binding of Isaac.

Al Kiddush Hashem—See *Kiddush Hashem*.

Alshech—Rabbi Moses Alshech (or Alshich) HaKadosh (1508–1593). Scholar, commentator, and mystic who lived in Safed.

Amcha—Lit. "Your people." Refers to the lay Jewish community.

Am Yisrael—The Jewish people.

Aron—See *Aron Kodesh*.

Aron Kodesh—An ark used to store Torah scrolls and other holy objects.

Asham—A sacrifice offered as expiation for sin.

Avadim Hayinu—The portion in the Haggadah during which the story of the Israelite slavery is recounted.

Bal Tashchit—The prohibition of wastefulness.

Bat Kohein—The daughter of a *Kohein*.

B'dikat Chameitz—The search for *chameitz* that is conducted the evening before the beginning of Pesach, to ensure that all of the *chameitz* has been removed from the house or building.

Beit HaMikdash—The ancient Temple that stood in Jerusalem.

Ben Azzai—Shimon ben Azzai, a second-century *Tanna*.

Bikkurim—The first fruits of the harvest, which in ancient times were brought to the Temple as offerings.

Birkat Kohanim—The Priestly Blessing, the text of which is found in Numbers 6:24–26. The blessing used to be offered to the people by the Temple priests and is now used at the synagogue for various ritual purposes.

B'reishit Rabbah—Collection of midrashim on the Book of Genesis.

B'rit—Covenant, contract, or promise.

Chacham—Jewish sage, wise person.

Chachamim—Plural form of *chacham*; see definition above.

Chafeitz Chayim—Also, *Chofetz Chaim*. Rabbi Israel Meir HaCohen Kagan (1838–1933), Polish rabbi, commentator, legal scholar and author of numerous texts about the harm of speaking gossip.

Chag—(plural "*chagim*") Holiday or festival.

Chameitz—Leavened food products, which Jews are forbidden from eating or owning during Passover.

Chatat—Sacrifice offered in order to make restitution for a sin.

Chazan—Cantor, or in ancient times, those who organized rituals in the Temple.

Chazanim—The plural form of *chazan*; see definition above.

Chazir—Pig.

Cheilev—Type of animal fat that is prohibited from consumption.

Chesed—Benevolence, kindness, charity, grace.

Cheshbon Hanefesh—Self-reflection and evaluation of one's merits and shortcomings.

Chok—Law, often one whose rationale is not understood.

Chukim—Plural of *chok*.

Davar Acher—Lit. "something else." Refers to a divergent opinion or explanation.

Davka—A versatile Hebrew word used to emphasize a point. It can mean, "specifically," "precisely," "for no real reason," "spitefully," or have other implications based on the context.

D'rash/a—Explanation or interpretation of the Bible; also refers to a short speech or article that teaches about the Bible and applies its lessons to daily life.

D'rashot—Plural form of *drasha*; see definition above.

Duchenen—The time in the traditional prayer service when *kohanim* offer the congregation the *Birkat Kohanim.*

Eichah—The Book of Lamentations.

Eidut—Refers to the *Aron Eidut*, the Ark of the Covenant that housed the Tablets of the Law in the *Mishkan.*

Eitz Chayim—The Tree of Life, often used as a name for the Torah.

Gan Eden—The Garden of Eden.

Geihinom—Or *Gehinnom*. In Rabbinic tradition, a place to which the soul descends after death, for a period of purgatory, before ascending to the spiritual Garden of Eden.

Ger—A stranger, one who is not a member of the community. Also the term for someone who has converted to Judaism.

Gerim—Plural form of *ger;* see definition above.

Ger v'Toshav—A foreigner who dwells temporarily in a community. Abraham uses this term to introduce himself to the group of Hittites in Genesis 23:4.

G'milut Chasadim—Benevolent deeds.

Haggadah—The book of texts, traditions, and songs that is used during the Pesach seder.

Hallel—A collection of psalms of praise that are recited during morning services on Rosh Chodesh, Chanukah, and *Chagim* and during the Pesach seder.

Har Sinai—Mount Sinai, the site at which the biblical story of revelation takes place.

Haz"al—An acronym for *chachameinu zichronam l'vracha*, or "our Sages, may their memories be for a blessing." This term refers to the greatly revered generations of rabbis from the time of the Second Temple until approximately the end of the sixth century C.E.

Hekhsher Tzedek—A commission that certifies food using the seal Magen Tzedek, indicating that the food is kosher according to dietary laws and according to ethical standards of labor, environmentalism, business, health, safety, and the humane treatment of animals.

Hineini—Lit. "Behold—here I am."

HUC—The Hebrew Union College–Jewish Institute of Religion (HUC-JIR). Established in 1875, The Reform Movement's graduate school and seminary for training rabbis, cantors, Jewish educators, and communal professionals.

Ibn Ezra—Rabbi Abraham ben Meir ibn Ezra (c. 1092–1167). A renowned scholar, biblical commentator, grammarian, and poet who was born in Spain and lived in many places in Europe.

Ikar—The principle, the main substance.

Ima—Mother.

Iturei Torah—A collection of ethical and Chasidic teachings, compiled by Rabbi Aharon Yaakov Greenberg (1900–1963).

JIR—The Jewish Institute of Religion. The American seminary founded in 1922 by Rabbi Stephen S. Wise, which later merged with the Hebrew Union College. See **HUC** above.

Kaftor—A decorative knop on the menorah in the *Mishkan*.

Kal Vachomer—Lit. "all the more so." If X is true, then *kal vachomer*.

Kaparah—Atonement or cleansing of sin.

Kaporet—The covering over the Ark in the Tabernacle.

Kareit—Discussed in Rabbinic tradition, a divinely ordained punishment whereby a person who deliberately commits certain sins is cut off from the Jewish community.

Kashiyot—Plural form of *kashya*; see definition below.

Kashya—A conceptual or interpretive difficulty.

Kavanah—Intention, meaningful focus.

K'dushah—Holiness.

Kiddush HaShem—The sanctification of God's name; often refers to martyrdom.

Kippur—Atonement.

K'lal Yisrael—The entirety of the Jewish people, worldwide.

K'li Yakar—A homiletical Torah commentary written by Rabbi Shlomo Ephraim ben Aaron of Luntschitz (1550–1609).

Kohanim—Plural form of *kohein*, see definition below.

Kohein—A priest who oversaw sacrifices and matters of purity and cleanliness in ancient Israel; also one who descends from priestly lineage.

Kohein Gadol—The High Priest, who had special privileges and responsibilities in the Temple cult.

Kol Yisrael—See *K'lal Yisrael*.

Korban—A sacrificial offering.

Korbanot—Plural form of *korban*; see definition above.

Kotzker Rebbe—Rabbi Menachem Mendel of Kotzk (1787–1859). A Polish Chasidic rebbe and teacher of ethics and spirituality.

K'tonet Pasim—The colorful garment that Jacob gives to Joseph in Genesis 37.

Kuzari—An Arabic philosophical treatise written by Y'hudah Ha-Levi, to explain and defend Judaism against other religions and school of thought.

K'vod—Or "*kavod*." Honor or glory.

Lashon Hara—Slander, gossip, and other forms of cruel speech.

L'dor Vador—"From generation to generation."

Leil Pesach—The evening celebration of Pesach, during which the seder is conducted.

Leket—"Gleaning." The law requires that farmers leave *leket*, small quantities of produce that have fallen to the ground, for hungry people to gather.

L'haskil—To gain knowledge.

L'havdil—"Not to compare the two." Used rhetorically to make a distinction between ideas, people, objects, or places that are unequal in quality or merit.

L'heifech—"Quite the opposite."

Likutei Moharan—A collection of teachings of Rabbi Nachman of Bratslav.

Maariv—The evening prayer service.

Machloket—A dispute among scholars over a legal point or textual interpretation.

Maftir—Refers to the concluding section of the weekly Torah reading, or to the final person called to the Torah, who then reads the haftarah.

Magen Tzedek—The seal offered by Hekhsher Tzedek; see entry above.

Maharal—Rabbi Yehuda Loew of Prague (1525–1609), a scholar, commentator, and teacher, who, according to legend, created a *golem* to protect the Jews of Prague from their enemies.

Maimonides—Rabbi Moses ben Maimon (1135–1204), a Spanish-born scholar, teacher, physician, philosopher, commentator, and codifier of Jewish law; also known as Rambam.

Makshim—A scholarly question or challenge to a text.
Malachim—Angels or messengers of God.
Malbim—Rabbi Meir Leibush ben Yechiel Michel (1809–1879). A Russian rabbi, teacher, and biblical commentator.
Maneh—A unit of gold or silver currency, referred to in the Mishnah and the Talmud.
Maror—Bitter herbs that are eaten during the Pesach seder and that symbolize the bitterness of the Israelites' slavery in Egypt.
Mayim Chayim—Fresh (literally "living") water.
Mei HaShiloach—A collection of Torah commentary written by Rabbi Mordechai Yosef of Izbitza (1800–1854), a Chasidic leader and mystic.
Merkavah—"Chariot" or "throne." Refers to a school of Jewish mysticism that is based on Ezekiel's visions of ascending to the heavens to view the divine throne.
M'forshim—Commentators.
M'gilat Esther—The Scroll or Book of Esther.
Midbar—The wilderness or desert.
Midrash—(pl. midrashim) Rabbinic lore, written to explain, interpret, or elaborate upon biblical or legal texts.
Midrash HaGadol—A thirteenth-century collection of earlier biblical midrashim, compiled in Yemen.
Mikdash—The temple in which the Israelites worshiped God.
Milah—Or *B'rit Milah*. The ceremony of entering a male into the covenant of Judaism through ritual circumcision.
Minchah—The afternoon prayer service, also a type of voluntary sacrifice to God.
Minhag—Custom.
Mishkan—The Tabernacle that the Israelites built to worship God in the wilderness.
Mishnah—Contained in six books or "orders," a collection of legal material that had previously been transmitted orally and whose redaction in written form was completed in 220 c.e.
Mizbeiach—The Temple altar.
M'tzora—One who is afflicted with *tzaraat*.
Musaf—The additional prayer service that is added on Shabbat, Rosh Chodesh, and *Chagim*.

Nachmanides—Rabbi Moshe ben Nachman Gerondi (1194–1270). A prominent Spanish scholar, biblical commentator, and mystic, also known as Ramban.

Nachman of Bratslav—A Chasidic rebbe from the Ukraine who moved to Breslov (19th cen.).

Necheuta—Lit. comfort. The concept of ending a portion of text or teaching on a note of consolation.

Nefesh—Soul.

Nega—Damage, affliction, or plague.

Ner—A candle or other source of light.

Nikud—A mark of vocalization, punctuation, or emphasis.

Ohel Mo-eid—The Tent of Meeting, a place in the Israelite wilderness camp where Moses, the priests, and the people would communicate with God.

Olah—A voluntary offering that is fully consumed on the altar.

Oleh—"Going up," or one who "goes up."

Or HaChayim—A Torah commentary written by Moroccan-born Rabbi Chaim ben Attar (1696–1742).

Orlah—1. The status of fruit from a newly planted tree. It is prohibited to eat *orlah* or derive benefit from it during the first three years of the tree's growth. 2. An impediment. 3. A foreskin.

Parashah—(Heb. "portion") The Torah reading for a particular Shabbat or holiday.

Parashiyot—Plural form of *parashah*; see definition above.

Pasuk—A scriptural verse.

Pei-ah—The corner of the field, which the Torah commands farmers to leave unharvested so that poor people can come and pick its produce.

Perek Shirah—An ancient book of biblical and Rabbinic quotations that praise God for Creation.

Pesach—The Festival of Passover; also the name of the sacrifice that was offered during this Festival during the time of the Temple.

Pesach Sheini—A secondary observance of Pesach (Passover) that falls a month afterwards. According to the biblical tradition, a person who was unable to offer the proper sacrifice during the week of Pesach can give the offerings on Pesach Sheini.

Pirkei Avot—A tractate of the Mishnah imparting ethical teachings, transmitted by generations of rabbis.

P'loni—An unspecified or generic name, "So-and-So" or "Such-and-Such."

P'rutah—A small coin, referred to in the Mishnah and Talmud.

P'sukei D'Zimrah—The psalms of praise that open the morning prayer service.

P'sukim—Plural form of *pasuk*; see definition above.

Rabbi Meir Yitzchak Rothenberg Alter of Ger—(1799–1866) A Polish rebbe, founder of the Ger Chasidic dynasty.

Rashi—Rabbi Shlomo Itzchaki (1040–1105). A renowned and influential French scholar and teacher, known best for his commentaries on the Bible and the Talmud.

Rav Avraham Kook—The first chief Ashkenazic rabbi of Israel and major religious Zionist thinker, born in Latvia, lived 1865–1935.

R'chilut—Gossip or tale-bearing.

Ruach—Wind or spirit.

Ruach HaKodesh—The divine spirit or inspiration.

Sdarim—Plural form of seder; see definition below.

Seder—A ritual meal for Pesach during which symbolic foods are eaten and the story of the Exodus from Egypt is retold.

Sefer Y'tzirah—The Book of Creation, a second-century-C.E. mystical text about God's creation of the world.

Seichel—Wisdom, insight, sensibility.

S'fat Emet—A Torah commentary written by Polish Chasidic rebbe Yehudah Aryeh Leib Alter of Ger (1847–1905).

S'firah—Counting, often refers to the daily counting of the Omer between Pesach and Shavuot.

S'firot—In Kabbalah (a large stream of Jewish mysticism), ten mystical attributes of God.

Sforno—Rabbi Ovadiah ben Yaakov (1475–1550). An Italian scholar, biblical commentator, and philosopher.

Shaatneiz—Forbidden mixtures of wool and linen fibers, as described in Lev. 19:19 and Deut. 22:11.

Shacharit—The morning prayer service.

Shaleim—Whole or complete.

Shamir—In Rabbinic tradition, a substance or worm used for carving stones for the Ten Commandments and for the Temple. Other implements were unacceptable for these holy tasks because they symbolized violence.

Sh'chitah—Ritual slaughter, necessary to produce kosher meat.

Shechinah—The Divine Presence, often in Jewish tradition connoting the feminine aspect of God.

Sheva Minim—The seven species that, in the Torah, are considered special produce from the Land of Israel. They are wheat, barley, grapes, figs, olives, pomegranates, and dates.

Shich'chah—A quantity of harvested produce that is accidentally left in the field and that the farmer is commanded to leave for the poor, rather than returning and picking it up.

Shidduch—A matched pair; often refers to arranging a couple for marriage.

Shirah—A song or poem; also refers to the Song of the Sea.

Shirat HaYam—The Song of the Sea. This is the poem in Exodus 15 in which the Israelites praise God for defeating the Egyptians.

Sh'liach Tzibur—A leader of communal prayer.

Sh'mitah—The Sabbatical year. The Torah teaches that in the Land of Israel, every seventh year the land should lie fallow and debts should be forgiven.

Sidrah—(Heb. "order") The Torah reading for a particular Shabbat or holiday.

Sidrot—Plural form of *sidrah*; see definition above.

Sifrei—Referring to one of two collections of midrashim: *Sifrei* to Numbers or *Sifrei* to Deuteronomy.

Sinat Chinam—Senseless hatred.

Sotah—The ritual found in Numbers that is used to determine the guilt of a woman accused of adultery.

S'udah Sh'lishit—The third meal eaten on Shabbat. It takes place shortly before the end of Shabbat and is often accompanied by singing and Torah study.

Sugya—A unit of Rabbinic discourse in the Talmud.

Sulam—Ladder.

Taam—Taste, reason, or point of linguistic accent.

Tachlis—Refers to practical or essential matters.

Tahor—Pure; in a state of ritual purity.

Tallitot—Prayer shawls with *tzitzit* on their corners.

Talmid Chacham—A wise and learned scholar of Torah and Jewish law.

Talmud—A compiled body of centuries of ancient Rabbinic legal discussion, lore, and religious thought. There are two Talmuds—the *Talmud Yerushalmi* (Jerusalem Talmud), which was compiled in the land of Israel, and the *Talmud Bavli* (Babylonian Talmud), which was compiled in Babylonia.

Tamei—A designation of ritual impurity.

Tamid—The burnt offering that was sacrificed daily at the Temple.

Tanach—The Hebrew Bible, consisting of three sections: Torah, Prophets, and Scripture.

Tanna—(pl. *Tannaim*) The term for a rabbi from the Land of Israel in the period of 70–220 C.E., who was involved with teaching and transmitting the Oral Tradition.

Targum—An Aramaic translation of biblical text.

Targum Onkelos—An Aramaic translation of the Torah.

T'filah—Prayer.

T'filat Geshem—The Prayer for Rain, which is traditionally recited by the *chazan* during the *Musaf* service on Sh'mini Atzeret.

T'filat Tal—The Prayer for Dew, which is traditionally recited by the *chazan* during the *Musaf* service on the last day of Pesach.

T'horah—See **Tahor**.

Tikkun—A completion, reconciliation, or repair.

Tocheichah—Rebuke.

T'reif—Non-kosher food. The term traditionally referred to animals that were mortally wounded and therefore prohibited from consumption.

T'rumah—Food or materials that are designated as offerings to God.

T'shuvah—Repentance.

Tumah—Ritual impurity.

Tzaraat—A disease of scales, sores, and discoloration that afflicts skin, garments, and buildings and renders them impure. The conditions and remedy are described in Leviticus 13 and 14.

Tzedek—Justice.

Tzitzit—The fringes that, according to the Torah, must be placed on the corners of a garment to serve as a reminder of God's commandments.

Ushpizin—The group of Jewish historical ancestors who are symbolically invited to meals during the weeklong Festival of Sukkot.

Vidui—Confession.

Yalkut Shimoni—A medieval collection of biblical midrash, drawn from a variety of rabbinic sources.

Yetzer Hara—The Evil Inclination. Jewish tradition teaches that every person is born with the tendency towards wrongdoing, which exists in tension with the *yetzer hatov*.

Yetzer Hatov—The Good Inclination. Jewish tradition teaches that every person is born with the tendency towards good behavior, which exists in tension with the *yetzer hara*.

Y'hudah HaLevi—Or Judah HaLevi (c. 1075–1141). A medieval Spanish philosopher and poet.

Yirah—Fear or awe.

Y'tziat Mitzrayim—The Exodus from Egypt.

Zayit Ra'anan—A commentary on *Yalkut Shimoni*, written by Rabbi Avraham Gombiner of Poland (1637–1683).

Zemer—A song, often used to refer to songs that are sung at the Shabbat table.

Zevach Sh'lamim—A voluntary sacrifice expressing gratitude or well-being.

Zohar—A collection of mystical theology and commentary on the Torah.

Permissions

Amichai, Hana: Excerpts from "Time #30" and "Miracles" by Yehuda Amichai. Used by permission of the Estate of Yehuda Amichai.

Cantu, Jean Shapiro: "Arabic Lesson" by Robert Friend from *The Next Room*, Menard Press, 1995. Copyright © Jean Shapiro Cantu.

HarperCollins Publishers: "The Gift" from THE FIRST FOUR BOOKS OF POEMS by Louise Gluck. Copyright 1968, 1971, 1972, 1973, 1974, 1975, 1976, 1977, 1978, 1978, 1980, 1985, 1995 by Louise Gluck. Reprinted by permission of Harper-Collins Publishers.

Houghton Mifflin: Excerpt from "My Parents' Lodging Place" by Yehuda Amichai in Open Closed Open, Harvest Books, a division of Houghton Mifflin © 2000.

Mintz, Ruth Finer: Translation of "Gleanings" by David Shimoni in Modern Hebrew Poetry: A Bilingual Edition, Ruth Finer Mintz, U. of California Press © 1982.

New Directions Publishing Corp: "Death Psalm: O Lord of Mysteries" by Denise Levertov, from LIFE IN THE FOREST, copyright © 1978 by Denise Levertov. Reprinted by permission of New Directions Publishing Corp.

Schwartz, Howard: Translation of "Biographical Note" by Gabriel Preil in *Modern Poems of the Hebrew Bible: An Anthology*, by David Curzon, Jewish Publication Society © 1994.

www.ingramcontent.com/pod-product-compliance
Lightning Source LLC
Chambersburg PA
CBHW060446170426
43199CB00011B/1114